ASIANS IN BRITAIN

400 Years of History

ROZINA VISRAM

Pluto Press

LONDON • STERLING, VIRGINIA

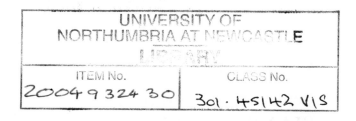
First published 2002 by Pluto Press
345 Archway Road, London N6 5AA
and 22883 Quicksilver Drive, Sterling, VA 20166–2012, USA

www.plutobooks.com

British Library Cataloguing in Publication Data
A catalogue record for this book is available from the British Library

ISBN 0 7453 1378 7 hardback
ISBN 0 7453 1373 6 paperback

Library of Congress Cataloging-in-Publication Data
Visram, Rozina, 1939–
Asians in Britain : 400 years of history / Rozina Visram.
p. cm.
Includes bibliographical references and index.
ISBN 0–7453–1378–7 (hb) — ISBN 0–7453–1373–6 (pbk)
1. Asians—Great Britain—History. 2. East Indians—Great
Britain—History. 3. Great Britain—Ethnic relations—History.
I. Title.
DA125.A84 V68 2002
941'.004914—dc21
2001005307

10 9 8 7 6 5 4 3 2

Designed, typeset and produced for Pluto Press by
Chase Publishing Services, Fortescue, Sidmouth, EX10 9QG
Printed in the European Union by Antony Rowe Ltd, Chippenham, England

For my sister,
NURBANU

Contents

List of Illustrations

Preface

Ayahs, Lascars and Princes: Indians in Britain 1700–1947, my pioneering work, was published by Pluto Press in 1986 at a time of growing interest in the history of black peoples in Britain. However, despite the fact that the past two decades have seen significant advances in research and writing in the history of African-Caribbean communities in Britain, the varied histories of Asians from South Asia (the present-day India, Pakistan, Bangladesh and Sri Lanka) – who have been in Britain for close on four centuries – remain little researched. Scholars have tended to underestimate the significant presence of Asians and their contributions to British society, and the perception that their settlement in Britain dates from the 1950s persists. Why so? Part of the problem may be to do with the availability of source material. Records, especially for the seventeenth, eighteenth and early nineteenth centuries, are fragmentary and scattered. There is, for instance, no comparable important source like slavery and abolition documents. The problem is further compounded by terminology. The terms 'coloured' and 'black' described Africans and West Indians as well as Asians. A further problem is the nature of Asian settlement, which was both transitory and permanent, including a diverse group of settlers. The lack of interest of researchers and academics, as well as at grassroots community level, is another reason. Research has tended to be concentrated more on the Asian communities who settled here after the 1950s and comes from academic disciplines largely based in university departments of social anthropology and sociology – not history.

And yet, as I have discovered, there is a vast amount of documentation available in the national and local archives in Britain requiring patient and rigorous search. The records of the East India Company and the government of India in the Oriental and India Office Collections (OIOC), form one major source for researchers, as do official British government records at the Public Record Office. But parish and local council records, newspapers and surveys, and contemporary literature, both by whites and Indians themselves, as well as visual sources provide another valuable source for reconstructing the history and experiences of Asians in Britain.

Ayahs, Lascars and Princes, researched and written during the two years of my ILEA teacher fellowship at the Centre for Multicultural

Education, University of London Institute of Education, was my pioneering shot at unravelling the complex history of Asians in Britain. During the course of my research for my present study on Asians and their descendants in Britain, I have been fortunate enough to come across several new sources at the OIOC and other repositories (I have by no means tapped every possible collection), as well as being given access to family memoirs, and these appear in the notes. I have not only re-examined the sources consulted previously, but have trawled through contemporary newspapers, journals and reports of various Christian organisations and other bodies, parish registers, Parliamentary papers, and writings by Asians themselves. This study has also benefited from the release in 1997 of the secret Indian Political Intelligence (IPI) records. Unfortunately, as an independent scholar, time and resources did not permit checking the holdings of many other repositories in Britain or the archives on the Indian sub-continent. Nonetheless, the mass of material uncovered has enabled me to trace the history of peoples from South Asia in Britain from 1600, when trading contact between Britain and India first began with the founding of the East India Company. An empirical study, the book examines the nature of Asian settlement, official attitudes to their migration, the varied reactions of the British people to their presence and the differing responses of the Asians themselves. It documents and analyses the economic, political, social and cultural lives of Asians in Britain largely through the experiences of various groups, individuals and their descendants, within the context of colonialism, race, gender and class. The record of their lives challenges accepted notions of migration and settlement patterns. The book also examines the anti-colonial struggle by Asians and their allies in Britain, Asian contributions to British society as well as their role in two world wars. A word about terminology: the terms 'Asian' and 'Indian' are used interchangeably to refer to the peoples of South Asia and their descendants, while 'black' describes both the peoples of African descent and more broadly, in a political sense, Africans, African-Caribbeans and Asians.

Much still remains to be researched and it is hoped that this new, expanded edition will re-awaken interest and stimulate further research to advance our knowledge of this important field of a little known aspect of British history and British identity.

Acknowledgements

I am much indebted to the curators and staff of the record offices, libraries and other repositories named in the bibliography who were invariably helpful and met my requests for information, photocopies, documents and books with courtesy and efficiency. My special thanks to Tim Thomas, Jill Geber and Tony Farrington at the OIOC for patiently answering all my queries and without whose help I would not have been able to locate some of the sources. I am most grateful to the several descendants for providing me with information, and giving me access to family papers and photographs: Shakun Banfield, George Chowdharay-Best, David Datta, Leena Dhingra, Anita Money, Jaya Nicholas, Sehri Saklatvala, Muriel Simpson and David Wilson; and Sqdn Ldr M.S. Pujji, DFC, for telling me about his RAF days. Many scholars, colleagues and friends who generously gave me information and references are specified in the notes. Many others kindly shared their knowledge with me and sustained me with encouragement and advice. I thank them all: Pauline Adams (Somerville College), Rohit Barot, Howard Bloch, Meghnad Desai, Audrey Dewjee, Anne Dunlop, Michael Fisher, Jeffrey Green, Jagdish Gundara, A.D. Harvey, Alistair Hinton (The Sorabji Archive), Vada Hart, Martin Moir, Jacquie Parkes, Vibha Parthasarathi, Ron Ramdin, Hazel Robertson (National Library of Scotland), David Selkirk and Marika Sherwood. I owe a particular debt of gratitude to Caroline Adams, for her faith in my work and helping with research in Norfolk; John Ballantyne, for sharing the tedious task of relaying the footnotes, and for being there; J. Stewart Cameron, for helping me to understand primary hypertension; Peter Fryer, for his interest and constant encouragement, and for taking on the onerous task of compiling the index; Anthony Batty Shaw, for checking the section on Frederick Akbar Mahomed; Christopher Fyfe, for kindly reading the draft chapters, for valuable suggestions, advice and words of wisdom, which steered me clear of pitfalls and helped to improve the manuscript; Peter Marshall, for all that and also for helping me to trim the manuscript further; Peter Fraser, for his advice and for being the final reader. My mother, sister and brothers, by letter and by phone, lent moral support. Finally, I am grateful to my editor, Anne Beech, at Pluto Press for being so understanding, and for her patience as an overlong manuscript had to be trimmed and trimmed again.

Every reasonable effort has been made to obtain permission for reproduction of the photographs. The author and publishers thank those that have given their permission.

The publishers and author gratefully acknowledge the financial assistance of the Thornley Bequest Fund Committee.

Rozina Visram
London

1

A Long Presence

On 22 December 1616, at St Dionis Backchurch in the City of London, in the presence of a distinguished gathering of the Privy Council, the Lord Mayor and Aldermen, and the Governors of the East India Company (EIC), an Indian youth, 'the first fruits of India', brought to Britain two years previously in August 1614, was publicly baptised. The church was packed and a crowd of curious onlookers was gathered outside. The Archbishop of Canterbury, who had been consulted, had given his approval, while the name given in baptism was chosen by King James I. The parish register records the ceremony as:

> 22nd December 1616. An East Indian was Christened by the name of Peter.[1]

This is the first known record of a baptism of an Indian brought to Britain, within years of the Charter being granted by Queen Elizabeth I to a group of London merchants, on 31 December 1600, establishing 'The Governor and Company of Merchants of London, Trading into the East-Indies'. Given the hazy notions of Elizabethan geography, the East covered a wide area, embracing the Indian sub-continent, China, Japan and the East Indian archipelago. The founding of the EIC and its exploits in India, first through trade and later through conquest and colonisation, leading to the British Raj, set in motion forces that would profoundly affect both India and Britain, altering their historical relationship and development.

Who was Peter and why the public baptism? Little is recorded about Peter's life. According to the EIC Court minutes, the Reverend Patrick Copland, the Company's Chaplain to Masulipatam on the Coromandel Coast in India, who had taught him to read and write English, was instrumental in bringing Peter to England in 1614. His aptitude for learning prompted the Company to vote '20 markes per annum' for his schooling in England, so that he could be instructed in religion and sent back as a missionary to proselytise his own people. Thus, under the influence and auspices of the EIC, Peter became the first Asian convert to Christianity on English soil.

Peter did not long remain in Britain. In 1617, within weeks of his baptism, and less than three years after his arrival, accompanied by the Revd Patrick Copland, he left on the EIC ship, the *Royal James.*

Nothing further is recorded about his subsequent career. However, the three surviving letters written by him in Latin in 1620, 'in the East Indies', to Sir Thomas Smith, the Company Governor and to Martin Pring, the commander of the *Royal James*, show that by 1620, Peter had acquired mastery of both English and Latin. Further, his letters, signed *Petrus Papa* (Peter Pope), suggest that he had gained a second name. What his original Indian name was, or his age, or where in India he came from, history does not record. His birthplace is mentioned simply as 'borne in the Bay of Bengala'.[2]

Peter was a transient. But other Indians settled here as evidenced in Parish registers:

> 26 May 1769. Flora an East Indian (buried at Woolwich).
> 5 October 1730. John Mummud a Larskar Indian died at Ratclif (St Anne's Limehouse).[3]

Starting in the seventeenth century, Indian servants and ayahs (nannies) were brought over by British families returning from India. Indian sailors, the lascars, crewed the Company ships and, later, the steam-powered liners. Some of these servants and sailors formed the earliest Indian working-class settlers in Britain. From the eighteenth century, a trickle of Indian emissaries, visitors and Indian wives of some European men and their children came to Britain.

From about the middle of the nineteenth century, a growing number of Indians began arriving in Britain. Some came as a result of the political, social and economic changes brought about in India under imperialism. Others came out of a sense of adventure or to see the land of their rulers. Exiled princes settled in Britain. Students, some on scholarships, came to obtain vital professional qualifications to enable them to secure entry into the structures of colonial hierarchy. Some stayed to practise their professions. Political activists brought the struggle for colonial liberation to London, the centre of imperial power. Businessmen and entrepreneurs came to seek economic opportunities.

By the mid-twentieth century, then, there was a small population of students and activists, petty traders and merchants, industrial workers and professionals, artists and performers, from different religious backgrounds and regions of the Indian sub-continent in Britain. More would come after the 1950s in response to the post-war labour needs of the British economy. Asian history in Britain thus, goes back almost 400 years.

2

Early Arrivals, 1600–1830s

Sir Thomas Roe, the first English ambassador to the Court of the Mughal Emperor Jahangir, in 1616, describing the 'curtesie' extended to him, wrote that an 'earnest' proposal had been made that on his return to England, he should be accompanied by an Indian 'gentellman to kysse his Majesties [James I] hands and see our countrye'.[1] The idea for an Indian ambassador came to nothing. But the founding of the East India Company (EIC) set in motion a chain of events leading to the movement of peoples in both directions. As trade expanded, the Company sent out a growing number of agents, both civil and military, to service its commercial enterprises, and its factories at Surat, Bombay, Madras and Calcutta consolidated, becoming little English enclaves on Indian soil.

THE COLONIAL CONTEXT

Young men, as young as 16, usually from the clergy and merchant families, through patronage or even by bribing their way, obtained posts as Company agents in India, a growing number of Scots among them after the 1707 Act of Union. Despite low salaries and hazards to health, employment in India was popular. Work was not arduous, hours were short and, with an army of Indian servants, agents were able to live like lords, adapting oriental conditions to suit English tastes and lifestyles. William Hickey, 'the gentleman attorney', the son of an Irish lawyer, vividly describes the opulent lifestyle of the European elite in eighteenth-century Calcutta: their clothes of velvet and lace, their coach and horses, their recreations, the enormous quantities of food – curried meats, rice and *pilaus* – and liquor consumed, their Indian mistresses, and their servants, some with titles like wig-bearers and *houccaburdars*. Hickey, by no means a wealthy man, had a staff of 63, including eight table servants, four grooms, one coachman, three grass-cutters for the garden, two cooks, two bakers, one tailor, one hairdresser, nine valets and two washermen. Alexander Mackrabie, who became Sheriff of Calcutta in 1774, shared the home of Philip Francis with two other friends. Their establishment consisted of 110 servants, while the Revd William Tennant, a chaplain, stayed with a private family who employed 105 servants.[2] Because wages were so low – one Indian visitor to England in the eighteenth century calculated that the cost of 'a common servant' in England was eight times more than in India – it was possible for the Company officials to employ many more servants than in comparable country homes in Britain.[3] Officers in the Company's army, too, were equally well provided, their servants never left behind, even during marches and battles. An English captain in the Mysore campaign of 1780, for instance, brought with him his steward, cook, valet, groom, groom's assistant, barber, washerman, and 'other officers', besides 15 'coolies' to carry his baggage, wine, brandy, tea, live poultry and milch-goats. If a gentleman of fashion really wanted to flaunt his status and wealth, then he could obtain the ultimate in luxury, an African slave, especially imported from Bourbon or Mauritius. Slaves could also be purchased in Calcutta.[4] But because African slaves were expensive, about ten times more than Indian domestics, most Englishmen preferred Indian servants. And it was these that they brought to Britain.

A grand lifestyle was not the only advantage of employment in India. There were also opportunities for making money by private trade, or by other means. And fortunes were made. For instance, Sir William Langhorne, the Governor of Fort St George, Madras from 1672, purchased Charlton House, a fine Jacobean mansion in Greenwich with the fortune he amassed through private trading. Another, Elihu Yale (1648–1721), also Governor of Madras, and later a director of the EIC, endowed the American University named after him. His collection of Mughal miniatures is said to have inspired John Vanderbank's designs for a series of tapestries, 'after the Indian manner', so popular in England at the time, and made at his factory in Soho.[5] Thomas Pitt made a fortune, first as an interloper in defiance of the Company's monopoly, and later as Governor of Madras, acquiring the famous Pitt Diamond, which enabled him to become a landed magnate and the founder of one of the most famous political dynasties of the time.

The years after 1757 (battle of Plassey), which virtually turned Bengal into a Company province, are particularly notorious for the plunder of India, as Company agents reaped for themselves wealth undreamed of, earning the title of 'Nabob' (*Nawab*, Muslim nobleman). Robert Clive, at the age of 35, extorted a fortune worth over £230,000 in settlement with Mir Jafar, in addition to an annual income of £30,000 from his *jagir* (land titles). This was by no means exceptional. John Johnstone, a Scot and the founder of the House of Alva, collected over £300,000; Sir Thomas Rumbold, having gained one fortune in Bengal, returned to make another in Madras.[6] Having made their money, these nabobs retired to Britain with their wealth, their Indian artefacts, their Indian servants and, occasionally, their Indian wives and children.

MAKING INDIA IN BRITAIN

Like the sugar barons of the West Indies, the India-returned nabobs settled down to the role of country gentlemen in Georgian society. They bought estates (and sometimes seats in Parliament), and built large mansions. As Head points out, it was Indian money that financed some of the most magnificent houses in eighteenth-century Britain.[7] Clive purchased an estate on the borders of Worcestershire and Shropshire, a house in Berkeley Square, London, and Claremont in Surrey, where, in 1769, 'Capability' Brown designed for him a mansion in neo-classical style. Woodhall Park in Hertfordshire, designed in Palladian style by Thomas Leverton, was commissioned by Sir Thomas Rumbold. Town Hill Park, South Stoneham in Hampshire was built for Nathaniel Middleton. Basildon Park, Berkshire, built in 1776 in Bath stone, and described by Nikolaus Pevsner, the architectural historian, as 'the most splendid Georgian mansion of Berkshire', was the home of Francis Sykes, who justified his loot from India as the question of choice: 'whether it should go into a black man's pocket or my own'. Stanstead Park in Sussex, built for Richard Barwell, Preston Hall in Scotland, Middleton Hall in Carmarthenshire and Gore in Kent are some other examples. Here the nabobs housed their priceless collections of Indian paintings, manuscripts, miniatures and other *objets d'art*. Newbridge House Museum, County Dublin, is a fine example of one such extraordinary collection of Indian *objets*, belonging to Thomas Alexander Cobb (1788–1836), who married Nazir Begum, the daughter of Aziz Jehan of Kashmir.[8]

Other nabobs brought India more directly to Georgian Britain, building homes in architectural styles reminiscent of India. William Frankland's modest two-storey house, Muntham in Sussex, with its portico and a verandah, hints at his Indian life. But the two most Indianised mansions were Daylesford House, commissioned by Warren Hastings, and Sezincote, built for Charles Cockerell. Both buildings in Gloucestershire were designed by Samuel Pepys Cockerell, the brother of Charles, and a descendant of Pepys, the diarist. Daylesford House, with its central dome and Indian motifs, costing over £60,000, was filled with Hastings' collection of magnificent ivory furniture, Mughal miniatures, oil paintings and Indian prints by Hodges and the Daniells. Even plants from India were introduced on his estate. And Sezincote, the 'Taj in the Cotswolds', is architecturally reminiscent of the Taj Mahal.[9]

The nabobs also brought their Indianised habits and tastes to cities such as London, Bath, Cheltenham and Edinburgh where they settled, adding to the Indian influences already becoming fashionable as a result of the trade with the east: Indian shawls, muslins and Madras prints for dress, changes in furnishing and furniture. For instance, as early as 1618, a 'Benguella Quilt' had been auctioned for a substantial price at a sale in London. At Kensington Palace, Queen Mary had a large collection of porcelain, lacquered screens, cabinets, chairs and textiles, including tapestries made 'after the Indian manner'. From John Evelyn, the diarist, we learn of a room in Lady Mordaunt's house, hung with Pintado (painted calico-chintz) with its extraordinary design depicting 'figures great and small, prettily representing sundry trades and occupations of the Indians, with their habits [costumes]', while Pepys wrote enthusiastically of buying some pretty 'chinte ... that is paynted calico' for his wife's new study.[10] Spices and new foods altered diet. As early as 1652, the first coffee house opened in London; by 1709, few had not heard of or tasted tea. The India-returned nabobs introduced their taste for 'curry'. By 1784 curry and rice had become house specialities in some fashionable restaurants in London's Piccadilly, the Norris Street Coffee House advertising it as such as early as 1773. How popular curry was among these India-returnees is seen from the fact that Sarah Shade, a widow, was able to support herself for 'a year and a half' by making curry, for which she was well known, for different East Indian families in London. Cheltenham and Edinburgh, where so many of the nabobs had settled, were famed for their delicious curries. The fact that Hannah Glasse's *Art of Cookery Made Plain and Easy*, published in 1747, contained a recipe 'to make a curry the Indian way' as well as for making 'a pellow' (*pilau*), further demonstrates that Indian cuisine was sufficiently well known to be included in an eighteenth-century cookbook.[11]

INDIAN SERVANTS IN BRITISH HOMES

Another distinguishing feature of nabob life was the presence of their Indian servants and ayahs. In his study of continental and colonial servants in Britain, Hecht has implied that the custom of importing Indian servants began in the eighteenth century, a thesis largely accepted by other historians.[12] But there is evidence to suggest that the custom may have begun a century earlier. Among the burial notices for the parish of St Botolph without Aldgate, 1618, mention is made of 'James (an Indian) servant to Mr James Duppa Brewer'. Further, from a small sample of the parish of St Olave, Hart Street, between 1638 and 1682, three baptisms and two burials of 'Indians', among them the 16-year-old Chirugeon, and a woman, Loreto, are revealed. The City of London, the heartland of the EIC, might be expected to show traces of Indian servants. But elsewhere, in Greenwich for instance, there are stray entries of baptisms and burials of Indians in the parish registers of the seventeenth century, including 'Sampson Samuell, an Indian' buried October 1680.[13] Another curious entry, the marriage of 'Samuel Munsur a "Blackamore" to Jane Johnson' at St Nicholas's Deptford, in 1613, might well be that of an Indian, giving us the first reference to Indian family life in seventeenth-century Britain. The Company Court Books for 1690–1702 contain several applications from EIC employees to return their Indian servants and ayahs in Company ships.[14] Another early piece of evidence is Peter Lely's *Lady Charlotte Fitzroy*, painted about 1672, which shows Charlotte, then aged eight, being offered grapes by a boy, identified by Professor J.D. Stewart as an Indian. This may well be the first portrait of an Indian page in England. Occasional advertisements seeking 'run-away Indian boys', like the one in *The London Gazette* for November 1685, for a 14-year-old 'Indian boy' with 'strait black hair', called Calib, too, testify to the presence of Indian servants in the seventeenth century.[15]

By the eighteenth century, the custom of employing Indian servants and ayahs in British households had become firmly established. For instance, in 1753, even before accumulating his legendary fortune, Clive, on a visit with his wife Margaret Maskelyne, was accompanied by his two Indian servants. Warren Hastings and his wife imported four maids, and two Indian boys, aged 13 or 14, described by one German visitor as having 'longish faces, beautiful black eyes, fine eyebrows, sleek black hair, thin lips, fine teeth, a brownish complexion and kindly intelligent faces'. Their four maids were sent back for refusing 'to work any harder than in India' and wanting to lead 'exactly the same life'.[16] Officials with lesser fortunes, too, imported their Indian servants. William Hickey, on a visit to London in 1780, brought his 'little pet boy', Nabob, and in 1808, he returned with the 13-year-old 'faithful little Munnoo', whose doting mother had only been induced to part with him after a payment of Rs 500. Munnoo accompanied Hickey into retirement at Beaconsfield, where, under an 'anglifyed' name, William Munnew, he was baptised. Claud Russell of Edinburgh brought back two Indians, a butler and a steward. Families, and even women, brought their personal maids with them. Fanny Burney, writing to Mrs Lock in 1789, described the arrival at Godalming, Surrey, of 'several post chaises containing East Indian [English] families with their negro [Indian] servants, nurses and children'. She considered their 'inhuman voices and barbarous chattering' unlike anything she had ever heard, but nonetheless felt sorry for these 'poor negro women' taken away from their own country. Their isolation and homesickness would account for the fact that one of them was seen on the stairs 'in tears'. Kitty Johnson attended Eliza Fay on her return from India, while a Mrs Gladwin, returning from Bengal on account of her ill health, was accompanied by two maids, who, it was later alleged, had poisoned her.[17] In 1784, a Captain Baker of the East India Regiment, on his return to Cork, Ireland, brought back with him Dean Mahomed, who had first entered his service as a youth of 11 in 1769.[18] Mahomed would later become famous as the 'Shampooing Surgeon to George IV' (see p. 37). But such fame was achieved very rarely and by very few. The majority of Indian servants in Britain simply eked out their anonymous existence.

Since domestic service was one of the largest classes of occupations in eighteenth-century Britain, why import Indian servants? Like their African counterparts, Indians served broadly similar functions. First, there was the practical aspect of convenience. Since the voyage home round the Cape of Good Hope was long and arduous, lasting six months or more, personal servants were essential to attend to the needs of the family on board the Indiamen. Second, children were often sent home for their education in the company of trusted Indian servants. William Thackeray, the writer, came home from India as a child, in 1817, accompanied by his 'Calcutta serving-man'. Then there were other reasons. The novel, *The Nabob at Home*, depicts a surgeon, after 30 years service in Lucknow, old and lonely, living in retirement on the family estate in Fernebraes, Scotland, with his old Indian servant.[19] A work of fiction, it nonetheless hints at an important reason for bringing Indian servants: a reluctance to leave behind a favourite, loyal servant, familiar with the routine and ways of the master. After years in India and returning to a changed Britain, the servant would be the one familiar figure round the nabob. Nostalgia for life in India might also be another reason. Then there was the economic aspect, a desire to enjoy the same cheap labour that had been available in India. But the most important reason was their value as an 'index of rank'. Just as having French servants reflected taste and status, Indian servants were a symbol of the exalted status of the newly enriched India-returned nabob. According to Mirza Itesa Modeen (I'tisam ud Din), a traveller to Britain in 1765, even the mere company of an Indian dressed in oriental clothes could add to the reputation of a man.[20] In an age when things oriental were desirable fashion accessories in the homes of the rich, Indian servants in their gorgeous costumes, added to this sense of oriental luxury. The presence of Indian servants and ayahs in eighteenth-century portraits of families who had made their careers and fortunes in India visibly emphasise this relationship.[21] Moreover, Indians were seen as exotic. William Hickey's 'little pet boy', Nabob, for instance, being 'an interesting looking handsome boy', must have cut a dashing figure when dressed in smart clothes as a hussar. No wonder he was such a 'little pet' with all the ladies. The strikingly beautiful faces of the Hastings' servants, too, must have drawn attention.[22]

How widespread the practice had become by the eighteenth century is seen from the fact that in a single year, 1771, for the two months of April and May, the EIC received 18 applications from its employees to return their servants to India: 15 of these were male, and 3 were females.[23] How long they had been in England is open to conjecture as no information is provided. Some Indian servants were sent back when no longer required, but an unknown number remained as personal servants. Numerous advertisements in newspapers of the eighteenth century record their lives in England. In 1750 an East Indian, fluent in six languages, including Portuguese and German, and who had been 'Christen'd according to the Establishment of the Church of England', was seeking employment as a footman. In 1775, an Indian servant aged 20, who had lived in Britain for 12 years in 'his present place', was advertising to serve 'any genteel family'. Another, in the same year, was looking for service as a footman with a single gentleman or in a small family. His list of accomplishments included shaving and dressing hair. He could 'read, write, and understand common accounts, clean plate and furniture well [and] look after a saddle horse or two'. In 1776 a native of the East Indies, experienced as a footman, and having an understanding of 'the nature of a table', was seeking a place 'to wait on a single gentleman or a family'. Having lately returned from America, this East Indian had no objection to travelling abroad. And in 1777, a 22-year-old, brought from Bengal by a gentleman whom he had served for 15 years in Britain, was seeking employment as a footman with 'any person of quality on reasonable terms'.[24]

Parish registers reiterate the same story. Parish records also tell us the areas where Indian servants lived, and, by inference, the favourite haunts of the India-returnees. Cities like Edinburgh, Cheltenham and Bath have already been mentioned. In London, it is highly probable that Indian servants were as familiar in East London as in St James's and the Mall or Marylebone. Gravestones in churchyards bear witness to the fact that many Company agents retired in the East End, forming a visible presence. Places like Stepney may be poor today, but in the eighteenth century these areas were gentrified and desirable residences, and it was this that attracted the India-returned nabobs. A random search of parish registers illustrates the point: the presence of Indian servants in places as far apart as Tooting, Marylebone, Whitechapel, Greenwich, Lewisham and Essex.[25]

Indian servants and ayahs were also popular with families going out
to work in India: many advertising for them in newspapers of the time as
maintaining English servants in India was expensive. Custom required
they be given their own attendants and accommodation. Besides, they
did not always prove reliable. Women servants left to get married, while
the men went off to set themselves up in trade. Their unfamiliarity with
the climate, the country and its customs, too, could be a trial.[26] The
status of the ruler over the ruled would be another factor in deterring the
employment of whites as the servant class in India. Indians, on the other
hand, were less expensive, had become accustomed to English ways and
whims, and knew India.

Sometimes, Indian domestics themselves sought placements with
families going out to India. In 1795, for instance, a woman servant from
Bengal, who had worked for a total of ten years for the mistress she was
leaving, two in India and eight in Britain, advertised to return to Bengal
with any family going out. A woman of many skills, she could 'dress
hair, cook plain victuals, make bread, wash well' and look after
children, as well as speak French, having served her mistress for a year
in France. The advertisement made clear the reason for her leaving: 'she
does not quit her place for any fault, but because it no longer suits the
Lady to keep her …'. Indeed, Indian servants of both sexes sought
positions with families going to India.[27] The reasons for their willingness to return home are not far to seek: Hecht suggests 'Nostalgia or
homesick longing' as the reason.[28] But that may provide only a partial
explanation. Lack of security and an unwillingness to be dependent on
those who had brought them may have been a far more important factor.
Other reasons, too, may account for Indian servants' eagerness to return
to India. An analysis of advertisements shows that they generally fall
into two categories: those looking for a position as a valet or as a lady's
maid to those going out, and those signifying a willingness to attend on
the passage without wages (customary for travelling servants and
ayahs). The servants in the second category might have been those
employed for the duration of the voyage only. Once in England, they
may have found that a return passage had not been provided, as is
suggested in the application from a man servant 'just arrived in England,
entrusted with the care of two children' and looking for a means of a
'speedy return' to India.[29] Working a passage home may have been
preferable to being destitute in Britain.

An important aspect in this complex web of importing Indian
servants to Britain was the practice of employing them for the duration
of the voyage home. Travelling servants and ayahs were indispensable
on the voyage. Once in England their engagement was over, and they

were returned to India at the expense of the family.[30] By the middle of the eighteenth century, however, an increasing number of families were discharging their travelling servants on arrival in Britain, leaving them to fend for themselves. Abandoned and destitute, they were forced to beg for a passage home, as the following letter from 'Truth' shows:

> ... but the number of those poor wretches who are daily begging for a passage back, proves that the generality of those who bring them over leave them to shift for themselves the moment they have no further occasion for their services. Many of them, I am informed, have been in England two or three years; and some of them must for ever remain here ...

In reply 'Oriental' disputed 'Truth's' facts, asserting that all Indian servants were provided with return passages. Notwithstanding such protests, evidence weighs in favour of 'Truth' as letters from the Court of Directors suggest. After several petitions for a passage home in Company's ships from 'forsaken' servants in destitute circumstances, the Directors had been forced to 'prevent reflection on us in this respect from the people of India', to provide passages at their expense. In order to save the Company any future expense, the Directors ordered that a bond of £50 be provided as a surety before any Indian servant was permitted to leave India.[31] But this measure failed to provide the desired security as, in 1782, the Company again complained to Madras that it had been 'put to considerable expense'. In a strongly worded letter, the Company tried to discourage the practice of sending Indian servants to Europe. Failing that, a bond of security must be obtained for their maintenance and repatriation. In 1783, regulations for the proper treatment of Indian servants and lascars (seamen) taken abroad came into force in India. By this edict, no servant or lascar was to be received on board a ship without proper indemnification bonds against the possibility of them being left destitute and becoming chargeable to the Company.[32]

Such regulations proved ineffective. Servants and ayahs employed for the duration of the voyage lacked any security: there were no contracts of employment. Some could even be dismissed and stranded during the journey, never reaching England.[33] Others were discharged on arrival and left to find their own return passage with another family. While awaiting re-engagement, they lived in squalid lodging-houses and were grossly exploited. This would explain why servants and ayahs became destitute long before they found a passage back and had to resort to begging. By the middle of the nineteenth century, concern for the ayahs would lead to the founding of the Ayahs' Home (see p. 51).

STATUS OF INDIAN DOMESTICS IN BRITISH SOCIETY

As personal servants Asian domestics may have led comfortable lives in the homes of rich nabobs. Treated as 'pets', they may have been pampered and well looked after. Some, like Hickey's Munnoo were even sent to school.[34] But evidence also suggests that they led lonely and rather sad lives, while their position in society remained lowly. The Indian page, Bimbi, brought to Britain by the Countess of Londesborough, throws some light on their lives. Whenever she gave a dance at her mansion in Mayfair, Bimbi would 'stand, in his native robes and high pink turban, on one of the landings of the marble staircase, directing the guests in the manner of an eighteenth-century page'. The life of Julian, another servant, further illustrates this. Stolen from his parents in Madras while still young, Julian was brought over by a Captain Dawes, and presented to a Mrs Elizabeth Turner, who, apparently, according to the records, treated him with 'the greatest Tenderness and Kindness', often calling him in 'to dance and sing after his Manner' in front of her guests. At 16, and said to be still retaining 'his *Pagan* ignorance in respect to our religion and our language', Julian finally decamped with 20–30 guineas, leaving a burning candle under the sheets, firing the house. Not much imagination is needed to work out the motive for this act of resistance. Julian ended his life on the gallows at Tyburn. Instances of cruel treatment were not unknown.[35]

Legally, the position of Indian domestics remained murky. As personal servants were they free or mere property? Like their African counterparts, Indians were sometimes publicly sold. An advertisement in 1709, in Steele's and Addison's *Tatler*, read: 'A Black Indian Boy 12 Years of Age, fit to wait on a Gentleman, to be disposed of at Denis's Coffee-house in Finch-Lane near the Royal Exchange.' Some rare advertisements even show Indian domestics with slave collars, while in a case that came up in Dublin in 1770 (*Armstrong v. Coffee*), the plaintiff charged the accused of 'stealing away his servant or slave, an East India Black'.[36] At baptism (which also implies prejudice against the 'heathen') Indians were sometimes given their masters' names with the words, 'belonging to', as: 'Peregine Hector, an Indian boy from Bengal. About 8 years old and belonging to the Countess of Abingdon. Baptised 19 December 1700'. They could be given away as presents as in the case of Julian, while Nabob was a present or a loan to Hickey from John Lewis Auriol.[37] All this would lead to a conclusion that Indian servants were treated more like property. This is reinforced by an advertisement in 1775 from a 'Slave Girl' brought from the East Indies whose mistress, 'having no occasion for her will give her over to any

Lady to attend her in the passage to India and to serve her for three years after the arrival there without wages, provided the Lady engages at expiration of the term to give her freedom'.[38]

Servants often ran away and the many 'hue and cry' advertisements in English and Irish newspapers would suggest that the only remedy for these aggrieved slave/servants was to abscond, some even taking their livery with them. In 1685, a Bristol man offered a reward of 20 shillings for his 14-year-old runaway 'Indian Boy'; in 1702, another was searching for an 'Indian Black' servant 'with long hair' called Morat, aged 15 years, who had absconded from Westminster. There had been sightings of the runaway in Hampstead, Highgate and Tottenham. Another advertisement, for an 'East India Tawny Black' was issued in 1737, and yet another tried to find a 'Run-away Bengal Boy' in 1743. In 1772, Thomas Hornsey, 'a Black, a Native of the Coast of Malabar' ran away from his master's house in Epsom. He was reported as having offered himself as a servant to several gentlemen in areas as far apart as Highgate, Deptford and London. In 1767, the *Dublin Journal* advertised for 'a mulatto East India Boy', eloped from Eyre Evans Crow at Aughrim near Ballinasloe, and in the same year the *Belfast Newsletter* was looking for a 'black boy', native of Bengal. In 1795, the *Morning Chronicle* carried the following notice from a Mrs Ramus in connection with her 14-year-old

> Black Servant Boy, a native of Bengal, called by the name of HYDER did on the eighteenth of this inst. February, leave the services of Mrs Ramus, no. 58, Baker Street, Portman Square, and had taken with him his livery and other apparel, the property of his mistress – This is therefore to forewarn all persons from hiring the said Hyder, or harbouring him in any manner as they will be prosecuted for the same as the law directs ... [39]

As for the working and family lives of Indian servants in Britain, very little is known. Those released, or left in freedom after the death of the family who had brought them, and runaways, would have continued in domestic service. Their range of skills and expertise as valets, footmen, cook, maids and nursery maids would have been a factor in their employability. Further, we know of a 'Gentoo coachman'.[40] But there are scant other records. Seafaring, if available, would have been another sector of employment open to these working-class Indians. Those who fell on hard times would have survived on the margins of society. Poor law records shed some light here. In 1770, John Thomas, described as a 'Gentoo' and brought to England by Captain Morris(on), is shown as having applied for relief in Greenwich. Some would have turned to begging or crime. The case of one Indian beggar, a sailor, so successful that he has become legendary, is recorded in an 1814–15 *Report on the State of Mendicity in the Metropolis*. A half-penny ballad seller, his takings from begging allowed him to 'spend fifty shillings a week for his board; he would spit his own goose or his own duck and live very well'. Some others were self-employed. Granee Manoo, for instance, sold old shoes.[41] There are other tantalising glimpses. The author of a manual on domestic servants described 'the wonted haunts of Moormen and Gentoos', which suggests that Indian domestics had their own meeting places.[42] As to their numbers, however, no contemporary estimate is available.

The fact that Indian servants were able to find employment not only implies their employability, but one might also infer from this that little hostility against them existed from within the servant class, as in the case of European domestics like the French. One writer suggests that the 'key to social security or advancement' in Georgian England was not based on skin colour, 'but the status and favour of one's master and patron'. As far as the Indian servants are concerned this might well be the case as there is no evidence to show that the hostility against the nabobs for their rapacious activities in India or their ridicule in the contemporary press, rubbed off on their servants.[43]

BRINGING CARGO HOME:
SAILORS WHO FILLED THE GAP

As a maritime country, India had a long tradition of seafaring and Indian seamen were well known for their skills. Portuguese accounts tell us that Vasco da Gama hired an Indian pilot at Malindi on the east coast of Africa, to steer the Portuguese ship across the Indian Ocean to the Malabar coast.[44] It is therefore not surprising that Indian seamen, lascars, came to be employed in naval and commercial vessels by European powers trading in the east. The Portuguese had a long tradition of using lascar crews on their ships.[45] When and in what numbers the EIC first began employing lascars on board its home-bound ships is unclear. According to Section 7 of the Navigation Acts in force from 1660, the master and 75 per cent of the crew of a British registered ship importing goods from Asia had to be British, thus restricting the number of lascars employed in European waters (i.e. west of the Cape of Good Hope). Some historians have assumed that lascars did not serve in Europe-bound ships in 'any appreciable numbers' before 1780, and have labelled them 'new arrivals'.[46] However, despite restrictions, between 1685 and 1714 it would appear that the number of lascars in Company ships was already higher than envisaged: each ship employing between 2 and 20. If one takes the Company directive of a vessel of 100 tons having a crew of 18 men, and another 5 for every additional 50 tons, the number of lascars being shipped was quite considerable.[47] In fact, by 1730, in the face of their mounting numbers in the Company's chartered ships, even exceeding the 25 per cent limit set by the Navigation Acts, and steady complaints from lascars, the Company urged its commanders to draw up contracts with their lascar crews, preventing them from being set adrift in England, and the Company having to shoulder responsibility for their maintenance and return to India. But even this did not prevent lascars being left in England without provision. By 1765, an Indian visitor to Britain noted that the English were not 'unacquainted' with 'Chatgaon [Chittagong] and Juhangeer Nuggur lascars', confirming the trend in the numbers employed, and stranded in London.[48] Two important points emerge from the complaints to the Company by stranded lascars. First, their ability under their *serangs* (boatswain) to organise in order to recover wages due to them and to press the Company to provide for them. Second, since lascar petitions sometimes reached as high an authority as the King himself, and the fact that the sight of lascars roaming the streets of London begging, cast 'great reflections' on its reputation, the Company was forced to take action to save its own political and economic standing, to deter lascars from 'making further clamour'.[49]

How had the need for lascar labour in Europe-bound ships arisen? Initially, the need arose because of the high sickness and death rates of European sailors on India-bound ships, and their frequent desertions in India, which left ships short of crew for the return voyage. Desertions became more prevalent once sailors, attracted by better prospects, began to join the armies of Indian princes. Obtaining a fresh supply of English sailors in India was expensive, costing 50–70 per cent more than sailors recruited in England.[50] And so, in order to bridge the labour gap, the custom of employing some lascars among the predominantly British crews began. Another reason was war. During the Napoleonic Wars, for instance, conscription of British sailors by the Royal Navy was particularly heavy from Company ships in India. Lascars were, therefore, recruited in larger numbers to supplement the European crew. Further, the requisition of Company vessels by the government as auxiliary ships led the Company's administration in India to allow private 'Country' ships to bring rice and other commodities to Britain. ('Country' ships, owned by British and Indian merchants engaged in the burgeoning 'Country' trade all over Asia, were crewed entirely by lascars, and hitherto not allowed to come to Britain and break the monopoly of Company freighted ships.) Between 1799 and 1800, 20 such 'Country' ships left for London, increasing the number of lascars employed.[51] The 'shipping interest' of the Company's chartered ships hated this and attempted to put a stop to it. As late as 1802, successive British governments forbade the employment of lascars on ships sailing west of the Cape of Good Hope, while the EIC itself, in 1808, possibly in response to the riot in 1806 between 200 lascars and Chinese sailors in Angel Gardens, Wapping, resolved that no lascars or Chinese were to be taken on Company ships.[52] Despite this, because of the war-induced shortage, by 1813, six times more lascars were brought to Britain as substitute crew than at the beginning of the century (in 1803, 224; in 1813, 1,336).[53]

With an end to the Napoleonic Wars, the 1814 regulations introduced for the registration of India-built ships decreed that 'no Asiatic sailors, lascars or natives of any territories ... within the limits of the Charter of the East India Company, although born in territories ... under the Government of His Majesty or the East India Company, shall at any time be deemed or taken to be British sailors'. The Regulation is significant: it excluded Indian seamen from British citizenship for the purpose of Navigation Acts, preventing the employment of all-lascar crews on ships bound for Britain.[54] In 1813, when the Company's Charter was renewed, faced with the continuing agitation from merchants, Parliament stripped the EIC of its monopoly of trade with India. And it was free trade, coupled with steam power, which ultimately proved crucial for the employment of lascars. As trade expanded and India became increasingly central to Britain's global trade and economy, lascars became the mainstay of the labour force in British-registered ships bound for Europe. Yet lascars have not received the place they deserve in studies of British maritime history.

CONDITIONS OF LASCAR LABOUR

Following the EIC directive in 1730, the Company's freighted ships began signing agreements with their lascar crews. Much valuable information is obtained from one such surviving document, *Articles with Lascar Crew on Tryal*, 23 October 1746, signed on behalf of the EIC by John Foster, President and Governor of Fort William in Bengal with the crew of 21 Indians, all from Calcutta, and all with Portuguese-sounding names. Their employment package included a monthly wage of Rs 15 (£1. 17s. 6d.) for the voyage from Calcutta to London, a weekly maintenance allowance of 7 shillings each in London, pending a return passage to Calcutta, and a requirement to perform duties in London as directed by the Company. Finally, lascars were bound by a promise not to remain in England once a return passage had been arranged for them.[55] But because of the nature of the Company trade, an imbalance of exports from Britain against imports from India, lascars were forced to remain in England for long periods of time before ships were ready to take them back. Two important facts arise: the first concerns responsibility for the provision of their maintenance in England pending a return passage. Was responsibility ultimately vested in the Company or the owners of chartered ships? This was to prove contentious, leaving lascars destitute, as will be seen. Second, the provision of a return passage, and repatriation of destitute Asians became part of Company policy, and would endure. In time successive laws made the policy stricter to prevent lascars settling in Britain.

Lascars were recruited in gangs through an intermediary, called the *ghat serang,* who, in the realm of Indian shipping, occupied a position akin to that of a labour agent, a lodging-house keeper and a money lender. The *ghat serang* made his own bargain with individual seamen for their services. The *serang,* who owed his job to the *ghat serang,* was responsible for lascar welfare and discipline and wielded tremendous influence. The whole system was so riddled with corruption, as each in turn made his profit from bribes and commissions at the expense of the lascar, that the amount received by the poor lascar was reduced to a 'mere pittance'.[56]

In 1783, under the Ordinances issued for recruiting and fixing the wages of 'native' seamen employed on 'Country' ships, Hastings attempted to reform the Indian system of labour recruitment. A western-style registration office was set up for lascars to sign on. Wages were fixed and paid directly to individual lascars through the registration office agent, cutting out the middleman. But the well-intentioned reform had to be repealed as it ran into difficulties from the vested interest of the *ghat serangs,* while in London, the Court of Directors, too, considered the regulation inconvenient and expensive for Europe-bound chartered ships, risking delay and the possibility of not obtaining good seamen.[57] And so the eastern system endured well into the twentieth century. As to their wages, a first-class lascar received much less than an equivalent British seaman, who, according to one ship-owner, earned between £4 and £5 a month on average during the Napoleonic Wars.[58]

LASCARS IN ENGLAND

In eighteenth-century England, according to one historian, lascars were 'in a more unfortunate position than the Negroes'. The extent of lascar distress and exploitation is described by one witness in 1757:

> The public has seen here some of them miserable objects about the streets of London, begging charity, and exposed to all the distress incident to persons so far remote from their native country, friendless and abandoned, for want of knowing the laws and customs here ... rendered them a prey to all the little low designing people, amongst whom their station in life and misfortune has cast them away.[59]

In the 1780s, public attention focused on the lascars as they roamed the streets of London looking for subsistence. In 1782, several who had been hired by Danish ships arrived from Denmark, presumably encouraged by the owners, and having 'been reduced to great distress', applied to the Company for relief. The Company, forced to foot the repatriation bill, complained bitterly to the President and Council at Fort St George, Madras, urging action to prevent future 'like inconvenience'. Then, in 1784, 'naked, pennyless and almost starving in search of subsistence', poverty-stricken lascars made their way from the riverside slums of Wapping, Shadwell and Poplar to the common lodging-houses in St Giles. A 1784 pamphlet, protesting about the beggars of Westminster and drawing attention to the particular plight of the lascars and their 'feeble but interesting efforts' at finding subsistence, commented: 'Their situation is as singular as it is deplorable; they have been brought into this country as the friendly assistants of natives ... [and] ... have been left a prey to melancholy and distress.'[60]

What had led to their destitution? Foreign shipping, as in the case of Denmark, was obviously one factor. The EIC, too, blamed foreign ships, prompting one correspondent, 'Humanus', to urge the Company to use its powers to stop 'foreign' captains dumping lascar crews in Britain, while at the same time imploring the public's charity. Others claimed that the lascars had been brought to England by the navy and blamed the government for neglecting them. In fact the Committee for the Relief of the Black Poor in 1786 counted 23 lascars brought over in the 'King's ships'.[61] But the most important factor was the question of responsibility for their maintenance in England. The EIC no longer built its own ships, but, from 1639, chartered vessels for its trade with India. Disputes frequently occurred between ship-owners and the Directors over the extent of their responsibility. The Company claimed that it looked after its lascars. After several negative letters in the press, a correspondent under the pseudonym 'Veritas', informed the public that the Company provided accommodation specially 'appointed for that purpose' in Stepney. He also claimed that lascars awaiting a return voyage received an allowance of 1 shilling a day.[62] Whatever the merit or otherwise of such claims, when disputes flared up, lascars, caught in the middle, were invariably the worst sufferers. Without maintenance, shelter or prospect of ships to return them to India, they were left destitute. Their poverty was further compounded by ship-owners who cheated them of their wages as seen in the 1785 case, when Soubaney and four other lascars successfully sued William Moffatt of Queen Square, 'managing owner' of the *Kent*, for a balance of wages owed to them since July 1784. Although Moffatt tried to evade responsibility by claiming he was not the sole owner, he was eventually forced to withdraw, the court awarding each of the lascars £20. 10s. These lascars were unusually lucky.[63]

Without networks, ignorant of the English language and customs which would have given them some prospect of employment, and unable to get parish relief as they did not come under the existing framework of Poor Laws, which arranged for the return of the pauper to his parish of settlement – and lascars were between voyages – they were forced to beg, 'in silent attitudes and gestures more eloquent than language'.[64]

By March 1785 their number must have risen, as a letter from 'Sennex', expressed shock 'at the number of miserable objects, Lascars', seen shivering and starving in London. He appealed to the 'good Mr Hanway' and other well-known philanthropists to promote a subscription to help these 'fellow creatures ... dragged from their warmer and more hospitable climates by our own avarice and ambition'. Several letters in a similar vein appeared in newspapers throughout December, some considering their abject misery a 'disgrace to humanity' and reflected 'the utmost discredit to a country universally distinguished for its humanity' and a reproach to the 'unsullied honours of Britain'.[65]

By the winter of 1785/6, the condition of lascars reached crisis levels. Without warm clothing – 'these wretched mendicants are in rags!' is one description – lodgings or provision, several lascars died. Ship-owners often skimped on lascar clothing. Joseph Emin, an Armenian, who worked his passage to England as a 'black lascar', records receiving only 'four shirts and four coarse drawers to wear in all weather'. The crisis prompted one newspaper to urge the public 'to consider their hard fate', and provide for their relief. Such sympathetic public reaction suggests that lascars were seen as deserving of charity. Correspondent after correspondent mentioned that they did service by navigating 'our vessels' trading in the East Indies; they were without adequate clothing and were strangers in a rich country.[66]

Nine months after concern first surfaced, on 5 January 1786, *The Public Advertiser* reported that a 'Quartern Loaf' was being provided to every distressed 'Asiatic Black' from the premises of Mr Brown, the baker, in Wigmore Street, Cavendish Square. And on 7 January, a subscription for their benefit had begun. Initially, the *ad hoc* Committee of Gentlemen aimed to provide temporary relief only. But the public's generosity prompted them to go 'much further', in order to prevent future suffering and a meeting was called for that purpose at Mr Faulder's in Bond Street. This was the background to the formation of the 'Subscribers for the Relief of the Distressed Blacks' (i.e. lascars). By 12 January subscriptions were being collected at four places in the City.[67]

Who were the 'Gentlemen' behind this initiative? They included businessmen of 'considerable standing in the world of finance', philanthropists like Jonas Hanway and MPs.[68] The majority of the subscribers were rich, but donations also came from the clergy, as well as ordinary people, male and female, some anonymously, all contributing their 'mite'. Subscriptions poured in, amounting to a total of £890. 1s. by 4 April 1786, when the appeal was wound up. Begun as a charity to help distressed lascars, by 16 January, the Committee having learnt of a 'considerable' number of African and West India blacks, it widened its scope to become the Committee for the Relief of the Black Poor.[69]

Who were the Black Poor? First there were the Asians: the lascars and servants abandoned without a return passage (the Company's bond scheme notwithstanding) and found 'daily begging for a passage back'. Second, the blacks: seamen discharged in Britain, the former (now free) slave-servants of planter families and the Black American Loyalists.[70] Humanitarian instincts aside, it is likely that the public's generous financial response had been prompted by the presence of black American Loyalists who had fought with Britain. One contemporary noted: 'the *Lascars* and other East Indian mendicants demand our pity only; but the *African negroes* have an actual claim on our justice … '. [71]

THE BLACK POOR:
WHATEVER HAPPENED TO THE LASCARS?

In their accounts of the Black Poor and the Sierra Leone Settlement scheme of 1786–7, organised by the Committee for the Relief of the Black Poor with financial support from the government, historians have tended to concentrate on the blacks of African descent, arguing over whether they were passive victims of a racist deportation, or whether they had a say in 'determin[ing] their own destiny'.[72] The 'Asiatic Blacks', whose destitution had first led to the setting-up of the Committee and a handful of whom were also transported to Sierra Leone, have received a passing mention only. But in the surviving records of the Committee and in contemporary newspapers, lascars are present and we learn something about their response to the Sierra Leone resettlement scheme, their relations with the Africans as well as the attitude of authority and the public.

Of the 250 Black Poor initially found to be in need of charity, only 35 were from the 'East Indies'. By April 1786, when the appeal closed, a total of 460 Black Poor had applied for relief. How many were lascars is not recorded. But the type of relief provided gives an indication of the extent of their destitution during the winter of 1786: food (distributed from two centres) and clothing – shoes, stockings, shirts, trousers and jackets. A hospital, with the necessary bedding and medicines, was set up and a place 'with straw and blankets' was made available for those needing lodgings. Some were kitted out for employment as seamen.[73]

But, as the Committee itself had realised, relief was no answer to the problem of black poverty. The solution, however, was suggested by some of the Black Poor themselves who expressed a wish to return to Nova Scotia or Halifax. From then on the Committee, too, appears to have embraced the idea of an overseas settlement, in 'some parts of his Majesty's Dominions' best suited to 'their constitutions'. At the same time, the Committee publicly announced that such a step would 'effectually relieve' the Black Poor, and simultaneously render 'considerable advantage to the Police of this country', a motive which appears suspect.[74] But whether the Committee really believed this, or used it to attract funds, is open to question. At this stage, though the lascars are not mentioned, it is assumed that the plan applied to them too.

In April 1786, when the Committee closed its appeal, the government became involved in the project. From then on, relief to the 'Blacks and People of Colour' came from the treasury in cash payments, of 6d. a day. By May 1786, 347 people had received daily cash payments, among them several lascars. By then, Henry Smeathman's scheme for the settlement of the Black Poor on the coast of Sierra Leone, first proposed to the Committee in February 1786, had been accepted, both by the Committee and the government. Preparations commenced with speed. By then, it was also understood by the Committee that the daily cash relief would only continue until such time as the recipients commenced on the voyage. This already implies conditionality. But as to whether the Black Poor themselves were aware of this or not, the minutes are silent. The Smeathman Memo, too, envisaged overseas settlement as 'removing such a burthen from the Public for ever'.[75] Since lascars were in receipt of the daily 6d., they too would have been included in the Sierra Leone resettlement plan. Such an assumption is confirmed in the Committee's proposal to divide the blacks into companies of 12 persons each under a chosen man, designated as a corporal, who could 'write or give account to our clerk by memory', and the list to include such details as ethnic origin (mulatto, East Indian), birthplace, medical record (e.g. smallpox), gender, length of time in Britain and the mode of arrival, as well as the allowance paid by the Treasury.[76]

Of the eight headmen (corporals) selected by Hanway, one was John Lemon, a 29-year-old Indian, born in Bengal. A hairdresser and cook, he had come to Britain as the captain's cook 'of a King's ship'. Lemon, together with three other headmen, was literate. As 'the most intelligent among the Blacks', headmen were responsible for the 'steadiness and good behaviour' of their company. Supervised by the clerk, they were responsible for payment of the daily allowance,[77] and on them depended the orderly organisation of the motley crew of the Black Poor. They also assumed the role of spokesmen for the Black Poor, as demonstrated when a disagreement arose between the Committee and the government on the one hand and the Black Poor on the other over the suitability of Sierra Leone as a destination, as it was notorious for slave trading. The blacks were only prepared to go to Sierra Leone provided they were given 'some instruments' to guarantee their liberty. It was at this juncture that Hanway is reported to have 'formed them into a ring and harangued them', to convince them of the government's 'pure and benevolent intentions'. Whether the 'Instruments of Agreement' given a 6d. stamp for 'legal sanction as ... a pauper's Indenture' legally entitled the Black Poor to a long-term guarantee of freedom is debatable. At the meeting where the Instruments were discussed and at which their representatives were present, 'a ninth man, said to be a person of weight among the Blacks left the room saying he would consider it'. But the other eight headmen approved it as 'the fairest and most just agreement that were made between white and black'.[78] This would not be the only time when the headmen, including Lemon, would act on behalf of blacks and people of colour.

Following the sudden death of Smeathman in July 1786, serious doubts arose over the suitability of Sierra Leone and the Committee chose the Bahamas. But now it was the blacks who remained steadfast to Sierra Leone. On 15 July, the Committee received a petition from the corporals on behalf of 'upwards of 400 people', informing them that the Black Poor viewed the prospect of being sent to the Bahamas with 'considerable unease' and that 'no plantation would be agreeable to them as Sierra Leone'. Of the 15 signatories to the Petition, John Lemon's name heads the list. This suggests that Indians, too, favoured Sierra Leone. It further suggests amicable relations between the Indians and the Africans, the Indians not seeing themselves as a separate group. It also shows a decision-making process involving a dialogue. This assumption is supported in a report of the Committee which informed the Treasury that the East Indians 'seem disposed to mix with the Blacks and to accompany them to Africa in case their Lordship should have no objection'.[79]

A list ordered by the Committee in July of 'Asiatic Blacks', with details of their age, employment and when and how they had come to Britain, with a view to communicating it to the EIC and the Navy Board, has not survived. But available information gives a total of 50 Indians among the Black Poor: 23 of whom had been brought over 'in the King's ships', another 23 in Company ships and 4 in 'foreign ships'. Their length of stay ranged from 2 to 4 years. Some, however, had lived in England for 8 years, others for 24.[80]

Why did lascars choose to go to Sierra Leone? The 'Back to Africa', appeal would not have cut much ice with them. The prospect of land and a better future might be one reason. Smeathman, after all, had painted a very rosy picture. Another reason could be the length of time spent away from India. Others, like John Lemon, the headman, were married to white women and a re-entry into India might not have been easy.[81]

By the end of October 1786, two ships, the *Belisarius* and the *Atlantic*, were ready. New agreements were signed with Joseph Irwin and the Black Poor, described as 'seamen, labourers and of various other descriptions' who had received 'charity from the humanity of British government' and 'in consideration of the several sums of money' and other 'Emoluments Liberties and Privileges', agreed to go as settlers to the 'Grain Coast of Africa'. A total of 675 names are recorded. Included is John Lemon (Leman), the headman. Several other lascars, only distinguishable by their Portuguese-sounding names, include Domingo Anthony, Emanuel Pardo (Parado), Anthony Sylva, Thomas Sylva, John Manuel, Joseph Domingo, Besantee Sylva, Martin Sevvantus and John Baptiseter.[82]

But embarkation was slow (only 259 by 22 November), further delayed by alarms over rumours that the Black Poor were destined for a penal colony. As weeks went by frustration mounted. On 6 October 1786, the Committee resolved that no further relief would be given to those who had signed the agreement. There are hints, too, of threats to induce them to embark on pain of being charged under the Vagrancy Act. On 14 December the Committee placed advertisements in the press, urging the public to 'suspend giving alms to the said persons, in order to induce them to comply with the engagements ... entered into'.[83]

December 1786 saw lascars once again 'on the point of perishing' begging in the streets of London, their 'emaciated figures' again rousing public concern. One correspondent wrote that from his conversation in Portuguese with 'two bare-footed' and almost naked lascars, he had concluded that 'some of them [were] quite ignorant of the arrangement' to send them 'to their country'.[84] On 1 January 1787, *The London Chronicle* reported that the Mayor had given orders 'to take up all the blacks ... found begging about the streets ... that they may be sent home, or to the new colony ... in Africa'. On 3 January the *Public Advertiser* went one better. It suggested that magistrates in Westminster, Middlesex and Surrey 'imitate' this measure. Recommending 'hard labour in Bridewell' instead of 'mere confinement in a gaol' for blacks found begging, the paper pronounced its view: 'The blacks, especially those of the East Indies, are naturally indolent ... '. Notwithstanding, blacks and lascars continued to roam the streets, begging. In the meantime, on 1 January 1787, an 'East Indian', employed by the Company as an interpreter, was sent to inform the magistrates at the Guildhall that the lascars seen begging around the City had, by the Company's orders, been put on a ship bound for India 'last year'. But 'because they would not go, they jumped overboard, swam to shore, and made off'. It was alleged that 'the great encouragement' given to these beggars by the public 'induced' them to remain in England. The Company spokesman claimed that he had himself seen them 'count over the money' at their lodgings at Saltpetre-bank, money amounting to 'six or seven shillings, and sometimes 10 shillings six pence a day'. The Company absolved itself of any blame and responsibility, as the lascars 'would not return when they might'.[85] Since ships arrived regularly from India bringing fresh crews, the question arises, especially in view of the fact that some lascars were unaware of the Sierra Leone scheme, whether those found begging in December 1786 had been in receipt of the bounty or were in fact new arrivals.

Finally, after a five-month delay, frustration, illness, difficulties and disagreements on board, 441 emigrants, black men, women and children; white men and women, and a handful of lascars sailed for Sierra Leone. White women, wives of lascars, included Elizabeth Lemon, Sarah Parad (Parado?) and Mary Dominic (Dominico?).[86]

Towards the end of May 1787, the settlers arrived in Sierra Leone. But a sad fate awaited them. In the words of Equiano:

> ... they reached Sierra Leone just at the commencement of the rains. At that season of the year it is impossible to cultivate the lands; their provisions therefore were exhausted before they could derive any benefit from agriculture; and it is not surprising that many, especially the lascars, whose constitutions are very tender, and who have been cooped up in ships from October to June ... should be so wasted by their confinement as not long to survive it.[87]

Another source, dated 30 December 1788, by Captain Thompson who had accompanied the settlers, shows that a few lascars, like their black colleagues, ran away; some died, while a minority, including John Lemon and Elizabeth Lemon, were still alive.[88]

Were the Black Poor 'ejected' from the country in a hurry? The balance of evidence suggests otherwise. The problem of lascars is more complex. As a matter of policy and for political reasons, 'to prevent reflections on us ... from the people of India', the Company, as a last resort, repatriated destitute Indians. Further, under the 1783 Regulation, the Company's administration in India insisted on 'proper indemnification bonds' for a return passage to prevent lascars (and Indian servants) remaining in Britain and being thrown on the Company's charge.[89]

Pending a return passage, lascars had to be maintained in Britain. The EIC claimed that responsibility lay with the ship-owners and the Company took charge only in case of 'necessity'. It also claimed that prior to 1795, 'the owners of the Company's ships were allowed £1 per ton' for the maintenance and return of lascars.[90] From 1795, however, as a result of complaints from the lascars – and from the public that lascars were not kept under control – the Company, concerned 'only' for the welfare of the lascars and the public's convenience, took over responsibility. Two procedures were introduced: first, instructions were drawn up for commanders of Europe-bound ships concerning lascar diet (rice, dal, spices, vegetables), medical care and clothing (two pairs of jackets and trousers, mittens, caps, shoes and bedding of three blankets sewn together). Second, premises were contracted in East London to house them. By 1801, during the Napoleonic Wars, three premises were used: Kingsland Road in Shoreditch, Hackney Road and Shadwell. However, complaints from the magistrates regarding 'the nuisance' caused by lodgings lascars 'so near the city', led to their removal to Shadwell. A medical officer, Hilton Docker, was also appointed.[91]

Did such regulations improve lascar life aboard ships? Indirect evidence suggests otherwise. Lascar sickness and mortality rates remained high. The first set of statistics relates to the 'Country' ships, wholly crewed by lascars, and allowed to bring goods to Britain during the Napoleonic Wars. The returns to the Bengal Board of Trade, dated 1800, reveal that of the total crew of 287 lascars on three ships, the *Cavera,* the *Gabriel* and the *Calcutta,* 73 died on the voyage to England, and 11 on the return voyage; 22 were discharged sick in England, while 36 deserted. Thus 145 lascars, just over 50 per cent, returned home to Bengal. In another instance, Joseph Hume, the surgeon on the *Houghton,* which left England for Bombay, in June 1799, complained that the ship was crowded, with 223 lascar passengers, 'many of them ... in a dangerous situation', suffering from fever, flux and venereal disease; others 'with ulcers on different parts of their body which remained obstinate ... '; 14 died during the voyage. Concerned at the high mortality rate among lascar crew, upwards of 50 per cent, on return voyages, William Hunter, the surgeon of the Company's Marine Establishment in Bengal, wrote a long essay to 'rescue' lascars from ravages of disease.[92] Further evidence, relating to the Company's own chartered ships, for the years 1808 and 1814, confirms the trend of lascar mortality and sickness arising out of neglect and mismanagement. In 1808, of the 86 lascar crew on the *Lucy Maria,* 22 died on the voyage, and 20 arrived sick in England, while in the case of the *Surat Castle,* which left India carrying 123 lascars, 36 died during the voyage, while 45 were landed sick in England. Six years later, in 1814, by which time Parliament had compelled the Company to take responsibility, records paint a dismal picture. The *Wellington,* which left Bombay with a crew of 71, recorded 4 deaths on the voyage, while 16 had to be sent to hospital in England. The resident surgeon at Gravesend reported that 'the whole number of sick in this ship are afflicted with berry-berry ... three of them have died since arrival in the Downs, and two or three others are beyond all human aid'. Had the ships been delayed any longer in the channel, then 'more than half of the crew would have been incapable of duty from this disease'. The burial notices of lascars in parish registers bear further witness to their treatment on board.[93]

Sickness and mortality rates were not the only indicators of the evasion of 1795 regulations. The 1802 report on two 'Country' ships, the *Union* and *Perseverance,* detailed such shocking treatment of floggings, beatings and ill-usage of their lascar crews that the Committee of Shipping could not 'help shuddering at the ... inhumanity' of those in charge. On the *Union,* a ship of 750 tons crewed with 74 lascars, 28 died during the voyage and several others arrived in England in a 'deplorable state of health'. The atrocities perpetrated on the orders of the captain on three lascars, Bolla, Boxoo and Dena, were such as never seen before on any ship, stated one witness. All three died. The ship had no surgeon or medicines. Without proper berths for lascars they were accommodated under the forecastle, and were continuously wet from the spray. The men on the *Perseverance* had fared little better: 14 out of 21 were found to be sick on arrival in Greenwich, 10 apparently so ill as to be incapable of any duties. Diet must have been inadequate, since Docker reported that lascars on the ship 'were absolutely starving for want of food'. Ship-owners often provided unsuitable diet: in the case of *Fort William,* Docker blamed sickness on the men 'having lived an unusually long time on rice, dall, ghee and salt fish'. No wonder then lascars deserted, both on the way and in England. Such desertions may account for the tiny sprinklings of lascar settlements in the islands of the Indian Ocean, and in Britain.[94]

Did lascars fare any better in England? Their barracks, described as of the 'lowest type', were according to Docker, in 1809, 'unwholesome' and because of overcrowding 'at the worst season of the year', he feared a high death rate. Although no direct evidence of lascars in the premises for the period 1795–1814 is available, the fact that a bill was rushed through Parliament without debate in November 1813, to compel the Company to provide for lascars, suggests that the Company's own arrangements had failed. Under the 1814 Act, no ship with a lascar crew was permitted to leave without a bond for their support until they were returned to India. It also empowered the Company 'at the ultimate expense of the owner of ships' to repatriate lascars left behind.[95]

But theory and practice did not match. As numbers rose towards the end of the Napoleonic Wars, by as many as 1,600 per year, overcrowding led to indiscipline and fighting. Some lascars were sucked into the criminal underworld of the East End of London. A trawl through the Old Bailey Sessions Papers reveals names of convicted lascars – Nowardin (Nur al-Din), Sack Mahomet, Sheikh Brom, Abdulah, Enacoe Caetano, Albion Gummes (Gomez?), Louis Francisco and Emanuel Antonio. As Duffield has shown, some were even transported to Australia. Historians who have analysed crime patterns suggest that the percentage of black crime was no higher than white crime, and the types of crimes were similar: poor people's crimes.[96] In winter the death rate in the barracks shot up, one estimate before 1810 suggests 130 died in Britain each year, while the lascars claimed the figure was double that. Another estimate was one per day. During the severe winter of 1813, nine died in a single day.[97] Reports that lascars were 'ill used' and underfed began to circulate. Information reached the Society for the Protection of Asiatic Sailors (set up in 1814), who began systematically collecting evidence. The Society met a lascar cook whose back bore marks of deep lacerations from a recent flogging. When the Company was informed of lascar complaints, the Directors 'resolved to send the grumblers off' by the first ship available. Such reaction was not new. In January 1712, the Company had ordered that two complaining seamen, a *serang* and a *tindall*, were never to be employed again on their ships.[98] The Society applied to visit lascar barracks, but access was only granted after several refusals. They met with a sorry sight:

> ...people were ill-fed and badly treated by a person (a superior lascar) who had command of them, both as to food, clothes and settling disputes among them. He frequently whipped them ... The buildings ... were like warehouses, very dirty, and ... without pavement – the floor consisting of earth ... There were two or three large cupboards of the height of sentry boxes.

When these were opened, 'out came a living lascar', put there for 'quarrelling and bad behaviour'. The Society's visit must have worried Docker because, while he wrote that he did not doubt the Society's 'benevolent' intentions, he nonetheless insinuated that their information was 'mainly, if not entirely, collected from the discontented and criminal' element among the lascars, so casting doubt on their credibility. The Society publicised their findings in *The Times,* and their report was sent to the government, and the Directors of the EIC.[99] The result was a Parliamentary Committee of Enquiry to investigate the workings of the 1814 Act.

The Committee made a surprise visit to the barracks and concluded that, although not crowded at the time of their visit, the barracks could in no way accommodate the 1,000–1,100 who were arriving regularly, with any degree of 'comfort, health and cleanliness'. They found the rooms dirty, without any bedding or furniture. Lascars slept on the floor. There were no fireplaces and the men received only one blanket each. The Committee learnt that stoves were provided for heating during the winter. What struck them most was the total absence of any accommodation for the sick: instead they saw 'several sick [men] ... lying on the floor, covered only by a blanket or rug, in a room which was open to the yard, and exposed to the entrance of all the persons in the barracks'. The Company justified such neglect, giving the excuse that the sick themselves objected to being separated, and that they 'will persist in laying or sitting on the floor, reclining against the wall, or a chest'. The Committee rejected this as 'a sufficient reason'. As for their diet, the Committee recommended replacing salt fish with fresh, 'so abundant in London as to be the cheapest article of animal food'. As regards the death rate, despite the Company's own admission that during the severe winter of 1813–14, five had died in 24 hours during one very cold day, and at least two per week was the usual average, the Committee concluded that the mortality rate was 'peculiarly small'.[100]

The Committee also accepted that the Company provided adequate clothing and bedding, but the lascars invariably sold these, exposing themselves to the rigours of winter. No one bothered to ask why lascars found it necessary to sell their clothes. To overcome demoralisation brought on by long periods of idleness, the Society for the Protection of Asiatic Sailors recommended that the Company provide temporary work. But the Directors justified their policy on the failure of a single experiment in the Rope Ground, in 1810. They also alleged that lascars were not inclined to work and lacked physical strength. But the crucial reason why no employment was provided had nothing to do with lascar character: 'there being always in the metropolis a far greater number of English and Irish labourers than find constant employment, consequently the employing of these men would be to the prejudice of our native population'. The Society's complaints of the way *serangs* maintained discipline was explained away, first, as being similar to shipboard discipline; second, as being more acceptable to lascars, since it had been arranged amongst themselves. Further, the Company painted an alarmist picture of what would result if the *serangs'* authority was 'annihilated': 'the evil' would then spread to the neighbourhood and courts would be overwhelmed. They even hinted that already, as a result of the Society's interference, the magistrates were finding how troublesome 'the natives of India [had become] ... to civil power'. Both the Company and the Parliamentary Committee took refuge in stereotypical explanations. The Directors blamed lascar promiscuousness and their 'native habits' which were 'so repugnant to Englishman's ideas of comfort', while the Committee attributed the clean and airy lodgings of the Chinese to the 'different character of the nations and habits', and not on overcrowding. Of the Asian sailors employed in British Merchant service, 60 per cent were lascars, 20 per cent Malays and only 10 per cent were Chinese. Finally, concluding that the 'greatest defect' in the existing system of managing lascars was a lack of a 'regular authority', the Committee saw a need for greater control, with policing powers, to prevent lascars leaving their barracks 'by day or night'.[101]

The Committee made four recommendations. First, given the large numbers, it considered the method of contracting individuals to house lascars as outdated. Instead it recommended setting up a 'regular establishment', strengthened by legal powers for better care and efficient policing of lascars. Second, it recommended relocating lascar barracks, away from the 'populous part of the town', to the area of the

docks. Third, it suggested keeping regular records of the numbers
arriving and leaving Britain, both in London and at the outports. Fourth,
ship-owners were made financially responsible for repatriating lascars
left behind. As for the authority of the *serangs* in the barracks, or the
method of recruitment in India, while the Committee considered the
system 'capable of improvement', it did not find cause 'to be
dissatisfied with the conduct of it'.[102]

The direct outcome of the Parliamentary Committee of Enquiry was
the 1823 Merchant Shipping Act ('Lascar Act'), which re-confirmed the
racial division between British subjects first introduced in 1814, that for
the purpose of the Navigation Acts, lascars were not British citizens.
The 1823 Act also abolished the system of bonding. Instead, any lascar
convicted of vagrancy was to be repatriated by the Company, and
reimbursed by ship-owners responsible for bringing the lascar to
Britain.[103]

The effect of the 1823 Act was to place lascars at the bottom of the
imperial hierarchy of maritime labour. According to several contemporary commentators, no similar enactments applied to 'the Krooman of
Africa ... the Negroes of the West Indies, and ... all other colonial
subjects', who were regarded 'as much British Seamen as a white man
would be'.[104] The racial division had several consequences: first, lascar
wages remained far below those received by British and other colonial
seamen. Second, lascars could not be discharged in Britain, but were
paid off in India. Further, as Dixon pointed out, because the 1823 Act
was not repealed until 1963, the legal minimum standard of
accommodation for lascars on board ships, their contractual position and
diet scales lagged far behind those of white seamen.[105]

What lay behind such a discriminatory treatment of lascars in law?
Contemporaries claimed that it was designed to protect lascars. They
claimed that the Act was passed in the 'spirit of humanity', the 'simple
confiding character of the Hindoo' making it necessary for legislation to
intervene on their behalf in a way 'no other class of our fellow subject'
required. They claimed that lascar constitutions were 'unfitted' to
withstand the winter cold, that their 'nature and habits' were formed in
warmer climates, and they made excellent sailors, but in hot regions
only.[106] No one, however, looked at the evidence on their own doorstep:
Indian servants in British households. Further, there were alarmist
claims that if lascars were discharged in Britain, they would become a
drain on the poor rate and the charity of the public. And if the public or
private charity did not provide for them, they would 'starve and die in
the streets'.[107] Finally, contemporaries claimed that ships crewed by
lascars sailed at 'a cheaper rate than a British ship', but only so long as

they remained in warmer climates. They claimed that since lascars did not possess 'the stamina of a British sailor', in colder seas more lascars were needed, as many as double the number of whites, adding to the expense. One witness to the Parliamentary Committee put the cost of victualling a ship crewed by Europeans at £1. 10s. per head per month, while lascar food, though costing only 6d. a day, 15s. a month, worked out more expensive because of the greater numbers employed. And yet, the same witness had complained that a European crew in Calcutta cost between 50–70 per cent more in wages than the wages current in England.[108]

But such claims to humanitarian motives do not really stand up. The main reason appears to be partly economic protectionism. As Hepple points out, the roots of discrimination lay in the 'relative cheapness per head' of lascars in the eastern seas. As early as 1711, one contemporary writer expressed his fear of competition on the Cape route. According to him, the 'most pernicious project' was 'such as learning the Moors the way about the Cape of Good Hope, which I look on as a blot, that, once hit, would give them a great deal of trouble to remove'. He warned merchants to be 'cautious, how they bring home the ships with lascars'.[109] There was also a political motive. The EIC's concern for its standing in India has already been noted. As the Company rule expanded and more of India came under British rule, the political motive of maintaining British prestige became even stronger, as illustrated in a letter from Henry Dundas to the Committee of the House of Commons. Recommending some means by which this 'feeble race' of Indian sailors might be prevented from being brought into the western world, he declared:

The contemptuous Reports which they disseminate on their Return, cannot fail to have a very unfavourable influence upon the Minds of our Asiatic Subjects, whose Reverence of our Character, which has hitherto contributed to maintain our Ascendancy in the East (a Reverence in part inspired by what they have at a Distance seen among a comparatively small society, mostly of the better ranks, in India) will be gradually exchanged for the most degrading conception; and if an indignant apprehension of having hitherto rated us too highly, or respected us too much, should once possess them, the effects of it may prove extremely detrimental.[110]

Ranked lower in the hierarchy of the imperial seafaring community, how were lascars seen by the public? As one source suggests, in London's working-class neighbourhoods diverse groups of people mixed freely together: at the All-Max Coffee House 'colour or country

considered no obstacle ... everybody free and easy ... The group motley
indeed – Lascars, blacks, jack tars, coal heavers, dustmen, women of
colour, old and young, and a sprinkling of remnants of once fine girls ...
all jigging together.'[111] But reality was somewhat different. An ambivalent attitude to lascars emerges. On one level, there was concern and
sympathy for the distressed lascars. On another, they were regarded as
'naturally indolent' and entirely 'destitute of moral capacity'.[112]
Criminal records provide an indication of the attitude of authority.
Interpreters were provided in court. But how low was the opinion of
some is seen in a comment by the magistrate, following licensing
scandals of public houses in Tower Hamlets: 'little good can be done by
taking away the licences of the houses in Shadwell for this reason, that
the population consists entirely [clearly an exaggeration] of foreign
sailors, Lascars, Chinese, Greeks and other filthy dirty people of that
description'.[113] Christian bodies, though concerned for their welfare,
saw lascars as the heathen other. In an address, highlighting the
'spiritual' state of lascars and Chinese, at a general meeting of the
London Missionary Society in 1814, for instance, lascars were described
as 'extremely depraved', idol worshippers and:

> deluded followers of the licentious doctrines of a false prophet ... a
> prey of each other, and of the rapacious poor ... of our most
> abandoned country women. They have none ... who will associate
> with them, but prostitutes ... no house that will receive them, except
> the public house and the apartments of the abandoned.[114]

As non-Christians, Asians were rated low according to western values
and civilisation.

How many lascars were brought to Britain? Any attempt at
estimating numbers is fraught with difficulties as no official data on a
regular basis exists, despite instructions from the Directors of the
Company to ships' commanders. A contemporary source, estimating
that 2,500 lascars visited England every year, 'expected [their numbers]
to be doubled' in the future.[115] The 1814–15 Parliamentary Committee
of Enquiry put the figure much lower, 'less than 1,000–1,100'. The only
reliable figure, 1,336, is for 1813, during the Napoleonic Wars. For
1814, Docker put the figure as 'near 1600', while another source
reckoned that 'there were 2,000 ... in the Company's boarding-
houses'.[116] Speculation is only replaced with certainty for the two years
between July 1821 and June 1823. In the seven ships that arrived
carrying lascar crews, of the total of 621 seamen, only 91 were British
and 21 foreign (other Europeans). The rest, 509, were lascar crews,
making 84.8 per cent lascars to 15.2 per cent British sailors.[117] By the

1850s, of the 10,000–12,000 lascars and Chinese seamen employed for service in the 'Country' trade, 50 per cent, 5,000–6,000, were brought to the United Kingdom every year. Of these, 60 per cent were Indians. This demonstrates how high the reliance on lascar labour was becoming in the age of British industrialisation, global trade and imperial expansion. With the opening of the Suez Canal and the coming of the steam-powered liners, the demand for lascar labour would increase even further.

VISITORS, EMISSARIES AND TEACHERS

Servants and sailors aside, other Indians to come to Britain during this period included individuals of diverse backgrounds and social origins. The reasons for their coming also varied. In 1723, the Parsi, Naorozji Rastamji, son of the factory broker, Rastam Manak of Surat, came to make a claim to the EIC against their factory agent in Surat. His mission was successful.[118] Some other early visitors were educated Muslims. Mirza Itesa Modeen came on a political mission in 1765 as an emissary of the Mughal Emperor Shah Alam, to get the support of King George III against the Company. Muhammad Husain, in 1776, came to learn western advances in astronomy and anatomy, while Mirza Abu Talib Khan, from Lucknow, was on a private visit. Between 1799 and 1803, he travelled around Britain and Ireland, and was lionised by upper class society. Munshi Ismail was brought to England in 1772 by Claud Russell, an employee of the EIC in Bengal, as his personal *Munshi* (teacher). All these scholar-travellers have left written accounts, which provide valuable information and rare insights into how educated Indians viewed British society of the time.[119] A record of a different kind comes from another educated Muslim visitor, and is in the form of an engraving of the view of the City of London. No name or other details of the visitor survive, but from the comments written in Persian, concerning the dimensions of St Paul's cathedral, Blackfriars bridge and wages of ferrymen on the Thames, calculated in *huns*, a coinage current in South India, historians have identified him as coming from the Carnatic region.[120]

In 1781–2, Ragunath Rao, the deposed Peshwa of the Marathas and an ally, sent his three agents, Humund Rao, a Hindu Brahmin, a Parsi, Manuar Ratanji and his son Cursetji Manuar, to seek military assistance from the EIC. One of them, Humund Rao, gave evidence to a Select Committee of the House of Commons in February 1781. The 'three ambassadors from India', in the words of the *Morning Herald,* were dressed in 'long rich habits, over which they wore a fine muslin in the form of a child's frock; their heads were covered with shoals [sic], the

corners of which fell on their shoulders'. Edmund Burke accompanied
them into the House of Lords. The newspaper report described the
scene: 'they were introduced to the upper part of the House and stood by
the fireplace to see his Majesty. The Indians bowed to the King most
respectfully.'[121] Their mission, however, was unsuccessful, and from the
correspondence of Burke, who befriended them, we learn that the
Company's treatment of them was shabby, 'unworthy of ourselves, and
unbecoming of their commission'. Burke even gave the Brahmin
sanctuary in his greenhouse at Beaconsfield, so that he could observe
religious and cultural rituals without constraint.[122]

Rammohun Roy (1772–1833), from a land-owning Bengali Brahmin
family, was the first Hindu of 'intellectual consequence' to visit Britain
in the nineteenth century.[123] A linguist, social reformer and one of the
pioneers of Indian journalism, Roy was selected by the Mughal Emperor
Shah Akbar II as his unofficial emissary (and given the title of raja).
Accompanied by his son Rajaram and two servants, Rammohun Roy
came to represent the Emperor's cause in London, to appeal for a more
generous rise in his annual stipend. But Roy's visit in April 1831 was
more than just a diplomatic mission. At a time when the EIC's Charter
was due for renewal, he submitted a memorandum representing Indian
views to the Parliamentary Committee on Indian Affairs. A campaigner
against *suttee*, Roy successfully argued his case before the Privy
Council for the retention of the 1829 legislation abolishing the practice.
That Roy was a man of wider concerns and interests is seen in his
enthusiasm for the 1832 Reform Bill. He hailed its success as 'the
salvation of the nation', proclaiming that he could 'now feel proud' of
being a British subject. He was enthusiastically received in Britain.
Presented to William IV, and seated amongst the foreign ambassadors,
he witnessed the coronation in Westminster Abbey. London society
lionised him. Lucy Aikin of Hampstead described him as a 'friend and
champion of women'. In Manchester, 'the great unwashed' rushed in
crowds to see 'the King of Ingee!' In early September 1833, Roy visited
Bristol to meet his Unitarian friend Dr Lant Carpenter. He made a deep
impression on Mary Carpenter, his daughter. This is seen from her
interest in Indian education and women. She visited India four times and
in 1870 the Bristol Indian Association was founded. Roy died in Bristol
in September 1833. The *Chattri* in Arnos Vale cemetery marks the spot
of his burial.[124] In London, a blue plaque marks the house in 48 Bedford
Square where he stayed.

Other Indians in this period worked in a professional capacity. There
are references to musicians employed by the Company to perform at
dignified gatherings at India House and to interpreters. After the death

of Rammohun Roy in 1833, his son, Rajaram, worked as an 'extra clerk' at India House for three years.[125] Then there were Persian language teachers. Claud Russell had engaged Munshi Ismail. In 1777, a London newspaper carried an advertisement from Moonshee [sic] Mahomet Saeed, 'teacher of the Persian and Arabick Languages'. Saeed had originally 'attended the Hon. Mr Frederick Stewart in that capacity'. For those aspiring to high office in India, knowledge of Persian was desirable, and employing personal teachers was, therefore, not uncommon. Once the Company opened its College, Haileybury, at Hertford, *munshis* like Mirza Khaleel began to be employed on a regular basis as teachers of Oriental languages.[126]

INDIAN WIVES AND CHILDREN

Another group during this period were the Indian wives and the children of English men. The Indianisation of nabobs in India did not stop at mere adoption of Indian habits and an interest in Indian culture and languages. One or two even became converts to Islam and Hinduism. Many others married or lived with Indian women. This was particularly the case during the seventeenth and eighteenth centuries. It was said at the time that every one of the Company's factories was 'surrounded by a ring of native substitutes for English wives and a swarm of Eurasian children'. The Society for the Promotion of Christian Knowledge put the annual number of births of Eurasian children in Madras and the Coromandel Coast at 700.[127] European 'adventurers' like Reinhardt and de Boigne, who commanded armies in the service of independent Maharajahs, also took Indian wives.

Indian wives sometimes accompanied their husbands back to England. Mention is made of a 'black Portuguese', wife of a Mr Peacock travelling on the same ship as Mirza Itesa Modeen. Colonel John Cockerell brought back his Indo-Portuguese wife, Estuarta. He may have initially planned to live with her at his estates in Sezincote, but this never came to pass. Even his will deprived her and her children of all claims to the Cockerell estate. But Estuarta remained under the guardianship of the family, sometimes staying with John Cockerell's sister, Elizabeth and her husband John Belli, in Southampton, where Colonel Cockerell often visited her. She was also, on occasion, seen as the guest of S.P. Cockerell in London.[128] Then there was Hélène Benoît (Bennett), the wife of General Benoît de Boigne, and the sister of *Bibi* Faiz Baksh, a Begum of Oudh and the 'dear companion' of William Palmer. In 1797, Benoît brought Hélène and their two children, Banu Jain (baptised Ann) and Ally Bux (Charles Alexander) to London. But

before long he had deserted her for Adèle d'Osmond, the daughter of
the French ambassador, and went to live in Savoy. Hélène Bennett
continued to live at their house in Enfield, north London, where Abu
Talib Khan visited her during 1801–2. After the death of her daughter,
Hélène retreated to the country, at Lower Beeding in Sussex and lived in
a cottage called Great Ground House. Little is now remembered about
her life, except that she smoked long pipes, wore magnificent rings, was
a devout Catholic and was 'exceedingly good' to the poor. She died in
December 1853, aged 81 and is buried in Horsham parish churchyard.
Hélène Bennett is said to be the Indian woman the poet Shelley referred
to as the lady wandering in the Forest of St Leonard.[129] Another Indian
wife of a European in London was Mrs Ducarel. The extent of her
European lifestyle and acculturation is seen from Abu Talib Khan's
comment that she was so 'accomplished in all English manners and
language therefore I was sometime in her company before I could be
convinced she was a native of India'. Her two children lived with her.[130]

The children of these unions, usually regarded as part of the family,
were often sent to England for their education. Jane Cumming Gordon,
the natural child of George Cumming Gordon and his 15-year-old
Indian mistress, was probably the first Anglo-Indian child in a Scottish
school. Brought to Britain after the death of Gordon by his mother, Lady
Helen Cumming Gordon, she was placed at a boarding school in Elgin
in 1804. In 1809, the 14-year-old Jane, described as 'a dark-skinned
girl, a native of India', was moved to a girls' school in Edinburgh, to be
near her grandmother. Here, in company with other students, Jane
achieved some notoriety when she became involved in a lengthy
lawsuit, arising out of an accusation against two teachers of having an
indecent relationship. What happened to her after this brief moment of
fame is unknown. John Campbell, the son of a Bengali mother and
Scottish father, was educated at Tain and Aberdeen University. He
returned to India as a missionary to the Bhowanipore Institution in
Bengal run by the London Missionary Society. 'Mr Tommy', the son of
Panna Begum and Colonel Pearse, was sent to England for his education
after his father's death. Whether 'Mr Tommy' is the same as
'Muhammad' in the Harrow school register is not clear. Colonel Green
of the Bengal Artillery had his two Indian sons educated at the Academy
in Canterbury. Many other Anglo-Indian sons attended Tait's School, in
Bromley-by-Bow, East London.[131]

How did eighteenth-century British society view such cross-cultural
marriages and their children? One American visitor to London,
describing the fact that one 'occasionally' met 'genteel' young ladies
born in London walking with their 'half-brothers', or 'more commonly'

with their nephews born in India, wrote: 'These young men are received into society and take the rank of their fathers ... It would seem that prejudice against colour is less strong in England than in America.'[132] To read into this observation that British society, at any rate compared to the American one, was free of colour prejudice would be to misread the Indian context and the complex attitude to colour in contemporary British society. This is evidenced by an exchange of letters between Hastings and William Palmer. Writing to Hastings, Palmer, who could mention the progress of his own 'natural children' without any embarrassment, commented that the two children of 'Julius' (whose case Palmer was dealing with at the time), who were 'almost as fair as English Children', were being sent to England for their education, while the third, though strong, was 'too dark to escape detection' and would be educated in Bengal.[133] A contemporary work of satire further illustrates English society's complex and ambivalent attitude to these children: 'Mind Old Pagoda the Nabob, with his piebald family. I wonder how much he will give [his daughters], those dingy devils *set in diamonds* there. They'll doubtless fall to the lot of some dished [bankrupt] guardsman.'[134] A combination of fair skin, the wealth of a nabob father and a claim to descent from Indian aristocracy, could allow them to win a place in English high society.

A fate of a different kind awaited the majority, who stayed in India. They were consigned to 'the life of clerks' in the lower ranks of government service, as second-class whites. A few managed to make a name for themselves: James Kyd, the ship-builder, Colonel James Skinner of Skinner's Horse, Charles Pete, the artist and H.L.V. Derozio, the poet.[135]

By the early nineteenth century, thus, a transitory and a small settled population of Indians formed part of British society. Thanks to official reports, like the 1814–15 Enquiry, something is known about the living conditions of transitory lascars in their London barracks. But little is recorded about the family and working lives of the settled population. One individual, Dean Mahomed, however, stands out. Mahomed's remarkable career in Britain, where he lived for nearly three-quarters of a century, gives us unique insights into how one early Indian immigrant managed to find a place for himself and his family, first in Georgian Ireland and then in England.

SAKE DEAN MAHOMED (1759–1851)

Born in Patna, Bihar in 1759, Dean Mahomed, according to his own account, came from an elite Muslim family, being related to the Nawabs of Bengal and Bihar, his ancestors having risen in the administrative service of the Mughal emperors. Faced with the altered state of politics in mid-eighteenth century Bengal, according to family narrative, the 'only refuge' for such Muslim families was to seek service, however 'lowly', in the Company's Bengal Army. In 1769, aged 11, Mahomed fulfilled his early ambition to enter a 'military life' when he joined Godfrey Baker, an Irish Cadet, as a camp follower, rising rapidly, first to the position of Market Master in 1781, then *Jemedar* (ensign) and finally *Subedar* (captain).[136] Such rapid promotion hints at Baker's patronage, whose own fortunes, too, rose. As part of Baker's battalion, Mahomed saw action (e.g. against the Marathas) and took part in several battles (e.g. against Cheyt Singh), which extended the Company's domination over India, a process completed during Mahomed's own lifetime.[137]

In 1782, Mahomed resigned from the Army to accompany Captain Baker to Ireland. What motivated him to abandon his career? According to his own testimony, curiosity to see 'that part of the world' and his conviction that without 'his best friend' he would 'suffer much uneasiness of mind' prompted him to accompany Baker. This suggests that the decision was his own. At the age of 25, in September 1784, Mahomed arrived at Dartmouth to start a new life in Britain.[138]

For the first several years Mahomed lived in Ireland with the Baker family, in a prosperous part of Cork, on the South Mall. His position in the Baker household is not recorded. His biographer suggests that he was 'most plausibly' a 'manager', 'not a servant in livery, but not an independent gentleman either'. An advertisement from Mahomed in a London newspaper, in 1813, in which he advertised his skills in 'marketing ... and conducting the business of a kitchen' confirms such an assumption.[139] Of Mahomed's life in Cork, very little is known except for a brief account from Abu Talib Khan's visit in December 1799 to the Baker household, where he met Mahomed. We learn that Mahomed was sent to school to learn English and where he met a young woman, 'known to be fair and beautiful', the daughter of 'a family of rank of Cork', with whom he eloped to another town, returning to Cork after their marriage. This was Jane Daly, whom he married in 1786. According to Abu Talib Khan, the Mahomeds had 'several beautiful children ... a separate house and wealth'; Mahomed had published a book, giving an account of himself and the customs of India. Inter-religious marriages would have been difficult enough in Ireland, requiring a bond, but inter-racial marriages would have been most unusual at this time. Negative images of Islam and India current at the time would have informed British consciousness.[140] How did Jane's family see their daughter's marriage? One can only speculate, but their elopement hints at a measure of opposition. Further, the absence of any likely Daly name in the official list of subscribers to Mahomed's book also hints at lack of support. But from the account of Abu Talib Khan there is no doubting that Mahomed had retained the patronage of the Baker clan.[141]

In 1794, Mahomed's book, The *Travels of Dean Mahomet,* written as a series of letters to an imaginary friend, was published in Cork. Written in the genre of eighteenth-century travel writing and for an audience of Anglo-Irish with India connections, seen from the subscribers' list, the narrative demonstrates how well he had mastered the English language and style. Mahomed's *Travels* is unique for several reasons. It is the first book to be written and published in English by an Indian. As a historical document, it provides a valuable 'Indian voice', describing India's conquest, which Mahomed witnessed as a member of the Company's army, and another version of the conquest, different from existing European accounts. Mahomed also describes the physical landscape of India, its cities and towns as well as Indian society, and Muslim life as an insider, giving us an Indian perspective to set alongside European contemporary accounts.[142]

Around 1807–8 Mahomed arrived in London. When exactly and why at 48, having lived in Cork for 25 years, he left Ireland is not recorded. The birth of his daughter, Amelia, in August 1808, locates Mahomed in London's Portman Square, a fashionable area and a haunt of India-returned nabobs. Here, Mahomed first found employment with a rich nabob, Sir Basil Cochrane, who had set up a vapour bath establishment in his huge mansion in Portman Square. Mahomed is said to have added an Indian treatment, 'shampooing' (*champi*) or therapeutic massage, to Cochrane's vapour bath, a treatment that would later make him famous in Brighton, under the name Sake Deen Mahomed.[143] But before that, he embarked on a different independent career, as a proprietor of the Hindoostanee Coffee-House.

The Coffee-House, established in 1810, at 34 George Street, Portman Square, is perhaps the first example by an enterprising Indian of economic survival through ethnic 'cultural entrepreneur-ship', as the advertisement in *The Times* illustrates.[144] Aimed at Anglo-Indians, Mahomed offered them the enjoyment of Hookha, with 'real chilm tobacco', and Indian dishes, 'in the highest perfection, and allowed by the greatest epicures to be unequalled to any curries ever made in England', in a setting decorated with Indian scenes. Thus, Mahomed sold what whites could not offer, authentic Indian taste in an oriental atmosphere. Further, his appeal to the wealthy 'Indian gentlemen'

[Anglo-Indians] shows that Mahomed's success was dependent on their patronage. The Hindoostanee Coffee-House must have attracted enough support for Mahomed to expand into 35 George Street. Given the strict licensing laws, managing a restaurant would not have been easy. Building up a loyal clientele, too, takes time. Coupled with that, breaking into an established market would have been difficult, regardless of how 'novel' his idea. It is also possible that Mahomed over-reached himself by too rapid an expansion; his 'purse' was not 'strong enough to stand the slow test of public encouragement', and he was forced to declare bankruptcy in the *London Gazette*, 1812. However, the Hindoostanee Coffee-House, furnished with 'Asiatic embellishments', offering 'dinners in the Hindustanee style', and other refreshments in 'the same genre', made enough of an impact on some Londoners to merit a mention in the nineteenth-century version of the *Good Food Guide, The Epicure's Almanack,* long after the Coffee-House had closed down.[145]

Having fallen on hard times, Mahomed advertised, in 1813, for a situation as a butler or valet, adding that he had 'no objection to town or country', in order to increase his employability. His son, William, aged 16, a postman in London, could not have earned enough to support the family. By then Mahomed was past middle age, and starting afresh could not have been easy. Is it any wonder then, that this painful episode has not been mentioned in any of his subsequent writings, except obliquely and in the most general terms as 'reverses ... attended with all the uncertainty, and precarious circumstances of struggling fortune'. The only direct mention, of 'the breaking of his Banker' comes to A.B. Granville much later, and Granville, who knew Mahomed in Brighton only, assumed it referred to his bank in Calcutta.[146]

Around 1814, Mahomed arrived in Brighton as a 'shampooing surgeon' at the Devonshire Place bath-house, possibly as a result of his advertisement. The date can be inferred from two sources: a testimonial from a grateful patient, dated 10 November 1814, and the baptism record of his daughter Rosanna, March 1815.[147] In Brighton Mahomed achieved fame.

Brighton at this time was a growing and fashionable health resort. Its population, about 2,000 in 1750, had grown from 4,000 in the 1780s to over 7,000 by 1801, and would shoot up to 65,000 by 1850. It attracted numerous visitors. The coming of the railway made Brighton accessible, drawing crowds from London and elsewhere. Significant among the reasons for its growth were the popularisation of the health-giving properties of sea bathing (and sea-water drinking) in the medical writings of Dr Richard Russell, and the patronage of the Prince of Wales

(King George IV), reflected in the building of the Royal Pavilion. As the fashion for sea bathing took off, many indoor (cold and hot salt water) baths were established, the first by Dr Awister in 1769.[148] Long before the arrival of Mahomed and his family, Brighton boasted a variety of bathing establishments, offering different cures.

Here Mahomed set up his own distinctive establishment: the Indian Vapour Baths and Shampooing Establishment. As with the Hindoostanee Coffee-House, he found a new way to cultural entrepreneurship, trading on his Indian-ness, emphasising the Indian qualities of his Medicated Vapour Bath: the use of special Indian oils in shampooing and herbs for the bath 'brought expressly from India'. Mahomed claimed that he was the first to introduce shampooing in Britain and his treatment was more powerful and 'superior' to other remedies for rheumatic aches and pains, and he alone, 'a native of India', possessed 'to an eminent degree' the art of shampooing. At Mahomed's Baths patients first lay in a steaming, aromatic herbal bath; having sweated freely, they were then placed in a kind of flannel tent with sleeves. They were then massaged vigorously by someone outside the tent, whose arms alone penetrated the flannel walls.[149]

At first he met with scepticism and ridicule. His son, Horatio, writes that there was 'tremendous opposition, the public press teemed with abuse, the medical faculty shook their heads and doubted' while 'ninety-nine in a hundred of the public at large' considered the cure to be nothing more than 'a cheat and a Hindoo juggle'. Undeterred, Mahomed offered to treat patients for free, and it was only after 'several gratuitous cures' to patients who had failed to respond to other treatments that interest was aroused, winning over the hesitant and bringing him recognition.[150]

Like any shrewd businessman Mahomed relied on marketing and publicity to build up a clientele, seen from the very many advertisements and the use he made of the numerous 'testimonials' praising his cure. In 1820, *Cases Cured*, a book of letters from grateful patients was published, according to Mahomed, at 'the pressing desire' of the nobility and gentry. In the vestibule of his establishments were 'hung ... crutches of former martyrs' of rheumatism, lumbago or sciatica, said to have been cured by Mahomed's 'vigorous and scientific shampooing'. He kept visitors' books (separate ones for men and women) for patients' comments.[151] Each new edition of his book, *Shampooing, or, Benefits Resulting From the Use of The Indian Medicated Vapour Bath, As Introduced Into This Country, by S.D. Mahomed (A Native Of India),* first published in 1822, carried the names of patients successfully cured and glowing notices from them. The book, largely consisting of descriptions of successful cures for asthma, paralysis, rheumatism, sciatica and loss of voice, reached a third edition in 1838. Mahomed attempted to demonstrate that what in India was regarded as 'a restorative luxury', in England worked as a 'most surprising and powerful remedy' for many diseases. The book also has a short biographical sketch of his life. Re-inventing himself, Mahomed edited out his period in Cork and London. He advanced his birth by ten years, to 1749, provided himself with medical training, claiming that he had been 'educated to the profession of, and served in the Company's services as a surgeon', a claim that is dubious.[152] As a self-publicist, and in the competitive environment of Brighton, Mahomed may have exaggerated the miraculous claims of his cures. The use he made of names on occasion, too, came in for questioning. But by the standards of the time, and before the law of 1858, which regulated the medical profession, Mahomed remained, according to his biographer, 'within the bounds of medical and advertising ethics of the day'.[153]

But a flair for marketing and publicity was not the only factor contributing to his success. The popularity of his Baths may also have been due to the fact that he was in the right environment at the right time. The Pavilion, Nash's oriental fantasy, was completed by 1821, a reminder, in the words of a contemporary in the *Monthly Magazine,* of the 'fairy palaces of the sovereigns of the Hindus', and in the context of the developing Raj, the Regent as a 'virtual sovereign of the East'.[154] Mahomed's Baths, with its associations of oriental luxury, would have blended in with such associations.

In 1821, his new premises 'Mahomed's Baths', a symbol of his success, opened on the sea-front at East Cliff, its decor suggesting 'oriental and classical Grecian exotica'.[155] Here, female patients were personally supervised by Mahomed's wife, Jane, as the expressions of gratitude in the visitors' books attest. Mahomed's Baths became famous, meriting a mention in Brighton guidebooks and in Brighton and London newspapers. According to one gushing notice: Mahomed's Baths were 'daily thronged, not only with the ailing but the hale … the powerful efficacy of [the Baths] … have brought foreigners to him from all quarters of the World'.[156] Indeed, the visitors' books bear testimony to how well the Baths were patronised. And success followed, guaranteeing his survival. His patients, from among the nobility and gentry, included Lords Castlereagh, Canning and Reay; Lady Cornwallis and Sir Robert Peel. Some patients declared their undying gratitude; amateur poets composed verses, one even crediting the growth of Brighton to Mahomed's reputation for curing illness. Princess Poniatowsky of Poland presented a silver cup.[157] Mahomed's highest achievement was to be appointed Shampooing Surgeon to King George IV, an appointment continued under William IV. In 1825, Mahomed installed the apparatus for an Indian vapour bath at the Pavilion and royal account books record baths given to the Royal household.[158] Such patronage enhanced his social standing and patient numbers rose. Mahomed opened a second establishment in London, at 7 Ryder Street, St James's, managed by his son, Horatio. The medical profession of the time, too, recognised his treatment. Dr John Gibney, the senior physician at the Royal Sussex County Hospital, sent him patients. As rival establishments, for example Molineux's, were set up, to prevent poaching, Mahomed made much of his Bath's Indian qualities.[159] But Mahomed was not without his critics. One contemporary, for instance, wrote: 'a dingy empiric has invented a new system of *humbug*, which is in great dispute here ... called shampooing; a sort of stewing alive by steam ...'. And in the verses parodying Brighton's characters, Mahomed's were not without overtones of negative images of Islam.[160]

Mahomed's Baths remained among 'the noted institutions of Brighton' and Mahomed one of its 'local celebrities', long remembered driving to the Races 'gorgeous in Eastern costume, with his pretty wife by his side, and a dagger in his girdle'. A kind-hearted and benevolent man, in his prosperous days, he was said to have 'a heart and hand ready to relieve the wants of others'. As a public figure patronised by Royalty, Mahomed often loyally illuminated his Baths (with gas lights) to mark royal occasions. From 1841, as a Brighton citizen, he was on the register of voters.[161]

Mahomed retired from active work in 1834, aged 75, handing over to his son Arthur. With Queen Victoria's accession to the throne in 1837, Brighton lost its favoured place, and Mahomed his prominence. A financial blow in 1841 spelled the end of Mahomed's Baths. He died in February 1851, his wife Jane, preceding him in December 1850. A simple tombstone in St Nicholas's churchyard records his identification with 'Patna, Hindoostan'. Today, Mahomed is merely remembered as an 'exotic and romantic figure' in Brighton's history and his Baths as providing an 'intriguing sensation' of 'voluptuous indulgences of the East'. His other achievements lie forgotten.[162] How his descendants and other British-born Indians attempted to find a place in Victorian and Edwardian society, and the changes and developments in Asian settlement in Britain, are considered in the next chapter.

3

A Community in the Making
1830s–1914

From about the middle of the nineteenth century to the beginning of the First World War in 1914, several hundred Asians lived in Britain. Some were born here; a few came from the Caribbean or Africa, but the majority came directly from the Indian sub-continent. They lived here permanently or stayed for varying periods of time. Further, every year, in response to the needs of the labour market, thousands of sailors and hundreds of ayahs continued to be brought to Britain. A growing number of students arrived to study at English and Scottish universities. Indian nobility, exiled from their kingdoms, also lived in Britain. They formed part of the growing multi-racial society, a result of the empire in India, Africa and the Caribbean. The Asians were a diverse group: some were working class, surviving on the margins of society. Others mingled with the English upper class. Then there were the professionals active in medicine, education, law, business, politics and the women's movement. Others were ministers of religion, sportsmen and entertainers. Their presence, whether as transients or as settlers, had a significant influence on British society and culture, an influence which has not received the attention it deserves.

The tradition of importing servants and ayahs continued. Mention is made, for instance, of a Madrassi ayah travelling with a civilian family going on furlough to Britain. The 1861 census for Croydon, Surrey, shows a footman and a nurse, both named as 'Mair Mooto', and born in Madras, living at Shirley Cottage. The family, Louisa Mure, and her sisters Isabella Trotter and Emily Strange, had also been born in Madras, as were Emily Strange's children, while her husband, Thomas, a judge in Madras, was born in Calcutta. Another, for Ealing, Southall in 1871, records Brinoo, a Calcutta-born 49-year-old widow in a combined role as a nurse and servant. In 1882, at Cheltenham, Christchurch, Ruth 'an adult Native of Madras', an ayah, in the service of Colonel Rolandson was baptised in the 'Tamil Language'.[1] It is unlikely these are isolated instances. According to the biographer of Sir Thomas Lipton, who owned tea plantations in Ceylon (Sri Lanka), Sinhalese servants attended him at his mansion, Osidge, in Chase Side, Southgate, London. Their presence would have added to Lipton's status as a Ceylonese tea planter, in much the same way as Lipton's Tea was advertised in the

1890s with sandwich-men dressed up as Indians parading through London's streets. In 1910 the *Committee on Distressed Colonial and Indian Subjects* heard of ayahs in Hornsey, North London, and in Hayward's Heath. Bimbi was brought over in 1911. Then there is Sundhi Din, from Balanda, a village in the Nakodar/Jagraon region of the Punjab. According to his testimony, he had come to Scotland, 'sometime before the First World War' as a valet to a Scots army officer whom he had served for many years in India. A 1925 photograph taken in Glasgow of two nannies from Madras, and a handful of surviving passports confirm the presence of ayahs and servants well into the twentieth century, brought probably for much the same reasons as in the Georgian period.[2] Very little, however, is known about their lives in Victorian and Edwardian households. A little more is known about Queen Victoria's Asian servants. As royal attendants, they were far more visible as photographs in the Queen's Collections show. One photograph, the 'Carte' of Alexandra, Princess of Wales, with the baby Louise and an ayah, most probably, Hurmat Ali, sold more than 300,000 copies.[3] But it was the *munshi* Abdul Karim who attracted the most attention and formed the subject of much debate in much the same way as John Brown, Queen Victoria's Highland servant.

AN INDIAN IN THE ROYAL HOUSEHOLD

In 1877, at a magnificent *durbar* (the Mughal ceremonial assembly was re-invented by the British) Queen Victoria was proclaimed Queen-Empress of India. Its effect on India and imperial relations aside, one of its immediate results was the addition of the Durbar Room at Osborne House, Isle of Wight. Designed by John Lockwood Kipling, the Durbar Room was the creation of the master craftsman, Ram Singh, who crafted the 'Indian extension' at Bagshot Park, Surrey, for the Duke of Connaught. Specially brought over from Lahore, in February 1891, he was paid £5 per week and given a cottage at Cowes to live in. He designed the intricate carvings and wooden moulds from which the plasterwork was cast by Jackson and Co. of London. Ram Singh spent Christmas at Osborne and was painted by Swoboda; the portrait is still at Osborne House.[4] Before that, in 1887, three days after the Golden Jubilee, several Indian servants with their wives arrived at Balmoral. The Queen was reported to be 'as excited about them as a child would be with a new toy'. Mohammed Bux, described as large, bearded and quite dark, was older, Abdul Karim, at 24 was 'much lighter, tall and with a fine serious countenance'.[5] Dressed in scarlet and gold in the winter and in white during the summer, they attended the Queen at table.

Two years later, in 1889, Queen Victoria promoted Abdul Karim, once a clerk in Agra, to the post of her *munshi* and began learning Hindustani, with 'instructive' discussions in Indian religion and culture thrown in. Soon she was able to greet visiting Maharanis in Hindustani. So pleased was the Queen with the *munshi*, described as 'really exemplary and excellent', and who was most useful to her 'with papers, letters and books etc.', that in July 1890, she asked Lord Lansdowne for a suitable grant of land for him in the Agra suburbs. She enthusiastically explained: 'it is the *first time in the world* that any Native has ever held such a position' and so she was very anxious to 'mark this permanently'. In the same year, Von Angeli was commissioned to paint another portrait of the *munshi*. He was given cottages: Frogmore at Windsor and Arthur Cottage at Osborne, where every Christmas, in keeping with English tradition, he gave a party for the children on the estate. In 1894, elevated to the position of the Queen's 'Indian Secretary', with the title, *Hafiz,* he assisted Victoria with her 'boxes', handling Indian petitions, requiring 'merely a civil refusal'.[6] The award of the Companion of the Order of the Indian Empire (CIE) followed.

All this may have been an expression of the Queen's delight and a royal lesson in race relations, but in an acutely race- and class-conscious imperial Britain it caused a great deal of 'court commotion', in the Household generally, but particularly among the private secretaries, who resented the 'social and official position' accorded him in the Court Circular and on all occasions by the Queen. The Royal Household retaliated. At first the *munshi* was socially snubbed: at theatrical performances he was placed among the dressers; his Christmas cards were returned. Then the Queen was given a report, especially obtained from India, to show that his father was not a 'hospital assistant', but merely an apothecary at the Agra Jail.[7] Queen Victoria, who condemned divisions based on class as 'the *one thing* which is most dangerous and reprehensible', was shocked. She wrote: 'to make out that the poor good Munshi is so *low* is really *outrageous* & in a country like England quite out of place ... She has known 2 Archbishops who were sons respectively of a Butcher & a Grocer ... Abdul's father saw good & honourable service as a Dr.' How Abdul Karim reacted to such insults can only be gleaned from Victoria's pen as no other record survives. He felt 'cut to the heart at being thus spoken of' and the Queen sympathised with 'the poor Munshi's sensitive feelings'. For the next two years, in the words of her biographer, there were 'running battles' between the Queen and her advisers, she determined to promote her 'excellent and much esteemed Munshi and Indian Clerk', and the Court putting him down. For instance, Sir Fleetwood Edwards, the Assistant Keeper of the

Privy Purse and Assistant Secretary to the Queen, refused to take tea with him, while Dr James Reid, the Queen's Physician, declined to show Karim's father round London hospitals.[8]

In the spring of 1897, ten years after his appointment to the Royal household, the whole affair reached a climax. In an attempt to discredit him further, the Court used a new weapon, politics. Suggestions were made that Hindus would resent a Muslim in the 'position of adviser' to the Queen and Indian Princes would not understand a *munshi* being given 'such a responsible position'.[9] Further, the Court alleged that giving Abdul Karim access to 'very confidential' state papers, including the Viceroy's correspondence, was dangerous for the safety of British rule, especially, it was insinuated, that as a 'thoroughly stupid and uneducated man', the *munshi* could easily be used as a tool by others. It was claimed that the *munshi*'s friends, described as 'untrustworthy adventurers', were in contact with 'disorderly elements in India', a reference to Rafiuddin Ahmed, a law student, said to be the 'the brains' behind Abdul Karim.[10] The situation was considered to be so serious that police were consulted. Reports compiled by the *Thuggee and Dacoity* Department, which investigated anti-British agitation in India, show that instructions had been sent to have the *munshi*'s movements watched during his visit, although the authorities stopped short of having him 'shadowed'. In March 1897, in a confidential telegram to the Viceroy, the Secretary of State for India requested particulars of the *Munshi*'s family background and his 'exact social position' at the time of his appointment to the Royal household. But nothing new emerged. His father, Sheikh Mohammed Waziruddin, was a hospital assistant on a salary of Rs 60 per month, and, although of humble origins, was 'respectable and trustworthy'. His eldest brother was employed at the jail and his four sisters were all respectably married. As for Karim, he had been a 'vernacular clerk' in Agra Jail at Rs 10 a month.[11]

But the persecution did not end. In a desperate attempt, Frederick Ponsonby, the Queen's Equerry, asked for gossip from the 'Native' or European press since the 'Hindoo papers' he had brought from India, and read to the Queen, had done 'very little good'. The Queen, in Ponsonby's words, accused them of 'race prejudice' and jealousy. But, within days, on 30 April 1897, the Secretary of State for India distanced himself from the 'court mud pies' and stopped the trawling of newspapers. Instead, Queen Victoria was 'plainly' spoken to by some 'old Indian officers' in her Court about the 'social and official position' given to the *munshi* and he was relegated to his 'proper place'.[12]

Was the *munshi* as 'dangerous' as he was made out to be? Or was it, as the Queen claimed, 'race prejudice' that caused the 'commotion'?

There is evidence that the *munshi* used his position to better his family's prospects. During his trip to India he was reported purchasing 'at his own price' a plot of government land adjoining the land presented to him. Evidence also suggests that he may have asked for favours for his family: his brother was promoted to *tehsildar* at the Queen's request. Beyond this there is no evidence of any impropriety or 'reprehensible' conduct, deserving of 'official stricture'. He came from a 'trustworthy' family. Even the India Office did not consider him to be as 'dangerous' as he was made out to be.[13] What then of the allegations that he read state papers? Like the Court at the time, some historians suggest that Abdul Karim saw 'more confidential papers than he should have' and 'probably influenced' the Queen's attitude to India and 'its problems'. But even the Secretary of State doubted this, while the Queen cleared him of the charge of spying. In July 1897, she informed Lord Salisbury that '*no* political papers of any kind are ever in the hands of the munshi, even in her presence'. He merely helped her to 'read words which she cannot read or merely ordinary submissions on warrants for signature'. Moreover, given that Abdul Karim could not 'read English fluently enough' he was unlikely to be able 'to read anything of importance' let alone pass it on to his friends. Even suspicions against Rafiuddin Ahmed were found to be 'unjust'. The editor of the *Nineteenth Century*, to which Ahmed was a contributor, vouched for his character, confirming he was 'much too honourable' a man to give information.[14] Therefore, one can only conclude that the furore over the *munshi* is more an illustration of race and class prejudice, a conclusion substantiated by Frederick Ponsonby. As he explained, Abdul Karim's elevation to a *munshi* was 'nothing wrong', because *munshis* were not 'very high up in the Indian world'. But the Queen's attempts at social engineering had gone further: 'If he had been kept in his proper place no harm would have been done, but ... from being Khitmagar the Queen made him a Munshi, and then Indian Secretary, giving him at the same time the CIE.'[15]

After Queen Victoria's death in 1901, on King Edward VII's orders, all *Munshi*'s papers were burnt at Frogmore Cottage. He returned to Agra. After his death in 1909, a second bonfire of his papers was ordered, his widow being allowed to retain only a few letters from the Queen. No royal servants were appointed. Instead, starting in 1903, each year, especially during the London season (April to August), four Indian Army Orderly Officers came to attend the King at court, at levees and at ceremonial occasions like the Trooping of the Colour, symbolising the grandeur and unity of imperial Britain.

More significantly, Abdul Karim's presence may have made Queen

Victoria 'more sensitive' to race prejudice, as a long letter to the future Viceroy in May 1898 demonstrates. Decrying the 'red-tapist narrow-minded' council, she encouraged him to be:

> more independent and *hear* for *himself* what the *feelings* of the Natives really are and not be guided by the *snobbish* and vulgar and overbearing and offensive behaviour of many of our Civil and Political Agents, if we are to go on peacefully and happily in India and be liked and beloved by high and low, as well as respected as we ought to be, and not trying to trample on the people and continually reminding them and make them feel that they are a conquered people.[16]

But such sentiments were already out of date. By the mid-nineteenth century, as more of India was conquered, race relations had undergone a change, from the 'ethnocentric' racism of the earlier period to a more aggressively 'strident racist stance', based on a doctrine of racial supremacy, biologically determined. Easing of access to India for missionaries after 1813 had altered the perception of Indians: as heathens, they were seen as morally bankrupt, 'obsequious, deceitful, licentious and avaricious'. The 1857 Rising, coinciding as it did with the rise of 'scientific racism' in Europe and America, further convinced the governing class in India that they 'belonged to a race whom God had destined to govern and subdue'.[17] In such a world, a letter, written in 1883, could make the astonishing claim: 'The only people who have any right to India are the British; the SO-CALLED Indians have no right whatever.'[18] A similar expression of cultural and racial arrogance finds an echo in D.H. Lawrence's vicious attack on Rabindranath Tagore, winner of the 1913 Nobel Prize for Literature. In a letter to Lady Ottoline Morrell, Lawrence observed:

> I become more and more surprised to see how far higher, in reality our European civilisation stands than the East, India or Persia ever dreamed of. And one is glad to *realize* how these Hindus are horribly decadent and reverting to all forms of barbarism in all sorts of ugly ways. We feel surer on our feet then. But this fraud of looking up to them – this wretched worship-of-Tagore attitude – is disgusting. 'Better fifty years of Europe' even as she is. Buddha worship is completely decadent and foul nowadays: and it *was* always only half-civilized.[19]

Such ideologies defined Britain's relationship with India and the view of Indians.

NURSES OF OCEAN HIGHWAYS

By the 1850s an increasing number of travelling ayahs were being brought to Britain by white British families. By one reckoning 140 were found in London's lodging-houses. Another source, in 1876, estimated the number to be 100. However, not all travelling ayahs were discharged immediately on arrival. Some accompanied the families to their homes and were retained for some time before being sent back as shown in the case of 'Topsy', who in 1871 came with Agnes Cayzer, the wife of Sir Charles, the Clan Line shipping magnate, and 'Jemima', taken twice to Langley during the 1870s by the Reverend Francis Kilvert's family.[20] If these ayahs are counted, then the numbers brought back annually would be higher.

What led to their increased employment? Two developments, one political and the other technological, were responsible for this change. First, following the 1857 Rising, the Government of India Act abolished the EIC and transferred the power of administration to the Crown. A host of Britons, both civil and military, went out to service the Raj. Businessmen, planters, engineers, teachers, doctors and nurses, too, went to further their careers. According to the 1901 census, there were 170,000 Europeans and members of 'allied races' in India, including 89,000 'Eurasians'. As wives, the *memsahibs* accompanied their husbands, family life became an important feature, and visits home more regular. Second, the opening of the Suez Canal in 1869 cut nearly 4,500 miles off the journey between India and England. Communications were further improved by the coming of the steam-powered liners and regular passenger services like the P&O. This in turn facilitated more regular visits home, especially between March and October, the travelling season. Ayahs, indispensable to the *memsahibs'* households in India, became even more essential for the annual seasonal visits.[21] According to one contemporary source, families either asked their own family ayah to accompany them or they engaged the services of experienced travelling ayahs, who were said to possess certain 'essential attributes in their make-up': they were honest, clean, capable nurses and made good sailors.[22] There are no testimonies from the ayahs. But it is not difficult to imagine why they agreed to travel. Economic necessity would undoubtedly have been one important reason. Their devotion to the family and children under their care would have also been a factor. Some ayahs may have been motivated by a sense of adventure and a desire to see the land of their rulers. On board they took complete charge: they cared for the babies, amused the children, and looked after the *memsahib* and the baggage. On arrival in England, their duties over, they were discharged to await a ship bound for India. Return passages, formally agreed in India, were not always honoured, and ayahs were stranded. Cases of abandoned ayahs in workhouses were occasionally reported. But it is difficult to assess the scale of the problem.[23]

Attention was first drawn to their plight in 1855 when it was reported that 50–60 ayahs were found in one disreputable lodging-house in Ratcliffe Highway in London's East End. In another 'low-order' slum, where as many as 140 were located, it was reported that 'the windows in the door' were 'all broken during the drunken riots of the ayahs'. They paid high rents, as much as 16 shillings a week, causing them 'most lamentable' hardship. Their earnings exhausted, they were thrown out and left to fend for themselves in the metropolis. The fact that men lodged in the same establishments was a further cause for concern. But what caused the most concern was that ayahs had not been befriended by any missionary and, in a 'Christian land', had learnt nothing of Christianity. Victorian paternalism combined with the moral imperative to rescue the heathen other, thus led to the establishment of a hostel for the ayahs, references to which first begin to appear in 1891.[24]

THE AYAHS' HOME

The Ayahs' Home was set up by Mr and Mrs Rogers at 6 Jewry Street, Aldgate. Within six years, however, the Home would have closed, but for the lobbying by a committee of concerned white British women. Its management was then taken over by the Foreigners' Branch Committee of the London City Mission (LCM). Around 1900, the Home was moved to 26 King Edward Road, Mare Street, Hackney; 20 years later, in 1921, it was re-located to bigger premises at 4 King Edward Road.[25] The Ayahs' Home provided accommodation for Indian ayahs and Chinese amahs sent there by the white British families. There were 30 rooms, and every year, over 100 women stayed there, their numbers fluctuating according to circumstances. For instance, after the Armistice, 223 ayahs were recorded, suggesting that families prevented from travelling during the war, had rushed home at the first opportunity; another 24 ayahs, with no return passages, had applied for assistance. In 1917, in fact, it was reported that three ayahs, unable to find a family travelling to India, had been stranded. During the depression in 1934, only 80 to 100 ayahs had lodged there. The Home also served as a refuge for ayahs who had been ill-treated, dismissed from service or simply abandoned. Such instances were by no means rare. The Home found them placements with families returning to India.[26] Here, too, came families needing ayahs for their journey to India.

How did the Ayahs' Home operate? The evidence given by Mrs Dunn, the matron of the Home to the *Committee on Distressed Colonial and Indian Subjects* in 1910, sheds some light. The system depended on the ayahs' return ticket, normally provided by the family arriving from India. When an ayah was brought to the Home, the return ticket was surrendered to the matron, who 'sold it' to another family needing the ayah's services. The money obtained from the new employer paid for the ayah's board and lodging: 14 shillings a week during the season, more out of season as the ayah was likely to remain longer. The ayah, thus, stayed at the Home 'free', but worked her passage in both directions. What the ayah earned is not recorded. Any shortfall in the Home's finances was made up by donations; one wealthy woman patron was said to be particularly generous. The fact that ayahs found a return placement without much difficulty suggests that a sophisticated network, equal to any modern-day employment agency, had formed around the Ayahs' Home. Such a conclusion is substantiated by the fact that shipping offices in the City provided information about the Home.[27]

The Ayahs' Home was more than just a hostel. The chief object of its philanthropic founders was to bring the ayahs under Christian influence. Experience of mission work in India and fluency in Indian languages was an essential requirement for the superintendents of the Home. Daily religious services, advertised as 'purely optional', were attended by 'almost all' the ayahs and, according to one source, were the main vehicle of 'eventually ... spreading our beliefs among the heathen' women. They were taught hymns and, whenever possible, taken to church. There were 'chats in the bedroom' on religion, which the matron considered 'productive of much good'.[28] In the absence of any data, however, it is impossible to measure the success of such evangelical zeal.

Described as 'a home from home', the Ayahs' Home would have improved the quality of their stay in England. Here, in an environment having 'something of the colour and atmosphere of the Orient', Indian languages were spoken and Indian food provided, qualities made much of in the advertisements for funding.[29] But it was an 'Orient' as imagined by others, the whites, where the lofty rooms with striking dadoes and gaily distempered walls, it was said, reminded one of the 'Eastern passion for colours', where the bedrooms were 'ticketed' according to cultural communities, Indians, Chinese, Javanese, Malay States, etc. In such surroundings, the ayahs whiled away their time, a few days, weeks or even months, doing embroidery, reading, playing *pachis* or going for walks to the local park, with an occasional organised outing to Westminster Abbey, the Houses of Parliament and the Palace, or the Zoo.[30] The ayahs must have felt isolated and lonely.

The Ayahs' Home in Hackney, the only such institution of its kind with a named building, was an important landmark. But it represented a symbol of empire, a colonial enclave in the heart of London, replicating many colonial attitudes and images. Referred to as the 'poor ayah' in contemporary literature, these women were seen as 'child-like' and as 'these children of the other climes'. Such perceptions are emphasised in events like the annual LCM Foreigners' Fete. In 1904, for instance, a group of ayahs were conducted before visiting dignitaries to sing a hymn, 'From Greenland's Icy Mountains', taught them by the matron, very much like school children, reinforcing the image of the child-like, happy ayah.[31] The Ayahs' Home represented an expression of Christian charity for the welfare of Indian womanhood, of the caring mother country, binding the colonised in a web of gratitude and loyalty. The ayahs, it was said, appreciated the public's kindness and 'seldom' gave any trouble, a view shared by the India Office. Therefore there was no need to investigate wages and conditions, for redress or intervention to reform the system, for laws to compel British families to honour their contracts – and this despite the fact that ayahs continued to be stranded, without any impunity, by their 'perfectly indifferent' employers.[32] And so the system endured to the end of the Raj in 1947.

The British public found the ayahs fascinating. Seen as 'picturesque', they were stared at, photographed and painted. One account in London tells of 30 ayahs photographed a 'dozen times': what had attracted attention was the 'glitter and colour' of their 'native' dress. Another recounts the amazement of the passers-by in the country at the sight of the ayah's 'brown face, nose ring, bangles and shawl'. Helen Allingham, a nineteenth-century painter, who first saw an English woman not long returned from India with her children in charge of their India ayah at a seaside holiday near Dover, was so fascinated by the ayah that she inspired several of her water-colours. Contrast this with Rebecca Solomon's *A Young Teacher,* which shows an ayah as a protective carer *and* an educator, a role seldom acknowledged by white society.[33]

No testimonies from the ayahs exist to provide us their version of their experiences. But they were not children of the colonial imagery. They were responsible women, mothers and grandmothers, trusted with children, and who, as their actions demonstrate, negotiated successfully both an Indian and an English world. Further, the view that ayahs were generally 'able to look after themselves pretty well', though advanced in favour of employers and against legislation to make them responsible for ayahs, supports the conclusion that ayahs were resourceful women. Instances of their initiative and pluck are also on record: ayahs who, on their own, delivered children left alone during voyages, through accidents or deaths of their mothers, to their relations in unfamiliar places in Britain and Ireland. Others were seasoned travellers. Mrs Antony Pareira journeyed 54 times between India and Britain, and once to Holland.[34]

LASCARS: SERVICING THE IMPERIAL TRADE ROUTES

By the 1820s, as has been shown, discriminatory legislation restricted the number of lascars on British ships. However, the economic reality of an industrial economy coupled with the needs of an expanding British shipping industry, forced Parliament in 1849 to revise the existing laws and lascars were redefined as 'British' for the purpose of shipping, enabling ship-owners to hire labour more profitable to them. The demand for lascar labour was further stimulated by two developments: the opening of the Suez Canal in 1869 and the introduction of steam navigation, which created totally new categories of labour in the engine room, those of firemen and trimmers needed to stoke the furnaces. And it was in this sector, shunned by European sailors in tropical zones, that lascars came to be concentrated. The fact that nearly half the total number of seamen afloat were firemen demonstrates the importance of this sector of labour, and of lascars. In fact, Broeze argues that without the stamina and sinews of lascars the British merchant fleet in the Indian Ocean would have ground to a complete standstill.[35] The P&O led the way in the 1840s, employing all-lascar crews on their passenger and cargo ships sailing to Britain, followed by its rivals, the Clan Line, Harrison's, Bibby and others. This had a knock-on effect on recruitment. Traditionally, lascars had been drawn mainly from the maritime areas of Gujarat and the Malabar on the west coast (from Ahmedabad and Surat to Bombay, Goa and Cochin) and East Bengal (Calcutta, Chittagong, Noakhali and Sylhet). But increased demand extended recruitment to the land-locked agricultural regions of the Punjab, Peshawar, the North-West Frontier Province, as well as Bengal and Assam. A majority were Muslims, but Hindus and Christians also formed part of this growing seafaring community.[36] By 1914, lascars, numbering some 51,000, formed 17.5 per cent of the total number of seamen employed on British registered ships.[37] They serviced not only the Indian Ocean trade, but also worked on the international trade routes, particularly to Britain.

The reason that the shipping industry found lascars attractive as a labour force was economic. In a fiercely competitive world of free trade, profit margins and rival companies, trimming costs made sense. In 1914, on an average, Indian deckhands earned Rs 16–22 (£1. 4s.–£1. 14s.), while firemen received Rs 20 (£1. 11s.) a month, compared to £5. 10s. paid to their white British counterparts, clearly unequal wages for equal work, to say nothing of the wage disparity between sailors engaged at Bombay and Calcutta.[38] Actual wage bills aside, further savings could be made from inadequate and often inferior quality food, both on board and in Britain. Internal minutes reveal cases of 'culpable carelessness and indifference' on the part of ship-owners, but the government of India was reluctant to prescribe standards in lascar diet similar to those governing European scale and quality. This was tantamount to legally condoning lower standards for lascars. Savings could also be made on lascar entitlement to space on board ships, 36 cu. feet in 1876, compared to 60 cu. feet for European sailors. By 1914, when accommodation for European sailors was raised to a minimum of 120 cu. feet, lascars still lagged behind with only 72 cu. feet. Even these changes had been achieved in the teeth of fierce opposition from the shipping companies.[39] What such cost-cutting amounted to in actual savings to the shipping industry was demonstrated at the East India Association lecture in London in 1910. According to this, even taking into consideration the larger Indian crews (of 92 against 46), the net gain to the ship-owner still amounted to £40 a month, or 14.5 per cent. Others revised the figure upwards, to 20 per cent on the scale of efficiency, two Europeans being equivalent to three lascars. If a ship made three voyages a year between India and Europe, then profits were considerable indeed.[40] Monetary savings aside, there were other gains. Lascars were renowned for their sobriety. They were seen as more manageable and amenable to discipline, 'as quiet as lambs' is one description. Even the different ethnic groups were stereotypically graded. Further, un-unionised, lascars were considered trouble-free, the more so, it was argued, if black and white were kept separate. Ship-owners contrasted lascar docility to European sailors' 'insubordination ... tendency to drunkenness ... and the interference of unionism'.[41] But these very same qualities conspired to keep lascars down: what was seen as strength might also, when required, be construed as weakness. In the shipboard mythology, the docile lascars became inferior, lacking in masculinity, self-reliance and initiative, and, although competent as sailors, could make excellent seamen only when led by European officers.[42] By such contradictory justifications, shipping companies played white against black, and in the process kept down wages of both.

The image of physical weakness of lascars was further reinforced in European eyes by larger crews, the high incidence of disease and death on board ships and on shore in Britain. This was attributed to their lack of stamina, not to their inferior rations or their appalling conditions of service. Further, the concentration of lascars in the engine-rooms gave rise to a complex mythology based on racist notions of genetic suitability for types of labour. Lascars were said to be more suited to the engine-rooms as they were able to withstand the heat better than Europeans. But such arguments are not borne out by reality: there are incidences of lascars overcome by heat, throwing themselves overboard in desperation.[43] The argument that Indian sailors were genetically 'unfitted' for colder latitudes, too, persisted, justifying latitude restrictions in Lascar Articles. Indians could only be employed for voyages between 60 degrees north and 50 degrees south. Therefore, latitude limits, taken together with Lascar Articles (under which they were discharged and paid off in India), coupled with the 'socio-psychological imagery' based on racist stereotype, not only justified and consigned Indian seamen to the bottom of the maritime labour hierarchy, but effectively ghettoised them as a labour force.[44] Lascars were thus less likely to be in direct competition with British seamen.

Racial discrimination against lascars was further strengthened by legislative enactments in Britain between 1855 and 1894, designed to prevent their settlement, and allegedly becoming chargeable to poor rates. For instance, under the 1854 Act, ship-owners were fined £30 if a lascar was left behind in Britain. In 1871, alleging that lascar desertions were on the increase, the Board of Trade appointed Lascar Transfer Officers at all major ports with powers to escort Indian crews to London for shipment back to India. But the most draconian was the Merchant Shipping Act of 1894, section 125, which empowered ship-owners to sign a further agreement with lascars binding them to proceed to any other port in the UK, and there sign a further agreement with a ship ready to sail to any port in India as part of the crew.[45] This was supposedly 'to protect' lascars from becoming destitute in Britain. Under this provision, Indian sailors, effectively, had no choice but to work their passage back on any terms and conditions offered. As Hepple points out, what was even more 'remarkable' about this 'unusual provision' was that, for breach of their 'contract', lascars were liable to criminal prosecution.[46] Legislation notwithstanding to escape cruel treatment, lascars sometimes jumped ship in Britain. One record tells of a harrowing tale of an entire crew of Muslims deserting on arrival in London. They had been 'hung up with weights tied to their feet', flogged with a rope and forced to eat pork. The 'insult' had been carried further: the tail of the pig had been 'rammed' into their mouths and the entrails twisted round their necks. Desertion was, then, akin to an act of resistance.[47] By 1914, small settlements of lascars had grown up in the dockland areas of major British ports: London, Glasgow, Cardiff and Liverpool.

LASCARS, UNIONS AND CHRISTIAN MISSIONARIES

The state's response to lascars was contradictory: to help the shipping industry, laws were modified to allow the employment of lascars within defined limits. At the same time, racially discriminatory legislation barred their settlement in Britain. What, then, was the reaction of British seamen and the National Sailors' and Firemen's Union (NSFU)? Evidence of anti-lascar agitation in this period (which would intensify after the First World War), suggests that Havelock Wilson, president of the NSFU, was not averse to using race as a weapon when it suited his purpose.

The twentieth century began with cries of 'Yellow Peril' directed predominantly against the Chinese, blamed for undercutting wages, but a term which often included lascars. In 1905, the Aliens Act was passed in an atmosphere of xenophobia against the influx of Jews fleeing persecution from Czarist Russia, and acrimonious debates over the issue of indentured Chinese labour in South Africa. Against this backdrop, began a wave of anti-Chinese agitation in British seaports, first surfacing as an English-language issue. Declaring that the safety of British shipping was at stake, Wilson campaigned for a language test, demanding that one lascar in every five should be fluent in English. However, behind claims for the safety of shipping lay economic protectionism. A letter in the *Glasgow Herald,* referring to the employment of 'our own jolly tars' declared: 'Fifteen thousand Scotch boys dying every year, and Scotch ships manned by Lascars. Is it satisfactory?' But the 1908 Act exempted lascars, unlike the Chinese, from the language test. Why? According to the official version, being British, lascars had 'special privileges and exemptions' under Lascar Articles.[48] In 1911 (when lascars, an isolated labour force, had remained neutral during the strike) and again in 1914, shortly before the outbreak of the First World War, union antagonism flared up once again. At a demonstration organised by the Clyde District Committee of the National Transport Workers' Federation held at the City Hall in Glasgow, and attended by 2,000, it was alleged that the employment of 'Asiatic and other Eastern labour' had increased to such an extent that there were 'ten times more eastern labourers on British ships' than at any time in the Chinese compounds in the Rand. To counter a charge of racism, the Chairman argued that they objected to Chinese and Indian labour not because of the difference in colour and race, 'but because they lowered the standard of life for white men'. Their resolution, pledging the meeting to use every means 'constitutional or otherwise', urged 'organised workers' to show 'in the most unmistakable manner' that they would not 'tolerate this collusion between ship owners and the Board of Trade in their attempts to lower the standard of life secured by years of trade union effort'. There was even a hint of threat: if Parliament would not stop the 'danger of this Chinese invasion', then to protect their standard of living, workers would be 'compelled ... to have one of the biggest fights that the country had ever known'.[49] But, with the outbreak of the First World War and the need for the labour of the vilified Chinese and lascars, opposition disappeared, to return after 1918.

What is significant in these anti-Chinese campaigns is, first, in many of the speeches and arguments: in *The Seaman*, the organ of the NSFU, and at meetings, Indians and Chinese were paired together as one monolithic 'Asiatic' labour force. Blurring distinctions could thus make the 'foreign' threat appear even greater. During the 1911 seamen's strike, Ben Tillett claimed that shipping companies had not only brought 'more Chinese coolies', but had engaged 'all possible Asiatics and foreigners, including negroes'. Quoting the figure of 40,000 'Asiatics', Tillett claimed that white labour, 'even white foreigners' were removed to make room for Chinese crews, forcing sailors and dockers to stand up for British citizenship and 'for British ships to be worked by British labour'. A figure of 40,000 could only have been arrived at by including Indian seamen on Lascar Articles and who *were* British citizens. Second, despite denying racism, the imagery and the emotive language in these debates, as historians have noted, was of 'racial and cultural difference'.[50]

Christian missionaries and evangelicals saw lascars as a moral challenge. Like the ayahs, they presented an opportunity for proselytising. It must be remembered, however, that evangelicals had begun by targeting European seamen. Seamen's missions organised Christian services, distributed Bibles and provided alternative accommodation and recreational facilities, which they believed would wean them away from 'crimps' and prostitutes. In the case of lascars, concerned clergy, especially the India-returnees (e.g. Revd James Pegg from Orissa) pointed to the paradox that thousands of pounds were spent on missionaries and Bibles in India, while the 'perishing heathen' on the doorstep received no spiritual and moral guidance. There was also an element of self-interest. Without adequate care, left to wander freely, associating with no one but 'prostitutes ... in the public house, and the apartments of the abandoned', it was feared that if tales of lascars having been fleeced in these 'abodes of infamy' reached India, the image of 'Christian England' would suffer as Englishmen would come to be seen as 'vicious or even worse' than Indians. This, it was suggested, would create distrust and retard the progress of Christianity in India. There was a further issue, first articulated as early as 1814, and graphically summed up by Joseph Salter, the missionary to the 'Asiatics': 'the heathen mind is dark, and the vices of the various heathen systems in which the Asiatic is so brought up, as to form part of his nature, are bad enough when unmingled with European sin in his own land of superstition; but here is an interchange of sin and an unholy compound of both'.[51] Hence, lascars were believed to be in need of spiritual and moral welfare, *and* needed to be contained.

As in the case of white sailors, philanthropists and Christian missionaries first campaigned for proper lascar accommodation with interpreters and attendants, and where 'native' and English police would exercise order and control over them. In the wake of the loss of the EIC barracks in New Road, St Georges-in-the-East, there was no proper accommodation and lascar neglect, disease, and deaths in London again hit the headlines. The National Appeal for East India and China Sailors, with graphic descriptions, drew attention to the squalid makeshift arrangements for boarding them. Those housed on board were 'crammed together between decks', without warmth in the cold damp weather, while those on shore lived in two 'wretched sheds scarcely fit for hogs', one having a 'common earth floor' and without glass to the windows or a chimney. In such surroundings scantily clad shivering lascars were said to huddle round two wood fires, with the room filled with such dense smoke that a 'stranger could not bear it'. The National Appeal campaign gained support from the Seamen's Hospital Society because of an outbreak of scurvy among Indian sailors. And the media took up the campaign.[52] However, lack of funds delayed the setting-up of a Home for lascars for over 10 years. It was only a generous donation of £500 from the Maharajah Duleep Singh, the 'Christian Prince', that made such an accommodation a possibility.[53]

THE STRANGERS' HOME FOR ASIATICS

Known as the Strangers' Home for Asiatics, Africans and South Sea Islanders, the Home, in West India Dock Road, Limehouse, opened in June 1857. It was the first institution of its kind to be established in Britain.[54] During the years of its existence, it served a triple purpose.

First, as a lodging house for Asian and black sailors, with 220 beds, it provided board and lodging on the 'most economical terms', about 8 shillings a week. Considering their wages, lascars would have found even this beyond their means. And, in the days of keen competition and cost-cutting, large ships with short turn-around periods preferred to keep their lascar crews working and on board, and only used the Home as an alternative accommodation. In fact, in the first 20 years, between June 1857 and December 1877, only 5,709 sailors had registered as lodgers. Second, the Home was a repatriation centre. The Lascars' Shipping Office and its officer, accredited to the Board of Trade, were housed in the Home. There was even a book containing names, addresses and the 'mode of living' of all Indians found 'wandering about London'. Ships' captains used the Home to find and engage lascar crews. Repatriation was further facilitated by the 1855 Act, and Colonel Hughes, the secretary of the Home, was most zealous in his pursuit of lascars and 'other natives' of India. In the first 20 years, 1,605 'destitute cases' had been provided for, and repatriated. The India Office contributed an annual grant of £200 from the 'revenues of India' (Indian tax-payers) for the temporary maintenance of 'destitutes', prior to their repatriation. Third, the Home was a centre for evangelising lascars.[55] Salter, fluent in Hindustani and Kiswahili, became their first missionary.

A separate Home for Lascars in Queen's Dock, Glasgow, 'the second city of the Empire', was not established until after the end of the First World War. But lascars and other colonial seamen were boarded regularly at the Glasgow Sailors' Home, opened in Broomielaw in 1857. As trade expanded, the number of lascars arriving in Glasgow rose. In 1903, of the annual number of nightly boarders at the Glasgow Sailors' Home, about one-third (5,500), were lascars.[56]

Christian missions also established lascar missions and recreational-cum-reading rooms for their moral and social welfare, and control. For instance, the Asiatic Rest, with its sign in Persian and Bengali, was started by Salter at 377 East India Dock Road; the London City Mission's Lascar Institute was at 164 Dock Road in Tilbury, while St Andrew's Waterside Mission set up St Luke's Lascar Mission in Victoria Dock Road in the 1880s, under a Bengali Christian, E.B. Bhose. Lacking any welfare facilities in port, lascars patronised reading rooms and institutions provided by the Christian missions.

Insights into lascar experiences in British ports are gleaned from the reports of various Christian organisations, including the perceptions of these caring agencies. Lascars were seen as children, who became easily excited, asked naive questions, were unable to amuse themselves and needed constant supervision. The reports also highlight divisions, emphasising that Indians from different regions did not mix. But this apparent lack of socialisation between men from Calcutta and Bombay could have been due to language. Dotted through these reports appear the concerns of Indians: the state of harvests in India, their need to know why their wages were so low compared to white sailors and their interest in politics of the day, the Boer War and the 1905 war between Russia and Japan. These reports also tell us that lascars frequented markets (e.g. Petticoat Lane) to buy gifts of toys; they observed religious and cultural festivals and carried out funeral rites when colleagues died here, not an infrequent occurrence. The lot of the lascars was not easy: they endured 'rough treatment', insults and robbery.[57]

Resident Indians, too, helped lascars. Duleep Singh's generous contribution has been noted. The Lascars' Club, at 313 Victoria Dock Road, was set up in 1909. K. Chowdry, one-time secretary of the Manchester Indian Association, and later assistant secretary to the British Indian Seamen's Institute, was behind this venture, while among its active subscribers were Princess Sophia Duleep Singh, Sir Ratan Tata and the Maharajahs Sindhia and Burdwan, as well as Anglo-Indian well-wishers, Lord Curzon among them. The Club's location, 'practically at the dock gates', was considered ideal, seen from the fact that in the six months between January and June 1910, a total of 4,180 lascars had used its facilities. There were some attempts at their political education too: in 1908 Indian students rented a room in Royal Albert Dock, while the activities of Rose Majumdar, described as an 'ardent nationalist', were noted by contemporaries.[58]

REVD E.B. BHOSE

Bhose was possibly one of the earliest Indians to be appointed missionary in charge of lascars by a Christian organisation in Britain. A Bengali Christian, Bhose, fluent in several Indian languages, was said to have done 'valuable work' among the 'coolies' (a pejorative term for Indian indentured labour), on sugar plantations in Demerara, in the West Indies. When Bhose and his family came to England is not known. He was said to be on the staff of the Society for the Propagation of the Gospel in London, and, in 1887, was appointed chaplain at St Luke's Lascar Mission in Victoria Docks, his stipend being paid by the St Andrew's Waterside Mission. In rented premises, Bhose set up a mission room, which doubled up as a Sunday school, and a club room for social and leisure activities. He visited lascars on ships and at the Seamen's Hospital, Connaught Road, and managed to baptise a few of them. His reports for the Lascar Mission, written in the mission style, are insightful, nonetheless, reflecting some lascar concerns: their poor labour conditions and isolation, their lack of literacy and the burden of taxation. He also explained Muslim festivals, like Mohrrum and Eid, observed by lascars in port. Bhose was said to talk little about his work, but so seriously did he take his duties that he was seldom absent, until illness overtook him. He died in March 1905. In 1909, Yusuf Sayah (baptised Luqa), another Muslim convert, a former *Imam* of a mosque in Bombay and a physician, who was well versed in Muslim law, became assistant at the Lascar Mission. But his appointment lasted only a few months as he died of TB.[59]

AZIZ AHMAD

While Bhose was accredited to St Luke's in London, Aziz Ahmad worked among lascars in Glasgow. An aura of mystery surrounds Ahmad: some official records are no longer available, and the little that is known arises from the fact that he was investigated by the Glasgow police on instructions from the Indian Criminal Intelligence Bureau.

When exactly Aziz Ahmad, from Lucknow, a Muslim convert to Christianity, first came to Glasgow is not recorded. According to an 1898 report, he had been sent by the Indian Missionary Society 'about 15 years ago' (i.e. 1883) to qualify as a 'native missionary'. Ahmad attended several sessions at 'the University', but was not known to have taken any degrees. Why had Ahmad not returned 'to the mission field' in India as had been intended? Records conflict. 'Want of funds' is one explanation, and this certainly would explain why his studies ended prematurely. Another account suggests that, despite the fact that Ahmad was anxious to go back as 'a missionary to his own people', the Committee would not send him because apparently 'only Europeans could be appointed'. Not unnaturally, Ahmad was a disappointed man, and wrote much on the desirability of Indians being allowed to work as missionaries in India.[60]

Ahmad lived on in Glasgow. The first mention of his address, 36 Bank Street, in the Hillhead district of Glasgow, comes from the 1887 Post Office directory. He supported his family – his Scots wife and three children – by lecturing and as a tutor of Hindustani. He also edited two papers, *Asia* and *Missions*. When lecturing on Islam and Islamic studies, he was said to wear his 'native dress'. Life could not have been easy for the Ahmads. His income from the door collection at his lectures and from tutoring would have been meagre. In January 1900, his neighbours confirmed that 'judging from their purchases' the family lived 'very sparingly'. His 'philanthropic and evangelistic' friends assisted with money and food. In addition, Ahmad contributed to several Indian newspapers in Lahore and Amritsar, for instance, *Vakil* and *Akbar-i-Am*. What he earned from this is unknown, but it was these articles, alleged to be 'objectionable' and 'seditious', that led to his investigation. An articulate and well-informed writer, Ahmad exposed the hypocrisy of Christian missionaries and was critical of British colonial rule. In one article, written in January 1897, he denounced the life of 'pleasure' led by the British in India, while Indian men, women and children died of starvation and famine. Another, in October 1897, demanded that the government of India should spend money on industrialisation and education to help the poor. Investigations by the Glasgow police, however, revealed nothing seditious: he was found to be conscientious and hardworking, but a 'very impractical man'. The constable on the beat reported that Ahmad was seldom away, and was often seen 'posting letters and papers', most probably his newspaper articles, while friends and neighbours spoke highly of him as a respectable man, the family living 'very quietly'. Scotland Yard concluded that Ahmad was harmless and 'not worth shooting'.[61]

Plans for mission work in India had not materialised, but Christian organisations retained their interest in Ahmad. Some, like 'Professor Bruce' of the Free Church College, wanted to set him up as a missionary adviser to Indian students; others proposed he should be appointed among the lascars in Glasgow. In November 1897 an Indian Mission run by Ahmad from his home was reported to have been founded. Many 'coolies' were said to visit him 'very often', referred to him by shipping companies. By 1900, the *Glasgow Post Office Directory* described Ahmad as 'superintendent missionary to Indian sailors, lecturer and tutor, editor'.[62] Ahmad's Lascar Mission was largely educational: he described his work as 'making lascars better men' and not proselytising. He wrote: 'As a layman I try to give the best advice to Indian seafaring men, for the good of their souls, minds and bodies.' He was said to meet them at the docks and provided counselling and aid. In the absence of welfare facilities, his institution must have provided a much needed service. By 1904, he was described not only as 'superintendent missionary to Indian sailors', but also as the 'only authorised collector for the Lascar Mission', which suggests that the Mission was an independent charitable institution, Ahmad raising funds locally. From the evidence in the *Post Office Directories*, the Mission survived the 1914–18 war, when his work would have been particularly demanding owing to the number of lascars recruited. The final fate of the Mission is unknown: the last entry describing Ahmad as superintendent missionary and authorised collector appears in 1919/20. Thus, for over 20 years, Ahmad had worked as a social welfare officer among the lascars in

Glasgow. What happened to Ahmad is unknown: he disappears from the directory after 1924/5.[63] Much remains to be learnt about his family and descendants. What this portrait of his life illustrates is the difficulties historians face in researching the lives of Asians in Britain in this period.

RESIDENT ASIANS: THE WORKING CLASS

Bhose and Ahmad were but two of the several hundreds of Asians in Victorian and Edwardian Britain. Some working-class Asians survived on the margins, earning a precarious living. Some were beggars or in occupations verging on begging. Ringa Swamee, a Hindu from Madras, a servant to an English 'sahib', after 15 years' service, finding himself destitute at the death of his master, supported his English wife and small daughter by begging. In a report on the poverty of the lower classes in Edinburgh, several Indians, described as 'professional beggars' were found in the lodging-houses in the West Port. Referred to as 'those Malays' (although some were from India), who 'shiver in turban and thin printed tunic', they earned a living selling religious tracts on street corners. Able to speak 'English fluently' (which suggests they had been living in Britain for some time), yet they communicated by making 'signs'. Why they had adopted this mode of living is not stated: it is possible that, unable to find work, they had resorted to this 'professional masquerade'. This sort of unflattering portrayal of the Asian poor was by no means uncommon. One generally held view was that Indians, or 'Hindoo beggars', were by nature full of 'artifice and deception'. Others referred to the 'extraordinary mendacity of this race' that 'never falters, hesitates or stumbles, but flows on in unbroken stream of falsehood'. Their portrayal in works of fiction, too, is akin to caricature.[64] Earning a 'spare subsistence' by selling Christian tracts appears to be popular: Buksoo of east London sold tracts arranged on a board suspended in front of him. In Henry Mayhew's survey, the first such inquiry into the state of the people by a private individual, mention is made of several Indian tract-sellers. Of the 50 at the time of the survey (1850s), more than half were stated to be 'foreigners such as Malays, Hindoos and negroes', some of whom spoke no English. Unlike the Edinburgh 'Malays', the London Indians might have been relative newcomers. For the cold and hungry, the slide from selling tracts to begging, even stealing may not have been too difficult, as can be seen from criminal records. Some earned a few pence as crossing-sweepers. The more enterprising were said to pitch a claim to a crossing 'proudly ... [as] their own' and were accused of depriving 'our own mendicants' of their livelihood. Others were alleged to be aggressive and 'impudent', demanding money by thrusting their hands into the faces of unescorted women passengers.[65] Such stereotypical views of Asians were not untypical.

But not all working-class Indians were paupers or lived by begging. Those who could, continued in domestic service. Thirty-year-old James Abdoolah from Bombay, who came in 1842, married and with an eight-year-old daughter, was a servant to a Bombay Artillery Major. Others worked as casual labourers. Sardulla Sandas, a sailor with a knowledge of gardening, having missed a ship in Glasgow, tramped the country for several months, supporting himself as a gardener. In Enfield he found employment in a nursery, only being discharged when business became slack. Francis Kaudery, from Goa, was employed as a steward at the Royal Sovereign, a public-house in Bluegate Fields in London's East End, patronised by many lascars. Ameen Adeen, from Bombay, lived in Westminster with his wife and two children. He had been employed as part of the retinue of the Queen of Awadth. He also hawked jewellery in the streets. Roshun Khan, a long-time Edinburgh resident, lived with his wife and two children in Gilmour-close, in the Grassmarket area. He was described as a well-known character, who had 'long enjoyed the fame of supplying savoury pipes to the lovers of smoke'. He sold pipes every Friday in the High Street, near Castle-hill and went to fairs and races at Mussleburgh. Another Edinburgh Asian was Khuda Baksh, an old man who lived at Canongate, earning his living making 'various articles in ornamental basket-work'.[66]

Some self-employed Asians made a living purveying Asian culture as peripatetic singers and musicians and vendors of Indian articles. Ram Sam, the 'tam-tam man' was well-known around London. For 15 years, he had entertained Londoners with his little drum. Another, a Hindu, a professional musician, carried his drum suspended from his neck. Beating a melody, he was said to sing and dance, 'his skinny legs, spinning round and round ... [performing] all the antics which only Asiatic exhilaration can produce'. Dermian was another drum player. Jhulee Khan, from Calcutta, who had jumped ship in 1841, earned a living with a fiddle, playing hornpipes and singing English songs, 'mostly in tap-rooms' around London and in provincial towns in England and Scotland. Sixteen years later, in 1857, influenced by a woman in Tottenham, north London, he embraced Christianity, took the name of John Carr and, abandoning the tap-rooms, turned to singing hymns and preaching the Gospel in the streets. In 1866, he returned to Calcutta with his English wife and five children as 'an agent of the Foreign Evangelists' Society' to work with a European missionary in the north-west of India.[67] Thus, Indians, like the Italian hurdy-gurdy players, used music to earn a living. What is significant is that, through such processes, Indian music would have become familiar to some people in Britain from the second half of the nineteenth century. In the East End of London, for instance, at the back of the dilapidated public-house, the Royal Sovereign, working-class Indian residents and others gathered to listen to an Indian sitar and tambour player. Asians are also documented as snake charmers and working in circuses.[68]

Other Asian street vendors hawked Indian cures and wares. Doctor Bokanky, the London street herbalist, sold 'Kalibonca Root', especially brought from Madras, for complaints ranging from toothache, headache to dimness of sight and giddiness. He advertised it as a cure 'never known to fail'. He must have been widely patronised for he had been a vendor for 26 years when photographed by Mayhew. Some sold curry powder, most probably to India-returned British families, in places as far apart as Dublin and London's East End.[69]

Like the Chinese, working-class Indians, helped by their English wives, ran lodging-houses for their compatriots. Meer Jan had a lodging-house in Liverpool, Jan Abdoolah one in Salford. In Birmingham Ram Jan and Dada Bhai ran two lodging-houses. In the Bluegate Field district of Shadwell, London, 'the Hindoo Piero and the Hindoo Abdoolah' (clearly Muslim names and therefore not Hindus) kept lodging-houses for lascars. 'Abdoolah' (Abdool Rhemon) from Surat, who had lived in London since 1830, had first swept a crossing in St Paul's Churchyard, picking up 'a little English'. Later, he had worked for the Nepalese ambassador, and then progressed to set up his own lodging-house with his English wife. It was alleged that the house was for 'degrading and wicked purposes' and he enticed lascars to come there. A woman from Calcutta, described as a 'dark girl of Indian Portuguese class', with her two or three English companions, kept a lodging-house. It was alleged to be a brothel for lascars and Chinese. However, the reference to an Indian working-class woman, usually absent from surveys, is significant as it suggests the presence of Asian women in Britain. References to Indian wives married to white men, too, are found in literature of the period. In 1871, the case of Elizabeth of 'Hindoo extraction', living in Artillery Place, in Greenwich, and mistreated for '20 years' by her husband, was reported.[70] At one time Indian oculists were popular. They were found practising in Edinburgh, Swansea, Bradford, Norwich, Croydon and London. Some advertised themselves with sophisticated handbills and testimonials of their successes.[71]

From the narratives of two Asians recorded by Mayhew, we learn something of their experiences in Victorian society. The first, a Calcutta

Muslim, had been brought to Britain as a servant by a military officer and taken to Scotland. Within seven months, his master having died, he had been left without employment. By the time Mayhew recorded his testimony, he had been in Britain for 10 years, including 5 in London. He was a Christian and married to a white woman who had been a maid. They had one 6-year-old son, to whom he sometimes spoke in 'Hindustanee', which suggests the child was bilingual. He had continued in domestic service for some years. However, despite references, unable to find work as a servant, and not wanting to beg, he had purchased a 'tom-tom' with his last 10 shillings. Playing the drum, he sang religious songs in his 'own language', while his son performed jumps 'in my contree's way'. At first, he had made good money, earning 3 to 6 shillings a day. But once the novelty wore off his takings dwindled. To supplement his income, he turned to working as a 'model' for two or three 'picture-men'. He summed up his philosophy as 'anything for honest bread. I must not be proud.' Life in Britain had not been easy. Food, especially rice, was expensive; he lacked adequate warm clothing. His wife, a good needlewoman, could not obtain work. He had experienced racism, been called names, 'black dis or de oder', and often beaten up. On the positive side, 'gentlemen' sometime saved him, and the magistrate punished one rough for a violent blow, which had left a scar on his chin. The 50-year-old Joaleeka was fluent in English and several Indian languages, having travelled all over India as a baggage servant to a European army officer. He came to Britain as an interpreter to the retinue of a 'great native prince'. In their hotel in Oxford Street, having formed an attachment with an English maid, he stayed on and converted to Christianity. He found white women kind and helpful. Joaleeka, married several times, lived with his three children and Irish wife of six years. The marriage was not without friction: he complained that his wife got drunk 'too often'. He earned his living by interpreting, sweeping the crossing and begging. After the 1857 Rising, life had been difficult, as 'no one would look at a poor Indian then – much less give to him'.[72]

What emerges from these accounts is the resourcefulness and adaptability of the Asian working class, of the variety of jobs they did in order to preserve their self-esteem. We also learn of their experiences of racial prejudice and violence, and of their unexpected geographical locations. In London, one contemporary found 20 'Asiatic vagrants' living within a 'short distance' of Parliament. The same writer recorded that, between 1867 and 1869, he had encountered Asians living in Edinburgh, Leith, Glasgow and Stirling in Scotland; at Cardiff in Wales. And in England, in the Isle of Wight, Southampton, London, Brighton,

Bristol, Bath, Peterborough, Hull, Sunderland, Durham, Birmingham, Liverpool and Manchester.[73] Contemporaries disapproved of their relations with white women:

> It would surprise many people to see how extensively these dark classes are tincturing the colour of the rising race of children in the lowest haunts of this locality; and many of the young fallen females have a visible infusion of Asiatic or African blood in their veins. They form a peculiar class, but mingle freely with others. It is an instance of depraved taste, that many of our fallen ones prefer devoting themselves entirely to the dark race of men, and some who are not married to them have infants by them.[74]

Their English wives were referred to merely as 'Lascar Sally' or 'Calcutta Louise', and only occasionally as 'Mrs Janoo, Mrs Peeroo or Mrs Mahomed'. Many of these women became fluent in Indian languages and acted as interpreters in police courts for Indian sailors. Their children, if they attended school, went to the Ragged School.

However unflattering the picture, it illustrates the level of their integration. Inhabiting the same spaces and sharing a similar subculture, the extent to which they had merged into the working-class population of their locality and the degree of acculturation of some is seen from the comment that 'the man spoke English like a cockney of the lowest order'.[75] Such a level of integration may suggest their acceptance in British society. But references to their offspring as 'an anomalous race of children', is revealing of other attitudes: of anxieties over racial 'purity' and meanings of Englishness. Contemporaries described the multi-racial areas of London's East End as 'the most awful places', of opium smoking and oriental depravity. The perceived connection between 'oriental quarters' and opium 'dens' in literature demonstrates 'the nineteenth century academic and imaginative demonology of the "mysterious Orient" '. The description of their wives as 'Lascar Sally' or 'Cheeney Emma' further conjures up emotive images of the 'orientalisation' of English women. In popular imagination, these women not only became half-orientalised, but were seen as innocent victims.[76] For instance, one reporter to a 'den' in Victoria Court, describing how Eliza, the wife of 'a black-moustached, swarthy Lascar' came to be addicted to opium, wrote: 'She says that she can speak Hindi and Hindustani, and used to be with those that spoke them, and one would say to her, "Have a whiff," and another would say to her, "Have a whiff," and she knew no better, so she got into the habit, and now she cannot leave it off.' Such imagery whipped up fears of oriental men's sexual powers over English women, corrupting the race and undermining the empire. Reality, however, was different: the so-called opium 'dens' were 'simply poorly fitted social clubs', free from even the 'vices' usually found in the 'public-houses of the same class'.[77] But in popular consciousness, lascars and Chinese appeared as morally corrupt outsiders, who needed controlling.

The state's policy, on the other hand, remained one of preventing the settlement of working-class Indians in Britain. In 1910, the Committee set up to investigate the 'problem' of relieving destitutes from India and the colonies, found only 250 Indians for the entire period 1888–1910. In its conclusion, it also admitted that 'there is unfortunately, a prejudice in the labour market against the coloured British subjects', making it difficult for them to obtain employment. Nonetheless, the Committee recommended repatriation as the best solution.[78]

Life for the working class in Victorian and Edwardian society was difficult enough, but, for the Asian working class, speaking a different language, having a different religion and faced with racial prejudice, life was even bleaker. But for the determined second-generation British-born Indian with working-class roots, social mobility might be possible, as the remarkable life of Albert J. Mahomet illustrates.

ALBERT J. MAHOMET

Possibly the first British-born Indian photographer, Albert Mahomet, a preacher and a teacher, is one of the few Asians in Britain in this period to have left us a record of their lives. *From Street Arab to Pastor,* first published in 1894, is an important piece of social history, describing the life of the poor in London's East End, in the workhouses of London and Norfolk, life in rural Norfolk and the state of race relations in Victorian Britain.[79]

Born in April 1858 in Sophia Street, Bow, East London, Mahomet had an English mother, a woman from Wells-Next-the-Sea, and an Indian father, from Calcutta, who may have come to Britain as a seaman and who became a pedlar, selling jewellery and watches, knives and scissors and other oddments at Fakenham, Norfolk. Eventually, the family moved to London. After some years, 'things being not so pleasant at home', the father deserted his wife and six children, signing on as a 'single boat-swain' on a ship bound for Calcutta, where he died. Ann Mahomet, struggling to bring up the family, scraped a living somehow and took to drink, devolving family responsibility to Rosa, the eldest, until her death at the age of 18.[80] Life must have been grim: Mahomet describes their poverty and dilapidated home in Bow, their hunger and scraps of food, and walking to the Ragged School barefoot in the snow.

At the age of six or seven, Mahomet began helping the family budget, earning a few pence selling newspapers. With a gang of eight to ten children – Mahomet as 'leader' – he banded together to obtain money by 'tippling', begging, singing, or pretending to be lost to gain a tram fare and even by stealing. The fact that Mahomet makes no mention of any taunts from the neighbourhood children, and the fact that he was accepted as 'leader' of the gang, suggests he merged into the world of the East End where inter-racial marriages were not so uncommon. What else emerges from the picture of poverty and deprivation is the support of their neighbours, Mahomet particularly commenting on how 'the poor' of the slums helped others 'handsomely despite being drunkards, criminals and unemployed'; and his fond memories of the care and shelter given to them by a woman chestnut-seller.

Some time in 1866, Mahomet's older brother, Eli was sent to the reformatory at Feltham for stealing. After his three-year sentence, he went to sea, eventually settling in Canada. Around 1867, after a street brawl and the imprisonment of their mother for 'causing obstruction and using obscene language', the four children were taken into Limehouse workhouse, where within 12 months, Sake Husson died of consumption. Because their mother was a Wells woman, and it was customary in Victorian times for over-stretched Parishes to send inmates to their place of settlement, Mahomet and his two sisters were moved to Thursford, nine miles from Wells-Next-the-Sea. Because of the rigid rules of separation of males and females in the workhouse, he and his two sisters were separated. After two years at Thursford Union, Mahomet was rescued by his uncle, William Jenkerson, who found him a job as a servant in an establishment in the High Street, Wells, cleaning cutlery and boots, polishing harness, grooming the pony, and running errands. His sister Louisa found placement as a maid, emigrating with the family to South America.[81] After several years in Wells, and a series of jobs, first for a doctor, then for a lawyer and finally for Samuel Gooch, farmer and superintendent of the Wesleyan Sunday School, Mahomet moved to Lincoln to work as a blacksmith's striker at Messrs Clayton and Shuttleworth's Works. He stayed here for three years. It was in Lincoln that Mahomet, aged 18, 'found peace with God'; this would launch him into his work as a Sunday School teacher and a lay preacher.

What were Mahomet's experiences as a young worker in Norfolk and Lincoln? Did he suffer from racial prejudice? There was much curiosity about his origins and family: whether his father was 'a black man', was frequently questioned. Though sparing in details, it was here, while working at the farm, and especially in Lincoln, that Mahomet records some of his most painful experiences, which he put down to his

'complexion being rather dark'. Taunted as a 'darky' and 'soot bag', he
was tormented and jeered at by his workmates 'nearly everyday'. Some
would hold a lump of chalk to his face, light a match or a jet of gas
when he was around to indicate darkness in the room. Bits of iron, coke
and greasy waste were hurled at him, causing injury. His conversion led
to further sneers: 'Darky has turned a Methody.' Christian stoicism and
a quick repartee helped him retain his dignity.[82]

After his conversion, Mahomet became a teacher in a United
Methodist Free Church Sunday School in Lincoln, and an evangelist
with the Christian Mission, preaching around Lincolnshire, Nottingham-
shire, Lancashire and Yorkshire. Mahomet was active in the temperance
movement. He compiled an essay on the use and abuse of tobacco. In
December 1881, he married Paulina Gill, a fellow evangelist, whom he
met at the Huddersfield Convocation. The Mahomets lived in Littlebor-
ough, in London and Elton, moving to Gorleston where, for three years
he was a pastor to the fishing community of Great Yarmouth. In October
1893, Mahomet and his wife returned to Wells-Next-the-Sea. His
autobiography written in Wells ends in 1894.

From his base in Wells, Mahomet continued as an evangelist with
the Primitive Methodists, assisting Sam Peel. He was one of their
recognised preachers, as seen from his name on the 1906 Plan.[83] He also
launched into a new career as a photographer, with a studio in Lugger
Yard, Theatre Road, first listed in the 1896 Kelly's Directory. He was
possibly one of the only two photographers in Wells around this time.
Mahomet specialised in family portraits (children given special attention), weddings and groups; he enlarged pictures at 'reasonable prices',
copied and renewed old photographs and undertook assignments to
photograph buildings. He was well known: booklets of his photographs
of town and country scenes, costing 2d., were sold by accredited agents,
at post offices and grocers in Norfolk. After his death, the collection of
his photographic plates was largely spoilt, but some of his photographs
can be found in the library in Wells.[84] Mahomet's studio flourished for
over 12 years, the last entry being in 1904.

What happened to Mahomet? No obituary with the Primitive
Methodists has been traced. In More Memories of Wells, mention is
made of 'his grandson' who 'came to teach at Wells Primary School for
a few years'. In October 1998, in response to my appeal in the Dareham
and Fakenham Times, the 79-year-old Mrs Kathleen Francis wrote to
tell me that her grandmother, Emily Jane Bishop's maiden name was
Mahomet. And that they 'have a book by a Pastor A.J. Mahomet and a
portrait of my father (taken during the First World War), which we
believe he did, and he may be my great-grandfather but we have no

proof'. However tenuous the evidence, Mahomet's descendants still live in Norfolk, and in other parts of the world.[85]

Mahomet's ministry as a Sunday School teacher and an evangelist lay preacher, during the 17 years covered in his autobiography, was entirely among white people. Much of his work in parishes like Gorleston consisted of visiting his 'folk' in their homes. As a photographer he recorded people and the topography of Norfolk. How was he perceived? The testimonials contained in his autobiography speak glowingly of his devotion as a preacher, his 'ready utterance' and his services as 'full of fire', of his zeal, energy, earnestness and the success of his work. Considered as having 'a remarkable history', he was seen as 'wonderfully successful in adapting himself to various classes of people among whom he laboured' – and, by inference, of his acceptance by the local communities. Mahomet makes no mention of any hostility during this period of his life. Totally committed to his work as a Christian, he immersed himself in the communities among whom he worked. For instance, he raised funds within the church for the Gorleston 'Voluntary Lifeboat Fund', even writing a poem to raise money. A testimonial and a purse given to him from the skippers and crews of the Short Blue Fleet of Fishing Vessels in Gorleston testifies to their regard for him. In Wells, he formed the Wells Mutual Concert Band for the youth and was appointed its president. How did he see himself? Without denying his history and identity, he did not dwell on it either. The autographed photograph in his autobiography shows a man dressed in western-style in the period of the time.[86] Mahomet appears to have merged into the English Christian community of his localities.

ASIAN PROFESSIONALS

Then there was the Asian middle class. Their diversity is illustrated from a small sample of 53 signatories, most from London, others from as far afield as Edinburgh, contained in the 1914 letter from Gandhi. Six described themselves as merchants and traders, another six as physicians and surgeon; three were barristers, two engineers, one a journalist; and many others were students.[87] This section considers the lives and achievements of some Asian professionals in Victorian and Edwardian society.

The rise to prominence of Sake Dean Mahomed was described in Chapter 2. The careers of his descendants (and some information is available) provide us with further insights into the experiences of Indo-Britons. William, the eldest (1797–1833) continued as a postman in London till his death. Three other sons followed in Sake Dean Mahomed's footsteps, but better equipped with 'modern' techniques. Deen Mahomed (?–1836) apprenticed to Thomas Mapleton to learn the medical practice of 'cupping' (bleeding a patient), ran the London bath house established in 1830, in St James Place. However, within a year of his death in 1836, the establishment was taken over by a rival.[88] Horatio Mahomed (1816–73), the manager of the Ryder Street Baths in St James's, London, established in 1838, was forced in the 1850s, by financial insolvency, to move to a smaller establishment at 42 Somerset Street, Portman Square. Horatio, too, made a social and professional name for himself, his second marriage to Elizabeth Pruday in 1848 being reported in the *Gentleman's Magazine*. As an author, he publicised the healthful qualities of bathing, and his own establishment.[89] Arthur Ackber Mahomed (1819–72), the youngest, inherited the much reduced, rented Brighton establishment at Black Lion Street. In keeping with the family tradition, his wife, Amelia, attended female patients. But, lacking his father's flair for self-promotion, Arthur could not compete with his rivals. Besides, times had changed. Brighton-born and having a white mother, he did not succeed in cashing in on the 'Indian-ness' of Arthur's Baths. Some English clients considered his establishment not authentically Indian enough. Others excluded him from English society for racial reasons, equating him with 'jettee [black] natives of India'.[90]

Frederick Mahomed (1818–88), unlike his brothers, branched out into an entirely new enterprise, establishing a fencing academy and gymnasium. Beginning as a dancing master in Liverpool at the age of 20, he returned to Brighton, and, in the words of the writer of his obituary, was the first man to open a gymnasium and orthopaedic establishment in 'his native town'. He became an accomplished fencing instructor and teacher of gymnastics, running daily lessons for young men and adults, while his wife, Sarah Hodgkinson, described as 'professor of girls' exercises', ran courses for young women, three days a week, in the popular 'Swedish musical exercises', designed to develop a graceful and healthy figure.[91] The middle classes patronised Mahomed's gymnasium. Private families, public schools and ladies' seminaries appointed him for instruction in 'gymnastics, orthopaedics and hygienics'. That he was successful and that the gymnasium, as the centre for fashionable exercise, made a mark on Brighton society, is seen from the fact that, by 1844, the gymnasium had expanded from its original premises at 8 Paston Place to three establishments, while the half-yearly exhibitions he organised were notable events in the social calendar of upper- and middle-class Brightonians, attended by over 300 spectators. An 'amiable and unobtrusive' man, he was well known among the fashionable gentlemen's clubs in London.[92]

How did Frederick Mahomed see himself? Unlike his father, he professionally advertised himself simply as 'Mr Frederick Mahomed (late Pupil of Mons. Hamon)'. Nonetheless, he took pride in some elements of his Indian Islamic heritage. One of his sons recalled that 'his family was very proud of their descent from the prophet Mahommed [sic]'. Further, Frederick and his wife combined their dual heritages in the names they chose for their children. Their five sons were given at least one Muslim name: Frederick Henry Horatio Akbar (1849–84), a distinguished doctor at Guy's; James Deen Kerriman (1853–1935), a graduate of Keeble College, Oxford and a Church of England Vicar, was for many years a minister in London's East End parishes, a chaplain to the London Hospital for eight years, and later Rector of Culford in Suffolk for 27 years. Omar Said (1854–?), was an architect, while Arthur George Sulieman (1857–1943) medical student at Guy's, later a doctor at Bournemouth and author of *The Treatment at the Bournemouth Mont Dore*, published in 1889, was well known in the British Medical Association. Their youngest son, Herbert Abdulla Selim (1860–?), was a dental surgeon for some years in Norfolk. Their daughters, on the other hand were given 'Anglo-Saxon' names: Florence Gertrude (1851–1945), Marcia Madeline (1856–?) and Adeline Alice Bertha (1859–1949).[93]

How was the family perceived in Brighton? Mahomed's gymnasium may have been patronised, he may have been accepted by fashionable society, but there are conflicting perceptions and meanings of Britishness. Some saw Frederick Mahomed as a 'much respected fellowtownsman', and a 'native' of Brighton. Others saw the family differently, as a comment from a contemporary of Mahomed's youngest daughter at the Brighton High School for Girls, who described Adeline Mahomed, as a 'dark and typical Eastern' girl, illustrates.[94]

FREDERICK AKBAR MAHOMED

A pioneer of clinical research, Frederick Akbar Mahomed (1849–84) changed our understanding of high blood pressure.[95] Born in Brighton and privately educated, Mahomed studied medicine at Sussex County Hospital and then at Guy's (1869–72). A student of 'exceptional ability', he carried off several prizes, including, in 1871, the Pupils' Physical Society Prize for his work in modifying the sphygmograph, an instrument for measuring blood pressure. Mahomed not only made it lighter, but, more crucial for the measurement of blood pressure, introduced the spring mechanism, controlled by a screw, with the help of his local watchmaker in Forest Hill, South London, to regulate the pressure applied to the artery.[96] He also published a series of papers on the sphygmograph in the *Medical Times and Gazette.*

In 1872, having qualified as a Member of the Royal College of Surgeons (MRCS), Mahomed joined the Highgate Infirmary (Central London Sick Asylum) in North London as an assistant medical officer. A year later, in 1873 (the year he married Ellen Chalk, the daughter of a Brighton solicitor), he was elected resident Medical Officer at the London Fever Hospital in Islington. Two years later, in 1875, having already gained Membership of the Royal College of Physicians (MRCP), with the support of Sir William Broadbent, he secured the appointment as medical tutor and pathologist at St Mary's Hospital, Paddington. The family then moved to 54 Norfolk Square, Paddington. In 1877, Mahomed's ambition to work at Guy's was fulfilled when he was appointed to the post of resident medical registrar. By then, although he had obtained an MD from Brussels, realising that a European qualification might not be enough for further promotion, he enrolled through Gonville and Caius College for a Bachelor of Medicine (MB) from Cambridge. 'To keep his terms' involved commuting twice a week to Cambridge. But by travelling on the last train, he was able to continue working at Guy's and fulfil University requirements. It is a tribute to his intelligence, energy, enthusiasm and determination that he completed his MB in October 1881. His thesis, 'Chronic Bright's Disease without Albuminuria', published in *Guy's Hospital Reports,* is his significant work on hypertension. In 1880, Mahomed was elected a Fellow of the Royal College of Physicians (FRCP), a tribute to his achievements, though lack of money for fees deferred his taking up the honour. In 1881, he was elected assistant physician at Guy's, the first member of staff to be recommended by his own colleagues.[97]

Mahomed's most notable contribution to British medical science is his work on hypertension. In Britain and elsewhere at the time almost every authority on the disease followed Bright's teaching that high blood pressure was caused by kidney damage. Mahomed was the first person to recognise that high blood pressure was a primary condition, and provided the first clear clinical description of it. Medical authorities today suggest that his description of 'essential hypertension' in a series of papers in the *Lancet*, would, 'after some modernisation of the terms used, find a place in any modern text book'. Mahomed also accurately described the history of the progression of the disease: how young people with high blood pressure showed little sign of illness, but with age it could prove fatal, thus recognising what today is considered to be a most important public health issue: the large numbers of apparently healthy people who could develop serious illness in old age. What caused hypertension? In Mahomed's view, high blood pressure was a 'diathesis', that is the result of the 'interaction of genetic and environmental factors'. He listed environmental factors as alcohol, good living, lead poisoning, hard work, mental anxiety and constant excitement. What Mahomed concluded in the 1870s anticipated conclusions confirmed by Pickering 70 years later.[98]

Mahomed's other project, even more remarkable for the time, was the Collective Investigation Record: gathering data by means of printed questionnaires sent to practitioners of medicine throughout the country, in order to build up a record of clinical, hereditary and anthropological features of disease. The Record set up by the BMA in 1880, with Mahomed as its secretary, was his brainchild. But the project was abandoned after only two volumes of the results were published. Why? Some doctors did not have time to fill the data, others, lacking training, sent inadequate information. Without computer aids, analyses and computation involved massive labour. Nonetheless, the value of Collective Investigation is recognised. As John Swales points out, it was 'an impressive monument to a brilliant concept many years ahead of its time'. With its abandonment progress in epidemiology and our understanding of disease was delayed until the large-cohort studies like those at Framingham, Massachusetts in recent times.[99]

Mahomed died of typhoid fever in November 1884. He was just 35 years old, at the beginning of his fame and on the ladder to a successful career. To help his wife and young family, a subscription was set up by the medical fraternity, both at St Mary's and Guy's, an illustration of the measure of their esteem.[100]

A man of prodigious energy and new ideas, Mahomed made important contributions to medical science. The *Medical Press and Circular* noted that 'his work on arterial tension gained for him a world-wide reputation, as well deserved as it was extensive', while the *British Medical Journal* considered his death 'a great loss ... great nationally and internationally'. In our own times, in 1995, speculating on the 'what if' of history, Swales suggests that if Mahomed had not died prematurely in 1884 'clinical research in Britain would have been both stronger and more highly developed at the beginning of the twentieth century'. Then why was Mahomed forgotten so quickly and his name left out from the pantheons of British medical science? And why are his important findings on essential hypertension are not acknowledged?[101]

Some writers cite the fact that Mahomed's own writing lacked clarity. Others suggest that his scrupulous retention of Bright's terminology, 'pre-albuminuric Bright's disease', unfortunately obscured the nature of his ground-breaking conclusions, which had moved beyond Bright. But this had not prevented his contemporaries from understanding the significance of his conclusions as seen from the tribute by his colleagues, Goodhart and Jacobson of Guy's. His early death, too, is cited as a reason. 'If Akbar had lived he would have made his name' is a constant refrain from professionals and friends, and, as Cameron and Hicks suggest, his early death prevented the growth of a school of thought round him with devoted pupils.[102] Was racial prejudice a factor? The fact that Mahomed succeeded in breaching the citadel of Guy's suggests otherwise. While his family had succeeded as self-employed entrepreneurs, Mahomed was in a white establishment. His enormous abilities were recognised. He gained promotions on merit – 'gave so much satisfaction', is one description – and he was awarded the FRCP precociously for his achievements. But racism cannot be ruled out altogether. Several obituaries in respected journals drew attention to his 'dark complexion'. Even Wilks and Bettany, in their history of Guy's Hospital written in 1892, comment on Mahomed's 'Oriental strain', while a student recalled that Mahomed's 'teaching and his methods seemed as foreign as his name to the atmosphere of the place [Guy's]'.[103] This would suggest that Mahomed remained an outsider in some eyes. An analysis of *Munk's Roll, 1826–1925,* is even more revealing: among the 864 FRCPs, there is no other Indian-sounding name. After his death, pride of place was given to Mahomed's work on the Collective Investigation Record (which was abandoned) by several distinguished papers and journals, including some medical ones, among them Wilks and Bettany. But they made no mention of his most revolutionary findings on high blood pressure, which changed our understanding of the disease – except as a mention to his writings on 'questions relating to kidney disease'.[104] Could this then mean that racist exclusion operated against Mahomed? This might explain why his sons changed their names to Deane in 1902 (see p. 78). But, even more crucially, was it because Mahomed's work was misrepresented by others, so depriving him of the credit? Several writers have pointed to the fact that Sir Clifford Allbutt (1836–1925), Mahomed's contemporary and the 'acknowledged' authority on hypertension, who outlived him, in his compendium published in 1915, *Diseases of the Arteries,* 'misquoted' Mahomed's conclusions. And this, despite the fact that Allbutt was present at the meeting of the Pathological Society in 1877, where Mahomed presented his findings. What is even more surprising is that, in 1895, Allbutt had acknowledged the influence of Mahomed's conclusions on his research. And so Allbutt gets the credit, but, as Cameron and Hicks point out, 'at the expense of occluding Mahomed's contributions' in his writings.[105]

Mahomed was a man ahead of his time. Nothing much of any significance has been added to his account of the clinical features of essential hypertension since his death in 1884.

Of Mahomed's five children (two sons and three daughters), only Archibald Deane (1874–1948), followed his father into medicine and research on arterial blood pressure. Born in Brighton in November 1874, he graduated MB, Ch B from Aberdeen University in 1902, obtaining his MD in 1910. Starting work as a house surgeon in the Children's Hospital at Paddington, and at the East Suffolk Hospital, he later moved to the Brompton Hospital as senior clinical assistant. Around 1912, he went into practice at Eastbourne, also acting as assistant medical officer to the Princess Alice Memorial Hospital, later becoming surgeon and physician there. In 1935 he moved to a practice in Abingdon. He was chairman of the Eastbourne branch of the BMA, worked as a police surgeon, and as medical officer to Morris Motors. He died in December 1948, aged 73. Of Mahomed's other children, nothing is known about Ellen (1876–?), and Dorothy (1880–?). Janet Pearson (1881–?) was alive in 1951, living with her family in Cornwall, and Humphrey Deane (1883–?), an architect, was then in Orkney.[106]

Indian students, having obtained their qualifications, sometimes stayed to practise their professions in Britain. Upendra Krishna Dutt, from a poor Calcutta family, whom a Gilchrist scholarship, won in 1876, had enabled to study medicine at London University, was one. But, despite brilliant qualifications (he won several prizes) and testimonials, Dutt found himself rejected, time and again. His persistence finally obtained him a post in Leicester. Eventually, lack of capital notwithstanding, Dutt managed to buy a medical practice in Cambridge, in a working-class district with an overwhelming population of railway workers. He married the Swedish writer, Anna Palme, by all accounts against the wishes of her family, and relations remained strained. But the Dutts were a close-knit family. As a doctor, according to his son, the future Communist, Rajani Palme Dutt (see p. 290), Dutt was popular, held in 'deep affection ... by all the workers and poorer sections in Cambridge'. But financially life was difficult. Dutt also encountered colour prejudice, particularly from 'the upper-class sections' of society. Like his relative, R.C. Dutt, the writer of the influential *The Economic History of India*, Dutt was an ardent nationalist and his Cambridge home became a meeting place for visiting nationalists. When the first Asian Students' Society (Majlis) was founded at Cambridge University, its meetings, too, were held at Dutt's residence. Indian politics would, thus, have had a formative influence on the Dutt children. Upendra Dutt died in 1938.[107]

Pulipaka Jagannadham, a student from Madras, after obtaining his MB, CM from Edinburgh in 1891, established his practice at 13 Rillbank Terrace. In the same year, Fram Gotla, after an outstanding career at Bombay University, came to London for further qualifications and experience. He, too, stayed to work as a physician in London. One of the signatories to Gandhi's 1914 letter, Gotla, married to an Irish woman, became an influential member of the Parsi community. Of their three children, Dudley became a doctor in Leicester, Irene was a nurse, while Micky established a minicab business. Dr Krishna M. Pardhy, a civil surgeon, had been sent to South Africa with the Indian army during the Boer War in 1899. In 1900, he came to England as a medical officer in charge of the soldiers. Having obtained his MRCS and LRCP, in 1904, he was appointed a House Surgeon at the Royal Cornwall Infirmary in Truro. Three years later, Pardhy went to London's Harley Street and in 1911, he moved to Edgbaston in Birmingham as a consultant surgeon. A sportsman, Pardhy won a gold medal for wrestling in the Midlands Championships in 1910. He founded the British India Association in Birmingham and in the 1920s and 1930s played an active role in Indian student societies. Married to an English woman, he had two children. Dr Bhattacharya, a Christian, on the other hand, worked as a factory doctor at Nunhead, earning £8 per month, with free board and lodging and an allowance for a servant.[108]

THE EDALJI CASE

George Edalji's name is synonymous with the infamous Edalji Case of 1903, involving a gross miscarriage of justice with overtones of racism. Born in 1876, in Great Wyrley, Staffordshire, George Ernest Thompson Edalji was the eldest son of Shapurji Edalji, the vicar of Great Wyrley. Educated at Rugeley Grammar School and Mason College, Birmingham (Birmingham University), in October 1893 Edalji began his five-year articleship with a firm of Birmingham solicitors. A brilliant law student, he won a number of Law Society prizes and, in 1898, he was Birmingham Law Society's bronze medallist for that year. In 1899, aged 23, he set up his own law practice at 54 Newhall Street, Birmingham. Edalji was also the author of *Railway Law for the 'Man in the Train'*, published by Effingham Wilson in 1901.[109]

Little is known about when and how Shapurji Edalji, an Anglican clergyman of Parsi origin, first came to Britain. In fact, had it not been for the wrongful arrest of his son in 1903, we would probably know even less. The first substantive record of his life relates to his marriage in 1874 to Charlotte Elizabeth Stoneham, said to be of genteel family background. In December 1875, through the patronage of his uncle by marriage, the gift of the living of the parish of Great Wyrley, situated six miles north of Walsall, was given to him. A rural mining village of 5,000 farmers, agricultural labourers, miners and small shopkeepers, it was not a rich living. Despite their slender means, their three children were given a good education. George became a solicitor, Horace, born in 1879, worked in government service and their daughter, Maud, born in 1882, was a botanist.[110]

Edalji, described as an 'amiable and devoted' clergyman, was said to conduct his ministry with 'dignity and discretion'. But he had not been fully accepted: some considered the appearance of a 'coloured clergyman' with 'half-caste' children in 'a rude, unrefined' English parish 'regrettable', and such 'experiments' should never be repeated. The family played down suggestions of prejudice, maintaining that, if it existed, it was 'confined to a very small section of the community'. Nonetheless, a series of malicious anonymous 'joke letters', the first reported case occurring in 1888, suggests that the family had long been the object of racial persecution, albeit intermittently. It is likely that racial prejudice was further compounded by Edalji's politics: he was a strong supporter of the Liberal Party. During the 1892 General Election, he lent the Vicarage schoolroom to the local Party, chairing their meeting. And for the next four years, between 1892 and 1896, the family was subjected to a spate of bizarre hoaxes and sinister anonymous letters; one even threatened: 'Before the year's end your kid will be either in the graveyard or disgraced for life.' The Chief Constable of Staffordshire, Captain the Hon. George Anson, investigating, however, alleged that the hoaxer was none other than the 16-year-old George Edalji.[111]

After a seven-year interval, on 18 August 1903, George Edalji, then aged 27, and a rising lawyer, was arrested. For seven months, between February and August 1903, a number of horses, cows and sheep had been found mutilated in Great Wyrley. Coincidental to this, sensational anonymous letters circulated, some implicating George Edalji as the culprit. And when, on the night of 17 August, yet another pony was found maimed the police accused him of the crime. Despite the fact that he had an alibi, that the crimes continued while he was in custody awaiting trial, and that he was so myopic as to make it impossible for him to find his way on a dark night to the scene of the crime, he was found guilty of the two charges:

mutilating a horse and being the author of the anonymous letters. He was sentenced to seven years penal servitude and struck off the register of the Solicitors of the Supreme Court. The Edalji family began a long campaign for his release. The Hon. R.D. Yelverton, one-time Chief Judge of the Bahamas took up their appeal. Three petitions signed by 10,000 people representing all professions, industries and trades in the Midlands and elsewhere, including 300 solicitors, were presented to the Home Office. But to no avail. To publicise his son's innocence, Shapurji Edalji wrote a 64-page booklet, *A Miscarriage of Justice: The Case of George Edalji*, rebutting, point by point, the prosecution's case. Published in 1905, it was sold for 2d.[112]

Then, in 1906, George Edalji, after three years in prison, was released without explanation. He was free, but without a pardon, and unable to practise his profession. To clear his name, he wrote a series of articles in the *Umpire*, a Manchester newspaper, and enlisted the help of Arthur Conan Doyle, who published two long non-copyright articles in the *Daily Telegraph*.[113] The case received wide publicity. Herbert Gladstone (son of the Liberal Prime Minister), the then Home Secretary, bowed to public opinion, and, in 1907, appointed a three-man Special Committee of Inquiry.

Was George Edalji guilty? The record of the trial at the Staffordshire Quarter Sessions no longer exists. In fact the 1907 Committee lamented its destruction. The depositions at the Magistrates Court survive. The only contemporary record appears in newspaper reportage, and in his father's pamphlet. There is no doubt that the conviction based on 'circumstantial evidence', would today be described as unsafe. The Committee of Inquiry found the conviction 'unsatisfactory'. In their opinion, the police and the Chief Constable, Captain the Hon. George Anson, had conducted their investigation not with a view to finding the guilty party, 'but for the purpose of finding evidence against Edalji who they were already sure was the guilty man'. Further, during the course of the proceedings the prosecution had changed the case presented to the jury. The Committee, therefore, cleared Edalji of the crime of maiming the horse. As for the anonymous letters, the Committee stuck to the verdict of the jury and in an extraordinary statement of blaming-the-victim, it concluded that Edalji, as the author of the anonymous letters, had 'brought his troubles upon himself'.[114] But why would Edalji, a rising lawyer, wish to ruin his own career by writing anonymous letters, accusing himself?

The Committee did not recommend a free pardon and Edalji's innocence was not positively established. Nonetheless, the Law Society re-instated him and a *Daily Telegraph* subscription raised £300 to help Edalji (which he used to repay the loan for his defence advanced by his aunt). Under further pressure, and placed under a great difficulty by the Special Committee's conclusion, Herbert Gladstone granted George Edalji a 'free pardon' – because his case was 'exceptional'.[115] But Edalji was never compensated for the three years he spent in prison, for the injury to his reputation and the loss of earnings.

According to one legal expert, in the case of George Edalji, 'justice doubly miscarried'. An innocent man went to jail, while the culprit remained free.[116] Why had the Chief Constable the Hon. George Anson, and the Staffordshire police, been so intent on prosecuting Edalji? Was it racial prejudice? In Shapurji Edalji's view 'prejudice and unfairness' had gained the upper hand, while George Edalji considered that the police had a 'pre-conceived and long-standing prejudice' against him. Conan Doyle condemned the police for 'accusing them beyond all sense and reason', instead of acting as the family's 'natural protectors'. Writing in 1996, Rosemary Pattenden concluded that Edalji's 'dark skin and unusual appearance had long made him the object of racial prejudice'.[117] Edalji had confounded the racial stereotype of a black man by being uppity: a grammar school boy and a brilliant student, he was a promising young lawyer, and had even dared to suggest to the police that they use dogs to track down the culprit.

The Edalji case, like that of Adolf Beck before him, became a *cause célèbre*. There were long discussions in the newspapers. Politicians demanded an independent court of criminal appeal, arguing that *ad hoc* committees were no answer to restoring the public's confidence in the British justice system. On 28 August 1907, the Criminal Appeal Act established the Criminal Court of Appeal. In this respect Edalji was an agent of change. And what of the family? Shapurji Edalji died in May 1918, having gone totally blind. He had been the vicar of Great Wyrley for 42 years. George Edalji, as far as is known, went to London where he continued to practise as a solicitor till his death in 1953.

GROWING UP IN BRITAIN

Womesh Chandra Bonnerjee, another Indian lawyer, first came to Britain in 1864 to study law at Lincoln's Inn, being called to the Bar in 1868. After a successful legal career in Calcutta, in 1902, Bonnerjee settled in England, joining his family living in Croydon. Between then and his death in 1906, he was a Privy Council lawyer in cases on appeal from India. A prominent Indian nationalist (he was the first president of the Indian National Congress), he pursued a political career, standing for

Parliament as a Liberal (see p. 132). An Anglophile and an unorthodox Hindu (he had refused the formal ritual of re-admission to caste), Bonnerjee had been charmed by Britain. He described it as a 'glorious country' and, in 1868, on his return to Calcutta, had brought his wife, Hemangini – whom he had urged to learn English – out of purdah and into wearing English dresses.[118] He gave his children Indian and English names: Kamal Krishna Shelley, born in 1869, was named after the poet, Ratna Krishna Curran (born 1883) after an Irish barrister, Nolini Héloise (born 1871) was called Nelly, Susila Anita was Susie and Pramilla was shortened to Milly. Determined to give all his children the 'privileges' of an English education from a young age, he sent the 4-year-old Shelley, young Nolini and baby Susila with Hemangini to Britain in 1874. They boarded with Colonel and Mrs Wood in Anerley, south London, and later in Croydon, the daughters attending the local Croydon High School. Over the years, Hemangini and Bonnerjee travelled back and forth until 1888, when Hemangini re-located permanently to live with their eight children in Croydon.

What would it have been like for the young Bonnerjees to be brought up in Britain during their most formative years? A family memoir, *Pramila*, by the youngest Bonnerjee, Agnes Majumdar, born in Calcutta in 1886, provides some glimpses of their lives and the choices made by one western-educated Indian nationalist.[119] Boarding with the Woods (who belonged to the austere Plymouth Brethren), was not only 'dull' – they were not even allowed to read novels – but by all accounts traumatic. The Woods, Majumdar writes, 'had a strong colour prejudice and disliked all orientals, classing them as "natives" '. They were 'never treated equally by the family' and were subjected to 'numerous indignities', ranging from ridicule for not getting their skin 'clean', to physical punishments. In 1888, Bonnerjee decided that Hemangini should have 'a home of her own', and a three-storied Victorian house 'complete with attics, basement and ten bedrooms, but alas, no bathroom' was purchased and altered to suit their requirements. Furnished 'beautifully' by the London firm of Fox and Co., the house was named Kidderpore, in memory of the ancestral home in Calcutta. Here the Bonnerjees lived for 18 years (1890–1908), and Bonnerjee himself died there in 1906.[120]

What kind of world did the Bonnerjees inhabit? Majumdar's Memoir is more a record of family events, their friends and education in England. Aware of the possibility that his daughters, 'brought up so differently' from other Bengalis, might not marry, Bonnerjee equipped them with 'a wage earning profession to fall back upon'. Nolini (at Girton) and Susie (at Newnham) both became doctors. Nolini (as Mrs

Blair) later practised as a doctor and welfare worker in Liverpool. What also emerges is their elite Victorian middle-class life, and the extent of their acculturation, reflected in their schooling, their literary and leisure pursuits, holidays in Europe (the continental tour) and at the English seaside with family and friends; Dorinda Neligan, the Head of Croydon High, joined one such holiday at Harlyn, Cornwall. Having 'lived so long' in England, the young Bonnerjees 'knew no Bengali', found their Calcutta cousins' ways 'trying', and were 'more at ease with the English-speaking Westernised Bengali girls'. Two Bonnerjees, Shelley and Nolini, chose English partners and had 'grand', 'lavish Church weddings'. The Bonnerjees entertained many visitors, English and Indian, conversation was 'lively and interesting', and the young were expected to participate, but if they got their facts wrong, they were 'sent straight off' to consult the *Encyclopaedia Britannica*. Bonnerjee is vividly recalled as 'a patriarchal figure with a long white beard' and Hemangini as 'a small figure' dressed in 'Victorian black silk dress and white lace cap'. Another visitor described Kidderpore as 'an oasis' for 'the dozens of young Indian students who came there on Sundays and were transported in spirit to their own country'. But Kidderpore would have been an India shaped by the dual world inhabited by Hemangini and Bonnerjee, as evidenced from a description of Sundays. After lunch came the obligatory visit to the cemetery with Mrs Bonnerjee (one son had died in England), followed by a 'spread of tea' and then 'Hymns' in the drawing-room, 'each in turn choosing our favourite hymn', while Nolini played the piano. The Christian 'ceremony' is explained by the fact that though Bonnerjee remained a Hindu, Hemangini converted to the Plymouth Brethren, as did some of the youngsters. In the evening the guests had a 'real Indian dinner' cooked by Hemangini. Even Bonnerjee was known to help in the kitchen. Majumdar describes how he and R.C. Dutt cooked them a 'wonderful duck curry'. Their English servants, too, acquired a taste for Indian food. The intellectual and cultural environment at Kidderpore would have reflected Bonnerjee's nationalist politics, and would have rubbed off on family and friends alike, and who helped Bonnerjee 'nurse' his parliamentary constituency of Walthamstow.[121] Home in Croydon thus was a hybrid world, reflecting choices made by two imperial citizens, Bonnerjee and Hemangini, at a particular historic time.

In 1908, two years after the death of Bonnerjee, Hemangini chose to return to India where the older Bonnerjees had set up their own homes. She died in 1910. Kidderpore was sold and, as Bedford Lodge, became an old people's home. Some of the descendants still live in London.

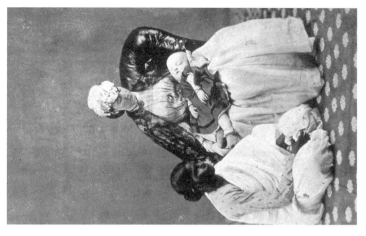

1. Charlotte Fitzroy with an Indian servant, c.1672, by Peter Lely.
(York City Art Gallery)

2. Carte de visite of Alexandra, Princess of Wales, with the baby Louise and an Indian ayah.
(Donated to the author by Noel Chanan)

3. Possibly the only surviving portrait of Dr Frederick Akbar Mahomed (1849–84). (*King's College, London (Guy's Campus) and Dr Anthony Batty Shaw*)

4. Lascars on board ship in the East India Dock, London, 1908. (*Museum of London, Docklands Collection*)

DOCTOR BOKANKY, THE STREET HERBALIST.

[From a Daguerreotype by BEARD.]

"Now then for the Kalibonca Root, that was brought from Madras in the East Indies. It'll cure the tooth-ache, head-ache, giddiness in the head, dimness of sight, rheumatics in the head, and is highly recommended for the ague; never known to fail; and I've sold it for this six and twenty year. From one penny to sixpence the packet. The best article in England."

5. Dr Bokanky, the street herbalist as depicted by Henry Mayhew, 1850s.
(Museum of London)

6. Britain's first Mosque, the Shah Jahan Mosque, Woking, built in 1889. (*Author photograph, 1998*)

7. W. C. Bonnerjee family and friends, 1900s. (*Jaya Nicholas*)

8. Frederick Mahomed Palowkar with his wife Elizabeth Woodgate and their children, c.1889. (David Wilson)

9. Sophia Duleep Singh selling the *Suffragette* outside Hampton Court Palace, 1913. (*Museum of London*)

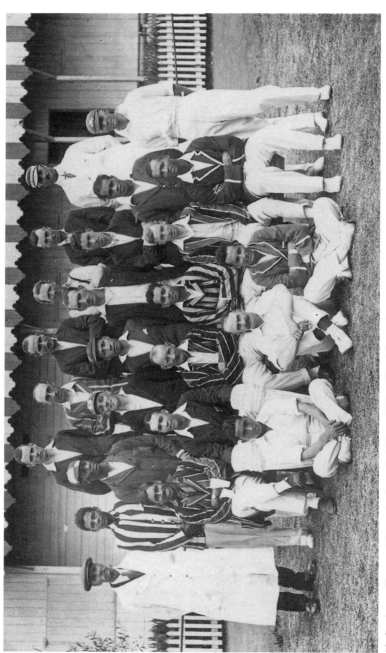

10. Gentlemen Players of Essex, the Essex 2nd Eleven, 1920s. (Muriel Simpson)

11. Group showing Dr Chunilal Katial, the first Asian Mayor (*right*), Pastor Kamal Chunchie (*left*), his wife Mabel (*centre*), daughter Muriel and friends in the garden of the Coloured Men's Institute, 1929. (*Muriel Simpson*)

12. A traditional Parsi ceremony: Shapurji Saklatvala, the Communist MP for Battersea, on his fiftieth birthday with his daughter, Sehri, aged 5. (*Sehri Saklatvala*)

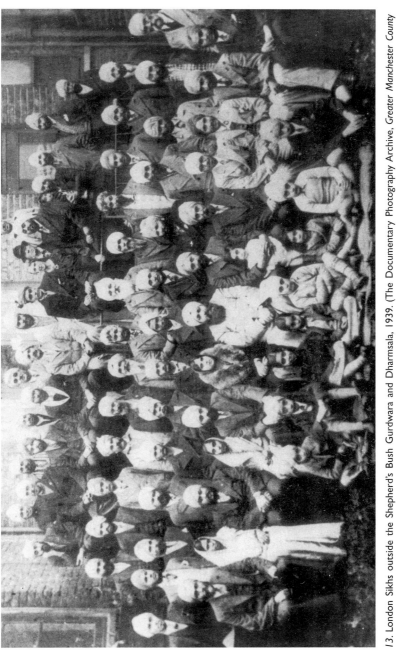

13. London Sikhs outside the Shepherd's Bush Gurdwara and Dharmsala, 1939. (The Documentary Photography Archive, *Greater Manchester County Record Office and Bhai Gurbax Singh*)

14. Lal Khan, ex-sailor and pedlar of Castlecaulfield, N. Ireland, with his wife, Mary, their three children and Mary's younger brother. (*Narinder Kapur*)

15. Dr Dharm Sheel and Savitri Chowdhary with son Vijay [George] and baby Shakuntala, Laindon, Essex, 1930s. (*Shakun Banfield*)

16. The first recorded Indian cremation in an open field on the outskirts of Londonderry, N. Ireland, 1940. (Narinder Kapur)

17. Dr Sukhsagar Datta on a TGWU march in Queen's Square, Bristol, mid-1930s. (*David Datta*)

"VOICE"—the monthly radio magazine programme in the Eastern Service of the B.B.C.

(*Left to right, sitting*) Venu Chitale, J. M. Tambimuttu, T. S. Eliot, Una Marson, Mulk Raj Anand, C. Pemberton, Narayana Menon; (*standing*) George Orwell, Nancy Barratt, William Empson.

18. London writers and poets reading from their work, 1940s. (*BBC and the British Library*, T 2497. PA. (101.) or Nº 00.E. 50388ᴾ)

ASIANS IN BUSINESS

Indian commercial activity is also evident in Victorian and Edwardian England. One of the earliest, Cama and Company, established by three Parsis, Dadabhai Naoroji (see p. 126), K.R. and M.H. Cama, was set up in London in 1855, with a branch in Liverpool. Tata Industries, founded by J.N. Tata in Bombay, had its branch in London, headed by Sir Ratan Tata, of York House, Twickenham.[122] There were other smaller enterprises. As early as 1905, an Indian restaurant was said to exist in Shaftesbury Avenue and another in Red Lion Passage in Holborn, described as 'small, extremely dirty', and frequented by students. Surveillance reports name several others: the Indian Catering Company at 36 Ledbury Road was managed by Nizam-ud-din, who also established the Eastern Cafe near Chancery Lane; the Coronation Hotel and Restaurant, founded by K.N. Das Gupta in 1911, was in Gray's Inn Road. Nitisen Dwarkadas established an export–import business in 1906.[123] The stability of these businesses is doubtful, however, unlike that of one small enterprise set up by Mahomed Ebrahim Palowkar.

Born around 1811 in Bombay, and from a Muslim family, Mahomed Palowkar came to Britain in 1834 with his father, Abu Syed, to petition the EIC in connection with their lands. In February 1835, he married an Irish-born woman, Eleanor Deegan, at St Leonard's, Shoreditch. By 1837, Palowkar was listed as a tobacconist at 20 San Street, Bishopsgate, a business that must have been successful enough to continue till his death at the age of 44 in July 1855. Of their three surviving sons, none, however, continued as a cigar manufacturer. William became a clerk to a general merchant, Ricky, a gas fitter and engineer, while Mahomed (Frederick), a hatter, migrated to Australia to seek his fortune, leaving his wife, Elizabeth, and children in England. During the First World War, because of the mistaken belief that Palowkar was a German name, Elizabeth and the family suffered much 'anti-social' behaviour, despite the fact that four of her sons were fighting in France. As a result, they changed their name to Wilson. The Wilsons and other descendants of Mahomed Palowkar still live in England today.[124]

STUDENTS IN BRITISH UNIVERSITIES

From the mid-nineteenth century onwards, a trickle of Indian students began arriving in Britain as a British qualification became essential for entry into the highest levels of public services created by the British in India. The examination for the Indian Civil Service (ICS) was only held in London. The Bar in Calcutta and Bombay was confined to barristers trained in England. Senior appointments in engineering, the police, public works or any other service, were all more likely with qualifications obtained from British universities, bringing Indians to study at English and Scottish universities. A few came on government scholarships, first established in 1868. But many more were private students, parents'sending their sons, and sometimes their daughters, at great cost and hardship. A British education conferred economic benefits and status. According to M.S. Khan, the prospect of 'good pay' and 'good living' had lured him to London for the ICS examination, while Bonnerjee considered a qualification from the 'English Bar' would give him 'a better position in life than as a mere Brahmin'. S.K. Bhuyan summed it up: 'A visit to England formed part of the future plans of ambitious children and youth of those days; and a man returned from abroad, known as *Bilat-Pherat*, commanded considerable distinction in society.' The quest for wider intellectual and cultural experiences motivated others. Dr Mehta in London advised Gandhi, 'we come to England not so much for the purpose of studies as for gaining experience of English life and customs'. Satthianadhan explained it as 'the desire to see the grand "old country", to fully understand what English life is, and form for himself an idea of English society and manners – in other words to share in the social life of the people'. According to N.S. Subbarao, the President of the Cambridge Majlis, 'sound education' and a professional qualification aside, Indian students were 'anxious' to 'mix freely with Englishmen and see English life, for which they come charged with an intense admiration of course'. How deeply colonial intellectual encounter had influenced this generation is seen from M.C. Chagla, who was so inspired by Morley's *The Life of Gladstone* that he chose to go to Christ Church, Oxford, Gladstone's college.[125] Many famous names form part of this roll call of British-educated elite: Gandhi and Jinnah, both law students; Nehru, who spent seven years in Britain, first at Harrow, then at Cambridge and finally at the Inner Temple, and his daughter, Indira Gandhi, who was at Somerville College, Oxford. There were hundreds of others, less well known. Some have left us records of their experiences, but the majority are merely names on the registers of their universities, or sometimes in official government records.

There were an impressive number of firsts: two of the earliest, Jehangir Nowrojee and Hirjeebhoy Merwanjee, from the famous Wadia firm of shipbuilders in Bombay, came to study shipbuilding at Chatham Dockyard. They stayed for nearly three years (August 1838–April 1841), and wrote a book describing their experiences. Another,

Ardaseer Cursetjee, their cousin, came in November 1839 to learn the latest developments in marine engineering, spending much time in scientific pursuits. He visited glass works and the East London waterworks, and was elected an Associate of the Institute of Civil Engineers in 1840. In 1841, he became the first Indian to be elected Fellow of the Royal Society. He also gave evidence to the Committee of the House of Commons on the opium trade. The diary of his overland journey records many of his scientific impressions.[126]

The first recorded Indian student to take up British higher education, Dhunjeebhoy Nowrojee, a Parsi convert to Christianity, came with Dr John Wilson in 1843, to study theology at the Free Church College, Edinburgh and was ordained in 1846. He was followed by the Muslim, Wuzeer Beg. Four Bengalis were the first to study medicine at University College, London in 1845. Two were financed by Dwarkanath Tagore, the grandfather of the poet Rabindranath, and the other two were sponsored by the EIC. One of them, Dr Surjor Coomar Chucker-butty, became the first to be awarded the MD in 1849. He also topped the list at the first open competitive examination of the Indian Medical Service (IMS), held in London in 1855. Comroodeen Tyabjee (Camrud-din Tyabji) the first to study law, was articled with a London firm of solicitors, and admitted to the Rolls of the Law Society in November 1858. Others chose the Inns of Court, the first being Ganendra Mohun Tagore of the Tagore family, in 1859, who was called to the Bar in June 1862. He settled in Britain with his Bengali wife, and was the first of the many Indians to teach at London University, Syed Abdoollah, a linguist being another. While Abdoollah was the professor of Hindustani, and coached students for the ICS examination, Tagore held the professorship of Hindu Law and Bengali language, from 1860 to 1866. Another, Syed Ali Bilgrami taught Marathi at Cambridge. The first Indians to study for the ICS examination were Satyendranath Tagore, the brother of the poet, and Manmohun Ghose in 1860. Tagore, at University College, London, became the first Indian to succeed in the examination in 1864, while the unsuccessful Manmohun Ghose joined the Inner Temple, being called to the Bar in 1866. Many others would follow. The poetess, Toru Dutt and her sister Aru, were probably the first women students to attend lectures for women at Cambridge in 1869. The Bonnerjee daughters, as noted, attended Cambridge university colleges. Probably the first Indian from the Caribbean was William Hewley Wharton from Guyana. The son of a Hindu indentured labourer, in 1893, at the age of 24, he joined Edinburgh University to study medicine, graduating in 1899.[127]

As the nineteenth century progressed, the trickle of Indian students showed a small but steady rise. A census taken by the National Indian

Association (NIA) counted a total of 160 in 1887. Three years later, in 1890, the number had risen to 207, and by 1894 the figure had reached just 308. The NIA lists, providing an analysis by region, religion, course of study and university, give us some insight into these students' social background. According to the 1890 list, of the 207 'Indian gentlemen in the west', 105 were Hindus, 53 Muslims and 45 Parsis. Bengal sent the highest number of Hindus (35) and Muslims (17), while Parsis were predominantly from Bombay (44). Law was the most popular course of study (100), followed by medicine. By the turn of the century numbers began to rise. By 1910, according to one official statistic, more than 700 Indian students, both male and female, were in the United Kingdom, while another put the figure at between 1,000 and 1,200. Although the number of students had increased, overall the numbers remained small, and the students were largely confined to London, Cambridge, Oxford and Edinburgh. The reason, according to one writer, was due to the fact that Muslims were slow to awaken from 'educational lethargy', while the Hindus were not 'emancipated' from caste restrictions.[128] But the cost of university fees, accommodation and travel would also account for the small numbers. The thought of separation from family and friends in a faraway, culturally different country might have deterred some others. Nonetheless, the determined came to advance their careers. In the hands of some of the educated elite, the nationalists, western education became a double-edged sword in their struggle for colonial freedom, justice and civil rights. Gandhi, for instance, used his legal training to outwit the Raj.

Although small in number, they attracted much attention and comment. Anglo-Indians deplored their 'lionising' by the sympathetic and well-meaning public. Others saw them as material for Christ. According to the president of the Cambridge Majlis, the Cambridge Inter-Collegiate Christian Union was so fervently enthusiastic for the 'salvation of the heathen's soul' that it sought him out even in his 'obscure lodgings'. Cornelia Sorabji (see p. 93) wrote: 'Dear old ladies were always trying to convert me – for instance – the heathen at their gates.' But Sorabji was a Christian and when she tried to explain this to one proselytising woman, she was informed 'reproachfully, "But you look so very heathen." ' Sorabji was under added pressure. Coming as she did from a reformist Christian family, with a father who was an agent for the Christian Missionary Society (CMS) and whose mother's school, the Victoria High for girls, was sustained by CMS grants, the CMS naturally had expectations of her. As an Indian and a Christian she was considered 'an advertisement in itself'. Although Sorabji helped raise funds all over Britain, in her letters she was critical of the misleading representations of Indian women and what she described as their 'brutal oppression ... which they label zeal for the cause'.[129]

At the official level, Indian students were seen as presenting a moral and a political problem, as evidenced by the tone of the special committee of inquiry set up in 1903 for establishing a hostel for their supervision. Witnesses claimed that the 'large numbers' of private students, unlike the government scholars, were not 'picked men'. As 'raw youths', lacking 'self-control', they were considered unable to withstand the pressure in British cities. It was alleged that they easily succumbed to the temptations of London life, and found 'attractions of a London brothel and intercourse with white women almost irresistible'. Some claimed that white women in England, unlike their sisters in India, found the 'Bengali Baboos' (a pejorative term for educated Indians) attractive, and so 'rushed at them', willingly becoming their 'victims'. Horror stories were recounted as evidence of their 'fast living' and 'downward' slide after just one night in London. One student was said to have killed himself with drink and fast living; another, having ruined his parents with his extravagance, had ended up by marrying a prostitute. However, the evidence provides a different picture: the 'majority ... [led] studious and decent lives', without succumbing to any temptation. This view was later confirmed by the Lee-Warner Committee, which concluded that the 'wrecks' constituted 'the exception'. Nonetheless, the authorities claimed that the 'large amount of leisure' enjoyed by Indians studying for the Bar, and the fact that most lived in private lodgings, made it easier for them to succumb to 'temptations' and a life of 'fast living' – justifying their supervision.[130]

Behind such views lay the fear of miscegenation, the loss of authority in India based on the mystique of the Raj, and the whole issue of race, gender and class in Victorian and Edwardian society. But in the case of students there was an added ingredient: a fear that they would be politicised and begin to question the legitimacy of the Raj, a serious consequence, as the educated elite formed an influential section of society. According to Lord Curzon most of the 'friends of India' in Britain were radical politicians, an exaggeration, no doubt. Therefore, to exercise control and supervision over these 'raw youths', a hostel was proposed. Some, however, doubted a government-sponsored hostel would be a solution: it might arouse suspicion in India. Further, it could easily become a focus for 'political agitators'. Plans for a hostel were therefore shelved. But concern did not go away. With growing political unrest in India during the early years of 1900, fingers were pointed at Shyamaji Krishnavarma, a graduate of Balliol College and a Barrister of the Inner Temple, accusing him of 'indoctrinating' students with a 'seditious virus' at his India House in Highgate. A long-time resident, Dr S.D. Bhabha, President of the Indian Christian Union, who had contacts with students, however, doubted Krishnavarma's influence. Nonetheless, so concerned was the India Office at the politicisation of students, described as 'already imbued with feelings of hostility' and resentful at 'imaginary slights', that in 1907 Lord Morley set up the Lee-Warner Committee of Inquiry to promote 'their welfare'.[131]

The Committee examined 100 witnesses, both Indian and English, students and tutors as well as representatives from resident Indians, and English officials. In the politically sensitive atmosphere, following the 1905 partition of Bengal, the government of India considered publication of its report would be 'nothing short of a disaster' and 'a grave blunder'. Publication was postponed. The Committee's report, couched in diplomatic language, recommended control by subtler means: rather than tying them with 'political leading-strings' or 'restricting their liberty', students would be provided with social opportunities hitherto not open to them, so removing a 'feeling of friendlessness'. By means of such socialisation, it was hoped, they would come under 'wholesome influences', which would 'check evil' and do good. The Committee made three recommendations: first, the establishment of an Advisory Committee of resident Indians and whites; second, a Bureau of Information under an Education Adviser to provide information on courses, lodgings and references for students. Third, cooperation amongst the three existing unofficial agencies connected with student welfare: the NIA, the Northbrook Society and the East India Association. In 1909, W.T. Arnold, a one-time professor in India, was appointed the first Adviser, and the Bureau was opened at 21 Cromwell Road in 1910. Local education committees were also set up in India to give the Adviser 'trustworthy and detailed' information on students. Identified 'correspondents' in universities kept contact with the Education Adviser.[132] In this way, a network was set up to control Indian students in England.

Of the unofficial agencies, the earliest, the NIA, was founded in 1870 by Mary Carpenter, in Bristol, to promote knowledge about India and understanding between Indians and Britons. By 1877, when its headquarters had moved to London, there were several branches, in England and India, and the NIA increasingly took on the role of a mentor. It issued an information *Handbook*, gave advice on clothing, lodgings, on 'exposure to English home life' and helped students find their feet on arrival. It organised social gatherings where Indians and well-meaning whites met. It also published a journal. The Northbrook Indian Society and Club was set up with the encouragement of Sir

Gerald Fitzgerald, the Political Aide de Camp (ADC). It, too, aimed to spread 'good influence' among Indian students.[133] After 1910, both these organisations moved to 21 Cromwell Road, the premises of the Bureau of Information. It is difficult from this distance in time to assess the influence of associations like the NIA, or how many used its services. Some certainly used the journal as a vehicle to write about life in British universities, and to give advice to prospective new students. Cornelia Sorabji spoke highly of 'Miss Manning', the secretary, and the assistance given her on her arrival in England. Other students, too, praised Elizabeth Manning's 'great service', helping them get over their initial difficulties. Many others attended the NIA socials where they met fellow countrymen and English friends and patrons. But not all spoke so 'gratefully' of the NIA or its parties. Some particularly disliked having to 'appear in Indian costume', complaining that they were 'treated as mere "spectacle" '.[134]

Indians themselves set up their own organisations and societies. These served as centres of social and cultural exchange, and intellectual and political discussions. The Cambridge Majlis has already been mentioned. The Edinburgh Indian Association was founded in 1883, when there were just six Indians at Edinburgh University. By 1900, membership had grown to 200, and included several Scottish student supporters. It held weekly debates, on social and cultural issues: the subject for the 24 June 1899 debate was, 'That the further social emancipation of Indian women is desirable'. In 1896, a concert, which raised £200, was organised for famine relief in India. By 1907, the Association had acquired its own premises at 11 George Square. The Indian *Gymkhana* in London was established in 1916.[135]

How did the Indian students view Britain? Separated by thousands of miles from family and friends, sometimes living on insufficient funds, life for the average student would have been hard, lonely and isolated, although small groups of Indians had lived in Britain before the arrival of students. Not only did they find 'everything strange – the people, their ways and even their dwellings', but diet, religious and cultural conventions would have further restricted their lives. Because of colour prejudice it was practically impossible for those in straitened circumstances to find a job as the *Committee on Distressed Colonial and Indian Subjects* pointed out. One undergraduate had to resort to acting as a 'showman to a tea company', standing in 'advertisement' in front of the door. How difficult it was to find apprenticeship in industry is seen from the experience of N.B. Wagle, who had come to learn about glass manufacture. He faced prejudice on two levels: colour and class. Unions wanted to ban him, as they feared competition from a future glass industry in India. Workers classed him a 'gentleman' in their struggle against capital. Reports from the Indian students' department, too, hint at the existence of racial prejudice.[136] Indeed, witness after witness, both students and tutors, in their evidence to the Lee-Warner Committee in 1907, testified to the increase in incidents of race prejudice in British universities. Examples cited in evidence ranged from offensive remarks, insults and a general feeling that the English were unfriendly, to the outright exclusion of Indians by English students and landladies. One English student reported that he was told by another that he did not 'like to see niggers in your room', while another would 'sport' the door if he invited an Indian to tea to his room to prevent anyone coming in. At Edinburgh, Indians were barred from certain university boarding houses, even though there were always vacancies as these houses were not popular among Scottish students. In Cambridge, a senior tutor reported that there was a reluctance to admit a 'black' man to a set of rooms in a house where other inmates were whites. The result was that Indians congregated in lodgings not of the 'better' sort. In London, most lodged in Bayswater, dubbed 'Asia Minor'. While Indians explained prejudice as the Englishmen's 'dislike' of having Indians in their midst, university tutors blamed the 'undeniable' increase in 'aloofness' of the English undergraduates on the 'influx' of Indians. To solve the 'problem' they proposed 'scattering' Indians among the various colleges. The Master of Balliol considered 'two Indians' per college to be a good number, as more would result in the college losing 'caste'. Oxford authorities opined that 'to admit as many as five or six would be fatal, and would at once give the College a bad name among other undergraduates'. But records reveal actual numbers at most Oxbridge colleges to be between one and four only. Yet there are hints of a quota system. Commenting on the fact that 'influence' had lately been brought to bear upon freshers to avoid certain colleges having 'too many Indians', the president of the Indian Majlis remarked: 'Good relations between the two peoples was not likely to be promoted by blunt declarations that at a particular college Indians are not taken as a rule', but as a 'special favour'.[137]

Nonetheless, their testimonies suggest that they found friendship and kindness from landladies, from some well-meaning and sympathetic families and such English students 'as chance throws in [their] way', as well as resident Indians. Some made lasting friendships with like-minded white students and the more liberal-minded families. Such experiences contrast sharply with their treatment in India, prompting one to comment that the 'English in India and the English at home are two entirely different people'. But this does not suggest that they were blind to the fact that an Englishman considered himself 'innately superior' and as belonging to 'a race the first in all the world'. But *'at home'* he was seen by some to be more 'natural and genuine'. Indians also saw their years in England and their English education as a formative influence in their intellectual development. Nehru acknowledged his debt:

> Personally, I owe too much to England in my mental make-up ever to feel wholly alien to her. And, do what I will, I cannot get rid of the habits of mind, and the standards and ways of judging other countries, as well as life generally, which I acquired at school and college in England. My predilections (apart from the political ones) are in favour of England and the English people, and, if I have become what is called an uncompromising opponent of British rule in India, it is almost in spite of these.[138]

Of the several hundred Indians in British universities during this period, two are considered in some detail because their careers have a bearing on British life. One, Cornelia Sorabji, was an Anglican of Parsi origin at Oxford; the other, an Indian Prince, Ranjitsinhji, was at Cambridge.

CORNELIA SORABJI

Social reformer and barrister, Cornelia Sorabji in 1889 was the first woman ever to study law at a British University. Her university career is an illustration of the very many hurdles women – not just Indian women – have had to overcome in order to win educational and academic equality. But it is well to remember that Sorabji was no feminist, either.

Born at Nasik in November 1866, Sorabji came from a reformist Parsi Christian family – her parents were active in educational and social work in Poona – and was deeply influenced by them. 'I am a child of my parents', she explained. The Sorabji children were 'brought up English', but they were also taught Indian languages and respect for Parsi culture and heritage. Indeed, Sorabji saw herself as 'Parsee by nationality', always wore saris the Parsi way, even in England, and, when presented at Court, Queen Victoria, in a 'gracious message' allowed her to wear a sari, 'one of my "pretty colours" '. In her autobiography, Sorabji recalls that she chose 'the law' in order that she might help *purdahnashin* (literally, behind the curtain), women secluded by religious customs and confined to the private domain. They suffered injustices: they could be cheated and deprived of their property rights.[139] Initially, though, Sorabji had wanted to be a doctor; the choice of law came later.

Considered 'too young' for admission to a college in England after matriculation, Sorabji enrolled at Deccan College, travelling five miles there and back every day. As the first woman student in a men's college she faced some opposition. Having gained a first in the finals, the Government of India Scholarship for study at an English university automatically became hers. But she was barred from the award, despite the fact that the University Constitution declared that 'women were as men' (i.e. eligible for scholarship). Undaunted, she applied successfully for the post of a 'short-term fellowship' in English Literature at a man's college at Ahmedabad in Gujarat, becoming at 18 the first woman to teach at an all-male college. In later life, Sorabji made light of her experience, describing it as 'quite good fun' from the 'point of view of hard work, and of absurd authority – of dealing with ragging, and making quick decisions'. But, as a lone woman in a male college, and in the context of the time, it would have been no easy task – but worthwhile: 'it would greatly benefit the cause of women generally, for a woman, even once, to have been entrusted with directing ... men's intellect'. Her savings, together with the 'substitute scholarship', launched in England by well-meaning British women led by Lady Mary Hobhouse, enabled Sorabji to travel to England in the autumn of 1889, to study medicine at Somerville Hall, Oxford, 'the town of my dreams', as she put it.[140] However, in England Sorabji was steered away from medicine. She wrote: Miss Manning and Lady Hobhouse 'rather expect ... me to keep to the Education Line', and at Somerville, she was 'to read two years ... for Literature Honours'. But by early 1890, she had changed direction to read for the Bachelor of Civil Law (BCL) course, becoming the first woman ever to do so.[141]

Sorabji's letters from Somerville Hall provide us with a witty and candid picture of female student life of the period. She wrote of the 'overwork': 'Dr Wright gives us much more Anglo-Saxon to do than we can manage without sitting up late at night', of freshers' parties, of college societies and the pleasures of Oxford. As the first Indian woman at Somerville (it was not until April 1890 that Bamba and Catherine Duleep Singh arrived), she was lionised and given privileges. 'Miss Maitland' let her have a fire to dress by in the morning, 'a very big privilege', she wrote. For the Halloween party in 1890, chaperoned only by her brother Dick (also at Oxford), she was allowed a key to let herself in, the earliest recorded instance of the loan of a college key, according to Somerville's biographer. Through Benjamin Jowett, the Master of Balliol, and other influential friends, Sorabji met many literary and political personalities, including Gladstone, Balfour, Max Müller and the aged Florence Nightingale, who had been one of the contributors to her 'substitute scholarship' fund. Such interchange gave her the opportunity to broaden her education, gain an insight into religion, English politics and culture, and the growing movement for women's rights, in short, 'getting England into ... [her] bones'. Years later, Sorabji would present 'a handsome' Indian carpet, copied from a Persian design, to Somerville for the new Senior Common Room.[142]

As the only woman law student at Oxford, Sorabji became the first woman to be admitted as a reader to the Codrington Library at All Souls. Here everyone was 'so kind' that men students even gave up 'a book if the librarian says I want it'. Considering this 'rather rough' on the men, Sorabji circumvented such privileged patronage by not asking for a book until it was 'disengaged'. She was patronised in other ways. Commenting on one of her tutors, she wrote: 'I wish he would treat me like a man and not make gallant speeches about my "intellect" and "quickness of perception" ... He is frightfully apologetic, too, and wonders if he is not wasting my time when he is coaching me!' She put up with such 'eccentricities' because of the 'mental value' of the teaching. But life for female students in Victorian Oxford was beset with barriers. Until 1893, they had to be accompanied to lectures by a chaperone. But her greatest struggle came when it was time for the examinations when it was proposed that she sit her BCL alone, at her own College, supervised by the Warden and not 'in the schools with the men'. When she inquired the reason, she was informed that 'the London Examiner for the BCL Examination refuses to examine a woman'. This was tantamount to devaluing her degree. She wrote: 'Some day when women are allowed to take degrees mine might be withheld because I had not sat in the schools with the men.' Such discriminatory treatment made her indignant and she put up a tremendous opposition. As late as May, we learn that 'owing to some mismanagement' the issue had not been settled, driving her 'nearly mad with distraction'. The only way out was to get the university to pass a special decree on the vote, 'that Cornelia Sorabji be allowed to sit for the BCL Examination'. Her tutor appealed to the Vice-Chancellor. It was an exhausting experience and it had come very close. But she succeeded. She informed her family: 'The difficulty about my schools was favourably settled the evening before I went in and settled far beyond my hopes – for I had a special decree and I could write in the schools; so that though the schools are not public, my exam was official.'[143]

Sorabji won the first round in her struggle against male exclusivity and for equality in education, pioneering the first step to the opening of the Bar. She passed her law degree, being placed in the third class, a disappointment. But she could not be admitted to the legal profession.

The Bar remained closed to women until 1919. And Sorabji had to wait until the Convocation of 1922, when she could come to Britain, to receive her BCL degree. In the same year she was admitted as a member of Lincoln's Inn and in 1923 she was called to the Bar. Her next hurdle after Oxford was to get professional training in the practice of law. This might have proved even more difficult for a woman, and an Indian woman for that matter. But through influential friends like Lord Aberdare, she obtained a pupilage with Lee and Pemberton's, a firm of solicitors at Lincoln's Inn (44 Lincoln's Fields), starting her apprenticeship as a clerk in 1893. But, as a woman, she was barred from the Solicitors' Examination. However, at the end of her training, which had equipped her with experience of attending court, training in draftmanship, estate management and client interview, Lee and Pemberton's gave her a Certificate. The firm even returned her fees because she had saved them money by detecting a flaw in some title deeds, which had escaped their notice. Most of her clients accepted Sorabji without comment. But two old ladies looked at her with awe, and asked, 'Are you a New Woman?'[144]

In 1894, Sorabji returned to India. Her struggles to help the *purdahnashin* continued. To gain professional standing she sat for the LLB of the University of Bombay and a high court pleader's examination at Allahabad. But she could not register as a lawyer. Eventually, in Calcutta, as a legal adviser, she was able to help women and minors under the Court of Wards with cases of property. She was also appointed a consulting counsel to the government of Bengal. In 1909, in recognition of her work for women, she was awarded the Kaiser-i-Hind gold medal. But Cornelia Sorabji was no radical, despite her tireless work for the *purdahnashin*. This is evident from her entry in the 1934 *Women's Who's Who*, where she lists her interest as 'protection of women in India'. This is not surprising. At Somerville, she had not been disposed kindly towards women active in the movement for women's emancipation, as her comment on Mrs Sheldon Amos 'but she is a *women's rights* person, a type I cannot appreciate', shows.[145] In the 1930s, she settled in Britain. An Anglophile, Sorabji was not in sympathy with the views of the Indian National Congress or the campaigns of Menon's India League in Britain (see p. 321). Described as 'a most ardent British Empire Patriot' and one who was 'well-known for her pro-British views and activities', Sorabji was a voluntary worker on the Ministry of Information panel of public speakers on India.[146]

Sorabji was also a writer, a journalist and broadcaster. Among her books are the two autobiographies, *India Calling* (1934) and *India*

Recalled (1936). *Between the Twilights* (1908) and *The Purdahnashin* (1917) reflect her life as a social reformer and her work with women. A prolific writer, she also wrote fiction and other works on India and her family, including *Queen Mary's Book of India*, to raise money for the Indian Comforts Fund during the Second World War. She died in Britain in 1954, aged 88.

K.S. RANJITSINHJI

Prince Ranjitsinhji, known popularly as Ranji, occupies a unique place in the history of English cricket. During the heyday of the Raj, seen as an English cricketer, he entertained and thrilled crowds with his style and flair. Born in 1872, Ranji, the Jam Saheb of Nawanagar, at the age of eight, attended the Rajkumar College in Rajkot, modelled on English public schools to prepare sons of Princely States to 'enlightened' government. At 16, he was one of the three to be selected for education in England. He studied at Cambridge from the Michaelmas Term, 1889 to the Easter Term, 1893. Admitted without passing the entrance examination, he left without graduating. He obtained his cricket Blue during his extra term at Cambridge, Easter 1893.

At Cambridge, at first, Ranji was said to be viewed as 'a curiosity', an Indian prince, but from an unknown Indian public school. However, he was not slow to adopt the trappings of 'an English country gentleman', living in style, playing cricket, fishing and shooting game. Whether he encountered any prejudice at Cambridge is difficult to judge. He was said to be often lonely. His biographer suggests that it may not be too 'fanciful to connect his later extravagant hospitality and generosity, as well as his determination to succeed as a cricketer, with his eagerness to break down social barriers'.[147] Eventually he came to be respected and admired. He played cricket for one season, 1893, was elected to the exclusive Hawks Club (the first Indian to become a member) and was a centre of the exuberant social scene at Cambridge.

In 1895, the year Ranji began to play regularly for Sussex County Club, he moved to Brighton, a town with many Indian associations and oriental influences. He was not the first Indian to play cricket on British soil. The Bombay Parsi Cricket Club had played in Britain in 1886. But it was Ranji who became the living legend of cricket in Victorian and Edwardian Britain. For a total of nine seasons, between 1895 and 1904, when he played regularly for Sussex, his name was synonymous with cricket, both at Hove and Lords. Commentators wrote many column inches trying to capture his extraordinary skill and artistry, describing him as graceful as a panther in action, with lean but steely muscles under his smooth brown skin; wrists supple and tough as a creeper of the Indian jungle, and dark eyes which see every turn and twist of the bouncing ball, he has adopted cricket and turned it into an Oriental poem of action.[148]

A tribute, but one not innocent of the stereotypical images of Indian masculinity. Ranji was so popular that he featured on cigarette cards, songs were written and music composed in his praise, and in capturing space on music albums of the day, he was second only to W.G. Grace. Crowds saw him as the 'people's darling'. During the disastrous match against Australia in 1896, it was Ranji, who, according to *Wisden*, 'punished the Australian bowlers in a style that, up to that period of the season, no other English batsman had approached', and in the 1899 test against Australia, placards all over London voiced their verdict: 'Ranji saves England.'[149]

Between 1895 and 1904 Ranji played regularly in English first-class cricket. A champion batsman, he scored huge number of runs and was the first cricketer to score over 3,000 runs in one year (1899), repeating the feat in 1900, with an aggregate of 3,065. He captained Sussex, represented England against Australia in four series of test matches between 1896 and 1902, and in 1897–8 he went to Australia as part of Stoddart's All England – and was let off the £100 entry tax imposed on all non-whites entering Australia. The diary of his tour, *With Stoddart in Australia* was published in 1898. 1904 was Ranji's last year as a regular player for Sussex, although he returned four years later, in 1908, and again in 1912 and finally in 1920.[150]

Cricketing hero, author and later owner of 30,000 acres in Connemara, he was a cricketing 'genius'. According to Neville Cardus, 'when Ranji passed out of cricket a wonder and a glory departed from the game forever'. But his achievement was greater: he challenged the accepted stereotype of India and the Indians. By becoming the first Asian to play for England, and that too, at the height of Victorian imperialism, Ranji, according to one sports journalist, 'demonstrated that a coloured man could not only be the equal of any Englishman in the field of endeavour but, in his case, indisputably superior'. Indian self-esteem rose. Satthianadhan, who saw him play at the Oval, wrote: 'the "native" is, after all, not the poor spiritless fellow that John Bull thinks him to be, and … is capable of holding his own with the Englishman, even on the playground'. Indians in the diaspora, too, were filled with pride. As Seecharan comments: 'the fact that he was a Hindu prince fed visions of divine rule and the India of the *Ramayana,* and his ennobling performances before White crowds in England and Australia heightened the enchantment, the mythical associations'.[151]

Ranji died in 1933. He was only the first in a long line of Asians to play cricket for England. His nephew, Duleepsinhji, educated at Cheltenham, followed the family tradition, playing for England in the 1930s. The Nawab of Pataudi became another well-known name in the 1940s. There were many others, like Subba Row, and some less well-known names, like Kamal Chunchie, who played for Essex in the inter-war years.

Ranji was not the only Indian prince to stir people's imaginations in Victorian and Edwardian England. From about the third quarter of the nineteenth century, many princes from the 600 princely states (covering about two-fifths of the sub-continent), hereditary rulers, owing allegiance to the Crown, annually visited Britain. Many column inches were devoted to them in the court circulars and in society magazines. Indeed, for some Britons India *was* the land of the Maharajahs. The Princes came to attend royal state functions, for example Queen Victoria's Jubilee celebrations or coronations, or they visited for pleasure. Some acquired a taste for foreign travel; others sent their children for education. At the official level, some may have condemned them as a bunch of 'unruly and ignorant and rather undisciplined schoolboys', deplored the attention lavished on them by the upper classes and worried about the 'woman question' and its effect on the standing of the Raj, but there is no doubting their presence at official functions was part of the pomp and grandeur of imperial Britain. They socialised with the upper classes, played polo and went to shooting parties. They attended state balls and dances, went to the races and gave extravagant presents and parties. Their wealth and splendour dazzled, and like 'orchids and champagne' they seemed indispensable in Edwardian England.[152] Not all members of the Indian nobility were itinerant visitors. Some, as victims of imperialism, having lost their kingdoms to the British, lived in exile in Britain. One such was the Maharajah Duleep Singh.

DULEEP SINGH

Born in 1838, the youngest of the acknowledged sons of Ranjit Singh, the founder of the Sikh state, Duleep Singh was officially proclaimed Maharajah of the Punjab in 1843. But he did not remain ruler for long. The Punjab was beset with conflict and the British, anticipating chaos, intervened, defeating the Sikhs in two Sikh Wars. The Punjab was annexed and Duleep Singh, then only 11, surrendered for himself and his successors 'all right, title and claim to the sovereignty of the Punjab', and the famous Koh-i-Noor diamond (now part of the Crown Jewels). To compensate for the loss of his kingdom, Duleep Singh was allowed to keep the title of the Maharajah, and awarded an annual pension of around 4 lakhs for himself and his relations and dependents. Lord Dalhousie considered this a good bargain for 'he would die in his bed like a gentleman'.[153] Deposed and deprived of his kingdom and separated from his mother, Rani Jindan, he was exiled to Fatehgarh (Futteghur), a small town on the other side of the River Ganges, and placed under the guardianship of Dr John Login, a Scot. In 1853, he converted to Christianity, whether of his own free will or through the influence of his English education and tutors, it is difficult to judge. However, officials viewed it as a step towards the destruction of his standing and influence in the Punjab.[154] In 1854, the EIC permitted him to visit England, which became his home for the greater part of his life.

Duleep Singh was presented at Court: Queen Victoria was impressed by the 15-year-old Maharajah. She noted his careful upbringing, refined manners, good looks, the fact that he was a Christian, and spoke 'English remarkably well' in preference to 'his own language, which he thinks he will forget'. With great sympathy, the Queen wrote: 'I always feel so much for these poor deposed Indian princes ... once destined to so high and powerful a position and now reduced to so dependent a one by our arms.' Queen Victoria took a great deal of maternal interest in him. He was invited to Osborne, accorded the rank equal to a European prince and Winterhalter was commissioned to paint his portrait. Meanwhile, his English education continued under Login. He studied photography and German and was said to have 'great facility in acquiring languages'. He was seen as industrious and truthful, qualities considered exceptional to the 'natural indolence ... inherent in all Easterners'.[155]

Although he had reached the age of majority in 1856, it was not until December 1857 that in accordance with the Treaty the EIC finally allowed him to manage his own affairs, granting him an allowance of £25,000 a year, an income which Duleep Singh considered smaller than he would have liked (i.e. £35,000) for the prosperous Punjab. But Charles Wood at the India Office considered his request 'unreasonable'. Further, £25,000, he opined, was 'far above average of peers and noblemen' in Britain, and even the 'overall income of the House of Lords [was] under £10,000'. Duleep Singh's financial grievances remained a festering sore. In 1860, he was permitted to visit India and bring his mother, Rani Jindan, then in exile in Nepal, back with him to England. It was from Jindan that he learnt of the private estates of his father, Ranjit Singh, to which he had claim, and which, because of the valuable salt deposits, had since risen in value. No wonder, then, the India Office considered Jindan a 'pernicious' influence.[156] Recovery of the estates became a contentious issue between him and the India Office.

In 1863, with an India Office loan, he purchased the 17,000-acre Elveden estate for the sum of £105,000. Situated four miles from Thetford on the borders of Norfolk and Suffolk, Elveden Hall was transformed by John Norton into a magnificent palace, Italian on the outside and with an oriental interior, its design derived from the palaces of Rajasthan, Delhi and Lahore. Here Duleep Singh settled down to the role of an English country squire, supporting local charities and socialising with the English upper class. Nicknamed the 'black Prince', he and his wife, Bamba Muller, the daughter of an Ethiopian mother and a German father, became great Norfolk socialites. All the important names of the day came to Elveden as shooting guests: the Prince of Wales, Lords Kimberley, Dacre, Ripon, Atholl, Balfour, Burleigh, and Londesborough. Duleep Singh was rated the fourth best shot in England. Fond of photography and music, he was said to have turned his hand to composing an opera. In 1873, with the support of the Duke of Richmond, Lords Walsingham and Colville, he was elected to the Carlton Club. He even considered standing for Parliament, which in the opinion of *The Times of India* would enable the people of India to get a voice in Britain, especially as Duleep Singh was so successful. But Queen Victoria did not favour Indian princes dabbling in English politics.[157]

Duleep Singh's lifestyle suggests that he played the role of a country squire effortlessly and felt 'at home' in England. A report in the London Society magazine, *Vanity Fair*, in 1878 noted: 'H.H. Duleep Singh was much aggrieved the other day at the absence of fish-knives at the Carlton club, and wrote a letter to the Committee petitioning them to allow him to introduce half-a-dozen for his own private use ...' However, despite his English lifestyle, Duleep Singh did not lose all sense of self. This is seen from the fact that, when Queen Victoria offered peerages to his sons, Victor Albert and Frederick Victor, Duleep Singh graciously declined, writing:

> I claim myself to be royal; I am not English, and neither I nor my children will ever become so. Such titles – though kindly offered – we do not need and cannot assume. We love the English and especially their monarchs, but we must remain Sikhs.[158]

An Indian Prince, he was not unconcerned at the plight of Indians in

Britain, seen from his generous donation for the Strangers' Home. But it was his financial dispute with the India Office that led him into his own history and the Punjab Question. The result was a long letter in *The Times*, stating his version and the wrong done to him as a child by the greed of the then British administrators. But his attempts to re-negotiate his allowance and regain possession of the Koh-i-Noor diamond were rebuffed. Instead the India Office condemned his extravagant lifestyle and an inquiry into his debts was set up. He was advised to sell Elveden, which he did not wish to do.[159]

Disillusioned, in 1886, after over 30 years in Britain, he gave up Norfolk and prepared to return to India with his wife and six children. He renounced Christianity and re-embraced his Sikh identity and religion. The rumours of his return created ripples in India. The British authorities became uneasy: it was a little more than 40 years since Ranjit Singh's death, and an entire generation was still alive who remembered the great ruler. The humiliation of the 1857 Rising remained part of the historical memory. Further, the Indian National Congress had been founded in 1885. The government of India considered that his return was likely to have a 'disquieting effect' and cause 'much anxiety to the government'. Orders were issued to detain him at Aden. This 'rather startled' Queen Victoria. She wrote: 'This is rather sharp practice', but concluded that 'better than if he went to India. He has brought it on himself.' From Aden, Duleep Singh sent his family back to England and he proceeded first to Paris and then to Russia, hoping with the aid of the Czar to raise the standard of rebellion against the British. In a letter from Paris, he declared that he had 'closed' all correspondence with the council of India, was no 'longer loyal to the British Crown', but 'a rebel … in earnest'. His Russian plans, however, collapsed and in 1888, he returned to live in Paris. According to one Sikh historian, 'the bout of megalomania' lasted till he found he was not taken seriously, many of the Sikh organisations advising him to seek forgiveness from the Queen.[160] Eventually, through his son's intercession, Duleep Singh made peace with the British government, but lived on in exile in Paris, where he died in 1893. His body was brought back to Britain and buried at Elveden.

Elveden was eventually sold. Of his six children by his first wife, Bamba, the eldest, Victor (1866–1918) educated at Eton and Cambridge and married to Lady Anne, the daughter of the Earl of Coventry, became a captain in the Royal Dragoons. Frederick (1868–1926), also educated at Eton and Cambridge, reached the rank of Major in the army, lived at Blo' Norton, was a popular Norfolk squire, a local historian and benefactor of the Ancient House Museum. Albert died in 1893, aged 13.

Of the three daughters, Bamba (1869–1957) and Catherine Hilda (1871–1942) were educated at Somerville, being contemporaries with Sorabji. Bamba, married to Dr Sutherland of the Lahore Medical School, died in Lahore. Sophia was a suffragette in London before the First World War (see p. 164), while less is known of Catherine, also a suffragette. The two daughters by his second wife were Ada Pauline (Mrs Torry) and Irene (Mme Villemant).[161]

PRINCESS GOURAMMA

Princess Gouramma, daughter of the Maharajah of Coorg, whose kingdom the British had annexed, lived in England from a young age. Born in 1841, she was brought up in England on the wishes of her father so that she could be given an education befitting an 'English child'. Described as an 'interesting and intelligent child', she was considered to be 'a little darker' in complexion than 'many Europeans'. In 1852, at the age of 11, she was baptised at St James's Chapel, and given the name Victoria, after the Queen, her godmother. Lord Dalhousie considered this 'a great mistake'. Queen Victoria hoped that she would marry Duleep Singh. But her attempts at matchmaking failed and Gouramma was placed as a ward of Colonel and Lady Catherine Harcourt at Buxted Park in Sussex. Far away from friends and family, and in the company of a 'strict and fussy guardian', the young Gouramma must have felt lonely. It is probable that this may have led to her romantic attachment to the young under-butler at Buxted, George Christinas. Her reputation compromised, eventually she was introduced by Duleep Singh to Lady Login's brother, Colonel John Campbell, a 'dashing' widower, 30 years her senior, with several children of his own. In 1860, the 19-year-old Gouramma married John Campbell, the Queen expressing satisfaction that her god-daughter had secured a 'comfortable', if not a 'brilliant' home. After a brief married life, and birth of one daughter, Gouramma succumbed to consumption and died at the age of 23.[162]

This then was the cross-section of Asians living in Britain on the eve of the First World War. Little reliable information is available as to numbers. Whether this diverse group of people, some born here over several generations, some settled permanently, others transients, could be considered to be a 'community', is debatable. Educated Indians, as we saw, gathered at several locations, in the homes of resident Indian leaders. Religious community organisations, too, were beginning to emerge. As early as 1861, the Religious Society of Zoroastrians was founded in Britain with its Communal House at Kensington. A burial ground was also acquired at Brookwood, near Woking. In 1889, the first mosque, the Shah Jahan Mosque, described by Pevsner as 'extraordinarily dignified', was built at Woking on the initiative of Dr Gottleib Leitner and funded by the Begum of Bhopal, and a cemetery was established in 1917. According to the *Illustrated London News*, Queen Victoria's *munshi* and several of her Muslim servants attended the mosque, it being near Windsor, suggesting Victoria's religious tolerance. The Woking Mosque is still in use. Then there was the short-lived Liverpool Mosque and Muslim Institute, established in the 1890s at Brougham Terrace under the leadership of Abdullah Quilliam, a Muslim convert of Manx descent. Built in Saracenic style, the complex housed a home for children, and a school. The majority of the faithful were converts from Christianity. Here the first Muslim marriage was celebrated in 1891 between a London Indian barrister and an English woman, Charlotte Fitch. The first Sikh society, the *Khalsa Jatha* of the British Isles, was founded in 1908, and in 1911, the first Sikh *Gurdwara,* the Bhupindra Dharamsala, was established at 79 Sinclair Road, in west London, with funding from the Maharaja of Patiala.[163] Such developments suggest that various Asian cultural and religious communities were beginning to put down roots in Britain. There are also occasional references to religious celebrations attended by Asians of all faiths, and joined by Christians. For instance, in 1891, Parsis gathered at Maidenhead for the Parsi New Year, the Sikhs met at Westminster Palace Hotel in January 1910 for the anniversary of Guru Gobind Singh, while the members of the Bramho Samaj celebrated its anniversary at Essex Hall.[164]

Indians combined several contending identities, devised their own strategies for living in the 'contact zones', negotiating their own way, and straddling different cultural heritages.[165] However, whatever their profession and contribution to society, and despite their small numbers, their experiences of British society were in some respects similar. Racial prejudice, indifference and patronising concern, or at times grudging acceptance, as well as friendship characterised their presence. In this respect the reception given to the post-1950s migrants from the Indian sub-continent has its roots in the treatment accorded to these early settlers. But, by their very presence in Britain, the heart of the empire, they posed a challenge to colonialism and struck a blow to its pervading ideology, which considered imperial citizens as inferior. Their achievements demonstrated the fallacy of that argument.

4

Through Indian Eyes

Travellers' Perceptions of Britain in the Eighteenth and Nineteenth Centuries

The genre of European travel writing is familiar. Less well known are the opposite accounts, going back to the eighteenth century at least, of peoples from the Indian sub-continent writing about London and British life. Reference has already been made to some of the early Indian Muslim visitors during the eighteenth century (Chapter 2). While the travel accounts of Mirza Abu Talib Khan in Europe, Africa and Asia from 1799 to 1803 appeared in an English translation in Britain as early as 1810, and that of Mirza Itesa Modeen's *Excellent Intelligence Concerning Europe* from 1765, in an abridged translation, accompanied by an Urdu version, in 1827, the Persian texts of other visitors, Munshi Ismail, who came to Britain in 1772 and Mir Muhammad Husain during 1776–7, are known only through the works of recent scholars.[1] In the nineteenth century, an increasing number of western-educated Indians travelled to Britain to learn from and see, in the words of Lala Baijnath of the judicial service, 'the home of [our] rulers … those lands of civilisation and liberty' about which they had read so much.[2] Some of them have left us records of their experiences and impressions of nineteenth-century Britain, the earliest of these being the *Diary of an Overland Journey from Bombay to England*, by Ardaseer Cursetjee, the marine engineer, published in London in 1840, followed by the *Journal of a Residence of Two Years and a Half in Great Britain* by Nowrojee and Merwanjee, the two ship-builders, published in 1841. Princes, too, turned their hand to keeping a diary of their impressions, some dedicating their works to eminent British personalities. A number of students published texts of their experiences and observations, offering guidance and advice to others.[3] However, it was between 1886, the year of the Colonial and Indian Exhibition, and 1911, the coronation of George V, that there was a flowering of travel accounts in English by Indian visitors, some of which had first been written as articles and letters in newspapers and magazines, or delivered as lectures, and later converted into books to inform and interpret Britain for their country-men and would-be travellers. Not all were literary men in the accepted sense of the term and the quality of their writing is variable. But there is a rich seam, witty, satirical and informative, revealing a keen eye and shrewd, perceptive impressions of Britain, London, the chief city of the empire – and by extension, of the empire itself. Their intellectual and cultural encounters also tell us that Indians could observe as well as be observed. This chapter looks at the observations and reflections of a few of these visitors to Britain, largely men, in the eighteenth and nineteenth centuries, isolating a few themes shared, to a greater or lesser extent, in their travel accounts.

OBSERVATIONS OF MUSLIM SCHOLARS:
THE EIGHTEENTH CENTURY

Mirza Itesa Modeen excited much curiosity. According to him, before his arrival in 1765, the English had never seen a 'moonshee' dressed in a *jamah* (long coat), turban, sash and dagger, being familiar only with poor wandering lascars, and so took him to be 'a great man of Bengal, if not brother to some noub' (nawab). Others considered his 'costume' to be 'the dress of the Harem and delicate females'. Crowds of people visited him: they were kind and friendly, but curious to examine his robe and other accessories. After one such experience when he had been invited to watch music and dancing at an assembly room, Itesa Modeen commented wryly: 'and it is singular that I, who went to see a spectacle, became myself a sight to others'. Such a remark is revealing: Itesa Modeen, the object of curiosity, turned the mirror round to comment on the 'natives'. A religious man, he was troubled by what he considered to be the neglect of compulsory religious duties and obligations. He wrote that in Britain villagers and people in the towns went to church only on Sundays. He remarked that intellect and reasoning received far more attention than traditions and sayings of learned men and prophets. He compared these with similar views of Muslim rationalists and materialists.[4] But his observations were not confined to religion. He wrote about the government, the law, agriculture and modes of travel. He described the education of the poor, his visits to the theatre, the circus, Oxford, commenting on its 'beauty and clean appearance', and the University, where he discussed some of the Persian manuscripts with 'Mr Jones' (Sir William Jones). London and its buildings, for instance, St Paul's, which he described as 'celebrated for its size and beauty', he considered 'deserving' of a visit. He could find no words suitable in praise of Georgian London, merely stating that 'on the whole face of the earth there is no other so large or so beautiful'. The houses, which were three to five storeys high, he considered so uniform in their build as to resemble 'the Calcutta barracks', and only distinguished from one another by a 'brass plate' of the owner fixed on the door. Munshi Ismail, on the other hand, during his stay in London in 1772, had found this uniformity so baffling that he feared losing his bearings and not being able to find his way again.[5] Itesa Modeen enjoyed the theatre, 'in a word the entertainment is excellent and wonderful', he commented. What particularly impressed him was the fact that the poor and the rich, paying different prices, saw the same 'spectacle which is fit for Royalty itself'. On the social mores of the upper classes in Georgian England, he tells us that the higher classes judged social background of men and women from certain social accomplishments, their knowledge of music or art and how well they danced or rode. He commented that 'ladies' who could neither dance nor sing, hence judged 'as descended from a mean parentage', had no chance of getting 'well married' as they were seen in 'a very inferior light'.[6]

These early Indian visitors to Britain at a time of the EIC's developing ascendancy in India, also tried to make sense of the reasons for Britain's power and prosperity. Itesa Modeen saw Britain's supremacy to be located in the strength and readiness of her navy, forestalling any hostile intentions of other European powers. Mir Muhammad Husain proffered a different explanation. Deeply interested in science, he came to Britain to learn more about new developments in astronomy and anatomy, although he was aware that to scholars versed in Greek sciences, this knowledge 'might cause immense amount of bewilderment'. In his view, the new European discoveries in science were correct despite the fact that they appeared to contradict cherished wisdom. Interestingly, Husain considered Europe's source of power to lie in its 'discovery' of the New World, which, in his view, had further stimulated advances in geometry and astronomy – an explanation that has a resonance with current debates in history.[7]

Abu Talib Khan stayed in Britain longer than the other three scholars. He was feted by high society and hugely enjoyed himself. Known as the 'Persian Prince' (he never assumed the title himself), his social appearances in public were the subject of press notices. According to him, after he was presented to the King and Queen, he received invitations from all the princes, and 'the nobility vied with each other in their attention to me', with the result, he was so much in demand that he was 'seldom disengaged', leading him to observe that 'hospitality is one of the most esteemed virtues of the English'. He charmed London society with his wit, repartee and poetry. Abu Talib's curiosity led him to look at everything: from newspapers, 'read by all ranks' of people, to the King's private library, which he noted had some 'choice' Persian and Arabic manuscripts, including the *Shahnameh*, to education, 'poor houses' based on the system of parish relief, and hunting with hounds.[8] The two-volume translation of his travels provides historians with fascinating observations ranging from the life of the upper classes in Ireland and Britain in Georgian times, to his views on the English national character. Abu Talib was as liberal in praise of English virtues, as he was critical of what he saw as their national 'defects'. Among these he mentions love of fashion, attachment to worldly affairs and material things, arrogance and contempt for the customs of other nations, however superior these may be to those of the English.[9]

London enchanted Abu Talib: he wrote about its houses, parks, streets and clubs which, according to him, were composed of 'society persons' of the same rank or mode of thinking. He attended meetings of the Royal Society, finding them mentally stimulating. He described London as 'the largest city' he had ever seen and considered its 'greatest beauty' to be 'its numerous squares', many of which were 'very extensive', but 'only inhabited by people of large fortune'. He went to the opera and the theatre, describing with great wit the 'amusement of masquerade' and the different guises – as Turks, Persians, Indians or mechanics and artisans – adopted by guests, who 'being thus unknown to each other' lost their inhibitions, speaking 'with great freedom' and eloquence.[10] From his account we learn of the various modes of travel in Georgian Britain. Abu Talib must have found noise pollution irksome since he remarked that in Dublin, London and in other European cities, there were so many carriages of different kinds that from the day he arrived in Dublin, till he left Paris, 'the sound of coach wheels was never out of my ears'. He visited Oxford, noting that the stone buildings 'much resembled in form some Hindoo temples'. Like Mir Muhammad Husain, Abu Talib, too, was interested in science. He described how one of the professors showed him every part of the 'anatomy building', explaining to him many of 'the mysteries of this useful science'. Unfortunately, his discourse comparing European and Islamic ideas on the science of anatomy is not contained in the English translation of the *Travels*. At Greenwich, he admired the Observatory and the scientific instruments. He visited the hospital for invalid seamen, describing it as a 'noble institution', 'worthy of imitation'. Abu Talib appears to have been impressed by various types of industrial machinery he saw. Following a visit to Woolwich to inspect the Arsenal, he wrote that he was 'particularly attracted by the mode of casting cannon-balls and shells'. Describing the mechanical processes for the shaping of arms, he noted that all was 'done by the motion of a wheel, which an old woman or child might have turned'. In a similar vein, commenting on the 'extensive manufactories' of England, and the spinning engines that he saw, he remarked that 'a few women or boys' were sufficient to attend to these machines.[11]

Abu Talib was not unaware of the connection between the fortunes of India and Britain. Explaining the EIC affairs, he mentioned that, as a consequence of 'their extensive conquests in India', the value of each share was 'now worth nearly twice the original subscription'. How did he explain Britain's success? Like Itesa Modeen, he too concluded that 'the greatest perfection' to which the English had brought their navy was 'doubtless, the chief cause of their prosperity, and the principal source of their wealth'.[12]

Abu Talib also commented on the social position of women in Georgian England. He was favourably impressed by what he described as the division of labour between men and women, noting that women were either assigned the 'internal management and care' of the house, or they worked in the shop where 'their beauty and eloquence often attracted customers'. He wrote, approvingly, that giving women 'sufficient employment' kept them away from idle gossip and temptations. He was also struck by the freedom with which women and men in England mixed socially. However, he was shrewd enough to observe that 'despite apparent liberty' and 'politeness and flattery' with which women were addressed, laws and social restrictions denied women equality. In his opinion, their Muslim sisters in India possessed more rights, despite their seclusion. Muslim women possessed right to property, while women in England had to wait until the Married Women's Property Act, 1882.[13]

This brief sampling, based on the English translations of the texts, can only provide a glimpse of the early cultural encounter and engagement between Indians and the British on their own territory. What these accounts reveal is the intellectual curiosity and wide interests of these men who came from roughly similar socio-cultural backgrounds and a family tradition of service in the administration of the Mughal Empire. The next generation of travellers was from the western-educated elite of the Raj.

OBSERVATIONS OF THE WESTERN-EDUCATED ELITE: THE NINETEENTH CENTURY

For the ordinary Briton, an Indian in Oriental dress was still as much an object of curiosity in the nineteenth century as in the eighteenth, when Itesa Modeen had visited Britain. Most visitors, regardless of whether they were princes or of less exalted status, recount similar experiences. In 1838, Nowrojee and Merwanjee had found that it was in the 'quiet spot' of Egham that their 'Eastern costume created a sensation'. On the other hand, Bhagvat Sinh Jee, the Thakore Saheb of Gondal, a visitor in the early 1880s, wrote how, while walking up Bond Street and through the Burlington Arcade, he sensed that 'a great many people' appeared to comment on his dress, which was 'a novelty to most of them'. With good humour, he observed, 'it would have afforded me great amusement to hear their criticisms on it'. He could not tell if their smiles pronounced 'their approval or disapproval'. 'At any rate', he wrote, 'it was pleasing to be told that the peculiarity of my dress made me for a time the cynosure of all eyes'.[14] Jhinda Ram, a Pleader in the Chief Court in the Punjab, also reported how he was made to feel conspicuous. When he arrived at his London hotel 'several hats were taken off by way of salute to me. Everybody's eye was turned on me, as I looked a stranger, being dressed in my big turban and enveloped in my big Multan overcoat.' Later, while sitting on a bench in Battersea Park, he had been surrounded by local boys 'who stood staring at me with as much indifference as if I were a stuffed figure'. It was not just small boys who behaved in such an intrusive fashion. T.N. Mukharji, one of the three supervisors employed by the government of India at the Colonial and Indian Exhibition held in London in 1886, commented that, to the exhibition visitors, Indians never 'ceased ... to be a prodigious wonder', and 'we were pierced through and through by stares from eyes of all colours', their every movement, 'walking, sitting, eating, reading, received its full share of "Oh, I never!" ' He wondered, 'would they discuss us so freely if they knew that we understood their language?' Ayahs, it seems, were not the only Indians seen as 'picturesque'.[15] Clothing easily marked them out. But in their accounts, with good humour, the mirror was turned to reflect the English at home, in a manner somewhat reminiscent of European accounts of the unsophisticated 'native'. Some, however, unable to stand such close scrutiny for long, made concessions, dressing European style, for some of the time at least, with rather curious consequences. Rakhal Das Haldar, a student in 1861–2, was mistaken for a Portuguese by Sir Charles Trevelyan, while Ram, dressed in 'European costume to such a fault' narrated that an Englishman who had known him in India missed him at the station in Liverpool. Others, however, refused to become 'a black Englishman', preferring 'a thousand' stares to 'a change in one's national habits'. Colour, too, could be an object of curiosity and amusement, even without the badge of Indian clothes, as G.P. Pillai, a writer, found.[16]

One other recurring theme in the observations of these nineteenth-century travellers was the difference they saw in the pattern of behaviour towards Indians between the English 'at home' and the English in India. Reverend P.M. Choudry, for instance, noted the 'remarkable cordiality and respect' with which he had been welcomed in English homes. N.L. Doss, of the London Missionary Society, who had been kept 'at arm's length' on board the ship by his fellow passengers, the returning English men and women, recounted how different was the behaviour of the English at home, untainted by 'nabob-ship' and Anglo-Indian 'vices so vigorously fostered by ... race-pride and despotism' in India. P.C. Mozoomdar had a similar experience, being treated like 'an excommunicated object' on board the ship, but welcomed by Christian friends in London. Others described that even some of the Anglo-Indians behaved differently towards them in England. Rao Bahadur G.N. Nadkarani was 'overwhelmed' by the 'unaffected hospitality and courtesy' of his friend Sir George Birdwood, while Mukharji, too, commented that the Anglo-Indians treated them 'as gentlemen would treat gentlemen' and that they saw English society in its 'best aspects'. Such observations were not confined to men from certain sections of Indian society, or like Mukharji, on official duty at the Exhibition. Others too, described how Anglo-Indians rushed to them like 'long departed friend or relation' to exchange a few words in 'broken or half-forgotten Hindustani', leaving Baijnath with the impression that in retirement, these old India hands retained 'an extraordinary fondness for India and its people'. He explained that they now saw India and Indians 'possess attributes which they would probably never have given them credit for in India – and others seem to pine for it more keenly than they did for England when in India'. Mehdi Hassan Khan, the Chief Justice of Hyderabad, regarded the 'privileged' treatment as 'a brother' given to Indians in England 'a recompense for the humiliations' they had to undergo in India. With irony he wrote that he would advise Indians 'who could afford it', to come to Britain 'every five years, to refresh their admiration for the English people'.[17] Such observations suggest that Indians could admire the British, but not their pretensions as an imperial power. This is aptly summed up by Behramji Malabari, poet, journalist and social reformer, who visited England in 1890 to campaign against child marriage and enforced widowhood. Commenting on the well-meaning friends who 'overdo their part of friendliness', he wrote, 'the patronising Englishman does us as much harm as he who disparages and decries our merits'. He pleaded: 'we should be treated exactly as equals, if we deserve to be. You must not give us less than our due – equal justice and no more.'[18]

But Indian visitors were also tourists. Their travelogues recount their experiences during the voyage and their observations of places they travelled through, such as Aden and Malta, their first encounter with the 'west'. In Britain, they travelled around the country, visited university towns – Oxford, Cambridge and Edinburgh. They went to the industrial cities of Birmingham, Manchester, Glasgow and Liverpool. They visited Bristol and Brighton, one commenting on the Pavilion's 'Mahomedan look', while another considering its ornamental style 'a sort of vulgarised Taj Mahal'.[19] They took a tour of the Scottish Highlands. But it was London that received pride of place. Drawn to the usual tourist sights, they visited Madame Tussaud's which even then had a few wax figures of Indians, Maharajah Scindia, the Nizam of Hyderabad and Begum Bhopal; the Zoological Gardens in Regent's Park, described by one as 'superior to any other of [their] kind in the world', Crystal Palace, the Royal Academy of Art and the museums. The British Museum, with its collections from all over the world, was, for many of these western-educated Indians, a symbol of learning and culture. They enthused that the British Library, 'the largest and the richest', with volumes of oriental literature, was open to rich and poor alike 'without favour and without charge'. Another visitor, the much-travelled Hajee Sullaiman Shah Mahomed, noted gender division with 'separate tables' for female readers. At the South Kensington Museum, they informed their readers, that 'one could learn much about India even in London'. The Tower of London, described by one as like 'an eastern fortress', prompted pride at the sight of its collection of Rajput and Sikh arms and armour. Ram remarked that the 'splendid' Indian pieces 'adorned with expensive gold and brocade' put to shame the arms and armour of England and noted that they attracted much attention of visitors to the Tower.[20] They went to St Paul's and to Westminster Abbey, described by many as 'unique' amongst the great buildings of England because, they explained, it combined both beauty and history, as well as being a place where English monarchs were crowned. They wrote that London was steeped in history, with its historical monuments, streets and squares named after some famous personality. They tried to convey the large expanse of London by giving facts and figures and advising that it was best to see London from the top of an omnibus.[21] Parliament both impressed and disappointed: Cornelia Sorabji was delighted, and described 'the ritual' of the House of Commons as 'lovely', but Nowrojee and Merwanjee were unimpressed. They had expected to see 'the representatives of all the wealth, all the talent, all the resources of the country, better dressed and a different sort of men'. They were surprised to see them 'with their hats upon their heads for the last two or three hours sleeping in all directions, and only opening their eyes now and then, when a cheer louder than common struck upon their ears'. Others still were saddened to see how thinly Indian debates on the budget were attended. They strolled round London's parks, taking pleasure in their beauty, describing them as the 'pride and glory of London'. And they visited Whiteley's, the famous department store, with its 'separate department for every human need'. They went to the theatre, the English national institution. As products of western education, Indians took pleasure in acting as guides and interpreters to London's theatre-land. They wrote knowledgeably about Shakespeare plays they saw and other productions they enjoyed, dropping the names of the stars of the time, Ellen Terry and Henry Irving.[22] Their writing reveals their familiarity with guidebooks, Baedeker, for instance, and their own knowledge of English history and literature through their English education in India, as well as their acute observation of people and places. Their accounts are also a testimony to the fact that they refused to be deterred by ridicule and the snobbish pretensions of others from looking at London and Britain, both as tourists and as imperial citizens.

As guides to Victorian Britain, they commented on everything from newspapers to the postal service and public transport to the bank holiday rush to leave London on excursion trains. With an eye for detail they described the interior of English homes and management of English households. Some noted seeing Indian objects in Anglo-Indian homes.[23] A few stayed in hotels. Most found lodgings with English families, naming Bayswater, the 'Asia Minor', as the locality. The writer, Pillai, alerted his readers to the idiosyncrasies of landladies; some, he warned, could be talkative, others nosy or even mean, charging 2d. for 'damidges'. He drew attention to the snobbery of women boarding-house-keepers, who pretended that Indian students were native princes because on them rested the foundation of their fame. They compared restaurant food with that of lodging-house fare, commenting on the indifferent curry and rice served in restaurants. The best curries and genuine Indian dishes with Indian chutneys and pickles, they wrote, were to be had at the East India United Service Club, the membership of which consisted mainly of retired Anglo-Indians, or were those served in Anglo-Indian homes.[24] For vegetarians, like Malabari, the sight of meat in butchers' shops was offensive: 'an exhibition of barbarism'.[25]

What did they think of London? There were of course several Londons. Amrit Lal Roy, a student turned tourist, who also visited America on completion of his studies at Edinburgh University, wrote:

London means the centre of a world-wide empire and a wonderful civilisation, a repository of wealth and a reservoir of energy ... a whirlpool of activity and a deep sea of thought, a point where the ends of the world may be said to meet.[26]

What struck a newcomer most was its rush and bustle, the incessant noise in the streets. 'Activity, thy name is London!' was one description, while another called it 'a city of brisk [and]... breathless activity'. All narratives comment with amazement, even bewilderment, at 'the bustling crowd', 'the surging traffic', 'the ceaseless stream of vehicles', the rushing pedestrians, 'as if racing with time itself'. They described the amazing mixture of transport: tram cars, omnibuses which ran day and night, four-wheeled cabs and two-wheeled hansoms, cycles, wagons and carts. They wrote of railways running overground and underground, for people wanting to go even faster. To Doss, the underground, the Metropolitan and District Railway, was the 'most wonderful English Railway', while Mukharji, who used it frequently to travel to the Colonial and Indian Exhibition, called it 'one of the wonders of London'. Others thought it a 'great triumph of art and engineering'. A dissenting voice came from Malabari, who considered it the 'least desirable' mode of transport and could not bear the dark, damp, smoke-laden tunnels.[27]

Amid this confusion of vehicles and humanity, they applauded the London policemen who controlled the traffic, discharged the functions of an inquiry office, kept order and acted as a protector and friend to lost tourists and Londoners alike. They observed that rowdiness outside the pub ceased, and the beggar pestering a foreigner scuttled away at the sight of the policemen. Ram described how, while walking in the street one evening, he was saved from the sexual advances of a 'stout girl' by the arrival of a policeman. In admiring the London 'bobby', they also revealed their views of the police in India. The London policeman was 'always courteous and polite', so unlike 'his brother European police-men' in the streets of Calcutta who, according to Doss, made 'too much of his little dignity' when approached by an Indian. The Revd T.B. Pandian contrasted the integrity and 'the incorruptibility' of the London police, 'the most conspicuous and the most commanding figures in every London crowd', with the corruption-ridden police in India. But it is Malabari's affectionate sentiment which sums up their view of the London police. 'Dear old Bobby; roughly tender in your attentions to all in need, seldom losing your temper, though distracted by a score of tongues at a time, or your presence of mind amid the confusion and clatter of a hundred feet!'[28] Would destitute lascars have seen the London police as favourably?

The frenzy of traffic and activity, the variety of jobs that London provided, the shops, selling 'everything that you could possibly need', made the commercial character of London visible to them and they, in turn, tried to explain it to their audience in India. They described the 'City' with its banks, offices and warehouses, which according to Mukharji was 'the heart which supplies life blood to commerce of the world', while Mahomed called it the 'first city in the world in wealth and commerce'. Ram tried to convey a picture of the City as a great business centre by providing a physical description, noting that nearly 800,000 people and 70,000 vehicles daily entered and left its area of 632 acres. At the other end of the scale, there were the 'street cries'. Like other contemporary commentators, Indians, too, wrote about London's costermongers with their barrows, the hawkers of fruit and vegetables, the shoe-black man, the paper boys and sometimes paper girls, and flower-girls, who were the most 'picturesque', being dressed differently and not in black as every man, woman and child, according to Pillai.[29]

Public advertisements also caught their eye, prompting amusement, and anger. They commented on the amount of money spent on advertising in order to push business. Malabari explained that every industry, every art, flooded the streets with circulars, handbills and advertisements in what he termed 'an inordinate desire to make the largest fortune within the shortest space of time'. Such a 'wilderness of advertisements', led 'A Hindu' to comment that the English were not only a nation of shopkeepers, but also a nation of advertisers. Another wrote that the English, not content with 'defacing' every available inch of space, and covering railway stations with bits of paper, hired men to walk with advertising boards on their chest and back, the 'sandwich men'. But it was the sensational claims of the advertisers, Pears' Soap, for example, 'professed to wash a black boy white', that raised many an eyebrow, while the Revd T.B. Pandian was startled by a dyer's firm's advertisement: 'Here we dye to live.' What Malabari found intolerable were advertisements posted 'here, there and everywhere', depicting 'figures of women', 'standing or sitting in various postures, all but naked'. He questioned its ethics: 'All this is done … to invite the lewd to the dancing or swimming bout … [and the] unwary to purchase of worthless articles. Oh London, What is to be the end of thy ethics in business?'[30]

Indians also commented on the extent of drunkenness in London, some considering it a 'great curse' of England. On Sundays, the day of rest, when the busy London streets, according to Baijnath, enjoyed 'a dead calm', only restaurants and gin shops were open in the afternoon. He observed: 'John Bull lets his people hear sermons in the morning, and get drunk in the afternoon', a contradiction that was also remarked on by Malabari, who wrote that, on the day of 'holy rest and living', there were 'many more liquor shops open than bread shops and Bible shops put together'. Again, it was Malabari who made the link between the number of liquor shops licensed by the state, and the interest of the government in revenue.[31]

Many Indians remarked on the cosmopolitan character of London. Satthianadhan, formerly a student at Cambridge, visiting London in 1896 with his family after a 14-year absence, thought the diversity was even 'more pronounced' than previously. According to him it was 'quite common' to see Indians in all the main thoroughfares of London. At the Oval, where he had gone to see the cricket match between Australia and England he counted 'nearly fifty Indians' come to watch the star player of the day, Ranji. Pillai, who had gone to Hyde Park one Sunday to listen to the soap-box orators, mentioned seeing an Indian, a Bengali Christian, addressing a crowd. To see Indians in London was not that surprising, as we already know. However, what had struck Satthianadhan, was the fact that 'all nations on the face of the earth' were represented in London, described by another as 'a world in a miniature'. Many others, too, commented on the diversity of London's peoples. Pandian mentioned the Jews, once refugees from persecution, Pillai listed the French and the Italians. Roy explained that the cosmopolitan character of London, Liverpool and Southampton was a result of Britain's 'world-embracing' commerce, which brought peoples, firms and agents of every nationality here. Because of this, Roy thought Englishmen in cities and ports were 'less provincial' in their ideas of other people, and particularly 'non-Christian' countries, than were the Americans.[32]

However, there were negative responses to London, too. Familiar with the architectural grandeur of buildings in India, they were unimpressed with the architecture and aspect of London. They compared London negatively with European cities they had visited, such as Paris, Venice, Florence and Milan. 'A dull monotony of ugliness, unrelieved by variety of construction or colour', was Malabari's verdict on an average London street. Baijnath saw 'no grandeur' in the houses, few public buildings that were 'handsome'. He informed his readers that in Britain 'ornament' gave way to 'utility'. He explained it thus: 'Their logic is, "Does it pay? If not, don't undertake it." ' Even cathedrals like St Paul's they considered inferior to churches in France and Italy. Pillai felt that what impressed one about London was its immensity, while the Scottish capital, Edinburgh, charmed one by its beauty. He summed London up for many when he wrote, 'To London for labour; to Paris for pleasure.' Indian visitors also remarked on the pollution in London:

'smoky and sooty' was the general verdict. To convey to their readers the extent of the pollution one visitor advised, 'wipe your face or furniture now and again, and in a couple of hours you will see your kerchief tinged with soot'. The Thakore Saheb of Gondal preferred the country to the capital city: it was not only the smoke and the soot that he found not to his liking, but also the 'unceasing din and rattle' that filled his ears 'all day long', echoing Abu Talib Khan's sentiment. But he decided not to be too hasty in his judgement. However, he was disappointed:

> I was labouring under the impression that of all the cities of the world London the metropolis of the vast English Empire must not only be a charming place to live in but that its lanes and by lanes must be entirely free of filth. The results of my personal observations, however, have been disappointing.

London was also expensive. Commenting on the high charges in hotels, Malabari concluded that the profit motive was largely behind it. He explained that the proprietor had to live, after enabling a multitude of servants to make a living. 'And he must live like a gentleman', and so 'fleecing' in England was done on 'a larger scale' than in India.[33]

The poverty and the glaring inequality between the rich and the poor came as a shock. Nearly a hundred years earlier, Abu Talib Khan had been appalled by the dire poverty of the Irish peasants, prompting him to remark that in comparison, the peasants of India were 'richer'. He had explained their hardship as the result of the cost of living and the cold climate, which necessitated additional expenditure.[34] Indian visitors to Victorian Britain commented on the condition of the urban poor. Pandian, for instance, in his chapter on working-class homes, described what he called the 'ever-changing "abodes" of the houseless poor' – the doorsteps of public buildings and open spaces of London. Life for these homeless poor of London, he wrote 'must seem nothing more than an intolerable condition of agonising cursedness'. He found it no surprise that 'so many of these wretched being' tried to end their 'earthly miseries by plunging themselves headlong into the unclean waters of their Father Thames'. Others described the 'poverty-marked' dilapidated tenements of the east end of London. Rao Bahadur G.N. Nadkarani thought that, in comparison, 'the most insanitary quarter' of Bombay might be described as 'homes of comfort'.[35] Malabari concluded that poverty in industrialised states like Britain could be far worse than poverty in non-industrialised countries like India. He was thankful that:

Poor as India is ... she knows not much of the poverty to which parts of Great Britain have been accustomed – the east end of London, for instance, parts of Glasgow and other congested centres of life. Men and women living in a chronic state of emaciation, till they can hardly be recognised as human, picking up, as food, what even animals will turn away from; sleeping fifty, sixty, eighty of them together, of all ages, and both sexes, in a hole that could not hold ten with decency; swearing, fighting, trampling on one another; filling the room with foul confusion and fouler air. This is not a picture of occasional misery, in some places it represents the every-day life of the victims of misfortune.[36]

Such reflections questioned the notion of progress and imperial claim to civilisation. As Roy wrote: 'Well might one regard civilisation a failure on seeing the condition of the poor in London.' Malabari thought that winter exacerbated the misery of the poor, though, proportionately, the extent of it was smaller. But Indians also felt that in Britain, far too often, such extremes of poverty contrasted starkly with immense luxury, and the indifference of the rich 'gorgeously dressed luxury flaunting the streets, dragged along by horses, better fed and better looked after than many a human family in the same neighbourhood'. Pillai saw the poor as the 'victims of fierce competition of the over-crowded labour market'. Malabari concluded that this 'cruel sacrifice' of humans was 'due to the arrogance of capital in its dealings with labour, especially unskilled labour'. The sight of working men's demonstrations and strikes led him to hope that the day for labour would come, as he doubted that capital would be able to resist the legitimate claims of labour for too long. 'The spirit of the age is crying out against such resistance', he wrote.[37]

Indian visitors to Britain, not unnaturally, were interested in the position and status of women, coming as they did from a society with sexually segregated roles, women occupying the private sphere. In Britain, they also met English women socially, an interchange that did not take place in India, given the context of the Raj. They liked the social role women played in Britain. Ram described women as the 'grace and ornament of English society', and he was sure that anyone who had been to England and mixed with men and women socially, was bound to rebel against the purdah system. Pillai added that in India a woman 'knows no society', but in England, society meant 'nothing' without women. Mary Bhore noted the time 'ladies' spent in works of charity. They also noticed how much freer women were in England: they used public transport as freely as men and went about their business just as men did. Satthianadhan noted the changes that had taken place since his student days: women 'as clerks in post-offices, as platform orators, as bicycle-riders in crowded thoroughfares of London, and experts even in hair-cutting and shaving'. Others were perceptive enough to see that there was another side to the picture: that freedom did not give women equality. They noted women's campaign for the right to vote. One visitor in 1911, mentioning the huge demonstration organised by the suffragettes in London, commented that it gave him 'an idea of the power and strength of British womanhood' that could organise and carry out such a programme 'without a hitch'.[38] But it is Malabari's observations on women's rights that are by far the most interesting and his views on gender equality far in advance of the time.

A successful journalist and an advocate of women's social reform in India, Malabari championed women's suffrage in Britain. In fact, he thought that the question 'ought' to be independent of party politics and 'ought' to be part of a common platform. 'Where is the danger in a number of well qualified women exercising the vote?', he asked. Malabari even argued that women's influence on social legislation would be 'more useful and salutary' than that of men. He was concerned about the exploitation of women at work. He wrote that he wanted to see 'movements got up to induce employers of labour, and particularly skilled labour, to observe the same scale of wages between men and women, where the quality of work done is the same'. He also commented on other aspects of gender inequality, for instance, the glaring absence of monuments to women in the 'sacred national valhallas'. After a sightseeing tour, he wrote:

> There was not a single bust in the Abbey or the Cathedral, that I could see, devoted to the memory of woman. This omission cannot be accidental. If it is designed, it may be taken as another instance of the disfavour with which Mother Church has viewed the liberation of her daughters from religious thraldom. Is it now too late to deny that there have been women in England worthy of a place side by side with some of their illustrious countrymen whom they have aided materially in winning a niche in the Temple of Fame?

In the third edition of *The Indian Eye,* published in India in 1895 (the first was published in Britain in 1893), Malabari, in a new chapter, entitled 'Sex', devoted considerable space to the question of women's rights and gender equality. In it he cautioned against the notion that there 'really' were 'two distinct' sexes in nature, arguing that 'Nature seems to love unity in multiplicity. The unit varies and multiplies, only that varieties and the multiples may return to the original unit ... May it not be more correct, then, to say that there is one dual sex in nature?' and consequently 'no higher sex to dominate a lower one'. Malabari also challenged the usual assertion that women's intellectual powers were inferior and they lacked originality. He pointed to strides in women's education and asked: 'What is originality? – and who fixed the standard of greatness? What opportunities have women been allowed of competing with their brothers or husbands, in this matter?' Malabari saw no reason why 'with a wholesome change in ideals, such as would meet the aspirations of men and women alike, a woman should not make herself as great a force in the affairs of life as a man'. Although he could not see many women wishing to leave the domestic sphere, he did not see why those wishing to do otherwise 'are to be cooped up in a political zenana, simply on account of their sex'. Hence his support for women's suffrage.

How did Malabari account for gender inequality and the subordination of women? He was critical of both the Church and the state. He castigated what he called 'man-made law' that treated women as 'inferior beings'. He thought some laws and customs were a caricature and women were rightly rebelling against them. He wrote that the time had gone for treating women 'as toys, as things to be played with and thrown away; or merely as breeders of the race'. An implicit criticism of Victorian sexual mores is seen in his denunciation of different standards of sexual morality. He warned that 'The wife of the future is not likely to stand for it.' For Malabari, the guiding rule of the future was to be 'sex equality before public morality'.[39] Malabari, the campaigner for social reform on behalf of Indian women, was arguing for reforms that were far ahead of its time – in India as well as Victorian Britain.

What other observations did these imperial citizens make? The relationship between the rulers and ruled features implicitly or explicitly in many of these accounts. Their visit to Britain gave them another view of Britain, the British, and their place as imperial citizens. This contrasted sharply with their experiences of imperial arrogance in India. These narratives also convey their admiration for the British people. Pillai, for instance, concludes his travelogue with a confession: that he was returning to India 'more deeply impressed than ever with the power and the glory, the ability and the uprightness of the British nation'. Ram, too, praised the British sense of justice and honesty. Another considered English qualities of enterprise, energy, ambition and drive 'worthy of imitation'. There is also a sense that they saw India's future to lie in the continuance of imperial relationship. Pillai summed up the sentiment when he wrote: 'India must stand or fall with Britain.' But they were also clear that the relationship had to be one of equals. To quote Pillai again, 'by removing the ... gap which separates the British and Indians in India ... by obliterating all distinctions of colour'. Others asked for 'justice' for India. Bhagvat Sinh Jee spelt out some of India's demands: higher posts in government and the military, reduction in taxation, respect for the rights of Indians and 'supplying their real wants'. Their unequal relationship was further evidenced in the contrast between Britain's economic prosperity and Indian poverty. It was in London that Malabari came to realise the havoc of famine in India, 'the semi-starvation of 40,000,000 in India year after year'. He denounced 'the unnatural economic conditions' imposed on India, which drained her resources. Those who suffered most from 'this process of depletion', according to Malabari, were the peasantry. He pointed out that India was not asking for Britain's 'superfluous wealth. But we do want her to manage our resources in India as carefully as she manages her own.'[40] India's potential for development and the importance of Indian resources for Britain's prosperity and elegant living were nowhere more visible than at the Colonial and Indian Exhibition, where Indian artists and craftsmen, her silks, jewellery and other commodities were on display. Mukharji wrote that he watched:

> with pleasure the anxious and inquisitive scrutiny to which the various raw products of India were daily subjected by thousands of visitors to the Exhibition. Merchants, manufacturers, and scientists flocked there to see what new sources of wealth and human comfort had been brought within their reach from Her Majesty's distant dominions ... Parents explained to their children, and young men to their sweethearts, the various points of interest found in the innumerable products and manufactures which India sent to the Exhibition ...

But this was only one side of the picture. As Mukharji pointed out, while India's economic products attracted 'the attention they deserved', 'half of India goes naked for want of means to purchase the necessary clothing'. Mukharji urged Indians to turn their attention to utilising India's resources for industrial development and Britain to help 'their fellow subjects' as 'the benefit will be mutual'.[41]

The travelogues of writers considered above remind us that 'writing Britain' is not new, merely that these works are not so well known. They provide an important contemporary voice, not only as travel guides and commentators, providing a detailed map of London, the imperial capital, but they reveal how Indians interpreted and explained Britain, and their place as imperial citizens, to their Indian audience. These texts also tell us something about the writers themselves: about their humanity and their refusal to be defined. Their concerns were not narrow or confined to struggles against colonial oppression. Malabari, for instance, had important things to say about the poor and women in Britain as well as in India. These accounts also reverse the ethnographic survey, telling us how Indians viewed Britons at home. It is possible that the accounts were written not merely for Indian eyes. N. Ghose, in his introduction to Mukharji's *A Visit to Europe* for the Colonial and Indian Exhibition, pointed to its wider value: 'The Hindu cannot fail to regard the account as something like a revelation; and the European will learn to see himself as others see him.' As Mirza Abu Talib Khan put it: 'He is a friend, who like a mirror, exhibits all your defects; not he, who, like a comb, covers them over with hairs of flattery.'[42]

5

Parliamentarians, Revolutionaries
and Suffragettes

In the struggle against imperialism, Britain, the centre of Imperial power, and the British Parliament as the instrument of legislative process, formed an important platform for Indian agitational pressure. But Indian concerns were not only confined to Indian issues. This chapter looks at how early nationalists and their allies brought their struggle for justice and reform to Britain, the diverse means they employed to influence Parliament and public opinion. It also considers Indian involvement in British political movements.

Long before the birth of the Indian National Congress in 1885, the first Indian to pioneer political activity in Britain was the Bengali intellectual, Rajah Rammohun Roy, who, as has been seen in Chapter 2, submitted a memorandum to the Parliamentary Committee on Indian Affairs during his visit to Britain at the time when the EIC's charter was up for renewal. Another was Dwarkanath Tagore, the grandfather of Rabindranath, and a leading businessman, philanthropist and India's 'first industrial entrepreneur', who visited Britain twice, in 1842 and 1845–6. According to his biographer, Blair Kling, in Calcutta Tagore was a 'bold and un-cringing political leader trying to whip up support for political action'. In England he 'was the urbane diplomat', who was lionised. He was presented to Queen Victoria, was present at a grand review of the troops, attended the Lord Mayor's banquet as a guest of honour, and met the Directors of the EIC. In Edinburgh, he received the Freedom of the City. Tagore was introduced to Charles Dickens, William Thackeray and Henry Mayhew. He sought out radicals and social reformers and in Glasgow witnessed the march of the Chartists and the unemployed.[1] Like Roy, Tagore saw the need for an Indian association in Britain and in 1839 the British India Society was founded, the guiding spirits behind the initiative being William Adam, a friend of Roy, and George Thompson, an associate of Tagore. This was one of the earliest organisations in England for improving the 'conditions of native population in India'. The Society, which obtained its information from Calcutta, had an additional aim: of 'advancing the prosperity of our own country', demonstrating that Britain's well-being was linked with India. At its crowded inaugural meeting at Freemason's Hall, of the several Indians among the 'array of

Indian notables seldom … seen in any London assembly', were Nowrojee and Merwanjee, as well as Nawab Eckbaloo Dowlah, Prince of Awadth, the Prince Imamudin, son of Tipu Sultan, Mir Afzal Ali and Karim Ali, agents in England of the Rajah of Satara. During the years of its existence, the Society brought together 'friends of India', organised branch societies and kept up agitation by means of speeches and in writing. But its influence was limited.[2]

In March 1865 at a meeting held at University Hall, Gordon Square, another organisation, the London Indian Society, was set up. Its initiators were Dadabhai Naoroji, who made England the centre of Indian agitational politics (see p. 126), Bonnerjee, G.M. Tagore, B. Tyabji and Indian students and businessmen in London. But the Society was short-lived, being superseded by the East India Association, formed in December 1866 by Naoroji, together with other Indians, in collaboration with sympathetic retired British officials from India. Given that the Association's aim was 'independent and disinterested advocacy of the interests of India and promotion by all legitimate means' its welfare, it provided Indians with a ready platform for discussions.[3] At its gatherings papers were read, 'grievances' aired, and remedial measures proposed. For instance, on 25 July 1867, Bonnerjee gave a lecture on 'the Representative and Responsible Government in India', which advocated an Indian constitution on the American model. Naoroji, in his paper on 'Expenses of the Abyssinian War', read on 29 November 1867, argued that England, not the Indian tax-payers, should be made to pay for the use of Indian troops in Britain's colonial wars.[4] The Association published a journal and lobbied MPs.

The Association was considered to be such an important political organisation for educating public opinion that, in 1868, Naoroji, in his capacity as its secretary, toured Bombay, Calcutta and Madras to set up branches and raise funds. His pamphlet, *On the Duties of Local Indian Associations in Connection with the London Association,* outlined their reciprocal needs, and information sent by its Indian branches was used in London. In Parliament several of its members, notably Henry Fawcett and John Bright, voiced India's concerns. Naoroji was even able to secure financial support from the Indian princes. The Association grew. Its membership of both whites and Indians was estimated in 1871 to be over 1,000.[5] However, by the 1880s, under the creeping 'shadow of jingo-imperialism', the Association had lost its edge, becoming a mere debating forum for Anglo-Indians less interested in Indian reform. Indians in England, however, kept Indian interests alive, seen from the inauguration of the Indian Constitutional Reform Association at the house of G.M. Tagore in 1884–5.[6]

Another organisation started by a Cambridge University student, Ananda Mohan Bose, was the London-based Indian Society. Founded in 1872, it aimed to foster a spirit of nationalism among Indians in Britain. Bose's activities aroused interest in the nature of British rule. For instance, commenting on his speech at Brighton, an MP is said to have observed that 'never in his life had he listened to a more eloquent description of the wrongs of India'. Another event of note occurred at Cambridge University Union, where Bose's speech was instrumental in the motion, 'in the opinion of this House England has failed in her duties to India', being won by 74 votes to 26.[7] For more than 50 years, the Indian Society carried on propaganda work on behalf of India. However, these early organisations, important as they were for pioneering agitational activity, did not achieve much.

After the founding of the Indian National Congress in 1885 (its members were from the western-educated elite), the need for an effective political platform in Britain became even more imperative. Once British officials realised that Congress was bound to become a focus for Indian nationalism, early sympathy was replaced with suspicion and even hostility. As early as 1887, despite the fact that Congress motions were couched in loyal terms, a government circular forbade officials from attending its meetings, even as visitors. Dufferin publicly ridiculed the Congress as a 'microscopic minority', claiming at the same time that he, as Viceroy, had a better understanding of what was in the 'best interests' of the 200 million illiterate peasants of India, his 'children', a sentiment shared by many British bureaucrats at the time. Nationalists then came to be dubbed as 'disloyal babus' and 'violent villains', and the Congress as 'a factory for sedition'.[8] Such criticisms made the Congress realise that a major obstacle for its aspirations and effective operation lay in the bureaucracy of Indian administration and hence the need for an effective voice in England. The first steps were taken in 1888, when Naoroji, supported by Bonnerjee, Eardley Norton and William Digby, set up the Congress Political Agency. This developed into the British Committee of the Indian National Congress in 1889, with Wedderburn as its chairman. The Committee aimed to enlighten the British public about the realities of colonial rule and Indian aspirations, to win their hearts and minds through public meetings, speeches and in writing, and to gain a voice for India in Parliament. Once the Committee had been founded, Congress spent more on propaganda work in England than in India, which further illustrates its importance.[9] From public platforms, in Parliament and through the press, including its own journal, *India*, the Committee kept up a steady campaign from its inception in 1889 to 1920. In 1893 it formed the Indian Parliamentary Committee. Among its 152 members in 1894, mainly Liberal MPs, was Naoroji.

DADABHAI NAOROJI

Academic, businessman and politician, Naoroji was the first Indian nationalist to be elected to Parliament in the heyday of Victorian imperialism. Born in 1825 in a poor Parsi priest's family in Bombay, and encouraged to study by his widowed mother, Naoroji was educated largely on charitable grants. One of the first Indians to graduate from Elphinstone College in 1845, he became the first Indian Professor of Mathematics and Natural Philosophy at Elphinstone. In India, Naoroji had been involved in a range of campaigns, including female education, Parsi religious reform and in politics, having set up the Bombay Association in 1852. A linguist and founder-editor of *Rast Goftar*, his political credentials are evident from the fact that he was appointed to the Bombay municipal corporation and town council, as well as being a member of the Bombay Legislative Council (1885). Described as the 'Grand Old Man' of India in the pre-Gandhian era, he was thrice elected president of the Indian National Congress: in 1886, 1893 and 1906.

In 1855, at the age of 30, Naoroji came to Britain as a business partner of Cama and Company. Within three years, however, he had resigned on ethical grounds, and in 1859, set up his own cotton company in London, Naoroji and Company. But in the 1881 crash his business collapsed. For Naoroji, however, business was secondary to his main mission: to expose injustices under what he called the 'un-British rule' of India. An active man, he was a member of several business, social and literary organisations, as well as being Professor of Gujarati at University College (1856–66) and a Member of the Senate of the University of London. He founded the London Zoroastrian Association in 1861, and was its first president (1861–1907).[10]

Seventeen years before the founding of the Indian National Congress, together with Bonnerjee, Naoroji had played a leading role in the East India Association, raising funds, reading papers, lobbying MPs and corresponding with Secretaries of State for India and others like the socialist, H.M. Hyndman, editor of *Justice*. In May 1868 Naoroji had submitted a memo to Sir Stafford Northcote on the Indian Civil Service. By 1880, as president of the East India Association, he had become the voice of India, not to be ignored, invited before Parliamentary Commissions to give evidence on behalf of India. But educating public opinion meant more than writing articles in newspapers, or reading papers at gatherings of the East India Association. Naoroji also had to challenge the pervading racial ideology which saw Asians as genetically inferior, as his paper, 'The European and Asiatic Races' read before the Ethnological Society in refutation of John Crawfurd's sweeping thesis which described Europeans as superior to 'Asiatic races', demonstrates.[11] But Naoroji's main campaigns on behalf of India centred around three main demands: first the Indianisation of the Indian Civil Service (ICS); second, the principle of equitable finance and trade; and, third, the introduction of the principle of representative government in India.

The ICS was largely closed to Indians. In theory, the ban on Indians holding higher posts in government service had been abolished when in 1833 Parliament ruled that race would no longer be a disqualification. The principal of equal citizenship was again enshrined in the 1858 Proclamation. Further, the introduction of a competitive examination meant that any bright Indian youth born in British India was eligible for any post up to the position of chief commissioner. But in reality Indians remained excluded from the administration of their own country. The age limit of 19 and the fact that the ICS examinations were only held in London effectively barred Indians, except those rich enough to afford the fare. Even then, most were failed, despite having high qualifications, as the case of Surendranath Banerjea (1848–1926) illustrates. A brilliant student and wealthy enough to afford the fare, having passed his BA in English Literature at Calcutta in 1869, he triumphed in the ICS examination, scoring higher than many of the English students in Latin, English Literature and moral philosophy, only to be disqualified on a technicality. Banerjea appealed successfully. But within three years he was dismissed. Back in London to plead his case, he lost a judgment which then even barred him from practising law. As Banerjea observed: 'I had suffered because I was an Indian.' In fact, during the first 15 years of open competition, only one Indian had passed, Satyendranath Tagore. After nearly 40 years, of the 1,000 higher-grade civil servants, only 20 were Indians; by 1900, Indians numbered just 60 out of a total of 1,142.[12] In England, Naoroji campaigned to loosen this grip on the ICS, canvassing to raise the age limit and for the principle of simultaneous examinations to be held in London and India. He reminded Britain that the pledges of equality remained unfulfilled.

NAOROJI'S ECONOMIC CRITIQUE OF COLONIALISM

Bipan Chandra has argued that 'of all the national movements in colonial countries, the Indian national movement was the most deeply and firmly rooted in the understanding of the nature and character of colonial economic domination and exploitation'. Its early leaders were the 'first in the

19th century to develop an economic critique of colonialism'.[13] R.C. Dutt, a retired ICS officer and lecturer in Indian History at University College, London, for instance, made a detailed analysis of the economic record of the entire colonial period from 1757 in his book, *The Economic History of India*, first published in London in 1901. He argued that the cause of Indian poverty lay in the way the economy was operated. But it was Naoroji, in his famous 'drain theory', who linked Indian poverty to excessive tax and the siphoning off of Indian trade surpluses. In 1876, in his paper, *Poverty of India*, he showed that it was the 'drain' of Indian finances to England, which was sinking India into poverty. In 1901 came the publication of *Poverty and Un-British Rule in India,* which developed the theory further.[14] Naoroji argued that under her former invaders, the Mughals, India's wealth remained in the country, but under British rule it was exported to Britain, 'draining' and 'bleeding' India of £30 million–£40 million annually, causing poverty, famine and misery. How? Naoroji pointed to the burdens placed on Indian revenues by the army, the expensive bureaucracy and other external remittances. The Indian Army, so vital for Britain's position east of Suez and her status as a great power, was maintained entirely by Indian taxation, which, in the words of a modern historian, C.A. Bayly, represented 'a huge hidden subsidy to the British taxpayer'.[15] Thus a large proportion of the Indian budget, instead of being spent on measures to relieve poverty, went on what Naoroji and the nationalists regarded as excessive defence spending. The 'Home Charges' represented another significant aspect of the 'drain'. These were payments made to Britain for the 'privilege' of British rule and consisted of high salaries and pensions for civil servants and administrators, the cost of running the India Office and its entire personnel (including the Secretary of State for India) in London and service equipment purchased from Britain. Then there were India's huge remittances to her British creditors. From the second half of the nineteenth century, India attracted an ever-increasing flow of capital investment from London, for railways, services and plantations, and Indian trade surpluses were soaked up to pay her creditors. Between 1858 and 1898, for instance, these payments averaged nearly half the value of India's exports: about 30 per cent of the total went in payment for private services, including interest on investments and repatriated profits and the rest, 20 per cent, went in the 'Home Charges'. Indeed, as early as 1867, in a paper, *England's Duties to India,* Naoroji questioned whether India derived any benefit from the expansion of Indian overseas trade.

India's incorporation into Britain's multilateral trade pattern and financial and service interests made her crucial to Britain's balance of payments. How vital India was to Britain's financial health, is summed up by one economic historian. According to him, before the First World War, 'the key to Britain's whole payments pattern lay in India, financing as she did more than two-fifths of Britain's total deficits'. Finance and investment apart, India was an important market for British manufactured goods, particularly textiles, British policy in the first part of the nineteenth century having largely destroyed the Indian textile industry. With the result, while British exports to India were worth £23 million in 1855 rising to a staggering £137 million by 1910, India's exports to Britain amounted to only £13.5 million and £86 million – the deficit being paid from India's surplus export trade with Europe and Asia. The lucrative opium trade with the Far East was a state monopoly developed primarily for generating revenue. Thus, in the words of another economic historian, 'not only the funds for investment in India but a large part of the total investment income from overseas, that gave Britain her balance-of-payments surplus in the last quarter of the nineteenth century, was provided by India'. Is it any wonder than that contemporaries considered India to be 'in truth the jewel in the imperial diadem'? And the twin policy imperatives that exercised the minds of British administrators revolved round holding India – at all costs – and India not defaulting on financial payments to her British creditors.[16] Indian nationalist economists condemned the subordination of India's economy to Britain's. To Naoroji, this 'bleeding' represented a 'despoilation' and 'exploitation', hitting the poor. He argued for equitable trade and finance. Naoroji's writings became an authority: Hyndman, for instance, acknowledged its influence.

What was more unjust, Naoroji argued, was the fact that Indians paid tax, but had no say in the expenditure of 'a single farthing' of Indian revenue, having no voice in the government in India, or a single representative in Parliament. He argued that taxation without representation was illegitimate and campaigned for more Indian members in the Legislative Council. He also considered standing for Parliament.

In speeches and in writing, in letters to the Secretary of State for India, Naoroji kept up a steady campaign, publicising 'injustices' and demanding reforms very much in the manner of the Anti-Corn Law campaigns. He did not lack for allies: many influential Englishmen joined the British Committee of the Indian National Congress. Radicals like John Bright of the Anti-Corn Law League, Henry Fawcett, Charles Bradlaugh, W.S. Caine, H.E.A. Cotton, Keir Hardie and the future Labour MP, Ramsay MacDonald, were among its members. The Committee organised public meetings, petitions and resolutions and sent news items to the press. By the end of 1899, for instance, 130 public meetings had been held around Britain, in Manchester, Edinburgh,

Liverpool and Lambeth, south London. Its journal, *India,* published weekly, carried articles by authoritative people like Dutt, Digby and Naoroji himself, and countered hostile propaganda in the British press. Described by George Hamilton as a 'pernicious little rag', *India* remained in circulation for over 30 years.[17]

However, the British Committee did not underestimate the importance of Parliament: 'the only way to Indian reforms runs through Parliament', urged Bonnerjee, Naoroji and Tayeb. In 1893, the Indian Parliamentary Committee was formed. It had 152 members in 1894, mainly Liberal MPs; Naoroji, who was in Parliament by then, was among them. In 1895, with the defeat of the Liberals, membership dwindled to 84, rising again to over 200 in 1906, after the Liberal landslide. By then not only Liberals but Labour and Radical MPs, Keir Hardie and N.V. Rutherford, belonged to it. The Parliamentary Committee asked questions, tabled resolutions and countered biased propaganda. Its importance as an Indian lobby is seen from the fact that its members were described sarcastically as 'our Indian members', or 'the Indo-phils' and 'Anglo-Indians'. Lord Minto's dispatch further confirms its weight. Writing in August 1906, he observed, 'Such support at Home does untold harm in India. It is exaggerated here and encourages a belief that the people of England are in full accord with the intention of the Indian National Congress.'[18]

From an India lobby in Parliament, the next logical step was an Indian MP. As Naoroji argued, if Indian reforms were to be a reality, it was necessary to give a voice to Britain's disenfranchised Indian subjects. This was not a new idea, being first voiced by Dwarkanath Tagore. In 1874, M.G. Ranade had suggested Indian delegates be sent direct to the British Parliament.[19] Nor was Naoroji the first Indian to stand for Parliament. That pioneering feat belongs to Lal Mohan Ghose (1849–1909), a London-educated barrister, whose attempt in Deptford, south London in 1885, also revealed the enormity of the task. Unanimously adopted by the Liberal 500 and endorsed without opposition at a public meeting of Liberals in Deptford, a new constituency, working-class and with a large Irish population, Ghose stood on Gladstone's programme which included Home Rule for Ireland.[20]

Despite opposition claims that the election would be conducted in a 'gentlemanly' fight, a reading of the local press reveals the depth of prejudice as the media tried to whip up a frenzy of hostility against Ghose. Described as an 'Indian Baboo', Ghose was reviled as a 'political adventurer', an 'Asiatic foreigner' and a 'stranger to English civilisation and Christianity', while his opponent, W.J. Evelyn, the descendent of the diarist, was lauded as an 'English gentleman of old and honourable traditions' with a name that was 'honoured wherever English literature and English civilisation' flourished. In an attempt to further discredit Ghose, one newspaper ran an article from the *Civil and Military Gazette* (the official voice of Anglo-Indians in India), which gave its opinion that the habit of drink in India was confined 'solely to the class known as the Bengali Baboo', the educated and 'semi-Europeanised native', and so, by association, branding Ghose, a Bengali, unfit as a candidate. Another local paper made much of the fact that Ghose, an 'Oriental', was 'the advocate of Mohamedenism' in a land of 'pure minded Christian Liberals', darkly hinting that while he stood as a radical reformer in Britain, in India he upheld and sanctioned 'the most abominable wrongs'.[21] This was a powerful imagery in western eyes, regardless of the fact that Ghose was not even a Muslim.

Ghose put up a dignified fight. But he lost by 367 votes. In a second election, which followed in July 1886, he stood again, once again losing to Evelyn.[22] Deptford was significant in that this was the first time the newly enfranchised masses (1884 Reform Act) could vote. Although Ghose's defeat ended his parliamentary ambition, he paved the way for other Asians, while in Deptford itself his popularity is evident from the turnout at his farewell. An Indian visitor described how, an hour before the meeting, the lane leading to the hall was so crowded that he had to push his way 'with the most difficulty', while inside there was not a single seat empty or 'a bit of standing place' which had not been occupied half an hour before the meeting was to start, many people having to be turned away for lack of space. Four years later, in 1890, when Surendranath Banerjea visited Deptford, he met people who still remembered Ghose's 'genius and eloquence', which suggests that Ghose had captured the imagination of some people in Deptford.[23]

The year 1886 was also when Naoroji canvassed for a British constituency. He was enough of a realist to know that to be accepted by an English constituency, a good deal of preparation on party and local issues would be necessary. Holborn, in central London, unanimously adopted him – just nine days before the poll. Undaunted, Naoroji threw himself into the contest. He was even bold enough not to hide from the electors what he saw as his most important task in Parliament: that of 'serving my countrymen'. But Holborn was unwinnable: a Tory stronghold, it was also against Home Rule for Ireland, supported by Naoroji and the Liberal ticket. The outcome was in no doubt, but he did better than expected, taking 35 per cent of the vote, which compares favourably with the 38 per cent Liberal share in 1885 and 33 per cent in 1892.[24] His next chance came in 1892 at Finsbury Central, a marginal.

Because he had been adopted as the prospective Liberal candidate as early as 1888, he had time to establish himself. A predominantly working-class constituency, consisting of Clerkenwell with its watch and jewellery trade, it also included 'a detached portion' outside the London Corporation (LC) boundaries, at Muswell Hill, where around 5 per cent of the electorate lived in a 'detached villa' area. Naoroji won the seat, with a slender majority of five, becoming the first Indian nationalist voice in Parliament. At the same time, at Barrow-in-Furness, Bonnerjee, also standing as a Liberal, lost to his Tory opponent, Charles Cayzer of the Clan Line, an employer of low-paid lascar labour.[25]

Naoroji's victory was a historic achievement. A predominantly white electorate had elected an Indian, a British imperial citizen, to Parliament. Does this then suggest that, unlike Ghose and Bonnerjee, Naoroji, standing in a winnable marginal, had an easier ride? And faced no opposition? Such a conclusion would be too hasty. Naoroji's candidature roused strong passions, gave rise to racist attacks and even opposition from his own party.

Indian nationalists naturally regarded the Liberals, their allies, as 'their' party. Commenting on the Conservatives, Gokhale observed: 'I confess, I did not at all feel at home with these men – their ideas about India being derived mainly from official and Anglo-Indian sources. It is only when you talk to these men that you realise the advantage of having to deal with the Liberals.' However, despite the sympathy of individual Liberals, Naoroji had at first met with caution, even evasion. John Bright warned that constituencies preferred 'local men or men of distinction'; others advised a Scottish seat as the Scots were apparently 'more liberal than English Liberals'. Presumably to counter racial prejudice and in order to appear 'altogether like an Englishman', he was advised to discard his Parsi head-dress for an English hat.[26]

The Liberals emphasised Naoroji's long residence in England (of 20 years), his English appearance, his mastery of the English language and his status as a British subject. But while the Liberals sold Naoroji, a Parsi, an Indian and a British citizen as 'a cultivated English gentleman', the Tories defined him as neither British nor even an Indian, but a Parsi, who could not represent anyone, English or Indian. For instance, 'Fairplay', in an Open Letter to Queen Victoria in 1893, wrote that Parsis, as settlers in India of 'comparatively recent times' (they had fled Persia to seek asylum in India during the eighth century), were not 'natives proper of India' and hence could not speak for India. Sir Lepel Griffin, chairman of the East India Association and one-time chief secretary in the Punjab, compared Parsis to 'Polish Jews settled in Whitechapel' and, as such, 'unsuitable' as India's representatives, adding that Parsis were 'as much aliens to the people of India as the English rulers can possibly be'.[27]

Not only was Naoroji's Indian identity questioned, he was also subjected to racist attacks, the first shot coming in November 1888, from none other than the Conservative Prime Minister himself, Lord Salisbury. Explaining Naoroji's defeat and Conservative victory at Holborn in 1886, Salisbury declared that 'however far we have advanced in overcoming prejudices, I doubt if we have yet got to that point when a British constituency will take a black man to represent them'.[28] According to Naoroji's biographer, the two words – 'black man' – made this 'hitherto little-known Indian' famous, because within 24 hours his name was 'on the lips of everyone'. Further, Liberal leaders like Gladstone and Morley seized the chance to make political capital out of the scurrilous attack. The National Liberal Club gave a banquet to 'mark their disapproval of Lord Salisbury's intolerant language'. Others invited Naoroji as a speaker for the Liberal cause. Supporters seized on the shades of pigmentation, to point to Naoroji's fair skin and 'Caucasian head'.[29] The *Glasgow Mail* suggested that to divide humanity into Englishmen and 'inferior races for Englishmen to rule' over was unjustified and bound to fan the flames of 'disaffection in India'. The *Newcastle Leader* reminded Lord Salisbury that 'by far the larger proportion of the British subjects are black men' and to condemn a man merely for his colour was reminiscent of the 'very worst days' of slavery. Others regarded Naoroji, the 'trusted representative' of the 'great Indian National Congress' as a suitable voice in the government of India. Predictably, the right-wing press sprang to the defence of Lord Salisbury. *St James's Gazette* suggested that if Naoroji had been a 'typical Indian' he would not object to being called a *'kala adami'* (black man). Others considered it unwise to let a man from a 'conquered country', a 'Baboo from Bombay' into the House of Commons. At Scarborough, Lord Salisbury himself, in an apology, hastened to clarify his position. He claimed that candidates like Naoroji were 'incongruous and unwise' because the British House of Commons was a 'machine too peculiar and too delicate to be managed by any but those ... born within these isles'. What the noble lord, however, forgot was that whites born in Australia, and the USA, not to mention India, were in Parliament at the very moment he was speaking. The 'incongruous' aspect about Naoroji could only have been his colour. The term 'black man', as used by Lord Salisbury, thus implied a differential citizenship, defining the colonised as second class. Naoroji's arrival in Parliament was viewed by the *Bristol Times* as an 'odd choice for an English constituency', while *St Stephen's Review,* thankful that Finsbury had not elected a 'Bengali

Baboo', at the same time suggested that Finsbury 'should be ashamed of itself at having publicly confessed that there was not in the whole of the division an Englishman, a Scotchman, a Welshman or an Irishman as worthy of their votes as the fire-worshipper from Bombay', a reference to Parsi religion.[30]

Locally, too, Naoroji had to fight his corner, revealing an undercurrent of latent, even overt, prejudice on the one hand, and, on the other, the ambivalent attitude of the Liberal Party towards an Asian candidate. What also emerges is that perhaps the most significant aspect of Naoroji's adoption at Holborn, a safe Tory seat, had been its timing, a mere nine days, too short for divisions to emerge and take root.

At Finsbury Naoroji found himself facing a rival candidate, Richard Eve, despite the fact that he had received more votes and had been assured by F. Schnadhorst, the highest organising official at the National Liberal Federation, that he had been 'fairly selected' and would receive full support. Schnadhorst had even suggested that, 'although a Parsee is much handicapped in an English constituency Naoroji is not only the best man and politician of the two, but ... more likely to win ... [and] become liked the better he is known', but 'Eve the opposite'.[31] What was, therefore, astonishing was that seven months later, in March 1889, both Schnadhorst and Arnold Morley, the Executive at the London Liberal and Radical Union, asked Naoroji to submit to arbitration. Why? Naoroji's biographer suggests that in the face of the 'strong caucus' opposing Naoroji, Schnadhorst and other party members believed arbitration as a means of 'healing the division'. But as long ago as September 1888 the original motion for arbitration had been thrown out, and in the intervening months Naoroji's hard work had built him sizeable local support. Is it any wonder that Naoroji regarded the suggestion an insult and resolved to stand firm and 'go to the poll'?[32] In June 1890, when Eve departed to Tottenham, Naoroji once again received assurances that no new candidate would be encouraged to oppose him. But, as Naoroji's correspondence with William Digby shows, these pledges, too, proved empty. In January 1891 handbills and posters announcing F.A. Ford's candidacy appeared, hinting support from Liberal headquarters. Naoroji was astounded: he had been nursing the constituency for three years. Ford even insinuated that Naoroji's selection had not been by 'a thoroughly representative body'; that Naoroji lacked 'the confidence of the Party in the division' and did not have 'the slightest chance' of winning, appealing at the same time to the headquarters to remove him as otherwise the Tories would have a gift of the seat.[33] The situation was considered to be so serious that Digby informed the Party that if Naoroji, as 'Lord Salisbury's black man', was made a 'victim of petty and wholly discreditable intrigue' as conducted at Finsbury, then the Liberal cause would be harmed. But while Schnadhorst proclaimed neutrality, resorted to delaying tactics, even returning letters unopened, Morley threatened that unless Naoroji went to arbitration, the Party would not be able to 'maintain a neutral position'. In the face of such tactics, Naoroji was forced to publicise his case, issuing the pamphlet, *Mr D. Naoroji and Mr Schnadhorst*.[34] Finally, Ford withdrew, only because Naoroji, supported by Digby, had stood his ground.

When the election came, in 1892, Naoroji received support from Josephine Butler and the bed-ridden Florence Nightingale, and active help from Digby, John Burns, Mrs Evans Bell and Mrs Bradlaugh-Bonner, as well as Keir Hardie. Indians too, came to his aid. Jinnah, it is suggested, 'caught up in the excitement' of Naoroji's campaign, was to become his political secretary in 1906 and joined the Congress on his return to India.[35] Naoroji's success at Finsbury vindicated his position.

A LIBERAL MP

MP Naoroji, then aged 67, worked hard. He sponsored bills in the interest of his constituency, among them the Lincoln's Inn Fields Transfer Bill and the Land Values (Taxation by Local Authorities) Bill. He supported Friendly and Temperance Societies, Working Men's Clubs and Trade Unions. He took up the cause of National Union of Women's Suffrage Societies, the Women's Franchise League as well as the Women's Liberal Federation. As a party man, he supported the Liberal programme, including voting for the Irish Home Rule Bill in 1893. His attendance and voting record was exemplary: of the 310 divisions in the 1893/94 session, he voted in 304, while of the 246 divisions in 1894, he had voted in 231.[36] As 'member for India', Naoroji introduced the Civil Services (East India) Bill for simultaneous examinations, while Herbert Paul moved the resolution. The resolution passed by a majority of 84 to 76. But victory was hollow: the resolution did not receive the Secretary of State for India's sanction, while the government of India considered it 'ill advised and dangerous'. To George Russell's charge that even those Indians 'most successful' in the ICS exams were not 'fit ... for high administrative posts', Naoroji vehemently retorted that this was adding 'insult to injury ... after stultifying our growth, our mental and moral capacity, we are told that we are not capable'. He accused the government of hypocrisy, of breaking pledges of equality given by Parliament, in the 1833 Charter Act, 1858 Proclamation and the 1887 Jubilee declaration. Such behaviour, according to Naoroji, smacked of a policy of 'a market for their goods and employment for their boys'.[37] Indians had to wait till 1923 for examinations to be held in India.

As for Naoroji's campaign for equitable finance and trade, he used every opportunity to show that Britain governed India for the 'material benefit of Britain'. In his address on the Queen's speech, pleading that Britain should share the burden of expenditure on civil and military services and of military operations beyond India's borders, he argued that the effect of the present system was to throw India's resources into the 'hands of British capitalists'. His efforts led to the setting-up of the Royal Commission on Indian Finance, the Welby Commission, on which he was appointed a member, together with Wedderburn and W.S. Caine. With other leading members of the Indian Parliamentary Committee, Wedderburn and Caine among them, Naoroji initiated debates and questions on India: in 1893 alone, 400 questions were asked by the Committee on subjects ranging from Indian reform, finance and the civil service.[38] But, because much parliamentary time was taken up with the Irish Home Rule Bill and the splits it generated, there was little time for other issues.

In 1895, although Finsbury re-adopted him, opinion had turned against the Liberals in the country, and, in a massive swing to the Conservatives, Naoroji's brief three-year parliamentary career ended. Ill-health prevented him contesting the 1900 election, but in 1906, he stood at Lambeth North, only to experience Finsbury-like divisions. In a four-cornered fight, standing as an Independent Liberal, he was defeated, securing only 733 votes. This was not the end of Asian candidates, however. In 1906, at St George's, Hanover Square, and in 1910 in Uxbridge, Manmath Mallik, the grandfather of Lord Chitnis, stood unsuccessfully as a Liberal. C.R. Morden stood unsuccessfully as a Labour candidate, first in Hammersmith North in 1918, and then in 1922 at Finsbury.[39]

Naoroji's election created great expectations. How influential was he at Westminster? *The Times* dismissed it as a 'romantic event' and did not consider he had made any 'distinct mark' in Parliament, attributing this to his 'lack of mental adaptation and narrowness of view'. Duse Mohamed Ali, the pioneering Pan-Africanist, too, was dismissive, seeing Naoroji as more of 'a born fighter' rather than a leader of men, 'somewhat inflated and over-weighted' by his election to Parliament. In Ali's view, Naoroji 'did not contribute anything of importance in the House to debates on India'. In fact, he considered Lord Sinha of Raipur to have accomplished 'a good deal more for India during his month or so' in the House of Lords.[40] (Satyendra Prasanna, given a hereditary peerage, had the task of piloting the 1919 Government of India Act through Parliament.)

However, given the context of the time, Naoroji faced an uphill task. Besides, he was in Parliament for only one term, and at a time when Irish Home Rule dominated the parliamentary timetable. But Naoroji and his allies cannot be dismissed entirely, as the official correspondence between the India Office and the Viceroy shows. Referring sarcastically to his association with what was described as 'the least reputable portion of the political world', George Hamilton, the Secretary of State, voiced his hope that Naoroji's 'influence will even more rapidly decay and vanish'. Further, commenting on the activities of the Indian Parliamentary Committee, Hamilton wrote, 'Wedderburn's motion was chiefly noticeable for the vigorous and effective attack from Mr Bhownaggree on the tactics of the Congress whose motion Wedderburn was engineering.'[41] The fact that the Conservatives introduced Bhownaggree as the Conservative voice of India (see p. 139), suggests that Naoroji and the Committee's constant questioning worried the India Office. The tactics of Irish MPs, especially Frank Hugh O'Donnell, who used Indian issues for filibustering in Parliament, also suggests Indian nationalists' influence. It was O'Donnell's friendship with G.M. Tagore which enabled him to come into contact with nationalists and to appreciate Indian concerns. But Naoroji's most effective contribution in Parliament, and outside it, was his economic critique of colonialism, which questioned the 'great blessings' of British rule in India. The effect of this, as Bipan Chandra writes, was to 'undermine the moral foundations' on which British rule rested.[42]

Naoroji's success, at the height of Victorian imperialism, was important for another reason. It contributed to 'a perceptible rise' in the national self-consciousness of Indians everywhere, but especially in India. He was enthusiastically welcomed on his visit to India and the appreciative citizens of Bombay presented the people of Finsbury with a wooden casket containing an album of photographs of Indian life. In 1946, a portrait in oils of Naoroji as 'the father' of the Indian National Congress was accepted by the Executive Committee of the India League from Naoroji's family for their offices in the Strand. For the present generation of British Asians, Naoroji is a symbol of their history in Britain; his importance in British history can be seen from the plaque erected at Finsbury Town Hall in 1993 and a street was named after him in 1996.[43]

Naoroji also helped others. He encouraged the political career of Henry Sylvester Williams (1869–1911), the Trinidadian barrister, introducing him to the National Liberal Club, and even tried to find him a constituency for the 1906 election. This was part of Naoroji's wider vision of influencing colonial policy from within Westminster. But it was too late to find a constituency. Williams and his friend, John Archer (1863–1932), the Liverpool-born black photographer, were then steered, under Naoroji's guidance, to serve an apprenticeship in local government. The strategy paid off, Williams being elected as a Progressive Councillor for St Marylebone in 1906 and Archer as a Progressive in Battersea.[44] Naoroji was also concerned about Indians in the diaspora. He persistently questioned the India Office about the high rate of suicides among Indian indentured labourers in the West Indian colonies. It was because of agitation by Naoroji and Bhownaggree that the India Office finally took some notice of suicide statistics. He also supported Gandhi's campaign on behalf of Indians in South Africa for equality and against racial legislation, for instance, the 1897 Natal Act, which placed restrictions on immigration based on knowledge of English and property qualification, and the 'Black Acts' of 1907.[45] In and out of Parliament he campaigned against the opium trade.

Although critical of certain aspects of British policy, Naoroji was no radical. His nationalism, like that of the early Congressmen, was 'moderate'. His criticism was not that British rule was alien, but that it was 'un-British'. He had faith in British justice and fair play – despite his own experiences and the evidence in his own writing. He therefore hoped to persuade Britain of the justice of Indian demands for economic and political reforms. But in the end Naoroji, too, lost patience. Developments elsewhere in the white colonies, for instance, self-government in South Africa and Australia, and the Partition of Bengal in 1905, may have contributed to his disillusionment. There is evidence to suggest that towards the end of his career in England, Naoroji was moving in a radical direction. In 1901, he joined the National Democratic League, which had as its programme universal adult suffrage, the payment of MPs and state funding of election expenses. He contributed to the fund set up to support Keir Hardie, the Labour parliamentary leader. Further, in an undated note, but which is believed to be from this period, Naoroji wrote, 'society is bound in its own interest to take such care of the individual as would render him a healthy and useful member', ideas that are akin to socialism.[46]

On India, too, Naoroji introduced a new note. Speaking on his usual theme 'the drain', at the 1904 International Socialist Congress in Amsterdam, he demanded self-government and for India to be treated 'like other British colonies'. And in 1906, at the Calcutta Session, as the President of the Indian National Congress, he firmly defined his goal for India. To quote: 'Instead of going into any further divisions or details of our rights as British citizens, the whole matter can be comprised in one word: "self-government" or *swaraj* like that of the United Kingdom or the Colonies.'[47] The use of that one word, *swaraj*, left no doubt in the minds of his audience, of whatever level of education, as to the direction of the national movement.

In 1907, Naoroji left England, living in retirement at Versova, where he died in 1917, aged 92. He had campaigned for the freedom of India for over half a century. His most important contributions to the anti-colonial struggle remain his pioneering analysis, the economic critique of colonialism, and later defining self-government as its goal.

MANCHERJEE M. BHOWNAGGREE

The 1895 swing to the Conservatives, which unseated Naoroji at Finsbury, brought Mancherjee Bhownaggree to Parliament. The son of a rich Parsi merchant of Bombay, Bhownaggree was born in 1851. After Elphinstone College and Bombay University, he began a career in journalism as a sub-editor of the *Bombay Statesman*, before succeeding his father to the agency of the Princely state of Bhavanagar in 1872. Ten years later, in 1882, aged 31, and with an allowance from the Maharajah, he came to England to study law, being called to the Bar in 1885. For his paper on women's education, Bhownaggree won the Royal Society of Arts silver medal. As one of the commissioners of the 1886 Indian and Colonial Exhibition, he was awarded the CIE (Commander of the Order of the Indian Empire). Bhownaggree donated a huge amount of money towards the Imperial Institute (the Commonwealth Institute) in London, as well as a window to St Luke's, Redcliffe Square in memory of his sister.[48] In 1887, as Judicial Counsellor of Bhavnagar, he drafted its constitutional administration, largely based on British lines, introducing reforms in the police and judicial departments. Considered far-reaching, the reforms attracted much personal criticism in the local press. In England, where he settled in 1891, Bhownaggree followed in Naoroji's footsteps, becoming President of the Parsee Association in 1908, a post he held for 25 years, and in 1895 entering Parliament, but as a Conservative, and for 11 years to Naoroji's 3.[49]

How did Bhownaggree come to be adopted by the Conservatives? As early as 1892, at the banquet to celebrate Naoroji's victory, Bhownaggree had suggested an Indian Conservative candidate to stop Liberals monopolising Indians.[50] It was Bhownaggree, too, who first approached the Conservatives. Describing his conversations with Lord Harris in a letter to George Birdwood, Bhownaggree wrote:

Now how to remedy this growing evil, which threatens to become serious, and make the Conservative Party unnecessarily odious in people's estimation here. Why will not the Conservative Party start me as their candidate for some constituency? ... The very fact of there being some one from India who is a Conservative would break the Radical theory like a house of cards. Then, it will make me free or rather justify me in declaring the opinions of conservative India from platforms, which will further dispel the Radical conspiracy.[51]

The 'evil' referred to by Bhownaggree was the low esteem of the Tories in India. What was his motive? Was it personal ambition? Again the clue lies in his letter. A Conservative by conviction and sympathy, Bhownaggree alleged that India was not 'athirst', as he put it, for the reforms advocated by Naoroji, Wedderburn and the British Committee of the Congress. Commenting on Naoroji's election and what he termed the 'dodges' used by the 'Indian Party in Parliament' and in their newspaper interviews, he accused them of 'palming off' a false impression of India as 'en bloc Liberal and Radical'. According to Bhownaggree, India was 'solid Conservative'. Furthermore, he wrote: 'Everyone of note or wealth and influence and most of all Parsees' and 'the older and the sounder thinking among the natives' wanted him to stand as a Conservative so that the 'Congress fad of Radicalism was laid bare' and their 'nonsense' challenged. Anglo-Indians, too, approved of his move. Bhownaggree deeply admired the British and considered British rule to be in the best interest of India, the India as represented by the 'powerful Rajah and contented sepoy ... the landholder, the shroff, the merchant and the trader ... the poor labourer and the ryot'. His was a view of British benevolent paternalism, and, as he saw it, the Conservatives offered the 'best promise of securing the union of India with Great Britain, and the best practical result of that union'. He argued that India was not 'ripe' for reforms demanded by the Congress as the conduct of other 'Oriental states from Egypt, Turkey and China' demonstrated. Such views were bound to receive a favourable response from the Conservative Party. His candidature was made public in the *Morning Post* by the end of August 1894 and Bhownaggree began carefully to prepare for his 'glorious fight'.[52]

As has been seen, the Conservatives did not view Indian candidates favourably. Further, as a Parsi, Bhownaggree, too, fell in the same category defined by Sir Lepel Griffin, as 'alien' to India. Why then the Tory turnaround? The answer lies in their unease at the influence of the Congress and its lobby in England. Referring to the debates on the budget in India and the use of the term 'an alien government' by an

Indian member of the Legislative Council to describe the Raj, the Secretary of State, Hamilton, observed: 'I think that this is the first time that the obnoxious expression has been used at any official gathering.' What he found even more worrying was that the speech appeared to have been 'a carefully prepared one ... not improbably ... written out or drawn up in England'.[53] It is also likely that some Tories perceived a threat to Britain's economic interests, as is evident from the sentiments of Sir William Hunter, who foresaw a 'conflict of mercantile interests' arising between the 'manufacturing classes' of India and Britain's own manufacturing interests as a new industrial era began in India. However, it is well to remember that there were many differing interpretations of British economic interests in India. The Tories therefore needed on the one hand a 'counterpoise' to Naoroji and the Congress, and on the other, a 'mediator'. And who better than Bhownaggree with his background and views? Having 'nothing quixotic or crusading' in his temperament, Bhownaggree seemed an ideal choice. Is it any wonder, then, that Conservatives were eager to make this 'sound and practical imperialist' their voice of India in Parliament, lauding him as a 'member of a numerically small but intellectually great Parsee race to whom Bombay owes its importance'?[54]

In 1895 Bhownaggree won the London constituency of Bethnal Green North-East by a small majority of 160 votes, a victory hailed as 'remarkable'.[55] Bethnal Green, a working-class constituency, had a 'uniformly Radical' tradition. Its sitting MP, George Howell, a well-known trade unionist, had easily won the seat as a Liberal-Labour candidate in three previous elections, in 1885, 1886 and 1892. Bhownaggree, on the other hand, was a Conservative, and a rich Indian. Howell himself was baffled by his defeat, as his letter to Charles Bartlett in December 1905 shows: 'After ten years of hard labour in Parliament ... I was kicked out by a black man, a stranger from India, one not known in the constituency or in public life.' He blamed his defeat on the complacency of his supporters, his ramshackle local organisation (he was even forced to act as his own agent) and the opposition of the New Unionists who refused to campaign for him.[56] However, there were other reasons for Bhownaggree's victory. The swing against the Liberals undoubtedly helped the Conservatives. Their policies, too, proved to be a winner among the working class of the East End, an area with a substantial Irish and eastern European Jewish settlement. The Conservatives were against Irish Home Rule and against 'alien' immigration. The support of the Party was another factor. Because Bhownaggree fitted Conservative Indian strategy, and the letter from Viscount Cross, 'I believe you would be a very useful MP from an

Imperial point of view' is a confirmation, the entire party machine, the senior Tory establishment, the Tory ladies and the Tory press, all swung behind him. Locally, the many Tory-dominated interests, the Licensed Victuallers, the City Goldsmiths and Fishmonger Companies and the Green Street Costermongers backed him. The *Eastern Argus* promoted him as a politician of 'wide experience', a lawyer and 'a true British citizen'.[57] But it was not all plain sailing. Opposition supporters tried to damage him by labelling him an 'alien' and a 'foreigner', knowing nothing of 'English life and political work'. Such criticisms were countered by the large number of 'lady friends' who canvassed for him. Bhownaggree had other qualities in his favour. An able speaker with a 'ready wit', 'in repartee' on a political platform, he 'always held his own'. His wealth, too, was an asset and his campaigners used it to his advantage, pointing out that he would be able to give a 'helping hand' to local charities. All this enabled him to overturn Howell's majority.[58]

According to Naoroji's biographer, Bhownaggree's election to Parliament was greeted with 'serious apprehensions' in India. Even his victory visit to India was a fiasco, in marked contrast to Naoroji's. Given Bhownaggree's views, this is hardly surprising.[59] Indian reaction is also significant in that it suggests that the Congress was much stronger and more popular, and that Bhownaggree was out of tune with elite Indian aspirations.

A CONSERVATIVE MP

Bhownaggree lost no opportunity to speak in the interests of his constituents. In 1896, he promoted measures to safeguard against deaths by accident in the 'East End portion of Regents Canal'. He tried to secure metropolitan borough status for Bethnal Green. He generously supported many local charities, keeping up his association with the borough even when no longer its MP. His benevolence earned him much popularity in Bethnal Green, where, it was said, 'his short, stout figure and smiling countenance were prominent in any gathering'. As a party man, Bhownaggree supported the party line: he opposed a Catholic University in Ireland and voted for 'alien' immigration controls against the Jews fleeing Eastern Europe. All this earned him popularity and he was re-adopted in the 1900 Khaki elections, winning the seat with an increased majority.[60] By 1897, Bhownaggree had also been promoted to the Knight Commander of the Order of the Indian Empire (KCIE).

On India too, Bhownaggree adopted the Conservative line. He helped Lord George Hamilton ward off criticisms from Wedderburn and the 'Indian Opposition'. In debates on the Indian budget, and on the 'condition of India', as death tolls rose among the masses during recurring years of famine, to laughter in the chamber, Bhownaggree laid into Wedderburn, ridiculing him as a member of 'that microscopic body the British Indian Committee', a phrase reminiscent of Dufferin's description of the Congress. In debates, Bhownaggree maintained that India was 'admirably administered' and Indians had confidence in British rule. He claimed that throughout 'the length and breadth of India', Indians were grateful for the government's famine measures. He alleged that what Wedderburn and 'a certain class of agitators' presented as public opinion was nothing more than what had been 'manufactured in a small room, not far from the House of Commons ... sent out ... to India ... brought back in the form of newspaper articles ... and passed off ... in the House ... as the public opinion of three hundred millions of people'. In a letter to *The Times* in 1897, Bhownaggree further accused Wedderburn and the Congress of 'maliciously misrepresenting' British rule in India, and of 'conjuring' up grievances which existed only in their own 'imagination'. He insinuated that the Congress representatives, in their evidence to the Royal Commission, merely echoed Naoroji and Wedderburn, grievances which the 'bulk of the population neither feels nor understands'. To counter what he called such 'sedition-mongers', Bhownaggree even went so far as to suggest action against the 'native press' in India.[61]

Although most vitriolic in his attack on the Congress during his first term in Parliament, Bhownaggree's defence of British imperialism and, by implication, criticism of the Congress, did not entirely cease. In April 1900, he claimed that a Famine Commission, as proposed by Wedderburn, would have an 'injurious effect' on the 'natives' themselves, while in 1905, speaking against an inquiry into 'Indian grievances', he compared it to a 'trial by impeachment'. Such an action, he contended, would only 'hurt the prestige' of the government of India and 'do no good whatever to the people'. The motion was lost both times.[62] Bhownaggree also supported the 1905 partition of Bengal by Lord Curzon. Deeply resented in India, it sparked off mass protests and boycotts all over Bengal and in other parts of India. The fact that, on his defeat in the 1906 parliamentary election, his effigy was burnt by the Bengalis, illustrates a measure of their feelings. It was not that he was a Conservative MP that riled Indian opinion, as Dinshaw Wacha explained. It was his behaviour in Parliament and his robust imperialistic opinions that caused alarm in Congress circles, who saw them as 'Anglo-Indianism run mad', and as such injurious to Indian interests. He was derided as 'Bow-and-Agree' and 'Bow-the-Knee'.[63]

Within the wider context of strengthening imperial ideals of equal citizenship, Bhownaggree spoke up to safeguard Indian interests. He joined with Naoroji to question the India Office about the high rate of suicides among indentured Indian labourers in the Caribbean and race discrimination in South Africa. But he was at his most vigorous in Parliament. As early as 1896, he queried the disabilities and indignities inflicted on British Indian subjects in Transvaal and Natal, demanding they should not be deprived of their 'rightful privileges'. Arguing that the people of South Africa, by their treatment of Indians, had 'torn into tatters all the pledges given by the Crown for fair play and equal justice in the British Empire', he proposed that not a single labourer from India should be sent to South Africa until such time as Indians there were treated properly as 'citizens of the British Empire'. He did not accept that, because self-government had been given to the colonies, governments could 'throw up their hands' and not act. Rounding on the Colonial Secretary, he pointed out that 'self-government had its responsibilities and limitations, and when a colony trampled on the elementary rights of British subjects and trailed in the dust the noblest traditions of British rule', then the imperial government must intervene to invalidate these Acts. Bhownaggree even charged that, despite repeated pledges of the Colonial Secretary, in the Transvaal the position of Indians was 'much worse' since the establishment of British administration than it had been under the Boers; and that there was a tendency in South Africa, with the 'countenance of the responsible administrators' there to 'tyrannise' over Indians and 'trample underfoot their few remaining rights'. Urging action, he pointed out that the issue was not 'one merely of the treatment of a few Indians in South Africa', but it was an 'Imperial question affecting 300,000,000 people in India'.[64] Such spirited performance and 'resourceful advocacy ... deeply impressed the House' and earned him praise. Gandhi, too, who was campaigning in South Africa on behalf of Indians, and who provided Bhownaggree with information, lamented the defeat in 1906 of their 'greatest champion' in Parliament.[65] In this advocacy, Bhownaggree's was an important Indian voice in Parliament and, as such, his significance should not be underrated. In condemning white racism in South Africa, Bhownaggree, Naoroji and Syed Ameer Ali (see p. 146), as well as many whites, Lord Curzon, among them, were upholding an imperial philosophy which was pledged to equality before the law, irrespective of religion, colour or ethnic origin, and the empire's good name.[66]

Historians have pointed out that Bhownaggree was 'not so abjectly pliant' and, recently, some have even argued that he was critical of the government's economic policy in India.[67] Certainly, evidence exists to show that he queried some aspects of the government's military spending in the House. In 1901, he warned that an 'additional burden' of £780,000 per annum on account of an increase in British soldier's pay, and another £400,000, to defray part of the cost of maintaining troops in South Africa, was unjustifiable and 'uncalled for' by military requirements of India, and bound to impact disastrously on Indian finances. Indeed, he was aware how unpopular military charges were in India, and like Naoroji, suggested that in justice to the people, the government 'seriously' consider lightening their burden. On broader questions of taxation, during the 1904 budget debate, reminding the House of the extreme poverty of India and the government's 'first obligation' in times of huge surpluses to cut tax, he pleaded for remission of land revenue in provinces hardest hit by famine. In 1905, he expressed his hope that the government would abolish the oppressive salt tax. During his second term, he championed the long-suffering Indians in the IMS, who after 30–40 years of service and despite their ability, retired on the 'same pay' as when they had joined. He proposed opening up avenues of promotion for Indians in the proposed reforms. Lascars, too, received his sympathy. Referring to a case in court involving lascars, he suggested that since it was profitable to the owners to employ them, he saw no reason why they could not be paid 'on terms which they themselves were willing to accept'.[68] But, above all, he demonstrated an interest in industrial education. Bhownaggree decried the fact that British education policies introduced 50 years ago had produced an 'immensely overstocked' market of learned professions, to such an extent that even the smallest articles of daily use were imported, a criticism that echoed Curzon. He pressed the government to speed up technical and industrial education. In 1901, for instance, praising steps taken by Curzon and local governments in India to foster indigenous industries and promote 'technical instruction', he proposed a public inquiry in order to devise 'a thoroughly regulated system of elementary, technical and industrial training' within the existing educational framework. He also prodded the government to spend more than the allocated £30,000 on industrial education. Bhownaggree's objective in advocating such measures was so that Indians would have 'a sense of containment and confidence' in the Raj.[69]

After 11 years in government, the Conservatives lost popularity, losing to the Liberals in the 1906 landslide. Bhownaggree, in Bethnal Green, did not survive. The campaign had been acrimonious: the *Morning Leader* attacked him for supporting Curzon's unpopular policy of the partition of Bengal, hinting that it was personal financial interests that prompted his support. His donations to local charities came under attack as vote buying, while his allowance, it was insinuated, came from the famine-ravaged people of India. Bhownaggree sued the paper and won. But this did not save him: he lost, taking only 34 per cent of the vote.[70] The defeat ended his parliamentary career.

In 1916, the War Publications Department and the India Office, worried by German 'propaganda', proposed a short popular pamphlet, to be written by an Indian 'cracking up' British rule. Its aim was, not so much to describe the loyalty of Indians in the war (India had come out wholeheartedly in support), but to emphasise Indian 'confidence' in British rule, the benefits of the Raj and the Indian 'wish for its continuance'. Designed for neutral countries, and especially for the American audience, the pamphlet, it was argued, would effectively counter German claims, and serve as a 'whipping post' for critics of the 'drain theory'. The choice of Bhownaggree by the India Office as the writer was significant: he was seen not only to carry 'greater weight' but was the more likely to be 'wholehearted' in defending British rule. Bhownaggree did not disappoint. In a 51-page brochure, he countered German 'falsehood', described what British rule meant to India, giving his verdict that British 'genius and statesmanship' had been directed for the 'progress and prosperity' of India. He concluded that Indians were 'proud of being British citizens ... taking their place in the community of nations ... with the other children of the Empire'.[71] That Bhownaggree remained steadfast to his political principles is further evidenced by his letter to Saklatvala in 1930, informing him that he 'never cared to shift ... the foundations of my beliefs in accordance with popular, that is mob moods'.[72]

Bhownaggree remained a prominent figure in Bethnal Green and in London for over 40 years, as well as within the Parsi community to which he gave a new direction (see p. 298). He died in London in 1933, aged 82.

SYED AMEER ALI

A jurist, educationist and activist, Syed Ameer Ali's work in India and England was largely devoted to safeguarding the political and cultural rights of the Muslims. Born in Cuttack, Orissa, Ameer Ali, from a poor but distinguished family, was largely educated with the aid of scholarships, being the first Muslim to gain an MA in law from Calcutta University. In 1869, he came to England on a government scholarship, and was called to the Bar in 1873. In India, he became the first Muslim judge of the Calcutta High Court in 1890, serving for 14 years, till his retirement in 1904. His political credentials are evident from the fact that he served on the Bengal Legislative Council and was a member of the Governor General's Council (1883–5). It was during this time that, after a personal appeal from Lord Ripon, the Viceroy, Ameer Ali negotiated a compromise over the Ilbert Bill, earning him much criticism as this was considered a surrender to the Anglo-Indians. In 1887, he was awarded the CIE. In England, where he settled permanently on his retirement, with his wife, Isabella H. Konstam, sister of the actress, Gertrude Kingston (they had married in 1884 at the Unitarian Church in Little Portland Street), he was appointed to the Privy Council and its Judicial Committee in 1909, the first Indian in that position. His judgements, said to be carefully prepared, had great literary merit, while his knowledge of Indian history and law was invaluable in cases on appeal from India.[73]

Ameer Ali's chief ambition, according to one source, was to advance Indian Muslims, 'both morally and materially, along practical and constitutional lines'.[74] While Sayyid Ahmad Khan (1871–98) channelled Muslim intellectual revival by founding Aligarh College, modelled on Cambridge, Ameer Ali worked for their political revival. In 1877, aged 28, convinced that 'Hindu organisations' gave them an 'immense advantage' over Muslims, he founded the first Muslim political organisation, the National Muhammadan Association, later re-named the Central National Muhammadan Association, which 'from loyal but independent standpoint' publicised Muslim aspirations and grievances, particularly in education and government service, as his memorandum to the government in 1882, shows. It was his energy that was largely responsible for the formation of the Association branches all over India. But his elevation to the High Court in 1890 led to its decline. Like other Indian organisations in this period, the Association was a moderate and constitutional body. Indeed, Ameer Ali saw self-government for India as a 'dream' of the future.[75]

Although the focus of Ameer Ali's campaigns was Muslim political aspirations, he saw their welfare to be 'intimately' bound up with the well-being of all other 'races' of India. The Association, as such, was not a separatist organisation. Indeed, it has been suggested that it had helped organise the first Indian National Congress meeting, and Ameer Ali had 'openly' welcomed it. A few Muslims joined the Congress, Tyabji being elected president for the 1887 session.[76] However, Ameer Ali and some others considered Muslims in India's pluralist society to have special needs. He feared that 'tied to the juggernaut of the majority' they would 'in the end ... be crushed out of the semblance of nationality'. From England, he urged Muslims to organize and unite for a 'concerted action'. In 1907, the All-India Muslim League was founded by a group consisting largely of landowners, ex-bureaucrats and upper-class Muslims, having its objective to promote harmony among different 'nationalities' of India, to work for their general advancement, and to safeguard Muslim 'special interests'.[77] Separate electorates formed one of its major aims for safeguarding Muslim interests. In May 1908, at a meeting in Caxton Hall, Ameer Ali, S.H. Bilgrami and other Indian Muslims in England formed the London Branch of the League, with Ameer Ali as its president.

During the Muslim League's formative years, it was the London branch that was the most effective, and in some respects its pacesetter, providing Muslim students in England with their political training. Ameer Ali worked with energy to put forward the Muslim point of view to the British public and Parliament. Through articles in journals and newspapers (he was a frequent contributor to *The Nineteenth Century*), through correspondence with the India Office, and meetings, he campaigned for separate Muslim electorates. As early as October 1906, 35 Muslims had met Lord Minto in India to lobby for a 'legitimate share' for the Muslim 'community' in any future expanded representation on official councils, a share that was 'commensurate' with their numerical strength, 'their political importance and the value of the contribution which they make to the defence of the Empire'. Lord Minto pledged his support.[78] But in the run-up to the Morley–Minto reforms, the battleground shifted to Britain. Morley did not favour separate electorates, offering instead joint electoral colleges with some reserved seats. Ameer Ali and the London League kept up a sustained pressure to convince Parliament of the justice of their claim, and the importance of Muslim loyalty, an important argument in the face of Pan-Islamic movements. In his letters, Ameer Ali argued that unless Muslims received 'distinct and separate ... representation', no reforms could do justice to Muslim aspirations. According to him, communal electorates were the only way Muslim representation could be 'real and not illusory, substantial and not nominal'. In May 1909, he issued a 60-page pamphlet, reminding the government of Lord Minto's pledge given in 1906. Following the assassination of Curzon Wyllie by a Hindu student (see p. 155), both Ameer Ali and the Aga Khan used the episode to remind the India Office of the 'advantage' of Muslim loyalty.[79] It was a struggle, but the 1909 Government of India Act gave them victory. Although they did not gain all the seats they had demanded under separate electorates, they won the principle.

Ameer Ali's campaigns for Muslim welfare extended beyond India's borders. In 1911–12 he was instrumental in setting up the British Red

Crescent Society, a Muslim version of the Red Cross. Like Bhownag-gree and Naoroji, he championed the cause of Indians in South Africa, warning of repercussions in India. For many years, he was the chairman of the Committee of the Woking Mosque and played an active role in the central London mosque trust (see p. 298). An eminent writer, he was an authority on Islamic law and history. In the opinion of *The Times,* Ameer Ali combined 'the best traditions of the east and west'. He died in Sussex, in 1928, aged 79, leaving his widow and two sons, Toric and Waris.[80]

STUDENTS AND REVOLUTIONARY POLITICS

The western-educated Congress and League leaders were constitutional in their approach and moderate in their outlook. While denouncing colonialism as a system, they remained loyal, demanding reforms and a share in the government within the continuing framework of British rule. But the youth of India did not stop at political and economic reforms: they campaigned to rid India of alien British rule. To achieve this, they were prepared to use physical force.

The turn of the century saw the emergence of 'revolutionary terrorism' in India, which was to culminate in London, in July 1909, in the first assassination of a British official outside India, that of William Curzon Wyllie, political Aide de Camp (ADC) to the Secretary of State, Viscount Morley, at the hands of Madan Lal Dhingra. Several factors, both national and international, contributed to this. Historians have pointed to the impatience of the youth with the politics of the Moderates and the failure of the Extremists to give them positive leadership.[81] The teachings of Hindu revivalists like Swami Vivekananda (1863–1902), the influence of Shri Aurobindo Ghosh (1872–1950) and the writings of novelists like Bankim Chandra Chatterji (1838–94), aroused intense patriotism. Other national developments, too, contributed to revolution-ary fervour. Curzon's scornful and insulting attitude to the Moderates, seen in his famous remark in 1900: 'The Congress is tottering to its fall, and one of my greatest ambitions is to assist it to a peaceful demise', was one. Another was the partition of Bengal, which sparked off, in the words of Wolpert, 'a half decade of intense revolutionary nationalist activity'.[82] As *swadeshi* (literally, of one's own country) and the boycott of foreign goods gained momentum in Bengal, drawing large sections of society in mass protests, the British authorities cracked down. The police moved in, protesters were arrested and civil liberties abandoned as 'emergency ordinances' were introduced, giving district officers powers to suspend public meetings, gag the press and arrest and deport leaders. Such violence by the State, argued Madame Bhikhaiji Cama (see p. 152), one of the leading revolutionaries in Europe, left Indians with little choice but to respond with violence, legitimising their use of force. Another important reason why the young turned to radical politics was white racism: the humiliating assaults on Indian subordinates and the scornful treatment of educated Indians reinforced a hatred of colonialism.[83]

Then there were the external factors. The victory of Japan, an Asian power, over Russia in 1905, inspired hope in the struggle against western domination. Ideas and techniques of European political movements, such as the Russian revolutionaries against the Czar, the Irish nationalists and the Italian *risorgimento,* provided inspiration, infusing them with a sense of idealism and patriotism. They were sufficiently attracted to these methods to copy them in the service of Mother India. Secret societies and revolutionary organisations were set up: the *Abhinav Bharat* in the Bombay Presidency and the *Anusilan Samiti* in Bengal. To escape the arm of the law in India, they established centres in foreign countries: the USA, Japan and Europe. In London, India House became the centre of radical nationalist politics.

INDIA HOUSE

India House was founded by Shyamaji Krishnavarma, described as 'the architect of the revolutionary movement in England'.[84] Born in 1857, in Kathiawar, western India, Krishnavarma, a linguist, first came to Britain in 1879 as an assistant to Sir Monier Monier-Williams, the Oxford Sanskritist. Graduating from Balliol in 1882, he was called to the Bar in 1884. After service in three Indian states, in 1897, Krishnavarma settled in England with his wife, Bhanumati. Little is known about his early years in England. One Intelligence Report suggests he ran an egg business, which earned him a sizeable fortune. He surfaced in December 1903 at the funeral of Herbert Spencer. Deeply influenced by Spencerian ideas, Krishnavarma endowed an annual lectureship in his honour at Oxford.[85]

In January 1905, at the age of 48, in the words of his biographer, Krishnavarma 'made his debut in Indian politics' by publishing a penny monthly, the *Indian Sociologist*, an Organ of Freedom, and of Political, Social, and Religious Reform, which came out regularly till 1914. The paper, dedicated to propagating Spencer's ideas, carried on its masthead two quotations: 'Everyman is free to do that which he wills, provided he infringes not the equal freedom of any other man'; and 'Resistance to aggression is not simply justifiable but imperative. Non-resistance hurts both altruism and egoism.'[86] In its very first issue, Krishnavarma warned that the paper would be a constant reminder to the British public that they could not be a 'nation of freemen and lovers of freedom' so long as Britain continued to 'exercise despotism' over the conquered peoples of the empire. Krishnavarma was dismissive of the London Indian Society and the British Committee of the Congress and its journal *India,* seeing them as institutions not controlled by 'Indians themselves'. He saw an urgent need for 'a genuine Indian interpreter', and in February 1905, founded the Indian Home Rule Society, a radical alternative to the Congress, having its objective Home Rule for India. Krishnavarma also endowed five fellowships worth Rs 2,000 each and another six valued at Rs 1,000, to enable bright young men to study in England. Officials, however, claimed they were recruits, who came 'to equip themselves … for the work of spreading … a knowledge of freedom and national unity'.[87]

In 1905, Krishnavarma established India House, at 65 Cromwell Avenue, Highgate, as a hostel for students in receipt of his travelling fellowships and for other visitors. Gandhi, during his visit from South Africa in 1906, for instance, was known to have stayed there. At its official opening by Hyndman, many prominent figures were present, including Naoroji, S.D. Bhabha, Charlotte Despard, the Irish Republican and Suffragette and Bhikaji Cama. O'Donnell sent a message of support. With this, Krishnavarma's self-appointed task of working for Indian freedom in Britain and Ireland was complete.[88] India House became a centre for meetings and the dissemination of revolutionary ideas. Many students came under its influence, drawn to it not only for Indian meals and lodgings, but also for the philosophy of radical nationalism preached there.

Of the several key personalities associated with India House politics, Vinayak Damodar Savarkar, a middle-class Brahmin, is considered to be its brain. Born in 1883, educated at Ferguson College, Poona and Bombay University, Savarkar came to England in 1906 as a recipient of Krishnavarma's Shivaji scholarship to study law. Described in Intelligence Reports as a 'youth of great talent', Savarkar's patriotic radicalism was already apparent. As a student in India he had organised protest burning of foreign cloth in 1905, been a leader of *Mitra Mela*, an organisation considered to be the 'beehive' of revolutionaries in western India, and in 1904, had set up Abhinav Bharat.[89] In England, Savarkar wrote two important texts: a Marathi translation of Mazzini's *Life,* and *The Indian War of Independence of 1857.* Translated from Marathi into English by several hands at India House, it was published in London in May 1909. Readings and discussions from the book formed an important feature at India House gatherings. Savarkar also founded the Young India Party, and after 1907 assumed the 'moral and political leadership' of India House, organising its activities. His 'extraordinary personal magnetism [and] ...an intensity of faith' was commented on by many.[90]

BHIKHAIJI RUSTOM CAMA

Two other prominent personalities connected with India House were Sardarsinghji Rewabhai Rana, who ran a jewellery business in Paris, and Madame Bhikhaiji Cama. Known as 'the Mother of Indian Revolution', Cama moved between London and Paris, until 1909, when she established herself in Paris, becoming prominent in French Socialist circles.[91] Born in 1861, in a wealthy Parsi family of Bombay, Bhikhaiji Cama, married to Rustom Cama, the son of the Parsi reformer, was a woman of independent means, her father having left her considerable property. Educated at Alexandra Girls' School and fluent in several languages, Cama is said to have worked as a social worker during the 1897 plague epidemic in Bombay and it is likely she met Shapurji Saklatvala, the future Communist MP (see Chapter 10) and another volunteer worker. Her experience among the plague victims would have been a formative experience, as was the Indian National Congress. She is said to have 'enthusiastically' followed the proceedings of the first session, held in Bombay, while her husband belonged to the 'Ginger Group' of the Congress. Around 1902, aged 40, Cama arrived in Britain, spending 'about a year each in Germany, Scotland, Paris and London', where she came under the influence of the radical Indian Home Rule Society. But her first political apprenticeship was under Naoroji, when he unsuccessfully contested Lambeth North.[92]

In 1907, Madame Cama, who was to become one of the best-known Indian women in European revolutionary circles, first arrived as a delegate with Rana at the International Socialist Congress at Stuttgart, and, with the help of Hyndman, of the Social Democratic Federation, proposed a resolution on India. Compared with Naoroji's at Amsterdam in 1904, the Indian resolution at Stuttgart was remarkable for its radicalism, as it categorically demanded the withdrawal of British rule: that 'no people should be subject to any despotic or tyrannical form of government'. Opposition from British delegates prevented its adoption. But Cama was allowed to address the delegates. In a passionate speech on behalf of the 'dumb millions of Hindustan', she exposed the 'terrible tyrannies' under British rule and, Naoroji-like, pointed to the '35 million pounds' taken from India annually 'without return'. She concluded her speech by unfolding the Indian National flag, a tricolour in green, yellow and red, with *Bande Mataram* on the middle band, and bearing emblems representing the three major religions of India. This was the first time an Indian flag had been displayed in a foreign country. Following Stuttgart, Cama embarked on a campaign tour, travelling to the USA in 1907, and then to London, and Paris, where she settled, but kept up her contacts with India House, attending its meetings.[93]

Beginning in September 1909, Cama, who had previously written for Krishnavarma's paper, published *Bande Mataram, Monthly Organ of Indian Independence,* a radical newspaper. Financed from her own resources, the paper, which appeared regularly till 1913, survived on her own admission, by denying herself.[94] To further the revolutionary nationalist cause, she funded the party, contributed money to print its literature and helped to smuggle revolutionary literature and explosives into India. She kept up a voluminous correspondence with Indian revolutionaries in different parts of the world, was a friend to Maud Gonne (who was close to her during her exile in Paris) and maintained her contacts in French socialist circles. Her house in Paris was a meeting place for budding nationalists and revolutionaries from India, Egypt, Turkey, and China.[95] A rare Indian woman in a leadership role, she inspired others with her zeal, being elevated as a heroine alongside the Rani of Jhansi. One of her close associates during this period, Perin Naoroji, the granddaughter of Naoroji, for instance, became active in the 1930s campaigns, and a member of the Bombay Congress.[96]

Profoundly influenced by the radicalism of India House, Cama admired Russian methods and advocated the use of force, pointing out that although repugnant to her once, 'why ... deplore the use of violence when our enemies drive us to it?' But she is also known to have advocated non-cooperation, which Gandhi would use so successfully. For instance, at a meeting in London in 1909, she told her audience that they could free themselves 'at a moment's notice' if they did not 'under any circumstances accept any offices, however high that might be under the present government'.[97] At a time when few Indian women were active in politics, Cama urged women to play an equal role in national life and in the struggle for national independence. In all her speeches she appealed to all Indian ethnic groups, denounced Indian 'slavery' under British rule and asked for 'human rights' and *swaraj.*[98]

The radicals at India House were uncompromising in their demands and methods: as Krishnavarma wrote, Indians wanted independence instead of the 'alien despotism', and they were prepared 'to resist violence by violence'.[99] By 1906, within a year of its founding, the Indian Home Rule Society had enlisted 119 members. At its meetings resolutions were passed, condemning arrests and punishments in India. They organized annual Martyrs' Day gatherings to commemorate the anniversary of the 1857 Rising, the first, in May 1905, taking the form of a dinner for Krishnavarma at an Indian restaurant in Shaftesbury Avenue, when, in a stirring speech, a Dr Pereira informed the assembled that India could only be freed by blood. From such beginnings, the annual Martyrs' Day celebrations grew into important events with invitation cards printed in red ink.[100] Such activities did not escape notice: Krishnavarma was condemned as 'anti-British', his paper labelled as 'extreme' and India House as a 'notorious ... centre of sedition'. Although officials saw him as the leader of 'a most dangerous, seditious movement', some contemporaries doubted his influence. Nonetheless, questions were asked in Parliament: in July 1907 and, again, in June 1908, a 'Mr Rees' urged action against him. But, seven weeks before the first question was tabled, Krishnavarma had fled to Paris, from where he kept up his attacks.[101] The *Indian Sociologist,* however, continued to be printed in London until 1909 when the government moved against the printers, Arthur Horsley and Guy Aldred. Krishnavarma, too, did not escape action: he was disbarred by the Benchers of the Inner Temple – for his 'seditious publications', while Oxford University tried abolishing the Herbert Spencer Lectureship he had endowed.[102] Krishnavarma retaliated by moving the paper to Paris and copies were smuggled into India, despite a ban on its importation under the Sea Customs Act.

According to his biographer, while Krishnavarma marked out 'the purely theoretical radicalism ... the abstract law on the subject', others at India House prepared for action.[103] Under Savarkar's leadership, campaigns gathered force. India was 'flooded' with smuggled leaflets. For instance, Cama's 1908 speech in London was sent out as a *Bande Mataram* leaflet over her own signature. Another, 'A Grave Warning', asking merchants to withdraw their investments, was intended to embarrass the government, while *'Khalsa'* was designed to 'seduce' the Indian army. Meetings in public venues generated a sense of excitement. At the celebrations to mark Guru Govind day, for instance, Caxton Hall was decorated with flags and audiences of over 300 attended. Patriotic songs were sung and stirring speeches, described as 'objectionable', were made by India House radicals and other leaders like B.C. Pal. At the 51st anniversary commemoration of the 1857 Rising, in May 1908, which lasted four hours, special Martyrs' Day badges were distributed. Two students, Hernam Singh and Rafik Muhammad Khan, who refused to remove them on their return to Cirencester Agricultural College, were expelled. Accounts of such public meetings were reported in Indian newspapers. At the private India House gatherings on Sundays no less 'seditious' speeches were made and tactics for liberating the motherland discussed, including the 'policy of assassination'. At one meeting in June 1908, a Dr Desai from London University gave a talk on bomb making; at another, Nitisen Dwarkadas proposed infiltrating the Indian Army. Chapters from *The Indian War of Independence* were read and discussed. Some students, it was reported, practised revolver shooting at a range in Tottenham Court Road, while even pistols and bombs, including cyclostyled copies of a bomb manual obtained from a Russian, were smuggled into India. International in their outlook, India House radicals joined hands with the Young Turks, made links with the Irish and the Egyptian nationalists. Plans were made to form an Indo-Egyptian Nationalist Association. In October 1910, Bhikaji Cama helped organise the Egyptian National Congress in Brussels, attended by Egyptians and Indians.[104]

The demand for complete independence advocated by India House radicals struck at the heart of the imperial system and alarmed the authorities. However small the movement, their activities, within the context of the unrest in India following partition of Bengal in 1905, appeared sufficiently 'grave' to prompt a communiqué to the Secretary of State, Viscount Morley, from the government of India. Describing measures already taken in India, Viceroy Minto urged action to end 'the evil' of India House. Drawing attention to the 'evil results' such 'malignant sedition' might have on the impressionable Indian youth in England and in India, he considered it 'intolerable that enemies of British rule ... should ... be permitted to use the headquarters of the Empire as the centre of a seditious and revolutionary campaign'.[105]

The government moved against the radicals. Scotland Yard planted informers at India House. Students were watched and dossiers compiled on them.[106] They were harassed in other ways. Their future careers, too, were at stake, as India Office used its muscle to influence academic outcomes. For instance, when it was learnt that the Benchers at Gray's Inn hesitated calling Savarkar and Hernam Singh to the Bar, 'incriminating evidence' linking Ganesh Savarkar's 'seditious activities' in India to Savarkar's in London was sent by the Viceroy, with the result the Benchers decided not to admit Savarkar to the Bar.[107]

Student anti-colonial agitation reached a climax on the night of 1 July 1909 at a social gathering ('At Home') arranged by the NIA at the Imperial Institute, when Curzon Wyllie was assassinated by Dhingra. A Parsi doctor with a practice in Shanghai, Cawas Khurshedji Lalcaca, was also fatally wounded. Wyllie, with a long family history of service in India, was not particularly high up as an official, his duties being connected with European visits of Indian Princes and other dignitaries from the Native States. He also doled out advice to students and other Indians in Britain. Dhingra, too, though connected with India House, was not considered a 'prominent' activist.[108] Why then had he been the first to fire a shot outside India for freedom of the Motherland? Did he act on his own, or was he used as a 'tool' as some contemporaries, notably the authorities and his own family, suggested? The trial transcripts and Dhingra's own statements provide some clues. But the most vital evidence is contained in the testimony of another India House inmate, H.K. Koregaonkar, a friend of Dhingra, who, after returning to India, turned 'approver' in the Nassik case.[109]

MADAN LAL DHINGRA

Born in Amritsar, Punjab in 1887, Dhingra came from an educated, professional family, who had made good under the Raj, were prosperous, influential and loyal, sincerely believing that Britain ruled India 'in the interest of the people and their enlightenment'. Educated at Municipal College, he then attended Government College, Lahore, but was withdrawn within a few months in favour of business. In 1906, Dhingra came to London to study engineering at University College, travelling on the same ship as Koregaonkar. According to family testimony, Dhingra was not involved in politics in India, which is not surprising given his background.[110]

Dhingra was said to have visited India House shortly after his arrival in London and to have lodged there on two occasions, once in 1908, for as long as six months. Not considered an activist, he attended India House Sunday gatherings, being first spotted in January 1909. Dhingra had also taken lessons in revolver shooting at the Tottenham Court Road rifle range for 'some months' and become 'very proficient'.[111] After his arrest, two loaded pistols, a knife and a written statement were found on him, which suggests the crime was premeditated, but not part of a conspiracy, since nothing of significance was revealed in the intercepted telegrams between London, India and Paris.[112] What had motivated Dhingra?

Officials saw the influence of India House, and especially the hand of Savarkar, in Dhingra's action. They alleged that Dhingra was 'the product of Savarkar's sound teaching'. Even his prepared statement was alleged to be unlike Dhingra's in style, but 'most probably Savarkar's'. They also alleged that Koregaonkar had gone to the Imperial Institute to 'watch and guide' the whole thing, encouraging Dhingra with the words *'Aji, jao na, kya karte ho'* (Well go on, what are you doing?), a statement that conflicts with another statement, where Koregaonkar was shown not to have 'any conversation' with Dhingra. The immediate causes leading to the assassination were alleged to be, first, the prosecution and transportation for life of Savarkar's brother Ganesh. Savarkar, it was alleged, had sworn to avenge his brother's life, had advocated the 'wholesale' murder of Englishmen in India, urging everyone to do their best to serve the country by 'sacrificing' their lives at the 'earliest possible moment'.[113] Second, the refusal of the Benchers to admit Savarkar to the Bar, and the disbarring of Krishnavarma, were alleged to be factors. Even the 'particular victim', Curzon Wyllie, had been chosen, according to the Director of Criminal Intelligence, not because Dhingra had any personal grievance against him, but 'to satisfy the private grudge of Krishnavarma', who had known Wyllie in Udaipur. Krishnavarma's approval of Dhingra 'as a martyr' was considered sufficient evidence of his complicity in the murder.[114] In this way, the authorities managed to incriminate those they considered to be ringleaders.

Dhingra's family, deeply shocked and ashamed of the stigma of the murder, also blamed India House, seeing Dhingra an 'excellent tool' for the 'evil purposes' of 'Krishnavarma and his lieutenants'. They had been sufficiently concerned at his residence at India House to request Wyllie to wean him away from 'such evil company'. Dhingra's family took pains to emphasise his 'eccentric' and 'wayward' behaviour, attributing this to his interrupted education in India, prompting him to run away to sea as a lascar. They cabled their younger son, Bhajanlal, in London, to instruct their solicitor to plead 'mental unsoundness from childhood', and express the family's abhorrence, possibly hoping to save Dhingra.[115]

Dhingra's action puzzled many contemporaries, his family background making his behaviour appear even more incongruous. Dhingra, it was suggested, had no 'personal grievance' against Wyllie, who had shown great kindness to the family. However, available evidence suggests that Dhingra's action had been premeditated. He had a prepared statement with him. After the murder, he had remained calm. At the Westminster Police Court, he had stood in the dock in apparent unconcern, with his hands in his pockets and had chatted in an animated fashion to the police, even with a smile on his face, after his remand. All this suggests that Dhingra had no fear of the consequences of his action. His refusal to have a solicitor at his trial and his conduct there, would further confirm this.[116]

In his prepared statement, Dhingra had written that he had tried to shed blood intentionally, as a protest against 'inhuman transportations and hangings'. He wrote that a country held down by force of arms was in a 'perpetual state of war' and since 'open battle' was not allowed, he had struck by surprise. This establishes the crime to be political. Dhingra claimed that he had acted alone, consulting none but his own conscience. As a Hindu, he argued that slavery of the Motherland was an insult to God, and he offered his blood on the altar of freedom. According to him, 'the only lesson required in India is to learn how to die, and the only way to teach it is by dying alone'. No wonder the authorities attempted to suppress his statement. It was refused in court. Eventually, with the help of David Garnett, it was published in the *Daily News* in August 1909.[117] The two postcards found in his room also affirm the political nature of the assassination. One was a reproduction of the famous scene showing 'Mutiny rebels' being blown from the mouth of a cannon, the other showed Lord Curzon, with 'Heathen Dog' written across it. His conduct at the trial, too, hints at his political self-sacrifice. Dhingra refused to accept the judge's description of his crime as a 'wilful murder'; instead he described it as 'an act of patriotism and justice' and as such, justified. When sentenced to death, he was reported to have thanked the judge and proclaimed that he was 'proud to have the honour of laying down my life for the cause of my motherland'.[118] In his court statement, Dhingra maintained that he was not speaking in defence of himself, but to prove the justice of his deed, explaining why it was patriotic and 'more justifiable' for an Indian to fight the English. He pointed to the horrors of British rule, the murder of 80 millions in the last '50 years', the exploitation and the draining of '£100,000,000 every year'. He said:

> In case this country is occupied by the Germans, and an Englishman, not bearing to see the Germans walking with the insolence of conquerors in the streets of London, goes and kills one or two of the Germans, and that Englishman is held as a patriot by the people of this country, then certainly I am prepared to work for the emancipation of my Motherland.[119]

His personal experiences under colonialism, too, are significant. Dhingra was said to speak little about his affairs. But he must have deeply resented his degrading experiences at the hands of some Englishmen. According to the evidence contained in Koregaonkar's statement, Dhingra had been 'treated badly' in the Settlement Department, which he had joined on leaving Lahore Government College. He had later travelled through Assam, and, working partly as a stoker on the P&O line, to Australia and as far as Eastern Turkestan. He had been thrown out of Australia and 'ill-treated' by his 'superior English officers' on the P&O. Travelling through Assam, Dhingra would have seen the poverty of the Assam tea pickers; as a stoker on the P&O line, he would have experienced lascar labour conditions. Is it any wonder then that Dhingra was said to speak 'bitterly of the Colonials?' Certain writings in English newspapers further fuelled his 'intense hatred'. He was said to read over and over again articles like 'Coloured Men and English Women' in *London Opinion* and 'Babu, Black Sheep' in *Cassell's Weekly*. Having experienced racism at a personal level, such articles would have made him even more 'wild'. According to Koregaonkar, Dhingra attended India House, but not that often, seeing it as 'mere talk', while Englishmen only understood force. He was said to have various schemes in his head, like blowing up a P&O ship. Koregaonkar testified that Dhingra admired Savarkar, spoke highly of Krishnavarma's paper, which he read avidly; that he had decided to 'sacrifice' his life as early as December 1908, and consulted Savarkar who had suggested Lord Curzon or Lord Morley or Lord Asquith as a target. Dhingra even joined the NIA for the express purpose of meeting important people.[120] Therefore, Dhingra's personal experiences are crucial in understanding his actions.

Wyllie, eulogised by *The Times* as a lover of 'justice and fair play', was not seen in the same light by the Indian students. They found his arrogant behaviour 'obnoxious'. Wyllie kept a close watch on them and had planted a number of detectives at India House.[121] Further, his memo to the India Office concerning a meeting of the East India Association at Caxton Hall and the reactions of Indian students – their deep distrust of India Office proposals for 'their betterment' as manifested there – shows what Wyllie really thought of them. He wrote that Indian students wished to be on the same footing with Englishmen, and wanted their entitlement to 'equal liberty of action and … freedom of speech'. Wyllie saw such aspirations as a 'demonstration of disloyalty', concluding that a majority were 'neither afraid nor ashamed to openly manifest their disloyalty'. Hence the need for an Indian hostel to 'make them loyal', in other words, under control and compliant. The hostel was said to be Wyllie's idea. Further, it was Wyllie who had gone to Paris to collect information against Savarkar, Hernam Singh and others.[122] They condemned Wyllie for wanting to keep them down.

All this would suggest that Dhingra had not been a 'tool'. His background, too, far from making his action a puzzle, explains it. He was from a western-educated family, loyal to the Raj, a family who had turned to Wyllie to lead him back to what they considered the right path. In London, under the heady ideology of India House, all this would have appeared in a very different light: a family of collaborators, they had appealed to Wyllie, the embodiment of the power of the occupier, under whose rule he, like so many millions of Indians, suffered. And so Dhingra had acted, in the name of freedom, justice and patriotism.

The assassination of Wyllie in the capital of the empire created shock waves. British opinion was scandalised. In Parliament, members of the British Committee of the Congress, Rutherford and Keir Hardie, deplored the deed and saw it as a setback for reform. Dhingra's action was condemned at two public meetings of resident Indians, attended among others by the Aga Khan, Bhownaggree, J.M. Parikh and B.C. Pal. Ameer Ali called it 'a national disaster', while Surendranath Banerjea, then in England, disassociated himself from violence. Gandhi, too, on a visit to London, considered Dhingra's defence as 'inadmissible'. To H.S. Polak, he wrote: 'Every Indian should reflect thoroughly on this murder ... He was egged on to do this act by ill-digested readings of worthless writings.' In his opinion, those who had incited Dhingra deserved to be punished. In Poona, Gokhale, denouncing the philosophy of violence, labelled Dhingra's act a 'foul deed', which had 'blackened' India's name.[123]

A few voices supported Dhingra. At a meeting attended by Aiyer, Savarkar, Haider Raza and S.M. Master among others, the radical students praised his action as a 'glorious act'. In Paris, Cama's paper, *Bande Mataram,* paying tribute to 'Dhingra the Immortal', wrote that in years to come, when the British empire in India was reduced to 'dust and ashes', it would be Dhingra's monument that would 'adorn the squares of our chief towns'. Krishnavarma saw him 'a martyr' in the cause of independence. Hyndman, in his paper, *Justice,* pointed out that he had long warned that if Britain continued its policy of 'despotism and bleeding' in India, terrorism would be the result. He wrote: 'That prediction has been fulfilled. Tyranny and torture ... have produced the same results as tyranny and torture in Russia.'[124]

Dhingra was hanged in Pentonville prison on 17 August 1909. To prevent his martyrdom, it was proposed that, if cremated, his ashes should not be sent back to India. It was only in June 1977 that his remains were finally returned home. Savarkar was arrested at Victoria Station on his return from Paris and eventually extradited to India. According to Garnett, the authorities were determined to have him tried in India where he was more likely to get a stiffer sentence. And so took place the farce of Savarkar being brought to Bow Street week after week and remanded, until the authorities were able to dig up some speeches made by him in India several years previously, and which could be used in evidence against him. They then applied for his extradition order and he was put on board a ship for India. At Marseilles, on 8 July 1910, by jumping through the porthole of a lavatory, he made his escape. But he was captured and handed back to the British by the French police. Cama, prominent in socialist circles, used her influence to such effect that socialist papers in Paris took up Savarkar's cause and strong articles were published in *L'Humanité* by Jean Longuet and in *Action.* But to no avail. The case even reached the Hague Tribunal. Savarkar was tried in India 'for abetment of murder' and in December 1910, he was transported to the Andaman Islands for life.[125]

India House was closed down and sold. Some of the remaining radical students tried keeping up their activities: a Martyrs' Day celebration was held on 10 May 1911 and attempts made to found new societies. But increased state vigilance dispersed the movement. In Paris radical activity centred around Rana, Krishnavarma, Virendranath Chattopadhyaya and Cama. Intelligence reports recorded their activities. Even King Edward VII viewed with 'apprehension' the Paris secret organisation and its literature, asking Lord Morley if it was not possible 'to prevent the dissemination of their pamphlets which must have a most injurious effect on the native mind'.[126] Cama, seen by the British authorities as one of the 'recognised leaders of the revolutionary movement in Paris', and described as 'anarchical, revolutionary, anti-British and irreconcilable', was considered dangerous enough to have dossiers consisting of details of her almost daily doings compiled. Fearful of her influence, in 1911, officials contemplated appropriating her property in India to cut off her source of finance. Finally, during the First World War, under pressure from the British government, the French put an end to the activities of the Paris group. Cama was interned in Bordeaux. Even after the war, and though broken in health, she was still considered important enough to have visits from associates of the *Ghadar* Party in the USA , and for Indian Political Intelligence to watch her activities.[127] She lived on in exile in France till 1936, when she returned to Bombay – to die. Rana was exiled to Martinique, while Chattopadhyaya went to Berlin and Krishnavarma with his wife to Switzerland. Chattopadhyaya died in mysterious circumstances in 1936. Bhanumati Krishnavarma died in 1930, and Krishnavarma in 1933.[128]

As a result of the assassination, Indian students came under increasing supervision and control. So concerned were the authorities that even the King suggested that Viceroy Minto take 'serious steps' to prevent men 'with no fixed occupation' leaving India since in England they only 'learn sedition and treason' which they infuse into the minds of Indians both in England and in India.[129] In 1910, as has been seen, the Advisory Committee, Educational Adviser and the Bureau of Information were set up. In the same year, to supervise Indian students, an Institute with accommodation facilities was also established at 21 Cromwell Road. Then, in 1920, the YMCA Indian Students' Union and Hostel was opened, first in Keppel Street, moving to 112 Gower Street in 1923.[130] Such were the measures and mechanisms devised to control and spy on them. In India, the government responded with repression on the one hand and concessions on the other (e.g. the India Council Acts). And although, after the First World War, Indian nationalist politics was dominated by the Gandhian philosophy of non-violence, the radical tradition remained influential among a minority.

On a wider front, as a result of 1909, at the suggestion of the India Office, the Department of Criminal Intelligence in Simla sent John Wallinger to London to set up a new intelligence section at the India Office, to snoop on Indian 'revolutionaries and criminals', that is to say any Indian engaged in anti-colonial activity or even voicing views sympathetic to Indian freedom. The section developed into the Indian Political Intelligence department (IPI), headed by Philip Vickery (in surveillance reports, he signed himself IPI, never by name), an Irishman, and supported by an army of detectives and informers, all paid for by Indian tax-payers, without their knowledge, and whose reports remained secret until August 1997, the 50th anniversary of independence, when they were de-classified.[131]

INDIANS IN THE SUFFRAGETTE MOVEMENT

At the height of the empire it is not surprising to find Indians in Britain involved in anti-colonial campaigns for Indian freedom. However, Indians were not narrow in their concerns: they participated in other contemporary political struggles for social justice. One such campaign was the women's right to vote. At a time when few men were sympathetic to women's franchise, Malabari's views and Naoroji's support of women's suffrage organisations have already been noted. Gandhi, too, admired the suffragettes, until their campaign turned violent. It was during his 1906 visit, when 11 women were arrested for demonstrating in front of the House of Commons and sent to prison for refusing to pay their fines, that Gandhi first became aware of the suffragettes. So impressed was he by the courage and strength of these middle-class women that he was moved to write an article for the journal, *Indian Opinion*, entitled, 'Deeds Better than Words'. He continued to follow their struggle and to write about them. This was the period when, under Gandhi's leadership, Indians in South Africa had participated in acts of civil disobedience and Gandhi was developing his own ideas of *satyagraha*; he is known to have discussed whether it was appropriate for men to embrace 'women's tactics' without appearing 'effeminate'. During his 1909 visit he met both the Pankhursts and Despard, president of the Women's Freedom League (WFL), who was looking for ways of demonstrating her disaffection with the government's lack of support for women's franchise. Despard, a pacifist, shared Gandhi's ideals and saw her refusal to pay taxes as a form of 'spiritual resistance'. It has been suggested that her meetings with Gandhi 'sharpened her awareness of the potential' of civil disobedience.[132]

Some Indian women, too, supported their sisters' aspirations, just as they campaigned for their right to vote in India. But little is known about Indian suffragettes: they remain largely outside the historiography of British suffragettes. However, evidence shows that some Indian women were involved in suffrage campaigns, and one in particular, Sophia Duleep Singh, was prominent in the Women's Social and Political Union (WSPU) founded in 1903 by the Pankhurst family, and was active as a tax resister in the Women's Tax Resistance League (WTRL), founded in October 1909 as an offshoot of the WFL.

The participation of Indian women in the suffrage campaigns in Britain is evident from a little-known photograph of the 1911 Women's Coronation Procession, which stretched 7 miles (11 kilometres), when 60,000 women, with over 1,000 banners demanding 'votes for women', marched from Westminster to the Albert Hall. The Indian contingent shows a small group of Indian women under the banner 'India', carrying their emblem, a model of an elephant.[133] Who were they? To answer the question we need to go back to its planning and organisation. In June 1911, when George V was due to be crowned, to publicise the women's campaign and their determination to win the vote, a procession, which was to include a foreign and an imperial delegation to demonstrate the strength of the women's movement world-wide, was organised by the WSPU. By 26 May 1911, a committee to organise the Indian contingent, comprising Mrs Fisher Unwin, Dr Helen B. Hanson and Mrs P.L. Roy, was hard at work amongst Indian women in England.[134] No details are given for 'Mrs P.L. Roy', but could she be an Indian and the mother of Indra Lal Roy, then a student at St Paul's School, and a pilot in the Royal Flying Corps during the war (see pp. 172–3)? The India representatives exhorted those not in receipt of a communication from the committee to contact them, at the same time inviting subscriptions for banners and emblems. By 2 June, it was reported that their emblem was being prepared. This hints at a network among Indian women in England, some of whom, students and residents, would have taken part in the preparations and the procession. Next, on 9 June 1911, comes a mention of the 'visitors from India', who had come to participate in the procession, suggesting links between the women's movement in England and in India. Among these were the Maharani and the Gaekwar of Baroda, who represented India at the mass meeting held at the Albert Hall following the procession.[135]

Although the Indian contingent in the procession was small compared with other sections of the imperial delegation, it was nonetheless considered to be impressive, not only because of the 'particularly striking and picturesque', 'beautiful dresses' of the women, but for what it demanded. A seasoned India hand, for many years governor of an Indian province, was so struck by the appearance of women 'in the Oriental dress' in the international procession, that he considered them to be 'the most significant feature' of the whole procession because they demonstrated that the 'Woman's Question' was 'without race, or creed, or boundary' and, as such, the extent to which the women's movement 'may influence the world of the future can hardly be dreamed of by the present generation'. In a similar vein, *The Star* agreed: 'Nothing can prevent the triumph of the cause which behind it has such reserves of courage and conviction.'[136] One such woman was Sophia Duleep Singh.

SOPHIA DULEEP SINGH

Like her older sister, Catherine, Sophia was active in the campaigns for women's right to vote. While Catherine was a member of the National Union of Women's Suffrage Societies (NUWSS) founded in 1897, Sophia was prominent in the WSPU and active in its Richmond and Kingston District branches, playing a significant local as well as a national role.[137] Born in 1876, Sophia Alexandrovna was the youngest daughter of Duleep Singh. She lived at Faraday House, Hampton Court and, like her sisters, had inherited the sum of £23,000 under arrangements made for Duleep Singh and his heirs. From the surviving personal letters written to her by her two sisters, Bamba and Catherine, and her brother Frederick, we get a few glimpses of their lives in Edwardian England.[138] From these we learn that Sophia played hockey, took music lessons and played in concerts. The family's taste for western classical music, too, is strongly apparent, as Bamba's comment on opera shows: 'I cannot understand the use of being in Europe if one hears no music.' Sophia was a keen photographer, kept pedigree dogs and may have exhibited them at Crufts. Like some of the middle-class women of the time, she rode a bicycle. And like the upper classes she travelled in Scotland and on the Continent, went to balls and dances during the season and supported various charities.[139]

What also emerges from these letters is a strong sense that the family of the Maharaja of the Punjab did not lose sight of their Indian/Sikh heritage. They travelled widely in India, commenting knowledgeably about its history, architecture and music. They kept in contact with friends and relations in the Punjab, being warmly received as Duleep Singh's children. A copy of the family tree compiled possibly by Sophia, a short history of the family written by Bamba in the preface to Frederick's *Portraits in Norfolk Houses,* as well as Catherine's comment 'she is very very lovely, rather like our grandmother Jindan', further illustrate that the Duleep Singh family, living the life of the English upper classes as they did, nonetheless retained a sense of family history. Such impressions are confirmed by Sophia's diary of her visit to India, November 1906–May 1907. Although difficult to read – witness her sister's complaint: 'but oh the writing' – it nonetheless provides historians with tantalising glimpses of Sophia Duleep Singh's personality and interests. Her strong character is evident from her complaint to the Viceroy for not being accorded courtesies she was given to understand by the India Office she would be entitled to 'as a traveller of position', as well as from her comment on a church service conducted by an American bishop, 'but I have never in my life heard such drivel, everyone was in fits … and I nearly got up and left'. Her pride in and sympathy with India and her own heritage are also apparent from observations such as: 'very delighted to be in India once again', or 'I was delighted to see the house of my ancestors, but oh dear how primitive it all is.' Of her visit to the Ellora caves, she wrote: 'it must have taken 1000s of men 100s of years to make all this and no ordinary men either but artists as all is beautifully carved and finished'.[140] In London, she maintained her links with Indians, seen from her subscription to the Lascars' Club. She was also present at that fatal NIA 'At Home' in 1909. During the First World War, she visited Indian wounded in hospital and entertained Sikh soldiers at her house in Hampton Court. Records also show that she gave them her photograph, which one soldier described as 'the photo of our King's granddaughter'.[141]

As a suffragette, Sophia Duleep Singh was mentioned by Mrs Blathwayt to have converted to the views of the WSPU at the home of Una Dugdale. First recorded as a campaigner in the fourth annual report of the WSPU, where she is listed among the card collectors for the self-denial week (the £5. 11s. pledged against her name is considerably more than some others on the list), she remained an active member from March 1909 till 1914, when the suffragettes called off their action. Her subscription to the WSPU, ranging from £6 to £30 per year, is substantial, indicating a strong commitment to the cause. Sophia was also a member of the WTRL, and is named as an active tax resister.[142] The WTRL combined direct action with non-violence, its main weapon being refusal to pay taxes: income tax, property tax and inhabited house duty; dog tax, servant insurance and other types of licences, including carriages and armorial bearings. With their slogan, 'No Vote No Tax', the WTRL members, drawn from various suffrage societies, both militant and non-militant, aimed to demonstrate the injustice of exacting taxation from women, while at the same time denying them political representation. Inspired by John Hampden, the seventeenth-century reformer, who in 1635 had refused to pay 'ship money' levied by Charles I, the WTRL claimed historical legitimacy for their action. Refusal to pay tax could lead to fines, even imprisonment, offenders' goods being impounded by the bailiffs under distraint and sold by public auction to recover the sums due. Such auctions provided great opportunity for publicity as WTRL members came out in support, often buying the articles under 'distraint', returning them to the owner, and organising meetings and protest demonstrations. Because these auctions were held in public places local to the tax resisters, a good deal of interest and sympathy was generated in the community for the cause. Of the over 220 active tax resisters in the five years of active campaigning before the war, a majority were middle class, many of them professional women. Only one was Indian: Sophia Duleep Singh.[143]

Our knowledge of Sophia Duleep Singh as a campaigner, both nationally, and locally in the Richmond and Kew branch as well as the Kingston and District branch of the WSPU, is derived largely from the pages of the weekly newspaper, *Votes for Women*, and the *Suffragette*. Evidence shows that she played a prominent role in the 400-strong demonstration to Parliament on 18 November 1910, 'Black Friday', marching at the head of the deputation, with Mrs Pankhurst, Mrs Garrett Anderson and Dorinda Neligan, the 76-year-old head of Croydon High School. She took an active part in the WSPU publicity campaigns, for instance, in July 1911, driving with 'Miss Shepherd', in the first cart in the parade of 'Press Carts', delivering copies of *Votes for Women* to various pitches in central London. 'Press Carts' were an important means of advertising. But they were also considered 'unwomanly' and as such created a strong, but often, unfavourable impression. From 1912, she was regularly seen selling the *Suffragette*, the new organ of the WSPU, at her 'pitch' outside Hampton Court.[144] An energetic fund-raiser, she contributed items for WSPU shops; for instance, in April 1911, she donated a cake and sweets at the opening of the Streatham shop, which are said to have sold 'instantly'. Listed as a collector, she sold the *Suffragette* at Saturday meetings, in addition to her regular 'pitch' outside Hampton Court. Locally, the branch reports are peppered with 'grateful acknowledgements' and 'special thanks' for her fund-raising activities, taking collecting boxes, and selling other items like sweets and children's clothes.[145] Sophia was active in the Richmond and Kew branch, described as an 'energetic union', as well as in the Kingston and District branch. She spoke regularly at meetings of the Richmond branch, addressing large enthusiastic audiences, and was also known to chair meetings of the Kingston and District branch. Among the five members of the Richmond branch in the 'Black Friday' deputation, Sophia Duleep Singh, as has been seen, was one.[146]

But, perhaps, it was as a tax resister that she made her greatest impression, arousing 'great interest', as *Votes for Women* wrote. Taking her stand on the principle that taxing women who had 'no voice in the management of the country' was unjust, she registered her defiance on several occasions. In May 1911, at Spelthorne Petty Sessions, her refusal to pay licences for her five dogs, a carriage and manservant led to a fine of £3.[147] A month later, in July 1911, against arrears of 6 shillings in rates, she had a seven-stone diamond ring impounded under Warrant of Distress and sold by auction at Ashford, attended by a large number of women supporters from different suffrage societies, including Madame Jenner d'Ermont of Rome and Mrs Madison Millard of Chicago. The bidding, according to the press report, was 'brisk' and the ring was 'knocked down' for £10, to Mrs Jopling Rowe, who returned it to Sophia Duleep Singh, 'the graceful little act' being greeted with applause. A 'well-attended' meeting followed, at which a telegram, expressing regret for her absence, was read out from Catherine Pankhurst. The significance of such a high-profile stand and the publicity surrounding it should not be underrated. This is evidenced by the fact that *Votes for Women* reported that by her action Sophia Duleep Singh had done 'her utmost' to impress an 'otherwise "Anti" neighbourhood' with the 'righteousness of the cause'.[148] In December 1913, she was summoned to Feltham Police Court for employing a manservant and keeping two dogs and a carriage without licence. In Court, sporting the WTRL badge, and accompanied by several members of the League, pointing out that 'taxation without representation' was a tyranny, she declared:

> I am unable conscientiously to pay money to the state, as I am not allowed to exercise any control over its expenditure; neither am I allowed any voice in the choosing of Members of Parliament, whose salaries I have to help to pay. This is very unjust. When the women

of England are enfranchised and the state acknowledges me as a citizen I shall, of course, pay my share willingly towards its upkeep. If I am not a fit person for the purpose of representation, why should I be a fit person for taxation?[149]

She was fined £12. 10s. with costs. Her refusal to pay the 'unjust taxes' and the fine, resulted in a necklace, comprising 131 pearls, and a gold bangle studded with pearls and diamonds (clearly family heirlooms) being seized under distraint and auctioned at Twickenham Town Hall, the necklace fetching £10 and the bangle £7 and both bought by the WTRL members.[150]

With the outbreak of the war in 1914, campaigning ceased as WTRL, WSPU and other suffrage societies called off action for patriotic war work. In July 1915, Sophia Duleep Singh took part in the 10,000-strong Women's War Work procession led by Mrs Pankhurst. After Mrs Pankhurst's death in 1928, she was appointed president of the committee responsible for providing flowers for her statue, demonstrating further her prominence in WSPU. After the war she joined the Suffragette Fellowship, remaining its member till her death.[151]

Sophia Duleep Singh's high profile in the WSPU and WTRL campaigns is significant and, although largely omitted from the historiography of the suffragette literature, her contribution to women's struggle before the war should not be underrated. In the collective memory of the inhabitants of Richmond and Twickenham district, which had its share of militancy, she is remembered for her prominent part in obtaining the vote for women. Her strong commitment to the cause of women is in no doubt, seen from the fact that in the 1934 edition of *Women's Who's Who* she listed 'Advancement of Women' as her one and only interest.[152]

In 1935 she lent her brother Frederick's collection of Stuart relics to the Inverness Museum. She died in 1948.

6

Indians in the First World War

The First World War brought the largest number of Indians to Britain. Historians have pointed to the fact that but for India's membership of the British Empire, Indians would not have been so directly involved in the war.[1] The Indian Army, raised for the defence of India, was required to keep internal peace and to protect its frontiers. On many occasions, it had also been used beyond India's borders as an 'imperial fire brigade', in Eastern Africa, Egypt and the Persian Gulf and against the 'Boxer rebels' in China in 1900, but in small numbers and for short periods of time, and never in Europe. In this context, the First World War marks an important departure: Indian troops fought with the British on the Western Front, and Indian wounded were brought to England. This chapter briefly examines Indian contribution to the war effort, and explores reactions and responses of Indians and the British, both at official level and at the level of ordinary people, to the presence of Indian troops in Europe and of Indian wounded in the hospitals on British soil.

INDIA'S CONTRIBUTION TO THE WAR

India's contribution to the war effort, in terms of men, materials and money, was huge. By 1918, India had sent over 1 million soldiers, more than from any other part of the empire, including the white Dominions. In addition, there were over 115,000 men of the Imperial Service Troops from seven of the Indian Princely States.[2] Further, starting in 1917, units of Indian Labour Corps were dispatched to the Western Front to load and unload ammunition, chop down trees, construct roads and aerodromes and to do other building work.[3] India also contributed medical personnel, field ambulances and hospital ships; supplied war materials, ammunition, plant and rolling stock, uniforms and boots, and vast quantities of raw materials like manganese, mica, saltpetre, jute and even food. In addition, India voted to bear the cost of the maintenance and provision of the Indian Expeditionary Force (IEF) sent overseas and those remaining in India. Over £100 million was given to Britain outright as a free gift and a further £20–30 million was raised each year.[4] The Indian armed forces saw active service in France and Belgium; in Gallipoli and Salonika; in East Africa; in Mesopotamia, Egypt, the Persian Gulf and Aden. They suffered heavy casualties. 53,486 died, representing 8.7 per cent of the total; 64,350 were wounded and 3,769 were missing or taken prisoner. They won many military awards and merits for bravery (12,908 honours in total), including 12 VCs, 6 of them on the Western Front, a very high number indeed.[5]

Then there were the sailors. Figures are difficult to obtain, but according to one government report 3,427 lascars lost their lives, representing between 5 and 6 per cent of the total shipped out from Bombay and Calcutta during the war; 1,200 were imprisoned in enemy countries. Awards for gallantry, too, are on record. Other individual Indians – one memo mentions 200 artisans and mechanics from Bombay and the Punjab – came looking for work, helping the war effort by working in munitions factories and industries around Britain.[6]

When Britain declared war on 4 August 1914, as loyal imperial citizens, Indians considered it their duty to help Britain defend international treaties. From the 'total support' wired by the princes as they placed their personal services, troops and resources at the disposal of the King-Emperor, to the willingness of the political leaders to sink their differences with the government, Indians urged fellow citizens to support the 'British fight' with their 'life and property'. A hospital ship, *The Loyalty*, fully provisioned by the princes, was made ready to sail for Europe with the first IEF.[7] The only dissenting voices were a handful in the radical movement, including Har Dyal, who saw war as an opportunity in the fight for freedom. But they posed no serious challenge: even the Extremist leaders, Tilak and Lala Rajpat Rai, did not co-operate with them.[8]

Indians also argued that this was their opportunity to prove them-selves 'worthy members' of the empire, in short a means of gaining respect as equal citizens, a status hitherto denied them, and possibly achieving their goal of self-government like the Dominions.[9] The issue of equality was compelling. In the words of the *Lahore Tribune,* if troops were to be sent to Europe, 'let Indian as well as British soldiers be sent without distinction of race and creed to serve side by side in defence of our united cause'. It warned, 'Let there be no question of "prestige" or the inadvisability of employing brown against white soldiers. Prestige must be based on conduct and on no other consideration.'[10]

At official level, there were divergent views. In Britain, the War Council decided to send the IEF to Egypt as a reserve force to replace British troops needed in France. Lord Hardinge, the Viceroy, advised otherwise, suggesting the IEF be sent to the Western Front. In his view, such a gesture would remove the 'stigma and a colour bar upon the Indian troops', would demonstrate Britain's appreciation of Indians as fellow subjects, appease Indian political leadership, strengthening British rule, and even making it possible to get Indian sanction in the legislature for the payment of the IEF. King George V, too, approved of Indians fighting. Others, like his secretary, Lord Stamfordham, and Sir Valentine Chirol, of *The Times,* shuddered at the implication of equal citizenship and what Indian politicians might demand in return for the contribution of the 'fighting races'.[11] In the end the contentious issue was decided by the crisis on the battlefields in France. And Lord Crewe ordered the Indian Army to proceed to Marseilles.

INDIANS ON THE WESTERN FRONT

When war broke out on 4 August 1914, there was no mass army in Britain, and no conscription. With the near decimation of the small British Expeditionary Force of two corps in the first few days of the war, reinforcements were desperately needed. So Indian troops on their way to Egypt were dispatched to France. The first to arrive, the 16,000 British and 28,500 Indian troops of the Lahore and Meerut Divisions and the Secunderabad Cavalry landed in Marseilles on 26 September 1914, where their arrival was greeted with great enthusiasm.[12] Having been equipped with new rifles, but still in their khaki drill uniforms, they were rushed to the front to face the full fury of the first German assault against Ypres in Flanders. Thanks to the Indian reinforcements the 'thin and straggling' line of the Allied troops guarding Calais and the Channel from the massed might of Falkenhayn's force, held firm. Indian soldiers were said to have arrived in the 'nick of time', preventing, according to some historians, an allied defeat in late 1914.[13] More reinforcements followed as the trench warfare took its toll.

Altogether 138,608 Indian soldiers, comprising two infantry divisions, two cavalry divisions and four field artillery brigades, saw action on the Western Front. In the 14 months of war between September 1914 and December 1915, when the infantry divisions were dispatched to Mesopotamia, they had taken an active part in major battles of the Western Front: the First and Second Battles of Ypres, and the battles of Festubert, Neuve Chapelle and Loos. The two cavalry divisions remained on the Western Front for a further two and half years and, fighting as infantry, saw action, notably in the Somme offensive in 1916, and in the battles of Passchendaele and Cambrai in 1917. Casualties on the Western Front were heavy: 7,700 Indians died, 16,400 were wounded and 840 were reported missing or taken prisoner.[14]

In Britain, Gandhi urged Indian students and residents to 'think imperially' and volunteer their services 'unconditionally' to the empire, an offer accepted by the India Office. And the Indian Field Ambulance Training Corps was organized, its personnel recruited as doctors, nurse orderlies and as clerks and interpreters on hospital ships and in the hospitals for Indian wounded in England (see p. 180). Indian women knitted 'comforts' for soldiers. For their magnificent record of service, some students, especially those who worked as house physicians and house surgeons, notably R.N. Cooper, G.C. Chatterjee and Cawas Homi, received a special mention in the annual report of the High Commissioner for India.[15] But Indians could not obtain commissions in the armed forces, despite being 'natural born British subjects'. Why? Under Naoroji's persistent questioning, the War Office was forced to admit that 'the intention of the military authorities is to exclude all candidates ... who are not of pure European descent' as 'a British private soldier will never follow a half-caste or native officer'. Nonetheless, some Indian students in British public schools and universities somehow managed to join the armed forces, as the case of Naoroji's grandson, Kershap, illustrates. A student at Cambridge, he saw action in France in 1915 as a private in the Middlesex Regiment, and later as a lieutenant in the Hazara Pioneers in Iraq.[16] The descendants of some of the families mentioned in Chapter 3 also fought in the war: Frederick Duleep Singh saw active service on the Western Front as did the four grandsons of Mahomed Ebrahim Palowkar, Edward, Herbert, Harold and Victor; the latter, having been gassed, was invalided out of the army. Two great-grandsons of Sake Dean Mahomed are known to have fought in France. Lt Claude Atkinson Etty Mahomed, a civil engineer, serving with the Scots Guards, died in France in August 1917; another was killed in the Royal Flying Corps (RFC).[17]

Four Indian students also managed to get temporary commissions as pilots in the RFC. 2nd Lt H.S. Malik, the only one who survived, was a student at Balliol. Initially, in 1915, he joined the French Red Cross. He transferred to the RFC from the French Air Service, being accepted only after the recommendation of General Henderson, the then head of the RFC. Malik was part of the crew of the five RFC squadrons sent to Italy during the battle of Caporetto. A Sikh, he was said to fly wearing a turban, instead of the regulation leather and fur flying cap.[18] The most important Indian pilot in the RFC, however, is 2nd Lt Indra Lal Roy, DFC, a fighter Ace.

AN INDIAN ACE IN THE RFC

Indra Lal Roy, born in Calcutta in December 1898, came to Britain for his education at the age of 10. Having joined Colet Court Preparatory School for the first three years, in 1911, he went to St Paul's. A foundation scholar and said to speak only English, having 'forgotten' his Indian language, he was a good athlete, played rugby, was captain of the swimming team, a motor cyclist and passionately interested in flying. In early 1917, anxious to do 'his bit' in the war, he applied for a temporary commission in the RFC. How difficult it had been for Roy to obtain a commission is hard to judge. A letter addressed to General Sefton Brancker from a Charles Roberts suggests it had not been easy. The 'best way', apparently, for an Indian, was to enlist as an Air Mechanic and then, if he proved worthy, become a 'Flight Mechanic'. However, as in the case of 2nd Lt S.C. Welinkar from Jesus College Cambridge, it is likely that it was Brancker's personal recommendation that eventually secured Roy the commission.[19] He joined the RFC in July 1917 and on 30 October, was posted to 56 Squadron.

But Roy's flying career did not begin well: on 6 November he crashed his aircraft and was returned to England for additional training. After some further flying, he was pronounced to be unfit by medical authorities and recommended for service only as an Equipment Officer. Roy managed somehow to get the decision reversed and, on 19 June 1918, he returned to France to join George McElroy's flight in 40 Squadron. Roy distinguished himself as a fighter pilot. In only 170 hours and 15 minutes of flying time, between 6 and 19 July, he shot down 10 enemy aircraft, claiming 10 victories, 2 of which he shared with Captain McElroy. But, on 22 July 1918, he was killed in a fight with Fokker DVIIs of Jasta 29, his aircraft, SE 5A (B180), going down in flames. He was just 19 years old.[20] In the history of British aviation, Indra Lal Roy's record of 10 victories at the very outset of his flying career is a unique achievement. W.A. Bishop, the Canadian Ace of Aces, claimed more victories, but only after long practice, while Roy was a beginner when killed in July. He was awarded a DFC posthumously.

THE INDIAN ARMY IN ACTION

The Indian Army was recruited heavily from northern India, the Punjab and the North-West Frontier Province. In the perceived hierarchy of races, the British classed them the 'martial races'. As a result, considering themselves superior to the alleged 'non-martial races', these men saw the army their special preserve, enlisted with enthusiasm and were rewarded. The theory of the 'martial races' thus became an instrument for mobilising men and a basis for developing a sense of loyalty, having a stake in the Raj.[21] Believing that one reason for the 1857 Rising had been British disregard for India's 'caste prejudice', the Indian Army was organised into class regiments, each from a single ethnic or religious community, led by an officer of the same class. At the top, the Indian Army was officered entirely by Europeans. Often there developed an intense paternalistic relationship (*Mai-Baap*) between the men and their officers.

The Indian Army, trained to fight tribesmen in the North-West Frontier region, was efficient at guerrilla-style warfare. But in no sense was it a modern army. To prevent another 1857-style uprising, its artillery units had been disbanded, and it was kept 'one generation behind in weaponry'.[22] By 1914, its main weapon remained the rifle. This was the Indian Army pitted against the German forces, possibly one of the most formidable armies, equipped with modern weaponry. How did Indian soldiers react to trench warfare on the Western Front? And how did they come out of the experience?

Official reports and war diaries of white British officers provide some insight, but from a European angle. Indian voices are found in Mulk Raj Anand's fictional account, *Across the Black Waters,* written at the time of the Spanish Civil War, which provides a vivid testimony of trench warfare, and in Chandradhar Sharma Guleri's *Usne Kahā Thā*, written in Hindi and published during the war.[23] But the most significant immediate records are the extracts from Censored Mails, the translated letters written by Indian soldiers in their own languages from the battle front and from the hospitals in England. The war censor's office was set up at Boulogne after a member of the Indian Revolutionary Party was found with pockets 'stuffed' with, allegedly, 'seditious literature', distributing it amongst Indian troops.[24] These extracts provide a unique glimpse of how soldiers saw the war and their sojourn in Britain, as well as their reflections and concerns. The picture that emerges belies the usual image of the 'simple' soldier.[25] The authorities' nervousness concerning 'seditious' literature and censorship of letters, however, needs to be placed in the wider context of pre-1914 radical activities: memories of Dhingra's assassination of Wyllie and the activities of India House and Cama were fresh in many minds. The Ghadar Party in the USA was another factor. Its literature, smuggled into India and designed to stir up anti-British feelings, targeted particularly the Punjab, the recruiting ground of the army. Already some Sikhs had been favourably impressed with the gesture of some retired Sikh soldiers in America, who had destroyed their medals and discharge certificates. Sikh passions had been further inflamed by the *Komagata Maru* incident of March 1914. The majority of the 376 emigrants to Canada, barred from landing because of the Canadian government policy to restrict Indian immigration, and forced to return to India, had been Sikhs. Indian Muslim reaction to the Pan-Islamic Movement also created unease, particularly as Turkey had joined the war on Germany's side. The amount of 'seditious' literature, however, proved to be negligible and as Pradhan has shown, Sikhs and Muslims enlisted in the army despite the existence of anti-British feelings in days before the war or Pan-Islamism.[26]

Accustomed to frontier skirmishes, trench warfare, not surprisingly, came as a shock, as their letters reveal. Standing knee-deep in mud, soldiers endured endlessly exploding shells and deadly machine-gun fire, and even aerial bombardment. Casualties were high. They met with experiences deeply offensive to their religious practices. Many were outraged to see dead bodies left on the battlefield, 'as stones lie in our country', wrote one.[27] The horrors on the Western Front appalled them, as did the use of poison gas, bombs and other military hardware. Indians could not believe that 'civilised and cultured nations of Christian faith' used such 'devilish ... modern and scientific process' to destroy each other. Struggling to convey the extent of the carnage, they resorted to using terminology of ancient religious epic battles: one described it as 'Kerbela', another as 'Mahabharat' and yet another wrote, 'I've heard that the Pandevs and Kauris had a great war, but that battle could not have been so great as this one.' Others used language nearer to their own everyday experiences. A Punjabi Muslim compared it to a butcher slaughtering goats; a Sikh, as 'dying like maggots'. To another, the dead lay like 'chaff upon the threshing floor', while a Pathan Muslim, giving an account of a battle where many of his comrades died, simply wrote: 'I cannot give you an account of this hurricane.'[28] Many others vividly described trench warfare:

> When our army attacks 600 guns fire for 35 minutes on the enemy's trenches. The very earth shakes. Then our men advance. Just like a turnip is cut into pieces, so a man is blown to bits by the explosion of a shell ... Day and night there is a rain of shells ... In taking a hundred yards of trench, it is like the destruction of the world.[29]

Faced with such experiences, the morale of some crumbled. From December 1914, a sense of unease became noticeable, as the wounded began to be returned to the trenches. In January 1915 the Censor reported the tendency of men to 'break into poetry', an ominous sign, according to him, of 'mental disquietude'. Some Indian soldiers even deserted, but the number was said to be surprisingly low.[30] As the onslaught continued and casualties mounted, some despaired. This is shown from the space devoted by the Censor to monitoring Indian morale, which is not surprising, since one of his tasks was to take the 'temperature' of the Indian Army.[31] Low morale would explain the incidences of self-inflicted wounds among some Indians, which was claimed to be noticeably higher than among the white soldiers, especially among those who had seen the first wave of combat – a claim, however, according to a recent study, that has been exaggerated. Furthermore, doctors made mistakes in their diagnosis of such wounds, Indians being condemned unnecessarily, further adding to their low morale.[32] By May 1915, as stalemate on the Front continued and the fighting became even more vicious, with the use of deadly scientific weapons such as poison gas, despair among some Indian soldiers became, in the words of the Censor, 'rife', tempered only with a sense of 'resignation' or 'belief in a Higher Power'.[33]

J.N. Macleod, Commander, Pavilion Hospital, Brighton, in his report to Sir Walter Lawrence, blamed the cold and 'the damned trench work' for 'paralysing' the Indian soldiers. Officers close to Indians on the battlefield tended to agree. To keep up their spirits, and to hustle them back into the trenches to have another go at the enemies of their 'Sahibs', a bulletin containing news of their successes (e.g. Neuve Chapelle), and glowing accounts of their regiment and *bhais* (brothers) was proposed. The result was the *Akbari i Jang*.[34] Indians certainly missed the sun and found the wintry trenches a trial, seen from sentiments like 'may the dear God … release me from the climate of this country'.[35] But their letters provide other explanations for their low morale and sense of fatalism.

Distance was one reason. Separated by thousands of miles from home, they keenly felt their separation from their loved ones. The news of inflation and of rising food prices worried them. As war continued and the prospect of a return grew even more remote, they feared they might not live to see their children again, that it was their fate to be 'buried here'.[36] Such fatalism is vividly illustrated by one Garhwali's comment, that only women would be left in India as all the 'men will be finished here'. Another, referring to the 'increasing violence' of war, wrote: 'One cannot tell who in this war lives or survives, the whole of India has become empty.'[37] Heavy casualties added to the fear, leading some to see themselves as mere cannon fodder. One explained that when a brigade attacked it was the Gurkhas and Sikhs who went first while 'the white troops [were] put in a second line'. Another shared the sentiment, writing that 'black men' were put in front and the second line was of 'white soldiers of complete regiments'.[38] Fearing censorship, others conveyed their message in code: the 'brave English' used little of the 'red pepper' while the 'black pepper' was being utilised daily to the 'extent of … a thousand maunds', leaving no doubt as to their meaning. Some even explained the reason: that 'black pepper' was 'hard' and there was 'plenty of it'. But perhaps the most important reason, and which may have helped to confirm their suspicion that white troops were spared at their expense, was the fact that they were returned to the trenches time and again, as a petition to the King in May 1915, from the hospital at Milford-on-Sea shows:

> Your Majesty's order was that a man who had been wounded once should be allowed to return to India or that if he had recovered should not be made to serve again ... the heart of India is broken because they inflict suffering on the sick ... The Indians have given their lives for 11 rupees [the Indian soldier's pay]. Any man who comes here wounded is returned three or four times to the trenches. Only that man goes to India who has lost an arm or leg or an eye.[39]

Mir Dast, who won a VC for his bravery in a gas attack, presented a petition to the King, making a similar request on behalf of Indian soldiers. Omissi has suggested that sending the wounded back into battle was 'without precedent in the recent past' of the Indian Army.[40] This would explain the Censor's recommendation that, as an 'act of perhaps tardy justice', Indian wounded should not be returned to the Front. But the Front needed more and more men. How keenly Indians felt their long separation from home is illustrated in a letter from Wazir Chand, a clerk in Rouen, who, in December 1915, informed his correspondent that the Viceroy had been petitioned that all Indians should be sent back as they had been separated from their families for so long.[41]

Unable to return to India unless crippled, men felt desperate as sentiments like 'we are trapped like animals' or 'tied up in the Sirkar's string' show. Some considered that even bravery was of no use.[42] Such desperation led some to circumvent the system: some feigned illness, others sent for herbs and medicines from India, which would produce sores and induce sickness.[43] And others still begged their families and friends not to enlist, entreating them in coded language, not to send any 'more rupees' to Europe. Such desperate sentiments would suggest that soldiers saw their loyalty as conditional. These attempts at subversion did not go undetected, the Censor interpreting them as an illustration of their 'low order' of patriotism and as sacrifice not being 'good enough for them'.[44]

However, literature of the First World War shows that Indians were not alone in reacting in this manner. Trench warfare took its toll on all, black and white, prompting different strategies for survival. Indian soldiers themselves mention seeing whites refusing to enlist or mutinying. A letter from Brighton hospital, withheld by the censor, described how an Indian tried to 'preach' to some whites, asking whether they felt no 'shame' that Indians had come to the aid of Britain, while they, men 'of the same race' refused to fight. Indians considered such behaviour as a 'scandal'.[45]

But, to concentrate only on evidence of despair and attempts at subversion as a survival strategy, is to distort the picture as it emerges from these letters. Such sentiments were counterbalanced by many genuine expressions of loyalty and prayers for Britain's victory.[46] There is no evidence that Indians wanted Britain to lose the war. As citizens of the empire, their honour was bound up with Britain's victory, a sentiment summed up by one: 'pray that victory may be given to our King so that we may return in safety and with honour to our dear country'. Another, wounded in a charge, wanted to rush back to the trenches 'to kill more bastered [sic] Germans', because they were not men, they used poisoned gas. Sikhs wrote that they were keen to fight the enemy and 'took pleasure in the battle'.[47] A strong sense of moral behaviour emerges from expressions like having 'eaten' the 'government's salt', it was their duty to 'repay' him with loyalty. Desertion was deplored as a 'disgrace to the regiment'.[48] Pride and honour and renown for family, village and country were also strong factors in their conduct, seen from a letter which exhorted a soldier to fight well and bravely so that 'India may not be disgraced'. Another was reminded that he must always bear in mind his own honour and the honour of his family, as there was 'nothing in life better than honour'. Military tradition, too, played a part. A Sikh wrote: 'Fighting and war are the Sikh's pap. Such hardships come upon brave men ... to die in battle is a noble fate.'[49] In time, Indians got used to trench conditions and mechanised warfare as this remark illustrates: 'No one considers rifles now-a-days [and] ... after two years' experience we have grown used to these troubles and think lightly of them.'[50] Further evidence of their loyalty to King and country is seen from the fact that in India recruitment was not seriously affected and, in the later stages of the war, even extended to 'non-martial races' to satisfy the army's growing need for more men. The Indian Army had increased five-fold by the end of the war.[51] Tributes paid to their performance on the Western Front, long after the war, are a further confirmation of their endurance. For instance, Lord Birkenhead, unveiling a memorial to the Indians at Neuve Chapelle in 1927, compared them to the Roman legionary, who had remained 'faithful unto death'. In Britain, unveiling a memorial in Brighton in 1921, the Prince of Wales reminded his audience that 'future generations should not forget, that our Indian comrades came when our need was highest', and that they gave their lives in a quarrel in which it was enough for them 'to know that the enemy were the foes of their sahibs'.[52]

Indian soldiers came out of their experiences with a heightened sense of their own soldierly qualities. The number of VCs they won on the Western Front alone, six in all, is one indication, especially as it was only in 1911 that Indians became eligible for this highest military honour. To be presented their awards by the King in Brighton would have added to their sense of self-esteem. Mir Dast, for instance, recounted the King's 'great pleasure' at the 'valour of the Indian Army', while another soldier, commenting on a VC awarded to a Garhwali, wrote with pride: 'the fame of the Garhwalis is now higher than the skies ... a havildar has won the honour of the Victoria Cross'. Such public ceremonies and pronouncements further emphasised their sense of worth. Some noticed how the British were 'extra polite' to them. A Sikh soldier recounted how, when the Sikh unit refused to wear the new steel helmet, seen as an insult to their religion, the British withdrew the order as a concession to them.[53] Their victories brought them renown. A Sikh, describing how, despite heavy losses, they fought on bravely, inflicting equally heavy losses on the Germans, capturing their trench, wrote: 'Our regiment is the first among all our regiments ... not only have we not tarnished our name but we have added lustre to it.' Publicity given to their regimental valour also helped their sense of esteem, seen by the comment, 'and its bravery has been published'.[54] Pride of regiment reflected pride in the entire Indian Army as a letter sent to a military newspaper shows, 'our Hindustani troops pursued the enemy with such spirit for three miles that the French begin to vaunt the name of the Indian Army'. The step from pride in the regiment to pride in the whole army and to race and country, too, might not be too difficult. Describing how Indian troops were accounted to be the bravest, another soldier wrote that he was fortunate to be engaged in this war, as there would never be another chance 'to exalt the name of race, country, ancestor, parents, village, brothers, and to prove our loyalty to the Government'.[55] To be fighting in a white man's war and have an opportunity of proving that they were equal to the whites, thus removing the stigma of racial inferiority and a blot on their manhood, was a matter of pride. A Muslim soldier described it thus: 'This is a fight of heroes ... On both sides are white troops. It is a place of courage. Men will remember this war all their lives, and say that so and so died in the German War.' Their experiences led one to conclude: 'what are the Germans in the face of Indian troops? They do nothing but run away in front of us ... Judged impartially, the Germans are not equals of the Indian troops.'[56] A couplet written by a Sikh is revealing indeed: 'A bomb from Bengal! A gun made in France! A Khalsa from India, Make Germany dance!' The Censor's comment that England's omission was 'interesting', and his dismissal of the verse as being 'typical of the Sikh in every way', suggests that such sentiments worried the authorities. Indian civilians took pride in the achievement of their soldiers, and felt that they, too, could hold their heads high as equal members of the empire.[57]

How did European soldiers react to them? The performance of Indian soldiers on the battlefield impressed many. The Germans, for instance, who had jeered at them in China in 1900 as an army of 'coolies', now looked at them with respect as they discovered fighting them was 'bitter hard work'. These 'brown rascals are not to be under-rated', commented one German.[58] H.V. Lewis, attached to the 129th Baluchis, wrote with relief that the 'men are very cool under fire, don't seem to mind a bit'. Another British officer was a little more cautious: though the Indian Corps 'put up quite a good show at first ... they could not stick it for long' was his verdict. Such an ambivalent view is confirmed by a second-in-command of the Garhwali regiment. According to him, although Indian soldiers had not been found 'wanting', the sensational press reports had raised impossible expecta-tions about 'the marvels of night scouting, surprise attacks and kukri work' done by the Indians. In his opinion officers might regard their Indian soldiers highly, but 'never for one instant imagine them equals of the British soldier'. A slightly different estimation came from an English soldier. Referring to the Gurkhas and Garhwalis, he commented that 'they are the chaps as long as a white soldier is going to be there, they fight like tigers'.[59] And this feeling that Indians were helpless without their British officers to lead them was repeated by the Censor as well as in dispatches from officers of the Indian Army as Lt R.L. Benson's letter to Hardinge illustrates. Commenting on the fact that Indians were 'of course splendid fighters', he went on, 'but [they] are very lost without their officers ... they were splendid in the trenches as long as their officers were there but afterwards did not know what to do', a sentiment reminiscent of the view held of lascars on merchant ships by their officers. The debates over granting the King's Commission to Indians in 1917 highlighted similarly divided views among officers and policy-makers.[60]

INDIAN WOUNDED IN ENGLAND

The intended plans for removing the Indian wounded to southern France and from thence to Egypt and India having fallen through, because, in the words of Lord Crewe, of the 'unwillingness or inability' of France to accommodate them, they were brought to England.[61] Here, on the southern coast of England, several buildings had to be hurriedly converted as military hospitals for the Indian wounded. In Brighton, for instance, the Royal Pavilion became the Pavilion and Dome Hospital, the Workhouse became the Kitchener Indian Hospital, and the York Place school was turned into the York Place Hospital. The New Forest had two, the Lady Hardinge and the Forest Park Hotel, both at Brockenhurst. There were also the Royal Victoria Hospital at Netley, Mount Dore Hotel in Bournemouth, Hotel Victoria at Milford-on-Sea and a convalescent camp at Barton-on-Sea, New Milton.[62] Unlike the very basic regimental hospitals for Indian soldiers in India, these hospitals were of a high standard with up-to-date medical facilities, and some, like the Kitchener, were equipped with the most modern scientific appliances.

To treat the wounded and the sick, white British medical staff having experience of India were recruited from the IMS, some from the ranks of the retired. Indians studying medicine in England were given temporary commissions in the IMS and brought to assist in the hospitals, and the Indian Field Ambulance Training Corps provided dressers and interpreters.[63] Other recruits from India included sub-assistant surgeons, ward orderlies, writers, clerks, store-keepers, cooks, tailors, barbers, washermen and even sweepers, creating miniature Indian towns in the English countryside. At the Royal Victoria Hospital, Netley, some of the cooks and ward servants and sweepers were lascars from the Asiatic Home in Limehouse, London.[64]

Indian Hospitals were organised on the same 'class' lines as the Indian Army and a special 'caste committee' was set up to supervise arrangements. In the Royal Pavilion and Dome Hospital, for instance, patients in the wards were grouped according to their religion or ethnic group and provision was made for the observance of their religious and social practices. Nine separate kitchens catered for their different dietary requirements and special effort was made to obtain ingredients like dal, ghee and spices. Even a special slaughter-house for the ritual killing of animals was organised. There were multi-lingual signs in Hindi, Urdu and Gurmukhi. Tents were erected in the grounds of the Pavilion to facilitate religious worship. Recreational rooms with a variety of games and entertainments, too, separated soldiers on ethnic lines. Special suites, reflecting the hierarchical structure of the army, were set apart for the Indian NCOs, and a signed photograph of the King decorated their sitting-rooms.[65]

Such arrangements would have required massive organisation and resources. How might this be accounted for? As noted earlier, the loyalty of the Indian troops was perceived to depend on the non-interference with their cultural practices. But an added factor, as a note by E.B. Howell the Censor reveals, was political: to frustrate the 'noisier classes' (educated elite) from influencing the peasantry and 'political agitators' fuelling anti-British sentiment, while at the same time using every opportunity to gain 'a far reaching political effect' in India.[66] The fact that some MPs considered that imperial considerations allowed Indians to be treated better than British soldiers, confirms the influence of political considerations.[67] Hardinge, the Viceroy, however, defended the treatment of wounded Indian soldiers on a scale far above the customary Indian Army practice, on grounds of 'gratitude and justice'.[68]

Other special arrangements, too, indicate political motivation. One of these was the provision of burial according to religious rites. To combat rumours, suspected of having been started by the Germans, that the Muslims were not given burial according to Muslim law, in a public relations exercise, a special cemetery on Horsell Common, near the Woking Mosque, was established. For the Hindus, crematoria were set up at Patcham, Netley and Brockenhurst.[69] Stephen White has argued that the arrangements for the burning Ghat at Patcham, five miles out of Brighton, in no way complied with the usual understanding of the Cremation Act of 1902. As internal minutes show, the Home Office was aware that the anticipated cremations were 'quite outside the restrictions of the Cremation Act and the regulations under it'. Nonetheless, hospital officers were asked simply to record cremations and the cause of death in a register.[70] Such an action by the Home Office is highly significant.

On leaving the Pavilion and Dome Hospital, each soldier received a souvenir copy of *A Short History in English, Gurmukhi, and Urdu of the Royal Pavilion, Brighton and a Description of it as a Hospital for Indian Soldiers*, illustrated with 'additional' photographs specially included to 'enhance [its] value in India'. A study of the *Short History,* the photographs, together with reports by the Censor, and the official correspondence, is revealing. The booklet, designed to show the King's caring concern, provides the impression that the initiative for converting the Pavilion into a 'great hospital' for the 'loyal sons of India of every caste and creed' came from the King himself.[71] The fact that, since 1837, the Pavilion had ceased to be a Royal residence, is glossed over, as was the role of the Mayor and Corporation of Brighton and Lord Kitchener. In defending his version of the account to Sir Walter Lawrence, Macleod explained that since he wrote the pamphlet 'solely for its effect *in India*', to have mentioned the prominent role of the Corporation or Lord Kitchener would have been confusing. And, more importantly:

It would also spoil the parallel I drew between King Edward's action at Osborne and that of the present King at the Pavilion. The fact of one Palace being for British *officers* while the other is for Indian *sepoys* seemed a useful point ... To give more details ... would minimise the political impression we want to make in India.[72]

Indian soldiers were certainly dazzled by the magnificence of the Pavilion. One wounded Sikh, referring to the famous Persian couplet on the wall of the Diwani Khas in Delhi – 'If there be paradise on earth, it is this, it is this' – even applied it to the Pavilion.[73] There is no doubt, too, that the government's *bandobast* (arrangement) produced the desired effect. One Muslim, commenting on the 'perfect' arrangements for kitchens and cooking, wrote that there was no fear as even the meat was 'halaled', while a Sikh expressed his happiness at the 'Sikh church' in each hospital, where the services were 'held just as in India'. One soldier even suggested that the care given them in the hospitals was such 'as no-one can get in his own home, not even a noble'. The burial arrangements, too, came in for praise: a letter describing the 'fine coffin' provided for a syce and the 'great honour and dignity' with which he was buried, remarked that 'in our country, doubtless, only the greatest in the land are furnished with coffins of this sort'. All favourable reports from the Indian wounded were widely circulated in India – to achieve 'good will' and loyalty.[74]

The Censor, too, monitored such sentiments, drawing attention to them in his reports. Any criticisms or adverse comments, and there were some of these too, received special attention and action. For instance, when in a letter from France, a Sikh soldier complained that he was forced to relax his religious duties since there was 'plenty of everything except *kachhehra* (drawers worn by Sikh men), *kanga* (comb) and *kirpans* (knife)', the Censor suggested that money from the Indian Soldiers' Fund might be better used purchasing items of religious significance, which would give 'more pleasure', rather than on 'personal comforts and indulgences', like sweetmeats and tobacco.[75] In a similar vein, the 'political importance' of permitting Muslim soldiers in England to observe the fast during Ramadhan was seen as overriding the 'military disadvantage' of postponing their return to the trenches.[76] Zealous attempts by Christian bodies at proselytising were judged 'ill-timed' and discouraged. Even the supply of free envelopes, bearing the inscription 'The Young Men's Christian Association of India', were considered by the Censor as likely to produce 'lamentable' results in India. He, therefore, requested that the Military Secretary at the India Office put a stop to it. Howell's real anxiety about the YMCA envelopes is revealed in a letter of a later date.

Describing how they spent hours cutting off such headings, he wrote: 'an agitator could make quite a capital out of it'. Similarly, letters from English soldiers containing racist references like calling Indians 'niggers' were also censored.[77]

Then there were the specially organised tours. Starting in December 1914, the India Office arranged for small parties of 24 at a time, either all Muslims or all Hindus, to be taken to London to see the sights: St Paul's Cathedral, the Tower of London, the Houses of Parliament, Buckingham Palace, Queen Victoria's Statue, the Natural History Museum, Hyde Park, the Albert Museum and the Zoo. An hour's shopping at Selfridges and a ride on London's underground train were also included. Such an itinerary could be on any tourist list. It might be argued that there was a genuine desire on the part of the India Office, expenses notwithstanding, to give some of the wounded a day out, away from Brighton.[78] The India Office might also have considered that the soldiers were missing out on an experience if, having been in England, they had then not seen the metropolitan capital, especially as some had shown a desire to do so. It could also be argued that this was their reward for their service to the King-Emperor and country. However, it is the outcome of the tours that is pertinent to the discussion. Commenting on the 'excellent effect' these 'joy rides' were having on the minds of Indian soldiers, R.C.F. Volkers wrote how, in 'sympathetic hands', these men 'expand wonderfully', so that while giving them a pleasant day out, it was possible to 'direct their attention and with it their minds' in such a way that 'they obtain an impression of England's greatness, wealth and power', which would not only remain with them, but 'through them react on other Indians of their class'. Major P.G. Shewell, too, supported them as having a 'good effect ... politically in India'.[79] In other words, the tours were worthwhile for generating loyalty and impressing Indians with the power and might of Britain. A letter from Lord Ampthill, in charge of the Indian Labour Corps, confirms this. Endorsing Charles Lyall's suggestion that some rank and file of the Labour Corps should be brought over from France to see England, he wrote: 'we must look ahead and take into account the future interest of the empire even in the midst of this war'. In his view, if these 'simple, strong-hearted men from the hills and jungles and plains' of India were given a 'joy ride' in England, it would have a 'far-reaching effect' and may very likely be of 'great advantage' to the British Raj in some 'serious emergency'.[80]

When the last hospital had closed in January 1916, Sir Walter Lawrence, looking back over the working of the hospitals and the policy decisions, wrote: 'In one instance only has opportunity been given to the agitator.' Such a statement shows that the authorities judged their objectives and propaganda to have succeeded. The 'one instance' referred to the Imam of the Mosque at Woking in connection with Muslim soldiers' burial arrangements.[81]

THE WOMAN QUESTION

But there was another, harsher side, to Indian hospitals in England. The very same 'loyal sons of India' were also branded a 'problem', especially in regard to what might be termed the 'woman question'. As far back as 1901 during the Coronation of Edward VII, Lord Curzon, in response to a request for 'Indian orderlies', had spelled out the 'difficulty', as he saw it, when he wrote: 'strange as it may seem, Englishwomen of the housemaid class, and even higher, do offer themselves to these Indian soldiers, attracted by their uniform, enamoured by their physique, and with a sort of idea that the warrior is also an Oriental prince'.[82] As already noted, similar sexual anxieties had been voiced over students and lascars. Indian Royalty, too, was similarly condemned as the case of the Rajah of Puddukotta shows: in Curzon's opinion, the only thing against Puddukotta, was 'that he wants to marry a white woman'.[83] During the Coronation in 1911, when Indian troops had been brought to Britain, 'scandals' were said to have occurred because of the 'perverted behaviour' of English women. Within the imperial context, the mystique of English womanhood and the prestige of the empire were interlinked. As the Censor explained: if a 'wrong idea' of the *'izzat'* of an English woman was conceived by the Indian male, then it would be 'most detrimental to the prestige and spirit of European rule in India'.[84]

Such obsession, combined with unprecedented numbers of Indian wounded and personnel (it is difficult to give precise numbers for obvious reasons) led to various measures of control to prevent 'scandals' from occurring.[85] In late October 1914, Sir James Willcocks, Commander of the Indian Army in France, telegraphed the India Office that he 'strongly deprecated' the employment of women nurses in 'any capacity' in Indian hospitals. Lord Crewe was of the same opinion. Accordingly, on 4 November 1914, the Army Council issued the directive that no English women were to be employed as nurses with Indian troops in the 'home' military hospitals.[86] But there was one exception. At the Lady Hardinge, English women nurses came to be allowed, but on the strict understanding that they would not be employed in 'menial' or 'nursing' duties, but would work strictly in a supervisory capacity only. Why the exception? Sir Charles Havelock, in his representation to the India Office, strongly recommended that in St John's Hospital female nurses could be employed 'without scandal' and with 'great advantage to efficiency'. According to him, Voluntary Aided Hospitals 'must' have 'one or two' women nurses per ward. (A marginal note corrected this to 'one woman for two wards'.)[87] The fact that the ground on which the Hospital was built was private property and given to the Indian Soldiers' Fund (ISF) would account for the exception, and women nurses, chosen by the St John's Ambulance Association for their knowledge of Indian languages, performed supervisory duties at Lady Hardinge, overseeing cleanliness of the wards, distribution of linen and medicines, supervising food and assisting in training ward orderlies, duties largely similar to those performed by women nurses in Civil Hospitals in India for the relatives of all fighting forces.[88]

However, it is evident that the original regulation of 4 November 1914 had not been acted on. English women nurses from the Queen Alexandra Imperial Military Nursing Service Reserve were also employed as supervisors at the Pavilion and York, and at Royal Victoria, Netley, but not at the Kitchener Indian Hospital. Indeed, at Netley, it had not even been found practical to limit the work of women nurses to mere supervision, as on occasions, in the 'absence of skilled male subordinates', nurses assisted medical officers in dressing wounds in serious cases of fractures.[89]

Eight months later, however, in June 1915, the Army Council issued an order to withdraw all nurses from the Pavilion, York and Lady Hardinge Hospitals. The Royal Victoria Hospital, Netley, was not mentioned, possibly because the nurses had already been withdrawn. What is significant, however, is why the order was issued. Brighton-based writer Joyce Collins states that 'no reason' was given.[90] However, although not stated in the Army Council's directive, the reason is given, though whether it can be classified as 'a scandal' is questionable. The reason is contained in the Proceedings of the Committee of the ISF, as well as in a letter from the eminent Bombay Parsi, Sir Shapurji Broacha, deploring what he described as official 'red-tapism' – although the facts concerning the place of the incident in his letter are a little muddled.[91] The offending reason was a photograph published by the *Daily Mail* on 24 May 1915, showing an English nurse standing 'behind a wounded sepoy'. This had resulted in a complaint from the 'Field Marshal C in C abroad'. The picture and the publication were then referred to 'an adviser' to the War Office on Indian Hospitals. Describing the employment of women nurses with Indian troops as a 'scandal' and not an 'Indian custom', he condemned the practice 'absolutely and totally'.

The Indian soldier in the photograph (Khodadad Khan) was certainly a VC, as stated by Broacha. But the 'incident' had not taken place at Lady Hardinge Hospital, but possibly at Brighton.[92] What is of significance, however, is the view taken of an innocent picture and the resultant action, the order to withdraw all white nurses. But the ISF Committee was adamant over its 20 nurses. Faced with a possibility of 'much trouble, irritation and scandal' were the ISF to take legal recourse (because of the status of the land on which the hospital stood), a compromise was made. Lady Hardinge kept the nurses in a supervisory capacity as before.[93] Elsewhere women nurses were withdrawn – for the protection of women and empire.

A compromise was also achieved on the question of allowing women visitors in Indian hospitals. Administrative and medical officers of the hospitals for the Indian wounded saw no objection for women, 'properly vouched' for, from visiting Indian patients since, in their opinion, Indian soldiers appreciated the interest taken in them. Such visits also relieved monotony. Sir Walter Lawrence, too, considered that women with a knowledge of India, or a direct interest in military regiments, might be permitted.[94] But others, like General Sir Edmund Barrow, the Military Secretary at the India Office, and Sir Alfred Keogh, head of the Medical Department at the War Office, in particular, were opposed. According to them it was unheard of for 'a lady' in India to visit a 'sepoy' hospital and the men themselves would 'not understand' it. Further, it was not desirable in the interest of 'discipline'.[95] But since well-meaning English women frequently visited English soldiers in hospitals, to exclude them from Indian hospitals, it was feared, would smack of a 'differential treatment' and as such Indians might feel resentful that, despite having shared the same dangers and hardships as white British soldiers, they were still looked upon as 'suspect' and 'even dangerous'. In the end precedent and policy were set aside in the interest of politics and diplomacy. English women 'properly vouched for' were allowed to visit the Indian wounded, as were Indian women resident in London.[96]

However, there was a limit even to diplomacy or expediency where women and empire were at stake: a colonised male needed to be controlled to prevent contact. Therefore, 'close surveillance' to keep a 'tight hand' was instituted by the Censor.[97] This is evident not only in the way the Censor watched out for letters from white women, or sexual allusions in Indian mail, but also in the way he deleted offending statements or withheld letters considered liable to give 'wrong' impression detrimental to the mystique of the Raj. Referring to one such letter, he wrote:

No 81 is indicative of the crude ideas of Orientals about European women; they cannot understand the freedom with which the sexes mingle. Hence when they are allowed unlimited freedom from the hospital etc. to go where they please, they are liable to gain many wrong ideas and impressions which might be difficult afterwards to eliminate.

There were even instances of writers of such letters being admonished. Further, a marginal note, 'I hope only children', appended to a letter which mentioned children and women getting hold of men's hands and wanting to kiss them, sheds another interesting light.[98]

Censorship apart, other harsher measures to prevent contact with women of the town were also put in place. Lord Crewe's comment to Lord Hardinge, that 'Arry' having enlisted left 'Arriet' 'more at a loose end and ready to take on the Indian warrior', is revealing.[99] Newspapers and contemporary accounts show that every possible entrance to the Pavilion ground was guarded by the police, and sometimes by the military, while carpenters boarded up all the 'possible crevices' where the curious might peer in. But the determined curious could not be deterred: it was considered 'worth a penny' taking a ride on the trams along the Steyne just to get 'a glimpse of the Indians' in the Pavilion grounds.[100] But the sepoy could not be confined all the time. In the interest of health he needed exercise. For this, there were route marches round Brighton, but accompanied by Colonel Coats, late Commandant of the 25th Punjab Infantry. In charge of British NCOs, small parties of sepoys, usually five, were taken for short walks along the sea front, while the severely disabled had car trips. There were also organised visits, to the theatre and the cinema and, as already shown, trips to London.[101] The wounded sepoy could be kept in the Pavilion grounds, or the recreational rooms, or shepherded round the town. But what about the hospital personnel? According to Sir Walter Lawrence's letter to a very nervous Viceroy Hardinge, Brighton had a 'very efficient plain clothes police system', and a track was kept of them.[102]

Fences were not only erected at the Brighton Pavilion and Dome Hospital. At Barton-on-Sea, despite the fact that the hospital, comprising two hotels and hutted accommodation was on sea cliffs and there were few houses, still it was surrounded by a wire enclosure. As for the men, they were allowed 'a certain amount' of liberty, but only 'under special precautions', and presumably because there were very few houses in the immediate vicinity.[103] But the strictest regime was at the Kitchener Indian Hospital, commanded by Col. Sir Bruce Seton. Ironically, it was at the Kitchener that no

English nurses had been employed from its very inception as an Indian hospital, because, in the words of Bruce Seton, 'women as nurses are out of place in an Indian unit'.[104]

So concerned was Seton to guard English womanhood's *'izzat'* that not a single woman in 'any capacity' was found on the premises and even the doctors' wives did not set foot inside the building.[105] Further, a military-style regime was enforced. Soon after his first visit to the Hospital, Seton predicted that 'drink and sex' would be the two 'problems', he would have to deal with. Why? Because, in his opinion, a large proportion of the followers, described as 'the sweepings of Bombay city' and 'a mob of bazaar coolies' were – allegedly – found to be 'habitual drunkards'. Then there were the women of Brighton whose 'ill-advised conduct', though 'partly innocent in intention', was 'bound' to result in 'the gravest scandals'. Determined to prevent these grave scandals, he imposed restrictions, in increasing degree of severity, and finally, in February 1915, drew up new and 'inflexible rules'. Under these, all Indian personnel were confined 'at all times' to the hospital area, the only exception being convalescent Indian officers and the sub-assistant surgeons, who could go out without a pass till dusk, and with a pass up to 'named hours' – 8.30 p.m., according to one source. As for the other Indian personnel, selected individuals in groups of three were occasionally permitted to go out for a walk, but always in charge of a private of the RAMC (Royal Army Medical Corps). It was reckoned by one Indian sub-assistant surgeon that such a strict regime confined men for anything up to two and a half months at a time before they got a chance for an hour's walk. Seton also began a regime of drill for all the personnel. For the convalescent patients there were the daily route marches in a party of 100, accompanied by members of the hospital. Further, a party of 24, either patients or personnel, in charge of a sub-assistant surgeon, were daily sent out for an hour's drive in a motor ambulance.[106] Finally, walls were supplemented by barbed wire palings to ensure that the staff of nearly 600 stayed in, and, from April 1915, a Military Police Guard was also organised to do sentry duty, as a 'further precaution against breaking out'. Punishments for any 'breaking out' were severe: some Parsis, who stayed out for two nights without permission, were confined to cells and asked to do fatigue duty, which they refused. They were then sent back to India.[107] The press reported only two cases of misdemeanour. One, in July 1915, was for liquor smuggling by Sandhu. It being his first offence, he was treated leniently. The other, in June 1915, was that of an alleged assault on a girl of 15 by Sohan Lal, a sub-assistant surgeon.[108]

For the authorities the desired objective had been achieved.

Reviewing the working of the Indian Hospitals, an element of self-congratulation is discernible. For instance, in his report on Barton-on-Sea, Lt Col. J. Chaytor White, commenting on 'the extremely good behaviour of the men', wrote: 'the attitude of the men, especially towards women, has been most correct'. The Chief Constable of Brighton considered the conduct of Indian sepoys could not have been 'better': they had behaved 'like gentlemen'.[109] If there was any unease over the tight restrictions, it was excused as being necessary, or as emanating from troublesome Parsees or 'English-speaking store-keepers and writers'.[110] However, not all opinion was so sanguine. Lt Charles Stiebel, IMS, laboured to get the 'irksome restrictions' at the Kitchener relaxed and it was largely on his insistence that the staff were allowed out onto the Downs. Another Englishman, condemning the precautions taken to isolate Indians from the 'indiscreet attentions of silly and ignorant women', wrote: 'It must not be forgotten that soldiers of a victorious army have seldom been chaperoned by sentries set over them.' And even the Censor was moved to write that though a 'certain amount' of restriction was necessary, for the men to feel that they were kept 'like prisoners' was 'dangerous', and urged that steps be taken to allay feelings of resentment.[111]

As the Censor's comment indicates, Indians were deeply critical of their loss of liberty, at the lack of trust, and of being punished if seen talking to any woman, young or old. Their letters – from soldiers, but particularly from the civilians – show a great deal of feeling at such stringent restrictions. Letters tell over and over again of their 'harsh treatment', at being treated 'like prisoners', of not being trusted to go out without an escort, being denied 'liberty', of being 'oppressed' and being 'powerless' to deal with it.[112] A letter from a store-keeper in Barton, describing the barbed wire, sentries on guard, and his own 'monotonous' life of a 'prisoner', reveals the extent of their feeling of alienation:

> If you ask me the truth, I can say that I have never experienced such hardship in all my life. True, we are well fed, and are given plenty of clothing; but the essential thing – freedom – is denied. Convicts in India are sent to Andaman Islands; but we have found our convict station here in England.[113]

At the Kitchener, anger at their treatment led to a complaint from the Indian inmates, but without result as the 'higher officers' were satisfied that the hospital had everything men could possibly desire: hockey, football, phonographs, games and free cinema. But, as Godbole, a sub-assistant surgeon pointed out: 'Has not God given the individual a right to go about and talk to others as he likes?' In the end, unable to bear any longer, what he described as the authorities' 'ungratefulness', and the conditions in the hospital, he attempted, as a protest, to shoot Col. Bruce Seton. He was caught, court-martialled and sentenced to seven years' imprisonment.[114]

How did the ordinary people of Britain react to Indian soldiers – this, for the majority, their first encounter with their fellow citizens? The people of Brighton quickly got used to their railway station being turned into 'an Oriental bazaar' as trainloads of wounded arrived from the Western Front. And just as the French at Marseilles had hailed Indians as liberators, Brightonians looked on the trainloads of Indians as warriors who had come in the defence of the empire, and to help fight their battles for them. They enthusiastically cheered and welcomed every train that brought the wounded. There is no doubting Brightonians' interest in the Indian soldiers, as a comment in the *Evening Herald,* at their departure, shows. Expressing a sense of regret, the paper wrote: 'one saw the last of the visitors who have brought so much unaccustomed interest and picturesqueness into our streets'.[115]

In their own letters Indian soldiers and civilians confirm their enthusiastic reception. For instance, a Parsi doctor wrote that people in Brighton were so friendly that 'everyone' wanted to speak with them, while another described how on their ship's arrival in England, people rushed to the steamer and mingled with them, and later when they went for walks, people rushed out of their houses 'to "salaam" ' to them.[116] Seeing such a welcome, one writer was even prompted to express the opinion that the 'English at home' were 'very good people', but it was 'the ruling class' that thought so highly of itself and stood in the way of 'any Indian reforms', a sentiment echoed by many other Indians, as has already been seen.[117]

But it was France and the French that captured the imagination of many Indian soldiers. One wrote that there is 'no country like the country of France', another told his countrymen that whoever had seen France had 'no need' to see England.[118] Such views are not surprising. In France Indian soldiers were billeted in French homes and got to know the people well; some even learnt to speak French.[119] No petty restrictions were imposed on their freedom of movement. The French regarded them highly: 'when once a Hindustani regiment rests in a village the people sing their praises', wrote one Muslim enthusiastically. They not only felt welcomed, but were treated with friendship, kindness and respect, 'just as their own people', 'as if we were their private guests'.[120] No wonder an English soldier was surprised that Indian soldiers were 'more chummy' with Frenchmen than they were with the

'Britisher'.[121] A few, especially the civilians, even formed lasting attachments with French women, and returned to India with French wives. The extent of mutual respect, admiration and feelings of gratitude can be demonstrated by just one letter from India. Thanking her son's 'French mother' for all the 'motherly affection' shown her son, the writer invited her to visit India, all expenses paid, so that they could 'pay our respects to such a God-fearing person as you are'. Is it any wonder than that Indian soldiers could write: 'after we are gone we shall mostly remember France very kindly'.[122]

AGENT OF CHANGE?

Writing in 1917, Madan Mohan Malaviya, an Indian political leader, suggested that war had changed the 'angle of vision' in India, as in England. It has 'put the clock of time fifty years forward'. For the majority of the Indians fighting on the Western Front this was their first experience of Europe. How did they react to European society? Were they changed by what they saw?

From a military point of view, Indians came out of the experience of war with a heightened sense of their own self-esteem, seeing themselves equal to any European soldier. The war shattered other accepted illusions. They saw that white men, Christians, were capable of brutal savagery, which they had been led to believe could only be committed by the allegedly inferior races. The stalemate on the Western Front shifted the European balance of power in their eyes. Though critical of Germany's use of poison gas, nonetheless they were impressed by her military and technological superiority in relation to Britain and her allies.[123] One writer, commenting on the power of the Germans, informed his reader that the English were 'much terrified', that all their munitions were 'spent' and they were beginning 'to quarrel amongst themselves', while another concluded, 'this is not such a king that can be defeated quickly'. The fact that the Censor not only drew attention to such sentiments, but was moved to write that 'the sooner the war is finished the greater will be the prestige of England', stresses this new assessment of Britain in Indian eyes, an assessment that was not welcomed.[124]

The standard of living and the way of life in Europe came in for much comment and led some to question Indian values. The independence of French women and how they coped in the absence of their men folk was greatly admired.[125] Absence of early marriage also drew comment and approval.[126] But it was education that found the most thoughtful mention in letters home and prompted reflection. Noting that education was compulsory in England and France, they wrote that both boys and girls went to school from an early age and could read and write. Expressing shame, one wrote: 'All the inmates of the house are educated and when they see our men going about with a letter in his hand [to be read] they are very surprised.' He urged, 'you must certainly send —— to school'. He was not alone. Others specifically mentioned wanting a daughter to be educated.[127] They were not slow to draw the connection between education and the standard of living in Europe. As the Censor commented: 'the cause of education has received a huge impetus'.[128]

Indian poverty in contrast with conditions in England and France depressed many. A sub-assistant surgeon remarked sadly that Indians only copied the faults of the British: 'merely by wearing trousers and hats and smoking ... and drinking wine', was no way to advance, he wrote.[129] A Maratha Brahmin, urging his fellow countrymen to work hard, concluded that looking to the 'deeds of our ancestors' would not lead to 'any improvements'. And the same writer, criticising Indian philosophy, religion and morality, felt it had only led them into being 'slaves' of others. According to him, listening to 'false doctrine' while remaining content with the present was 'no civilisation'.[130] A Pathan, commenting on an article he had seen in an Indian newspaper which favoured segregated compartments for the higher castes on Indian railways, expressed his disgust that Indians could be ashamed of sharing the same compartments with their lower-caste countrymen. 'What progress can you expect of a people like this!' he demanded, at the same time writing that, 'In Europe, sweepers, chamars, bhatiyars, Nawabs, Rajas are all one and sympathise with each other ... Here labour is not a disgrace, but a glory.' He may not have quite understood Europe's class distinctions, but there is no doubting his sentiment. As war dragged on, religious and caste barriers amongst Indians themselves relaxed as they mixed together 'like brothers'.[131] Some thought travel might help their countrymen 'appreciate knowledge' and profit from the experience.[132]

Did such sentiments lead to a questioning of British rule in India? It is difficult to reach a definite conclusion. The majority of the extracts deal with the men's own concerns: experiences of battle, worries about family and impressions of life in Europe. Moreover, Indian soldiers had little education, and were traditionally loyal. But there is a hint of political consciousness, if one looks at questions like 'does a man who is another's servant ever live in comfort?' or the statement that 'we are the slaves of the English'.[133] Further, an interesting letter comes from a Hindu store-keeper at the Kitchener Hospital. Writing to a Jacques Devel in France, the writer asked three very pertinent questions regarding their Algerian 'subjects or fellow citizens' then fighting in France. First, when off duty, were they at liberty to go out without guards? This, according to the writer, showed trust in their character as human beings – clearly a reference to the restrictions at the Kitchener hospital. Second, did they receive the same rate of pay as a French soldier, or was it different, and if so why? Third, was their uniform different from the French soldiers'? According to the writer, when fighting under the same flag, there should be no 'distinction'.[134] The Censor withheld the letter. Another, narrating the tale of an Indian sepoy, accused by a colonel of 'malingering', and then beaten up by some English 'Christian ward orderlies', till 'blood ran', described how a 'native officer of India' reported the 'unjust beating' to the colonel in charge, only to be told: '"Subedar Sahib, I cannot say anything to a white man on account of a Sepoy."' The writer continued:

> It is time to reflect ... We have crossed the seven seas, left our homes, and our dear ones and our parents, and for the honour of such an unjust and false-promising King we have sacrificed our lives. And now this is the honour we get ... We are regarded as inarticulate animals, but who can say that to oppress and dishonour us is good?[135]

This letter, too, was withheld. A Rajput expressed the sentiment differently. According to him, if Indians brought back to India the 'flag of victory which we have helped to win' for the King, then Indians would have proved their 'fitness' and would be 'entitled to self-government'. In a similar vein a store-keeper gave his view that the public was sympathetic to India because of the war and their 'invaluable services'. But what will they 'do for India after the war', was his question.[136]

Such a sample may not amount to much. But in his interviews with the Sikh war veterans, Pradhan came across views that show there was a feeling that Indians were being denied their rights by the British. One veteran mentioned that soldiers realised that the British had no 'respect' for the Indians, regarding them as their 'servants'. He described how the British soldiers received a salary 'four times more' than an Indian, and that their 'sepoy' did not salute 'our subedar-major or any NCO'. Another veteran mentioned that, before the war, they had been content with the 'existing circumstances'. But, having met various peoples and got their views, they began 'protesting' against the 'inequalities and disparities' created by the British between 'the white and the black', and they had learnt about 'the cunningness of the British'.[137]

The First World War marked a turning point in Indo-British relations. It loosened the bonds of colonial rule and helped to destroy the myth of Indian inferiority. It released many aspirations and aroused many expectations, quickening the pace of anti-colonial struggle.

7

Citizens or Aliens?

Racism, Repatriation and Passport Control

The period after the First World War found Indians disillusioned. And with much cause. In India, the Montagu principles for self-government, first announced in Parliament in 1917, and promulgated in December 1919 under a constitutional system known as 'dyarchy', fell far short of expectations. The Rowlatt Acts, 1919, known as the 'Black Acts', rushed through the Legislative Council against all-out opposition from the Indian members, violated their civil rights. The massacre at Amritsar and the martial law in the Punjab brought repression rather than peace or the promised change. Their loyalty and sacrifices in the war brought no reward. In Britain, too, no heroes' welcome awaited the Indians. Instead they found their British nationality and citizenship questioned and their rights under threat. Under a series of measures, including the racially discriminatory 1925 Special Restriction (Coloured Alien Seamen) Order, black peoples saw a steady erosion of their rights and their exclusion from the labour market. This chapter considers Indian experiences of these measures, their resistance and attempts to frustrate the state in order to defend their rights.

INDIAN LABOUR IN THE CONTEXT OF WAR

As we have seen, during the late eighteenth and early nineteenth centuries war had led to increased employment of Indian sailors. The First World War proved no exception. In fact, so acute was the shortage that the Board of Trade, under pressure from ship-owners, even considered modifying Section 125 of the 1894 Act governing lascar transfers to facilitate their employment on the South American route by shipping lines not hitherto employing Indians, or operating the eastern route. In 1916, in response to the demands of war, lascar contracts were extended to 18 months.[1] In addition, lured by opportunities for higher wages, some jumped ship in Britain in the hope of obtaining better pay and conditions under European articles. Others found employment on shore in industries around London, Merseyside and Clydeside. Some may have left their ships voluntarily, but firms in desperate need of labour enticed sailors away by offering higher wages than under ships' articles. For instance, in May 1916, reporting 'several cases' of desertion, the Anchor Line informed the India Office that 'certain parties' were canvassing 'Eastern Crews', an allegation supported by the powerful Liverpool Steam Ships Owners' Association. In its letter of complaint to the Board of Trade in July, the Association, too, blamed the increase in lascar desertions on 'organised attempts' to lure them into 'more remunerative employment on shore'. Warning of 'serious consequences' to shipping unable to fill vacancies in war-time, the Association pressed the Board of Trade to act to end the 'growing evil' and have lascars returned to sea. The Board of Trade, with India Office concurrence, responded quickly: within a month, in August 1916, a tough public notice warning against 'enticing and harbouring' deserters was issued.[2]

Attention was drawn to a 'large' number of Indians employed in factories around London, the Tate sugar refinery at Silvertown, being one. But it was Lever Bros in Merseyside who were revealed to be the most 'serious offenders', employing a 'considerable number' at Port Sunlight, Cheshire.[3] However, when Lever appealed to the Board of Trade that they would be seriously inconvenienced without their Indian workers, especially at a time of labour shortage, both the Board of Trade and the India Office, despite their tough public notice of warning, decided against taking legal action. Instead, a year later, in August 1917, a formula was devised, whereby Lever Bros, in consultation with their local Mercantile Marine Office (MMO), would gradually discharge their lascars when they could be 'spared' and as opportunities arose for securing them employment on ships bound for India.[4] Lever Bros could thus keep their Indians until such time as whites were once again available. Lascars would then be dispatched to India as ships' crew, saving the India Office the cost of maintenance and return passage. By then Indians were reported to be working in sugar refineries, in shipbuilding firms and in engineering in Clydeside as well as in Sheffield and Greenock, 'most' of them having registered 'in the usual way' with the Labour Exchange, and having been given clearance by the Mersey Dock Board. According to John Walker, sugar refiners at Greenock, even the 'Military Authority' had showed no objection to their employment. Again, these firms were not required to discharge their labourers forthwith. In January 1918, for instance, John Walker agreed to make arrangements with the local MMO for the gradual release of their firemen as and when they could be 'spared' for employment on ships bound for India.[5]

What is significant in this episode is that in time of economic crisis, and when need arose, different measures and solutions could be applied,

permitting Indians to remain in Britain to help service the needs of
domestic industries. However, by no means all Indians employed in
factories were seamen. At least 200 artisans and mechanics from
Bombay and the Punjab, working their passage as sailors, were known
to have come to Britain, helping the war effort, working in munitions
factories and in other industries. The situation was further complicated
by the fact that those seamen employed in Britain for a long time – and
settled – had no wish to return to India, preferring to go to jail rather
than accept employment on Lascar Articles on India-bound ships.
Commenting on their 'stubbornness', in February 1918, the MMO at
Greenock suggested that the men be compelled to go. But compulsion
was ruled out of order by the legal adviser at the India Office because,
after such a lapse of time, and since the men refused to identify the ships
on which they had first arrived, they could not be classified as deserters
and handed back to any ship bound for India. Further, the India Office,
regarding itself as 'the custodian of the interests of Indians', refused to
countenance the use of 'any exceptional pressure' likely to hinder the
employment of Indian seamen and others, who, in their opinion, had
'committed no breach of agreements, and who [were] endeavouring to
earn a living in this country in a legal manner'.[6] Such an intervention on
the part of the India Office, albeit for its own agenda and possibly with
an eye to the future recruitment of labour in India, is nonetheless
significant for the legal rights of Indians in Britain. Thus, by the time
war ended in November 1918, there was already a pool of Indian labour
in Britain, which was further increased by sailors discharged in England
after the war.[7]

RACE RIOTS, 1919

With a return to peace and an end to the war-induced shortage of white
labour, the position of Indians in Britain became vulnerable. In the
summer of 1919, riots broke out in some major seaports, including
London, Glasgow, Liverpool and Cardiff. Although much still remains
to be researched, scholars have documented details of events surrounding the 'race riots'.[8] Explanations for the immediate and the more
'deep-rooted' causes have also been discussed, notably, sexual jealousy
and the fear of miscegenation, competition for jobs and white hostility
to black labour, as well as the 'underlying link' between 'the experience
of Empire and the manifestation of racial antipathy in the metropolis'.[9]
Contemporaries also noted the increasingly indiscriminate attacks by
whites as they 'vent their spite on any darker skin'. As Fryer has shown,
Africans, Arabs, Chinese, Filipinos, Greeks, Somalis, West Indians and
Indians – no one was safe. In London in May 1919, *The Times* reported

that 'large crowds assembled outside the Strangers' Home for Asiatic Seamen in West India Dock Road and any coloured man who appeared was greeted with abuse and had to be escorted by the police. It was necessary at times to bar the doors of the Home.'[10] At the Manchester Assizes, in early June, three white men were sentenced for robbing £100 – no mean sum – from an Indian. In Cardiff, the damage done to Abdul Satar's shop was reckoned to be 'pretty considerable'. In Bute Street, a small crowd 'assailed' a Malay boarding-house which was wrecked, and the Malay boarders, who escaped through the skylight on to the roof, were subjected to 'a volley of stones'. Later, the appearance of a 'solitary' Malay sailor, who ventured into the city at dusk, 'immediately' caused a riot.[11]

Physical attacks aside, in a competitive job market, Asians, to their cost, now found their labour to be surplus to requirement, further illustrating their vulnerability in peace-time. For instance, the artisans and mechanics from Bombay and the Punjab, welcomed during the war, found themselves thrown out as demobilisation progressed. Another example is that of an Indian, who had served in the Navy for four years and was then employed on a river hopper on the Mersey. Given 24 hours' notice to quit, he was told: 'You were quite efficient but there are 11,000 demobilised soldiers to be re-instated and they must have first chance.' Searching for other jobs, and despite his war service, he even found Scandinavians being given preference over blacks, leading him to complain that 'the white men must be re-instated first, the unions insist on it'. By 1921, the fact that the India Office saw no need for printing more 'warning' handbills (against 'enticing and harbouring' seamen) as they had 'no reason to suppose that employers [were] now offering work' on shore, confirms the trend that once war was over Indians were dispensable.[12]

But it was in Scotland that working-class hostility towards Indian labour was perhaps most acute and, as argued by Dunlop, 'racialised' in its discourse.[13] Pre-war attacks on Indian and Chinese seafarers in British shipping on Clydeside have already been mentioned. With a return to peace and an end to the short-lived boom in shipping in 1920, coupled with the onset of recession in the iron and steel works in Lanarkshire, another spate of labour hostility surfaced in Scotland, first coming to notice in March 1920 when four Indian seamen, all from Bombay, were sent by the Labour Exchange to the Kingshill Colliery in Lanarkshire, as casual surface labourers. Protesters alleged that the Coltness Iron Company, which owned the mine, employed 'cheap lascar labour to the detriment of the British miner', forcing the Coal Association to refute 'inaccurate allegations ... against the methods of capitalism'. Their press release stressed that the men worked the same number of hours and received the same wages as other workers. However, what the protesters overlooked was the fact that Indians, too, were British, had loyally served in the war, and, as the press release pointed out, possessed 'certificates entitling them to wear war medals'.[14]

Over the next 12 months union agitation against Indian labour in the collieries and iron and steel works of Lanarkshire intensified. In June 1920, raising the question of numbers and terms of employment of Indian workers in Motherwell and at Wishaw, the MP for Leyton East, L'Estrange Malone, asked whether the Minister of Labour, Dr Macnamara, was aware of the complaints at the employment of Indian labour made at the local Labour Exchange. MPs were informed that around 20–30 lascars worked at the Etna Steel Works at Motherwell, while a further 20 were employed at the Stainton Iron and Steel Works and the Glasgow Iron and Steel Company at Wishaw, that Indian labourers not only received the same standard rate of wages, but were employed under similar conditions as 'British workmen'. Further, that a protest resolution over their employment had been 'passed by the local employment committee at Motherwell'.[15] But such assurances were not enough. Against a backdrop of mass unemployment in Lanarkshire, the local media, in January 1921, drawing attention to their presence in the locality, reported that since the end of the war, the district had been 'literally besieged' with Indian labourers looking for work in various 'local industrial centres' and that, despite their inability to speak 'the national tongue', they had 'taken to living in the model lodging-houses in the district'. Such allegations – and in such emotive terms – were bound to inflame passions. But Asians too were caught in the cycle of recession: unable to find work on east-bound shipping laid up in Glasgow, and in 'a serious plight', they struggled to find employment in industries, as is shown by the media's graphic portrayal of 'a "bunch" of six of these "dusky ones" ... eagerly and anxiously intercepting foremen in various departments muttering in broken English "me want a job"'. But their efforts, too, were 'doomed to disappointment'.[16]

Not only did the unions accuse Indians of lowering standards by undercutting wages, taking jobs and housing from 'local' working people, but their morals, too, were perceived to be a threat. For instance, a member of the Motherwell Trades Council, describing Indians as 'these aliens', alleged at a meeting in February 1921 that they were 'a menace to the social and industrial amenities of the community'. His authority was apparently a ship's steward who, at a union meeting in Glasgow, claimed that 'the conduct of lascars around the docks ... was disgraceful in the extreme' and if allowed to 'settle in the industrial centres' their conduct would 'probably be much worse'. But such stereotyped arguments were nothing new. In 1916, reporting lascar employment in the factories around London, N.A. Lash, secretary to the Strangers' Home for Asiatics, had voiced similar fears, warning: 'their sojourn in this country does not tend to improve the morals of their surroundings'.[17] Others, however, considered it unfair to condemn Indians for 'their colour', arguing that 'if the workers were looking after their own interests they would see that the Lascars were in the trade unions and imbued with the spirit of the trade unions' for a decent standard of living. The allegations that Indians were a 'menace' to the public, too, were disputed, as is evident from several letters in the Scottish press in defence of their 'work and habits'. One, referring to 'a little Asiatic colony' of Punjabi Muslims, glowingly described them as 'steady and industrious'; they 'keep good time' and are 'quiet, clean, temperate, thrifty citizens' who paid their taxes. They were even held up as 'models' to be recommended to the community. Others condemned the 'outrageous statements' made by the 'Labour men' in the Trades Council.[18] But such voices were a minority. It was alleged that 'thousands of [Scottish] workers' were suspended, while 'a large number' of lascars were 'still' employed in certain steel works in Lanarkshire, which resulted in the local Trades Councils making representations to the Ministry of Labour to have 'Lascars repatriated'.[19] This was not the first instance of such demands, however: in February 1918, the MMO at Greenock had urged their compulsory repatriation.

REPATRIATION

Elsewhere in Britain, calls for the repatriation of black peoples had come in 1919, in the wake of the 'race riots', and from the police. For instance, following a 'serious encounter' resulting in a 'negro' being thrown into the docks and drowned, the Assistant Chief Constable of Liverpool urged that 'unless a drastic and quick clearance' was made, disturbances would result in 'loss of life'. Similarly, in his report to the Home Office on the riots where a large number of Arab and Somali seamen had been the target of white anger, the Chief Constable of Cardiff, describing the 'aggressors' as those 'belonging to the white race', had nonetheless recommended that the Home Office 'give serious consideration to the advisability of immediate steps being taken to repatriate all the unemployed coloured seamen at this port'. If not, he warned that 'faced with destitution', they 'may become desperate', a commonly held view of black peoples' volatility and their threat to public order.[20] From the Home Office letters to the Chief Constables in Liverpool and Cardiff, and from the Conference report which followed, it is evident that at ministerial level, while ruling out compulsion to deport any 'coloured' men who were British subjects, repatriation was, nonetheless, considered a 'desirable' option. Further, local committees, described as useful, were to be set up – first in Liverpool and Cardiff and to be extended to all major ports – to collect information, arrange publicity, interview individual men to urge on them 'the advisability' of accepting repatriation, while at the same time pointing out the difficulty of obtaining work if they remained in the UK, as well as to advise the Home Office on 'other steps' to deal with the 'problem of coloured labour'.[21] At the same time, to facilitate repatriation, it was decided that 'monetary inducement' on the model of the resettlement gratuity offered to Australians and other colonial munitions workers (i.e. free repatriation, £5 gratuity plus £2 voyage allowance) would be extended to all black seamen, including the lascars. By mid-July 1919, in seven of the large seaport towns – Cardiff, Hull, South Shields, Salford, Liverpool, Glasgow and London – repatriation committees, with representatives from the NSFU, were in existence.[22] And in mid-July 1919, the *SS Porto* set sail for the east to repatriate a party of 205 black seamen from Cardiff, including 15 'Hindoos'. But the fact that only 205, out of the 450 identified as unemployed 'Asiatic seamen and labourers' at Cardiff, had availed themselves of the 'inducement' offered demonstrates the lack of enthusiasm for repatriation. As Jenkinson shows in the case of the West Indian seamen, black peoples long settled in Britain were not willing to uproot themselves.[23] By November 1919 the monetary offer was closed.

In economically difficult times, caught up in a cycle of recession, destitute and struggling to find work in local industries, Indians had come up against union hostility. With shipping still depressed and only a few jobs available, the pattern was repeated. On the Clyde, in March 1921, when a ship bound for Colombo signed on a crew of 'Asiatics', hostility boiled over in the form of a demonstration at the Mercantile Marine Office in Glasgow, leading to the intervention of the police.[24] But it was not in Glasgow alone that shipping was laid up. In other ports, too, 'coloured' seamen found themselves squeezed out of jobs on any vessel still sailing. In March 1921, Raymond Oliver, the solicitor to the Islamic Society, on behalf of his Muslim clients, 'Arab, Malay, Somali and Indian seamen', complained to the India Office of their deliberate exclusion from jobs 'on account of their colour'. He argued that as 'British subjects' who had served 'most loyally' in the war, they were 'entitled to employment in British ships, in preference to seamen of alien nationality'. With the onset of the coal strike and as shipping shrank further, their plight worsened, as the letter of appeal from several Indian and Adenese sailors from the Sailors' Rest in Swansea shows. On 'the verge of starvation' and in 'desperate condition', protesting that 'every ship which sign on gets all whites and nothing else', they asked the India Office to 'do something'.[25] Discrimination based on colour was not merely a black perception: the Swansea MMO, recommending the repatriation of 'about 50 Indian seamen' unemployed in Swansea, confirmed that the white men were 'strongly opposed' to 'coloured men of any nationality' being engaged on ships. An India Office minute of a later date, referring to the strength of feeling among the seamen's union, also noted that 'it is quite true' that the men had been 'handicapped in looking for work by reason of their colour', especially when 'English seamen' were unemployed.[26] Blacks also detected collusion at higher levels for the 'obstacles' that denied them jobs. Protesting on behalf of his Muslim clients, Raymond Oliver wrote that 'some kind of understanding had been arrived at between the Board of Trade, the India Office and the Firemen and Seamen's Union, to exclude the aforesaid men from all mercantile ships'. An internal minute, while denying complicity by the India Office, nonetheless admitted that the Board of Trade, 'acting in deference to the views of the Seamen's Unions, have taken a strong line with regard to "Coloured Seamen"'.[27]

By the summer of 1921, by one reckoning, 1,110 'coloured British seamen' – Indians, Arabs, Somalis, West Indians and West Africans – and around 300 'coloured aliens' were unemployed at Cardiff.[28] Only 'a very few' received any benefit under the Insurance Act. The majority, classified as not 'domiciled in Great Britain', and hence ineligible, survived on relief provided by the Lord Mayor's Fund, King George's Fund for Sailors, the British Foreign Sailors' Society (BFSS) and the NSFU. Threatened with bankruptcy, the boarding-house keepers, who had sheltered their compatriots out of solidarity and without payment for over five months, could no longer afford to keep them, while the BFSS was £200 in debt. Officially, it was still alleged that the 'problem' had arisen either because of 'wholesale' desertions or 'most probably' because of the disregard of the Indian Merchant Shipping Act by Aden authorities in allowing the men to ship on European Articles.[29] The peculiar circumstances of the war when, for instance, for strategic reasons the status of British subjects had been extended to trans-border 'Arabs', were conveniently laid aside. Repatriation was the proposed solution.

At Cardiff, the momentum for repatriation is traceable to a recommendation from the Town Clerk in April 1921, that the destitute 'may be either repatriated forthwith, or accommodated in a concentration camp'. The Immigration Officer added that, though 'quiet and patient', the coloured seamen were of an 'excitable temperament and it only [needed] one malignant spark to make a blaze' – a contradictory, if inflammatory image. The idea of a concentration camp was ruled out, but support for repatriation gathered force: the Home Office making overtures to the India Office and the Colonial Office responsible for their maintenance. The report from King George's Fund for Sailors in June also relayed the message that 'the distressed coloured seamen' were considered to 'constitute a very serious danger to the public peace'. The Chief Constable of Cardiff warned the Mayor that 'rioting must be expected at any time', and that 'undesirables' had been 'imported' into Cardiff.[30] By the time of the ministerial conference in late June 1921, repatriation to save on maintenance cost had been accepted.[31]

Responsible for Indians and Arabs, the India Office began preparation for their repatriation in September 1921. How many were Asians from the Indian sub-continent is difficult to know since, in official dispatches, the term 'Indian' is used in an administrative sense, rather than geographically. Undoubtedly, a large majority were Arabs, but a sprinkling of Indian names, identifiable by their place of birth, are contained in the BFSS communications, and amongst those boarding at the Strangers' Home for Asiatics and at Nairoolla's lodging-house in Poplar. And at a massive cost from the revenues of India, three ships were commissioned: *SS Kurmark*, having a capacity for 800 passengers, cost £14,316, *SS Diyatalawa*, £8,671 and *SS Frankenfels*, £4, 272.[32] But the project was a spectacular failure. The majority of the men refused to go, and, legally, could not be compelled to do so – consent of 'the destitute' being required for repatriation. But there is no doubt that the authorities wished to see them go. Referring to over 1,000 unemployed Adenese and the number that 'should be' considered domiciled in England, C.E. Baines at the India Office, in an internal minute, wrote: a 'great majority of the men do not wish to be repatriated but it is obvious that in a great majority of cases their wishes must be disregarded'. Further, the proposed 'diminishing scale of maintenance', also implied a logic of coercion, and the fact that any one refusing the offer was to be placed 'at once' on the 'minimum rate', confirms such a conclusion. But even this did not persuade men long domiciled in Britain to give up their citizenship rights and be repatriated, leaving families behind, in some cases.[33]

The first ship to sail from Plymouth on 12 September 1921, the *SS Kurmark*, could muster only 63 Indians and 150 Adenese.[34] Who were the Indians? An analysis of one surviving list compiled by the BFSS, dated August 1921, of 54 destitute Indians, shows that the men, all ex-firemen, had been in Britain between one and three years, the majority having been discharged by their ships in 1920–21; 48 were from the Punjab, 4 from Bombay and 2 from Peshawar. All were Muslims. Thirty-six came from Wishaw and 18 from Motherwell. Undoubtedly, these were the industrial workers who had been the object of labour hostility. Most of the rest too, according to the India Office, were subsequently repatriated.[35]

COLOURED ALIEN SEAMEN ORDER

Attempts at repatriation in 1919 and in 1921 had failed. But administrative measures to restrict the admission of 'coloured seamen' into Britain, 'in view of the unemployment among British seamen', begun in 1920 and initially aimed primarily at 'Arabs', but later revised to include all without 'unimpeachable' documentary proof of British nationality or domicile (Circular SI 284, October 1920 and December 1920), culminated in 1925 in the Special Restriction (Coloured Alien Seamen) Order.[36] Issued by the Home Secretary, William Joynson-Hicks, as an Order in Council under the 1919 Aliens Act, which had extended the 1914 Act into peace-time, the Order unequivocally stated:

> Notice is hereby given that, in accordance with the Special Restriction (Coloured Alien Seamen) Order, 1925, made by the Secretary of State for the Home Department, coloured alien seamen are required to register with the Police, whether or not they have been in the United Kingdom for more than two months since their last arrival. Any coloured alien seaman who is not already registered should take steps to obtain a Certificate of Registration without delay.[37]

The Order thus removed at the outset the 60-day period of grace normally granted under the Aliens Act. The 1925 Order was a blatantly racially discriminatory measure – even officially admitted as such, years later, when it was described as 'apparently the only enactment in this country constituting a colour bar'.[38] Initially restricted to 13 ports (Barry, Penarth, Port Talbot, Newport, Swansea and Cardiff in Wales; Liverpool, Salford, Newcastle, South Shields, Hull and Middlesbrough in the North and North-east), the Order was extended throughout Britain in January 1926. The Home Office claimed that the Order was necessary: first, to facilitate control of alien seamen already in the United Kingdom; and, second, to prevent more effectively the entry and 'accumulation' of 'coloured seamen' who, it was alleged, 'competed in the overstocked labour market' causing 'serious discontent' among British sailors – thus to all intents and purposes placing a bar to their settlement. But in view of the fact that by the mid-1920s shipping was beginning to pick up, such a claim is dubious. Further, even the 'Adenese' sailors had already been placed under Lascar Articles, preventing their discharge in Britain.[39]

The Order, initially aimed at 'alien Arab' seamen, came to be applied to all 'coloured seamen' not able to provide acceptable proof of British nationality.[40] This was for two principal reasons: first, sailors were not required to carry passports for their calling. Second, 'coloured' seamen's continuous discharge certificates, unlike those of white sailors, were not accepted as proof of nationality, it being alleged that 'trafficking' in discharge papers took place. This was yet another example of differential treatment based on race. In the event, establishing British nationality for the ethnically diverse seamen was bound to prove difficult. The Home Office was not unaware of the problem. But it claimed that those affected would 'not be numerous', and though registration under an Order meant only for 'coloured' aliens, 'might be unwelcome, they would acquiesce in an arrangement which was designed largely in the interests of British seamen'.[41] Did the Home Office seriously believe that 'coloured' British seamen would consent to their own registration as aliens or their own deportation? Thus the definition of who was British and who an alien became widened from alien 'Arab' seamen to all 'coloured seamen' – Indians, Africans and West Indians – not in possession of documentary proof of British nationality. Such a definition would eventually have implications for non-seamen, too, as the distinction between 'coloured seamen' and 'coloured' residents was fudged, treating all undocumented 'coloureds' in Britain as aliens, regardless of whether they were seafarers or not, born in the British empire or not – and in the process de-nationalising them.

Historians of black history have hitherto, tended to explain the erosion of the rights of black peoples under the 1925 Special Restriction (Coloured Alien Seamen) Order on two agencies. Some see it as a result of the action of overzealous 'local police' who 'high-handedly and quite illegally' overstepped their duties by placing 'their own interpretations' on the Order.[42] Others have seen the prominent hand of the NSFU (NUS), blaming it on the pressures exerted by the union and their 'fierce attack' on the employment of black seamen.[43] Recently historians have questioned these versions. They see the role of the union as less central, and focus instead on the role of the state, and the part played by the officials of various departments in initiating policy. In fact, Tabili argues that 'identifying local officials or the unions as the perpetrators ... has absolved the central government' of responsibility.[44] The view that the state played a more central role certainly receives support in official documents.[45] The 1925 Order had not come suddenly. It had been preceded by much debate, pressures from various state agencies, and administrative measures from the Home Office and the Board of Trade, going back to 1919. As such, the role of the state is crucial to the understanding of the Order and its application and implications for black peoples. What then of the NSFU? Among the archival papers is a letter from the Home Office to the Colonial Office dated August 1925, outlining the circumstances leading to the Order. According to this: 'strong representations were made by the National Sailors' and Fireman's Union, and supported by the Board of Trade that steps should be taken to restrict ... admission'.[46] Where both official versions are in agreement is in the role of the Board of Trade. No other record of 'strong representations' from the NSFU for the 1925 Order is contained in the official papers. However, as has been seen, demands for the repatriation of lascars in Scotland had come from the local Trades Councils in 1921. Then there was the perception among the sailors themselves, communicated in the letter from the Islamic Society's solicitor in 1921 and confirmed by the India Office minute, of the influence of seamen's unions on the Board of Trade. This therefore suggests that, by 1921 at least, the unions were playing an influential role. Such a role is further seen in a deputation to the Board of Trade from the Seafarer's Joint Council in 1923. Opposing the employment of 'Arabs' to the 'detriment of British subjects', the deputation in strong emotive terms expressed the view that an Arab seaman who 'claims to be a Britisher', was 'today' competing against the Britisher and getting employed while the Britisher was 'walking about and starving'. Therefore, worker agitation to exclude 'coloured' seamen, questions in Parliament and media publicity, would all have been important ingredients lending legitimacy to state action.[47] However, it must not be forgotten either that unions themselves were not averse to playing a double game when it suited their purpose. Referring to the domiciled 'Arabs' in Cardiff, in 1921, the Secretary of the Seamen's Union, Cardiff, gave his view that 'wholesale repatriation' would be bad for the shipping industry as 'this class of men ... do work which the white seamen will not do'.[48]

FROM CITIZENS TO ALIENS

In early March 1925, 16 Indian seamen on the *SS Tenbergen*, on arrival at Leith, left their ship because of a dispute with their ship-owners. They had a cause: contrary to their agreement signed in Karachi, the owners required them to sail to New York. The immigration officer at Leith, using the 1920 Aliens Order, ordered their removal because the lascars were unable to produce passports as proof of their British nationality. But the lascars were on transfer and, as such, the Order did not apply to them. Further, lascars were not issued with passports and, under Asiatic Articles, even their discharge certificates were retained under lock and key on board the ship until their return to India.[49] The men were helpless. After two months and with the aid of the solicitors employed in the interest of the agents, they succeeded in proving their British nationality by virtue of birth and residence in Karachi. The Home Office attempt may have been frustrated by the Scottish lawyers, but the fact that the India Office protested strongly that it was 'undesirable' for lascars to be treated as aliens even 'temporarily', and that a civil servant was moved to minute that the Home Office policy of 'worrying coloured seamen is being pushed to indefensible limits', suggests that this was not the first attempt to deport them as aliens, confirming widespread harassment of Indians under the 1920 and 1925 Orders.[50]

In an attempt to bar their settlement even Indian seamen domiciled in Britain lost their nationality, as the treatment meted out to Jan Mohamed illustrates. Discharged by a Finnish ship at Antwerp, Jan Mahomed, travelling at his own expense, arrived at Harwich on 1 April 1925. But he was refused entry as an 'alien passenger', and was forced to return to Antwerp. His funds exhausted by the enforced double trip, Jan Mahomed appealed to the British Consul at Antwerp. Yet both his discharge book and the rejection notice presented to him by the immigration officer described him as a 'subject of Punjab, India', and so legally British. Even the reason cited for his refusal, 'No. 15', according to a rather puzzled British Consul, did 'not figure in the list of immigration regulations'. In addition, according to his discharge book, Jan Mahomed lived in England, had signed on at South Shields in October 1918 and been paid off at Swansea in April 1919. Further, in conspicuously placing the 'refusal stamp' where usually only particulars of employment were entered in a discharge book, the immigration officer had made Jan Mohamed's future chances of employment more difficult, illustrating how the heavy hand of law was used to prevent Indians from obtaining employment on European Articles in Britain.

The fact that Jan Mohamed's case had embarrassed the British Consul at Antwerp points to the suspect behaviour of the immigration officer. But the Home Office insisted that under Article 15 (1) 1920 Aliens Order, Jan Mohamed, unable to produce a 'passport or other document' had failed to establish 'his identity and his claim to be a British subject'. Further, Sir William Joynson-Hicks claimed that, because Jan Mohamed had last been paid off in the UK 'as long ago as 1919', he had 'little claim' to return and resume the practice of signing on British ships at ports in Britain. But the reason why Jan Mohamed had been away from Britain was the fact that, having been paid off at New York in 1919, and unable to find another ship, presumably because depression had hit the industry, this resourceful man had worked as a labourer in Detroit till 1923.[51]

Jan Mohamed, however, was not to be deprived of his rights so easily. Stowing away on a ship to Leith, he then walked to London to lodge his claim for war risks compensation against the India Office and the Board of Trade, and to the American Consul for his savings deposited in New York. As a British subject, he even applied for a passport for travel to America to draw on his funds. Thus, Jan Mahomed, by his determined action, succeeded not only in sabotaging the 1920 Aliens Order, including the newly introduced 1925 Coloured Alien Seamen Order, and entering Britain to establish his rights, but by his action also managed, according to the India Office, to assume 'an interdepartmental, if not international importance'. The fact that the India Office found Jan Mohamed's ingenuity in 'eluding the legal obstacles' as 'disturbing' and indicative of 'serious trouble', illustrates how stringent were the regulations to prevent Indian seamen settling down in Britain – and it was this that ultimately defeated Jan Mohamed. Without means of support, as a destitute lascar, in September 1925, he was put on a ship bound for New York and Singapore and thence back to India. Thus Jan Mohamed was returned to India under a scheme euphemistically described as 'voluntary repatriation'.[52]

Inability to produce 'good evidence of British nationality' acceptable to the Home Office had defined Jan Mohamed 'an alien' under the 1920 Order.[53] But it was under the 1925 Special Restrictions (Coloured Alien Seamen) Order that more Indians, seamen and non-seamen, found themselves registered as aliens. Within months of the Order, the India Office received a letter from a distressed Mary Fazel, the wife of the 39-year-old Fazel Mohamed, a Peshawar-born British Indian fireman, resident at Bootle, who on 1 August 1925 had been registered as an alien on his disembarkation at Cardiff from his ship, SS Derville. Pleading for help, she explained that his 'Mercantile Marine Book', bearing his certificate of nationality as a British citizen, signed by the Mercantile Marine Superintendent in August 1919, had been 'ignored as documentary proof' of nationality. What Mary Fazel wanted to know was whether the authorities were right in taking this action and where she could obtain her husband's birth certificate, which would 'definitely establish his identity'. Mary Fazel was a worried woman. She wrote:

> I have been married to him for seven years, and we have three children, therefore the knowledge that my husband is not a recognised British subject, causes me much consternation, as should anything happen to him in a foreign port his rights as a Britisher would be jeopardised, and consequently my own and our children's.[54]

In reply, all that the India Office could suggest to reverse this injustice was to ask Fazel Mohamed to provide himself with a passport as a 'satisfactory evidence of British nationality'. But obtaining a passport was no easy matter: it first required verification of birth and other details in India, a process that took 11 months. In the meantime, without acceptable evidence of British nationality, Mohamed, unable to obtain a ship, had become unemployed and been subjected to other indignities. For instance, on 6 August 1926, the police had detained him for an hour just because he had 'an alien's book' on him. Mary Fazel could not understand why he had to carry such a book: he was a British subject, born in Peshawar, and had lived in Britain for nine years. By now, with four children to support, life must have been grim indeed for the Fazel Mohamed family.[55]

Thousands of seamen born in India, Malaya, Africa, the Caribbean and the Middle East were re-classified as aliens, their British nationality and their rights of domicile snatched away – with bureaucratic logic. In February 1927, writing to the India Office from the Sailors' Home in Belgium, two seamen, P.C. Fitzgerald, a Calcutta-born Anglo-Indian ('Eurasian'), with a father living in Liverpool, and Abdul Gani, a Bombay-born Indian, complained that they had been refused landing at Harwich and sent back to Antwerp, where they had been discharged by the SS Australind. They pleaded that as 'dark people' they had no prospect of employment in Belgium and wanted to return to England. The Foreign Office ruled that neither came under the category, 'domiciled in England and in the habit of signing on from British ports'. The Home Office agreed: they could only be permitted to land in England 'as aliens' for repatriation to India. But Abdul Gani, according to the Registration Book issued to him on 8 July 1925 under the Aliens Order 1920, and impounded by the Immigration Officer, had been in

England since 1914, had served in the war and lived at Newport. Absurdly, although his place of birth was shown as 'Bombay' in the Registration Book, his nationality had been entered as 'Doubtful', while the column 'previous nationality' had been cancelled and left blank.[56] This was no idiosyncratic whim on the part of an immigration officer. Nor was it a manifestation of a local official 'high-handedly and quite illegally' placing 'their own interpretations' on the Order. To prevent 'possible prosecution' immigration officers had been instructed that 'it would be wiser to leave the entry blank or insert "Doubtful" '.[57] Thus by the stroke of a pen, a Bombay-born British citizen had been registered an alien. And yet only '16 months' previously, he had signed on in England on the *SS Holy Park* bound for New York and from where he had been discharged at Antwerp. Fitzgerald, on the other hand, who had served in the navy during the war, and left Calcutta in 1919 for New York, while waiting in Antwerp had, on 28 March 1927, received his baptismal certificate issued at Calcutta, establishing his British nationality beyond doubt. Yet both British seamen were only allowed to enter Britain if they agreed to be repatriated to India.[58]

As a final example I cite the case of seaman William James Poynter, another Anglo-Indian, who lost his rights through a combination of bureaucracy and police recommendation. Resident in Limehouse, London, for many years, and married to an English woman, though separated from her, in January 1926, when the 1925 Order was extended to London, Poynter was classified as of 'Doubtful' nationality and registered as an 'alien'. Having signed on a ship at London, he was stranded at Marseilles, his application for the Special Certificate of British Nationality to enable him to have his wrongful 'alien registration' cancelled, rejected by the British Consul. Born in India, torpedoed twice in the war, and incensed at such treatment, Poynter demanded that an 'Indian Consul' be employed to represent 'Indian people', which suggests he had no confidence in the Consul. Not only was Poynter born in Calcutta and known to the Shipping Master at that port, but, according to information received from Calcutta, he possessed a British seaman's 'Discharge A Book', was normally employed on European Articles on Chief Steward rating, for £14. 10s. per month, and entitled to discharge in Britain or the Continent, all of which confirmed his domicile and citizenship. But the Limehouse police, who described Poynter as 'altogether a very undesirable character', strongly expressed the view that they did 'not wish to see him again in the Limehouse district'. This sealed his fate. The India Office, not wishing to 'embarrass the Police Authorities by enabling a person of undesirable character' to live in Britain, showed willingness 'to co-operate' with the

Home Office to arrange for Poynter's return to India when he arrived as a seaman on a ship to England.[59]

What emerges from these case studies is that state officials, in their determination to deport Asians, stuck rigidly to the rules of the 1925 Order, an Order that treated black citizens differently from whites, depriving them of their rights of citizenship and their livelihood. Moreover, some zealous officials, determined to deport all black British peoples whom they considered 'undesirable', used the Order for their own purposes – even against non-seamen, seen from the case of the Glasgow Indians.

In January 1926, Robert Gloag, solicitor, asking for clarification on points of law on behalf of 40 Indians forced to register as 'aliens' by the Aliens Officer, demanded to know whether it was only in Glasgow that Indians, British subjects, were required to register or 'if a similar practice' was pursued in London.[60] Clearly the Glasgow police, who, in September 1925, had urged the Home Office to extend the Coloured Alien Seamen Order to Glasgow, to enable them to register 'approximately 100' Indians, had wasted no time, seizing their opportunity as soon as the Order was extended throughout Britain in January 1926. In their original report to the Home Office, back in September 1925, the Glasgow police had informed the Home Office that these Indians had come to Glasgow 'several years ago', and had formed their own Indian Union. The police claimed that they sheltered other 'deserters', taking them to the industrial regions for employment in mines and iron works. Having mastered the English language, they applied for pedlars' licences which 'invariably' they obtained, being of good character and British subjects. The police also insinuated that four of the Indians had 'prostitutes on the streets in Glasgow for immoral purpose'. Insisting that the Indians were 'deserters', the police proposed registering them once Glasgow was made a specified area under the Order.[61] Within a matter of days, the number registered had gone up from 40 to 56. Of these, 19 lived in Glasgow and the rest in Lanarkshire.[62] By February 1926, according to the Alien Registration Department of Glasgow police, 73 had been registered: 18 of them seamen, the rest industrial workers or pedlars. Six, having produced their passports, had their registrations annulled. The police, in registering individuals who clearly fell outside the 1925 Order, justified their action by alleging that the men were 'lascar seamen', working in collieries and steel works. They also claimed that although some had at first objected to the word 'ALIEN', on being explained to them that they would find it easier to get work as 'seamen or ashore', no further objections had been raised, except by one, 'who is really the Babu', who had engaged two solicitors to take up their case with the India Office. But since the fees of the solicitors were raised by contribution from 'all the lascars in Glasgow and District', it is hard to accept the view that 'none of them raised any further objections'. Further, the fact that they had also approached their own union to protest to the India Office on their behalf, and sent a statement of their grievances to the Indian press and to the Members of the Legislative Assembly in India, confirms the view that they objected strongly enough not to let the action of the police remain unchallenged.[63]

In his letter of protest to the India Office, P.S.R. Chowdhury, secretary of the Glasgow Indian Union (GIU), formed sometime in the early 1920s, condemning Home Office action in 'arbitrarily' registering 63 Indians as aliens, as 'harsh and unwarranted', demanded that the India Office 'remedy this injustice' and protect their rights as British subjects in Britain. What irked the GIU most was the fact that in the 'Identity Books' issued to the men, their nationality and birth place were 'left blank', effectively making them stateless.[64] This was a point also made by the *Negro World*, when it commented that 'according to John Bull's new strategy, his black subjects in England have no nationality'. In India, the GIU letter was published by several newspapers, including the Madras *New India,* which ran the story under their political campaign, 'Agitate for the Commonwealth Bill', with the headline, 'Are Indians Aliens?', while the Calcutta *Forward* headlines read: 'Glasgow Ban on Indians' and 'Arbitrary Registration as Aliens', generating much publicity and outrage.[65]

The names of the 63 Glasgow Indians registered as aliens show a majority of them to have been born in the Punjab and as having lived in Scotland between 3 and 14 years; 37 were pedlars, 24 labourers and only 2 described themselves as seamen – which does not tally with the Glasgow police claim that as many as 18 were seamen.[66] The fact that the Home Office admitted to the India Office that 'some confusion' had occurred, and in an internal minute noted that the police had seized 'the occasion of the application of the Coloured Alien Seamen Order to Glasgow for a vigorous enforcement of the Order, 1920', suggests an excess of deliberate police zeal. But the status of the registered Indians remained unchanged: the 1920 Order still effectively re-classified them as aliens.[67]

In Parliament, George Lansbury, drawing attention to the registration of the 63 India-born British subjects as 'aliens' asked whether steps would be taken to reverse their registration and notify Glasgow that British subjects 'need not come under these alien restrictions'. J.S. Wardlaw-Milne inquired if lascars were now required to produce passports to show their British nationality, forcing the Home Office to admit in a letter, and later publicly in Parliament, that lascars on 'Asiatic Articles', did not come under the Aliens Order.[68] But it was in India that the Glasgow episode, revealing a 'systematic exclusion of Indians' from places of public entertainment, created the greatest outcry. Indians wanted to know whether the policy of treating Indians as aliens in 'British colonies' (i.e. white Dominions) was now part of the 'British government's "domestic policy", to treat Indians in Great Britain as "aliens"', too. Such publicity worried the government of India, prompting a flurry of letters.[69] Although the Home Office refused to withdraw their registration, William Joynson-Hicks nonetheless was forced to admit privately that the Glasgow police had 'exceeded their instructions in carrying out the rather wholesale round-up of coloured men'. But face had to be saved: officially the government of India was informed that the Home Office did not intend to 'order any wholesale' registration of 'coloured persons (other than seamen)' unable to produce satisfactory evidence. But a private letter summed up the situation: 'The intention of the Home Office put shortly is … not to disregard what was done at Glasgow but to see that it does not happen again.'[70]

The protest of Indians in Britain continued. At a mass rally on May Day 1927, in Cleveland Square, Liverpool, Indians called for the abolition of the 'Alien Certificate' for Indians, replacing it with a 'certificate of identity'. They demanded that police harassment of Indians, of summarily stopping and searching them, be stopped. They appealed to the Indian National Congress 'to investigate the status of Indians in England and to give them every possible assistance in securing the political and social equality which [was] their right as British subjects'. And they gave notice of their intention to found a Liverpool Indian Association under the leadership of N.J. Upadhyaya, secretary of the Indian Seamen's Union (see Chapter 8), for the defence and promotion of their 'political, social and economic rights'.[71]

By their determined stand, Indians had challenged the state's attempts to redefine them and deprive them of their rights. They reminded British people of India's 'signal services' during the war.[72] By enlisting the aid of solicitors to fight on their behalf, through letters of protest to the India Office and to the press in India, by mass demonstrations and by appealing to their own political leaders in India, they put pressure on the metropolitan and imperial governments. And they succeeded, if not in having the racially discriminatory Order in Council revoked, in tempering its outcomes.

Faced with protests from aggrieved Indian and Adenese British citizens 'subjected to unnecessary harassment' as aliens, an embarrassed and concerned India Office acted. Declaring that it could 'not disinterest' itself in a policy 'of worrying coloured seamen ... being pushed to indefensible limits', the India Office reprimanded the Home Office, pointing out that Lord Birkenhead was unable 'to accept the suggestion that this Order [was] of no concern to the India Office'.[73] To help seamen substantiate their British nationality, the India Office went so far as to propose issuing them with passports, a suggestion squashed by the Home Office. The reason is not difficult to imagine. Passports would undermine what lay at the heart of the 1925 Order, as an internal India Office minute indicates. Noting the 'adverse' reaction of the Home Office, it recorded: 'its real ground is a fear that such a step would knock a large hole in the administration of the 1925 Order'. A Home Office memo is even more outspoken:

> It seems very undesirable that additional encouragement to leave their ships and settle in this country should be given to coloured seamen, from whatever part of the Empire they come, by providing them with passports which would be 'an open sesame' to the United Kingdom.[74]

The upshot was a compromise: Indian and Adenese 'lascars' registered as aliens could apply to the India Office to have their 'claims to British nationality' verified. They were then issued with a Special Certificate of Identity and Nationality, enabling them to have their registrations cancelled, a procedure formalised by May 1926. Verification, undertaken in India, however, was a long and involved process, taking an average of three to four months.[75] In 1931 the Special Certificate of Identity and Nationality was extended to all 'coloured British seamen' of the British Empire, Colonies and Protectorates. Issued in place of passports, valid for five years and with a limited endorsement, it was colour-coded to distinguish between the two categories of nationality, British subject and British Protected Person.[76]

This was not the only instance of the India Office acting against Home Office policy in the interest of Indians. In 1930, to prevent Indian seamen who had jumped ship in Britain from getting employment on ships in the United Kingdom, the Home Office ruled that before a lascar could be employed, he had to produce his *nully* (seaman's continuous discharge papers), a procedure not required of white British seamen. The India Office refused to uphold such a policy, which imposed a 'differential treatment' based on 'racial discrimination'.[77] A final example relates to the Home Office policy of withholding Special Certificates of Identity and Nationality to Indian seamen known to be British. After several cases had come to light of seamen whose nationality had been verified but who had not been issued with their Certificates, the India Office objected in the strongest terms on the grounds that it exposed British subjects to the 1925 Coloured Alien Seamen Order.[78] India Office objections forced a retreat in both instances.

Such a stand by the India Office is significant and runs counter to the accepted notions of a monolithic racist state. Under pressure from imperial citizens and for reasons of imperial politics, the India Office (and the Colonial Office) during the inter-war period at times acted in ways that conflicted with the Home Office policy intentions and as a result of its oppositional role, worked as a check on 'domestic racism'.[79]

The 1925 Coloured Alien Seamen Order in the last analysis was a failure. In its first year, 7,408 'coloured alien seamen' were registered. In July 1931 the total stood at 4,846. Of these, 383 were 'Indians and Singalese', 8 per cent of the total, and mainly British Protected Persons (BPP) from Indian States (Princely states).[80] Accorded a status on a par with British Indian subjects for political reasons since 1891 and, in 1916, under an agreement with the Home Office, exempted from the Aliens Restriction Order, nonetheless, under the 1925 Order, seafarers from the Indian States were defined as aliens on British soil.[81]

The 1925 Coloured Alien Seamen Order remained in force for 17 years, until 1942, when, under pressure from the Colonial Office, it was finally revoked – it is said for 'sentimental' reasons, 'since it applied to African seamen who are British Protected Persons'. The India Office shared the sentiment.[82] However, such a reason is hard to credit. Could the motive be the need for recruits at a critical stage in the Second World War?

Thwarted in their attempts to curb immigration under the Coloured Alien Seamen Order by the Special Certificates of British Nationality issued to Indian seamen, the Home Office alleged that the India Office made it easier for Indians to remain in Britain. It was further alleged that the grant of the Certificates, together with the ease with which pedlar licences were available, encouraged desertions by creating an 'impression' that all a man had to do was apply for the Certificate, 'bide his time' earning a 'makeshift' livelihood as a pedlar, later obtaining employment on European articles.[83] The Home Office accused boarding-house keepers of profiting from 'corrupt practices' by smuggling Indians among 'Arab stokehold crews' or by supplying them as crews to newly built steamers at Glasgow.[84] It argued that in a competitive market if 'every opportunity' was not taken to repatriate Indians, the unions would 'soon make themselves heard'.[85]

What is significant is that arguments once used against 'Arabs' were now applied to Indian seamen. To prevent their settlement the Home Office placed new obstacles in their way. Police were instructed to withhold their Certificates as evidenced by the cases of Budhua, Ulla and the Khan brothers in the Cardiff/Glamorgan area, even though they were known to be British. But the India Office vetoed such practice.[86] Another device was the practice known as 'deferred' registration – of 'habitually discouraging' registration under the Coloured Alien Seamen Order of men who were BPP by 'placing difficulties' in their way, as highlighted in the case of Ghulam Rasul from Jummu and Kashmir. As an India Office minute wryly commented, 'the point [being] that the man is more likely to return permanently to his own country', since he was not allowed to get work, prompting India Office intervention.[87] In March 1929, for instance, referring to the case of Ashraf Khan, from Kashmir, F.J. Adams asked the Home Office that he may be viewed with a 'friendly eye', allowed to register and remain in Britain 'practically' as though he were a British subject.[88] But the most significant step taken by the Home Office came in May 1930 in the form of a notice in the *Police Bulletin*. Under this, police were instructed to examine applications for pedlar licences from Indians with 'special strictness' and to go slow in granting certificates to applicants suspected of being 'deserter[s]'.[89] The reasons for such an instruction are obvious: deprived of the means of employment while awaiting verification for the Special Certificate of Nationality, and faced with destitution, they would be forced to seek repatriation.

Was lascar desertion such a 'rapidly growing ... evil'?[90] Such alarmist claims are not substantiated by evidence. Desertions fluctuated. Taking the number of Special Certificates of Nationality issued by the High Commission as a guide, records show that in the six months between July and December 1930 only 40 Certificates were issued, which, in the opinion of the High Commissioner, was 'a steady but not unduly large stream'. The majority of the shipping lines surveyed by the Board of Trade, too, reported that desertions were not 'numerous', rejecting any need for a 'concerted action'.[91] What this suggests is not that Indian seamen did not desert in Britain. They did, as evidenced by small settlements of Indians in the port areas of Cardiff, South Shields, Glasgow and London, but the 'problem' was exaggerated. The June 1936 census of seamen, for instance, showed only 840 Indians on British articles. What is more compelling, however, is not the number who deserted, but why men from Sylhet, the Punjab or the North-West Frontier Province took the risk. And the reason, as discussed earlier, was their inferior Lascar Articles, a grievance not addressed by the India Office. Instead, 'in the interest of the lascar himself', the India Office, raising the spectre of the possibility of 'local ill-feeling', even 'active hostility', against Indians in the 'over-crowded' labour market, urged the government of India to warn them of their 'wholly erroneous' belief that there was opportunity for 'lucrative employment' as a pedlar or as a seaman under European articles in Britain. The result was a public notice in India, posted at shipping offices, post offices and other public recruitment offices, as well as supplied to the seamen's unions, warning Indians of the perils of settling in Britain.[92]

But with the outbreak of the Second World War, Indian labour was once again in great demand. And enticed by the prospect of higher wages on land, some jumped ship and were absorbed in the war-related industries in London and the Midlands. Ironically, once again the pool of Indian labour in Britain prompted much debate about ways to repatriate 'Indian seamen deserters', who, in the words of the police, constituted 'a social evil of increasing seriousness'. At a high-level conference in Birmingham in March 1943, it was proposed that the only way to 'break up these colonies' was to alter the wording of the Merchant Shipping Act of 1894 and the Defence Regulation Act, to allow repatriation by 'any ship' bound for India – an amendment known to discriminate against Indians, as the India Office, in a letter to the government of India, acknowledged. Nonetheless, there are indications that such a regulation was approved in early 1945.[93]

HIERARCHY OF CITIZENSHIP

Meanwhile, as the Depression continued, and faced with competition from German and American shipping, in 1935, the British Shipping (Assistance) Act, subsidising Tramp Shipping, was passed.[94] A measure introduced to help British shipping (a private industry) and safeguard British seamen's jobs became an instrument of discrimination, emphasising yet again a hierarchy of British nationality and rights of citizenship. The fact that payment of a subsidy to ship-owners was dependent on the employment of 'British seamen' soon led to a rush by ship-owners to clear their vessels of all but white British seamen, as evidenced by a spate of letters of complaint from Indians living in South Shields who worked as seafarers. Some were British subjects, others from Indian States were BPP, all were replaced by whites. Several had their passports tampered with, the word 'subject' scored out 'with red ink'.[95]

Not only did the men concerned make representations to the India Office to have their rights restored, but the threat to their jobs brought resident blacks and Asians together, galvanising them into action, leading, in mid-1935, to the formation of the Colonial Seamen's Association (CSA) in London, an organisation of 'Indians, Negroes, Arabs, Somalis, Malay and Chinese'. Led by the Barbados-born Chris Jones (Chris Braithewaite), its secretary was Surat Alley (also referred to as Surat Ali in official dispatches). Born in Cuttack, Orissa, and married to a white woman (Sarah Reder), Alley was also the honorary secretary of the Hindustani Social Club in the East End, and general secretary/founder of the Oriental Film Artistes' Union (see Chapter 9).[96]

The CSA, at its first Annual Convention in London in November 1936, attended by 51 delegates and representatives from the Negro Welfare Association, the India Swaraj League, the League Against Imperialism, the Cypriot Club and the League of Coloured Peoples, denounced the Shipping Assistance Act, reminding its audience of black people's service in the war. At the Fifth Indian Political Convention organised by the India Swaraj League in July 1936 and attended, among others, by George Padmore and Rowland Sawyer, the conference denounced the 'insidious colour discrimination', and the 1935 Shipping Assistance Act. A year earlier, in May 1935, in South Shields, the Coloured National Mutual Social Club – membership drawn from West Africans, West Indians, Indians and Malays – had heard an emotional Saklatvala speak out against the discriminatory treatment in the Shipping Assistance Act.[97] The CSA remained active through the 1930s, Alley, its secretary, featuring in several Scotland Yard Reports. In 1937, for instance, he was recorded as one of the marshals at a May Day rally, and as having published a circular in English and 'the vernacular' urging the 'many coloured' workers in London to join the rally, 'the day of the working people … for their rights'. In July 1939, Alley planned an Indian Workers' Conference at the United Ladies Tailors' Union Hall in Whitechapel, to be addressed by R.S. Nimbkar, the general secretary of the Textile Workers' Union in Bombay and Aftab Ali, president of the All-India Seamen's Federation (AISF), then in London for the International Labour Conference in Geneva. At this two-day conference, open to Indians and non-Indians, a substantial amount of time, a day and half, was set aside to discuss the problems of Indian seamen in Britain.[98]

In India, too, strong opposition was voiced against the Shipping Assistance Act by the trade unions and in the Legislative Assembly. Despite assurances that the government did not support racial discrimination, feelings ran high. In a bitter denunciation of a subsidy that imposed a principle of racial discrimination between Indian and white British subjects, Jamnadas Mehta warned of retaliatory measures against whites employed in India in engineering, railways and telegraphs.[99]

Who had ordered the differential treatment between white British
and black British seamen? Mohamed Star [sic] of South Shields, barred
from employment, informed the India Office: 'They, at the Shipping
Offices, meaning Union Office, Shipping Federation, the Board of
Trade, give us to understand that no Aliens, no British Protected Indian
seamen, or even British Indian seamen, can sign on a ship.' The claim
that there was a definite policy of racial exclusion was not without
foundation. Even a debate in Parliament hinted at its existence.
Reminding the President of the Board of Trade of the 'great uneasiness
and resentment' among British seamen who saw 'their jobs' being taken
by 'foreigners and coloured seamen', Mr Nicolson pressed for action. In
reply, Runciman, explaining that 'some steps' had already been taken,
indicated that more would come to increase employment of 'British
seamen', to the 'exclusion of others'.[100] Further confirmation was
provided by J. Henson, Chairman of the seamen's section of the
International Transport Worker's Federation (ITWF) at his meeting with
F.J. Adams, the India High Commissioner. According to him, the
Shipping Federation, having learnt from the Board of Trade of the
Subsidy Committee's recommendation to employ 'British subjects', had
issued a confidential circular laying down the order in which men were
to be taken on. First on the list came 'English, Scotch, Welsh and
Northern Irish', followed by seamen from the Irish Free State. In third
place were 'British subjects from other parts of the Empire' and lastly,
'Aliens'. Henson, who had had sight of the circular, also revealed that
there had been 'something about the BPP', but he could not remember
what.[101] Given that Vernon Thomson, one-time Chairman of the Tramp
Ship-Owners' Committee of the Chamber of Shipping, a leading
negotiator for the subsidy, who leaned towards the view that only
'United Kingdom seamen' should be allowed on ships in receipt of the
subsidy, was now the Chairman of Tramp Shipping Subsidy Committee,
it is not surprising that the Shipping Federation had been influenced to
recommend the order of employment.[102]

Faced with letters of protest and evidence of discrimination against
Indians, the India Office asked for clarification from the Board of Trade.
Reiterating official statements that the subsidy rule imposed no
discrimination between black and white British subjects, the Board of
Trade nonetheless admitted that the selection of the crew was a matter
for the owners. As for the BPP from the Indian States (and elsewhere),
the question, in the Board's view, was 'obviously a troublesome one'.
After further representations, in July 1935, the Subsidy Committee,
sticking to its position that priority was to be given to British seamen
offered a concession: provided no British seamen were available, then

and only then, 'natives' of Protectorates living in the UK could be employed on ships qualifying for subsidy.[103] But such a concession did not remove discrimination against the BPP. It merely strengthened the hierarchy between British subjects and the BPP in respect of employment on certain classes of British ships. The irony of the situation was not lost on the India Office: 'It means apparently that a subject of the Indian State ... will be liable to be refused a job which apart from the subsidy rules he would have obtained.'[104]

The India Office was deeply perturbed by the implications of this. In redoubling their efforts, the India Office (and the Colonial Office) argued that Protectorate citizens were British nationals in the 'widest sense of the term'. They pointed to their long tradition of employment in British shipping, their record of service in the Indian Army and in the Mercantile Marine during the war, noting that many had been domiciled in Britain for many years and that they rightly felt a sense of injustice. But, most importantly, the India Office played its imperial card. Explaining that discrimination against Indian State Subjects was certain to rebound and bring protest from the Indian Princes, they wrote: 'there will be difficulty in dealing with such protests, since it is our practice to secure Indian State Subjects the same benefits as British Subjects in Commercial Treaties.... It is a bad policy to introduce economic discrimination against Indian States if it can be avoided.' Furthermore, such prohibition on the employment of BPP was bound to react 'unfavourably' on shipping; as lascar gangs on Asiatic Articles consisted partly of British subjects and partly of BPP, it was not 'practicable' for the employer to take one and not the other.[105]

In March 1936, discrimination was finally removed, the BPP being accepted on the same footing as all other British citizens for employment on ships in receipt of the subsidy.[106] Victory was achieved. Intervention by the India Office (and the Colonial Office) had succeeded in moderating a racially discriminatory practice. However, in this instance, their arguments, powerful though they were, may not have been the deciding force. Evidence suggests that other factors may have influenced the Tramp Shipping Subsidy Committee. As early as June 1935, for instance, the NSFU was beginning to have 'some misgivings' about the 'effects of too stringent' an application of the principle of an 'all-British crew' on subsidised vessels. They accepted that 'coloured seamen', including the BPP had 'some claims to employment' on British shipping. There were signs that, as shipping picked up, ship-owners found it difficult to keep to the principle of an 'all-British crew'. And the unions, too, were no longer averse to 'a certain proportion of non-British subjects', long domiciled in Britain, being given jobs to relieve their hardship – and presumably to save union funds.[107] Such views would have paved the way to achieving change.

As a postscript on the subsidy payment it may be added that, according to records, in 1936, the owners of vessels employing lascars received £170,000 from the Subsidy Committee. As a condition of subsidy, the 1935 Act stipulated that seamen and officers employed on subsidised shipping had to be paid wages set by the National Maritime Board (NMB), which had been revised upward. But since Lascar Articles were signed in India, they were not entitled to wages under the NMB rates. However, as employment of lascars on British shipping was deemed to be a 'long-standing' tradition, it was argued that Lascar Agreements did not 'afford any grounds' for withholding subsidy from ship-owners employing lascars. Such a logic meant that ship-owners gained the subsidy, while Indians, unlike other British seamen, lost out, remaining at the bottom of the hierarchy of wages. When the British Shipping (Assistance) Bill 1939 re-introduced subsidies, lascars employed 'in accordance with established practice' and paid 'customary rates' under Lascar Agreements, once again missed out on the NMB wages – but ship-owners received their subsidy.[108]

PASSPORT CONTROL

Indian seamen in Britain, however, were not the only British citizens to be discriminated against or to see their rights eroded after the First World War. Beginning in the 1920s, Indians, particularly from the Punjab, began to come to Britain in search of employment. They arrived with regular passports and usually turned to peddling as a means of earning a living, some returning to India after a few years, others choosing to settle permanently. As itinerant traders, they travelled around the country. The police reported 'little colonies' in Chatham and London, while other sources mentioned Indian pedlars living in Glasgow. Evidence suggests that, to control immigration to Britain of these 'agricultural and labouring classes', after discussion at ministerial level in Britain, steps to restrict the issue of passports were taken in India in April 1930 and amended in September 1931.[109] Since these instructions applied to non-seamen, it is worth quoting the relevant paragraph in full:

> Indian British subjects of a low standard of education and limited means, who wish to travel to the United Kingdom in search of employment or to engage in petty trade, should not be granted passports, or an endorsement on a passport, valid for the United

Kingdom, unless they can produce evidence that they have a definite offer of employment or that they are unlikely to fall into a state of destitution in the event of their being unsuccessful in obtaining employment.

Indian British subjects of 'good character and established position', however, were not affected: they remained eligible for 'ordinary British passports of full validity … bearing the usual endorsement for the British Empire'.[110] How was 'low standard of education' defined? Initially, according to the circular issued in 1930, literacy was measured by the applicant's ability to 'understand and complete unaided' a passport application form in English. However, in 1931, the instructions were revised to cover the applicant's employability in Britain and 'ability' to speak English.[111]

Why the restriction? Passport control may have been introduced in response to several factors, the 'woman question' undoubtedly being one. Police also complained to the Home Office of the difficulty of keeping track of pedlars, some described as 'doubtful seamen'. Control over Indians in Britain was an important plank in imperial policy, as was seen in connection with Indian students and soldiers. Similarly, an important argument against sending Indian cadets to Sandhurst was stated to be: 'control over Indian boys in this country is more difficult than it is in India'.[112] Police allegations, without much evidence, that pedlars were 'rampant propagandists … speaking for India' at meetings and by 'remarks and innuendoes' on the doorstep around the country as they hawked their wares, may have been a contributory factor. Given the upsurge of the anti-colonial movement in India under Gandhi and the campaigns in Britain of the several organisations such as the India League, the Indian Workers' Association and the Indian Freedom League, keeping a check on itinerant traders would have been an important consideration in controlling their settlement. The fact that police filed regular reports on pedlars and seamen in their districts would confirm this assumption.[113]

Thus, once again, British nationality and rights under citizenship were redefined to exclude yet another group from its privileges. Seamen were eligible for Documents of Nationality and Identity only; others denied passports included individuals who were placed on 'stop lists' for periods of time and for reasons described as 'special' – that is, political.[114] In 1931, to close the 'open door', passport controls were widened to embrace another category of 'undesirables' – the working class from rural backgrounds. This foreshadows steps taken in the 1950s and 1960s.

How far the 1931 restriction on passports succeeded in controlling immigration of Indians of 'low standard of education and limited means' is difficult to judge. Evidence suggests that determined men by-passed regulations by working as 'one-voyage' seamen. This is seen from the fact that the Home Office embargoed issue of the Special Certificate of Nationality on the grounds that they were not 'genuine' seamen, and instructed instead that they be provided with an 'emergency certificate' to return home as provided under the 1931 circular. Some men may also have come to take up a 'definite offer of employment' from compatriots who had set up successfully in business. Others may have even obtained passports in India by different means. In 1939, the Hunter Inquiry reported that a number of 'semi-legal passport traders' in large ports in India provided passports at 'exorbitant charges' to their customers, described as 'lower classes ... generally illiterate'. The fact that Hunter, concerned at the growth of the Indian working-class population in London and what he described as the 'problem of the half-caste child', recommended that they should be prohibited from settling in Britain 'without special permission', similar to the 'embargo' introduced in the 'colonies' (white Dominions), suggests that determined men by-passed regulation to re-claim their citizenship rights somehow.[115]

Despite the fine rhetoric of equality pledged by Queen Victoria in 1858 and renewed by every successive monarch, for Indian imperial British citizens, equality remained illusory.

8

Lascar Activism in Britain, 1920–45

In 1919, at the end of the First World War, Indian seamen comprised 20 per cent of the British maritime labour force. Ten years later, the percentage stood at 23.5, rising to 26 per cent in 1938, a total of 50,700.[1] But despite being indispensable to British trade in a global economy, their conditions of employment, enshrined in the 1923 Indian Merchant Shipping Act, which replaced the 1823 Act, and its various amendments, lagged far behind conditions of labour for British seamen. In fact, while maritime labour conditions for sailors in Britain, Europe and the USA improved steadily (the founding of the International Labour Organisation (ILO) in 1919 was one important factor in raising standards) there were no comparable gains for Indian seamen employed in British shipping. This chapter considers how Indian activists in Britain tried to organise and unionise seamen to campaign for their rights, and how seamen themselves attempted to force a change in their conditions of employment.

Why did Indian seamen's labour conditions remain so impervious to change? One major reason was the power and opposition of the Shipping Federation, formed in 1890, and described by Broeze as the 'most aggressive and unscrupulous of all employers' organisations'. Together with the equally powerful Employers' Association of the Port of Liverpool, the Federation wielded an enormous influence in the City and in government.[2] The fact that British shipping dominated the Indian overseas carrying trade, controlling 64.2 per cent (by comparison the Indian share was a mere 1.15 per cent, the rest, 34.55 per cent, being in the hands of other European powers), and was the largest employer of Indian seamen (of the 59,000 Indian seamen in employment in 1935, a staggering 42,000 worked on British ships) gave it a huge advantage. And the Federation used its power to manipulate both the British and Indian circumstances in its own favour. Nothing illustrates this more aptly than the negotiations in 1938 over the proposals to regulate lascar hours as recommended by the 1936 Convention of the International Labour Conference.[3] It was common knowledge that Indian seamen worked considerably longer than European seamen. But ship-owners did not favour fixed hours and cash payments for their overtime on ships and on shore in Britain. The Board of Trade, therefore, decided on a strategy of counter-concession: tying reform of lascar hours to relaxing latitude limits for which ship-owners had long lobbied the government of India, allowing them to employ Indians beyond 38° N in the Atlantic, a move hitherto opposed by the Board of Trade, ostensibly 'to protect' their health, but mainly for fear of a 'very strong' challenge from the NUS opposed to any modification that would displace white seamen. Such a strategy, the Board hoped, would placate the unions, avoid political repercussions and keep the 'troublesome matter' of lascar employment conditions from being raised in Parliament.[4] But no such trade-off took place. Why? The Federation, using the Royal Seamen's Pension Fund (originally the 'Lascar Fund') as its weapon, succeeded in neutralising the NUS. Under the 1911 National Insurance Act, ship-owners contributed two pence (2d) a week for every lascar employed. But since non-domiciled seamen were not entitled to pension benefits, 'lascar money' was used for white seamen's pensions. Since around four-fifths of all non-resident seamen were Indians, their importance to the Fund's healthy balance should not be underestimated. Knowing the union's concern for their pensions, the Federation quietly let 'Mr Spence' understand that 'any action taken by, or on behalf of the NUS which might lead to the diminution in the number of Lascars employed, would adversely affect the Fund ... It was the case of "no Lascars no Pensions".'[5] In May 1938, the government of India lifted latitude limits for an experimental period of three years. As for the measure to regulate lascar hours, ship-owners put forward their own proposals. Meant to be seen as an 'improvement', the scheme was so complex that even the Board of Trade considered it would need careful handling, while the Federation itself predicted protracted negotiations and delays in India. Nothing further was heard: lascar hours remained unregulated and overtime unremunerated. Further, the oft-repeated argument that any legislation that pushed up costs would be detrimental to jobs, the shipping industry and the British economy, was powerful enough to stall any reforms.[6]

The Federation could also easily counter the 'cheap lascar labour' charge by recourse to the accepted notions of their capabilities based on the mythology of racial stereotypes, arguing that their lower wages were counterbalanced by heavier manning and the 'special conditions' attached to their employment. One ship-owner, described as 'experienced' in carrying both 'native' and European crew, even accounted £1 per month per head repatriation cost for lascars! Claims that Indian seamen were not employed for 'reasons of economy', but necessity, were known to be spurious, as the comment by a civil servant, 'what is the reason then for employing them in the North Atlantic?' demonstrates. Some authorities estimated a saving of £45 per month in wages, even after increasing crews by 20. But, in the last analysis, the myth that lascars ultimately cost more had to be maintained. Any public acknowledgement by ship-owners and the government of race discrimination or exploitation of black labour would have meant a complete reversal of the Federation's policy, leaving ship-owners guilty of the charge of undercutting, with serious repercussions, both in Britain and in India.[7]

Another obstacle was the lack of will at the India Office, the custodians of Indian interests in Britain. As a result, lascar accommodation and welfare provision in ports, a responsibility of ship-owners, remained grossly neglected. Kept on board ship in cramped accommodation (72 cu. ft space for lascars compared to 120 cu. ft for white British seamen), they were boarded in inferior lodgings when necessary, and during transfers from port to port. A 1922 inspector's report described their accommodation as the 'exceedingly poor class' of common lodging-houses and a 'public scandal ... actuated by no other motive than making a profit'. In Parliament, Lord Winterton admitted that there was 'room for considerable improvement'. Some claimed that shipping agents deliberately arranged to house lascars in common lodging-houses in Stepney and Poplar and at Carrington House in New Cross, south London, because these establishments were cheaper than the Strangers' Home in Limehouse. An inspection revealed that lascars had to guard their luggage stored in the kitchen, 'taking their rest on the boxes', a practice contrary to by-laws. Lacking privacy, it was said men had been seen praying looked on by a 'jeering crowd of Britishers'. The P&O 'go-down' (warehouse) in Albert Docks, consisting of an 'old hulk' and described as an 'abomination and a by-word in the Dock neighbourhood for filth and unsuitability' for housing human beings, lacked sufficient cubicle space, was badly heated and possessed no proper cooking facilities.[8]

Stirred by questions in Parliament, in February 1923 the India Office called a conference to discuss possible legislation and establish standards of accommodation.[9] However genuine their concern for Indian seamen's cultural and religious welfare, from the discussions it is evident that the most important priority, for both the state and the ship-owners, remained social control. As Captain T.G. Segrave (India Office) explained: common lodging-houses were unsuitable because their clientele was 'mixed ... and it is not desirable to mix Europeans and Asiatics'. Why? First, the authorities feared damaging publicity in India should a 'fracas' between black and white occur. Second, in the words of Captain Brett (Shipping Federation), 'the more they mix with the European, the more ambitious they become to obtain European wages'. Further, it was alleged that touts lured men to common lodging-houses with promises of European wages, encouraging desertions. The Revd George Dempster (BFSS), emphasised that once a lascar had deserted, he was 'no longer a lascar', as he 'trafficked' as a 'British seaman'.[10] The conference, therefore, recommended the Strangers' Home in London and the Asiatic Home in Queen's Dock, Glasgow as approved lodgings for lascars, and notices drawing attention to these 'recognised Homes' were to be posted in shipping offices in India and in London. The recommendation that common lodging-houses send regular returns of all Indian seamen on their premises to the High Commission, within 24 hours of their arrival, further illustrates that, in the post-1918 context, the state's priority was control. Further, the only action over the P&O 'go-down' was a private letter, 'in the interest of the Company's good name', to Lord Inchcape to 'see what steps are feasible to improve the state of affairs'. Without legislation, even the voluntary arrangements for 'approved' accommodation lapsed.[11] In 1937, when the Strangers' Home closed down because of a crisis in funding, the amenities provided by the Home disappeared. Cramped on board ships, lascars continued to live in miserable surrounding in Britain – in contravention of the ILO recommendations.[12]

The government of India, responsible for policy, also failed them. Delhi, like London, recognised only too well the value of a strong and powerful merchant fleet. Examples of collusion with the shipping industry are legion. In May 1934, for instance, following an outbreak of beri-beri, the medical officer, commenting on their 'ill-balanced and inadequate' diet, recommended an increase in the ration of condensed tinned milk from 4 ounces to a third of a pound per man per week, in line with the 1906 British Merchant Shipping Act. But the government of India refused to implement it for no other reason than the 'extra cost' to the ship-owners, which, according to the Board of Trade, amounted to no more than 'half a pence' (½d) per man per week. Three years and much correspondence later, in June 1937, India finally agreed, possibly because, in view of the trifling cost, the P&O had adopted the 'more generous ration'.[13] The government of India's procrastination is nowhere more evident than in reforming the system of labour recruitment, which left seamen at the mercy of corrupt brokers and *ghat serangs*. The Clow Committee, appointed in 1921, in the wake of the government's non-ratification of the 1920 ILO Convention on Placement of Seamen, was so outspoken in its criticism of shipping companies and their agents, and so radical in its proposals, that the first three paragraphs of the report, dealing with the current abuses, were suppressed. According to Broeze, one reason for this might have been the Committee's public condemnation of Lord Inchcape's British India Steam Navigation (BISN), which was asked to dismiss its *ghat serangs* and *ghat butlers*. The Clow Committee, urging immediate adoption of the ILO Convention, recommended setting up a public employment bureau at Calcutta and Bombay. But, despite the fact that seamen's unions were willing to cooperate, the government shelved the report. And while the ILO Convention was ratified by countries as diverse as Germany, Holland, Italy, Spain, Norway, Sweden, Japan and Finland, the government of India, in the words of Maulvi Abdul Chaudhury, in the Legislative Assembly debate in 1927, had 'for the past seven years been incubating upon it'.[14] The 1931 Royal Commission on Labour found bribery to be as rampant as ever. Similarly, draft conventions and recommendations adopted variously at Maritime Sessions of the International Labour Conference on pensions, workers' compensation and sickness benefit, remained largely unratified. Expressing 'full sympathy' with the objectives of the Convention, the government nonetheless adopted a position of neutrality or vetoed recommendations either as being impracticable, or because India was 'not ready', or because they remained 'under consideration'. Is it any wonder then that Dinker Desai, joint secretary of the Bombay Seamen's Union (BSU), concluded that the policy of the government of India had been not to do 'anything which would not meet with the approval of British Shipping Companies'.[15]

Given such conditions the only remedy was to organise. But the birth of trade unionism in India was a slow process. Various factors contributed to this, not least being the fact that it was only in 1926 that trade unions were legalised, allowing registered unions to act collectively. In addition, seamen were drawn from two major centres, Bombay and Calcutta, with the result that Indian unions were bedevilled by rivalries and splits, making the emergence of a united national organisation difficult. Poverty, illiteracy and insecurity of employment compounded the problem. Nonetheless, seamen's unions, which began to emerge after the war, successfully struck at Calcutta (1919) and Bombay (1920) to gain a 35–50 per cent wage rise, the only rise to be conceded by the ship-owners before the Second World War, bringing the Calcutta rate to Rs 22–5, and Rs 26 for seamen at Bombay (an average of around 35 shillings or £1. 17s. 6d. a month). By 1937, the four major unions at Calcutta (the Indian Seamen's Union (ISU), Indian Quartermasters' Union, Bengal Mariners' Union and the Seamen's Welfare League of India) and the Bombay-based National Seamen's Union of India (NSUI), together with the Karachi Seamen's Union, had combined to form the All-India Seamen's Federation (AISF) with its headquarters at Calcutta. Aftab Ali, a one-time seaman himself and the general secretary of the ISU, was its president. By 1939, the only union remaining aloof from the AISF, the BSU, had also joined. When war began in September 1939, the AISF was in a stronger position: membership of individual unions was healthy, the NSUI having 20,000 members and the ISU, 23,494. But ship-owners refused to recognise the AISF and remained openly hostile to the unions. Cases of intimidation of activists and even bribery by agents to deter strikers or buy off union leaders were not unknown.[16]

Life for the Indian seamen in the economically difficult climate following the First World War was grim. There was a large surplus of labour, a result of over-recruitment during the war, leaving men more than ever at the mercy of brokers. Poverty, indebtedness and low wages forced some to jump ship in British or foreign ports, hoping to earn higher wages on British articles to pay off debts and help families. But this was no easy matter. Lascar Articles bound them in a form of indenture, which was tantamount to 'a short term of enlistment', with penalties of a 'deserter': forfeiture of all or part of their wages, imprisonment up to 12 weeks, followed by repatriation. Is it any wonder then that a 'deserter' attempted to change his name, temporarily, in order to avoid imprisonment?[17]

UNIONISATION IN BRITAIN, 1920s–1940s

Attempts to unionise Indian seamen in Britain were first begun by the Workers' Welfare League of India (WWLI), a labour organisation formed in 1916 by Saklatvala. The first mention comes in a letter, dated November 1922, from Saklatvala to H. Pall in Berlin, of a committee of eight set up 'to investigate the needs of lascars and to organise them'. By December 1922, the Lascars' Welfare League (LWL) was in being and an 'active committee' of six had been formed to visit boarding houses to collect statistics on their conditions of labour. By February 1923, the 'extremist' members of the LWL were said to have formed the Indian Seamen's Association (ISA). Saklatvala was its president. In April 1923, the ISA changed its name to the International Oriental Seafarer's Union (IOSU), also known as the Union of Eastern Seamen. Whether the IOSU affiliated to the Red International of Labour Unions (RILU), or was its 'Oriental Branch', or was funded by it, is not clear. British intelligence reports conflict. Information on the activities of the IOSU is limited. Intelligence reports indicate that it was handicapped by lack of funds. There were plans to raise funds from resident Indians, to establish branches in India and enlist the help of Sir Ali Iman and Sir T.B. Sapru, to put pressure on the government to improve conditions of lascar lodging-houses. Reports also admit that the Communists did not succeed in influencing seamen.[18]

Did the IOSU achieve any result? There is little evidence to suggest that it succeeded in recruiting members, or raising consciousness. Times were hard and shipping slack. By 1924, surveillance reports suggest that, on Bukharin's orders, control of the Union of Eastern Seamen was to be transferred to 'IKKI'.[19] In early 1925 there are references to the Indian Seamen's Union (ISU) with Saklatvala as president, Clemens Palme Dutt coordinator of its activities, and N.J. Upadhyaya its organising secretary.

NATHALAL JAGJIVAN UPADHYAYA AND THE ISU

Upadhyaya (known as Paddy), activist and secretary-organiser of the ISU, was born in 1895 to a poor Gujarati Brahmin family. A teacher and a journalist on a Gujarati newspaper, he had been employed at the Bombay Stock Exchange before coming to England in October 1922. He first came to notice in December 1924, when Scotland Yard intercepted a letter to Saklatvala from Adela Knight, at whose house in Abbey Wood, south London, he was a lodger. Said to have been influenced by Knight, and described as 'an ardent communist' and 'promising specimen of younger workers', he addressed meetings from Communist Party platforms in Scotland and locally at Woolwich.[20]

But it was as the ISU secretary-organiser that Upadhyaya was most energetic. He visited London docks, addressed meetings, urging lascars to form a union 'like their capitalist employers'. He distributed literature, such as 'To all Lovers of Freedom' and 'What Will Be the Benefits of the Union?', translated into several Indian languages by Abdur Rahim Dard, the Imam at the Ahmadiya Mosque in Southfields (Putney). His own circular, 'The Indian Seamen's Union: Our Grievances and How to Remedy Them', summed up simply and succinctly their 'many injustices'. Upadhyaya demanded an end to race discrimination, compensation by law rather than charity and a Provident Fund, like the Railway Provident Fund, for retired seamen.[21]

By October 1925 the ISU executive of nine, with three lascars, three members from the National Minority Movement (NMM), and another three from the Indian Bureau, including Upadhyaya, had been formed. By then, weekly meetings, attended by 50–60 Indian seamen, were held at the London Dock gates. Following a public meeting in September at Poplar Town Hall, 20 joined the ISU. By August 1926, when its office, two rooms in a basement, was opened at 88 East India Dock Road, membership was estimated at 310, and Upadhyaya prepared the first issue of the *Seamen's Bulletin*, in Urdu and Bengali. By the time of the first social evening in November 1926, membership had reached 400. The following year, 1927, saw Upadhyaya extend his activities to Liverpool, Glasgow and Cardiff. In Liverpool, reports indicate that he had attempted to get on board a troopship and mustered 'a large number of coloured sailors' to participate in May Day celebrations. On May Day, at a mass protest meeting in Cleveland Square, he denounced police harassment, and Indians having to register under the 1925 Coloured Aliens Seamen's Order. It was also reported that Upadhyaya was visiting lascars in lodging-houses, 'stirring them up' to strike for better conditions, recruiting 200 to the ISU. Police claimed that, when questioned 'discreetly', Indian seamen revealed that plans were afoot for a strike in Britain for equal rates of pay. This was a clever strategy: a strike in Britain was likely to paralyse shipping, as lascars could not be replaced easily.[22]

But organising seamen was an uphill task. In July 1925, accused of trespassing on private property, the port police 'moved on' his meeting. One Sunday, he was 'forcibly ejected' from the Strangers' Home and, by December 1926, barred altogether. Early in 1928, while addressing seamen at Tilbury docks, he was thrown out for not having a dock permit. At another time, police interrogated him as he left the CPGB (Communist Party of Great Britain) headquarters.[23] In Parliament, Sir Frederick Hall, MP, accusing Upadhyaya of 'fomenting revolutionary plots among coolie seamen' and behaving in an 'undesirable manner', asked the Home Secretary whether Upadhyaya would be allowed to remain in Britain. He was assured that Upadhyaya's activities were known, and action was under consideration. Upadhyaya did not let such accusations under parliamentary immunity go unchallenged, however. Demanding that Sir Frederick either withdraw the charge or substantiate it, he informed the MP that he was engaged in a legitimate trade union activity. In a long letter highlighting lascar hardships, he drew attention to the fact that in Britain they paid British prices but did not earn British wages. But the most pitiful was the case for compensation by the family of a lascar killed in mid-ocean three years previously, and whose claim for a meagre Rs100 (£6.60) remained unrecognised by the company.[24]

Despite setbacks, Upadhyaya struggled on. He frequented docks, posing as a missionary, carrying 'Communist leaflets' concealed in religious tracts. ISU branches were opened in Cardiff and Glasgow and, by July 1927, membership was said to have reached 1,500: 900 in London, 400 in Liverpool and the rest in Glasgow, Cardiff and elsewhere. But by May 1928, it had dropped to 1,400, rising again, reportedly, to an all-time high of 6,000, three years later, in 1930, and including many Indian workers. By then the ISU office had moved to 1A Drew Road, Silvertown, E 16. 'Reliable' contacts had reportedly been established at Calcutta, Chittagong, Bombay, Karachi, Lahore, Peshawar, Madras and Colombo, and proscribed literature smuggled 'without a hitch'. A flag, with the inscription, 'The Workers of India Demand Complete Independence' was also designed.[25]

How effective was Upadhyaya? Evaluation of his work is problematic. Much of the evidence is contained in surveillance reports gathered from informants and in summaries compiled by the Political Intelligence Department. It is suggested that he succeeded in helping individuals: an injured cook refused permission to leave his ship was transferred after Upadhyaya had intervened.[26] Evidence also suggests he had a rapport with seamen. The fact that port police dispersed his meetings, and he was barred from the Docks and the Strangers' Home, suggests that he was perceived to be successful in his attempts to organise seamen. The delay, which several companies complained of in Liverpool, caused by Indian engine-room crew refusing to set sail by bringing their grievance at the 'last minute', shows Upadhyaya's influence.[27] There is indirect evidence, which by inference, hints at his effectiveness. He worried the India Office enough to be labelled 'an agitator and a nuisance', and in April 1925 to be put on the passport 'stop list'. Classified as 'distinctly a dangerous man', the India Office even instructed the Passport Office, in 1926, to cancel his endorsement for Europe, though this did not prevent Upadhyaya secretly travelling to Paris in October 1926 for a meeting with Roy, Mohamed Ali [Sepassi] and Clemens Palme Dutt.[28] The fact that dossiers were compiled on him shows that his activities were certainly perceived to be a threat. Even his deportation was seriously entertained, seen from the careful political calculations in lengthy correspondence between the various branches of the India Office and the government of India. Although not classed a leader of the same calibre as Dutt, Upadhyaya's deportation was considered desirable because as 'a very useful subordinate' and 'not an unimportant figure' in the 'M.N. Roy, C.P. Dutt and Sepassi organisation', it was concluded that he was likely to be 'less effective' in India than in Britain. He only escaped deportation because of the politics of the Princely States *vis à vis* the Raj. If Upadhyaya, from Nawanagar, and a BPP, was deported as 'an alien', it was feared that the 'Chiefs' might use this as an argument in support of their claim to be 'independent sovereigns'. But he remained under surveillance.[29]

In the last analysis, given Upadhyaya's own sympathies and the context of the time – fear of Communism as an ideology and the upsurge of nationalism in India – it could be argued that his achievements were exaggerated: official concern was not matched by results. Membership of the ISU remained unstable and tiny in relation to the number of Indians arriving in Britain. At a time of over-supply and under-employment, their reluctance to unionise is understandable. Lascar illiteracy and lack of industrial consciousness compounded Upadhyaya's difficulties: he lamented their reluctance to exert themselves in their own interests and to strike. Both he and Saklatvala saw the difficulty of organising Indians independently of other unions in Britain. Their efforts in India met with little success. Finance was a problem. Attempts to raise funds by interesting wealthy Indians like F.J. Bhumgara, an oriental curio merchant, were unsuccessful. There were never enough workers, despite help from several Indians and Britons. And Upadhyaya could not be in several places at once. The CPGB may have had a hand in setting up the ISU, but, beyond urging the seamen's section of the NMM to 'give much greater attention' to Upadhyaya's work and 'assist him in developing the union', there is no evidence of much practical help.[30] The aims of the ISU remained unrealised. Upadhyaya's struggles provide a measure of the difficulties involved. More than a decade would elapse before lascars would use their industrial muscle for change.[31]

LASCAR MILITANCY IN WAR

Between the end of the First World War and the start of the Second World War on 3 September 1939, little had changed. While white seamen in Britain earned £9. 12s. 6d. a month, lascars' wages averaged only £1. 17s. 6d. (35 shillings). The war transformed the situation. After decades of racial discrimination, facing the same risks in war, Indian seamen in Britain refused to sail without a wage increase, basic provisions and security for their families. Within weeks, strikes had spread from London, Glasgow, Liverpool and Southampton to countries as far apart as South Africa, Australia and Burma. By December 1939, hundreds of Indian seamen were in prison in Britain and elsewhere. Their compliance could no longer be taken for granted. Scholars today are beginning to overcome the tendency to regard the Second World War as a 'People's War'. They have shown that the picture of a harmonious Britain with all social classes united in the face of the common enemy to be nothing more than war-time propaganda and a myth.[32] Strikes and desertions by imperial seamen – Africans, Chinese and Indians – can be read in the same context. Ironically, the most 'docile' of the imperial maritime labour force, the Indian seamen, were the first to grasp their opportunity to use their indispensable labour power as a bargaining counter to win equal rights.

The speed with which Indian seamen were able to organise themselves caught the government by surprise. But 'trouble' was not unexpected. As war threatened, they had been induced to sign contracts with promises that they, too, would benefit from any bonuses or compensation scheme introduced in Britain. Indeed, to forestall difficulties in recruitment, on 30 August 1939, just four days before war was declared, a telegram announcing a 'war bonus' of 50 per cent, agreed by 11 major shipping lines, including the P&O, BI, Ellerman, Brocklebank, Clan, Harrison and Anchor, had been rushed to India and endorsed in new contracts.[33] But news of the bonus and its possible effect on the wage levels of white seamen alarmed the Cabinet. An internal Board of Trade minute cautioned: 'It was not the government's business to attempt to stop an increase of lascar wages or any other wages that might perhaps be low ... Government's policy was to stabilise prices.' Nonetheless, the Board intervened and a second cable was rushed to India cancelling the offer. This was bound to further inflame militancy. As Indian seamen in Calcutta refused to sail without the new terms, and the seamen's unions met the Minister of Labour, it was reported that a 'mass meeting' was called by the ISU, to ask all unions to unite to demand a 75 per cent war bonus. The Shipping Master at Calcutta, warning that promises must be honoured as 'any breach of faith at the present stage' would be disastrous, urged the necessity of offering 'some inducement' to get Indians to sign for foreign voyages. By 6 September difficulties were so serious that the government of India cabled: 'urgent consideration essential'.[34]

Meanwhile in Britain, on 1 September 1939, the same date as the Board of Trade intervened to stop the promised bonus, the Clan Line agreed to a wage rise of 100 per cent to the striking Indian crew of the *Clan Macallister,* requisitioned by the government. This prompted the crew of another government-chartered ship, the P&O *Strathaird,* to demand a similar rise. Requiring ships to sail on time, the Board of Trade instructed ship-owners that crew must be obtained even if it meant 'doubling' wages, while at the same time insisting that 'the extra payment' was not to be described in their agreements as a 'war bonus' or 'bonus for government service', thus, construing it as 'blackmail or bribe'. The government was not alone in giving the rise such a twist. The owner of the Clan Line, Lord Cayzer, 'just down to Glasgow from my shooting season in the north', wrote that 'to give lascar labour what it wants' would be 'the same' as giving in to 'Hitler's demands'. Accusing Indian seamen of 'really only' wanting money, he claimed that their action was nothing but *'profiteering of unskilled British lascar labour of the worst sort'* (italics in the original). Clan Line owners would later claim that early rises had only been given 'under duress'.[35] Such emotive rhetoric aside, in the early anxious days, in a frenzy of meetings, the government and the industry cast around for ways of cowing lascars. The Shipping Federation suggested the government of India use 'emergency powers' to compel them to 'engage at current lascar rates'. There were even hints of a 'possible use of force'. However, the authorities knew that prosecutions would fail. Further, in the politically explosive situation in India (feelings had already been incensed at Viceroy Lord Linlithgow's declaration of war on behalf of the peoples of India without consulting Indian political leaders) force 'might have awkward repercussions'. Some owners even tried to frighten lascars: the crew of the *Birchbark* was given 'until 9 a.m. tomorrow' to sign at 'ordinary rates', or face being replaced with white seamen. Lord Cayzer, to 'put the wind up' other Clan Line ships in Glasgow, went so far as to threaten sending a ship from Glasgow to Liverpool manned by officers and apprentices, 'and leave the crew ashore, who will be left on the quay and left to the authorities as deserters'.[36] But white sailors were not available and strikes escalated.

Three days into the war, by 6 September 1939, as many as eight ships were on strike, Indian seamen demanding, in some cases, a 200 per cent wage rise, including essential provisions like soap, warm clothing and bedding, which suggests that ship-owners neglected to honour their contractual obligations. As the government was not in a position to risk any delay to the sailing of requisitioned ships, the Board of Trade was forced into negotiations, enlisting the help of the India High Commissioner, Sir Firozkhan Noon, to act as a mediator in order to minimise concessions. In the Board's view, demands for a '100 per cent increase, plus in one case £10 extra for the voyage, plus two new suits, plus a bar of soap', were 'quite unreasonable'.[37] But neither Noon's strategy to persuade lascars to see reason by frightening them with the spectre of high unemployment in India, nor his frantic meetings with their representatives, nor even his rather farcical attempts to prevent two sets of waiting representatives communicating with each other, by putting them in separate rooms in his office, succeeded in budging lascars from demanding their rights. While seamen on the *Clan Morrison* accepted terms, which the Board considered 'rather better', that is, '100 per cent, one suit and three months advance in wages', a different settlement had to be negotiated with the crew of the *Clan Macbrayne*.[38]

Ship-owners, having refused the Board's suggestion that they 'seriously consider' negotiating with Aftab Ali, the AISF president and secretary of the Calcutta ISU, decided not only to bargain separately with each individual ship in Britain, but, on 15 September 1939, announced a mere 25 per cent rise in basic wages.[39] Such a callous attitude was not new. Noting how the Clan Line representative had gone back on the terms agreed in the High Commission's office, an internal Board of Trade memo continued:

> Mr Lall's chief difficulty, however, was the way in which the officers of the *Clan Macbrayne* were treating the Lascar crew. He said that they were extremely impatient with them and that even when he was explaining matters to the crew and was dealing with questions which the crew were quite entitled to put, the officers of the Clan Line wished to stop the proceedings. Mr Lall impressed on me that it was absolutely essential that in these times the officers of vessels carrying Lascar crews should treat the Lascars properly and above all should listen patiently to what Lascars had to say.

Both Noon and Lall predicted that unless Indians could 'rely on decent treatment' there was bound to be 'more and more trouble'.[40]

Given the context of war, broken promises and the rises already won in London, Liverpool and Glasgow, a wage increase of 25 per cent, although backdated to 1 September 1939, seemed derisory. Further, white British seamen received a 'war risk' bonus of £3 a month, on top of their considerably higher basic wage, thus once again demonstrating that a black life was worth less than a white life. Lascars were not alone in seeing the settlement as inadequate. An internal minute recorded that Captain Kippen of the Ellerman line had 'always held' that a 25 per cent rise was 'not enough', and that it would be 'necessary to go as high as 100 per cent'. But the majority of the lines, led by the P&O, instead chose to prosecute lascars as a deterrent, a strategy that backfired, as foreseen by Captain Kippen.[41]

On 17 October 1939, the crew of *SS Oxfordshire*, of the Bibby line, being fitted out as a hospital ship in King George V Dock, struck. The dispute took a tragic turn when the captain, informing the men, 'no work, no food', cut off steam in their quarters and shut up the galleys. One seaman died. But the men stood firm. The strike lasted nine days, ending only when they won a wage increase of 100 per cent and £10 war bonus for the round trip. Within two days of their settlement, on 28 October, 44 lascars on the Clan *Alpine*, which had arrived from South Africa on 20 October, refused to sail to Glasgow without a full settlement of a claim they had negotiated at Cape Town on their voyage to Britain. Forty angry men proceeded to the offices of the Board of Trade to lodge their protest, only leaving the premises when the police were called. The company, however, refused to settle their full claim and instead prosecuted them for 'wilful disobedience of lawful commands'. They were sentenced to two months' imprisonment. Thus, in the words of their solicitor, war had turned a 'normal ... industrial dispute' into a criminal offence.[42]

Indian seamen, hearing of the 100 per cent rise plus £10 bonus given to the crew of SS *Oxfordshire*, began demanding a similar rise, a concession invariably granted in ships requisitioned by the Admiralty, but not in the company-operated ships, who charged them with breach of contract. For instance, on 2 November 1939, the crew of the Anchor line's SS *Britannia* were prosecuted and sentenced to four weeks' imprisonment. On the same date, the crew of SS *Somali*, on arrival at the Port of London, refused duty: 39 were arrested and jailed for one month, with hard labour. On 7 November the owners of the SS *Manela* agreed to give each lascar warm clothing and a 100 per cent increase, including a £10 bonus. On 11 November, the crew of the Ellerman City line *City of Manchester*, about to sail from Tilbury Dock, went ashore, refusing to sail without the rise given other ships; 76 were arrested and sentenced to one month's imprisonment and forfeiture of two days' pay each. Strikes spread to other City lines. On 14 November the crew of *City of Capetown* at Royal Albert Dock went to the offices of the company to demand a £15 war-risk payment as the ship carried ammunition. The company having agreed to a 125 per cent increase in wages, the lascars dropped their demand. At Southampton, on 15 November, 153 members of the crew of the SS *Dorsetshire*, which was being converted to a hospital troop ship, were fined 5 shillings each for refusing duty unless granted the same rise as the hospital ship, *Oxfordshire*.[43]

By mid-November some 391 lascars had been convicted in Britain. But their militancy showed no sign of abating. Trouble was reported on the SS *Mulbera* on 17 November; *City of Agra* on 18 November; *Clan MacNab* on 21 November, SS *Burdwan* on 22 November and SS *Nirpura* on 28 November. Concerned at the propaganda effect, and to prevent information falling into enemy hands, the courts began taking evidence *in camera*, even refusing crew access to their union (AISF) representatives in court. Harsher sentences were combined with an appeal to lascar traditions of loyalty and service. On 17 November, for instance, when 100 members of the crew of the SS *Mulbera* struck for the by now standard demand, 100 per cent plus £10 and warm clothing, the four alleged ring leaders, Fyez Ahmad, Mokoo Mian, Mahamed Jan and Fazik Ebrahim, were sentenced to 12 weeks' imprisonment with hard labour and a fine of six days' pay each. But, appealing to their patriotism, the magistrate informed the 96 lascars that if they agreed to take the ship to sea, the case would be adjourned *sine die*. They refused and were sentenced to eight weeks' imprisonment with hard labour and fined six days' wages. Similarly, 55 crew of the *SS Nirpura*, arrested on 28 November, were told how grateful the British were to them for their 'hazardous work'.[44]

SURAT ALLEY AND THE CAMPAIGN FOR RIGHTS

The strikers received much publicity and sympathy. In India the *Statesman*, the *Jugantar* and the *Advance* supported their cause 'without reserve'.[45] In London, Surat Alley, the secretary of the CSA and the Hindustani Social Club (HSC), and by now the London representative of the AISF, who together with Tahsil Miah, had already reportedly given 'considerable assistance' to the strikers, organised meetings to publicise their grievances and campaigned for their release. At a public meeting on 15 November 1939, in Whitechapel, the audience learnt that, since the outbreak of the war, 150 Indian seamen had lost their lives as a result of enemy action, while 500 were imprisoned in various parts of the empire. And their 'crime'? A claim to 'reasonable wages to cover war risks'. Alley urged 'just treatment' for Indian seamen. At another meeting, on 16 November, lascars pledged their willingness to go to prison if ship-owners refused to agree to their demands. Over 200 leaflets signed by Alley, Miah and M.A. Jalil, from the *SS Somali*, explaining the strikes and appealing for public support, were distributed. Krishna Menon, secretary of the India League, took up their cause with MPs and the British trade union movement. In November, Reginald Sorensen, MP, an ally of Menon, and Thomas Johnston, made strong representations to the ministry on behalf of the imprisoned men.[46]

But at official level and in shipping circles, there was a reluctance to accept lascar activism as an industrial dispute over a long-standing economic grievance. Instead, it was insinuated that the men had been 'got at'. Some saw the hand of Indian political 'agitators', others of 'foreign agents', the Communists, the Germans or the IRA. Others still alleged that Alley and Miah were endeavouring to make every Indian seaman 'break his contract' in order to create 'such a contretemps at the eleventh hour' that the vessel would miss its place in the convoy.[47] But the news of strikes and imprisonment was politically damaging, causing alarm in India. The India Office acted to remove Tahsil Miah. The only offence they could pin on him was desertion. Menon tried his utmost to prevent his deportation, but to no avail. On 8 December 1939, Miah was deported.[48] Ultimately, however, the need for lascar labour, combined with the damaging publicity, forced ship-owners in late November to concede a 25 per cent war-risk bonus on pre-war wages, retrospective from 1 November 1939.[49]

On 1 December 1939, in a cable to Surat Alley, Aftab Ali, advising all seamen to return to work, warned: 'unauthorised stoppage is strictly forbidden'.[50] Given that the November agreement represented no real victory, why did Aftab Ali accept the settlement and call off strikes? It is possible that the agreement, negotiated with the shipping agents through the mediation of H.S. Suhrawardy, the Bengal Minister of Commerce and Labour, was seen by Aftab Ali as 'planting the first seed' of union recognition and a step towards an amicable settlement 'by the same process', of other points in dispute, including recruitment by 'open muster', pending the establishment of a Recruitment Bureau. Ship-owners, however, maintained that the increase was 'simply an act of grace', not a recognition of the AISF.[51] Further, it is possible that, committed to fighting Fascist dictatorship in defence of democracy, Aftab Ali agreed to a modified settlement to do 'our mite' in the war. Already, in October 1939, on his return to India from Europe, he had urged seamen to support the war effort while continuing to seek redress for their grievances. In September 1941, the ISU dis-affiliated from the All-India Trades Union Congress (AITUC). Aftab Ali remained strongly committed to the Allied cause, joining the Royal Indian Navy (RIN), reaching the position of Lieutenant Commander by the end of the war.[52] Indian seamen's unions strongly supported the war: over 59,000 lascars served in the British Mercantile Marine.

Privately, civil servants acknowledged that the 'owners were unwise' in not granting a second increase at 'an earlier date', thus averting much damage. Their priority now was to secure lascar 'good will'. A Ministry of War Transport letter urged, 'in view of our present urgent need' for lascars 'everything possible' must be done.[53] British prisons still held 152 lascars (100 in Liverpool, 49 in Brixton jail and the others in Cardiff). Overtures for their release had been made by Suhrawardy, and the Governor of Bengal. Surat Alley, too, organised an appeal to the Home Secretary. Further, acting on instructions from Aftab Ali, on 2 December 1939, he approached Sir Walter Citrine, the TUC General Secretary, to intervene with the Home Office and the Shipping Federation to get the men released and re-employed, and to secure facilities for Alley to personally recommend to them the acceptance of the agreement negotiated by the AISF. Following Alley's interview at the TUC, on 11 December, Citrine and W.R. Spence, the NUS General Secretary, appealed to the Home Secretary and the Shipping Federation.[54] However, the India Office was anxious to prevent Alley getting 'any credit' which they insisted must go to the shipping companies and Noon. Deft footwork by the state sidelined Alley. On 20 December, the Home Office informed Citrine that all lascars had been released, the decision having been taken 'some little time before' Citrine's letter, and 'in these circumstances no question any longer arises' of Alley visiting the prison. Yet lascars in prisons in the UK (and Australia, Burma and South Africa) were not released until February 1940.[55]

But the state's need for a negotiator remained as 'troubles' were by no means over, further aggravated by the action of the Shipping Federation. Having conceded a war-risk bonus of 25 per cent, owners expected crews to transfer to ships other than those proceeding to India (as under the 1894 Merchant Shipping Act) without the additional 'monetary inducement'. But such transfers being entirely voluntary, lascars refused. Nonetheless, the Federation pressed for a change to the law to make transfers compulsory, to allow for 'disciplinary action', should lascars refuse. The Board of Trade advised ship-owners to settle for a uniform monetary reward and even the government of India, fearing serious repercussions on recruitment, cautioned against changing the law.[56] The state, therefore, recognising an urgent need for 'some channel of negotiation' decided it was 'worthwhile' to use Alley's services, despite their reservations about Alley, rationalising their decision as 'testing [his] good faith' as Aftab Ali's representative.[57]

As a proper union man, regardless of his private views, Alley observed the settlement loyally. On 19 December 1939, he persuaded the crew of *Clan MacNeil* against striking for more favourable terms, urging them to abide by the Calcutta agreement. Similarly, he calmed the unrest on the *Clan MacInness*. He visited ships to reassure crew released from prison, informing them of the AISF settlement. Shipping lines willing to negotiate with him found him 'not unsatisfactory'. Indeed, Stokes of the Clan line informed the Ministry of Shipping that Alley was 'in fact carrying out Aftab Ali's instructions and ... not going beyond them'.[58]

Nonetheless, on the question of recognising the union 'which Aftab Ali leads', the ship-owners remained divided. Captain Kippen and the agents of the Ellerman line strongly favoured recognition, but the P&O and BI were opposed. The Shipping Federation, adamant that union recognition could only be determined in consultation with their agents in India, finally in March 1940, ruled against recognising the AISF 'as a body representing all seamen', alleging that such a claim was 'without foundation'.[59] Even the position of Surat Alley remained ambiguous. As the AISF representative, his cooperation had been invited. He had proved 'reasonably satisfactory'. But the Ministry continued to query his position: whether, when he had 'come into the picture', had he acted for 'Calcutta seamen only or with the Bombay seamen also'?[60] By 1940, there are hints that the state was ready to drop him. He had outlived his usefulness, as an internal India Office minute indicates: 'Are his services on Lascar matters now of any value?' By then, the government of India had approved the appointment of Lascar Welfare Officers (LWOs). And Alley, the union voice of Indian seamen, was once again sidelined.[61]

Recognising the need to win lascar compliance, the state embarked on a public relations campaign. Following the publication of the Hunter Report in November 1939 on seamen's welfare in ports (prompted in response to the ILO recommendation), the Ministry of Labour, ultimately responsible for the welfare of all seamen, set up port Welfare Committees, including a central Seamen's Welfare Board in London. Indian seamen thus indirectly became beneficiaries under the Hunter recommendations. At the same time, LWOs, as 'Lascar Friends', were appointed to ensure lascars received 'sufficient care', especially since war forced their extended sojourn abroad in Britain. The task of LWOs was to listen to the lascars' complaints, and explain their contracts, wages and conditions of service. Responsible to the High Commissioner, and appointed in mid-1940, the LWOs were all Indians: N.D. Tangri (at Glasgow), S.M. Sayeedulla (London) and M.J. Bukht (Liverpool). They visited hostels, boarding-houses and clubs to investigate lascar treatment, catering arrangements and the general standard of accommodation.[62] But this was not their only brief, as can be seen from a letter to the High Commissioner, following a suggestion by the government of India, that LWOs use their 'good offices' to facilitate lascar transfers without 'increase in wages'. Cautioning, India Office warned: nothing should be done to stigmatise LWOs as agents of ship-owners or the government. 'Once the impression were created, there would surely be no chance of the Officers obtaining the confidence of and influence over lascars, which it is hoped they will be able to secure.' Further, at the time of their appointment, LWOs were briefed that they might find 'subversive influence' and the 'best method' of countering it was to make lascars appreciate the state's concern for their welfare and to 'keep them contented'.[63] Evidence shows that, acting as the eyes and ears of the state, LWOs reported on trade union activity among Indian seamen and, on occasion, even gave their assistance to 'smooth over' difficulties encountered by ship-owners with their crew. But the fact that suggestions were made to replace Tangri, a barrister, with a more 'willing' man, suggests that not all LWOs were so compliant.[64]

As part of the welfare provision, hostels, clubs and other recreational facilities, hitherto woefully lacking, were now established, financed by the War Relief Fund, the King George V Fund for seamen and other private charities. Voluntary organisations too, helped to improve their sojourn. The Indian Soldiers and Sailors Comforts Fund sent parcels of warm clothing to every seaman coming ashore in Britain, supplying, during one winter alone, on average, 465 parcels weekly. The British Council, together with the Indian Comforts Fund and Mission to Seamen, provided a variety of entertainment, Indian film shows, and parties during religious festivals. At one such festival, a telegram reaffirming Indian seamen's loyalty was sent to the King-Emperor.[65] Lascar accommodation was regularly inspected. In Glasgow, the Trades Hotel at Coatbridge, a six-storey building with over 500 beds, established by Syed Tofussil Ally, one-time owner of the British Indian Sailor's Home in Canning Town, London (see Chapter 9), came in for special praise. But inspections also exposed the long-standing problem of sub-standard lascar accommodation.[66]

The paternalistic welfare policy was further buttressed by an appeal to lascar patriotism and traditions of service. This is demonstrated not only in the content of the 'Comprehensive Statement' issued to explain 'lascar troubles', but particularly in the way it was done. Initially planned to synchronise with the release of lascars from British prisons, it was issued, not as an official communiqué, but as a personal statement from the High Commissioner's office. The several drafts of the document to achieve the 'right balance' between the India Office view, that lascar wages ought to have been upped 'even before the war', and the instinct of the Shipping Federation, to stress lascar opportunism in causing difficulties at a time of war with 'the object of securing better conditions', shows the motive to be more a public relations exercise than anything else.[67] The final version, issued on 22 December 1939, expressed the 'hope and expectation' that lascar service will be 'no less' in the present war than in the last. Fulsome in its praise of the '30,000 Indian seamen' (actually 45,000) in the British Mercantile Marine, the statement recorded 'warm appreciation' of the 'peoples and governments of both Britain and India' for their service. Similar statements, issued periodically throughout the war, further illustrate attempts to win their hearts and minds. A memo, *Indian Seamen in the British Merchant Navy*, published by the Information Department in December 1941, highlighted the many acts of bravery and 'dangers and sufferings' borne by them. But emphasising, as it does, the 'extended' facilities for their welfare by the Ministry of Labour, leaves us in no doubt as to the motive.[68] By then a shortage of white seamen had led to the permanent lifting of latitude restrictions in the North Atlantic zone – a vital life-line to Britain, serviced by thousands of lascars. In a similar vein, in January 1942, on the occasion of laying the foundation stone for the first Indian Seamen's Home in Calcutta, the Viceroy, acknowledging the hard and dangerous work which took them 'far from home', spoke in their praise:

> there can be no example of devotion to duty more heartening and more inspiring to all of us engaged in this stern struggle than that of men, shipwrecked more than once by enemy action, seeking without hesitation a further opportunity of employment on the high seas.

The shipping media, too, glowingly described their 'courage, devotion to duty and sense of discipline', and their 'very creditable' part in the face of enemy attacks. Individual stories of their bravery were widely publicised. For instance, the *Journal of Commerce,* reporting the award of OBEs to Tuber Ulla, *serang* and Abdul Latiff, deck *tindal*, described the scene of their welcome after they had been decorated: they 'marched through Coatbridge, Lanarkshire, preceded by a ladies' pipe band, and followed by about 700 Indian seamen, some carrying flags and others banners on which were written "Welcome these heroes", "Decorated by the King", "Proud Sons of Empire" '.[69]

However, such enthusiastic praise, no doubt prompted by official prodding, and justly deserved, provides only one side of the picture. As Tony Lane has shown, the Admiralty's survivors' reports, our main source of evidence on crew behaviour, are so cluttered with 'ethnic stereotypes and evaluations' as to make them 'virtually impossible to interpret because for every report critical of Indian behaviour it seems there is another praising it'. Similarly, the work of the charitable organisations and the LWOs, appointed to listen to their complaints, was limited to their welfare in port. Such amenities undoubtedly improved the quality of their lives. Nonetheless, as Surat Alley pointed out, they left their core grievances unremedied.[70] A reading of the diaries and reports of LWOs, and action taken by the state in response to complaints, confirms Alley's claim. For instance, one entry in Tangri's diary records Indian seamen's monotonous diet: 'every day they had to eat mutton till they were sick and tired of eating it'. In response, in August 1941, a conference at the India Office of Welfare Officers recommended better and more rations, including 'Indian food' in seamen's hospitals. The same meeting urged that 'under present war conditions', engineers and shipping companies should not 'give trouble' by ill-treating lascars. However, on their grievances concerning wages and long hours, the conference merely noted that an approach was to be made to the shipping companies, 'if necessary'. Similarly, on the question of the war-risk bonus, we learn that as rates were agreed in India, 'no further steps' need be taken.[71]

Indian seamen themselves knew that, regardless of the fulsome praise and notwithstanding the dangers they faced, their race barred them from equality of treatment. A black life was valued less than a white one.[72] A further rise awarded in September 1940, and described as 'generous' by the Shipping Federation, amounted to no more, since the outbreak of the war in 1939, than a total of a 25 per cent increase in their basic wage and 75 per cent in the war-risk bonus, well below the £5 per month war-risk money paid to the white British seamen. The wide gap between wages for white and other seamen was highlighted further following strikes by Chinese seamen in their bid for a £5 bonus. Ship-owners' refusal to negotiate with the Chinese Seamen's Union brought the intervention of the Chinese ambassador in early 1941. As a result, their wages rose by a total of 400 per cent on pre-war rates.[73]

Disparity in wages, the 'niggardly manner' in which ship-owners interpreted rules governing the increase already granted, coupled with incidents demonstrating their deceit, drove lascars to further action.[74] Strikes broke out, intermittently, in Britain, Burma and elsewhere. A minority simply voted with their feet and were absorbed in industries in Birmingham, Nottingham, Wolverhampton or London, at wages they could never hope to earn as seamen. In 1943, according to Major Smith of MI5, 'reported' desertions amounted to 200–300 annually.[75] At the same time, Indian seamen's unions continued to campaign for redress of their grievances, a task made more difficult in view of the Shipping Federation's refusal to recognise the AISF. They forged alliances with the labour movement in other countries, and enlisted the support of the International Transport Workers' Federation (ITF). As long ago as 1928, a joint conference of the International Mercantile Marine Officers' Association (IMMOA) and the Seamen's Section of the ITF had instituted an inquiry into the working conditions of all Asian seamen on European ships. Its report, published in 1930, came out strongly in favour of equality of wages and treatment, as the work done by both classes of seamen was the same.[76] Given the circumstances of the war, Britain provided an important platform for negotiations and Surat Alley, despite being sidelined as the AISF representative, continued the campaign for Indian seamen's rights and to raise their industrial awareness.

In May 1940, for instance, in a bulletin issued under the auspices of the HSC, he urged lascars to join the AISF if they wanted their 'hardships ... overcome'. He argued that, given the cost of living, Indian seamen could not live on their current wages. In January 1941, together with the Colonial Seamen's Welfare Association, the AISF organised joint protests against the 'shocking' conditions of hostels for foreign seamen. Alley planned a 'full enquiry' to be presented to the Ministry of Labour and the Ministry of Health. It is possible that it was as a result of the AISF inquiry that Sorensen raised the matter in Parliament on 2 March 1941. Later, two pamphlets to publicise accommodation conditions in seamen's hostels were produced. One was written by Alley himself, the other, by Abdulla Khan, an interpreter at the Seamen's Mission in Glasgow.[77] In September 1941, at a two-day conference of Indians at the Central Hall, Glasgow, convened under the auspices of the India League, Alley presented a compelling picture of Indian seamen's conditions of labour. Praising their 'great bravery and sacrifice', and urging seamen to join their union to fight side by side with British workers against their 'callous' treatment, he reiterated their long-standing grievances. According to Alley, the worst injustice was that Indian seamen, torpedoed on British ships, could remain in Britain for up to five months without wages or compensation; in the meantime their wives and children 'had to starve'. He demanded that full compensation be paid 'forthwith'. This was no idle claim. Four months after three Indian seamen were badly injured in an air raid at Greenock in May 1941 – one of them totally incapacitated from severe burns – only one had received any compensation, £8, for loss of clothing. Their wages stopped, they subsisted on public assistance, ship-owners disclaiming any responsibility until they were fit for service again.[78]

Three months later, in December 1941, Alley issued a memo, *Indian Seamen in the Merchant Navy*. The memo was timely. Parliament had been debating the problems of seamen in the Merchant Navy and steps were being taken to improve their labour conditions. According to Alley, therefore, it was 'in keeping with the time and place', to draw attention to Indian seamen in the British Mercantile Marine.[79] As at the Glasgow conference, outlining their working conditions and the history of labour relations thus far, Alley pointed out that incorporating all the rises since September 1939, Indian seamen, in December 1941, earned on an average a mere 70 shillings (£3. 10s.) per month, including war-risk bonus, which in no way constituted a 'living wage', given the inflationary cost of living. Working hours remained long and unregulated and overtime unremunerated, while under the plea of 'tradition and *buxish*' (tips) the system of recruitment remained unreformed. Compensation for loss of effects and injuries sustained in war, paid in India, was inadequate, and the government scheme for compensation to families of seamen killed in action, paid not as a 'life pension' but as a lump sum, was 'very meagre'. The Indian seaman's old age, too, remained unprovided for. The memo ended with the same six points put forward at Glasgow as a basis for negotiation. In imitation of the government's own propaganda, Alley, too, used Indian seamen's war service to make an emotional appeal – but for a different purpose. Referring to thousands who had sacrificed their lives, he wrote:

> Indian seamen want to be useful in this fight against the forces of evil. It is for the authorities and ship-owners to take advantage of this eagerness and encourage them by making things easy for them. It is high time that Indian seamen were treated as human beings, and their usefulness recognised for the common victory over the forces of evil and Fascism.[80]

Alley contacted the media to publicise their demands and sent copies of the memo to the Shipping Federation, the India High Commissioner, the Ministry of Shipping and the Ministry of Labour and National Service. In Alley's view, given the hazards of war, Indian seamen's demands were not 'exorbitant' and could be met without 'any difficulties' by ship-owners. He urged the Ministry of Shipping and the High Commissioner to intervene.[81]

But to no avail. The Federation insisted that policy could only be decided in India 'through the recognised channels', a claim that was less than honest. The Ministry of War Transport adopted the same line, while the High Commissioner dispatched Alley's memo to India and to the ministry for their observations.[82] And, once again, attention focused more on the position of the AISF as the representative of Indian seamen and the status of Alley, rather than on lascar labour conditions. The ministry insisted that the question of recognition must be 'cleared up', as did the India Office, while ship-owners insinuated that the AISF was not 'a very respectable organisation'. They warned the NUS that 'European unions should go carefully in dealing with Mr S. Alley' as it was not 'always' easy to know whether Alley 'in fact' represented a 'substantial body' of Indian seamen. They reported that they were negotiating with 'four reputable unions in India', Alley's not among them.[83]

Undaunted, Alley appealed to the ITF. Considering the AISF claims to be legitimate, and alarmed at the Ministry's stand, the ITF threatened to consult with all its affiliated unions. Finally, five months and much correspondence later, in May 1942, having regretted so openly siding with the Shipping Federation, the Ministry agreed to receive a delegation.[84] Comprising Alley, Charles Jarman (NUS), J.H. Oldenbroek (acting general secretary, ITF) and P. Tofahrn (ITF), the deputation met P.J. Noel-Baker, Parliamentary Secretary, for an 'informal exchange of views'. As such, no conclusive outcome was possible. Nonetheless, the meeting opened with Oldenbroek informing the ministry of the ITF's concern at the conditions of employment of 'all coloured seamen', and his view that the 'only satisfactory solution ... was the recognition of the principle of equal pay for equal work'. Oldenbroek argued that ship-owners' insistence on settling matters in India rather than the UK was a ploy to keep lascar wages low. Jarman, fearful of Indian seamen's reaction to the 400 per cent wage rise, plus £5 war bonus given to the Chinese, stressed that it was imperative to remove grievances to forestall such troubles. But the NUS did not favour 'absolute equality' of wages. Alley, on the other hand, wanted lascar wages adjusted to the cost of living in Britain. Noel-Baker, wise to the importance of securing Indian seamen's cooperation, nonetheless stuck to the line that policy could only be decided by the government of India. Privately, however, the Ministry conceded that the AISF claims were 'reasonable'. An internal minute, dated 6 January 1942, noting that the £5 war allowance paid to the Chinese had been made applicable 'world-wide without zone limits' and extended to white British seamen, acknowledged that a lascar's total wage, though 'double' the pre-war rate, was still only Rs 49.12 for a deck hand and Rs 46 for a fireman.[85]

As a result, ship-owners were advised 'to act generously' and 'make a gesture without waiting for a demand' from Indian seamen. Noel-Baker went so far as to suggest that the delegates' case 'should be put sympathetically' to the India Office with emphasis on the 'importance of their views', rather than the status of Alley, which 'might perhaps be disputed'.[86] In June 1942, ship-owners announced a wage rise of 75 per cent, bringing the total wage packet, inclusive of war bonus, to Rs 78 (£5. 17s.), a development which perturbed the government of India, concerned at the impact on RIN wages. But the Ministry of War Transport, fearing 'crew troubles', especially in the USA (25–30 per cent of the personnel of the British merchant fleet being Indian), 'where we would get no help', warned against any delay in implementing the rise.[87] The ministry also admitted that the rise, exactly three times the pre-war basic wage, was 'not large in money' and 'the total ... still very low compared with the total wage earned by Chinese seamen'. Confessing defeat, an internal memo noted: 'but I suppose we can do no more, since the consensus of opinion among the experts seems to be against any larger increase'.[88] Once again, Indian seamen were outmanoeuvred. In the summer of 1942, while they earned £5. 17s., including war-risk bonus, a Chinese seafarer was paid between £13 and £16, and a British sailor's wage amounted to £22. 12s. 6d. in May 1942, and £24 by February 1943. Even the principle of equal war bonus for equal war risk did not apply. To quote Alley: 'Indian seamen ran the same risks to their lives and render the same valuable service to the cause of the United Nations as other seamen', yet their war bonus amounted to as little as £1. 15s., or a third of their total wage. White seamen, on the other hand, received £10 bonus a month.[89]

Indian seamen's unions re-doubled their efforts. Coincidental to the rise, Alley presented their case at the June 1942 session of ILO's Joint Maritime Commission (JMC) held in London. His plea for equality of treatment between the Indian and Chinese seamen received support from, among others, Joseph Curran, president of the National Maritime Union of America (NMU). The JMC resolution, unanimously adopted, recording admiration at the war effort of the Chinese, Indian and colonial seamen 'in the fleets of the United Nations', urged governments and organisations to take 'all practical steps' to ensure that there was 'no unfavourable comparison with crews of vessels in similar trades and under the same registry'. On 17 October 1942, Alley forwarded the JMC resolution to the Secretary of State for India, suggesting that India Office call a meeting of the representatives of British and Indian ship-owners, seamen and governments to 'explore the possibilities' for its implementation. The India Office reply was predictable: only the government of India could take appropriate action from 'the Indian point of view'.[90] Alley refused to be defeated. In October 1942, he updated the AISF memo, *Indian Seamen in the Merchant Navy*, to incorporate the new wage structure, and sent it to the ship-owners and the government.

In September 1943, under the auspices of the ITF, Alley launched the All-India Union of Seamen Centred in Great Britain, known as the All-India Seamen's Centre (AISC). Around 90 seamen and members of the local Asian community attended its inaugural meeting held at the British Council House in Liverpool. There were speeches from Alley, Percy Knight (the NUS District Secretary), J.H. Oldenbroek (ITF), Mr Braddock (member of the Liverpool City Council and a trade unionist), S.E. Teh (Secretary, Chinese Seamen's Union), and the secretary of the Dutch Seamen's Union. Such an array demonstrates Alley's success in enlisting support from a broad section of the labour movement. Expressing common cause with Indian seamen, Knight urged all seamen to seize the opportunity to make their demands 'when the world is saying what wonderful men they are'. After the war, he warned, the public would forget them. Indians voiced their own by now familiar demands, including wages 'nearly as high as the others' and better medical care, before enrolling in the union.[91]

Why did Surat Alley launch a new organisation? Was it because he had 'changed his allegiance', as the High Commissioner claimed in December 1943? The clue lies in the inaugural speeches. The AISC aimed to provide a united voice. Both Alley and the ITF knew that the AISF had disintegrated. Alley's position, too, notwithstanding the High Commission's insinuations, is clear from the intercepted letters relayed to the India Office. Aftab Ali viewed the AISC as a 'big mistake', likely to create 'more confusion' among seamen, especially at a time when the ISU membership of 34,000 (40,000 in the Director of the Intelligence Bureau's [DIB's] report) was growing and the ISU assuming an India-wide role, enrolling seamen at Calcutta, Bombay and Karachi. He urged Alley to submerge his AISC into the ISU, becoming its representative in Britain. By December 1943, a censored cable from Oldenbroek and Alley to Aftab Ali shows that the AISC had indeed converted itself into a section of the ISU with Alley as its London representative, his salary being paid by the ITF.[92]

By 1944, as a branch of the ISU, the AISC had established three offices: in London, Glasgow and Liverpool. Membership grew. Under the new scheme instituted by Aftab Ali, Indians could join the ISU in any of its branch offices, in India, Britain or the USA. There were plans to open offices in Canada, South Africa and Australia.[93] Alley's work grew. Based in Glasgow, he travelled the ports, visiting Indian seamen and dealing with their grievances – medical, legal or social. He encouraged them to join the union, removing their fear of being victimised by pointing out that this was their 'legal right'. He organised meetings to hear their concerns and periodically issued news bulletins in Urdu, Bengali and English to inform them of the work of the AISC/ISU. He brought to the attention of the India Office practices in breach of the Indian Merchant Shipping Act.[94] But campaigning remained the most important aspect of his work. Supported by the international labour movement, he exerted pressure at the centre of government in Britain, despite India Office attempts to confine discussions to India.

In October 1943, Alley circulated a new six-page memo, *Indian Seamen in the Merchant Navy*. Providing comparative statistics on conditions of black and white labour, it was a compelling statement in favour of the need for change. Referring to Indian seamen's 'fortitude and valour' in carrying out 'an essential war job', Alley warned that Indians had shown 'great patience', but could not be 'expected to acquiesce indefinitely in this discrimination'.[95] Keeping up the pressure, in December 1943 he forwarded a resolution passed at the International Seafarers' Conference, convened jointly by the ITF and IMMOA in London, 13–14 December 1943. The resolution urged ship-owners and the government of India, in consultation with seamen's organisations, to take 'immediate steps' to better Indian seamen's conditions of labour. He followed this up with a request that the High Commissioner and the Secretary of State meet a five-man international deputation to discuss implementation of the conference resolution.[96]

But to no avail. Alley ran into the same old obstacles. First, there were the inter-departmental wrangles over whether Alley should be accorded recognition as the ISU representative. Second, Alley ran into that by now familiar argument: India Office had 'no authority' to discuss policy which was decided in India, subject to approval by the government of India; that only 'local matters' of accommodation and welfare could be discussed in London. But such arguments were a ploy to buy time. What is even more revealing is the utter contempt with which India Office regarded the Indian and the International organisations. Noting that the AISC and the ITF had no *locus standi* in this matter', an internal minute dismissed Alley as 'not an entirely satisfactory person', and the ITF as 'these people do not really count for much and are unlikely to make trouble'. It was the NUS that was considered 'much more important'.[97] By early 1944 Indian seamen were becoming restive. The DIB reported a 'growing discontent', fuelled by ship-owners' rejection of the '16 demands' put forward by the ISU in 1943, and exacerbated by the delays in payment of pensions to relatives of seamen who had lost their lives in the war.[98]

The government of India, meanwhile, put together a package of wages based on India Office proposals, which would make extension of seamen's contracts more palatable (a proposed total rise of £4 per month: £2 war-risk bonus and £2 war credit). Determined to give ship-owners the credit, in February 1944, the government of India wired: 'avoid claims for increases in wages from other quarters', at the same time proposing that the measures, 'should be so carried out as to make it appear that shipping companies have spontaneously decided to grant the increase'. What of the AISC demands, then, contained in the 1943 memo and discussed with the High Commission and Lord Munster? According to the government of India, these 'very important points' could not be dealt with 'piecemeal', and, as a 'substantial increase' was 'under active consideration', it was 'unwise to complicate the issue by bringing in other reforms'. And so, in the time-honoured British fashion, the government of India proposed 'a review', to be undertaken after the ship-owners had agreed a wage increase.[99] In June 1944, their offer was unveiled: a rise in war-risk bonus of 50 per cent on a 12-month contract and 100 per cent after 18 months – but seamen would have to agree to a two-year term of service. This was the much-heralded 'substantial increase'. There was no rise in the basic wage, merely a temporary increase in the war-risk bonus, and that, too, still less than the £10 received by white British seamen. The proposals even flew in the face of parity of wages and war bonus on the Asiatic scale decided at the London Conference in 1943. Is it any wonder, then, that Aftab Ali called it a 'gross iniquity' and proposed to launch agitation, even strike action, if no satisfaction was received? The American NMU pledged its support. What action was taken is not clear: the official India Office file notes that, at the Copenhagen Maritime Conference, the Indian and UK delegates discussed the possibility of setting up an Indian NMB. In December 1945, Aftab Ali and Dinker Desai visited Britain for talks with Charles Jarman and the Ministry of War Transport.[100]

Just as the ship-owners took advantage of Indian seamen and out-manoeuvred them, the state, too, attempted to contain the unions. In December 1945, after discussions at the Ministry of War Transport with Jarman and the British lines employing Indian labour, George Reed, the assistant general secretary of the NUS, flew to India to help secure 'some federation, however loose', of the different unions as a 'preliminary step' to setting up a British-style NMB. The move was seen as a 'good thing' in principle and it was suggested that the Indian unions would benefit from British expertise. Ship-owners, too, who for years past had refused to recognise unions on the excuse that there was no strong union capable of speaking for all, agreed to participate, provided the unions represented on the Indian NMB were 'fully responsible unions'.[101] The India Office agreed. In their opinion, since Indian seamen's unions had not reached 'a sufficient stage of development', there would be a need for a representative of the government on the Board to secure 'proper conditions'. In a sanctimonious tone the minute continued: 'Actually under the UK Merchant Shipping Act [Indian Merchant Shipping Act] lascars' articles of service require the approval of the Government of India.'[102] The irony is inescapable. The whole history of Indian seamen's relations with the ship-owners and the state has shown that 'protection' had tended towards a strong British merchant fleet, not lascar conditions of labour.

And what of Surat Alley? There are suggestions that by the end of 1945 he was contemplating returning to India. How far did he and Aftab Ali succeed in bettering Indian seamen's conditions of labour? Given the obstacles, their influence was limited. War, however, finally brought some improvement in their welfare on shore. By November 1947 their wages, too, had risen by five times the pre-war rate to Rs 130 a month (£6. 15s. to £9. 7s).[103] But in comparison to the £20–24 earned by white British seamen, this gain too, is a qualified gain. By 1946, the All-India

Seafarers' Federation had been set up, and as such it could be argued that the unions were accorded recognition at last. But the story of success is patchy: bribery, poverty and irregularity of employment persisted, and wages remained low. The next stage of their struggle is beyond the scope of this book, which now looks at the lives of Indian workers, professionals and their families in Britain.

9

Asians in Britain, 1919–47

By the early years of the twentieth century Asians from the Indian sub-continent had been living in Britain for generations. In the period between 1919 and 1945 migration and settlement continued despite government attempts at restriction. What led to the growth? What kind of lives did Indians lead as imperial citizens, at the heart of the empire, at a time of growing nationalism in India, the economic turbulence of the Depression years and when the national self-confidence of the Victorian and Edwardian era had been jolted by the events and aftermath of the First World War? What changes, continuities and developments are discernible and was there an 'Asian community'? This chapter documents and analyses the experiences of Indian settlers, their manifold economic activities, their family lives and networks and institutions they established. It also rescues the work of some individuals and their significant contributions to British life and society. The Asians were not a monolithic group. A sprinkling of women, wives and children was represented in this diversity. The picture of their lives that emerges is complex and varied, and belies the traditional notions of the process of migration and settlement.

Estimating the size of the total population, however, is fraught with difficulties. Estimates of working-class Asians in certain locations, notably in London and the Midlands, are contained in some official records. But there are no global statistics. The only available data comes from the Indian National Congress survey of all 'Indians outside India'. According to this, in 1932, an estimated 7,128 Indians lived in Britain, the total UK population being over 44 million (the last census in 1931 before the outbreak of the war). Another writer estimated the number in 1945 to be 5,000. More recently, Hiro has suggested the figure of 'no more than 8000', possibly still an underestimate of the actual numbers.[1]

Despite government attempts to bar working-class Indians from Britain, the period between 1919 and 1945 witnessed an increase, though numerically still insignificant, of both the Asian working class and professionals. Motivation for migration remained varied and personal. Mention has already been made of seamen's poverty wages, prompting some to jump ship in Britain. The needs of British industries in war-time brought some Indian workers to Britain. A sense of adventure and the lure of the West enticed others, especially those who had worked overseas or heard stories from friends and kinsmen. Wali Ahmed Khan from the Punjab, for instance, who had been in the Shanghai Police force, migrated to Scotland in 1937 and joined a friend of his father's in Edinburgh. Charlie Verma (Pyare Lal Bucher) from Jullundur, who had once worked in Kenya painting and repairing railway wagons, went to Londonderry, Northern Ireland, in 1929, to join his two uncles there. His letters to his father in the Punjab, in turn, encouraged some members of the Vij family, who lived nearby in their village, to go to Northern Ireland. Anant Ram, another Sikh, was inspired to migrate by the example of 'three to four Muslims who had made a fortune' in England. Others were sponsored by relations. Then there were the Indian civil servants at India House, the Indian programme organiser and assistants at the BBC, and students, numbering 1,600 in the academic year 1932/3 alone, and still the largest group of colonial students in British universities. As in the earlier period, a few, having qualified, stayed on to practise their professions in Britain as is seen from the case of R.B. Jillani, a civil engineer in London in 1935. Of the many doctors who came for further training or additional qualifications in the 1920s and the 1930s, some stayed on to set up their own practices in Britain. Economic opportunities drew merchants and businessmen. Finally, the period witnessed the arrival of a distinct group of settlers, young males, largely from the Punjab, described as agriculturists in their passports and who in Britain became itinerant traders, selling ready-made clothes door to door.[2]

Why the Punjab and why Britain? The underlying reason was economic. Primary-producing countries like India, dependent on agriculture, were hit hard by the world-wide Depression. With a high population density and intensive cultivation, the problem in the Punjab was further aggravated by the fact that traditional subdivision of land among children left land holdings small and unable to sustain extended families. Even in the canal colonies, where, under a scheme to boost agriculture, thousands of peasants had been settled on irrigated virgin lands, families were in debt to moneylenders. Further, an important recruiting ground for soldiers and seamen, the Punjab had suffered over-recruitment during the First World War, leaving many unemployed. Migration within the empire, to East Africa, South-East Asia, Fiji and the Caribbean provided one outlet, some enterprising artisans, craftsmen and labourers even venturing to Australia and as far as the west coast of North America. But under the 'white dominion' policy, the 'open door' had closed. Enterprising young men from Jullundur, Hoshiarpur and Ludhiana began a steady trek to Britain.

THE INDIAN WORKING CLASS

Given the context of the time, the Depression years, the discriminatory Coloured Alien Seamen's Order, the racial hostility and the increased political surveillance over Indians, how did the working class manage to earn their living and what were their experiences? In a survey of social conditions in London, Liverpool and Cardiff in the mid-1930s, Captain F.A. Richardson, commenting on the 'hundreds of coloured men' living in the vicinity of the docks, wrote: 'the number of Indians is increasing weekly, attracted by the possibility of an easy life of idleness and the comparative wealth that is presented to them by the money obtained from unemployment benefit or public relief'. However, he cites no evidence. The police, on the other hand, complained of the 'growing evil' of Indian pedlars in 'all the villages and suburbs'.[3] What was the reality? Given that destitution meant repatriation, Indian seamen without wages (they were paid off in India) and itinerant traders with limited means had to find work quickly. Starting a new life was made somewhat easier by the fact that Indians were already living and working in Britain. But more importantly, in the dock areas of the major ports, there existed a complex but familiar set of institutions and networks, which offered succour to the newcomer. These were the common lodging-houses and cafes run by Arabs, Indians, Malays, Chinese or Maltese. Of a total of 51 seamen's boarding-houses in Cardiff, Little identified 17 run by Arabs, 4 by Somalis, 1 each by an Indian and a Malay and another 4 by West Africans and West Indians. According to a newspaper report, there were 40 cafes kept by 'Indians and Maltese in one area of the docks' in Cardiff. In Liverpool, a Chinese lodging-house (Ah Wah's), employing a Muslim cook, was patronised by Indians. In London, A.J. Perera's Oriental Cafe de Colombo is named in West India Dock Road, while a 1944 survey listed 32 cafes in Stepney alone, run by 'coloured' men or men from Malta, in addition to lodging-houses like Nairoolla's in Poplar. There were several others run by the Chinese in Limehouse and Somalis in Cable Street and one by a Sylheti, Muktar Ali.[4] Then there was Syed Tofussil Ally's British Indian Sailor's Home at 32–3 Victoria Dock Road, Canning Town. According to reports, Ally, a Sylheti seaman on British ships from 1913 to 1919, had run the lodging-house in Canning Town since 1923, in addition to his seamen's outfit shop. Shipping companies patronised Ally's Sailor's Home, boarding their lascar crew there when on transfer. In 1940, when the blitz made London increasingly unsafe and the shipping companies moved their base to Glasgow, Ally followed, establishing the Trades

Hotel at Coatbridge, and, in 1942, the Sailors' Home in Victoria Dock Road was closed down. Ally acquired a 'notorious' reputation amongst his compatriots as 'an informant' as he was said to report lascar deserters to shipping agents.[5]

Officials accused boarding-house keepers of encouraging desertions and profiting from seamen's advance notes. But there is no doubting that benefits were mutual. Men were boarded and maintained free of charge during periods of unemployment. Mrs Mahomed Ahmed of Cardiff, for instance, narrated how in 1921, during the recession, unemployed Indians, Arabs and Somalis had lived for six months at their expense. In these lodging-houses Indians found friends and compatriots who helped them to negotiate their way round the complex bureaucracy of documentation. Here, too, they found a system of obtaining seafaring jobs not too dissimilar to the one 'back home'. According to Mrs Nairoolla's testimony, they arrived at the boarding-house 'through friends' and were found jobs on English articles 'as soon as possible', thus replicating a version of *barriwallah* and *ghat serangs.*[6] Indians themselves confirm reports of mutual benefits. For many a Sylheti sailor, the house of Ayub Ali, in Sandy Row, east London, known simply as 'Number Thirteen', was a place of refuge and help, as well as a lodging-house. Born in Sylhet in 1880, and an ex-sailor himself, Ali, who had jumped ship in the USA in 1919, came to London in 1920, and set up a café (Shah Jolal Restaurant) at 76 Commercial Street, east London. Generous and helpful, he provided shelter and food without charge, 'for as long as was necessary'. He took men to India House and did their paper-work. When they had found jobs they continued to lodge at his house. Popularly known as 'Master' (teacher) because of his education, in the time-honoured village tradition, he acquired the status of a leader, later being made President of the UK Muslim League. Abdul Mannan's Basement Cafe at 36 Percy Street, established in 1944, was another well-known meeting place for Sylhetis, where news of jobs, friends and family were exchanged. Even S.T. Ally, despite his reputation, was known to be useful to those wishing to find jobs on English articles.[7] Kinship ties and village bonds provided another network of support for the newly arrived. Kartar Singh Seran, a Sikh from Ludhiana district, who came to Glasgow in 1932, for instance, was helped by a Muslim, Ali Mohammed Painter, a friend of his father, from the same village and whose house he shared. He described how newcomers were initiated into the craft and language of peddling by old hands, given moral support, 'fed, clothed and looked after ... without regard to caste or creed' until they were 'able to stand on [their] own feet'. Men lived communally, took turns to cook for all and ate 'together at table from one pot'. In Spitalfields, east London, the lodging-house of Kartar Singh Nagra was patronised by Sikhs. A 'cloth-hawker' himself, Nagra was helped by his English wife. In Londonderry, 4 Simpson's Brae, the house rented by Mohabat Rai Vij in 1936, long remained the meeting place of Indians in Londonderry and Northern Ireland generally. Religious institutions were another link in the chain of networks for those without connections. Sikhs, for instance, headed for the Bhupindra Dharamsala in west London.[8] Finally, mention must also be made of the many white women, friends, wives and helpmates, without whose support these migrants would not have been able to establish themselves so successfully. As partners, they helped to run businesses and kept accounts. P.D. Kapur, ex-president of the GIU, ran a boarding-house for Indians in Glasgow with his Scottish wife. Ethel Mohamed, the wife of Noah Mohamed, not only ran the tea shop in Pitt Street, Liverpool, where Indian and Arab seamen lodged, but helped lodgers with their application forms. Lal Khan, an ex-seafarer from Mirpur, who worked as an itinerant trader, relied on his Irish wife, Mary, to keep accounts and note his clients' requirements. Illiterate himself, though having a 'remarkable memory', it was said that Khan carried details of orders and payments in his head; but it was his wife who wrote these down at the end of each day and every month visited his customers with him to check the tally.[9]

Still, men had first to find work, master the geography of their environment, cope with a different currency, learn to recognise bus numbers and operate in a new language, a difficult task at the best of times, but more so for the many illiterate Indians. Jobs were scarce. 'In those days there were not many jobs even for English people, never mind the foreigners', is an abiding memory.[10] As such, they had to be resourceful and flexible if they were not to go under, earning a living in a variety of ways. Those who could, continued as seafarers when shipping returned to normality, and especially during the Second World War when demand was high. Others resorted to self-employment as hawkers and petty traders. Many firemen tell stories of how they became 'Indian perfumiers' selling cheap 'oriental fragrances' they had concocted in their own lodging-houses, or became purveyors of Indian herbal medicines. Others sold 'real Indian toffee' (spun sugar) from a 'metal carrying box' slung over their shoulder. Such experiences once again remind us that, as in the earlier period, 'selling culture' remained an important way of earning a living.[11] Others still turned to casual work as labourers in catering or the clothing trade. Hamdu Mia found employment as a cook, first in Glasgow for two years, then in Liverpool's Pitt Street, where he helped in a tea shop. Later, he was reported to be selling toffee in the streets of Liverpool. Nawab Ali worked at an Egyptian Coffee shop in Cannon Street Road, London, cleaning, washing dishes and peeling potatoes. Haji Kona Miah was employed in a Greek restaurant 'somewhere in Tottenham Court Road', washing dishes for £2 per week. Shah Abdul Majid Qureshi obtained work at the Bengal Restaurant in Percy Street. Cafes in docksides, said to make 'large' profits and pay decent wages, were a mainstay for many. A survey conducted in 1944 recorded an Indian employed to manage a cafe, earning £9 a week, plus a percentage of profits. But this would not have applied to waiters and kitchen staff. Catering was by no means the only avenue providing casual work. A 1930 report records Indians in Glasgow working as dock labourers and 'firemen in the flour mills'. Others took up employment as unskilled labourers in shops or as porters in small Jewish tailoring firms in the East End of London and elsewhere. According to a 1938 east London newspaper, such jobs paid 17s. 6d. to £1 a week, wages whites considered too low. Moreover, being 'blind alleys', porterage jobs did not attract local 'juveniles'. But given how low Indian seamen's wages were, even this would have appeared a relatively attractive wage to them. While the newspaper reassured its readers that Indians were not depriving them of jobs, a government report in 1939 noted that, when 'they can obtain employment', Indians often worked for 'wages which would be refused by a white man'.[12]

Such a statement illustrates the difficulties Indians faced in the job market during the inter-war years. What also emerges from their pattern of employment is their resourcefulness and flexibility. Further, by this period, catering and clothing appear to have become 'traditional' areas of employment for Indian migrants. Occasional work as film 'extras' in grand epics of the empire like the Korda brothers' *The Four Feathers,* ironically, provided many working-class Asians (and Africans) a means of casual employment, however irregular. Evidence shows that film companies hired Indians for 'crowd scenes' through local merchants. Said Amir Shah, of Shah Brothers, silk merchants and warehousemen of 8 Whitechurch Lane, for instance, acted as a film agent and contractor. It was to protect the interests of 'Indian and Asiatic people' employed as film 'artistes and crowd', that Akbar Ali Khan, also known as Chaudhri Akbar Ali Khan (see p. 271) and Alley, the trade union activist, set up the Oriental Film Artistes' Union (OFAU). Established in early 1938 as the Asian and African Film Artistes' Association, OFAU had 194 members by the end of the year. By 1939, there were two organisations, OFAU for 'all Asians', and the Coloured Film Artistes' Association, led by J. Cox and Peter Blackman, for 'all other coloured people, including Asians born in the West Indies'. The two organisations, though independent of each other, worked in close cooperation.[13]

But for many working-class Indians in the 1920s and 1930s, seamen or agriculturists from the Punjab, self-employment as pedlars, hawking 'cheap Japanese goods', as one report described, and popularly known as the 'door business', became their main profession.[14] Remembered in British folk memory as 'turbaned Sikh Pedlars', historians too, suggest that pedlars were Sikhs.[15] But pedlar testimonies recorded in Scotland and Ireland, and supported by McFarland's analysis of pedlar licences for the period 1939–40, show that pedlars were both Sikhs and Muslims. For instance, of the 97 licences issued, 35 per cent were to Sikhs and 65 to Muslims. Further confirmation that both Sikhs and Muslims 'peddled haberdashery' is contained in official records. The India Office distinguished between the Punjabis, who looked to 'peddling only' as a means of self-employment (indeed it was said that they travelled to Britain for the 'purpose' of carrying on business in second-hand clothing), and other Indian hawkers, particularly Sylheti seamen, who also took to peddling, but as an 'interim measure' to seafaring on European wages.[16] However, cases of seamen, both from Sylhet and from western India, abandoning seafaring altogether were not unknown. Ghulam Rasul, having jumped ship in London in 1929, 'travelled the country' as a pedlar. He was in Kirkcaldy for two years, then in Edinburgh for a year. Finally, in 1933, living in the West Holborn district of South Shields as a pedlar, he was reported to be attempting to return to seafaring, having applied for a Special Certificate of Nationality. Lal Khan, the Mirpuri seaman, on the other hand, having jumped ship in Glasgow in 1938, went to Ireland in 1939, and settled down at Castlecaulfield, selling clothes door to door. Joffer Shah sold scarves in St Helen's market.[17]

Peddling was easily accessible. Anyone over 17, of good character and with the intention to trade as a pedlar, could apply for a licence valid for a year throughout Britain and Ireland, the only condition being one month's residence in a police district. It required little capital. 'Just £3' filled a suitcase with new clothes.[18] Oral testimonies of these early pedlars provide glimpses into their lives. Like the Jews before them, Indians sold ready-made garments. With a suitcase containing items of light clothing, shirts, socks, ties, scarves, lingerie and aprons, working six days a week, in all weathers, they travelled miles to establish their own patch and build up a regular clientele. Ram Gupta in Omagh, Northern Ireland, recalled covering 10–15 miles in a day; Nizam Dean in Belfast travelled 5–10 miles, balancing his suitcase on his bike, while

Anant Ram walked 6–7 miles around London. Some travelled on foot, others used buses or bicycles, a few learned to drive cars, or, like Fakir Chand Sumra in Londonderry, even bought a van. Evidence suggests that new arrivals, not wishing to encroach on an established patch, branched out further afield, settling in new areas. From Glasgow and its environs, for instance, a few went to Edinburgh, Stirling, Perth, Dundee and Aberdeen. Others travelled to the west coast, to Paisley, Dumbarton or other little towns and villages, and even as far as the Outer Hebrides, as the story of Buttha Mahomed illustrates. He had come to a Depression-hit Britain in 1931. From Glasgow, selling clothes door to door, he travelled all along the west coast, arriving in Stornoway on the island of Lewis in 1935, where he decided to settle. While living at a guesthouse, he cycled round the island selling his wares, only returning to Glasgow to replenish his stock. The only Asian on the island for years, he was joined by a few friends from Glasgow, and in the 1950s by his two brothers. Today the family still lives on the island. Itinerant traders led monotonous lives, working long hours, to support families in India. For those living away from the urban centres of Glasgow, London or Londonderry and boarding with white landladies, life would have been even lonelier and more isolated, without even the company of fellow Indians in a communal household. In time, however, they managed to establish a clientele. Their customers, the poorer working class, who paid by small weekly instalments, came from the urban housing schemes and communities in outlying rural and fishing villages.[19] One important reason why Indians were able to get custom was the fact that they sold goods on interest-free credit to those unable to afford cash purchases at regular shops. A further factor was their willingness to branch out to outlying rural villages, where shops were few and far between, and few people had their own means of transport. Here, Indians, bringing necessary items of clothing to the doorstep, would have been welcomed for providing a vital service. A form of trust, too, would have developed between them and their clients, irrespective of race, culture and language.

Trading in such different geographical locations, separated by language barriers from white merchants, and not deemed credit-worthy, how did these early itinerant traders get their stock? Supplies were obtained by post or rail from the several Indian silk merchant firms based in London, for instance, Qureshi and Company, established by Ahmad Din Qureshi, at 36 Church Lane, Aldgate, or Shah Brothers at 8 Whitechurch Lane, run by Said Amir Shah and Fazal Shah. Other suppliers included C.L. Nayyar Brothers, at 30 Church Lane, and Fazal Ali, 'a tie manufacturer', at 44 Clifton Street, Shoreditch.[20] Evidence suggests that some even appointed their own agents in London: for instance, Nathoo Mohammed, from Jullundur, a farm worker and a stoker on a ship, who had been an itinerant trader in the Port Dundas district of Glasgow since 1920, dispatched his brother to London. Fateh Mohammed not only acted as an agent for his brother, but became a market trader in his own right. Gulam Mohammed was an agent for some Indians based in Ireland until they felt confident enough (and were deemed credit-worthy enough) to buy from Irish suppliers in Belfast or Dublin.[21] The pattern of supply between the London merchants and the pedlars is demonstrated by the business enterprise of Hashmatrai Rewachand, artificial silks and hosiery merchant, trading from 135 Grunding Street and 94 High Street, Poplar. Said to employ agents to collect orders from Indians in 'all parts' of the United Kingdom and Ireland, his parcels dispatch book reveals that Rewachand sent goods within an area bounded by Inverness in the north, Ramsgate in the south, Torquay in the west and Norwich in the east. Such a piece of information – preserved in police records because Rewachand was alleged to encourage lascar desertion to help his business, an allegation that proved groundless – not only shows the pattern of trade and spread of Indian itinerant traders around the United Kingdom, but also demonstrates Rewachand's flourishing enterprise. The fact that Rewachand sponsored, in the words of the police, 'a large number' of Indians, paying their fares to Britain, costing around £16–£18 each, confirms his business success. In the early 1930s, enterprising itinerants, who had prospered, opened their own draperies, for instance, Mohammed Kaka (96 Brunswick Street) and G.M. Sharif and A.M. Ashraf (Oxford Street), of Glasgow, thus extending choice of suppliers for Indians based in Scotland and Ireland.[22]

Scholars of black history have tended to underestimate, even ignore, the presence of Indians in areas traditionally described as multi-racial.[23] The working lives of these working-class Indians, seamen, labourers and itinerant traders, inform us of the geographical location of their settlement. Evidence of their presence is also found in Valuation Rolls, police records and official reports and surveys. Here I briefly map the main areas of clustering. In Scotland, Glasgow, with its long trading connection with India and the shipbuilding industry on the Clyde, the number of Indians was said to be growing. By 1923, Indians had formed their own union, the GIU, which had vigorously protested against the registration as aliens of over 60 pedlars and labourers (Chapter 7). A study of Glasgow Valuation Rolls indicates that working-class Indians tended to cluster in the districts of Port Dundas, Anderston and the Gorbals. The reasons for this are not far to seek. In the slum conditions of the older parts of the city, according to Maan, houses were not only cheaper, but available to rent even by Indians, one describing such properties as 'dilapidated ... in a state of utter disrepair'. How large Glasgow's working-class Indian population was is open to question. Based on Valuation Rolls, Maan has calculated that, by the mid-1930s, there were 'nearly 175' Indians, the number rising to 400 in 1940 as some men from the outlying regions moved back to Glasgow. The *Glasgow Herald,* on the other hand, put the figure as 'perhaps' 600 by 1941.[24] In 1937, on the initiative of S.N. Joshi, Bishen Singh Bans and Abdul Ghafur, the Hindustani Majlis was formed in Glasgow, illustrating that Indians felt settled. Initially formed to make arrangements for burial and cremation rites, the Majlis widened its scope to improve Indian workers' welfare and labour conditions in Scotland.[25]

In Wales, in the cosmopolitan district of Cardiff's Butetown, an area, in the words of one report, where 'almost every nationality and colour' in the world was represented, a sprinkling of Indians lived amongst Arabs, Africans, Chinese, Maltese, Somalis and West Indians. Several other seaport towns in England had a clustering of Asian inhabitants. In Liverpool, for instance, by this period, the Indian population was reported to have increased, although no figures are available. In the dock district, Pitt Street and George Square were said to be home to 'a considerable number of Chinese, Indians and Negroes'. The multi-racial district of Holborn, in South Shields, inhabited by many Adenese and Somalis, also had a clustering of Indian seamen and pedlars. A 1937 report counted 21 men in one lodging-house run by an Indian. According to the police, a 'little colony' of Indian pedlars lived in Chatham, Kent.[26]

But it was London, the metropolitan capital and the chief port of Indian and global trade, that naturally had a significant clustering. The dockside boroughs of Poplar and Stepney were described as having a 'good percentage' of Indians. According to T.E. Bugby, LCM's Lascar Missionary, Spitalfields and Poplar had a 'small Sikh community', numbering about 150, mainly 'pedlars of silks and fancy articles'. He identified 'several' boarding-houses where Punjabi Muslims lived, and 'a number' of places for Sylhetis. Further east, in the region around Canning Town, Customs House, Tidal Basin and Plaistow, 'many lascars' had settled amongst the 'appreciable' number of 'coloured people' of African descent. In fact, the 1939 Hunter Report, estimating London's Indian population to be 2,000–3,000, noted that while the Chinese and 'Negro' population appeared to be decreasing, that of the

Indians was on the increase. The Report further noted that Indians had limited earnings and lived in 'communal fashion' in 'overcrowded and sparsely furnished' housing.[27]

As in Glasgow, several organisations had been formed to protect their interests and meet their needs. Some, like the Indian Seamen's Welfare League, catered for a specific group. Established in 1943 by Shah Abdul Majid Qureshi and Ayub Ali, the League, a social welfare organisation based at 66 Christian Street, east London, aimed to provide seamen with social amenities, help with paper work and serve as a means of communication with relatives in India in the event of misfortune during the war. Its membership was largely Sylheti.[28] The HSC, established around 1934/5, survived well into the 1940s. Established for social and educational work among seamen and pedlars living in London's East End, its honorary secretary was Alley, the trade unionist. Among the few surviving pieces of evidence to inform historians of its actitivies is an advertisement for a special matinee performance by the celebrated dancer, Ram Gopal and his troupe at the Vaudeville Theatre in December 1939. The charity performance organised by Alley and the treasurer, Mrs Dutt, the wife of D.N. Dutt, a medical practitioner in north-west London, was to raise funds, war having added to the HSC's welfare work.[29] Mrs Dutt's involvement in the HSC suggests that contact was maintained between the Indian professionals and the working class in Britain. Indeed, this was not a solitary example, as will be seen. According to the recollections of Qureshi, an associate of Alley, the HSC was not 'much political'. It 'mostly' organised social gatherings with Indian songs, to which the High Commissioner and 'other big people' were invited, suggesting that such gatherings not only kept alive elements of Indian culture, but acted as a meeting place for Indians and English men and women. However, a rare translation of a newsletter, issued in Urdu and Bengali in May 1940 by Alley, provides a somewhat different picture and shows that Alley also aimed to raise the political consciousness of the working-class Indians for freedom of India, enrolling them to the Indian National Congress.[30] The Hindustan Community House (warden Kunda Lal Jalie) opened in 1937. It provided food and lodging at an affordable charge, ran classes in English and a medical clinic staffed by Indian doctors, who gave free medical advice. The House also served as a social centre, having Indian and English newspapers, a wireless set, a gramophone, Indian records and a variety of games. The House was razed in the blitz.[31]

The settlement of working-class Indians was by no means confined to the multi-racial settlements in dockside ports and cities. Given the social and economic conditions, and their occupations, Indians tended to move around internally. Personal decisions may also have governed their choice of location. There were Indians in Kent, in Ireland, especially around Londonderry, in smaller cities and rural areas of Scotland, including the Hebridean Island of Lewis. The outbreak of the Second World War would further shift their settlement pattern as some long-time residents and new arrivals moved to the Midlands to work in factories and in war-related industries. Our knowledge and understanding of the geography and sociology of Indian settlement pattern between the wars, however, remains incomplete. More research at regional and local level is needed.

How did the communities among whom Indians lived and worked perceive them? Many instances of kindness and friendship are remembered. 'Lots of English ladies helped us', is a sentiment of one Sylheti seafarer in London. An Irishman was said to have taught Lal Khan how to drive; another, Marcus Martin, acted as a guarantor for Ram Gupta, enabling him to get supplies locally from a Belfast warehouse, rather than from Glasgow. The Scottish group recall that the attitude of the Scots, particularly in the rural areas, was 'very good' towards them.[32] The very many examples of mixed marriages (see p. 273) provide another indication of absence of prejudice. But negative responses to such marriages demonstrate that racism was not absent. There were other humiliating experiences. In Scotland, the derogatory term, 'Johnnie the darkie', referred to the Indian itinerant traders. Finding 'good' housing was another problem, landlords blaming 'promiscuous living' as a reason for their reluctance to rent to 'coloured' people. But justifying racism by blaming the victim hides the nature and ideology of 'colour bar' in Britain, as will be seen. A case of violence in May 1925, in the Port Dundas district of Glasgow, when Sundhi Din and Mohammed Bakhsh were assaulted and the 27-year-old Noor Mohammed was murdered, reveals overtones of sexual and economic jealousy. Noor Mohammed was the brother of the successful itinerant trader, Nathoo Mohammed, who lived with his common law Scottish partner, Louise. The crime was widely reported in the media and the perpetrators found guilty. Some white British people alleged that Indians posed an economic threat to their livelihood; others accused them of importing diseases. In war-time Ireland, for instance, some Dublin wholesalers threatened to remove their patronage from W.B. McCarter's factory, Fruit of the Loom, if he continued to supply textiles to the successful retailer, Charlie Verma. McCarter, however, refused to be bullied.[33]

In the 'cotton town' of Bolton, tradesmen alleged that Indian itinerant traders, described as 'a small army of pedlars', by importing textiles made in India 'to sell cheap', hurt the Lancashire cotton industry, depriving industrial workers of their means of livelihood. According to an outraged Councillor Herbert Eastwood, secretary of the Bolton Labour Party and a member of the Bolton Watch Committee, given the attitude of the Indian government to imported Lancashire goods, allowing Indian pedlars to sell Indian textiles was 'adding insult to injury'. Some expert voices in Lancashire, however, dismissed the suggestion that Indians could possibly make a living hawking clothes. In the opinion of W. Coucill, director and manager of a Blackburn mill with 13 years' experience as a weaving master of the Muir Mills in Cawnpore, itinerant traders were only 'posing' as pedlars, but in reality they were 'emissaries' of Swarajists, engaged in peddling 'insidious' propaganda in favour of Indian independence, thus echoing views similar to those of the police (Chapter 7). The threat posed by the pedlars to the Lancashire cotton industry was considered to be so serious that the Bolton Chamber of Trade took the matter up. However, an examination of textile samples showed 'Indian cottons' to be French imports, forwarded from London. The Chamber of Trade concluded that 'public protest' had had the desired effect and 'Bolton and Lancashire wives will look at the matter in the right light.'[34] A final example of racial hysteria comes from the *Glasgow Weekly Record* in 1930. Warning Scottish housewives against being 'duped' into believing that they were acquiring 'contraband' beautiful, 'genuine silks' at 'rock-bottom prices', the reporter informed its readers that the merchandise peddled by these 'oily tongued, suave' Indian (and Arab) pedlars was no different from that sold by local stall-holders and purchased from the very same London and Manchester warehouses. Proclaiming that Indian pedlars were a 'positive peril' to the purse of the housewife, the *Record* sounded further alarm bells: 'the health of her family' was at risk. The reporter alleged that in the opinion of 'several' Medical Officers of Health, the outbreak of skin disease among the 'eight young men and four girls' was traceable to the garments purchased on the door-step, and, but for early consultation, there was 'no saying what lengths the disease might have run'. Scottish housewives further learnt that these pedlars were not sailors on a day's leave from their ship as they 'pretended to be', but 'deserters'.[35] The juxtaposition of the innocence of British womanhood, the family protector, with wily deserters not only brings out the ideology of 'difference', but emphasises the point made earlier: gender as the guardian of home, nation and empire.

How successful were these working-class itinerant entrepreneurs? Available evidence does not allow for a definite conclusion. According to one police report, a pedlar in Chatham, described as 'a man of good character', and once 'a cultivator by trade', who had been encouraged to come to Britain as a result of reports from friends of 'good business' prospects, was so successful that he had not only discharged his debt of Rs 400, borrowed from a moneylender at 25 per cent interest per annum, to pay for his fare from his village in Jullundur to England via Bombay and Marseilles, but had managed to make 'some profit' as well. Ram Gupta, in Ireland, reckoned that he made a profit of 'around £3–4' per week. Another report also suggests that Indians who obtained pedlars' licences were 'fairly successful', selling 'cheap Japanese goods'. However, this success was cited relative to the 'less fortunate' Indians, who found employment as porters.[36] The fact that news of good opportunities encouraged kinsmen or friends to come to Britain, suggests that pedlars managed to earn a decent living to support families in India. This, therefore, leads to the conclusion that some Indians prospered. However, there is also evidence to the contrary. Indian ex-seamen in Cardiff were said to merely 'eke a living' peddling 'cheap silk goods'. The suggestion that ex-seamen and Punjabi pedlars were remuneratively employed as 'unskilled labourers' in factories during the war, by inference, points to a precarious living as itinerant traders. Evidence from Indians themselves confirms that factory work was 'better paid and more secure'. Further, not all made a success at peddling: personal characteristics or shyness would have been inhibiting factors.[37] Set against the monotony of their lives, long hours and living conditions, the picture of success looks different and mixed. It is possible that compared to a seamen's wage on Lascar Articles, or what they would have earned from the land in India, their earnings selling clothes door to door represented a better living wage.

With the outbreak of the Second World War the lives of the working-class Indians underwent a change. Ex-seamen, earning a precarious living on land, found seafaring jobs were now plentiful. Factories and war-related industries in London, Glasgow, but particularly in the Midlands, needed labour. Indeed, demand was so high that even their lack of English language was, apparently, no longer considered a handicap. The fact that they were strong was all that mattered.[38] Some gave up peddling for more secure factory employment. Many others moved to the Midlands, where previously only a few Indians, mainly doctors and some pedlars, had lived. Evidence suggests that the labour shortage in factories was so acute that even seamen who jumped ship were absorbed, the Labour Exchange accepting men without even the documentary proof of British nationality. Further, the fact that police complained that men 'travelled from India' to the Midlands, attracted by 'high wages' and with the idea of 'deserting ship' in the United Kingdom, suggests that newcomers came to earn a living, helping the war-effort. The two most numerous ethnic groups engaged in industries in war-time Britain were Bengali Muslims, largely ex-seamen, and Punjabis, both Sikhs and Muslims. By mid-1942, it was estimated that over 3,000 Indians were employed in various industries in Britain, in Birmingham, Bradford, Coventry, Huddersfield, Nottingham, Newcastle, Manchester, Sheffield and Wolverhampton; and in Southampton, Glasgow and London. The largest clustering in the Midlands was in Coventry and Birmingham, where, by April 1943, it was estimated that there were around 1,500–2,000: 800 in Coventry and 800–1,000 in Birmingham, with at least 112 Indian houses.[39] In the light of this, some early studies of Indians in the Midlands need revising.

Indians worked as labourers on the construction of aerodromes, ammunition dumps and militia camps; as unskilled workers in aircraft factories and in other war-related industries. Thakur Singh Basra, for instance, was first employed as a labourer on the site of an aircraft factory in Coventry. In 1941, he fetched up as a bench-hand with Clark, Cluley and Company. But low pay forced him back into labouring. Charan Singh Chima began as a builder's labourer, next he moved to an aircraft factory in Coventry, later being transferred to Gloucester. Kartar Singh Nagra, from being a builder's labourer in Coventry, went to Chiver's Works, at Gaydon in Warwickshire. Akbar Ali Khan moved from London to Birmingham and then to Coventry as a labourer with Daimler's. Nawab Ali, an ex-Sylheti seaman, began at the American Dunlop factory in Coventry, moving to an aircraft factory, working in an all-female section with 600 women, wheeling a trolley, providing nuts for assembly work. Later he went back to seafaring. Mohammed Hussain, from the Punjab, who arrived in Scotland in 1939, was sent to work in the Royal Ordnance Factory at Bishopton. In east London Indians worked at Beckton Gas works in Newham, or as stokers in factories.[40] Factories employed men in shifts and wages were paid on piece rates. One industrial worker on night shifts remembered earning around £7 a week. At Beckton Gas Works, which at one time operated seven shifts a week, men received 13s. 8d. per shift and could total around £4–5 a week. However, to suggest that all working-class Indians moved to the Midlands in unskilled manual jobs is to distort the picture of their lives. Some ex-seamen returned to seafaring on English articles, while some Punjabis and Bengalis continued as itinerant traders. There were allegations that some were involved in black marketeering.[41]

Evidence suggests that, even when their labour was in demand, Indians only qualified for unskilled labouring jobs. To dismiss all working-class Indians as illiterate peasants is to do them an injustice.

Craftsmen, artisans, and some with education even, had all turned to peddling in Britain. Karam Singh, known as Karam Singh Overseer amongst his compatriots, for instance, was not only 'fairly' educated, but had acquired 'technical engineering' knowledge and worked as a foreman in India, while Muhammad Fazal Hussain had been a school teacher.[42] Indian students, unable to continue at universities (there were problems dispatching funds) also found work in factories. However, regardless of qualifications, ability or willingness to learn, they got shunted into unskilled manual labour, thus prefiguring the experiences of the post-1950s migrants. Abdul Hamid's experience is a case in point. Despite the fact that he produced a 'good number of shells', he was not allowed to continue, but was relegated to a labouring job. The reflection of one ex-pedlar, that men did jobs that were 'below their dignity', provides another example. Their complaints to the management did not receive a fair hearing: the white man, they found, was 'invariably' 'in the right'. In July 1940, the case of M. Deva, an Edinburgh resident, hit the headlines in Britain and in India. The War Department, urgently needing a clerical worker in a Scottish office and having applied to the local employment exchange, received Deva's application. But this 22-year-old MA graduate did not qualify for the clerical post. The Department could not employ a 'coloured man'. What amounts to a double discrimination against this British citizen, is revealed in a cancelled draft of a letter from the India Office to the government of India. Justifying blocking Deva on the grounds that he 'would have had access' to 'secret Defence Plans' were he to have been employed, Deva was labelled both an 'idle never-do-well' and an 'associate of political extremists'.[43] What episodes like this also reveal is the ability of the state to use careers as a weapon to stifle dissent. Finding 'decent houses', too, remained a problem. Mention has already been made of the attitude of landlords and the type of accommodation available to them. The result was overcrowding and unhealthy living conditions. Police in their reports damned Indians in the Midlands, complaining that '100s' of them were living 'in filth and leading dissolute lives', and there was 'drunkenness and gambling'.[44] But such reports merely describe the effect, and not the cause. In order to protect their rights and to cater for their needs Indian workers formed organisations like the Indian Workers' Association.

THE INDIAN WORKERS' ASSOCIATION

The IWA or *Hindustani Mazdur Sabha* (known as the Indian Workers' Union in its early days), formed in the inter-war years, has survived to the present day. Essentially a working-class movement, the IWA was open to all Indians, regardless of 'class or creed', and subscription was set at an affordable one shilling per year. Indeed, both Punjabi and Bengali ex-seamen living in the Midlands joined, and references to students and professionals in intelligence reports suggest a wider membership. Its aims and objectives were twofold: first, to organise Indian workers in Britain for the freedom of India; second, as a mutual welfare society, to protect the interests of its members. A bi-monthly bulletin, in English and Hindustani, the *Indian Worker*, was also published, its editor being Mohammed Fazal Hussein. However, the war-time paper shortage prevented regular publication. In 1945, *Azad Hind*, in Urdu and Punjabi, edited by Vidya Parkash Hansrani and Kartar Singh Nagra, was launched. But piecing together IWA's early history has been problematic owing to paucity of documentation. Even the names of its founding fathers and the nature of its membership are disputed. However, the IPI file sheds some light on these conundrums.[45]

The IWA had its beginnings in 1937 in Coventry, where, according to official sources, a 'number of disaffected Sikh pedlars', some with '*Ghadar* connections', lived. Surveillance reports name four individuals as founder-members: Charan Singh Chima, said to be 'largely instrumental' in its formation, Thakur Singh Basra, described as 'one of the most prominent figures' in the Sikh community in the Midlands, as its 'unofficial secretary', Ujjagar Singh, its treasurer, said to hold 'extreme views', and Kartar Singh Nagra, a 'keen supporter of the *Ghadar* Party'. Another report cites Karam Singh Chima (Overseer, also known as Babu Karam Singh) as being one of the original leaders, who in 1941, while living in Bradford, played a prominent role in organising Indian workers there. The IWA's early activities revolved around canvassing subscriptions for the Amritsar-based *Desh Bhagat Parwarik Sahaik* Committee (Patriots' Relief Fund) to help families and dependants of *Ghadarites* and other Punjabi 'patriots' jailed for life. And this remained an important activity throughout the IWA's existence. When war broke out and Indian workers moved to the Midlands, conditions for their 'political education' were said to be 'ideal', and, by the summer of 1941, IWA branches had been formed in Bradford and Birmingham. According to Dhani Prem, a doctor in Birmingham since 1939, the initiative for the Birmingham branch had come from him. As secretary of the local branch of the India League and a member of the Labour Party, Prem worked hard to integrate Indian workers into British society and, after the war, he was elected Labour Councillor in Birmingham. According to official sources, the IWA at this time existed 'little more than in name', and even the Coventry branch functioned 'lamely'. Several reasons were advanced for its slow progress: first, there were the air raids over the Midlands in the winter of 1940/41, which disrupted normal life. Second, 'general illiteracy' among the Indian workers, and third, lack of a 'capable directing hand'. By 1942, however, the IWA had been transformed, the change being attributed to one man, V.S. Sastrya (Sastri or Sastry), elected secretary of the Birmingham branch, following the dismissal of Mohammed Amin Aziz, its 'inefficient' first secretary. Vellala Srikantaya Sastrya, an educated Madrassi journalist, married to an English woman, and alleged to be 'a convinced Trotskyist' and a member of the ILP, was described as 'extremely able', with 'considerable' organising ability and capable of 'infecting' others with his own enthusiasm. At a meeting held in Birmingham in January 1942 and attended by delegates from Birmingham, Bradford, Coventry and London, the structure of the IWA was formalised. A Central Committee, elected yearly, based in Birmingham (25A Paradise Street), was set up. Its members, drawn from the IWA branch leadership, met monthly, in rotation, at Birmingham, Bradford or Coventry.[46]

By the summer of 1942, IWA branches had been formed in Manchester, Newcastle and Wolverhampton. Six months later, by early 1943, there were eight branches, seven in the Midlands and one in Dundee. Commenting on the progress achieved in the 'past six months', intelligence reports named Sastrya, Thakur Singh Basra, Kartar Singh Nagra and Akbar Ali Khan, as the 'driving force' behind the IWA. Khan, a man of 'superior education', an active fundraiser for political causes, and influential among Muslims, was said to hold 'advanced political views'. The IWA was 'loosely-knit', with self-contained branch organisations, functioning 'more or less' independently, electing their own office-bearers, the Central Committee maintaining contact through visits and monthly meetings. Coventry, with seven office-holders, was the largest, and Liverpool the smallest, with Dr G. Abbas, its secretary, the sole post-holder. As on the Central Committee, branch office bearers were Punjabi Sikhs and Muslims.[47] Membership figures available for 1945 show that Coventry, with 230, was the most active, followed by Birmingham, with 200. Bradford had 100 members and Wolverhampton 50. However, these figures provide no guide to its overall strength. Further, by 1945, some Indian workers were beginning to return to India. By then factions, too, had begun to appear.[48]

As a social/welfare organisation, the IWA helped its members with registration and National Service papers during the war. In his capacity as general secretary, Sastrya investigated cases of accident and injury at work, taking up claims for compensation with appropriate authorities. The IWA provided a platform for grievances concerning work and housing. It ran classes in English and Hindi and remitted funds to *Desh*

Bhagat Parwarik Sahaik Committee. As an organised movement of Indian workers, it enabled its members to participate in the British labour movement. For instance, during the 1942 May Day celebrations in Coventry, over 100 Indians took part, marching with their banners, winning the trophy for the most striking display that year.[49] The IWA was also a political movement, one of the several in Britain campaigning to raise political consciousness for Indian freedom. According to one IWA voice, Indian workers, with their village background, possessed 'very poor knowledge of the world', and it was at the IWA meetings that they learnt concepts like 'freedom and slavery'. Branch meetings, conducted in Indian languages, were held regularly on Sundays. Open meetings in English were held at Coventry, Birmingham or Bradford every two months.[50] In April 1943, the IWA joined with Swaraj House to form the Federation of Indian Associations in Great Britain (FIAGB), with Surat Alley as president, Sastrya secretary and Balram Kaura of Newcastle IWA the treasurer. As a result, intelligence sources suggest, the activities of the Central Committee of the two bodies became 'increasingly indistinguishable'. Nonetheless, individual IWA members, Charan Singh Chima, president of the Coventry branch, for instance, joined the India League, and there is evidence of joint meetings.[51]

Surveillance reports provide a flavour of IWA meetings, attended by both Sikhs and Muslims, and individuals from sympathetic organisations; the names of Fenner Brockway (ILP) and Vic Yates (India League) are cited. Important events in the Indian historical calendar, like Jallianwallah Bagh Day (Amritsar massacre) were marked with national songs, speeches and poems, described as 'ultra patriotic', 'inflammatory' and 'most objectionable'. The Indian National Congress flag and the framed photograph of Udham Singh were often in evidence. Singh, a political activist with *Ghadar* connections, having a record of smuggling revolvers into India and under Special Branch surveillance for some years, had rocked the political establishment when in March 1940, at a meeting of the East India Association at Caxton Hall, in London, he had shot dead Michael O'Dwyer, the governor of the Punjab at the time of the Amritsar massacre. Singh, answering to the name of Mahomed Singh Azad when arrested (signifying Sikh-Muslim unity and freedom), was hanged in July 1940. He acquired the status of a martyr and legends surround him. The IWA targeted the Secretary of State for India, L.S. Amery's constituency, interrupting meetings. At one such meeting of the Sparkbrook Division of the Conservative Party in October 1943, when Amery spoke on the situation in India, 30 Indians led by Sastrya unfurled a banner proclaiming 'Churchill and Amery are killing men, women and children.'[52]

India Office viewed the politicisation of working-class Indians with alarm. In an attempt to kill the movement, its leadership was dispersed. For instance, Sastrya was ordered to London for training, and Charan Singh Chima's employers posted him to Gloucester. Further, social clubs, staffed by retired Indian servicemen and missionaries, were proposed to entice them away from the IWA. Even a secret list for the internment of ringleaders was prepared.[53]

How effective was the IWA? Given the international context of the war, its activities may have appeared 'disturbing'. But the authorities admit that it was not an organisation of a 'terrorist character', posing a threat to Britain's 'internal security'. By 1945, the IWA was beginning to disintegrate under the strain of splits and faction fighting. Prominent leaders, Akbar Ali Khan, for instance, left to form a rival IWA in London. By 1947, IWA branches were seriously depleted and by 1950, it had almost disappeared, to be revived again by the post-1950s migrants. However, the IWA remained true to its vision of the unity of India, protesting against plans to partition India.[54]

WORKING-CLASS FAMILY LIFE

Indians in Britain during this period were overwhelmingly male. But women were not entirely absent. For instance, a 1940 photograph shows a Sikh with his wife and child sheltering in the crypt of Christ Church, Spitalfields, east London. Mention is made of the arrival in 1937 of Mrs Vidya Wanti Chada, perhaps the first Indian woman in Northern Ireland, and of Mrs Bal Krishna to Scotland in 1939. Dr Diwan Singh lived with his Indian wife in Birmingham, while Savitri Chowdhary joined Dr Dharm Sheel Chowdhary, in Laindon, Essex, in 1932. Dr Faridoon Boomla, who came to Britain in 1926, lived with his Parsi wife and three children in Plumstead, south London.[55] However, given the sexual imbalance, out-marriages by both the professionals and the working class would not have been unusual. That such marriages and relationships were not uncommon is evident from references in contemporary literature, but particularly as a 'social problem' with regard to working-class family life. The 1939 Hunter Report, commenting on the growth of a working-class Indian population in Liverpool and London, warned that Indians were creating a 'social problem' 'comparable to that of the negro', and the 'problem' of 'half-caste children … increasingly difficult', added to the 'already complex colour problem'. Police in the Midlands voiced similar anxieties, stressing that the 'numbers of young girls' associating with Indian men was a 'serious social evil'.[56] Historians of black history have commented on a spate of reports in the

1930s which portrayed 'half-caste children' (of African parentage) within a 'hereditarian and eugenical' analysis and the racialised view of society that they contributed to a 'process of moral decline'.[57] While Hunter, and others before him (e.g. Christian bodies), saw English women who married or lived with Indians as women of the 'worst type', the police added another ingredient. These women were said to be not only of 'loose character' who 'sold their favours' to different Indian men, but young women of 'low intellect' who 'made a habit of seeking out' Indians. Raising the spectre of 'half-caste' children and the resulting 'grave consequences', the police urged that such women needed protection against 'their own foolishness'. The view that women of 'low mentality' married 'coloured men' is echoed in the 1944 Report on Stepney, London, by a group of residents 'seriously concerned' for the welfare of 'coloured people'. It even suggested that such marriages were not an equal partnership, the wives having the 'distinct feeling' that they had 'lowered' themselves. However, examples of women like Mary Fazel or Mary Khan and others, regardless of class, do not fit the image portrayed. Such marriages were an act of love and not a matter of colour, whatever the societal view.[58]

Racist and gendered views aside, these reports document the extent of inter-racial relationships. In the absence of detailed census data of households and families, a global picture cannot be drawn. But, a snapshot is contained in the 1944 Report on a small area of Stepney. Without claiming that the study is representative, and however crude and unscientific the method of data gathering, nonetheless, it provides a useful starting point. The Report counted 400 'coloured people', including 12 women and 136 children, living in Stepney. Of these, almost half, 49.2 per cent, were Indians, 45.4 per cent 'Colonials', comprising West Africans, West Indians and men from Ceylon, Malaya and Aden. The rest, 5.4 per cent, came from the Sudan, South Africa and Egypt. Of the 75 married men, 32, slightly under 50 per cent, were Indians, of whom 14 were not legally married to the mother. The study found 136 'coloured or half-caste' children. Of these, 61 (45 per cent) had Indian fathers, comprising 33 families. The age range of the children sheds some light on the length of the marriage/relationship. Of the 61 Indian children, 38 (62 per cent) were under 5 years old, 22 (36 per cent) between 5 and 14, and one was aged 15. Interestingly, one mother, with 4 children, was classified as a 'half-caste Indian', who, after the death of her Indian husband, married a West African. There were also 4 'pure race' Malay among the 'Colonial' children. What emerges from this small sample is the multi-racial nature of Stepney and marriages across the racial divide. Nancie Sharpe's report on 'coloured' people of African descent in Stepney and Canning Town in the 1930s also bears this out.[59] What such reports further reveal is the deep-seated pattern of prejudice and poverty, which blighted their lives. As mentioned earlier, Indians who could find employment worked for wages refused by whites. Sharpe, too, confirms the low wage rates, as low as £2. 15s. a week. Housing was another problem. Landlords did not want 'coloured' men as tenants, with the result that families lived in one or two 'poorly furnished' rooms in dilapidated, overcrowded houses. Those able to rent a house usually let rooms to friends, living in one or two rooms themselves, further confirming poverty and the need to take in lodgers. The Indo-Briton (and Afro-Briton) offspring of these cross-cultural marriages, too, faced an uncertain future, caught in a cycle of prejudice and poverty. According to Young, 'few, if any' were able to stay on at school beyond the age of 14. In the labour market they faced race discrimination. Even in war-time Britain, when jobs were plentiful and labour scarce, they could only get unskilled work, perpetuating the cycle. To quote Sharpe, 'The whole economic situation of these families is an indictment of the society in which they live.'[60]

COLOUR BAR

Working-class Indians were not the only British citizens to be racialised and viewed as a problem in the inter-war years. A colour bar was experienced by all Asians (and blacks) at different levels and areas of life, as can be seen from their memoirs, their letters of protest in the media and to the India Office, and from questions in Parliament. It was as a student at Oxford in the 1930s that D.F. Karaka became conscious of his colour, more than 'any other classification'. He wrote: 'Then I forget that I am a Parsee, or an Indian or anything else, and I realise that the most significant fact about myself is that I am born dark.' Elected first Indian President of the Oxford Union, his achievement was marred by a leading London paper's comment that his election 'made the office ... no longer what it was'. Karaka made 'colour bar' the theme of his farewell speech to the union, and wrote articles on it. He described the 'aloofness' he encountered from undergraduates, an experience shared by A.S.P. Ayyar, a student at Oxford in the 1920s. Ayyar describes the subterfuge practised by landladies to keep Indian students out. When he confronted one 'in the centre of Oxford', he was informed that it was because 'other lodgers' 'objected to coloured gentlemen'. In May 1927, following reports that Indian, African and Chinese students in Edinburgh were being barred by a number of dance halls and restaurants, Saklatvala, the Battersea MP, twice urged Sir John Gilmour, the Scottish

Secretary to take action to prevent the 'obnoxious' practice of exclusion of a whole community 'on account of their racial origin'. George Lansbury added his voice in support. But while the affair was 'much regretted', both Gilmour and the Secretary of State for India deemed the matter to be outside their control and 'for decision on the part of the private enterprise ... concerned'. That this was not an isolated incident is seen from discussion in the local press. Indeed, several dance halls had operated a policy of 'colour ban' from the day they opened; others introduced it later. Some dance halls even operated complex rules: one permitted 'coloureds' on the premises, but only during the afternoon and only if accompanied by a 'white resident'; another allowed 'Asiatics or Africans' to 'partake of refreshments but not to dance'. And the reason? Objections from Scottish patrons to 'coloured visitors on the dance floor'. One restaurant manager, claiming that whites would not patronise his restaurant if 'Asiatics or Africans were permitted to frequent the premises', introduced a mini-apartheid, segregating 'coloured' students in one section of the restaurant set aside for them. To show what they thought of such discriminatory patronage, the 'coloured' patrons organised a deputation to the Lord Provost and a telegram of protest to the King.[61] Whether a 'colour ban' operated in flats and lodging-houses, restaurants and hotels or dance halls and dancing schools, the justification was always the same. Owners denied they were personally biased against Indians, but blamed their 'other' patrons. Phillipa Peeler, at the Ruby Peeler School of Dancing in Oxford, explained that the ban on Indian undergraduates had been forced on the School as white undergraduates objected to her 'dancing with Indians'. Hotels claimed that it was 'other guests' – 'Americans from Southern States or ultra-sahib Anglo-Indians' – who objected to Indians and Africans.[62] Underlying such claims, two issues concerning the state of race relations emerge: first, is the 'woman question', fear of sexual relations between black men and white women, a theme constant in British imperial history, as has been noted; and second, a general aversion to social intermingling between the races.

The Hotels and Restaurants Association of Great Britain denied there was any prejudice against Indians. H.S. Townend, its general-secretary, claimed that 'the matter really concerns the class of Indian rather than the hotels', a classic ploy of blaming the victim.[63] However, from the voluminous correspondence in the files marked 'Colour Bar' and 'Accommodation for Indians in England', we get a measure of how pernicious was the practice.[64] J.R. Shah, unable to get accommodation in a boarding-house or with a family, tried renting a flat. But invariably, the house agent informed him the very 'next morning' that the flat offered him was already let. Sir T. Vijayaraghavacharya, Commissioner for India at the 1924 Wembley Exhibition, narrated similar experiences, but with hotels in South Kensington. He commented wryly that 'that half-hour', between his phoning and arrival in person, 'must have been an unusually busy time for them'. Saliq Ram Kakar, a businessman, resident in London for 13 years, found that despite 'unimpeachable' references from bankers and solicitors, his offers for flats were rejected. Yet the same flat refused him was available 'for hire' to a friend, a French national. Such 'insult' led Kakar to consult his solicitors. But there was no redress in law. The final example comes from Agatha Harrison. When trying to obtain a flat in 1938 for Nehru and his daughter then at Oxford, she was shocked to find that even 'a distinguished' Indian like Nehru, a 'Cambridge graduate and ex-President of the Indian National Congress', was 'not acceptable' at St Ermine's Mansions by Sloane Avenue. In 1938, 11 years after Saklatvala had raised the matter in Parliament, Sorensen, too, found Parliament unwilling to make the operation of a colour bar in hotels a 'penal offence'. According to the Home Secretary, under the common law, inn-keepers (proprietors of public institutions) were under 'certain obligation' to receive and entertain 'all travellers', so ruling out legislation. But, as the India Office legal adviser noted, no proprietor would be 'foolish' enough to admit discrimination.[65]

But the fact that Sir Findlater Stewart, Permanent Under-Secretary of State for India, admitted that he was 'rather exercised' by the 'not infrequent' instances of Indians refused accommodation 'apparently on racial grounds', suggests that the India Office considered the publicity damaging. Further, as it was known that Indian businessmen received a far more 'cordial welcome' in Paris and Berlin, it was feared that the 'colour bar' would ultimately rebound on British business.[66] In an attempt to shield Indians from the crude racism in hotels, restaurants and boarding-houses, Sir Findlater Stewart met the general-secretary of the Hotel and Restaurants Association. After 'much persuasion' and several draft letters, in late December 1938, the Association issued a circular, approved by the India Office, to its 1,550 members, informing them that Lord Zetland and the British government wished Indian visitors to be 'treated ... *on their merits*' (italics in the original). Replies to the circular were monitored, so that Indians could be directed only to hotels and boarding-houses willing to take Indians, thus avoiding 'awkward "contre-temps" '. The India Office considered this a 'good beginning' and the 'best' solution 'so far' to the problem.[67] But the colour bar was not outlawed. By a cosmetic exercise it was merely made to appear that it did not exist. The hollowness of the pretence was soon exposed: of the five listed hotels tried by one Indian, three refused to take him. In 1941, no less a person than Sir Hari Singh Gour, a lawyer, a member of the East India Association, deputy president of the Indian Legislative Assembly, a member of the Simon Commission's Indian Committee, vice-president of Delhi and Nagpur Universities and a Fellow of the Royal Society of Literature, was refused accommodation by a West End hotel. The snub caused a sensation, especially when thousands of Indians soldiers and sailors were fighting against Fascism and Nazism. Questions were asked in Parliament. But while the government maintained it had no powers to intervene, an embarrassed India Office, in a flurry of cables, tried to prevent the Indian press from capitalising on the publicity given in the British media.[68] Two years later, when the Imperial Hotel in Russell Square turned away the well-known Trinidadian cricketer, Learie Constantine, he sued the hotel and won.

INDIANS IN BUSINESS

Indian businesses linked with white companies having interests in India, or with Indian merchant-houses and industries, like Cama and Company or Tata and Company, had been set up before the First World War (see Chapter 3). A 1933 survey of Indians overseas mentioned a number of firms located in London and Manchester, including two firms of accountants. A total of 48 such businesses were classified as 'Indian'. A random search, under the rubric, 'Merchants-East India', in the 1938 *Kelly's Directory* for London, shows Bakubhai and Ambalal Limited at 14–20 St Mary Axe, EC 3, and Cama, Surosh K.R. and Company at Philpot Lane. Surveillance reports list Ram Chand and Son, Oriental Importers, Bevis Marks, London E3 and Rohai Singh of New Indian Sports Limited at 57 St Paul's Yard, EC 4. D.S. Erulkar was another well-known Parsi merchant. In 1927, the Indian Chamber of Commerce was founded; in 1931, K.P. Mehta of Tata was named its president. Indian draperies supplying pedlars have already been noted. In 1935, Shahibdad Khan, a Punjabi Muslim living in Romford, Essex, with his English wife and two children, established the Egyptian Perfumery Company at 9 Assam Street, London. By 1938, Khan was trading under his own name. In 1943, in Northern Ireland, the Chada brothers opened the Corner Boot Stores in Waterloo Street, Londonderry.[69] Dr Sasadhar Sinha, an economist, a writer, and member of the Indian Progressive Writers' Association, ran the Bibliophile bookshop, at 16 Little Russell Street, near the British Museum, supplying new and second-hand books. Sinha had come to Britain in 1925 to study at the LSE, obtaining a BSc in 1928, and later a doctorate. The Bibliophile, opened in 1935, was a meeting place for the many politically minded Indians in London. Active in the Indian independence movement, Sinha, married to Marthe Goldwyn (Goldberg), a teacher at Prendergast Girls' School in Lewisham, was an LCC panel lecturer in sociology, current affairs and Indian history at Eltham and Plumstead Literary Evening Institute, and the Lewisham and Dulwich Literary Institute, south London from the 1940s. The range of Asian enterprises is further illustrated in a 1937 advertisement in the *Indian Student*, the quarterly Journal of the Federation of Indian Students' Societies in Great Britain and Ireland, which drew attention to 'the only Indian estate agency in England'. Possibly the earliest such agency, Nitra and Company (42 Mornington Crescent) arranged accommodation for Indian students and visitors to London. The Arya Bhavan, 30 Belsize Park, London (manager, M.U. Patel), billed as the 'only strictly vegetarian guest-house', was advertised in the same journal.[70]

What is perhaps more noteworthy is the appearance of Indian grocery stores. The Bombay Emporium (BE), 70 Grafton Street, Tottenham Court Road (and at 3 Leicester Place), London, importers and manufacturers of Indian groceries and condiments, was established in 1931. The first such enterprise, BE specialised in a range of 'ethnic' foods: Indian spices, Bombay and Madras curry powders, sweet mango chutney, hot pickles, papadams and a variety of rice, dhalls, betel leaves and nuts, Indian oils, and teas and coffees. In a tiny warehouse, in London's Portobello road, a 'Mr Mistry', described as 'a wonderful old chap', hand-prepared the tins of curry powder and *haldi* (turmeric). Seven decades later, BE, trading as Bombay International is still with us, managed by Raymond and Antony Chatwell, the sons of the Indian founder (died in 1973) of this family enterprise. Its well-known brands (e.g. Rajah, Lotus and Amoy) are stocked in many supermarkets. Suleiman Jetha, at 117 New Cavendish Street, London W1, was advertised as a supplier of the 'best quality curry powder' in the *Oriental Post*, 'an independent monthly organ of the Oriental Colony of Great Britain'. The first Bengali food shop in London's East End, Taj Stores, opened in 1936. In Glasgow in 1932, Sher Qadir and his Scottish wife, Mary, established Scotland's first Indian grocery. By 1935, according to the Valuation Roll, there were at least three Indian grocery/general stores in Glasgow.[71] Serving the culinary needs of Indians in Britain and Northern Ireland, these 'ethnic' groceries were patronised by white families with Indian army and civil service connections. What is even more significant, however, is that the emergence of 'ethnic' shops suggests that an 'Indian community' was already established in Britain, long before the arrival of the post-1950s

Asian migrants. Indian social and religious organisations and institutions, too, support such a view.

Indian restaurants, so popular today, were also part of the British restaurant scene before the 1960s. This is evident from contemporary memoirs, advertisements and references in Scotland Yard reports. Cafes catering for Indian seamen often served 'curry and rice'; their Indian cooks were usually Sylheti galley chefs who had jumped ship. From cafes the next step was Indian restaurants. By the early years of the twentieth century, restaurants like the one in Red Lion Passage, patronised by Indian students, were already in existence (see Chapter 3). During the inter-war years a different class of restaurants, with distinctive Indian names, employing Indian cooks and under Indian management were established, one Indian visitor in 1937 listing 16 in London alone. One, The Indian Restaurants Ltd, described as 'THE place for curries to suit all tastes', possibly established before the war (see Chapter 3), was annually advertised in Ward Lock & Co.'s guide to London from 1920/21, while Ayyar mentions having 'discovered' it in 1919. The two West End Indian restaurants usually cited are Shafi's and Veeraswami's. Shafi's, at 18 Gerrard Street, had its origin in the 1920s when, it is said, two brothers from north India, who had come to study in Britain, noticing a demand for Indian food, bought a cafe and turned it into a restaurant. Shafi's first appears in the Post Office London Directory in 1934. Veeraswami's in Regent Street (now owned by the Group Chutney Mary) was in a totally different class. Established in 1926 by Edward Palmer, a descendant of William Palmer and Begum Faiz Bux (see Chapter 2), it was patronised by royalty. Edward VIII dined there, as did Indian maharajahs.[72] Other restaurants in London's West End, perhaps not as well known now, but popular with contemporaries, include the Taj-Mahal (India) Restaurant in West Street, Cambridge Circus, advertised in the *Indian Student* in 1937 as 'newly opened', and the same journal recommended the Koh-i-Noor in Rupert Street for its 'finest Indian food'. Rajah Restaurant, 17 Irving Street, was named by Scotland Yard as was the Cafe Indien (re-named the India and Burma Restaurant, proprietor D.P. Chaudhuri) at 7 Leicester Place, Leicester Square. 'Outside catering' undertaken by some West End restaurants, notably the Taj Mahal and the Koh-i-Noor, suggests the popularity of Indian cuisine at private functions. The Oriental Restaurant, 192 the Broadway in south-west London, and Singh's Restaurant (proprietor Narain Singh) in Whitechapel, Aldgate, east London, are both mentioned in the *Oriental Post*. Some enterprising Sylheti seamen living in the East End and employed as cooks, sometimes set themselves up as restaurant entrepreneurs. Mosharaf Ali and Israel Miah are named as pioneers, who clubbed together savings and loans from friends to open the Anglo-Asia in Brompton Road, the first of their many enterprises. But in war-time Britain, savings could be as easily lost in the restaurant businesses. Qureshi's Dilkush in Windmill Street was razed to the ground in the blitz, in 1940, within two years of its purchase.[73] By 1946, Adams suggests, there were 20 Indian restaurants in London. Outside London, there was the Taj Mahal in Glasgow, advertised in the 1938 Empire Exhibition *Official Guide*, its proprietor identified by IPI as 'Bidhu Busan De'. Koh-i-Noor, at 12 St John Street, Cambridge, was a sister to the London restaurant.[74] Restaurants dating from the inter-war period afforded training and inspiration to the post-1960s 'Indian' restaurants, a majority Bangladeshi-owned.

INDIAN DOCTORS

One of the most distinctive features of the NHS since its inception in 1948 has been the large number of Asian doctors in the medical service. Indian doctors, however, as has been seen, have been around since the time of Sake Dean Mahomed. In fact, scholars have commented on their numbers in the inter-war period, one historian estimating that by 1945 there were 'no less' than 1,000 throughout Britain, 200 of them in London alone. Indeed, the Indian Medical Association was founded in the early 1930s.[75] These inter-war doctors were the first Asians to service the NHS, some having come for further studies and settled here in the 1920s and 1930s. Since qualifications obtained from universities in British India were not recognised, they had first to undergo further training to obtain a conjoint diploma from British universities. The nature of the available demographic information makes mapping difficult: names of some feature regularly in intelligence reports, not for their medical work, but for their politics, being active in the anti-colonial movement for Indian freedom. Others are listed in the medical directories. A few have left us landmarks of their contribution to British life, but today they are largely forgotten. By all accounts, Indian doctors were popular with their patients, drawn largely from working-class backgrounds in urban centres. Their devotion to their patients and the communities they served is evident from some of the available documentation. Apart from doctors, there were Indian ophthalmic surgeons, Rochi Hingorani at Harley Street and Ganpat Rai Bhatia at 112 Gower Street, London, for instance. Abdul Majid Khan was a veterinary surgeon in west London.[76]

There are instances of sons and grandsons following the family tradition. For instance, in 1928, when Dr Faridoon Boomla arrived from

Bombay to 'set up shop' in a basement surgery at 291 High Street, Plumstead, little did he know that the Boomla medical 'dynasty' would endure for over 60 years. After his death in 1940, his sons, Rooin and Darius, continued the Plumstead practice well into the early 1990s, until their retirement. His grandson is a GP in east London today. Working-class Cardiff, too, has a tradition of Indian doctors going back to the 1920s. Others led multi-faceted lives. K.S. Bhatt, whose surgery was in working-class Rotherhithe, at 61 Southwark Park Road, was known to speak on poverty and malnutrition. He was also the secretary of the WWLI and later the secretary of the Hindu Association of Europe (see p. 298).[77] The life of another, Dr Sukhsagar Datta (1890–1967) of Bristol, whose connection with that city spans over half a century, and who was active both in the British Labour Party and in the anti-colonial movement, provides a vivid illustration of the interaction between these two movements, and the involvement of both Indians and whites in India's freedom struggle.

Born in Bengal, Sukhsagar Datta, from a family with a known record of nationalist activity – his older brother was imprisoned for his part in bomb-making that had ended in the accidental death of two English women (the Alipore Conspiracy case 1908), an experience which affected the young Datta deeply – was packed off to England, in 1908, so that the family would not 'lose another son to the Raj'. Secret police followed his movements, recording his association with the India House 'extremist gang'. In London, he met and married Ruby Young of Bristol. He joined Bristol University Medical School, graduating in 1920. He was one of the first to study for the new Diploma in Psychiatric Medicine, qualifying as an MD in 1931. Appointed House Physician at Bristol General and then Southmead Infirmary in 1922, Dr Datta became a Senior Medial Officer at Manor Park Hospital, till his retirement in 1956. For 'many years' he was the 'only doctor' responsible for the care of patients in Stapleton Institution, described in the 1920s as having '600 imbeciles and a few chronic aged infirm cases', and of Downend Children's Home and Snowdon Road Children's Home. Like many Indian doctors at the time, Datta worked as a volunteer in the St John's Ambulance Brigade from 1937 and, in 1959, in recognition of his services, he was appointed Officer Brother. During the war, he played an active role in the Bristol Civil Defence programme.[78]

Attracted by socialist ideals, Datta joined the Bristol Labour Party in 1926. He became an active member, speaking at political rallies on Clifton Downs, and writing in the *Bristol Labour Weekly*. In 1946, he became chairman of the Bristol North Labour Party, and later Chairman of Bristol Borough Labour Party. In 1946–7, he became president of Bristol Trades Council. Given his commitment to Indian freedom, he joined the India League in the 1930s, and worked to educate Bristolians, and the local Labour Party in particular, about conditions in India and the justice of India's fight for freedom. With Mrs D. Parker-Rhodes, Datta, described as Menon's main contact in the League's Bristol Branch, organised meetings addressed by Menon, Bhicoo Batlivala, as well as Datta himself, Jim Baty and other activists in the Bristol Labour Party and the trade union movement. His efforts contributed to the Bristol Labour Party's pledge to support the NUR resolution on India calling for the formation of an independent Indian National Government at the 1944 Labour Party Conference. And it was Datta who, in a speech described as 'his finest', seconded the 'historic' NUR resolution. In 1947, when India became independent, at a gathering of the many Indian and white activists who had campaigned with him, Datta founded the Bristol Indian Association (BIA), a fitting memorial to their work. A lively multi-racial organisation, in 1983 the BIA organised the 150th anniversary celebrations of Rammohun Roy's death in Bristol. Sukhsagar Datta died in Bristol in 1967. His descendants still live in England.[79]

Some Indian doctors made distinctive contributions to British life, locally in the communities where they worked. Dr Baldev Kaushal (1906–92), born in the Punjab, had a large general practice in working-class Bethnal Green. In 1945 he was awarded an MBE for his 'gallant conduct' on several occasions during the heavy blitz over east London, but particularly for his act of courage on 20 September 1944. According to the official citation, although injured himself, he 're-mained at an incident attending to casualties until all had been removed'. Dr Kaushal continued working in Bethnal Green for well over half a century, into the 1980s.[80] A memorial of a different kind is left us by Dr Jainti Saggar (1898–1954), one of the longest-serving members of the Dundee Town Council, who first came to Britain from the Punjab in 1919, to study medicine at St Andrews University. Graduating as a Bachelor of Medicine and Surgery, he went on to take diplomas in public health and ophthalmic medicine and surgery. In 1923, he set up as a doctor in Dundee. One of the first, and perhaps the only Indian in Dundee at the time, he not only managed to win the confidence of his patients, but also the hand of Jane Quinn, the daughter of a bailie and town councillor of the City of Dundee. A member of Dundee Labour Party, in 1936, Saggar contested Ward 8. Topping the poll, he became the first Indian to be elected councillor in Scotland, an achievement which shows the respect he had earned within the community, and confirmed by the fact that in each subsequent council election he was re-elected. In 1939, preferring to remain on the council, he turned down an opportunity of a parliamentary seat. A councillor for 18 years, Saggar devoted an ever-increasing amount of his leisure time to public service: he was secretary of the Dundee Town Council Labour Group, convenor of the Public Health Committee and Chairman of the Public Libraries Committee. But it was education that was one of his chief interests, as can be seen from his membership of the general committee of the local branch of the Nursery Schools Association of Great Britain. With the coming of the NHS, he was appointed member of both the Eastern Regional Hospital Board and the Board of Management of Dundee General Hospitals. A factual account of his activities in public life conveys neither the measure of Saggar's achievements, nor the level of his work in the community. This is evident from the tributes on his death at the age of 56. The Lord Provost of Dundee, in publicly acknowledging his work, put on record the sentiment of many when he said that Dundee was 'much poorer by his passing'. The fact that 20 years after his death, in the 1970s, a street was named Saggar Street by Dundee Corporation, and in 1974, a public library was opened in memory of Dr Jainti Saggar and his brother Dr Dhani Ram, demonstrates Dundonians' esteem.[81]

Chowdhary County Primary School in Markhams Chase, Laindon, Essex, was named in memory of Dr Dharm Sheel Chowdhary, (1902–59), born in the Punjab and a doctor in Laindon for over a quarter-century. Graduating with an MBBS from Lahore University in 1927, in 1928, Chowdhary came to London for postgraduate studies, obtaining the conjoint qualification in 1930 and diplomas in Public Health (London) and in Tropical Medicine (Liverpool) in 1931. He then joined the rural practice of Dr Gilder in Laindon, purchasing the practice in 1933, on Gilder's retirement. In villages like Laindon, country doctors had to be more than a family doctor, Chowdhary having to adapt to become their GP, dentist and counsellor. That he won their trust and respect is seen from the fact that not only was he affectionately called 'Doc' by young and old, but his practice, too, grew, expanding into three surgeries and he had to advertise in the *British Medical Journal* for an assistant. In addition, he was a Divisional Surgeon of the St John's Ambulance Brigade. In 1953, for his 29-year record of voluntary service, he was appointed a Serving Brother in the Order of St John of Jerusalem. During the Second World War, he served in the Civil Defence and was in charge of Laindon First Aid Post and a captain in the Home Guard. Chowdhary was also involved in the welfare of the elderly, and for many years was vice-president of the Laindon and District Operatic Society. A generous man, knowing how poor some of his patients were, he was known to tear up the bill and dispense medicine free of charge in the days before the NHS.[82] How deep an impression he had made is seen from the fact that, when he died in December 1959, aged 57, Laindon mourned him, patients paying their last homage by 'standing perfectly still' on the pavement. It was said that 'no one had ever seen the church so full', and there were many letters of sympathy and donations to his favourite charities. But it is the Chowdhary County Primary School, built in 1966, seven years after his death, and named after him by popular demand, which stands as a memorial to his service to Laindon as the inscription on the brass plaque records: 'To honour the memory of Dr Dharm Sheel Chowdhary who gave devoted service to the people of Laindon and the local schools throughout the period from 1931–1959.' The school maintained contact with the Chowdhary family, until its final closure in July 1996, due to falling rolls and decay of the 1960s building.[83]

Dr Harbans Lall Gulati (1896–1967), the pioneer of the 'meals-on-wheels' service, was also a London County Councillor, and a magistrate. Born in the Punjab, he was educated at Lahore University. Joining the IMS in 1916, he was posted on the North-West Frontier. In 1920, working his passage to England, he came for further studies. Without funds, taking menial jobs, often at night, he put himself through Charing Cross Hospital Medical School to re-qualify, obtaining the conjoint diploma in 1926. Such experiences shaped his outlook and philosophy of public service. Gulati was on the management committee of the Indian YMCA. But it was as a GP in the working-class district of Battersea for over 40 years, and as a surgeon at the Royal Westminster Ophthalmic Hospital (having taken the DOMS in 1945) that he is better known. Popular with his patients, it was said that even after they had left the district, they travelled miles to see him. During the Second World War, he was in the St John's and Red Cross organisations, but it was as a social worker with children and old people that he is best remembered, pioneering the widely used 'meals-on-wheels' service. Gulati was active in Conservative politics and, in 1934, elected to the Borough Council, he served on various committees, including health, libraries and national savings. He resigned from the Conservative Party in 1947, on principle, over its hostility to the NHS. He joined the Socialist Medical Association (SMA), becoming its secretary. He also joined the Labour Party, and such was his personal appeal, that he was soon back on the council. In 1955, he contested the LCC elections, winning as a member for South Battersea. A prospective parliamentary candidate, pressure of work prevented him from fulfilling his political ambition. In 1940, Gulati was appointed a magistrate for the South-Western Petty Sessional

Division, possibly one of the first Asians to serve in that capacity. He died in June 1967.[84]

But it is Dr Chuni Lal Katial (1898–1978), Britain's first Asian Mayor and the driving force behind the Finsbury Health Centre, who is perhaps the most significant of the inter-war generation of Indian doctors. An activist in the India League and one of the Trustees and Directors of the Hindu Association of Europe, Katial was born in the Punjab. Educated at Punjab University, he graduated with an MBBS in 1922. For the next five years, as captain in the IMS attached to the RAF, he served in Baghdad. In 1927, he came to Britain, obtaining, in 1928, a Diploma in Tropical Medicine from Liverpool University and an LM from Dublin University. He was elected Fellow of the Royal Society of Tropical Medicine, and was a member of the SMA. Katial established his first medical practice (with Dr Satis Chandra Sen) among the poor in Victoria Dock Road, Canning Town.[85] And it was here that in 1931 he arranged a meeting between Gandhi and Charlie Chaplin during Gandhi's visit to the East End. Influenced by Gandhian philosophy of service for the benefit of humanity without personal reward, Katial's 23 years of public service in London reflected that spirit. In 1934, he moved to Finsbury, the borough that had elected Naoroji MP. Katial's surgery at 4 Spencer Street became so well known throughout the borough that it was said that 'the difference between east and west did not exist there'. In 1934, Katial entered on a public career when he was elected Labour Councillor for St John's Ward, Finsbury. And, as the Chairman of the Public Health Committee, he became instrumental in giving Finsbury a public health centre far in advance of the time, and which became 'almost universally famous'.[86]

Like many contemporary London boroughs, Finsbury, an industrial borough, described as '100 percent working-class', suffered from overcrowding and poor housing. There was poverty and ill health: children were malnourished, prone to TB, bronchial diseases and pneumonia. Medical facilities were fragmented and inaccessible, spread over the borough in 'a maze of dispensaries, voluntary hospitals, private contracts, clubs and clinics'.[87] Despite several reports nationally (e.g. the 1926 Royal Commission on National Health Insurance and the 1937 report by the SMA on health services), governments remained reluctant to embark on a revolutionary reform, requiring huge public expenditure. At Finsbury, however, in 1931, the Labour Council, led by Alderman Harold Riley, drew up the 'Finsbury Plan', a comprehensive programme for health and housing, with a new health centre at its heart. But by 1933 the Plan had been abandoned. In 1935, as the Chairman of the Public Health Committee, Katial not only revived the Plan, he pushed for a rationalised health service. In the event, the only project to be built before the war was the Finsbury Health Centre, despite opposition from some council members. It was Katial, too, who commissioned Berthold Lubetkin (1901–90), of the Tecton Group, as architect, so impressed had he been with Lubetkin's design for a TB clinic unveiled at the BMA in 1932.[88] Opened in October 1938, the Finsbury Health Centre in Pine Street, revolutionary architecturally, introduced a new concept in medicine: a centralised health service. There was a TB clinic, a foot clinic, a dental surgery, a women's clinic, a solarium as well as disinfectant rooms and a mortuary. Administrative offices, case records and statistics were all under one roof. At its opening, Katial predicted that the Centre marked 'the dawn of a new era' in public health service.[89] Its achievements may appear 'diminutive' today but, in the words of Lubetkin's biographer, in 1938 it marked 'a conspicuous advance in social policy and administrative co-ordination', anticipating the NHS reforms by 10 years.[90]

Today Katial's role in the Health Centre is all but forgotten. But, in the words of Alderman C.H. Simmons in 1948, Katial was acknowledged as:

> an institution in Finsbury local government, especially in connection with our almost universally famous health centre and the work he put into it – not only structurally ... on what form it would take, but also ... with regard to the various services that were constituted.

Indeed, for the November 1937 council elections, the *Finsbury Citizen*, which publicised the health centre as a vote winner (almost two pages were devoted to it), had Katial appealing for votes. Under his strikingly handsome photograph, which described him as the 'Labour Chairman of the Public Health Committee ... who has been untiring in his efforts to bring into being the new Health Centre', his personal message urged: 'I sincerely hope that all who care for the health and well being of the people of the borough will see that a Labour Council is returned ... in order that we can get on with the good work which we are doing.' Thus linking the Centre with its creator in a bold publicity campaign. Labour won the council elections with an increased majority.[91]

In 1938, Katial was unanimously elected Mayor of Finsbury, becoming Britain's first Asian Mayor. During the war, his public duties on the council increased. He was Chairman of the ARP Medical Service and Food Control Committee. He was a Civil Defence First Aid Medical Officer and a member of the City Division Medical Emergency Committee. He was said to be 'completely fearless' in the blitz and 'never had his clothes off for a week'. He was also on the BMA executive committee.[92] A Councillor and Alderman, in 1946, Katial was elected to the LCC, one of the two members from Finsbury. In 1948, in recognition of his services to public health, housing and social welfare, Katial was made Freeman of the Borough, only the third person to receive the honour at the time. It was typical of the man that even the casket presented to him, expressly by his own wishes, was made of wood (not silver or other precious metal as was customary) and crafted by the council's own carpenters, a real 'piece of Finsbury'. In 1948, Katial returned to India to become Director-General, Employees State Insurance Corporation of India. He kept his links with Britain and in the 1970s returned to live in London. He died in 1978.[93]

OTHER PROFESSIONS

Medicine apart, the range and variety of occupations of Indian professionals is astonishing, especially given the total number of Asians in Britain. There were academics, journalists, and accountants, barristers and solicitors, writers and editors, poets and musicians, political thinkers and men of religion. Dr M.D. Ratnasuriya lectured in Sinhalese at the London School of Oriental Studies (now SOAS); Dr Radhakrishnan was Spalding Professor of Oriental Religions at Oxford. Diwan Tulsi Das (1882–1951), a high-caste Brahmin, was a lecturer in Hindustani at Aberdeen University. Das had fetched up in Aberdeen, in 1903, in romantic circumstances. He had come to London in 1900 to study medicine. Having fallen in love with the daughter of Dr Charles Maxwell Muller, to escape parental wrath the couple eloped to Gretna Green, but instead arrived in Aberdeen, where they married and settled down. After several careers, including in the armed forces in the First World War and a taxi business, in the 1920s, he was appointed lecturer at Aberdeen University. Of the barristers and solicitors, we have P.V. Subba-Row, President of the Indian Social Club, who lived in Croydon and Jinnah, who between 1931 and 1934, had his chambers in King's Bench Walk and lived with his sister Fatima and daughter Dina at Hampstead. R.S. Nehra, who had come via East Africa and was for a brief period on the executive of Harold Moody's League of Coloured Peoples (LCP), was a Privy Council solicitor, and Krishna Menon with a reputation in Indian circles as 'a good lawyer' did much legal work without payment.[94] B.B. Ray Chaudhuri, Sunder Kabadi (*Amrit Bazaar Patrika*), and V.R. Karandikar were among the several Indian foreign correspondents in London. Pulin Behari Seal, a maths graduate from Cambridge, married to Judith Stuart and father of three children, reported for the Calcutta daily, *Forward* (later, *Liberty*). He was founder member of the Oriental Press Service, established in 1926 at 92 Fleet Street, to supply Indian news to British and American publications and British news to the Indian media. M.A. Khan, a political activist, was publisher/editor of the *Oriental Post*, founded in 1930.[95]

Of the several literary personalities, the poet, J.M. Tambimuttu, a Tamil from Ceylon, all but forgotten today, was well-known in literary circles as the founder-editor of *Poetry London,* a bi-monthly, started before the Second World War, in February 1939. *Poetry London,* 'an enquiry into Modern Verse', a journal devoted entirely to poetry and criticism, was an exciting venture. Over the 12-year period of its existence (1939–1952), beset by financial difficulties, it nonetheless succeeded in providing an 'intelligent platform' for poets of many talents and traditions. Contributors included W.H. Auden, Stephen Spender and William Empson. Tambimuttu, who also read his own work on the BBC's Indian programme throughout the 1940s, re-emigrated to America, in the 1950s, from where he edited *Poetry-London-New York.* Cedric Dover, an anti-imperialist, the author of *Half-Caste,* who during the war served in the Royal Army Ordnance Corps, also contributed to the BBC Indian programme. His books and essays, for instance, 'The Importance of Minorities', 'Race Mixture and World Peace' 'Freedom and Cultural Expression', remain as topical today.[96] Aubrey Menen (1912–89), the London-born writer, was the son of an Irish mother and Indian father. Mulk Raj Anand, the novelist and critic, also a contributor to the Indian programme, lived in London for almost 20 years. Born in 1905 in Peshawar, he was drawn into nationalist politics in Amritsar, and imprisoned for taking part in non-violent civil disobedience. In 1925, he came to London to study philosophy at University College, obtaining his PhD in 1929. A radical philosopher, an activist in the India League and a member of the Indian Progressive Writers' Association, Anand was briefly a member of the International Brigade in the Spanish Civil War. In London, he became acquainted with the 'Bloomsbury group', including Leonard and Virginia Woolf, worked 'off-time' as a proof corrector at the Hogarth Press and associated with some of the leading writers and intellectuals of the early twentieth century, E.M. Forster, Bonamy Dobrée and Laurence Binyon. Some of Anand's early novels were written and published in Britain, including *Across the Black Waters*, sketched as a rough draft in Spain in 1937 and re-written in Oxfordshire in 1939, and *The Untouchable.* Literary giant and Nobel laureate, Rabindranath Tagore, during his visits to Europe, was lionised in British intellectual circles. Krishnarao Shelvankar (1906–96), writer and journalist for the *Hindu* newspaper from 1942–68, was the author of the classic, *The*

Problem of India, described as 'a brilliant critique' of colonial rule, analysing the case for Indian independence. Published as a Penguin Special in 1940, it was banned in India.[97]

The work of Krishna Menon as an editor is also of note. Author of innumerable pamphlets, for three years, starting in 1932, he worked for Bodley Head. He edited the Twentieth Century Library, a series of serious books of social and topical interest, as well as editing another list, Topical Books, for Selwyn Blount. But Penguin–Pelican remain his most significant publishing contribution. With a colleague at Bodley Head, Allen Lane, Penguin Books was founded in 1935, its first premises in a church crypt. While Lane edited the Penguin fiction, Menon became the first editor of the Pelican Series, more educational in content. Its first title, George Bernard Shaw's *The Intelligent Woman's Guide to Socialism, Capitalism, Sovietism and Fascism*, for which Shaw wrote the section on Fascism specially for this edition, was published in 1937. Modestly priced, Pelicans made scholarship accessible to a wider audience – an extension of Menon's vision seen in the development of the library service when a Labour Councillor in St Pancras (Chapter 10). Menon's choice of the first 20 authors and titles, in the words of *The Times,* still provides 'an intellectual thrill'.[98]

The Dutt brothers, Clemens and the younger Rajani, both writers, were active in radical causes. Rajani Palme Dutt, born in Cambridge in 1896, had been attracted to Marxism as early as 1915. Marxist theoretician, and, in the words of his biographer, 'arguably, the most important figure in the CPGB', Rajani was a founder member of the CPGB and editor for more than 50 years of the journal *Labour Monthly*. A Stalinist, he was the party's intellectual thinker and analyst. Dutt strongly identified with Indian nationalism. His analysis of the condition of India contained in his book, *India Today*, was banned in India. In the 1945 general election, Dutt contested Sparkbrook, Birmingham, as a CPGB candidate against Leo Amery. Ayana D. Angadi, who came to Britain in 1924 to prepare for the ICS examination, instead became a political activist. A Trotskyist, he joined the Labour Party and was the author of several pamphlets under the pseudonym, Raj Hansa. However, it is for introducing western audiences to Indian culture, art, dance, music and yoga that he is better remembered. In 1946, he set up the Asian Music Circle, persuading musicians like Yehudi Menuhin to his cause. Angadi, his wife Patricia Fell-Clarke, together with many volunteers, made Ravi Shankar, Ali Akbar Khan and Alla Rakha, among other notable Asian musicians, more widely known in Britain. Angadi died in 1993.[99]

In the performing arts Kaikhosru Sorabji (1892–1988), composer, pianist, critic and writer, is described as a 'unique figure' in the history of music. Myths and rumours surround Sorabji. It was alleged that his music was unplayable; that he had banned public performances of his music. Recently, writers have set the record straight by pointing out that the 40-year ban amounted to no more than a stipulation that his music could only be performed with his 'express consent'. Concerts and recitals since the mid-1970s by international musicians such as Yonty Solomon, John Ogdon and Donna Amato have demolished the second myth, paying tribute to his unusual gifts as a musician.[100] Born in Essex in 1892, Sorabji's father was a Parsi engineer from Bombay and his mother, a gifted soprano, of Spanish-Sicilian origin. Proud of his ancestral and cultural roots, Sorabji identified himself as a Spanish-Sicilian Parsi. Sorabji, however, was an 'outsider' in another sense. A 'coloured' man, he was also a homosexual. He began composing music from around 1915 and continuing well into the 1980s. His prodigious output for piano and keyboard – he completed over 100 pieces – is remarkable for its rich complexity and length, varying from only a few seconds to 20–30 minutes, to works that lasted entire programmes. His most celebrated early work, *Opus Clavicembalisticum*, a solo piano work, is said to be the longest piece of piano music ever composed, lasting some four and a half hours. Sorabji rarely gave public recitals of his own music, his last appearance being in Glasgow in 1936. Described as 'a virtuoso pianist of international standards', his music is considered 'a seminal force in twentieth century music'. He was also a writer and a critic. Apart from his two-volume collected essays, *Around Music* and *Mi Contra Fa,* he is said to have written over 1,000 pages of reviews, essays, articles and 'letters to the editor' in the *New Age* and the *New English Weekly*. Additionally, he was a reviewer of recordings and recorded performances. A 'trenchant and sensitive' critic, Bhimani argues that a study of Sorabji's musical criticism is 'of fundamental importance for what it reveals both about musical activities in England between the wars and about Sorabji the composer'.[101] A man ahead of his time in musical tastes, he championed composers neglected by others, but whose works he found appealing. Sorabji was a man of many interests, seen from the range of his writings, from economics and unemployment to racism, both of which he hated – his own most painful experience occurring in his teens, when travelling with his mother in a first-class underground carriage, he had been called 'a Black Boy', by a 'Church of England dignitary'. Occasionally, Sorabji wrote about the unfair treatment of homosexuals, arguing for legal reform. His views on colonialism, however, are more ambivalent: critical of British rule, he was equally scathing of Indian activities.[102] He died in Dorset in 1988. The founding of the Sorabji Archive has re-kindled interest in the man and his music.

The Revd Pitt Bonarjee (1868–1948), cousin of W.C. Bonnerjee, and whose own father was one of the early converts to Christianity, came to England in 1911. In an 'exceptionally active' life in the Congregational world, Bonarjee held appointments in six churches, was instrumental in starting two day schools (at Reading and Walsall) and worked hard to improve relations between India and Britain. During the 35 years of his ministry in England, he became 'increasingly well-known as the only Indian Christian minister' in Britain. A member of the Liberal Party, he was adopted prospective candidate for Brighton and Hove in 1943, but he never contested the seat. His son, Lieutenant Stephen Bonarjee, educated at St Andrews University, was a journalist on the *Manchester Guardian*, before joining the army.[103]

Another man of religion, Pastor Kamal Chunchie (1886–1953), a Muslim of Malay origin, born in Ceylon, was a pioneer race-relations campaigner. Educated at Kingswood College, Kandy, after a career in the Ceylon and Singapore Police Force, in 1915, travelling at his own expense to Britain, he joined the Public Schools Battalion (3rd Middlesex Regiment) and fought on the Western Front, where he embraced Christianity. In March 1918, he came to England and in 1920 he married Mabel Tappen, his life-long companion and helper in his work among the docklands Asian and black population.[104] An Asian convert, fluent in four languages, Tamil, Singhalese, Malay and English, in December 1921, the Wesleyan Methodist Missionary Society (WMMS) appointed Chunchie to the Seamen's Mission for evangelical work among the black and Asian seamen, and dockland's small resident population. He visited sailors on ships, in lodging-houses, hospitals and prisons. He provided material relief to the needy seamen and resident families. In 1923, in a rented hall in Swanscombe Street, Canning Town, used by black people for 'jazzing', he set up London's first black church. In the same year, he organised the first of the annual summer outings to the seaside, Reigate in this instance. Confronted by the deprivation and discrimination which blighted black people's lives, he campaigned for a separate institution, which he was convinced would bring dignity to their lives and counter racism.

In 1926, his vision was realised when the WMMS established the Coloured Men's Institute (CMI) in Tidal Basin Road. A religious, social and welfare centre for both the sailors and residents, Chunchie became its pastor and warden. Here, too, he organised a Sunday school. To raise funds for the CMI's work and for overseas missons, he addressed Methodist gatherings all over Britain. Exposing the hypocrisy of Christian England where black peoples faced discrimination, while the missionary message 'back home' painted a different picture, he denounced racism, urging Christians to act in the 'spirit of brotherhood' and show that there were 'real Christians' who accepted black peoples as equal. A popular speaker, a bit of a showman even, he drew large audiences. For Chunchie the CMI was 'a monument of the love' of English people for 'the coloured folk in their midst'.[105] Black peoples saw him as their friend, who did so much good on their behalf. Their letters and the petition organised in his support provide some measure of the value of his welfare work. But others were more critical. The East End branch of the Universal Negro Improvement Association (founded by Marcus Garvey in the USA), accused Chunchie of patronising black peoples and fostering segregation 'under the guise of Christianity'.[106] There were disagreements over Chunchie's pastoral and financial management. Mission House alleged that he was 'overgenerous' and his success as having been 'bought – an English version of rice Christians'. But as Chunchie saw it, it was 'no use talking about religion to a man with cold feet and an empty stomach'.[107] In 1930, when the CMI was demolished in a road-widening scheme, no plans were made for another CMI, instead Chunchie was retained on Missionary Deputation for the Home Church for two years.

In 1933, Chunchie re-launched the CMI independently. He established a multi-racial council with Harold Moody of the League of Coloured Peoples (LCP), Shoran Singha, a Christian Sikh, who was a long-standing YMCA worker, Canon H.R.L. Sheppard, Professor R.K. Sorabji and Lady Lydia Anderson among them.[108] He raised funds by means of appeals, lectures and weekend Missionary Deputations. Throughout the Depression and the war years, until his death in 1953, using the Presbyterian Church in Victoria Dock Road as a centre and his own home as a base, with a band of loyal helpers, his wife among them, he continued with his social welfare work. Needy families received Christmas dinners. At New Year he hosted a party, distributing gifts of clothes and toys. A thrift club run by Chunchie and his wife provided clothes and shoes for the poor. Children attending Sunday school received breakfast and the seaside summer outings continued, sometimes in collaboration with the LCP. Some 3,000 scriptures were distributed annually. Chunchie extended his work to include Colonial and Indian students, the CMI being listed as an institution providing hospitality. According to the West African van Lare, without the 'privilege' of meeting a different class of Englishmen, they would have gone home with 'a poor impression of England and Christianity'.[109] Chunchie was Vice-President of the LCP (1935–7), patron of the Ceylon Friends' League and a member of the Royal Empire Society. He played cricket for Essex during his early years in London. During the war he was a member of the Voluntary Fire Fighting Party in Lewisham.

Chunchie laboured under great difficulties. Despite generous donations there was never enough money. As deficits mounted, he advanced funds from his own resources, resulting in his personal account, at times, becoming heavily overdrawn, an 'alarming state of affairs', according to the auditors.[110] Dependent on his zeal and energy as the Superintendent and General Secretary, the CMI did not survive him. A generous man, outspoken in his condemnation of racism, the solutions he offered were conservative. His daughter and grandson still live in London.

HOME LIFE

Living and working amongst white communities, what was 'home' in Britain like for middle-class Indian families? Of the few voices available, Savitri Chowdhary's *I Made My Home In England* provides valuable insights. A Hindu Punjabi woman, Savitri Devi, a teacher at a girls' high school before her marriage to Dharm Sheel Chowdhary, joined her husband in 1932, after a near five-year separation, in Laindon to start a 'new life' in surroundings that were 'unfamiliar'. Without suggesting that her life was typical of all Indian middle-class families/ homes, her narrative, nonetheless, helps us understand the Indian presence in Britain and the creation of a 'home' in another culture at a particular historical time. An educated woman, Savitri Chowdhary had read and heard much about the 'British people', and held them in 'high esteem', especially their women. But, neither in her husband's village of Murdapur, nor in her own birthplace in Multan, had she been in close contact with the British. Her first observation was how England had changed her husband in his near five-year residence, first as a postgraduate student and then a junior doctor. As she put it, he had become 'accustomed to their way of life', mixed 'mostly' with English people, and even spoke with her in English, to 'accelerate' her command of the language. As she struggled to understand a new way of life, she determined to adapt to her husband's life and his expectations of her. This meant discarding some elements of Indian culture, adopting western-style dress, reserving her beautiful saris for evening wear in Laindon or for when they went to see 'Indian friends' in London, cutting her waist-length hair short and learning to give up being a strict vegetarian. Independent-minded as she was, for an 'orthodox Hindu' woman like Chowdhary, such adaptation was meant partly to gain her 'proper' place in her husband's heart, and partly as a matter of being 'practical' in a busy surgery. In the early days, apart from being a wife and looking after a bigger house/surgery, Daisy Bank, she helped to get the three surgery rooms cleaned and ready, acted as an unofficial receptionist, taking telephone calls, and even handed over 'several bottles' of different medicines to the patients at the door. But she cites other reasons for making such a choice. To quote her husband: 'Besides, it is best not to make oneself conspicuous in Laindon.' It was not just a matter of being conspicuous in a country village in Essex, where the Chowdharys were the only Indian family. Others, too, had had to make painful choices, some having to shave off beards, others to become 'thoroughly' anglicised in order not to 'look conspicuous' or avoid being stared at, or laughed at. Interestingly, a Punjabi pedlar on his rounds mistook the 'olive-skinned' Mrs Chowdhary, dressed in western-style clothes and with 'plenty' of make-up, for an English woman.[111]

The 13 years covered in Chowdhary's narrative illustrate other aspects of home and work, for instance, learning how to deal with an English resident maid. Doctors in inter-war Britain, as has been seen, were popular with their patients. Chowdhary's account illustrates how hard they had to work to gain their patients' confidence and respect, to keep the practice together (purchasing a surgery meant a huge financial outlay) and to succeed. The three assistants to Dr Chowdhary mentioned in the text, Drs Banarji (a Bengali), Naqvi (a Muslim) and Madan (a Punjabi), were all Indians who shared 'Daisy Bank' with them, a pattern that suggests that Indian doctors possibly found it easier to find placements with compatriots. (Dr Chowdhary himself had come to Laindon as an assistant to 'Dr Gilder', a Parsi.) According to Savitri Chowdhary, not only did her husband gain the respect of his patients – even being 'idolised' – but the community accepted them. The friends they made showed no 'colour-or-race-bar', and she could not recall 'a single incident' when she was 'made to feel inferior ... because of the darkness of my skin'. She offers two explanations: first was Chowdhary's position as a respectable doctor, and, second, a genuine Christian belief among their friends that they were 'all ... God's children'.[112] During the war, the Chowdharys shared the sorrows and sufferings of their neighbours, helping each other. A strong woman, Savitri Chowdhary, in the period covered in the narrative, succeeded in creating a home and becoming part of the Laindon community.

Westernised, integrated and immersed in the life of the community among whom they lived and worked, the Chowdharys did not lose their sense of self as Punjabis and as Indians. They kept in touch with India, taking their two children to visit the parental village when they could. The first of these trips occurred in 1945, when the war ended, when she took her 10-year-old son, born in Laindon, to visit the Punjab. They joined the Hindu Association of Europe (see p. 298), kept in contact with Indian friends and Indian social life in London. Dr Chowdhary, who had trained at the Gurukul Kangra, also performed Hindu wedding ceremonies. Giving up being a strict vegetarian, too, did not mean discarding Indian cuisine, but embracing both. Mrs Chowdhary served an English meal for lunch, but cooked curries for supper. As her daughter recalls, after long hours in the surgery, Indian meals were a 'high point' in her father's day, and for her as a child *Pakoras* provided a 'warm, savoury comfort and had a magical effect', raising her spirits when she was feeling 'below-par'. They kept 'open house' and many an Indian visitor and student to their home, in this rural English setting, was entertained to an Indian meal on a Sunday. In the early 1950s, Savitri Chowdhary wrote the successful *Indian Cooking,* used in many cookery courses at the time.[113] India was part of their lives and present in other ways too. A desire to see India free drew many Indians (and their white allies) into the anti-colonial movement. Savitri Chowdhary, encouraged by her husband, met a young school teacher, 'Miss Cresswell', a patient, 'a real friend of India and Indians', who was active in the India League. As a result, she was drawn into the League's activities, attending meetings and campaigns and even occasionally spoke from its platform. Such actions posed no conflict: Indians were against the imperialist system, not the British as people. As Savitri Chowdhary wrote: 'If these fair-minded British people were trying to get together and press on for India's Independence, then was it not an urgent duty of us Indians in this country to join hands with them and carry the work much further?'[114]

Indians in Britain operated on many levels. As Savitri Chowdhary summed it up, it was 'like having two mothers to love and care for ... a heavier responsibility'. That Indians refused to be defined by others, saw themselves as people with plural identities, is further evidenced in a letter to the Home Secretary in 1935, when the Asiatic and Overseas Home for seamen (the Strangers' Home) was up for closure. Pointing out that the Home had been built by an 'Indian Prince', Syed Fazal Shah, the secretary of the Jamiat-ul-Muslmin (Muslim Association, see p. 298), writing on behalf of 'the representatives of the peoples of Asia resident in Aldgate, Poplar and other parts of London', expressed 'grave concern' at the disappearance of 'a place of refuge for the peoples of Asia in London'.[115]

Commenting on Indians in Britain during this period, Sheila Allen writes: 'The professional groups did not form separate geographical or social units and many became anglicised, practising in white communities.'[116] Anglicised and integrated, nevertheless, evidence of professional, social and religious organisations suggests a social identity and networks. The Indian Social Club, founded possibly just before the First World War, had a membership drawn largely from wealthy merchants and professionals, irrespective of religion. A surviving 1938 letter shows that of its five vice-presidents, two were doctors (Saeed Mohamedi and Fram Gotla), one an academic (Professor Varma) and of the two others, J.M. Parikh and Thakurdas Fatechand, one was a barrister and the other a merchant. Its honorary treasurer, C.B. Vakil, was a doctor, while the honorary secretary, M.L. Bhargava, was an accountant. Of its 21 life members, the majority were merchants, and 5 were women, including Lady Dhunjibhoy Bomanji, the wife of the Parsi shipping magnate, Sir Dhunjibhoy (died in 1937) who had homes in Bombay, Windsor and Harrogate, where she lived from 1939 till her death in 1986. The Club's life presidents were both members of the Indian nobility. One of its activities was an annual banquet, usually at the Savoy Hotel, to celebrate the Indian New Year. In 1933, at Saklatvala's instigation, the Club also organised a New Year party for the significant, but less fortunate, community of working-class Indians living in the East End. Held at Poplar Town Hall in October 1933, an estimated 280 working-class Indians, together with the Mayor and the Town Clerk, attended. An indication of the flavour of this cultural festival, with welfare overtones, is seen in the singing competition, presents of 'piles of toys and toy balloons' for the children and a gift of 'a tea caddy' for every woman. Some 100 children and 200 adults attended the function, which was to become an annual event. In Birmingham, Indian doctors, businessmen and students set up the Birmingham Indian Association.[117]

The Indian Social Club was not the only agency through which middle-class and working-class Indians came together. The IWA and HSC have already been mentioned. The India League's East End branch (meetings were held at Ayub Ali's cafe), organised education classes, run by Mrs J. Handoo, Asha Bhattacharya and Indian students. Dhani Prem worked hard to integrate Indian workers into British society. The Indian Social Conference (trustees Drs K.M. Pardhy and V.M. Lambah, and a committee composed of Indian students) annually organised a summer social conference for Indian students, usually on the Isle of Wight, when Indian sports teams held tournaments with the Isle of Wight teams.[118]

Evidence of an organised religious life is also evident from the several institutions. The Shah Jahan Mosque in Woking and the Zoroastrian Association were established in the nineteenth century, while the Bhupindra Dharamsala in west London, supported by the Maharaja of Patiala, was set up sometime before the First World War (see Chapter 3). This period saw other developments. Dr Diwan Singh was the president of the *Khalsa Jatha* of Great Britain. The Zoroastrian Association, under the presidency of Bhownaggree, became the Incorporated Parsee Association of Europe. The Zoroastrian House, a social and religious centre established in Kensington, also provided facilities as a guesthouse. Such infrastructure in the 1920s, as Bhownaggree's biographers suggest, was ahead of its time. The Association, in addition to its religious, educational and welfare role, organised social outings, river trips and banquets, bringing Parsis together.[119] The Ahmadiya Mosque in Putney, south London, was built in 1926. In 1941, at a multi-faith gathering, the East London Mosque and Islamic Centre at 446–8 Commercial Road was opened. Plans for a London mosque in the capital of the empire, initiated by prominent Muslims, the Aga Khan, Syed Ameer Ali and Sir Abbas Ali Baig, date back to 1910 and money was raised from influential Muslims all over the world. By 1926 a Trust Deed had been instituted. But funds were insufficient for a large project. Given the fact that a substantial number of Indian Muslims lived in the East End, in 1939, the Trustees decided to utilise some of the capital for the mosque in east London. The Jamiat-ul-Muslmin, based in east London, was founded in 1934. A charitable society for the promotion of Islam, it gave aid to needy Muslims, and served as a social organisation, bringing resident Muslims and visitors together. Official reports also mention the existence of the Glasgow Jamiat-ul-Muslmin.[120] The Central Hindu Society had been in existence for some years. Then, in December 1935, following a meeting at the Arya Bhavan, the Hindu Association of Europe was founded. A religious, social and welfare organisation for Hindus resident and visiting Europe, the Association aimed to spread knowledge of Hindu culture and civilisation, and promote 'friendly feeling' amongst the followers of different faiths. A list of its office bearers and subscribers in 1937 indicates the Association to be largely middle class. Its president, K.M. Pardhy (Birmingham), secretary, K.S. Bhatt (London) and vice-president, P.C. Bhandari (Brentford) were all doctors. The Association organised lectures on religious, cultural and economic subjects. Hindu festivals like 'Dha-shara' were celebrated at restaurants in the West End, notably, Veeraswami's.[121] Religious festivals and social outings often brought all faiths in Britain together. Ayyar, the Hindu student, mentions the Eid Festival at the Woking Mosque attended by over 200 Muslims, some Hindus and Christians.[122]

Such organisations and networks illustrate that an Asian community was already in existence in Britain long before the post-1950s migrants from India, Pakistan and Bangladesh came. This chapter has also shown that institutions and infrastructure usually associated with the post-war generation of migrants, were already firmly in place. An integrated and a richly diverse community, with plural identities, what also emerges is Asians' from the sub-continent over-riding differences of religion, language, and ethnic origin, which the government of India stressed so much. A resourceful and vibrant community, engaged in a variety of professions and careers, Indians made notable contributions to British life – contributions that remain obscured.

10

Radical Voices

The anti-colonial movement for Indian freedom entered a new phase in the years after the First World War. By 1906, Naoroji had defined 'self-government or *swaraj* like that of the United Kingdom or the Colonies' as their aspiration. In 1916, following the Lucknow Pact, in a joint declaration, Hindus and Muslims united to reaffirm India's goal to be Home Rule within the British Empire. This was a significant landmark. Indian aspirations received a boost in 1917, when, in response to the Indian contribution to the war, Edwin Montagu, the Secretary of State for India, announced in Parliament the government's policy as: 'the increasing association of Indians in every branch of the administration and the gradual development of self-governing institutions with a view to the progressive realisation of responsible government in India as an integral part of the British Empire'. However, 'responsible government' was not defined and Britain remained the sole judge of the nature and timing of India's advance towards 'responsible government'. Further, the system of 'dyarchy' under the 1919 India Act fell far short of expectations. The repressive Rowlatt Acts and the massacre at Amritsar shattered any illusion that the empire might become one of equals. As Gandhi called for a nation-wide campaign of non-violent civil disobedience, Indians abandoned cooperation. The national movement was transformed into a mass movement as Indians joined together in protest against the government. In December 1929, under Nehru's presidency, the Congress at Lahore called for *purna swaraj* or complete freedom from British domination and imperialism. In Britain, politically minded Indians and their allies stepped up their campaign – within the framework of Parliamentary institutions – to educate the British people about the effects of colonialism and to enlist their support. This chapter considers the work of anti-colonial organisations formed by Indians, how they tried to influence change, the difficulties they encountered, and focuses on two radical individuals: Shapurji Saklatvala and Krishna Menon.

Early in 1925, every Sunday from a platform in Hyde Park, M.A. Khan, a former employee of a provincial prison department, began addressing meetings on Indian affairs and India's need for self-determination. He was joined by a South Africa-born Indian Muslim, Sulaiman Katwaroon, married to an English woman and father of three, a former shipping clerk in a French company in London, and R.E. Franklin, a 'Eurasian' owner of a bookshop. Together they issued a manifesto. And so began the Indian Freedom Association, with its motto, 'Freedom within the Empire if possible - outside if necessary'. Both Khan and Katwaroon were described as individuals lacking a high social status and without previous experience of political work. By June 1928, the organisation had changed its name, first to the Indian Home Rule League, in line with the Indian National Congress policy, and then to the Indian Freedom League (IFL).[1] The Sunday Hyde Park meetings became more regular as new recruits, some of them students, others professionals, joined the IFL as speakers and supporters. Scotland Yard named P.C. Tarapore, a Parsi barrister, I. Singh, also a barrister, S.A. Huq, a Bengali Muslim, I.D. Dharadwaja (Das) and C.S.K. Pathy, clerical workers at the Indian High Commission, T.P. Boyce, a Parsi businessman, Nirendra Dutta Majumdar, and Don Philip Rupasangha Gunewardena, a Ceylonese student, among its diverse members. A few others regularly attended its meetings. An organisational structure was also apparent: members met weekly to discuss details of Hyde Park meetings; the executive committee and membership were open to both Indians and whites.[2]

Keeping pace with developments in India, the activists spoke of broken promises, lack of civil liberties and imprisonment of thousands without trial. They condemned the exploitation and poverty of Indian workers. They demanded self-government as India's 'lawful heritage' and appealed to the British working class to fight for their common interest against capitalism. They made alliances with other oppressed peoples: Garvey, president of the UNIA, spoke from its platform, as did Arnold Ward of the Negro Welfare Association (NWA) and Thomas Ashe, the Irish Republican. Evidence shows that prominent Indian visitors such as S.J. Iyer, a member of the Indian Legislative Assembly, too, sometimes used the IFL platform.[3] The IFL, however, did not make much headway. Membership fluctuated as recruits came and went. Only Khan, Katwaroon, Franklin, and later Huq, Gunewardena and Adrian Cola Rienzi, a Trinidad-born Indian law student, remained constant. Funds were short and the IFL failed to get recognition from the Indian National Congress.

However, what is significant is that a small band of determined individuals used Hyde Park, a public space, to expose conditions in India and campaign for self-government, attracting a floating audience estimated to be between 100 and 600.[4] Whether their speeches made any impression on their audience is open to question. But the IFL did not escape official notice, illustrating the difficulties Indians faced in their struggle against colonialism, even in the metropolitan capital. In March 1927, Colonel P.W.O. Gorman, in a letter to M. O'Dwyer, denouncing 'unscrupulous' preachings of 'youngish men … of extremist faction' against the government of India, alleged that such speeches did 'quite a lot of harm' to young students and could not be 'tolerated quietly'. He urged O'Dwyer to hear them, 'incognito'. IPI agreed. What appears to have worried the India Office was their language, described as 'freely interlarded' with 'the revolutionary propaganda of the Communist press', and the turnout at meetings of a fair number of 'labouring classes', Communists and Indian students. Therefore, to frustrate them, officials initiated a more organised strategy of heckling by a band of 'carefully chosen' persons possessing 'correct' information on Indian affairs. To avert suspicion, it was proposed not to use the same person 'too frequently'.[5] As a result, the incidence of heckling showed a marked increase, on occasion becoming so pronounced that meetings had to be abandoned. Fascists, too, interrupted IFL meetings. They were harassed in other ways: secret police compiled detailed reports on them. There are hints, too, of other, subtler, means of control. Their careers were at stake.[6] By the summer of 1930, the IFL had become an offshoot of the London Branch of the Indian National Congress (LBINC), and by March 1933, the Hyde Park speeches had dwindled.[7]

The LBINC was founded in 1928, at a meeting in Caxton Hall, called by 'several enthusiastic' Indians in London and chaired by Sreenivasa Iyengar, then on a visit to England. That a political organisation to educate public opinion was urgently needed was recognised. The vast majority of the British people remained ignorant of the political happenings in India. The media and the government's propaganda machine emphasised communal divisions, but the national movement was largely unknown and unrecognised. Affiliated to the Congress, the LBINC was open to Indians, Burmese and Ceylonese. By 1930, there were 380 members.[8]

But, like the IFL, the LBINC found campaigning for Indian freedom in Britain fraught with difficulties. Premises were difficult to rent as proprietors imposed restrictions: they would not allow what they described 'anti-British propaganda'. Funding was another problem. As an affiliate, the LBINC received some help from the Congress. But its main source remained membership subscriptions and donations from rich Indians. Increased surveillance made them cautious. To avoid getting into trouble, some made their donations clandestinely.[9] Students on government scholarships, or aspiring to future careers in the government, feared taking part in politics and were even actively discouraged. The Indian Students' Hostel in Gower Street was said to be 'full of spies'. The secretary of the Hostel would not permit any material and lectures considered of 'inflammatory nature'. Evidence shows that appointed supervisors to Indian students in universities exerted control to prevent them from being 'captured' by groups having 'advanced political views'.[10]

Undaunted, the LBINC organised public meetings, kept an eye on the press to counter injurious propaganda, and campaigned among students. Surveillance reports show branch membership among the Edinburgh Indian Association, the GIU, the Oxford and Cambridge Majlis and the Dublin Indian Association. It made links with other organisations, for instance, the Egyptian Association and the NWA. Annually, it organised the Indian Political Conference, the first being held in the summer of 1930, when, condemning the 'inhuman exploitation of masses in Asiatic and African countries' under the British Empire, the LBINC affirmed the 'legitimate right' of all nations to be free, and India's claim to full independence.[11] Then there were specific campaigns. In April 1929, the LBINC planned a demonstration to greet the Simon Commission's return from India. The seven-man fact-finding Commission, led by Sir John Simon and including the Labour MP, Clem Attlee, had been appointed by Parliament in 1927 to assess the appropriateness of extending further the principles of 'responsible government' as required by the 1919 Act. The fact that there was not a single Indian on the Commission caused uproar in India, and the Congress and the AITUC appealed to the Labour Party not to support the Conservative-appointed Commission, but Attlee stayed on. Nationalists boycotted it and demonstrators with black flags and placards proclaiming 'Simon, Go Home' greeted the Commission. In London, following a rally in Trafalgar Square, led by Saklatvala, over 200 Indian demonstrators and their sympathisers, some carrying little black banners, handbills and Indian national flags, marched to Victoria Station. But the peaceful demonstrators, picked out from the crowd of sightseers, were roughly hustled away by the police. In Parliament, Saklatvala, who demanded whether the police had been authorised to remove 'from a public crowd ... persons of a certain nationality or political view regardless of their individual behaviour', was informed that a 300-strong force, detailed for duty, had been sanctioned by the Home Secretary, Joynson Hicks. In the 1929 Parliamentary elections, the LBINC planned to campaign for candidates who pledged 'unequivocally' to work for India's claim to complete independence.[12] Among them was Saklatvala.

SHAPURJI SAKLATVALA

A radical left-winger, who campaigned against imperialism and capitalism for a classless society, Saklatvala, the third Parsi, and the last Asian MP until the 1980s, was the first to be elected as a member of the Labour and Communist parties. Born in Bombay in 1874, Saklatvala, from a merchant family, was related to India's pioneering industrial family, his mother, Jerbai, being the sister of J.N. Tata. Brought up in the 'grandeur' of Esplanade House, the Tata residence, he was educated at the Jesuit St Xavier's school and college. While still a student, during one of the worst outbreaks of the bubonic plague in Bombay (1895–1902), Saklatvala was a welfare worker among the poor in the squalid slums and tenements of Bombay. This would have been a formative experience, as was his first encounter with race relations under the Raj. Years later in Parliament, he described his degrading experience of being barred from entering the 'white man's club' to see Waldemar Haffkine, the leading bacteriologist, and ultimately of being led to the basement via the 'back yard ... through the kitchen and an underground passage'.[13] Joining the Tata Industries in 1901, he spent three years prospecting for iron ore, coal and limestone deposits in the remote regions of Bihar and Orissa, resulting in the Tata Iron and Steel Company at Jamshedpur. Significantly, it was during this period that he first met with practices such as villagers being impressed into service, and saw their poverty when sharing their 'meagre hospitality' in their huts and hovels. This aroused his concern and interest in labour conditions.[14] It was in England, however, that his ideas on industrial questions would develop, drawing him into the labour movement and working-class politics.

In 1905, aged 31, Saklatvala arrived in England as a departmental manager in Tata's Manchester office. In Matlock, Derbyshire, where he first went to recuperate from illness, he met his future wife, Sarah Marsh from a working-class family. Why was Saklatvala edged out of the 'centre of activity' in Bombay and Jemeshedpur and sent to England instead? His daughter cites rivalry between Saklatvala and his cousin Dorabji as the reason. Some historians suggest his 'outspoken' criticism of British authorities, a possible source of embarrassment to the Tata business, as another reason. But there is little evidence of Saklatvala's political involvement at this stage. In 1912–13, his presence in India was certainly unwelcome. By then he had been involved in left-wing politics and it is likely, as Saklatvala claimed, there had been pressure to 'throw [him] overboard and make an example of [him]'.[15]

A Liberal at first, according to Reg Bishop, his future parliamentary secretary, Saklatvala was quickly disenchanted with the Liberal 'mausoleum', as his politics underwent a radicalisation. He had begun to ponder labour questions at Matlock, attending union meetings.[16] In 1907, in London, he joined the small Marxist party, the Social Democratic Federation and in 1909, in Manchester, he became a member of the Independent Labour Party (ILP), founded in 1893 and affiliated to the Labour Party, which it had helped to form in 1900. Saklatvala also joined the General and Municipal Workers' Union, the National Union of Clerks and the Cooperative movement. Not so well known is his membership of the London section of the Home Rule for India League, founded by Annie Besant in 1916, which theosophist Labourites, like David Graham Pole, George Lansbury and John Scurr (the last two also anti-war ILP-ers, like Saklatvala) had joined, and which later, under Menon's direction, would be transformed as the India League (see p. 321).[17] Following the Bolshevik Revolution in 1917, Saklatvala played a prominent role in establishing the People's Russian Information Bureau and became active in the Left-Wing Group of the ILP. A leading exponent of affiliation to the Communist International, he was among the 159 signatories to the Left-Wing Group's declaration, *The Call of the Third International*. When the resolution was defeated at the 1921 conference by 521 votes to 97, Saklatvala was among the 200 who left the ILP to join the newly founded Communist Party of Great Britain (CPGB).[18]

But, as early as 1909, Saklatvala had attracted the notice of the Criminal Intelligence Office. A 1910 report, for instance, drawing attention to the fact that B.C. Pal had stayed with him in Manchester, noted that Pal's lecture on 'Socialism and Empire', given under the auspices of the Social Democratic Party, had attracted 700 people, most of them employees of the mill machinery manufacturers, Messrs Howard and Bullough, with significant business links in India. By 1911, labelled as 'one of the most violent anti-British agitators in England', Saklatvala was recorded as taking a 'considerable' interest in the 'extremist movement', communicating with both Pal and Madame Cama in Paris.[19]

Saklatvala's campaigns to improve Indian labour conditions began while a member of the ILP. In March 1911, for instance, at a conference of British labour leaders and 'representatives of Indian workers', he initiated a movement to form a labour organisation to help Indian workers. A committee, which included Saklatvala, was formed to draw up a proposal for submission to trade unions in England. But his efforts came to nothing. However, what is significant are Saklatvala's views on labour, and his belief that the interests of British and Indian workers were mutual, a theme to which he would return again and again. Five years later, in 1916, came the WWLI, Saklatvala being one of its founder members.[20] In 1918, the WWLI published a Statement of Principles, a document in which Saklatvala's hand is much in evidence. Based on the principle that Indian workers had the same right to general welfare and labour protection as the working class in Britain, the WWLI aimed to organise British workers to help Indians gain similar rights for their mutual benefit. To investigate labour conditions, Saklatvala urged a trade union commission to India.[21] But a decade would elapse before the TUC would send a fact-finding delegation in 1927.

Perhaps the most significant outcome of Saklatvala's initiative and WWLI's work was its Statement to the Joint Committee on Indian Reforms. In January 1919, deploring the total absence of the representation of organised British labour on its Committees, the WWLI protested that Parliament would learn nothing of the appalling conditions of labour in India:

> of a totally inadequate rate of pensions, of from 12 to 18 pence a week ... accorded to the widows of Indian soldiers who sacrificed their lives in France and other parts of the world. Nor will the Report enlighten them on the wages of from six pence to 12 pence a day in factories, mines and docks, and on merchant vessels; of the long working day of 12 hours, of the absence of insurance and compensation for accidents; of the employment of child labour from age 10, and of women's labour, at a still worse pay. One looks in vain for some reference to the wretched conditions of housing for the workers in places unfit for human habitation ... [22]

Written by Saklatvala, the Statement submitted in July 1919 exposed some of the 'fallacious contentions' in the government's proposals: that because Indian workers were illiterate they should not get the right to vote; that their low wages reflected cheap living in India. Saklatvala argued that Indian workers' cheap living was not based on 'actually being able to obtain articles of lower values but [was] literally based on his doing without everything that constitutes a worker's healthy and happy life'. He proposed a series of amendments for the 'progress of the masses': introduction of popular franchise, setting up of an Indian Labour Ministry in Parliament, the right to unionisation, the abolition of old laws such as indentured labour, the practice of impressment and recruitment by agents of private companies, as well as proposing reforms relating to wages and hours of work for government employees (the government being the largest employer). In addition, Saklatvala offered himself as a witness before the Committee, an offer that was rejected. His proposals, too, went no further.[23]

Nonetheless, the Statement is an important landmark. This was the first time a labour organisation had attempted to influence legislation at the level of the British Parliament. The fact that the Committee deemed it wise not to call Saklatvala as a witness, preferring its own representative, shows the radical nature of his amendments. The Statement is also an affirmation of Saklatvala's internationalism. He warned 'of the disastrous consequences ... to the progress of Labour and ... the material well-being of the masses in Great Britain and the British colonies by the continued degraded conditions of their fellow-workers in India'. The emerging working-class organisations in India recognised the important groundwork done by Saklatvala and the WWLI. In 1920, when the AITUC was founded, the WWLI's work was publicly acknowledged. In 1921, Saklatvala was appointed its representative in England, a post he held until 1928, enabling him to raise concerns of Indian workers at the TUC conferences in Britain.[24]

An eloquent speaker, described as 'India's finest orator', Saklatvala's campaigns intensified after 1916. As a member of the flourishing City of London Branch of the ILP, he addressed meetings around the country to communicate his vision. To paraphrase his own words in 1918, he only wanted to do one thing, and that was to spread socialism from one end of the world to the other. It was Saklatvala's influence, too, that made the City Branch 'a bastion of anti-imperialist solidarity'.[25] In April 1917, for instance, in a speech on 'Socialism and Racialism', Saklatvala emphasised that within the 'inseparable economic unit' of the empire socialism had to be international to benefit all, a message repeated in an article in July 1918.[26] In 1919, delegates from the Indian National Congress attended a conference organised by the City Branch on labour conditions in India; at another, representatives of the South African Native National Congress (the future ANC) addressed the public meeting. Saklatvala's campaigns, however, did not stop at branch level. He took India to the ILP conference floor itself. As a delegate to the 1918 conference, he urged members to be more 'definite' in their commitment to internationalism. To John Scurr's motion for granting a measure of self-government to the Indian people, he moved a supplementary, imploring the Conference to persuade the Congress to be more socialistic in their political programmes, advocating nationalisation. Speaking out against 'capitalist exploitation', which in his view lay at the root of Indian poverty, he urged solidarity of labour in Great Britain with labour in India. This was his attempt to link the left of the British labour movement and the Indian national movement to a radical programme of political and economic change. By 1919, he was recognised as the ILP expert on India, a role he performed until 1921, the year of his resignation.[27]

Like Naoroji, Saklatvala took his campaign for Indian independence and international socialism into Parliament. In 1921, the year he joined the CPGB, he was adopted as a Labour candidate for Battersea North, and between then and 1931 he contested five general elections, winning two. Given the context of the 1920s, how was it possible for an Indian and a Communist to be elected to Parliament? The choice of the constituency is one factor. Battersea, a predominantly working-class borough with a large Irish population, famous for its fiercely independent radical tradition, has been described as 'a place where the Left Wing took root and flourished exceedingly'. John Burns, the first working-class man to enter Cabinet in 1910, had been its MP from 1892 to 1918 and an important force in its political development. Battersea had a strong tradition of unionisation, high by the standards of London at the time. It was also known for its anti-imperialism and toleration of minorities. It was the first London borough to elect a significant number of Catholics to its council and two Catholic mayors, one of whom, elected in 1913, was John Archer, the Liverpool-born pan-Africanist, the first black mayor in Britain. During the jingoism of the Boer War, 1899–1901, Battersea became notorious for espousing the 'Boer Cause', with huge turnouts at protest meetings in Battersea Park organised by its Stop the War Committee, addressed by Burns and Keir Hardie, as well as by Afrikaners. In 1918, Charlotte Despard, suffragette and Sinn Fein-er, was its Labour candidate.[28] Saklatvala was thus in tune with the Battersea tradition. His own personal qualities and the support he received from a number of important Battersea figures, provide a further explanation. During his 12 years in the ILP, he had become well known, and admired for his oratory. For instance, Aberdare miners congratulated Battersea for choosing 'Comrade Sak'. Several of his supporters, Arthur Field, the ex-secretary of the City of London ILP branch and a fellow activist on the WWLI, and Duncan Carmichael, treasurer of Battersea Labour and Trades Council, the body responsible for choosing parliamentary candidates, lived in Battersea. Charlotte Despard was another supporter. Then there was Archer, who according to a Battersea councillor was his 'most loyal and doughty champion'. It was Archer, at the 1921 London Pan-African Congress, as chairman of the session on colonial freedom, who had introduced Saklatvala as the prospective Battersea candidate. Here Saklatvala, on behalf of the Indian National Movement, had made an important statement of solidarity with the 'Coloured World'. More importantly, Saklatvala, who made no secret of his CPGB membership, was willing to stand on the Labour Party Manifesto, accepting its constitution and its whip in Parliament. J.R. Clynes, chairman of the Parliamentary Labour Party, even considered Saklatvala's knowledge of Indian economic conditions an asset, as it would 'compel' attention to the 'neglected ... millions of our fellow subjects in that part of the Empire'. Selected by the Labour and Trades Council with an 'overwhelming majority' at a full meeting of the delegates, Saklatvala received official endorsement from the Labour Party.[29]

Thus, standing as a Labour candidate at the 1922 general election, on a turnout of 56.6 per cent, and in a three-cornered fight, he won, taking 50.5 per cent of the vote, a majority of 2,000, more than doubling Despard's 1918 vote, becoming one of the two Communists to win (Newbold at Motherwell was another). In 1923, however, despite increasing his vote on a 62.4 per cent poll, he narrowly lost to his Liberal opponent, by 186 votes. In 1924, contesting the seat as a Communist (Labour had outlawed dual membership) but still with the endorsement of the Battersea Labour and Trades Council, and on a record turnout of 73.1 per cent, Saklatvala defeated his Constitutionalist opponent by a majority of 542, winning 50.9 per cent – the only Communist to succeed, becoming a one-man Party in Parliament.

How did he manage such a feat? Part of the explanation lies in Saklatvala's personal popularity. A reporter from the *Daily Graphic*, on the eve of the 1924 election, found 'a Battersea charwoman ... almost in tears because she lived on the wrong side of her street and could not vote for Saklatvala'. He described seeing 'excited women waving his election handbills and actually kissing his portrait pinned on them'. A voter told another reporter that 'women of Nine Elms' were responsible for Saklatvala's success. But he was equally popular with working-class men. According to a reporter 'a burly taxi-driver' stood arguing for 'twenty minutes, politely but stubbornly' with 'Colonel H.V. Combs ... up from the country to help his friend Hogbin' (the Constitutionalist candidate). One of the taxi man's arguments was that he had fought with Indian regiments in the war, and 'their' soldiers were 'as brave as any white soldiers'. Such a remark suggests that, for Battersea, Saklatvala's ethnic origin was not a problem, an observation confirmed by the fact that, during a 1923 election meeting when a Captain Godfrey, representing Hogbin, was reported as saying that 'the electorate have an instinctive preference for an Englishman', he was howled down with cries of 'shame'. What was also irrelevant to the voters was Saklatvala's Tata family connection and his employment in the firm, said to pay 'very capitalistic dividends'.[30]

However, what was even more crucial was the support from the Battersea Labour and Trades Council. Malcolm Thompson of the *British Weekly* found no 'serious alarm' among Saklatvala's supporters at the 'Communist label of their champion'. What mattered to them was that he had declared himself 'willing to accept the Labour whip'. The Battersea Labour and Trades Council, too, despite being torn by conflicting loyalties following the ban on dual membership at the 1924 conference, had decided to stand by Saklatvala. By a clear majority of 114 votes to 14, he was adopted as their candidate in 1924, in defiance of Party headquarters. Saklatvala himself explained his success as due to the loyal support he received from 'all sections of the Labour Movement'. He wrote: 'The comrades of the ILP ... of the Battersea Labour League [a creation of John Burns] ... of the Trades Unions and Labour Party Wards and the Irish Rebels stood solid as a rock without one woman or one man in the active Labour ranks making an exception.'[31] Indeed, in all the three elections: 1922, 1923 and 1924, he was the only CPGB member not to face an official Labour opponent. By 1929, however, Battersea had rejected Saklatvala, and, in line with the national Party, adopted William Sanders, the veteran socialist and a product of Battersea's pioneering Labour days. Why?

One major reason for Saklatvala's rejection was his attacks on the Labour Party. As early as 1925, in a letter to the CPGB's Political Bureau, he argued that, in view of the 'great attraction' of the masses of Britain to 'Parliamentary customs and traditions', there was a danger of the CPGB being 'submerged into insignificance', unless 'merciless measures to fight the Labour Party' were adopted, thus anticipating the 1928 'New Line' of 'class against class'. He attacked the Labour leadership and the trade unions (the TUC's calling off of the General Strike in 1926 had been seen as a sell out), alienating Battersea politicians. Further, his increasingly flamboyant and unrealistic class rhetoric, so out of touch with Battersea issues and concerns, disillusioned his supporters.[32] All this, coupled with his unwise remarks, such as calling Sanders 'a murderer', on account of his war service, did not help matters. According to Sanders, Saklatvala's 'perpetual attacks on local, as well as national Labour leaders, have wearied Battersea workers, and his avowed object of smashing the Labour Party is only too obvious. If he has any support, it will only come from a few disgruntled elements.' As Kosmin concludes, Saklatvala's 'abandonment of the local spirit of 1922, and the Communist Party's growing intolerance and cynical manipulation of people and events in response to Moscow's directives', proved to be his undoing.[33] And so, to save the labour movement, Battersea fell in line. Even Archer, now the secretary of the newly formed North Battersea Divisional Labour Party, abandoned him. Faced with an official Labour candidate, he had no chance. In the 1929 election, on a turnout of 69.7 per cent, Saklatvala came third, polling only 18.6 per cent of the vote. This ended his parliamentary career. He unsuccessfully contested a by-election in Glasgow, Shettleston, in 1930, and attempted a comeback in his old Battersea seat in 1931. But he polled a mere 9 per cent of the vote. In 1934, he stood for council elections in St Pancras (Ward 4). But while he failed, Menon won for Labour.

If Battersea accepted Saklatvala as 'Labour's United Front' candidate, how did the media and his Liberal and Tory opponents view him? Some politicians, as seen above, tried to whip up race prejudice. Rajani Dutt, whose parents then lived in Battersea, years later described how a Tory candidate told his Swedish mother, 'Of course you will not want to vote for the black man.' There are references, too, in the media to Saklatvala as the 'Indian Communist' or the 'Parsee Communist'.[34] But race never made much of a running. A reading of the newspapers shows that the right-wing press hit upon a weapon it considered far more potent in the context of the time: Communism. Headlines like 'Red' Battersea were common. One paper described Battersea as 'little Moscow', one of the 'nerve centres' of the Communist movement and Saklatvala as the 'avowed apostle of Bolshevism'. Editorials implored Battersea to choose between 'constitutional progress and frank and flagrant Communism'. They reported scare stories of 'children of Russia' inviting the 'children of Battersea' to help destroy the old world and reconstruct the new. They accused the Communists of 'terror tactics', of denying free speech and causing rowdyism, allegations denounced as a 'stunt' by the *Daily Herald*. Saklatvala appealed for calm and invited his Liberal and Tory opponent to share his platform – a public meeting acknowledged by the Tories to have given 'a very fair and considered hearing' to all parties.[35]

THE COMMUNIST MP

Saklatvala's maiden speech in Parliament on 23 November 1922 set the tone of his campaigns when he exhorted MPs 'to burst out of these time-worn prejudices and boldly take a new place ... to push forward not only the good but the rights ... of the masses of humanity'.[36] In long and eloquent speeches he attacked British imperialism to expose the workers' plight under the capitalist system. For instance, in a debate on India in July 1923, he told the House that, of the 74 jute mills established in India by British companies, he had studied the records of

41, to find that in the four years between 1918 and 1921, on a capital investment of £6,140,000, these companies had earned £22,900,000 as dividends and, besides their profits, had managed to set aside £19,000,000 as reserves. How? By paying Bengali workers a pittance. And what was the result? While the wealth of a few Scottish families had increased, the closure of jute mills in Dundee, capital of Scotland's jute industry, had caused unemployment and misery among thousands of Scottish workers. But Bengalis had not benefited either. Low wages condemned them to a life of poverty, ignorance and squalor. Urging equality of wages between the British and Indian workers in the same industries, Saklatvala appealed for a Committee of Investigation. That workers' emancipation remained at the heart of his concerns is evident from the paper he wrote for the Labour Party Advisory Committee on International Questions (the Imperial Sub-Committee) in July 1924 (the Party consulted him until the rule change governing dual membership). The document, 'The British Labour Government and India', also submitted to the Joint International Department of the TUC and Labour Party, reiterated his argument that 'coolie' wages in the empire affected workers' wages in similar industries in Britain. He implored Labour to 'abate this exploitation', which in his view, they could do 'without affecting their administrative responsibility under the existing order of things'. His 11-point plan of reform repeated demands made in his 1919 Statement. He also proposed a commission for mass education, judicial reform and labour representation on councils and municipal bodies.[37] But Saklatvala found the Labour Party, in power and in opposition, as reluctant to act as the Tories. He complained that his parliamentary allies came from the extreme Left of the Party, and, on Indian questions, on occasions he mustered the support of 'people like Wedgewood or T. Wheatley'. Such was his frustration that he gave vent to his fury in a letter to Bhownaggree, denouncing Labour as 'worse Impostors even than ... Liberals, and in so-called Left-wing ILP-ers we reach the maximum of political hypocrisy of present day'.[38]

Saklatvala questioned whether British imperialism was 'at all permissible to exist' in the twentieth century. He mocked Britain's claims to be 'trustees of the people' and 'protectors of the undefended' in India where the Crown enjoyed 'a power so despotic and arbitrary'. He opposed the Simon Commission, ridiculing the need for a mission to test 'whether Indians should rule in their own country'.[39] Other causes, too, received his attention. He voted against the ratification of the 1922 Irish Free State Treaty, predicting that it would bring no peace. He raised the question of housing in Battersea. He helped the Edinburgh Indian Association's campaigns against the colour bar. When a 'Mr Singer' organised an 'African Village' as part of an exhibition at Newcastle, Saklatvala added his voice to the protests of the West African Students' Union (WASU), urging the Secretary to the Overseas Department to make sure the exhibition did not 'bring the Negro population into contempt or ridicule'. He also used the House as a platform to publicise international socialism, 'to Bolshevise' the hearts and minds of the MPs.[40] And as many of his speeches in Parliament and around the country show, he championed the working class in Britain, speaking up for their rights to employment and better living conditions. During the 1926 General Strike, he became one of its first victims.

On the eve of the Strike, at a May Day rally in Hyde Park, Saklatvala, whose meeting was 'much the biggest', acclaimed the Strike as the 'definite rising of Labour against their oppressors', amid shouts of 'Good old Saklatvala'. Next day he was arrested. At Bow Street Police Court, Detective Sergeant Arthur Davies read out extracts of the speech from his shorthand notes: 'We want to tell the Army boys that they must revolt now and refuse to fight, and then they will be the real saviours of their homes and the workers.' The speech was alleged to be 'dangerous and inflammatory'.[41] Saklatvala was charged with sedition and bound over to keep the peace and be of good behaviour for 12 months in the sum of £500. He refused to be bound over, defiantly informing the court that 'in the circumstances such as those existing today, I shall refuse to be silenced except by *force majeure*'. He was sentenced to two months in Wormwood Scrubs. But prison did not dampen his spirits: within hours of his release, he was back in Parliament making a speech. Under the Emergency Powers Act, however, Saklatvala found himself restricted. Police cancelled, often at the very last minute and with crowds already gathered, any meetings addressed by him.[42]

This was not the only penalty paid by Saklatvala. As an anti-imperialist *and* a Communist, he was under surveillance. His mail was censored; in 1925, when the police moved against the Communists, Special Branch raided his house.[43] In the same year, on orders of the American Secretary of State, Frank Kellogg, he was banned from the USA, preventing him from attending the Inter-Parliamentary Union Conference in Washington with 41 other MPs. Conservative MPs, who had threatened to withdraw from the delegation, were jubilant at this turn of events. Sir Robert Horne, the delegate leader, even used the episode to warn Battersea that by electing 'such a notorious person' as Saklatvala they brought 'disgrace' on themselves and their 'fellow subjects'.[44] But the ban did not go unchallenged. The *New York Times,* not an overtly radical paper, described Kellogg's action as over-zealous. There were protests from the

American Workers' Party, and the Civil Liberties Union staged a huge demonstration to greet the Parliamentary Union. Even the Republican Senator William Borah, chairman of the Senate's Foreign Relations Committee, condemned the ban. But it was the *Daily Herald* that reminded the British public that Saklatvala's views were 'the result of his country, India, being under the domination of Britain, a domination of which the mass of the American people strongly disapprove'. The USA, however, was not the only country to curb his freedom to travel. In 1929, as a delegate to a meeting of the League Against Imperialism (LAI), founded in Brussels in February 1927, Saklatvala, who was a member of its international executive and active in its British section, and his colleague Maxton were arrested and detained at Ostend and returned to Britain. Even the India Office attempted to prevent his tour of India, delaying his passport on the pretext that they needed to consult the government of India. Saklatvala protested to Stanley Baldwin, the Prime Minister, demanding he stop interfering with his 'legitimate' duties as an MP.[45] The passport was issued.

In January 1927, Saklatvala, 'Member for India', arrived in Bombay for a three-month working tour. Like Naoroji, he was enthusiastically received, the *Bombay Chronicle* comparing his reception to that given to Gandhi. In an intensive schedule he travelled all over India, visiting most of the major cities: Bombay, Delhi, Calcutta, Karachi, Madras, Ahmedabad and Surat, as well as his birthplace, Navsari. He visited Gandhi at his ashram.[46] He spoke to large gathering of students, textile and industrial workers. He addressed the AITUC, the newly founded Communist Party of India, and the Indian National Congress. He spoke at a Muslim rally, attended by over 6,000, urging Hindu–Muslim unity, and to the Indian Cultural Association in Bombay. Everywhere his message was the same: 'socialism had come to free mankind'; 'imperialism was running down human life', and he wanted to see 'India free because on her freedom depended the freedom of Egypt, Arabia, Africa, China and Japan'. He spoke of the international unity of the working class and exhorted Indian workers to organise trade unions. He chided the Congress for neglecting workers and peasants, urging the formation of an all-India workers' and peasants' party, which, in affiliation with the Congress, would make the national movement, in his view, 'truly national and really powerful'. He urged Indians to demand 'freedom from all foreign control' and not Dominion Status. Saklatvala, however, did not spend all his time making speeches. At a meeting with the AITUC, he stressed such practical measures as the need to keep careful accounts, to make sure that union members received its publications and urged research into workers' conditions in industries.[47]

How successful was Saklatvala's visit? The fact that large crowds attended his meetings and his speeches received a wide coverage in the media, suggests that he was well received. According to the *Bombay Chronicle,* he was given the welcome of 'an illustrious Indian and an indefatigable worker' for Indian freedom. That he was the only Indian in the British Parliament certainly gave him status. But the tour did not pass off without criticism. Indians hotly disagreed with his assertion that the boycott of foreign cloth was 'miscalculated' because it hit the poor in Lancashire. The Bombay Corporation argued over whether Saklatvala really had done anything for India, some Parsis denouncing him 'as a fanatic and a Bolshevik', epithets perhaps understandable from a community that was rich and successful under the Raj. It voted by a majority not to present him with an address. Whether his message of international socialism had any lasting influence is doubtful. At a meeting in Manchester after his return, Saklatvala claimed that 'I have successfully sown the seeds of Communism in India.' But in India, in some quarters, there were 'mental reservations'; others urged caution.[48] His attack on Gandhi went down badly. The Saklatvala–Gandhi correspondence (published in the Indian newspapers and later by the CPGB as a pamphlet, *Is India Different?*) reveals basic disagreements over methods. Saklatvala opposed Gandhi's *charkha* and *khaddar* campaign (calling on Indians to spin and weave their own cloth), seeing it as a retreat from industrialisation. He was critical of Gandhi's non-violent strategy, wanting Gandhi to organise peasants and workers and support strike action. His attacks increased after the 'New Line' seen from an article written in July 1930 for the *Labour Monthly.* An enthusiast for industrialisation, Saklatvala was one of the earliest to draw attention to the growth of industries in India, following the 1916 Industrial Commission's recommendation. In an article in the *Labour Monthly,* in 1921, he rejected the accepted view that India was 'industrially dormant': he showed that 15 per cent of the population, 45 million Indians, lived by 'industrial and commercial activity'.[49] He saw great similarity between India under the Raj and Czarist Russia, hence his advocacy of mass revolutionary struggle on the Bolshevik model. However, Saklatvala appears not to have understood the complex character of British imperialism. As Bipan Chandra points out, while there is no doubting the 'exploitative and dominational character of colonial rule', nonetheless, British rule was 'semi-democratic and semi-authoritarian' in character. It also relied 'very heavily' on the collaboration of Indians, and pursued the policy of 'the carrot and the stick'. Another historian, B.S. Josh, commenting on Saklatvala's analysis, makes a similar point.[50]

How did the government of India respond to Saklatvala's visit? There was nervousness about his 'preaching' of Communism. He was closely watched and his speeches monitored throughout his tour. And although the Viceroy dismissed the visit with the view that 'the Orthodox Swarajists and Congress people entertained much the same opinion of his activities as orthodox Labour entertains of their own extreme left wing', Saklatvala's presence must have been considered undesirable enough for him to be banned from visiting India again.[51] Later in 1927, the Foreign Office cancelled the endorsement for India from his passport. That such an action was against the accepted principle that 'no country can refuse to accept back one of its own inhabitants if his nationality is not in doubt', is evident from the fact that the Foreign Office was uneasy with the India Office request. The correspondence between Lord Birkenhead and Lord Irwin, the Viceroy, further reveals the dubious argument used by the India Office to deprive Saklatvala of his right to visit India: that Saklatvala regarded himself as 'a fully domiciled British subject' having had 'no connection with India for nearly 20 years'. It comes as no surprise to find that the real reason for the ban on 'empire-wide' endorsement was Saklatvala's membership of the CPGB. Even a Labour Secretary of State for India, William Wedgewood Benn, did not lift the ban. Saklatvala did not let the cancellation go unchallenged: he used an adjournment debate in the House to complain and letters of protest were sent by Saklatvala, C.B. Vakil, the LBINC secretary, as well others in the labour movement. But without result.[52] However, this did not prevent him from denouncing British imperialism or advocating Communism.

Back in England and no longer an MP, Saklatvala continued campaigning for international class solidarity. The 1920s and 1930s were a time of economic troubles, a government policy of retrenchment, unemployment and hunger marches. In rousing speeches, he denounced 'imperialist policy' as the 'root of the evil' in Britain, Africa, China and India. He proposed solutions, exhorting unions to demand, backed by a general strike if necessary, a universal seven-hour day, no overtime and two paid holidays a year, which, he argued would give the unemployed work. Explaining how cheap labour in the empire caused unemployment in Britain and misery for both he demonstrated that their interests were inextricably linked. A populist speaker, Saklatvala's services as a 'public propagandist' for the Party, according to Thomas Bell, were 'in continuous demand' and he gave them 'unsparingly'. This would explain the hectic schedules of his meetings, involving miles of travel.[53] In 1935, for instance, according to the events advertised in the *Daily Worker,* he was said to have spoken at 19 public rallies and meetings, undertaken a speaking tour of West Fife as well as campaigned for William Gallacher and Harry Pollitt, candidates in the general election. Pollitt's tribute to Saklatvala sums up the sentiment:

> Night after night, year after year, in all parts of Britain he carried out his task of working-class agitation, education and organisation ... No comrade ever did ... his work so uncomplainingly ... No call was ever made ... to which he did not respond. Be the meeting large or small, it was always the same. Be it near or far, it was always the same.[54]

Saklatvala continued campaigning for Indian freedom through the WWLI, LAI, the CPGB, and as an active and prominent member of the LBINC. He was untiring in protesting against the 'unjust' Meerut trials. The Meerut Conspiracy case, as it was known, became a *cause célèbre*: in 1929, in the wake of the successful textile workers' strikes in Bombay, 31 people, all active trade unionists, including two Englishmen, Philip Spratt and Ben Bradley (CPGB members), were arrested on charge of a Communist plot. The trial, without a jury, dragged on for four years, while the accused, defended by Nehru, were kept behind bars. A National Meerut Defence Committee was organised in Britain to collect money for the prisoners and their families. Saklatvala spoke at meetings and rallies organised by the LAI, WWLI, the Meerut Trade Union Defence Committee and the Meerut Prisoners' Release Committee.[55]

But Saklatvala also had a destructive influence. His authoritarian attempts to control and dominate the LBINC, and dictate policy to the Congress in India, alienated some members, who severed their connection. The Congress disaffiliated the LBINC. His attacks on the Congress as a 'bourgeois' body, in line with the 'New Line', too, increased.[56] Tension within the LBINC, apparent as early as 1929, reached a climax at the second National Political Conference in July 1931, when the chairman, V.J. Patel, ex-president of the Indian Legislative Assembly, was forced to step down after Saklatvala's resolution was defeated 2 to 1, the conference ending in uproar. Such antics and attacks were divisive and damaging to Indians in Britain. This marked the end of the LBINC. Some made overtures to Menon and joined the India League.[57]

With a small clique of Indian radicals, Adrian Cola Rienzi, I.K. Yajnik and Ajoy Banerji among them, Saklatvala formed the rival New Indian Political Group.[58] He also continued to champion other oppressed minorities, as can be seen from his prominent role in the Scottsboro Boys case and the meeting organised at Essex Hall, in collaboration with the NWA, to protest against the flogging of the

Paramount Chief Tshekedi in South Africa by Vice-Admiral Evans. After Hitler's rise to power in Germany, an appeal issued by the Workers' International Relief Organisation in March 1933 and signed by him was headed: 'Help Workers and Jews under Fascist Terror'.[59]

In April 1934, as part of a workers' delegation, Saklatvala went to the USSR, his third trip (the two previous being in 1923 and 1927), visiting factories, collective farms and spending time touring the Far Eastern Soviet Republics. Saklatvala was highly impressed. His letter to the *Daily Worker*, written in July on his way back, described 'New Russia' as a 'wonderful place but new Soviet Asia even more so'. Some members of Saklatvala's family have suggested that he returned from Stalinist Russia with 'a number' of reservations. His letter certainly gives no hint of that. On the contrary, his sentiment that 'No worker who sees for himself can leave anything but a friend of the Soviet Union, and one who is anxious to spread the news among his work mates', suggests his enthusiasm was undimmed. Further, an 18-page document, 'A Few Thoughts on Party Work', written in June 1934, while still in the USSR, provides a different angle and also illustrates Saklatvala's efforts to move the CPGB to take a more determined stance on the freedom of India, Africa and other colonies.[60] The document, not uncritical of the CPGB, especially in regard to its anti-colonial policy, gives Saklatvala's thoughts, in the light of his observations on the success of Party Control and Party work in the USSR, on how the British Party could tackle its work of propaganda and education more successfully among the workers in Britain and the colonies. Commenting on the 'great contrast' in the 'Asiatic' USSR where Party members were cautioned against 'chauvinism', Saklatvala pointed to what he saw as 'certain defects' among the British Party members towards 'the Asiatic, African and colonial problems'. He highlighted their tendency to treat the 'colonial problem' as 'a mere side issue'. He lamented the lack of funds for work among colonial students, African and Asian sailors and workers in Britain's ports. He complained of 'bourgeois colonials being ignored', given no representation on 'united front work' such as on anti-war, anti-fascist or German relief committees. Saklatvala saw such neglect as having a detrimental effect. He castigated Party members for their 'adverse comments about Negroes and Indians'. He further revealed that his suggestions were ignored by the Party and that he had, in the past, 'suppressed and moderated' his criticisms. But having toured the USSR, he was convinced that the 'defect' needed remedial action. He urged that the 'method of handling the problems of nationalities by the various Communist Parties in the USSR be fully expounded and given to the British Party'. To advance the cause of

Communism, Saklatvala then listed practical suggestions for India. These included entertaining Indian and African students in Party members' homes on a 'semi-bourgeois' scale – not so unlike what retired civil servants did for Indian students. He suggested sending young Communists to India 'smuggled' into the Salvation Army ranks to work in villages, as well as encouraging sympathetic working-class employees of British firms in India, Africa or China to organise trade unions, demanding equal rights for their colonial workers. He even suggested how propaganda postcards and literature could be utilised to demonstrate industrial and agricultural progress under the Soviet Union. The document, critical of the CPGB, leaves no doubt as to his admiration for the USSR and his belief in international socialism. It also shows Saklatvala's attempts to move the CPGB to a more vigorous policy of anti-colonialism.[61]

Within months of his return, in January 1936, Saklatvala was dead. His funeral at Golders Green crematorium highlights some of the contradictions in his life. A Communist, he nonetheless remained true to his Parsi faith. In 1927, after his return from India, he had his five children, two daughters and three sons, publicly initiated into the faith, the Navjote ceremony being held at Caxton Hall, earning him the censure of the CPGB. An anti-capitalist champion of the workers, Saklatvala remained the departmental manager of Tata's, the family firm of India's pioneering capitalists, only resigning in 1925.[62] An anti-parliamentarian, he represented the CPGB in Parliament. When he died there were tributes from all strands of his political career: from the leading figures in the Labour Party, Lansbury and Attlee, from the Communist International, and from Rajani Palme Dutt, who described him as 'a revolutionary tribune of the people', from Nehru, who lamented his passing as a blow to 'the Indian Freedom Movement' and 'the workers and peasants of India'. George Padmore, the left-wing Pan-Africanist, writing in the 1950s, called him the 'most independent-minded Communist ever. A Titoist before Tito.' The fact that Bengali workers, in 1937, celebrated a Saklatvala day and British volunteers fought in a Saklatvala Battalion in the Spanish Civil War shows how some contemporary workers regarded him.[63]

Saklatvala had been involved in left-wing working-class agitation for nearly a quarter of a century, active in the movement against imperialism and in trying to forge unity between the working class in Britain and India, by demonstrating that their interests were indivisible. But there is little evidence that he had any influence on his Party or on India. He remained on the margins.

VENGALIL KRISHNAN KRISHNA MENON

The driving force behind the India League, Menon, a socialist, was also a constitutionalist. Born in 1896 at Calicut, into a prosperous, educated, cultured family, he graduated from the Madras Presidency College in 1918. Even as a student, his interest in politics was apparent: he risked near expulsion by hoisting the red and green flag of Besant's Home Rule for India League from the college roof top. After a brief spell at the Madras Law College, it being his lawyer father's ambition that Menon follow in his footsteps, he abandoned law for the National University at Adyar, joining Besant's 'Brothers of Service', an organisation for national work. Annie Besant was thus an early formative influence. In England, it was Harold Laski's teaching at the LSE that contributed to the maturing of his socialist ideals and political philosophy.

In 1924, Menon came to England for an educational conference at Letchworth. A six-month stay, he was told, would enable him to obtain a teaching qualification. He was to remain for over a quarter-century. For a year, he taught history at St Christopher's School, Letchworth, Hertfordshire, gaining a teaching diploma; then at the LSE he studied political science, obtaining a BSc in 1927. By then, political work for the freedom of India had become a total absorption and education a spare-time activity. He obtained his MA in 1930 (University College London), and MSc in 1934 (LSE), being called to the Bar in the same year.

Professionally, Menon's career falls into three strands: legal, publishing and journalism. As a barrister, he did much work without payment, defending Indian sailors in magistrates' courts (he also represented Udham Singh), which earned him their gratitude, but was hardly likely to advance his professional reputation. He was also said to have 'made something of a name for himself' in Privy Council cases. Menon's legal career, however, did not advance. His biographer, quoting the view of one leading MP, ascribes this to 'colour prejudice'. As a publisher and editor, however, Menon shone: the Penguin-Pelican series with its concept of good, 'worthwhile books' at affordable prices in paperback editions, being his important contribution. Menon was a London correspondent for several Indian newspapers, including the Lucknow *National Herald*. But his life's main work was politics.[64]

THE INDIA LEAGUE

In 1925, within a year of his arrival in England, Menon joined Besant's Home Rule for India League (British Auxiliary), founded in 1916. Re-named the Commonwealth of India League (CIL) in 1922, it aimed to lobby MPs in support of self-government within the empire, or Dominion Status. More a debating forum than a campaigning organisation – even the India Office described it as 'not an extremist organisation' – Menon did not consider the CIL an effective 'second front' for India in Britain.[65] He therefore began injecting new ideas into the League and in the process transformed it into a formidable pressure group at the heart of British politics. Elected joint secretary in 1928, within two years, with the support of fellow radicals like Fenner Brockway, he had won the argument against Dominion Status and for *purna swaraj*. The elders, Besant and Polak among them, had resigned. The CIL became the India League, with its objective: 'To support the claim of India for Swaraj' in line with the 1929 Congress resolution.[66] But it remained an independent organisation. With its new headquarters at 146 The Strand (later, 165), increased membership (200 additional members were said to have joined within days of the name change) and a network of branches, the League became a national organisation. By the early 1930s there were 13 branches in London alone and another 13 around Britain: Bournemouth, Birmingham, Bradford, Bristol, Cardiff, Hull, Leeds, Liverpool, Manchester, Southampton and Wolverhampton among them.[67] And the League began to be noticed. How did it achieve such a transformation?

Enlisting public support was not easy. A majority of the British public was apathetic, or ignorant of Indian developments. Censorship in India prevented news reaching Britain. Further, organisations like the Indian Empire Society, founded in 1930 by some retired India hands – Winston Churchill, a prominent recruit, was its principal speaker at its first meeting – kept up a barrage of propaganda against what they called the 'ever more extreme' demands from the Indian political elite, emphasising India's unfitness for self-rule on the one hand and the benefits and benevolence of British rule on the other. The degree of their opposition is summed up in Churchill's words: sooner or later, 'we shall have to crush Gandhi and Congress and all they stand for'. The Society even had links with the India Office.[68] To counter such propaganda, the League began an intensive information campaign. There were meetings, lectures, courses and conferences on topics ranging from 'politics and economics of the empire in India' to 'women and India', 'the National Movement' and 'Political and Civil Liberty in India'. There were gatherings to mark special events like Amritsar Day, or 'Independence day', proceedings often opening with national songs. There were press conferences to put the Indian point of view on events in India. Cultural events, film shows, and readings from works of literature were organised to keep India in the public eye, and alter audience perception. How intense was the campaign is seen from a Scotland Yard report for October 1930, which noted that 'a dozen lectures' had been arranged in London 'within the present fortnight'.[69]

Described by Chagla as a man of 'formidable' intellect, and in an official report as 'a demonic worker, an able organiser, a powerful orator and a piercing critic', Menon addressed gatherings of students, factory workers and miners; spoke to women's groups, church groups and youth groups; at meetings of trade unions, local Labour Parties, the Fabian Society, Peace groups and the Communist Party, in short to anyone who was prepared to listen to him. He even spoke from a platform in Hyde Park. Indeed, surveillance reports on Menon for the 1930s and 1940s (the number of files on the League indicate the extent of surveillance), provide some insights into the League's method of campaigning and its supporters. These reports also show that although India was the centre of Menon's activities, his concerns were wider. He campaigned for all colonised peoples.[70] His dedication is seen from the fact that no gathering was considered small or trivial. Reginald Sorensen, MP, recalled how as a minister of a small Unitarian Church at Walthamstow, having learnt of the League from an 'old lady' who distributed leaflets on India, he invited Menon to address a small mid-week discussion group he ran. Menon's 'characteristic intensity and fervour' made this small audience 'almost' feel he was addressing 'the whole British people'. Sorensen was won over to 'the moral significance of India's cause', becoming a staunch supporter. Another, an 18-year-old girl, describing her 'first account of a real political meeting', and contrasting the 'insignificant mediocrity' of the local organiser with 'the greatness of the Indian', enthusiastically noted that she found Menon's speech 'really enthralling from beginning to end'.[71]

Menon's forte was facts. And in Chakravarty's words, he 'juxtaposed statistics in such a way as to make them stand up and raise their arms in social protest'. For instance, highlighting government spending in India, Menon showed that while 84.3 per cent went on defence, law and order, salaries and pensions, mostly for the British, only 5.7 per cent was spent on education and 10 per cent on social services. He provided charts to compare social service provision between Britain and British India: 1 nurse for every 435 persons in Britain compared to 1 for every

86,000 in India; 1 doctor for every 776 in Britain, but 1 to 9,000 in India. Education spending per head in Britain was £2. 9s. 8d., but only 10d. in India. He pointed to the shocking infant mortality rate and life expectancy, cut from an average of 30 years in 1881 to 23.5, and all this after nearly 150 years of British rule. He pointed to the low wages, wretched conditions of work and poverty of the masses. Such facts revealed the stark reality of life for the majority under colonialism and were powerful arguments against the view that the Raj was beneficial.[72] Even seasoned civil servants were sometimes persuaded, as the resumé of a talk to the Youth Advisory Committee of the Civil Service Clerical Association in June 1937 shows. Commenting on Menon's 'plain statement', the writer, noting that it 'caused some uneasiness in the minds of those of us who still believe in the "civilising mission" of the British empire', concluded: 'we shall endeavour to study events in India with open mindedness and insist that justice be done in our time'. Personal letters to Menon, regardless of whether the motive of the writer was a genuine desire for information or merely to ridicule him, received lengthy replies, packed with facts.[73]

The League also countered mis-information through a stream of literature, information sheets, pamphlets, circulars, articles, the League's organ *Indian News* (*Newsindia*), the *Information Bulletin* and other topical publications, most of it written by Menon himself, and all designed to keep members and the public abreast of happenings in India, current campaigns and more facts. Newspapers were bombarded with letters from India League-ers, a rapid response to hostile reporting. Liberal newspapers and journals such as the *Manchester Guardian* and the *New Statesman and Nation* carried articles by Menon. So successful was Menon in obtaining information from his contacts in India (he described his sources as 'secret channels') that the head of the Intelligence Branch wrote despairingly: 'We do all we can to prevent such information as is published in Congress bulletins reaching England, but the energetic editor of the *Information Bulletin,* Menon … is quite cunning in arranging post-boxes in England.' Commenting that a 'certain amount' of it reached Lansbury, the Intelligence Branch explained that 'we have so far refrained from tapping the correspondence of the Leader of the Opposition'.[74]

A member of the Labour Party, and regarded as an authority on India, Menon cultivated his academic and Labour connections to persuade sympathetic leading personalities to join the League. Bertrand Russell was its chairman, and J.F. Horrabin its vice-chairman. Such names gave the League status. Its executive committee in 1932 listed Brockway, Frieda Laski, Fred Longden and Dr Saeed Mohamedi. Its

Committee of Action named Lansbury, Harold Laski, H.N. Brailsford and Dorothy Woodman among them, the last-named providing a link with Kingsley Martin, the editor of the *New Statesman and Nation*. There was a women's committee with Mrs Nehru and Winifred Horrabin, a Labour Committee with A.A. Purcell and Menon himself. There was a strong Parliamentary Committee. At the time of the National government in the 1930s, 40 Labour MPs were identified as having League connections. The Committee asked questions on India, put the League's point of view and arranged for leading Indians to meet MPs. Official sources named Sorensen, William Dobbie and Alex Sloan, among others, as indefatigable Parliamentarians on behalf of the League. Other committees were added as need arose. In 1943, a Central Indian Committee was inaugurated with Rewal Singh, Mrs M.F. Boomla, Mrs Jai Kishore Handoo, Mulk Raj Anand, whose *Letters on India* provided the Congress view of the Indian situation, and Drs Katial and Saeed Mohamedi, among others. One of the aims of the Indian Committee was to maintain contact with Indians in Britain.[75] Over the years of the League's existence, supporters and speakers drawn from a wide spectrum of the Left of British politics, included Reginald Bridgeman, Rajani Palme Dutt, Sir Stafford Cripps and J.B.S. Haldane, Krishna Shelvankar, and Bhicoo Batlivala, a barrister married to Guy Mansell and living in Cobham, Surrey with her two children.[76]

Some Indian and Ceylonese students joined the League. Student interest in 'nationalist ideas', apparent as early as 1914, had by the late 1920s, according to the DIB, become 'more revolutionarily active'. S.M. Kumaramangalam and Rajni M. Patel, described as 'two leading spirits' in the Cambridge Majlis, for instance, were alleged to have 'very definite Communist affiliations'. They were also named as 'leading lights' in the Federation of Indian Student Societies in Great Britain (founded in 1937), and to have 'close associations' with the Colonial Bureau of the Communist Party. Then there was the Central Association of Indian Students Abroad. The Oxford Majlis programme of lectures on Indian affairs listed Gandhi, Ellen Wilkinson (of Jarrow Crusade fame) and Dutt among its speakers.[77] Like the LBINC, Menon too, campaigned among students and was said to have built up a position among them. Some became activists, addressing envelopes, dispatching League literature, distributing leaflets, pasting publicity posters, arranging and addressing meetings. They took part in demonstrations and meetings, usually identified in surveillance reports as 'student types'. Activists included: Rajni M. Patel at Cambridge, Ahmed Hoosain Sader in Birmingham, K.L. Haravu, P.N. Haksar, T. Subasinghe, who as a friend of Padmore also helped to organise the Pan-African Congress in

Manchester in 1945 and was secretary of the Subject People's Conference, Firoze Gandhi, described as Menon's satellite, and Dayanand Naidoo in Edinburgh.[78]

Thanks to its publicity campaigns, the reality of the condition of life of the majority of Indians under colonialism, the government's policy of repression during the 1930s and 1940s, and the stalemate in the constitutional advance, reached a much wider audience. By the 1940s, 14 branches had been formed, from Edinburgh and Glasgow to Birmingham, Bristol, Coventry and Wales. In London, branches were spread from Harrow to the East End, and membership of the London headquarters branch was estimated to be 510. Some politically minded Indians, irrespective of religion or class, joined. But the majority of its supporters were whites. There were affiliated organisations, trade unions, trades councils and cooperative societies. Internationally, there was a branch in the USA. But, as with most pressure groups, actual membership remained small, the team of active workers fluctuated and Menon remained its organiser and 'life blood'.[79]

But the League laboured under difficulties. At a time of economic depression and during the Second World War, sustaining interest in the Indian freedom movement was not easy. Turnout at meetings fluctuated. Some branches were more active than others. Finance remained a major problem, most of its income being derived from subscriptions, collections at meetings, sale of literature and donations from Indian and white British sympathisers. The fact that the workers at its headquarters in London were unpaid volunteers, Bridget Tunnard, Menon's secretary, included, helped the League to survive, while in the provinces many India League-ers were associated with other movements. Menon took no salary, even ploughing his earnings from publishing and journalism into the League, living an austere life in a garret at 57 Camden Square. Still, shortage of money resulted in publications being suspended. How unstable its finances were is seen from the fact that, in 1943, to put the League on a sounder footing, Mrs Handoo instituted a scheme for a fixed annual subscription from wealthy Indian supporters, mainly doctors and businessmen.[80] Another problem was Menon's own personality. A hard task-master, his irascible temper and biting tongue did not make for harmony. His single-minded vision and ideas of how to achieve it, led him to keep the strings of authority in his own hands and behave in autocratic ways, alienating even friends. Then there were schisms, common to most radical political movements, and jockeying for position and influence, giving rise to rival Indian organisations. While the goal of freedom remained common and their outlook international, Menon and the League did not escape criticism. Saklatvala established the New Indian Political Group. Another rival was the Friends of India Society (under A.S. Kamlani). In 1942 several other organisations were formed, among them, the Committee of Indian Congressmen (CIC), under the leadership of Amiya Bose, the nephew of Subhas Chandra Bose and P.B. Seal; and Swaraj House, a breakaway from the CIC, with Suresh Vaidya, the journalist for the US *Time and Life*, married to an English woman, and said to have been a 'great admirer' of Menon, Surat Alley and C.B. Vakil. With a policy of unqualified support for the Congress, membership of Swaraj House was open only to Indians, a position at odds with the League, which was independent and open to whites and Indians. Swaraj House and several IWA branches, together with the Glasgow Indian Majlis, affiliated to form the FIAGB. These organisations, though brushed aside by Menon, were damaging and added to the confusion in the minds of British sympathisers. But the greatest stumbling block remained British imperial authority and policy, particularly within the dominant Conservative Party.[81] Undeterred, throughout the 1930s and 1940s, in response to events and policy developments in India, the League kept up an intensive campaign to mobilise support of the British public against colonialism, and influence Parliament.

Before the outbreak of the war in 1939, on one level, the League agitated against the repressive ordinances which deprived Indians of their civil liberties, and, on the other, on constitutional developments, lobbied Parliament to secure amendments in line with Indian aspiration for *purna swaraj*. The Simon Commission had been greeted with hostility. But in 1929, Lord Irwin and the Labour government officially acknowledged that Britain's India policy was for Dominion Status, and the Round Table Conferences were called to consider a proposal for federation, to bring the Princely states and British India together. But, with the collapse of the Gandhi–Irwin Pact following the inconclusive Second Round Table Conference in London in the autumn of 1931, and the revival of civil disobedience, Gandhi was arrested within a week of his return to India. The Conservative Lord Willingdon (a Tory-dominated coalition had replaced Labour) more inclined towards repression than negotiation, issued tough ordinances. Congress was outlawed and activists arrested. Boycott spread. The press was muzzled. Peasants, hit by the fall in agricultural prices and refusing to pay taxes, found coercive ordinances extended to economic agitation. Within four months an estimated 80,000 Indians were in jail.

In Britain, the League protested against such coercive measures and demanded resumption of negotiations. At a meeting of the Leytonstone branch on 23 February, for instance, Revd A.D. Belden queried how

Britain could condemn Japanese repression in China, when it resorted to governing India by 'Ordinances of brutal character'. In March 1932, in a letter to the Joint Council of the Labour Party and the TUC, Menon and Horrabin urged the council to make a declaration against the 'wanton and unprovoked repression', and to receive a deputation from the League.[82] The response of the Joint Council is not on record, but, in 1932, the League organised a delegation to investigate conditions in India.

MISSION TO INDIA

The delegation consisted of Labour MPs Ellen Wilkinson and Monica Whately, Leonard Matters, a freelance journalist and ex-Labour MP, and Menon. They spent 83 days gathering evidence in provinces as far apart as the North-West Frontier Province, Bengal, the Punjab and southern India. They visited cities, villages, factories and prisons. They met Indians of all walks of life, religion and political opinion. They talked with businessmen, trade unionists, workers and members of the British resident population. They interviewed government officials, both European and Indian, and met the Viceroy. They came across humiliating and intimidating treatment of men, women and children and gross violation of human rights, all committed by the servants of the Crown. In Bengal, for instance, women resisters taken into custody were driven miles from their homes or places of arrest to island *chars*, 'small islands thrown up in the middle of the rivers of eastern Bengal', and in many cases 'uninhabited and full of jungle' and left there at 'dead of night'. They heard of women 'savagely set upon', beaten or insulted by the police, who used foul and filthy language to frighten them. They witnessed 'excessive force', the use of *lathis* (metal-tipped wooden staffs), bayonets and rifles, to disperse peaceful crowds and civil disobedience processions.[83] They learnt of strange offences and punishments of unspeakable cruelty. The fate of the 19-year-old Mohan Kaul in Rajshai jail is a case in point. He was put in 'standing handcuffs' for refusing to salaam at the call of *Sarkar Salaam* (salute the government), a compulsory disciplinary measure in all prisons. He suffered five and a half months of solitary confinement. After three months, and still adamant, he was put into a cage, only 7 foot by 5 foot. Here, 'with his hands fettered behind his back', Kaul 'spent all hours of the day and night … was obliged to take his food and answer the calls of nature'. At Madura, on the other hand, the delegation heard that on 28 August 1932, a group of 15, aged 15 to 20, gathered at an open public space 'to salute the Congress flag' (a custom on the last Sunday of each month), were 'set upon by the police who encircled them and beat the boys and men, until they fell on the ground'. Thousands were imprisoned. By the Secretary of State's own admission, in April 1932 there were 26,000 men and women in jail. Prisoner classification, as A, B or C category, was arbitrary, the 'bulk' of civil disobedience prisoners being in class C and treated as common criminals. Food was half-cooked and often insufficient.[84]

But the Viceroy appeared sanguine, even unaware of the conditions. When informed by the delegation of famine in the Uttar Pradesh and Allahabad, and villagers surviving on 'berries', the Viceroy denied its existence. Why? Because it had not been reported to him and 'by law' famine had to be proclaimed. As to the extent of the terror, according to the Viceroy, 'everything was peaceful in India', 'everything was 100 per cent better than 18 months ago'. On this Matters could only comment: 'If the people he met were 100 per cent better off than 18 months ago then God help them indeed ... India is a lawless country with a lawless government.' As for the political sophistication of the people in the villages, the Simon Commission had been dismissive: 'while abstract political ideas leave him unaffected, the personality of a leader such as Gandhi will make a great appeal'. But the League delegates found that the villagers were neither 'apathetic on great issues before the country' nor 'unintelligent or unreceptive to ideas'.[85]

The delegates' findings stunned British audiences. At one packed conference on 26 November 1932 in Kingsway Hall in London, the meeting unanimously demanded the immediate withdrawal of repressive measures and the transfer of power to the people, which was 'theirs by right'.[86] But the state was dismissive. In Parliament, the Secretary of State cast doubt on the reliability of the League's findings, alleging that demonstrations were 'stage managed'. Much was made of the fact that the Congress had partly paid their travel expenses. But, as Morgan Jones, the Member for Caerphilly retorted, 'if that argument is to be relied upon then every member of the Round Table Conference has his expense paid by the government'. However, the government's allegation of bias was a disingenuous attempt at damage limitation, as evidence shows. Lord Lothian had himself provided Whately with a list of 'reliable' contacts. India Office received weekly intelligence reports of the delegates' progress, their interviews with government officials and the police. Internal minutes even record disquiet.[87] A memo, dated 16 October 1932, entitled 'tentative suggestions', noted that, since the delegates were 'in a strong position of eye-witness ... it may do little good if not some harm to indulge merely in public attacks upon bona fides and veracity of the delegates'. Instead, the tour was to be discredited for being 'hurried' and their information as 'untrustworthy'.

A week later, a telegram informing the Viceroy that the Secretary of State was 'anxious to be in a position to issue a counter-blast at once', requested the 'fullest' information on 'bias and unreliability'. And so, by the time the delegates returned, India Office had decided how the government's 'counter propaganda' was to be 'managed': by alleging that they had 'allowed themselves to be "run" by Congress sympathisers', that 'persistent endeavours' had been made 'from one end of the country to the other to stage "incidents"', and that their 'minds were closed'.[88] How rattled the government of India had been is further evident from the reaction to the publication in the *Hindustan Times* in December 1932 of the League's initial report. Complaining to the India Office that 'so little' had been done by way of 'a counter-blast', the Director of Public Information in the Viceroy's office, wrote: 'The Nationalist press here have been pretty full of unpleasant articles ... and it has been difficult for me to do much to counter them.' When *Condition of India* was published, the India Office having failed in its attempt to prevent its publication, the government of India banned it, afraid that it might do 'much mischief', the Chief of Intelligence admitting that 'very many of the allegations are or may be true'.[89] *Condition of India* remains a searing indictment of the Raj.

This was the League's most important achievement in the period before the war. As Bertrand Russell wrote: 'so long as the British insist upon governing India, they have no right to ignore what is done in their name by the Government which they have elected'.[90] As a campaigning organisation, the League also provided a platform for visiting politicians, Gandhi and Nehru among them. This brought Menon and Nehru closer, strengthening Menon's link with the radical wing of the Congress. Thanks to Menon and the League, contact between the Labour Left and the Congress, especially its socialist wing, was re-established. As a result, at a meeting with Nehru, Attlee and Cripps conceded, subject to minority representation, to the Congress demand made in response to the 1935 Act, that India should be allowed to make its own constitution through a Constituent Assembly elected by universal suffrage.

With Fascism on the rise, at the World Peace Congress in Brussels in September 1936, which Menon attended as a nominee of the Congress, it was evident that, as an internationalist, he spoke as much for the people of Abyssinia (Ethiopia), Spain and other colonised peoples as for Indians when he said: 'Free peoples liberated from domination and thus themselves averse to conquests are the best guarantees of peace.' Indians could not remain passive in the face of Fascist aggression.[91] Indeed, the League's annual National Independence Demonstration on

30 January 1938 became an expression of solidarity with Africans, Chinese and the Spanish Republican people. A 1,200-strong procession, accompanied by four bands, marched to Trafalgar Square, carrying national flags and portraits of Nehru, Gandhi, Tagore, Haile Selassie, Chiang Kai Shek and La Passionara. At Trafalgar Square, Lieutenant Commander E.P. Young, Sorensen, Maude Royden and Dr D.H. Liem, among others, addressed a crowd 3,000 strong. The resolution, denouncing imperialism and Fascism as 'blood brothers', called on the British people to unite against the common foe. That summer, Menon and Nehru visited Spain. Their five-day visit convinced them that 'freedom was indivisible, and the world could not continue ... part free and part unfree'.[92]

At the India League meeting in Kingsway Hall on 27 June 1938, Nehru and Paul Robeson, the black American singer, actor and political activist, whose help Menon had enlisted before, spoke on internationalism and the need for unified action against Fascism. Some blacks at the time keenly followed India's struggle. According to Robeson they were 'conscious of its importance for us'.[93] At a delegates' conference organised by the Harrow and Wembley Branch, the South African, Peter Abrahams, declared that India's fight for independence had become 'a test case in the eyes of all coloured people', a sentiment echoed by the West African Wallace-Johnson in 1946. Indeed, black radical intellectuals like Jomo Kenyatta and C.L.R. James in Britain in the inter-war years attended some League meetings. In 1938 and 1939 there were more rallies against Fascism under the auspices of the League. There was also practical aid. At an 'Indian evening' organised by the India-Spanish League to raise funds, Indira Gandhi, then a student at Oxford, spoke and over £80 was collected.[94]

It was not only at the international level that the League campaigned against Fascism. Menon tried to remove Fascists from Britain's streets. According to a police report, Menon played a prominent role in the Campaign of the St Pancras Joint Council of Labour to persuade the council to 'take steps to cause the recent British Union of Fascists march from Kentish Town to Trafalgar Square, to be prohibited'. At another demonstration, in March 1938, to protest against the local council's decision to allow the German Nazi Party in London to hold meetings at Seymour Hall in Marylebone, Menon was among the speakers. How strong was Menon's abhorrence of Fascism and all that it stood for is seen from his statement to the teachers at the first meeting of the India League Teachers' sub-committee on 22 January 1944 at Alliance Hall, Westminster. Suggesting that education in the past had 'largely' been responsible for the 'chaotic' state of the world, he informed them that the object of the meeting was 'to show teachers the need for educating the rising generation so that Nazism in any shape or form would not raise its head again in the future'.[95] Such statements mark Menon out as an early advocate and pioneer of what today is termed anti-racist education.

ST PANCRAS COUNCILLOR

Menon had joined the Labour Party at the LSE. In November 1934, he was elected Labour councillor for Ward 4 in the Borough of St Pancras. He proved to be such a dynamic councillor that at each subsequent election he was re-elected with an increased majority, serving a total of 14 years, voluntarily resigning in 1947 on being appointed independent India's High Commissioner. Councillor Menon plunged into work with enthusiasm, equalling his work for India. This is not surprising. Menon, it is said, saw the slum dwellers behind King's Cross station in the borough to be just as 'cruelly exploited as the oppressed in India' and part of the same struggle to improve living conditions for the disadvantaged.[96]

During his 14-year term Menon served on all the major committees: Baths and Cemeteries, Sewers and Public Works, Highways, and General Purposes Committees. But it was as the chairman of the Education and Public Library Committee that he is best remembered. Appointed chairman in 1945, his passion for education and books was such that his term saw the extension of the library service throughout the borough. It is said that Menon would count the pubs in the borough and remark: 'We must have as many public libraries here as pubs.' For Menon, libraries were not big buildings, but a large central collection of books. To popularise the library service, he organised conferences for teachers, voluntary groups and cultural organisations. He began a travelling library, a gramophone records section, arranged exhibitions and concerts on Sundays. A local information centre was set up at the Town Hall; there were lectures for children on topics of educational interest, and a Book Week. But his greatest contribution, and legacy, to the cultural life of the borough remains the St Pancras Arts and Civic Council, established in 1944, with Menon as chairman and launched by Dame Sybil Thorndike, an India League supporter. Under its umbrella, Menon inaugurated the St Pancras Arts Festival, an annual programme of cultural events for the enrichment of its citizens, the forerunner of the Camden Arts Festival.[97]

The Second World War saw Menon, as one of the three-man team on the reduced council, rise to the challenge of enemy bombs and provide leadership. He served on the Food Control Committee, was a civil defence worker and an air-raid warden. He improved safety standards and conditions in the air-raid shelters and wardens' posts. For instance, seeing that the government was dragging its feet over the application to construct 'two-stage concrete shelters' as recommended by the local Civil Defence Committee, he got round the problem by moving a resolution in the council which would allow the Committee, in the interim, to build shelters in 'monolithic concrete' and not brick (already proved unsafe), while a deputation was sent to the ministry. Menon's own personal courage and devotion to duty as an air-raid warden, too, is still remembered. How great was his contribution to the borough is seen from the fact that in 1955, in appreciation of his 'eminent services' to local government and the 'very high regard and esteem' of its citizens, the council honoured him with the Freedom of the Borough. Menon was only the second person to be made a 'Freeman' of St Pancras, the first being George Bernard Shaw.[98]

In July 1939, sponsored by the Jute and Flax Workers' Union, by 60 votes to 33, Menon was elected prospective Labour candidate for Dundee, receiving the Party's endorsement. But within months, in April 1940, the executive of the Dundee Trades and Labour Council cancelled Menon's candidature, citing the reason that he had 'violated the loyalty pledge' by speaking from public platforms 'in opposition to official Labour Party policy', a possible reference to his participation in a *Labour Monthly* conference in London on 25 February 1940. The IPI 'history sheet', on Menon on the other hand, offers the explanation that he had 'identified himself largely with the Communist Party attitude in regard to Finland and with activities of Peace Councils whose views are not of the Labour Party'.[99] Menon categorically repudiated the charge. But, in response to his demand for an inquiry, the Executive of the Labour Party, while upholding the decision of the Trades Council, made no mention of Menon's alleged Communist identification. Instead, in January 1941, G.R. Shepherd, National Agent of the Party, wrote: the Executive 'recognises you as a representative of an important section of Indian public opinion', but 'it feels sure that you would not claim that, owing to your natural allegiance to India, you can give full support to Labour Party policy'. Shepherd at the same time declared that the Party did not 'whittle down in any way its own keen desire for the welfare of India'. Despite this claim, the reason seems clear: Labour, in coalition with the Tory government, disowned Menon for standing firm on Indian freedom.[100] Nonetheless, the claim that he had been dropped for being a Communist has stuck. The reason for this is not far to seek: Menon was an irritant and the easiest way of discrediting him was to brand him a Communist, as is evident from India Office manoeuvres. A telegram informing the Viceroy that: '[the] Labour Party Executive for reasons better known to themselves chose to inform Menon that his removal ... was because ... his particular association with India would not enable him to give full support to Labour Party policy', repeated the allegation that the 'real reason' was his 'association [with] and loyalty to Communists'. Further, at India Office 'instance', in a long 'useful message' sent by Byrt, the London Correspondent of the *Times of India,* much was made of Menon's statement concerning 'principles of freedom and social justice basic to international socialist movement'. The implication is clear.[101]

But Menon was no Communist. And the India Office knew this. Describing Menon as 'anti-British' and 'an extreme socialist', IPI, in his 'history sheet' on Menon, wrote disparagingly: 'He is not a Marxian Communist, having neither the brain needed to work out Marxian dialectics for himself, nor the type of character which would enable him to accept spoon-feeding from those who have.' Elsewhere, a scribble by a civil servant in the margin of a confidential letter written for counter-propaganda purposes which labelled Menon as 'an avowed communist', reads cryptically: 'he isn't'. There is no denying that Menon had many and frequent contacts with the Communists, something not unusual in the context of the time. Further, as an uncompromising fighter for the emancipation of India, Menon welcomed anyone willing to support India's cause. But, as his contemporaries confirm, Menon, 'a fiercely passionate and independent socialist', was a firm believer in constitutionalism.[102]

However, by its very decision that an Indian socialist's commitment to the Indian freedom struggle was incompatible with membership of the Labour Party, the Labour Executive had set up, in the words of the *Manchester Guardian,* an 'extraordinary proposition', implying Labour's unquestioning acceptance of the coalition government's India policy. The *Daily Worker* described the Executive action as 'one of the most shameful decisions ever taken by the party'. Menon saw it as the 'introduction of a national and racial bar' into the Labour movement.[103] He resigned from the Labour Party, after 16 years' membership. But this did not end his career on St Pancras Borough Council. He sat as an Independent. And he threw himself into the campaign for the freedom of India with greater energy, until the fight was won.

MENON AND THE LEAGUE IN WAR-TIME

When Linlithgow declared India a belligerent country without consultation and despite the pledge that Indian troops would not be sent abroad without first informing the Central Legislature, Indians felt outraged, the

more so as all the white Dominions had been consulted. Notwithstanding Indian abhorrence of Fascism, the Congress resolved that India
would not collaborate to 'rescue ... a tottering imperialism', and instead
demanded that Britain declare its war aims in regard to democracy and
imperialism and how these would apply to India. Britain refused.
Deadlock resulted. Indian constitutional advance remained a bone of
contention throughout the war, though millions of Indians fought with
Britain against Fascist dictators and for democracy.[104]

To Britons fighting against Hitler, the attitude of the Congress
leaders did not make sense. It therefore fell to Menon and the League to
explain that India was totally opposed to Fascism and was a willing
partner in a war for democracy, but India needed a pledge from Britain
on India's freedom. As he argued: 'A free India is a potent ally. A
subject India is a weak spot in Britain's moral armour and a weak link in
the chain of the battlements of world freedom.' In Parliament, Attlee
attacked Linlithgow's lack of sensitivity and pressed 'for an act of
statesmanship', while Cripps, a friend of Menon, lobbied Amery, the
Secretary of State for India, for a proposal based on post-war Dominion
Status, a Constituent Assembly and a treaty. But Churchill remained
adamant. In his diary, Amery records Churchill's vehement opposition:
'He said he would sooner give up political life at once, or rather go out
into the wilderness and fight, than to admit a revolution which meant the
end of the Imperial Crown in India.'[105] In India, Gandhi initiated his
individual *satyagraha* campaign, resulting in 20,000 convictions by
mid-1941. In Britain, Menon and the League mounted an intensive
campaign.

By the summer of 1941, France had fallen, Russia had been invaded
and in August 1941, Churchill and Roosevelt issued the famous
eight-point Atlantic Charter. But in India there was disunity between the
government and the people, and, under the repressive Ordinances,
thousands were in prison. Because of censorship and news blackout,
precious little was heard from India. To publicise the 'barbaric and
medieval' jail conditions and campaign for the release of political
prisoners, Menon launched a 'Release Nehru' Campaign, targeting his
appeal to organisations like the Howard League, while H.G. Wells, with
evidence supplied by Bhicoo Batlivala of Nehru's circumstances in jail,
protested to Amery.[106] To demand a settlement with India, on Sunday
10 August 1941, under the banner: 'Let the People of Britain Speak to
the People of India, Now', Menon called a Conference at Holborn Hall,
with MPs Sorensen and Dobbie in the chair. The ethical dimension was
underlined by the theme, 'The Issue is Freedom'. Supported by MPs,
academics, intellectuals and men of religion, the programme listed the

names of 46 sympathisers. Around 750 people attended, a third from the provinces. The 400 delegates, from 226 organisations, represented an estimated million people, ranging from trade unions, cooperative guilds and colonial organisations, to peace groups and political parties. In his opening speech, reiterating India's readiness to fight in 'the world front against aggression', Menon asked: since Britain had given a promise of self-government to Syria, to restored Abyssinia, Poland, Czechoslovakia and other occupied countries, should not Britain give a similar promise of self-government to India? For Indians, this was the 'acid test' of the sincerity of Britain's claim that the war was a 'war for democracy'. These were powerful arguments. That they carried weight is evident from the reports of the conference and by the fact that the four-part resolution was carried, in its original form, by an overwhelming majority.[107] A month later, on 6 September, at a two-day weekend conference of Indians in Scotland and Northern England, drawing attention to the Atlantic Charter, which affirmed 'the right of all peoples to choose the form of government under which they will live', and the 'wish to see sovereign rights and self-government restored to those who have been forcibly deprived of them', the Conference demanded negotiations with India based on the Charter. But, three days later, Indians learnt from Churchill's speech in the House that the Charter did not apply to 'India, Burma and other parts of the British Empire'. As S.O. Davies, MP, commented: 'if this was a war of liberation, why was India denied freedom? Was the Atlantic Charter an honest statement, to be honestly applied, or was it merely a piece of cheap rhetoric?' And Menon seized the opportunity to expose British double talk.[108]

As the international conflict widened – America had entered the war, Singapore had fallen and the Japanese were at India's backdoor – Cripps was sent to India in March 1942, with a Declaration prepared by the Cabinet Indian Committee (Attlee was its chairman). The Cripps offer was based on the broad principles discussed between Nehru, Attlee and Cripps in 1938, but with modifications in the light of the Muslim separatist movement under Jinnah. India was to be offered self-determination as soon as war ended, and an elected Constituent Assembly to frame a constitution. States and provinces not wishing to belong to the Indian union could 'opt out', effectively conceding the concept of partition. In the interim, Cripps was to negotiate a plan allowing Indian parties to participate in the Viceroy's executive. But the mission, dependent on the cooperation of the Viceroy and all the Indian parties, failed. Cripps blamed Gandhi and Attlee laid the blame on communal impasse. But, as Moore writes, American and Indian opinion 'guessed at the truth, that Cripps was undermined by colleagues who did not want to bring the Raj to an early end'.[109] In August 1942, Gandhi launched his 'Quit India' campaign and the government responded with repression, effectively ending further constitutional negotiations. Relations between Labour and the Congress became strained. All this made Menon's task even more difficult.

Menon intensified the League's campaign to re-open negotiations, arguing that a provisional government that commanded the respect of Indians would more effectively mobilise resources against Japan. He condemned the Cripps offer as 'Balkanising' India. The League publications publicised the Indian view, such that, by July 1942, leaflet distribution was 'approaching a million', some organisations even regarded the League, to the chagrin of the India Office, as 'a semi-official' organisation for providing information on India. Requests for speakers rose. By December there were 'an average of 25' per week, and Menon and his small band were kept busy addressing groups all over Britain. How intensive were Menon's own schedules is seen from his diaries, reproduced in surveillance reports. One such itinerary in 1942 recorded a total of 23 engagements in one month, and these were only the 'more important' ones.[110]

As the situation deteriorated, Menon hammered away, exposing grave human rights violations. The League meetings heard of innocent unarmed crowds having been machine-gunned by low-flying RAF planes to disperse them. Such revelations, hushed up so that the British public were left in ignorance, earned Menon the wrath of officialdom, seen from a venomous little minute: 'It's time Menon was machine-gunned.'[111] He publicised the famine in Bengal and organised fundraising. There were meetings in key areas to mobilise opinion to demand a settlement, release of prisoners, immediate negotiations and a National Government. One such meeting proclaimed '400,000,000' potential allies against Fascism. At another, in Central Hall in London, in 1942, described as 'perhaps the largest ... in recent years', the Dean of Canterbury, without exonerating the Congress, castigated Britain's 'stubborn imperialist policy', demanding that Indian people must be rallied to the allied cause. Another, at the Coliseum in January 1943, attracted 2,200 people. Apart from speeches and resolutions, the audience was entertained with a concert of Indian national songs, Negro Spirituals and poetry and prose readings by Rudolph Dunbar, the Guyanese musician and journalist, and Dame Sybil Thorndike.[112] At the same time, the Birmingham branch of the League targeted Amery's constituency, mounting an intensive campaign. Factory ballots were organised by the Shop Stewards' Movement in Birmingham and London. The grassroots of the labour movement and the Labour Party, too, received particular attention from the League, as did the churches.[113]

Menon's efforts did not stop at meetings, publications and grassroots campaigning. He lobbied MPs and there were questions in Parliament by MPs sympathetic to the League, especially Sorensen. In 1944, Menon produced a memo for a 'workable plan' to end the deadlock and install a transition government to a future free India. The plan, with guarantees for minorities, envisaged a power-sharing arrangement among all the parties in India.[114] Further, aware of the importance of American opinion – Bhicoo Batlivala had had a successful six-month lecture tour in America in 1940 – Menon made contact with the American ambassador in an attempt to persuade Roosevelt (and Stalin and Chiang Kai Shek) to urge Britain to acknowledge the independence of India. Menon's 'sufficiently cordial' relations with the Americans and his interviews with the ambassador, particularly at the time of Wavell's appointment as the new Viceroy, in September 1943, so worried the India Office that IPI suggested 'someone' in the Foreign Office 'casually' drop a hint to the ambassador about 'the character and background' of Menon to warn him off. The fact that this note is still not in the public domain suggests the scurrilous nature of the official version.[115]

Indeed, the India League's growing activity became the target of India Office action. Concerned at its effect on public opinion in Britain and the USA, the government, with its control of communication channels, hit back.[116] How wide-ranging was official propaganda to discredit, and frustrate, Menon and the League is seen from the Information Department file marked 'Anti-British Propaganda'. A twin-track strategy designed, on the one hand, to starve the League of publicity in the media and, on the other, to produce 'determined and aggressive' propaganda to counteract its message, was stepped up.[117] To prevent coverage of League meetings in the provinces, 'friendly and responsible' newspaper editors were persuaded that they would be doing 'real war service' if they got their staff to 'soft-pedal the utterances of ... fanatical and ... mentally dishonest' India League members. In addition, 'no less' than 850 newspapers and publications in England, Scotland and Northern Ireland were circularised with an article from the journal *Great Britain and the East*, written by that 'doughty fighter in our interest', Sir Alfred Watson, the editor, together with a letter, warning editors against the League. While purporting to have been sent personally by Watson, in actual fact the missive was sent from the India Office, which bore the entire cost. Faced with such a newspaper ban, is it any wonder that Menon could rely on the sympathy of only a handful of editors, the *Daily Worker* among them? Even the League's paper quota was reduced by the Paper Control authority, on official instructions, severely restricting the output of *Newsindia*. In order to remove Menon's parliamentary support, the possibility of approaching Amery to 'drop a hint' to Bevin to induce Labour to take 'firm disciplinary action' against MPs like Sorensen, too, was discussed.[118]

Then there was relentless propaganda. Every League meeting was carefully covered so that, in the words of one civil servant, 'specific mis-statements', could be countered with a 'correct' view in letters to the press, articles, addresses and official publications like: 'Has Britain exploited India?' and the 'Problem of Education in India', distributed free at meetings. Amery's own book, *India and Freedom* and Professor Coupland's piece on the failure of the Cripps Mission, were held up as 'sound' texts on the Indian question.[119] A team of 'old servants of India' kept a vigilant eye and a busy pen. The most prominent was the India–Burma Association, described as an 'unofficial body', but having links with the India Office. Formed in 1942, Edwin Haward was its most prominent member. Questions, prepared by civil servants, were planted to give the League meetings 'a knock'. Even Indians, for instance Cornelia Sorabji, described as 'a servant of India' and an outspoken critic of Menon and the League, were roped in.[120] Throughout, the official version stressed that the recognition of independence was 'not in doubt', that 'actual independence ... only' awaited the decision of Indians, who were divided, and that the Muslims, the Sikhs and the 'Untouchables' were 'only minorities' in numbers, 'otherwise they are separate constituent factors in the Indian polity'. While Churchill welcomed the 'Hindu-Muslim feud as the bulwark of British rule', the India Office, too, did not hesitate to play the religious card. For instance, Yusuf Ali, a Muslim barrister, ex-ICS, was approached to lecture and write from 'a Muslim standpoint' to counteract the 'growing Congress propaganda'. Although agreeable to the suggestion, Ali would not 'when it took forms which ran counter to his own ideals of a united India'. How seriously the India Office tried to exploit religious differences is seen from the fact that when the Imam (of the Woking Mosque) appeared on the same platform as Menon, A.H. Joyce, referring to the occurrence as 'strange', asked Sir Hassan Suhrawardy, OBE, whether in his opinion the Imam could be relied on to put the Muslim case against the Congress 'with force and conviction'. His reply is not on record. And the reason for such a question? That 'we are of course extremely anxious to widen the presentation of the Muslim point of view'. To that end Suhrawardy was asked for names of 'good speakers'.[121]

The state did not scruple from slandering Menon. In confidential letters from the Ministry of Information, Regional Officers were detailed to 'carefully watch' Menon's meetings on the grounds that he was 'an avowed Communist'. From India the Viceroy, too, urged action to put Menon 'out of temptation'. In a private letter to Amery, in June 1942, Lord Linlithgow, reminding him that Menon and 'his little group of somewhat malcontent people in the Commons, like Sorensen, give rise to quite a disproportionate amount of difficulty here', asked whether it was not 'possible to do something to impede his freedom of action ... and bring him under a little closer control'. In November 1942, the Viceroy again regretted that it had not been possible to accept the 'suggestion to break up Krishna Menon and the India League with him'. Early in 1943, IPI contemplated action under Defence Regulation 18 B. But Menon never overstepped the bounds of law.[122]

Undaunted, he continued campaigning for a negotiated settlement. In December 1944, at the Labour Party Conference, the NUR resolution that 'granting of freedom to the people of India to establish an Independent National government will be a decisive factor in the fight against Fascism', proposed by C.W. Bridges and supported by Sukhsagar Datta, was overwhelmingly carried. Menon re-joined the Labour Party.[123] Events moved to a climax: war ended in Europe, the coalition government fell and, in the July 1945 elections, Labour came to power with a huge majority. And the rest is history.

For Menon and the League it had been an 18-year hard struggle. How influential was the League? What was the effect of the thousands of campaigns, meetings, letters, resolutions and publications? According to Nehru, the India League had 'done yeoman service in the cause of Indian freedom'.[124] Menon himself claimed that the League wielded 'considerable' influence with the British public. He cited the increase in the number of resolutions forwarded to the India Office, forcing it to cease its practice of replying to such communications by letter, instead resorting to acknowledging them by means of 'specially printed post cards'. Menon claimed that the League prepared 95 per cent of the questions raised in the House of Commons on India. He also pointed to a change in public opinion among 'the more powerful' union representatives, sections of the professional classes and religious organisations as well as among some Liberals.[125] There is no doubting the League's broad-based appeal and the support it gained in the labour movement and among a core of Labour MPs. Further, the fact that the Viceroy urged action against Menon and the India Office issued a carefully orchestrated propaganda campaign against the League and kept Menon under constant surveillance, suggests that the League's activities and revelations were seen as injurious to the

Raj's image in Britain and India, and, by extension, supported anti-colonialism. Menon's membership of the Labour Party and access to persons of influence in the Party, and his relations with the left wing of the Congress, especially Nehru, made contact between the two movements possible. However, though not 'a one man show' as IPI claimed, there is need for caution. The League remained a small organisation. Numbers attending meetings fluctuated; turnout at times was confined to the same loyal core. Further, decisions and actions were taken on other, different levels, in India and in the Cabinet. In the last analysis, there is little evidence that the League's influence on policy at high level was significant. Nonetheless, as an active pressure group, the League is important and merits serious study.

In the year leading to 1947 freedom and partition, Menon turned negotiator as an intermediary between the Congress leaders and the Viceroy. According to Viscount Mountbatten of Burma, Menon was 'invaluable as a "go between" ' and a 'valuable contact' with Nehru.[126] He was also India's representative at the UN General Assembly Meeting at Lake Success in 1946–7. But the League's campaigning role, too, was not over, witness its condemnation of the use of British arms and Indian troops in Indonesia and Indo-China (Vietnam). In alliance with the Burmese, Indonesians, Chinese and West Africans, Indians protested that they would 'not tolerate' their troops being sent to 'prevent the birth of a free Indo-China or a free Burma'. Well-known Pan-Africanists, Kenyatta, W.C.B. Dubois and Padmore joined in the protest.[127]

In 1947, Menon became independent India's first High Commissioner to Britain, a post he held till 1952. As High Commissioner, he was instrumental in establishing the India Club in Craven Street (now in the Strand), its vision going back to 1943. The India League was reconstituted, Menon remaining its president until his death in India in 1974.

For nearly a quarter of a century in Britain, Menon had worked untiringly for India and for Camden (St Pancras then). His contributions to the educational and cultural life of that borough are still visible. Such was the esteem in which he was held in Camden that, apart from the honour of being given the 'Freedom of the Borough', Menon became the first person in Camden to have a special brown plaque put up in his memory by the council, outside the house, 57 Camden Square, where he had lived for many years.[128] As secretary of the League, his most important contribution remains as an activist and a publicist against anti-colonialism in general and for Indian freedom in particular.

11

Contributions in the
Second World War

Generations of school children have been brought up on Winston Churchill's statement that the British people 'stood alone' against the might of Hitler's Germany after the fall of France and before the USA came to Britain's aid in 1941, following Japan's attack on Pearl Harbour. And yet, in 1939 Britain declared war on behalf of India, Burma and the Colonies, or to put it another way, for approximately 48 million people in Britain, 63 million in the colonies in Africa and the Caribbean, 370 million in the Indian sub-continent and 15 million Burmese. People of all these countries fought *with* the British forces against Germany, Italy and Japan. In addition, Australia, Canada, New Zealand and South Africa, too, fought alongside Britain. But the myth of 'Britain alone' persists. And the contribution made by India in the defeat of Fascism remains unacknowledged, at best, marginalised, at worst, simply forgotten. This chapter briefly examines India's global war effort and focuses on the contributions of Indians in Britain.

Given India's vast reservoir of manpower, including a standing army, its huge variety of raw materials and central geographical location in the Indian Ocean, the Indian contribution to the defeat of Fascism was pivotal, particularly in the Middle East and the Far East. As in the First World War, Indian contributions in terms of personnel, resources and money were massive. The statistics speak for themselves. By 1945 India had sent an army of 2.5 million men, a number larger than the forces from the Dominions or the Colonies. In a war of conscripted armies, the Indian army was the largest volunteer army on the battlefield. Its naval force increased from 2,300 in 1939 to 30,000 by 1945, its fledgling air force of 13 officers and 260 airmen in 1933, expanded to over 20,000 by 1944 and the Women's Auxiliary Corps to 10,000, all recruited for the war. India provided doctors and nurses, personnel for armoured units, gunners, signallers, sappers and miners, air mechanics and wireless operators. More than 8 million were engaged in auxiliary work for the armed forces and another 5 million in war industries, producing machine guns, field guns, bombs, mines and small arms. At 18 different centres, aircraft were assembled and maintained by Indian engineers. In addition, the Princes placed their 'personal services' and their resources at the disposal of the King-Emperor. In material terms, India not only provided a large proportion of war requirements for its own forces, but kept up a regular supply of vital materials for the allies. All the jute for sandbags, most of the mica and shellac and a high proportion of manganese and cotton came from India, in addition to tea, foodstuffs, steel, timber, hides and skins. In 1944 alone, for instance, India provided American forces with 78 million yards of cotton cloth. All the cotton parachutes, totalling 4 million, used for dropping supplies to Burma, were produced in Indian factories. Its cotton mills supplied most of the tropical uniforms, producing 400 million tailored items, and 50 million pairs of boots were manufactured by Indian workers from Indian leather. Indian industries received a huge boost, developing faster than in any comparable previous period. But the switch from civil to military production on such a scale, coupled with war-time shortages, rise in prices and limitation on imports, also resulted in great hardships and disasters such as the Bengal famine.[1]

Yet more was needed. To accelerate India's munitions production and meet the demand for technical personnel, the Bevin Training Scheme was set up. Initiated by Ernest Bevin, the Minister of Labour, it planned to bring 'a number of Indian manual workers' to Britain for a period of six months' industrial training (later raised to eight) and to provide them with an 'appreciation of the British method of industrial co-operation ... and the value of sound trade union principles'.[2] Starting in May 1941, at regular intervals, Indian 'Bevin Boys', as the volunteers were called, began arriving in batches of 50. After a three-month initial training at the Centre in Letchworth, they were placed in various factories and industrial establishments in Manchester, Bedford, Birmingham, Rugby and Glasgow for practical work, and billeted with English working-class families. A majority of the Bevin Trainees were already skilled workers with technical and workshop experience, some with engineering degrees. Altogether, the scheme envisaged bringing 2,000 volunteers to Britain.[3]

India also donated large sums of money as gifts and in other forms of aid. By 1941, for instance, approximately £50 million was subscribed to war loans and another £3.5 million donated to the Viceroy's War Purpose Fund, half of which was sent to Britain for causes such as the Lord Mayor's Fund for the victims of air raids, St Dunstan's Fund for the blind and King George's Fund for sailors. Money was donated for the purchase of aircraft. The sums must have been substantial as, by 1942, there were at least six RAF fighter squadrons bearing names of Indian provinces, Hyderabad, Madras and East India. The Women's Silver Trinket Fund provided blood transfusion plants, motor ambulances, mobile canteens and mobile hospitals for the various theatres of the war.[4]

THE ARMED FORCES

The Indian army saw action in all theatres of the war: in the Middle East, North and East Africa, in Singapore, Malaya and Burma, and in Europe. By August 1945, India had sustained 180,000 casualties, including over 24,000 killed and 65,000 wounded. They won a total of 4,028 awards, including 31 VCs, 201 DSOs, 1,033 Military Crosses and other medals.[5] In the Middle East, the Indian Army helped to safeguard vital oil supplies. In East Africa it played a prominent role in the destruction of the Italian Empire. Battles such as Sidi Barrani, Keren and Amba Alagi record their gallantry.[6] India played a key role in the eastern theatre of war. An assault base for operations, India was transformed into a colossal military camp for the South-East Asia Command (SEAC). How huge was its contribution in the defeat of Japan is seen in the number of men supplied. Of the 1 million employed in the land forces, 700,000 were from India; of the 16 Divisions which formed the 14th Army in Burma, said to be the largest single army in the world, 11 were Indian, 2 came from Britain, 2 from West Africa and 1 from East Africa. Of the 27 VCs awarded in the Burma Campaign, Indians won 20, illustrating their important role in the SEAC victory against Japan.[7]

The Indian Army also fought in Europe, a fact not always remembered. As early as the winter of 1939–40, four animal transport companies of the Royal Indian Army Service Corps (RIASC) as part of the British Expeditionary Force (BEF) saw action in France, playing, in the words of one report, 'a worthy role' in the battle of France. After the German breakthrough and the British retreat to Dunkirk, three of the four Indian companies were evacuated together with the BEF, and brought to Britain. According to one military historian, in the chaos of retreat and evacuation, the Indians 'maintained the discipline, turnout and self-respect which many around them lost', 'greatly enhancing' their reputation. The fourth Company of 300 men, fighting behind the Maginot Line, was taken prisoner, the first of the many Indian POWs in Germany. The three evacuated Companies, later reinforced by three more, were stationed in Britain. But little is known of their role. However, they would have formed part of the defence of Britain. Apart from several tantalising visual images, and references to the 'Indian contingent' in some official literature, and the Indian Forces Club at Thetford, Norfolk, information is hard to find.[8] More, however, is known about the Indian army in Italy and its role, in cooperation with the American, the British and the Canadian forces, in the battle of Cassino, the capture of Rome, the Arno Valley, the liberation of Florence and the Gothic Line, paving the way for the final defeat of Fascism in Europe.

In May 1943, after the surrender of the Italian Army in North Africa, Indian troops, who had distinguished themselves in this mountainous region of Africa, formed part of the allied advance army of invasion of southern Italy. Three Indian Divisions, the 4th, the Red Eagles, who had first gone into action in December 1940 and had fought in the Middle East, the 8th and the 10th, together with a Gurkha Lorry Brigade, saw action in the mountainous terrain of the Apennines and over river valleys, leaving a trail of glory. The Italian campaign, in the words of one historian, was 'a stubborn fight', battles such as Sangro, Volturno and Cassino conjuring up 'memories of grim fight'. In the six weeks of bitter fighting around Cassino, for instance, the 4th Indian Division, who played a 'notable part' in the battle, suffered over 4,000 casualties in officers and men.[9] There are many stories of their courage. For instance, Subedar Subramanyan, Queen Victoria's Own Madras Sappers and Miners, who was awarded the George Cross, posthumously, for 'an act of unsurpassed bravery', by flinging himself on top of a mine in the four seconds before it exploded, saving the lives of his comrades. Naik Yashwant Ghadge, who captured single-handed a machine-gun post, and dying in the event, also earned a posthumous VC. The 19-year-old Kamal Ram in action for the first time, who, in what is described as an 'unsurpassed' day's work, saved the day by wiping out four machine-gun posts, opening the line of advance for the army. He won a VC. Others, like Namdeo Jadheo and Ali Haidar were awarded VCs in almost identical instances of 'superb gallantry'. Haidar, who died in July 1999, won his VC during the crossing at the Senio River in April 1945. According to the official citation 'with a complete disregard for his own life ... in the face of heavy odds ... his heroism saved an ugly situation which would – but for his personal bravery – have caused the battalion serious casualties at a critical time and delayed the crossing of the river'.[10]

Yet these were men in an army which only saw the beginnings of modernisation and mechanisation in early 1939, following the Chatfield Committee's report, and, as one historian points out, were 'often convenient' scapegoats for disasters like the early reversals in Malaya, Singapore and Burma. Furthermore, they did not receive equality of treatment. Indian officers received the Viceroy's Commission, not the King-Emperor's, were segregated in separate units and, compared with their British officers, received 'differential treatment' in respect of pay and terms of service. Commenting on their conditions of service, Field Marshall Sir Claude Auchinleck was to write after the war 'the prejudice and lack of manners by some, by no means all, British officers and their wives, all went to produce a very deep and bitter feeling of racial discrimination in the minds of the most intelligent and progressive of the Indian officers'. Reflecting on the Indian Army and its contribution, Auchinleck concluded that Britain 'couldn't have come through both wars if they hadn't the Indian Army'.[11]

According to records, 'large' numbers of Indians and Ceylonese came to Britain to join the RAF, and to look for adventure. After a rigorous test, some qualified as pilots, others served 'in most trades', as ground crew, as navigators and gunners, helping to relieve the RAF personnel. In addition 'a number' of Indian pilots were seconded to the RAF, and, after a period of advanced training, took part in 'operational flights' over enemy territory in European theatres of war.[12] Indeed, as early as August 1940, mention is made of the arrival of the 24-strong Indian contingent in response to Britain's urgent call for qualified pilots.[13] One such volunteer was Mahinder Singh Pujji. Born in 1918 in Simla, he qualified from the Delhi Flying Club in 1937. In 1940, at the call of the Air Ministry, he joined the Air Force (IAF) and was immediately seconded to the RAF for two years. He arrived in London in 1940 to a 'VIP's welcome' by the Secretary of State. After a two-week period of training, awarded the RAF wings, he joined a Fighter Squadron of the RAF. He still remembers those dangerous times when so many pilots lost their lives. Pujji took part in many air battles over German occupied territory, twice narrowly escaping death. In 1942, he was posted to the Middle East, and, from 1943 to the end of the war, as a Flight Commander, he was in Burma. In 1945, he was given the special assignment of locating a contingent of 350 American troops lost in the jungle. This was the last of the several unsuccessful earlier sorties. He succeeded in rescuing them. In 1945, Pujji was awarded the DFC. He now lives in retirement in Kent.[14] Karun Krishna Majumdar, born in Calcutta and trained at Carnwell, first served in Burma. Awarded the DFC, and promoted to Wing Commander, he was posted at Air Headquarters in Delhi. In 1944, he volunteered for service in Europe. Attached to the RAF, just before D Day, he joined Squadron 268, assigned the mission of providing air cover and visual reconnaissance. He saw service throughout the Northern European zone, at the beach-heads at Falaise, at Argentan, at the crossing of the Seine and in Holland. Majumdar's aerial photographs of the Falaise Gap contributed to the Allied breakthrough. He was awarded a Bar to his DFC.[15]

THE MERCHANT MARINE

Then there were the Indian seamen. Before the outbreak of the war, in 1938, 26 per cent of the labour force (50,000) in British shipping was Indian. The war led to their recruitment in even larger numbers and employment in all zones, including the North Atlantic, shortage of white seamen resulting in the permanent lifting of restrictions in the Atlantic Zone. Indian seamen helped to transport food, troops, munitions and essential raw materials without which the Allied war machine would have ground to a halt, in waters infested with mines, in the face of submarine attacks and aerial bombings. It must be remembered that seamen in the merchant fleets were largely without even the rudimentary means of self-defence and with totally inadequate means of protection. Indian seamen shared with white British seamen the perils in the landings on the coast of Africa, the shores of Italy and on the beaches of Normandy, although their part in the Normandy Landings has received 'inadequate publicity', evident from 'some criticism' in the House of Lords.[16] How vital was their work, is summarised by Alfred Barnes, the Minister of War Transport. Paying tribute to British seamen in 1945, he wrote: 'The Merchant seaman never faltered. He sailed voyage after voyage ... changing the North Atlantic for North Russia or Malta. To him we owe our preservation and our lives.' And to this can be added the words of the government of India in 1947: 'it was in no small measure due to the courage and devotion to duty' of the Indian seamen that 'the job was well done'.[17]

Thousands braved the hazards of aerial bombing and U-boats, were shipwrecked more than once in the icy waters of the Baltic or the north Atlantic, and the Indian Ocean. Religious faith, patriotism, a sense of wanting to be useful, or simply poverty, must have driven these lascars to conquer fear and keep going, as they now recount. Many lost their lives, or only reached freedom or captivity after great hardships. As Attar Ullah, narrating how he had jumped into the cold waters on hearing the shout *'pani pagro'*, recalls, 'I was in the water, swimming around and holding on to a piece of wood for twelve hours before somebody came and picked us up.' In another instance, in 1944, after the sinking of the *Sutlej* by a Japanese submarine, the two rafts adrift for 49 days 'in the shark infested-waters' of the Indian Ocean, survived largely because of the skill of two Indian seamen. According to the chief engineer's account, it was Fazle Huq Mangloo, General Service 'boy', who had not only volunteered to accompany 3rd Engineer A. Bennett to collect the 'provisions dropped by the Catalina aircraft', but had brought

Bennett, who was in 'a weak condition', back to the raft. And it was Huq's 'skill and diligence' at catching birds, and the First Tindal, Shahib Sadick Sardor's 'outstanding ... perseverance' in catching fish, which had augmented their food supplies and kept the men 'fit healthy ... in good spirits', and alive.[18] Such stories of comradeship and courage are also recorded in the annals of shipping lines. According to the Clan Line historian, when the *Clan Fraser*, loaded with ammunition, had been bombed in Piraeus, 'the wounded were got off the burning vessel by dragging them through the water on a line made fast to an overturned crane by a plucky Indian quartermaster who swam ashore with it'. When the Indian-manned British India Company ship, *Erinpura*, which sailed in a Malta convoy, was sunk in 1943, it was Motiur Rahman, among the few survivors, who had dragged the unconscious captain on to a raft. BI's Indian seamen were awarded nine British Empire Medals, two Albert Medals and two Commendations. Memories of horrible deaths encountered in war still form part of their folklore: 'I have seen many people die in wartime, some with no head, some with no leg, some ships blown in half ... '.[19]

From the available records, an estimated 6,600 Indian seamen lost their lives, 1,022 were wounded, many so badly as to be permanently disabled, and 1,217 were taken prisoners of war.[20] But no memorial to them exists. The monument at Tower Hill, which records the names of 26,833 seamen of the British Merchant Navy killed in two world wars, has only a few Asian names: Miah, Latif, Ali, Uddin. These are part of the tiny percentage who lived in Britain and served on British Articles. The vast majority in British ships on Lascar Articles, however, perished unnamed, as if they never were. Even statistics of the actual number employed in the Second World War conflict, and are incomplete. One India Office estimate puts the number before the war as 'some 33,000', while the estimate from the Indian government Bureau of Public Information records 45,000, an underestimate. The available figures for the war, from the same authorities, are given as 'approximately 40,000' for December 1941 and '59,000' in February 1943. Secrecy in war apart, the responsibility for the collection of all data, according to the government of India lay with the 'shipping masters in India'. And, by the government's own admission in 1945, they feared that accurate information was unlikely to be available 'from this source'. Indian seamen thus remain the 'forgotten men' of the British merchant marine.[21]

INDIANS IN BRITAIN

It was not only seamen living in Britain who contributed to the war effort, others, too, volunteered for war work in various capacities. Further, as British subjects living permanently in Britain, Indians would have been liable for national service in the same way as white Britons, except for those resident for 'less than two years, students and other temporary residents'.[22] Information about their war work, however, is difficult to find. Some data is contained in the records of the Education Department of the High Commission. Available family records and intelligence reports are also useful. But, none of these provide a comprehensive picture.

When war broke out, Indian students were quick to volunteer. One report, noting their promptness, wrote that 'many' of them had qualified as ARP wardens before hostilities began. An Indian ambulance unit consisting of 80 individuals was formed under the London County Council, with Dorai Ross in charge. A second corps under Dr C.S.K. Pathy followed, enrolling another 40.[23] Students were said to have earned 'high praise' for their work as ARP wardens, as Fire Watchers and in other areas of Civil Defence work. Some were sent to work in the factories. Some others joined the Army and the RAF. Joseph Lobo, a Ceylonese engineering student from Kandy, hoped to become a pilot. But he did not qualify, instead being selected as a navigator. He lost his life in an air raid over Germany. According to the Education Department's report, between September 1939 and October 1940, 18 students gained commissions in the RAF, whilst another 35 'also entered the service'; 16 are recorded to have joined the Army, 3 enrolled in the Navy, and 'no less' than 146 were put 'in touch' with the Ministry of Labour and National Service and other Home Civil Departments for appropriate work. Another 84 graduates volunteered for practical training in engineering and technological factories producing materials of war. W.J. Zorab, a Sussex Trust Scholar, is named as having obtained a temporary commission in the Royal Army Medical Corps.[24] Although only for the academic year, 1939–40, and however patchy, the Education Department report provides some indication of the extent and type of contribution made by Indian students. The case of the 26-year-old Pyare Lal, a graduate from the Punjab, provides a further illumination. Arriving in Oxford in 1941 to study for a certificate in public administration and social science, in February 1942, having completed his course, he enlisted in the British Army, joining the ranks of the Royal Fusiliers, while continuing to read for the Bar in his spare time. After 15 months, Lance Corporal Pyare Lal was commissioned Second Lieutenant and posted to the 1st Battalion, Worcester Regiment. But we learn that the Indian Army had 'suddenly' expanded to 'giant proportions' and being 'badly' in need of officers, after only six months with the Worcesters, Lal was transferred to the 5th Marattha Light Infantry, serving with this regiment throughout the Imphal campaign.[25]

Under the National Service Act, both students and residents were enlisted in the Indian Company of Pioneer Corps. In 1940, for instance, 250 to 300 were said to have joined.[26] Several others, including Drs Katial, Kaushal and Datta, Menon, Chunchie and Surat Alley did 'their bit' as ARP wardens, in Civil Defence in charge of local First Aid Posts and training residents in first aid. Working-class Indians filled the labour gap in construction of aerodromes, ammunition dumps and militia camps, in aircraft and tool factories and other war-related industries in London, Glasgow, but especially in the Midlands. How short was the labour supply, and by inference, how essential was their labour, is hinted in a report, which suggests that if the 2,000–3,000 Indians were to leave, they would be 'a loss to the defence programme' in Britain.[27]

Indian women helped their white British sisters to run the Indian Troops Comforts Fund, a charity established in 1939 by the Dowager Viscount Chelmsford and Firozkhan Noon, the High Commissioner. It provided woollen garments and other items of 'comfort', like tobacco, and arranged entertainment, outings and tours for seamen, soldiers and the Bevin trainees. They dispatched warm clothes and food parcels to Indian prisoners of war. Between 1940 and 1945, the names of Lady Bomanji, Lady Chatterjee, Mrs D.N. Dutt, Mrs Gupta and Mrs Hussain appear on its Council. To raise funds, Cornelia Sorabji edited *Queen Mary's Book of India*, published by George Harrap in 1943.[28] Another Indian woman, Assistant Section Officer Noor Inayat Khan, was a secret agent with the Resistance in enemy-occupied France.

NOOR-UN-NISA INAYAT KHAN

Born in Moscow in January 1914, Noor-un-nisa was the daughter of Inayat Khan, a musician and teacher-founder of the Sufi Movement and Order in the West, and Ora Ray Baker, cousin of Mary Baker Eddy, the American founder of Christian Science. In London, where the Khans lived with their four children, they are said to have suffered 'untold humiliation' from prejudice against cross-cultural marriages. In 1920, the family moved to France, establishing itself in Fazal Manzil, a house in Suresnes, a quiet suburb of Paris. Khan studied child psychology and music at the Sorbonne and the École Normale de Musique de Paris. As a young woman, she became known for her children's stories published in *Le Figaro* and broadcast in the Children's Hour on Radio Paris. Shortly before the war, Harrap in England published her *Twenty Jataka Tales Retold*.[29]

In 1939, when war began, Noor Inayat Khan trained as a nurse with the French Red Cross. In June 1940, with France about to fall, the family (their father had died in 1927), catching the last boat, evacuated to England. In November, under the name of 'Nora Inayat Khan', giving her religion as Church of England, she joined the Women's Auxiliary Air Force (WAAF). According to Fuller, what had led her to re-invent her identity was to remove anything that could 'appear exotic or "interesting" from her personality', her brother's experience with the RAF recruiting sergeant further confirming her urge to simplify things for bureaucracy. Trained as a wireless operator, one of the first 40 or so women to do so, Khan had already reached a high level of proficiency with 'a speed of 20 or 22 words a minute' by the time of her interview in the autumn of 1942 at the War Office with Selwyn Jepson, who was in charge of recruiting for the French Section (F) of the Special Operations Executive (SOE).[30] The SOE, an independent British secret service, established in July 1940, aimed to sabotage the German war machine by arming and building up resistance movements in enemy-occupied countries. As such, it needed bilingual agents. What had first brought Khan to the attention of the F section was her fluency in French, although she was said to have a slight accent.[31]

According to Jepson, Khan 'stood out as almost perfect' as a candidate for the SOE: 'She was obviously careful, tidy, painstaking by nature and would have all the patience in the world.'[32] Without hesitation, Khan volunteered. What motivated her? Evidence suggests that she volunteered out of conviction that Nazi values were 'wrong'. She also wanted to help liberate France. Indeed, in 1940, she had promised that she would be back. According to her biographer, Khan's commitment to Indian freedom was another factor. She had become 'more conscious' of India in London and is recounted to have said that if 'some Indians' were to win 'high military distinctions ... if one or two could do something in the Allied service which was very brave and which everybody admired, it would help make a bridge between the English people and the Indians'.[33]

Recruited for the SOE, F section, and seconded to FANY (Women's

Transport Service First Aid Nursing Yeomanry), as a cover, in February 1943, she was posted to the Air Ministry Directorate of Air Intelligence. A four-month period of intensive training in codes and general field security, including how to shoot, followed. But Khan never completed her training. Paris was in desperate need of fully trained wireless operators; being already proficient, she was commissioned for duty as Assistant Section Officer. Wireless operators played a crucial role in the resistance movement, relaying messages, requesting weapons and receiving instructions for arms drops from London. But as they ran greater risks of detection and capture, women, hitherto, had only worked as couriers. Khan became the first woman wireless operator to be infiltrated into occupied France. Under the code name 'Madeleine', and cover as Jeanne-Marie Regnier, a children's nanny, on the night of 16/17 June 1943, she successfully landed in the Loire Valley – on the mission that would end in her death.[34]

Controversy has dogged Noor Inayat Khan. Some in the SOE considered that she should never have been recruited. As a fellow agent put it, she was 'a splendid vague dreamy creature, far too conspicuous – twice seen, never forgotten – and she had *no* sense of security; she should never have been sent to France'. Colonel Frank Spooner, head of the Beaulieu group of training schools, years later, told her biographer that he had made an 'adverse' report on Khan because he considered her to be 'too sensitive and easily hurt … her inexperience … rendered her too vulnerable from a security point of view'. In his 1943 report Spooner had written: 'Not overburdened with brains but has worked hard and shown keenness, apart from some dislike of security side of the course. She has an unstable and temperamental personality and it is very doubtful whether she is really suited to work in the field.'[35] Colonel Maurice Buckmaster, head of the F section, on the other hand, had been impressed with her quiet confidence. In 1949, he publicly confirmed that Khan 'was chosen … because she had "guts" and because she had the indispensable quality of remaining unnoticed'. After the war, when the British authorities grilled the Gestapo, they learnt that she had indeed been 'braver than they had thought'. As the official historian of the SOE writes: in her short operational career, she was 'exceptionally gallant and was valuable to the section … and when she fell into German hands behaved with integrity'.[36]

But the timing was bad: the British team headed by 'Prosper', had already been given away and, in the week immediately following her arrival, mass arrests began, which, in the words of Fuller, 'constituted collectively the biggest coup ever made by the Gestapo in France'. The post to which she had been detailed had become 'the most dangerous post in France'.[37] Still, she immediately made contact with the 'Prosper' team, and settled down to transmit messages from the Agricultural School at Grignon, their headquarters. As arrests followed – the first wave began on 23/4 June – and narrowly escaping capture, she was ordered to lie low. Emerging when things had calmed down to inform London of the decimation of the British teams, 'Prosper' and 'Chestnut', she was given the chance by Buckmaster to return to England. Khan refused. As the only wireless operator left in the Paris circuit, she did not wish to abandon her remaining colleagues.[38]

Contact with London re-established, she continued with her operational work, providing that vital link for the Paris SOE. All through the late summer and October 1943, she continued to transmit messages for arms, arranging for arms drops to be collected, taking many personal risks. It was this work that would posthumously, in 1946 earn her a mention of 'distinguished service' in the Despatches.[39] But the Germans were on her track and, in the words of the official citation, deploying 'considerable forces' to catch her. Still she evaded them: her swift reflex evident from a report that when she 'caught sight of the first couple of SD men sent to arrest her … [she] simply vanished from their sight'. Some time in early October 1943 the Gestapo caught up with her when she was betrayed by someone who sold her address for a mere 100,000 francs, £500. She was arrested and imprisoned at the Gestapo Headquarters in Paris, 84 Avenue Foch.[40] Her toughness is seen from the fact that, within hours of capture, getting on to the roof from the bathroom, she made her first attempt at escape. As a prisoner, according to one account, she was 'superb', refusing to divulge any information. Tragically, however, when she had been captured, the Germans had taken her transmitter, and her codes, a school exercise book in which she kept a record, both in cipher and clear, of the messages exchanged with London. Why had she not destroyed them? One can only speculate: it is possible that she misunderstood, or took literally, a rather curiously worded vital sentence in the operating instructions: 'We should like to point out here that you must be extremely careful with the filing of your messages.'[41] The Germans now worked back her station. London, not entirely convinced with the tone of the touch, tried a few security checks which, according to Foot, 'no one had remembered to pre-arrange', by asking random questions about her family. They received the right answers. Khan had been tricked into talking of her family to an apparently sympathetic un-uniformed interpreter who told her he was Swiss.[42]

Later in 1943, while still in custody at the Gestapo Headquarters, she made a second unsuccessful attempt at escape and refused to sign a declaration that she would make no further attempts. Considered a 'particularly dangerous and uncooperative prisoner', towards the end of November 1943, she was transferred to Karlsruhe for 'safe custody', the first agent to be sent to Germany, and imprisoned at Pforzheim in solitary confinement and, for a long while, in chains. But neither isolation nor chains cracked her. She remained uncooperative to the end. On 11 September 1944, 11 months after her arrest, with three other women prisoners, she was taken to Dachau concentration camp and, next morning, shot dead. For the French, Khan remains one of the foremost heroines of the Resistance. In 1946, she was posthumously awarded the *Croix de Guerre* with Gold Star. Four years after the war, in 1949, she was awarded Britain's highest award for bravery, the George Cross.[43]

12

Conclusions

The presence in Britain of people from the Indian sub-continent did not begin in the 1950s when the post-war labour demands of the British economy encouraged their arrival, but stretches back to the founding of the East India Company in 1600. This small, but enterprising community of professionals and working-class Indians, was not a homogeneous community. There were different religious, linguistic and ethnic groups from the sub-continent and the diaspora, in Africa and the Caribbean. Others were born in Britain, some having families across the racial divide, over several generations. Although largely a male population, women were not absent. Over the time span of their settlement, what did it mean for Indians to live in Britain and for the British people to have Indians living among them? Generalisations are fraught with difficulties. However, several themes are discernible. Indian encounters and cultural interchanges with the metropolitan society were without doubt governed by the power relationships of colonialism and race, but class, gender and religion were also important determining factors. The picture of their life is complex, with a diversity of experiences, reactions and responses.

Living and working among white communities, Indians did not form separate social units, although there is some evidence of clustering of working-class Indians, particularly seamen, in the multi-racial port areas of Glasgow, London, Liverpool and Cardiff. These were the entry ports for Britain's global trade, and the existence of familiar economic and social networks such as cafes and lodging-houses run by compatriots provided social support and employment prospects for the newcomer. Here working-class Indians became integrated with the local working-class port communities, forming inter-racial relationships, the extent of which is apparent only from official concern in reports which referred to the existence of 'a social problem' and their children as an 'anomalous race of children'. Inhabiting the same spaces, Indians shared a similar sub-culture.[1] Professional and middle-class Indians, too, were integrated within their geographical local communities. Some were married to white women, perhaps a more common occurrence than the accepted notion of Asian exclusiveness suggests. With their colonial Western education, what is also apparent is the degree of their acculturation.

Creating a 'home' in another culture involved making choices and compromises. It meant discarding some elements of Indian 'culture', for instance, adopting Western-style dress. However, straddling two cultures, Indians inhabited a dual world and saw themselves as having a plural identity. Westernised, and immersed within their local communities, they also retained a sense of their Indian-ness and community solidarity, seen in the existence of social networks and the emergence of places of worship as early as the nineteenth century, and the growth of religious infrastructure in the inter-war years. The establishment of Indian social and professional organisations and institutions, for example the Indian Social Club, the Indian Workers' Association, the Indian Chamber of Commerce and the Indian Doctors' Association by the inter-war years, also points to an Indian identity. Identification with India is discernible in other ways, for reasons of family, but also because of the status of their country. Admiring the British and British culture, they were also aware of what the 'empire' did to India. What drove the political elite was anti-colonialism (and anti-fascism), and the desire to see India free, giving rise to Indian campaigning organisations, which drew whites as allies.

The development of social and professional organisations, religious infrastructure and networks demonstrates that, by the inter-war years, Asians had put down 'roots' in Britain and that an 'Asian community' was already established. The existence of 'ethnic' shops, for example, the Bombay Emporium (still with us) and restaurants provides a further indication of the same development. Leadership roles assumed by prominent Indians, Naoroji, Menon or Prem, are another indication of a community. Contact, too, was maintained between the working class and the professionals, as can be seen in the organisation of educational and welfare work or the annual social event at Poplar Town Hall.

A few Indian-style buildings dot the country. Elveden Hall, Duleep Singh's Norfolk residence, is Italian on the outside, but its interior is 'pure Indian ornament', reminiscent of Indian palaces in Rajasthan, Lahore and Delhi. The Village Pump, built by the Maharajah of Benares for the people of Stoke Row, Oxfordshire, is, according to one architectural historian, 'by far the most fascinating Indian monument' built in Europe at this time.[2] A handful of religious monuments, too, date from this period. The Chatri in the style of a Hindu temple in the Arnos Vale cemetery, Bristol, is a memorial to Rammohun Roy, who died there in 1833, while a carved pillar in the Kensal Green cemetery is a monument to an unknown Indian, 'Daboda Dawajee'. Britain's earliest mosque, the Shah Jahan Mosque in Woking, built in 1889, still serves as a mosque today. Then there are the First World War memorials: the Chattri at Patcham, designed by an Indian, E.C. Henriques, the memorial gateway at the Pavilion

in Brighton and the domed arch which marks the entrance to the
cemetery on Horsell Common, Woking.

Bounded by the ideology of colonialism, another theme that emerges
is the attitude of authority and official policies of control, which
restricted their lives, discriminated against them and had the effect of
depriving them of their rights as citizens. The 1823 'Lascar Act' and the
draconian 1894 Merchant Shipping Act, for example, prevented Indian
seamen from settling in Britain. The 1925 Order had the effect of
de-nationalising them, while passport restrictions introduced in the early
1930s took away the right to travel of working-class Indians of small
means. Britain's ascendancy in India was maintained, to a large extent,
on the mystique of racial superiority, the 'Reverence of our Character'.[3]
Within this context, the taboo against sexual relations between white
women and Indian men in Britain is a significant thread throughout the
period. Supervision and control of students and others, designed partly
to restrict sexual relations with white women, but also to prevent their
politicisation, and so keep them loyal, increased as anti-colonial
organisations developed. To stifle dissent, the India Office did not
scruple to frustrate their activities. A new intelligence section, the IPI, at
the centre of the imperial metropolis, extended the tentacles of control
with an army of detectives and informers. By the same token, for
imperial and political considerations, and as a public relations exercise,
the state could 'buy off' trouble by concessions, seen for instance during
the wars in the treatment accorded to soldiers and sailors in Britain, a
ploy that would be familiar to the present generation of migrants.
Theoretically equal as imperial citizens, equality proved illusory.

Racially discriminated against at official level, what about the
ordinary people in Britain? Indians' experiences reveal a pattern of
prejudice, hostility and racism. The colour bar blighted their lives and
was experienced by the working class and the professionals, to a
varying degree and at different levels, in hotels and restaurants, in
housing and in jobs. Stereotypical assumptions about their capabilities
were not absent either. Hostility and racism become particularly
apparent from the nineteenth century, and more marked as attitudes
hardened with the development of the Raj and the rise of 'scientific'
racism, which saw 'coloured' humanity as the inferior 'other'.
However, to see British society and the British state as monolithically
racist is to oversimplify a complex situation. There were many
instances of genuine friendships and acceptance. Inter-racial relationships provide another indication of absence of prejudice, just as
negative societal responses demonstrate racist aversion to such
relationships and social intermingling.

What did their encounter and cultural interchange with Indians mean to the British people? Answers are difficult. For the large majority, there would have been little or no contact. But for some, for instance, academics in universities, a British student having an Indian friend, or being an admiring cricket fan of Ranji, it would have been an enriching encounter. Responses of patients who had an Indian as a doctor, and the relationship of trust between itinerant traders, who offered interest-free credit, and their clients, further suggest that it is possible to transcend barriers of race, culture and class.

Over the years of their settlement, Indians were engaged in a variety of economic activities, demonstrating their resourcefulness and adaptability. In the eighteenth and nineteenth centuries working-class Indians were predominantly found in domestic service and in seafaring. But even then, other occupations, largely self-employment, are in evidence: as keepers of lodging-houses and cafes, as purveyors of Indian culture, playing music or hawking Indian cures and wares, reminding us that earning a living catering for compatriots or 'selling culture' was as important in the nineteenth century as in the twentieth, and did not begin with the post-war generation of migrants. By the twentieth century some working-class Indians worked as itinerant traders selling textiles door to door, or in the restaurant trade. Seafaring, however, remained important throughout. The middle classes were engaged in a variety of professions, mostly self-employed as doctors and lawyers, in journalism and as merchants and businessmen. There were educationists, and men of religion, too. A few stand out for their distinctive contributions to British society.

First among these are the ayahs, the travelling nannies, usually dismissed, but who cared for and mothered the children on land and sea and who played an important, but unquantifiable role, in the comfortable living of so many British families. Then there were the Indian seamen in the British maritime labour force, responsible for transporting raw materials and manufactured goods, and passengers across the world within Britain's global economy. Technological changes in the nineteenth century and the economics of cost made their labour indispensable to the British shipping industry. It can be argued that these poorly paid lascars contributed to the profits and prosperity of the British merchant marine. During the two world wars, they, too, helped to win the war by keeping British supply lines open, as did the Indian Army, the largest volunteer force.

Individual Indians in Britain, too, played their part in both world wars. The all too brief career of Indra Lal Roy, the RAF fighter pilot, the Indian Ace of the First World War, and the heroine of the

Resistance, Noor Inayat Khan, secret agent in France during the Second World War, stand out. Another, Dr Baldev Kaushal in Bethnal Green, awarded the MBE for his 'gallant conduct on several occasions' during the blitz, worked in the East End of London.[4]

Then there are the careers of several other outstanding individuals. Sake Deen Mahomed, the shampooing surgeon to George IV, was the earliest known Indian entrepreneur in Britain, with his short-lived Hindustanee Coffee House, the first Indian establishment with an Indian ambience, serving Indian cuisine. He later established the successful Indian Shampooing Baths in Brighton. His book, *The Travels of Dean Mahomet*, published in Cork in 1794, is the first book to be written and published in English by an Indian in Britain. Perhaps the only known Indian account in English, describing Indian society and the role of the East India Company's army in the conquest of India during the last days of the Mughal Empire, it forms a valuable historical source. The East End-born Albert J. Mahomet, from a deprived home, who became a Methodist preacher, was possibly the first Indian photographer in Britain. Among the medical men was Deen Mahomed's grandson, the Brighton-born Frederick Akbar Mahomed who worked at Guy's Hospital and is only now being re-discovered. His contribution to British medical science is his path-breaking discovery that high blood pressure was a primary condition, changing our understanding of hypertension. Little of any significance has been added to his conclusions since his death in 1884. Another Indian doctor to make a distinctive contribution was Chunilal Katial, a Labour councillor and the first Asian to be elected mayor in 1938. As chairman of the Finsbury Health Committee, he was instrumental in setting up the Finsbury Health Centre in Pine Street (still with us), a radical concept of integrated health service before the days of the NHS. In mathematics, the work of Srinivasa Ramanujan (1887–1920), distinguished as a pure mathematician, particularly 'for his investigations in elliptic functions and the theory of numbers' is of note. A research student at Trinity College, Cambridge between 1914 and 1919, he was elected Fellow of the Royal Society in 1918.[5]

During the era of colonialism, it is not surprising to find Asians in Britain actively involved in the movement for colonial freedom and social justice. As political activists and in alliance with Britons, especially in Liberal and Labour parties, they campaigned to publicise inequalities of colonialism, educating public opinion to achieve change through intellectual arguments. In the process, however, some became involved in British national politics. Dadabhai Naoroji, author of the economic critique of colonialism, *Poverty of India*, was also a member of the Liberal Party. He made history by being elected MP in the heyday of Victorian imperialism. The Conservative, Bhownnaggree, followed him. Saklatvala, active in trade union and working-class politics, was the only Communist in the 1924 Parliament. One Indian, Satyendra Prasanna (1863–1928), was elevated to the House of Lords in 1919, as Baron Sinha of Raipur. As the only Indian to receive a hereditary peerage, he was entrusted with the task of piloting the 1919 Government of India Act through the House of Lords.[6] Some Indian women, too, were active in politics. Bhikhaiji Cama, journalist and campaigner for Indian freedom, who featured in many intelligence reports for her 'subversive' activities, and became well known in European revolutionary circles. She took a prominent part at the International Socialist Congress at Stuttgart in 1907, demanding the complete withdrawal of British rule. But Indian political involvement was not exclusively concerned with the freedom of India. Indians also aimed to achieve change beneficial to the wider community. Some campaigned for women's right to vote. Sophia Duleep Singh, active in the WSPU, and a tax resister, is remembered as a campaigner in the Richmond suffrage movement.

Others were active in local politics. Dr Katial at Finsbury and Dr H. Gulati in Battersea, both councillors, were also elected to the LCC. Dr Jainti Saggar was a Labour councillor in Dundee and Dr Dhani Prem in Birmingham. He was also the author of *The Parliamentary Leper*, a pioneering study of the state of race relations in Britain in the 1960s. Krishna Menon, political activist in the anti-colonial movement for Indian freedom, and an early advocate of what today is termed anti-racist education, was a St Pancras councillor, remembered for his services to the arts in Camden. A multi-talented intellectual, he was the editor of the Pelican imprint.

Cornelia Sorabji challenged another male preserve, the law. The legal profession then was not open to women. Indeed, it was not until 1919 that women became eligible to the Bar. Sorabji was the first woman ever to study law at a British university, Somerville College, Oxford, in 1889. But when the time came for her to take her examination, she found that she could not sit her BCL 'in the schools with the men'. Her challenge to this ruling was successful, a pioneering step towards opening up the Bar to women in Britain.[7]

In the arts and sports some Indians, with their distinctive talents, have enriched British cultural life. Ranji, who played cricket for Sussex and England, entertained and thrilled crowds in Victorian and Edwardian England. He was recognised as a star of cricket by his British fans. Ranji was the first in a long line of Asian cricketers. His nephew, Kumar

Shri Duleepsinhnji in the 1930s and the Nawab of Pataudi in the 1940s are also well-known names. The talent of others is evident in literature. Rabindranath Tagore, awarded the Nobel Prize for Literature in 1913, was lionised in English and European literary circles in the first two decades of the twentieth century. What is today, perhaps, even more remarkable, is the fact that much of his poetry reached Western audiences in translation, often poor in quality. Yet his talent shone through and was acknowledged. Mulk Raj Anand was another literary talent in 1930s and 1940s London, as was the poet, J.M. Tambimuttu, the founder-editor of *Poetry London*. Ananda Coomaraswamy's writings on Indian art and sculpture, for example, *Dance of Shiva*, form an influential interpretation of Indian art and sculpture for both Indians and Europeans alike. He was later for many years Director of the Museum of Oriental Art in Boston, USA.[8] Finally, in classical music, we have the pianist, composer and critic, Kaikhosru Sorabji.

What Indians in Britain and their contributions to British life tell us is that migration has been part of Britain's history and society, and that British culture has never been a homogeneous product of indigenous origins as some nationalist ideologues would have us believe.[9] And so the process continues. Asians from the sub-continent, like other settlers who have come to Britain, bring with them their rich and varied cultures, elements of which, in the course of time, they bestow on their adopted country for its development and enrichment, and in the process they, too, change and develop through the influences they encounter.

Notes

1 A LONG PRESENCE

1. Guildhall Library, MS17602; IOR: B/5, f. 202, 19 August 1614 and f. 448, 18 July 1615; Edward D. Neill, *Memoir of Reverend Patrick Copland* (New York: Charles Scribner & Co., 1871), pp. 11–12.
2. IOR: B/5, f. 202, 19 August 1614 and f. 448, 18 July 1615; Revd Patrick Copland, *Virginia's God be Thanked* (London, 1622); Neill, *Memoir*, p. 75; Revd Frank Penny, *The Church in Madras* (London: Smith, Elder & Co., 1904), pp. 13–16. Peter's letters are in Copland.
3. Greenwich Local History Library; London Metropolitan Archives.

2 EARLY ARRIVALS, 1600–1830s

1. William Foster, ed., *The Embassy of Sir Thomas Roe to India, 1615–19* (revised edition, London: OUP, 1926), p. 212.
2. Alfred Spencer, ed., *Memoirs of William Hickey*, vols i–iv (London: Hurst and Blackett, 1913), vol. ii, pp. 138–40 and vol. iv, pp. 396–8; Dennis Kincaid, *British Social Life in India 1608–1937* (London: Routledge and Kegan Paul, 1938; 2nd edn, 1973), pp. 93–4; T.G.P Spear, *The Nabobs* (Oxford University Press, 1932), pp. 52–3; Eliza Fay, *Original Letters from India*, ed. E.M. Forster (London: Hogarth Press, 1986 edn); Suresh Chandra Ghose, *The Social Conditions of the British Community in Bengal 1757–1800* (Leiden: E.J. Brill, 1970), p. 111; Revd William Tennant, *Indian Recreations* (Edinburgh: John Anderson etc., 1803), vol. i, p. 62. Family portraits, too, illustrate their life of grandeur and comfort, e.g. John Zoffany's paintings of Warren Hastings, his wife and her maid; group comprising Sir Elijah and Lady Impey with their children, ayahs and servants.
3. Abu Talib Khan, *The Travels of Mirza Abu Talib Khan*, Charles Stewart, trans. (London: Longman, Hurst, Rees and Orme, 1810), vol. i, p. 242.
4. Kincaid, *Life*, pp. 83, 101; Fay, *Letters*, p. 284, note 47 for 1781 sale of 'two Coffree boys' of a Portuguese Padre; H.E. Busted, *Echoes from Old Calcutta* (Calcutta: Thacker, Spink & Co., 1882), note 120; D.R. Banaiji, *Slavery in British India* (Bombay: D.B. Taraporevala Sons & Co., 1933). Export of African slaves to India was prohibited under the 1789 Proclamation.
5. Edith Standen, 'English Tapestries "After the Indian Manner"', *Metropolitan Museum Journal*, 15, New York, 1981.

6.   P.J. Marshall, *East India Fortunes* (Oxford: Clarendon Press, 1976); Philip
      Lawson, *The East India Company* (London: Longman, 1993). Nabob was
      used pejoratively, see, Samuel Foote's play, *The Nabob or Asiatic
      Plunderer*, 1768; and satirical cartoons by Rowlandson and Gillray.
7.   Raymond Head, *The Indian Style* (London: George Allen and Unwin,
      1986), p. 7.
8.   I am grateful to Mira King for telling me about Alexander Cobb.
9.   This section on the Nabobs is based on J.M. Holzman, *The Nabobs in
      England* (New York, 1926); Michael Edwardes, *The Nabobs at Home*
      (London: Constable & Co., 1991); Raymond Head, 'Sezincote, a Paradigm
      of the Indian Style' (MA thesis, Royal College of Art, 1982); Head, *Indian
      Style*; Paul F. Norton, 'Daylesford: S.P. Cockerell's Residence for Warren
      Hastings', *Journal of the Society of Architectural Historians*, vol. xxii, no.
      3, October 1963; M. Archer, C. Rowell and R. Skelton, *Treasures from
      India* (London: The Herbert Press in association with the National Trust,
      1987).
10.   Quoted in J. Irwin and P.R. Schwartz, *Studies in Indo-European Textile
      History* (Calico Museum of Textile, Ahmedabad, 1966), p. 48; Head,
      Indian Style, p. 4; Evelyn's diary, 15 September 1663; Pepys, December
      1665, as in J. Guy and D. Swallow, eds, *Arts of India 1550–1900* (London:
      Victoria and Albert Museum, 1990), p. 158.
11.   *Public Advertiser*, 6 December 1773, in Holzman, *Nabobs*, p. 90; *A
      Narrative of the Life of Sarah Shade* (London, Knight & Compton, 1801),
      p. 27; Head, *Indian Style*, p. 7; John Heiton, *The Castes of Edinburgh*
      (Edinburgh: John Menzies, 1859), pp. 158–71; *Morning Post and Daily
      Advertiser*, 20 November 1786 for Patna rice and curry powder advertise-
      ments.
12.   J.J. Hecht, *Continental and Colonial Servants in 18th-Century England*
      (Smith College Studies in History, vol. xl, Northampton, Massachusetts,
      1954), pp. 50–6; F.O. Shyllon, *Black People in Britain 1555–1833* (Oxford
      University Press, 1977), p. 122; Peter Fryer, *Staying Power* (London: Pluto
      Press, 1984), pp. 77–8; Rozina Visram, *Ayahs, Lascars and Princes*
      (London: Pluto Press, 1986), pp. 11–30; Norma Myers, *Reconstructing the
      Black Past* (London: Frank Cass, 1996).
13.   8 September 1618, quoted in Thomas Roger Forbes, *Chronicles from
      Aldgate* (Yale University, 1971), p. 4; quoted in *A History of the Black
      Presence in London* (GLC, 1986), p. 13; GLHL, St Alphege's, Greenwich,
      burial 8 October 1680; see also, St Nicholas's, Deptford, burial 1692; St
      Margaret's, Lee, burial 1683.
14.   IOR: B/40, 25 April 1690–19 April 1695, ff. 25, 46, 176, 180; B/41, 24
      April 1695–26 April 1699, ff. 249, 342; B/43, 27 April 1699–27 April
      1702, ff. 135, 360.
15.   *The London Gazette*, 9–12 November, 1685; see also, *LG*, 1–5 March,
      1687; 9–12 April 1688; 7–11 June 1688; 29 November–3 December 1688;
      3–6 December 1688; and 4–7 February 1688.
16.   Archer, *Treasures*, p. 18; Sophie von la Roche, *Sophie in London 1786*,

trans., Clare Williams (London: Jonathan Cape, 1933), pp. 257.

17. Spencer, ed., *Memoirs*, vol. ii, p. 228; vol. iv, pp. 376, 405, 473. Munnoo was baptised on 27 February 1809 in the parish of Beaconsfield, and is described as 'a native of Madras'. Munnoo married Ann and, in 1814, their daughter Anne was christened in the same parish; Simon Digby, 'An Eighteenth-Century Narrative of a Journey from Bengal to England: Munshi Ismail's *New History*', in Christopher Shackle, ed., *Urdu and Muslim South Asia* (London: SOAS, University of London, 1990), pp. 50–2; Duchess of Sermoneta (V Caetani), *The Locks of Norbury* (London: John Murray, 1940), pp. 53–4; Fay, *Letters*, p. 242; *Annual Register*, 1773, pp. 110–11.

18. Dean Mahomet, *The Travels of Dean Mahomet* (Cork: Printed by J. Connor, 1794), pp. 17–19.

19. IOR: B/41, f. 342, dated 20 October 1699; B/48, f. 820, dated 16 January 1707; B/53, f. 226, dated 17 December 1714; f 230, 22 December 1714; and E/1/55, f. 278, dated 3 April 1771; W.M. Thackeray, *The Four Georges* (Leipzig, 1861), p. 71; *Morning Chronicle*, 8 June 1797; as in Head, *Indian Style*, pp. 9–10.

20. Hecht, *Servants*, pp. 7 and 36; James E. Alexander, *Shigurf Namah i Velaet ... the Travels of Mirza Itesa Modeen* (London: Printed for Parbury, Allen & Co., 1927), pp. 195–6.

21. For example Lely's *Charlotte Fitzroy*; John Mortimer's *Portrait of a Young Man with Servant*, reproduced in David Dabydeen, *Hogarth's Blacks* (Manchester University Press, 1987), p. 35; Joshua Reynolds, *The Children of Edward Holden Cruttenden with an Ayah*, 1759, reproduced in Rozina Visram, *The History of The Asian Community in Britain* (Wayland, 1995), p. 7; the painting by W. Thomas of William Hickey in 1819, with Munnoo and his dog, is in the National Portrait Gallery Collections; a painting by Thomas Roberts showing 'an East Indian Black' holding a pony belonging to Gerald Fitzgerald, is mentioned in Narinder Kapur, *The Irish Raj* (Northern Ireland: Greystone Press, 1997), p. 50.

22. Spencer, ed., *Memoirs*, vol. ii, pp. 228, 262, 275. Hickey was explicit that Nabob was of no use to him as a servant; von la Roche, *Sophie*, p. 272.

23. IOR: E/1/55, Misc. Letters received, 1771.

24. *Daily Advertiser*, 31 January 1750, in Hecht, *Servants*, p. 50; *MP&DA,* 10 February 1775; *DA*, 3 March 1775, 29 November 1776 and 12 July 1777. See also ibid., 26 August 1776; *MP&DA*, 11 June 1777.

25. For Indian servants in eighteenth-century Tower Hamlets, see Charles McNaught's articles, *East London Advertiser*, 29 October 1910, 25 February 1911 and 21 January 1914. For parish registers, see, Tooting Graveny Records, 26 December 1790, baptism Mooty Sam, native of Madras; St Mary's Whitechapel, 8 November 1786, baptism George Alfred Creighton, 'about ten years of age, born in Arcot in the East Indies'; St Marylebone, 15 April 1787, Mary Ann Flora, a native of the East Indies, aged 19; Great Easton, Essex, 1 October 1786 baptism a 'negro boy from Bombay belonging to Mr George Gooch gent by the name of Thomas

Easton'; Wethersfield, Essex, 8 April 1787, baptism John Mingo?, native of India, aged about 12; St Margaret's, Lee, Lewisham, 17 July 1771 baptism 'Lee, Thomas, Indian black servant of Governor Verelst'; St Alphege's, East Greenwich, 2 May 1782 baptism 'John Edwards son of John, an Indian, supposed to be born at Madras about the year 1754'; St Nicholas's, Deptford, 3 May 1768, baptism 'Thomas, an Indian boy belonging to Mr Currey in Lower street'; Woolwich, 2 July 1762, baptism Thomas Cato, an East Indian aged 11 years and burial Flora, an East Indian 26 May 1769.

26. *DA,* 4 April 1771, 21 August 1776 and ibid., 24 November 1790, in Hecht, *Servants*, p. 52. For a discussion on the relative merits of English and Indian servants in India, Spear, *Nabobs*, p. 53.

27. *MC,* 1 April 1795; *DA*, 4 July 1777, 10 October 1786 and ibid., 17 November 1773, in Hecht, *Servants*, p. 52; *MP&DA*, 31 January 1777, 15 October 1777, and ibid., 20 November 1777; *MC*, 8 June 1797.

28. Hecht, *Servants*, p. 52.

29. *MP&DA*, 31 January 1777, 15 October 1777, and ibid., 20 November 1777; *DA*, 4 July 1777; *MC*, 8 June 1797.

30. IOR: E/1/55; *Kilvert's Diary*, chosen, edited and introduced by William Plomer (London: Jonathan Cape, 1969 edition). The ayah, Jemima, was sent back on both occasions, vol. i, pp. 138–43 and vol. iii, pp. 178–92.

31. *PA*, 2 December 1786, and ibid., 5 December 1786; IOR: *Fort William–India House Correspondence*, vol. v, 1767–9, p. 186, letter to Court, 17 March 1769.

32. IOR: H/Misc/163, ff. 181–2, July 1782; IOR: *Fort William–India House Correspondence*, vol. ix, 1782–5, letters to Court, p. 374, dated 5 April 1783.

33. Letter from Syed Abdoolah, 16 February 1869, IOR: L/P&J/2/49, No. 7/281; Fay stranded Kitty Johnson at St Helena, Fay, *Letters*, pp. 242, 284.

34. Spencer, ed., *Memoirs*, vol. iv, p. 473.

35. Bimbi was brought after the *Durbar* in 1911, Osbert Sitwell, *Great Morning* (London: Macmillan & Co. Ltd, 1948), p. 217; *Lives of the Most Remarkable Criminals ... from 1720–1735, from Original Sources and Memoirs* (1874), vol. i, p. 264; also in *A Biographical Dictionary of Foreigners*, BL Ad MS 34, 282, vol. 3; *The London Chronicle*, 11–14 October 1800, p. 363.

36. *The Tatler*, 9–11 February 1709; *LG*, 1688, as in Shyllon, *Black People*, p. 11. The inscription on the collar of the 'black boy, an Indian', from Putney, reads 'The Lady Bromfield's black, in Lincoln's Inn Fields'; *Dublin Mercury*, 10–12 July 1770, as in Kapur, *Irish Raj*, p. 50.

37. Margaret Sparks, *A Study of the Registers by J.R. Scarrin in the Parish of Hytham, Oxford*, Appendix. I am grateful to Lucy Mackeith for this reference; Spencer, ed., *Memoirs*, vol. iii, p. 150.

38. *DA*, 1 February 1775; Bob Hepple, *Race, Jobs and the Law in Britain* (London: Allan Lane, The Penguin Press, 1968), p. 40.

39. *LG*, 9–12 November 1685; *Flying Post*, 11–14 July 1702, as in A.F. Scott,

Every One a Witness: The Stuart Age (London: White Lion Publishers, 1974), pp. 231–2; *DA*, 11 June 1737, and ibid., 4 November 1743, in Hecht, *Servants*, p. 53; *PA*, 29 May 1772, and *MC*, 17 February 1795. For more advertisements of absconding servants, see, *LG*, 1–5 March 1687; 9–12 April 1688; 7–11 June 1688; 29 November–3 December 1688; 3–6 December 1688 and 4–7 February 1688; *PA*, 16 March 1772; and *MC*, 6 October 1795; *Dublin Journal*, 7–10 February 1767, *Belfast Newsletter*, 25 September 1767, both in Kapur, *Irish Raj*, p. 50; Mary McNeill, *The Life and Times of Mary Ann McCracken, 1770–1866* (Dublin: Allen Figgis, 1960), p. 294, for a runaway 'Indian Black' in 1781. I am grateful to Lyn Innes for this reference.

40. Holzman, *Nabobs*, p. 25.

41. GLHL; BPP No. 471 (3), 1814–15, p. 84; J.M. Smith, *Mendicant Wanderers through the Streets of London* (Edinburgh: William P. Nimmo & Co., 1883), pp. 21 and 24.

42. *The Servants' Pocket-Book*, 1761, p. 18, quoted in Hecht, *Servants*, p. 54.

43. Hecht, *Servants*, p. 23 and 54; Douglas A. Lorimer, *Colour, Class and the Victorians* (Leicester University Press, 1978), p. 22; *PA*, 14 January 1786.

44. Justus Strandes, *The Portuguese Period in East Africa* (Dar es Salaam and Nairobi: East African Literature Bureau, 1968), p. 26.

45. From the Urdu, *Lashkar*, meaning an army or camp, the term, corrupted through the Portuguese *Lashkari* to become lascar, a soldier, as in gun-lascar, also applied to Indian sailors. See H. Yule and A.C. Burnell, *Hobson-Jobson* (London: Routledge & Kegan Paul, 1986 edn), pp. 507–9; IOR: L/E/7/936, No. 2435 for the usage of the term in British Law. *Khalasi* is the preferred term for a seaman in various Indian languages.

46. Conrad Dixon, 'Lascars: The Forgotten Seamen', in R. Ommer and G. Panting, eds, *Working Men Who Got Wet*, Proceedings of the Fourth Conference of the Atlantic Canada Shipping Project, 24–6 July 1980 (Maritime History Group, University of Newfoundland, 1980), p. 265; Fryer, *Staying Power*, p. 194; M. Dorothy George, *London Life in the Eighteenth Century* (London: Penguin Books, 1979 edn), p. 143; Visram, *Ayahs*, p. 34; and Myers, *Black Past*, p. 105.

47. IOR: B/38, f. 155; B/39, f. 77; B/40, ff. 94, 173, 177, 181, 191 and 301; B/43, ff. 48, 66, 90 and 122; B/44, ff. 173–4; B/47, f. 226; B/48, ff. 92, 102, 115, 147, 178, 360, 389, 409, 449–500, 506 and 910; B/52, ff. 194, 266, 293, 295, 466, 498, 516, 527, 536, 549, 580, 583 and 592; B/53, f. 195; and IOR: *Fort William–India House Correspondence*, vol. ix, letter from Court, 28 August 1782, p. 74 for crew regulations.

48. See the case of *The Greenwich*, reported on 26 September 1730, cutting, GLHL collection; IOR: B/61, f. 161, 6 November 1730; Alexander, *Shigurf*, p. 39.

49. IOR: B/40, f. 181, 29 March 1693; B/48, f. 409, 11 December 1706; B/52, f. 293, 21 January 1712; f. 516, 23 October 1713, f. 527, 4 November 1713; f. 579–80, 23 December 1713 and f. 592, 6 January 1713; B/53, f. 195, 24 November 1714.

50. David Hannay, *The Great Chartered Companies* (London: Williams & Norgate Ltd, 1926), p. 116; John-Henry Grose, *Voyage to the East Indies* (London, 1757), p. 176; T. Blanshard, 'Burials in Calcutta: 1782–1788', *Bengal Past and Present*, vol. 32, nos. 63–4, July–December 1962, pp. 109–32; BPP, No. 431 (20), 1848, Q. 4669.

51. IOR: L/MAR/C/902, vol. i, f. 69, letter 22 February 1815; BPP, No. 279 (10), 1816, pp. 2–3; BPP, No. 357 (5), 1810, p. 46; Evan Cotton, *East Indiamen* (London: The Batchworth Press Ltd, 1949), p. 45; Appendix 47, pp. 68–9, BPP, Nos. 151 and 182, 1812; R.A. Wadia, *The Bombay Dockyard and the Wadia Master Builders* (Bombay, 1935), pp. 173–80.

52. Act 42, Geo. III c. 61 of 1802; the preamble to Act 34 Geo. 3 c. 68 (1794) decreed that within six months of the end of the 'present war', no goods were to be imported into Britain on a British ship unless navigated by a master and 75 per cent of crew who were British subjects; Lascar riot, 11 October 1806, cutting, Museum of London Docklands Collection; IOR: L/MAR/C/902, f. 23, Company's resolution, 13 April 1808.

53. IOR: L/MAR/C/902, ff. 120–121.

54. BPP, No. 281 (2), 1814–15 and BPP, No. 360 (2), 1814–15, which repeats the provision.

55. IOR: L/MAR/B/580 B (2). The *serang* and the *tindal* received 20 and 17 rupees respectively.

56. IOR: P/4/24, 18 November 1793; *The Times*, 9 December 1814.

57. IOR: H/Misc/190, ff. 65–103; IOR: *Fort William–India House Correspondence*, vol. ix, Letters to Court, pp. 432 and 583.

58. BPP, No. 690 (6), 1833, pp. 229–30, evidence Robert Gray.

59. George, *London*, p. 143; Grose, *Voyage*, pp. 176–7.

60 IOR: H/Misc/163, ff. 175–85; at the request of the Council, the King of Denmark issued an edict compelling Danish ships to provide maintenance and return passage for their lascars, IOR: *Fort William–India House Correspondence*, vol. ix, p. 374; *A Letter to Archibald Macdonald Esq.*, 1784, p. 17, in George, *London*, pp. 143–4.

61. *Morning Chronicle & London Advertiser*, 22 December 1786; *PA*, 7 January 1786, letter signed 'Veritas'; PRO: T1 634, No. 2012, 4 August 1786.

62. *Archibald*, p. 17, in George, *London*, p.144; *PA*, 7 January 1786.

63. *MC*, 30 November and 1 December 1785 in Shyllon, *Black People*, pp. 123–4.

64. *MC&LA*, 22 December 1786.

65. *PA*, 16 March 1785, 21 December 1785; *MC&LA*, 26 December 1786.

66. *PA*, 15 March 1786, 7 January 1786 and 5 January 1786; Amy Apcar, ed., *Life and Adventures of Joseph Emin, an Armenian* (Calcutta: Baptist Mission Press, 1918), p. 26; *MC&LA*, 26 December 1786, letter signed, 'Youth'.

67. *PA*, 5 and 7 January 1786. A Quartern Loaf is a four-pounder loaf; *PA*, 10 and 12 January 1786.

68. Stephen J. Braidwood, *Black Poor, White Philanthropists* (Liverpool

University Press, 1994), p. 64. The Committee list is in copies of the *PA*, and PRO T1 630 series.
69. *PA*, 27 January 1786, 17 February 1786, etc.; *PA*, 11 February, 4 March, 15 March, 21 March, 18 April 1786; *PA*, 16 January 1786.
70. *PA*, 2 December 1786; Prince Hoare, *Memoirs of Granville Sharp* (London, 1820), p. 263.
71. *PA*, 19 January 1786.
72. Shyllon, *Black People*, p. 117; Braidwood, *Black Poor*, p. 1; Fryer, *Staying Power*, pp. 194–202.
73. *PA*, 3 and 11 February 1786; and ibid., 15 March and 18 April 1786; *Morning Post*, 15 March 1786.
74. *PA*, 10 and 21 January 1786; PRO: T1 630, 24 April 1786; *PA*, 27 January, 3 February, 11 February, 24 February, 15 March and 21 March 1786.
75. PRO: T1 630, 17 May 1786, No. 1333; PRO: T1 631, 24 May 1786, No. 1334 and Memo from Smeathman, 24 May 1786, No. 1304.
76. PRO: T1 631, 24 May 1786, No. 1334.
77. PRO: T1 632, 7 June 1786; PRO: T1 633, 15 July 1786; and T1 635, accounts for payments to the corporals.
78. PRO: T1 632, 7 June 1786; Hand Bill and Instruments in the same file.
79. PRO: T1 634, 4 August 1786, No. 2012; PRO: T1 633, 15 July 1786, No. 1815; a beautifully drawn up petition is in PRO: T1 638.
80. PRO: T 634, 28 July 1786, No. 1903 and 4 August 1786, No. 2012.
81. PRO: T1 643, Gustavus Vassa (Olaudah Equiano) list for the *Vernon*, 27 February 1787, has John Lemon (Lemmon) and Elizabeth Lemon (Lemmon) under 'white women married to black men'.
82. PRO: T1 638, Agreement, 6 October 1786. The names are difficult to read. But at least 20 are Portuguese-sounding ones.
83. PRO: T1 636, 6 October 1786; PRO: T1 638, 6 December 1786, No. 2864; T27 38, Letter from the Treasury to the Committee, No., 412; *PA*, 14 December 1786.
84. *MC*, 22 December 1786, signed 'Humanus' and ibid., 26 December 1786, from 'Youth'; *MC&LA*, 28 December 1786.
85. *PA*, 3 January 1787; *PA*, 1 January 1787.
86. PRO: T1 643, 27 February 1787, lists compiled by Vassa.
87. *The Interesting Narrative of the Life of Olaudah Equiano* (London, 1789), 2nd edn, vol. ii, pp. 248–9.
88. Sheila Lambert, ed., *House of Commons Sessional Papers of the 18th Century*, vol. 67, 1789, p. 255, Captain Thompson to Mr Stephens, 23 January 1888, No. 9.
89. Shyllon, *Black People*, p. 1; Braidwood, *Black Poor*, pp. 136–43; IOR: *Fort William–India House Correspondence*, vol. ix, letters to Court, 5 April 1783, p. 374.
90. IOR: L/MAR/C/902, f. 69, 23 February 1815 from the Directors to Rt Hon. Nicholas Vansittart; and f.33, Statement of Circumstances, 11 February 1811.
91. BPP, 1816, No. 279 (10), p. 3; IOR: L/MAR/C/902, for instructions

regarding diet, clothing and accommodation.

92. H/Misc/501, 26 May and 2 June 1802; IOR: F/4/89, file 1834, Petition 7 May 1800; William Hunter, *An Essay on the Diseases Incident to Indian Seamen, or Lascars, on Long Voyages* (Calcutta: Printed at the Company's Press, 1804), Appendix, No. ix.

93. *Reports and Papers on the Policy of Employing India Built Ships* (London 1809), p. 197; IOR: L/MAR/C/902, 11 December 1814; see also BPP, No. 279 (10), 1816, p. 11; e.g. St Nicholas's Deptford, GLHL.

94. IOR: H/Misc/501, ff. 1–133; IOR: L/MAR/C/902, 26 July 1813; Docker had noted scars on the backs of several men; Khan, *Travels*, vol. i, pp. 33–4; Alexander, *Shigurf*, p. 14.

95. Dixon, *Lascars*, p. 267; IOR: L/MAR/C/902, 28 November 1809; *Hansard*, vol. 27, cols. 214, 225–8, 29 November 1813; Act 54 Geo. 3, c. 134, 1814.

96. Ian Duffield, 'London's Black Transportees to Australia', paper presented at a Conference on the History of Black People in London, University of London Institute of Education, 27–9 November 1984 (unedited version with tables and appendices); Norma Myers, 'The Black Presence through the Criminal Records, 1780–1830', *Immigrants & Minorities*, vol. 7, no. 3, November 1988.

97. IOR: L/MAR/C/902, 7 February 1814; *Lascars and Chinese: A Short Address to Young Men* (W. Harris, 1814), p. 17.

98. *Life of William Allen* (London: Charles Gilpin, 1846), vol. i, p. 188; R.I. and S. Wilberforce, *Life of William Wilberforce* (1838), vol. iv, p. 154; IOR: B/52, f. 295, 21 January 1712.

99. Quoted in J. Salter, *The Asiatic in England* (London: Seely, Jackson & Halliday, 1873), pp. 4–5; J. Salter, *The East in the West* (London: S.W. Partridge & Co., 1896), p. 13; *William Allen*, vol. i, p. 189; IOR: L/MAR/C/902, 28 February 1814; *The Times*, 9 December 1814.

100. BPP, No. 471 (3), 1814–15, p. 5; IOR: L/MAR/C/902, 5 December 1814; BPP, No. 279 (10), 1816, pp. 13–14. The Company's defence was based on arguments supplied in Docker's letters.

101. BPP, No. 279 (10), 1816, pp. 6–7; IOR: L/MAR/C/902, vol. ii, ff. 104–14; BPP, No. 471 (3), 1814–15, p. 5; R.M. Hughes, *Laws Relating to Lascars and Asiatic Seamen Employed in the British Merchant Service* (London: Smith, Elder & Co., 1855), p. 5.

102. BPP, No. 471 (3), 1814–15.

103. Act Geo. 4 c. 80, 1823; BPP, No. 281 (2) and No. 360 (2) 1814–15, pp. 3–5.

104. BPP, No. 431 (20), 1848, Q. 4640; BPP, No. 340 (20), 1848, Q. 67.

105. Dixon, *Lascars*, p. 268.

106. BPP, No. 431 (20), 1848, Qs. 4640, 4657 and 5639; BPP, No. 122 (7), 1801, 'Report of the Special Committee to whose consideration the letter from Mr Henry Dundas referred', p. 35; BPP, No. 646 (6), 1830, Evidence Richard Alsager, p. 489.

107. BPP, No. 431 (20), 1848, Q, 4645 and 4646.

108. BPP, No. 646 (6), 1830, evidence Richard Alsager, p. 489; BPP, No. 545

(8), 1844, evidence Joseph Soames, Qs. 618–31; BPP, No. 431 (20), 1848, evidence David Cooper Aylwin, Qs. 4664–70.

109. BPP, No. 122 (7), 1801, letter from Dundas, p. 36; Hepple, *Race*, p. 43; for wages, see, IOR: H/Misc/190. f. 85; Charles Lockyer, *An Account of the trade in India* (London, 1711), pp. 260–1.

110. BPP, No. 122 (7), 1801, letter from Dundas, p. 36.

111. Pierce Egan, *Life in London* (London: Sherwood, Heeley & Jones, 1821), p. 286.

112. *PA*, 3 January 1787; BPP, No. 279 (10), 1816, p. 16.

113. *First Report from the Committee on the State of the Police of the Metropolis* (1817), p. 195.

114. *Lascars and Chinese*, pp. 3–10.

115. *Lascars and Chinese*, p. 5.

116. BPP, No. 471 (3), 1814–15, f. 45; Hannay, *Chartered Companies*, p. 116.

117. BPP, No. 491 (17), 1823.

118. Harihar Das, 'Early Indian Visitors to England', *The Calcutta Review*, vol. 13, 3rd series, October–December 1925, p. 85.

119. Alexander, *Shigurf*; Khan, *Travels*; Digby, 'Narrative'.

120. The engraving, 'A General View of London and Westminster – Printed for R. Sayer and J. Bennett – January 1777', see Digby, 'Narrative', p. 51 and f/n 21.

121. *Morning Herald*, 30 March 1781.

122. John A. Woods, ed., *Correspondence of Edmund Burke* (Cambridge University Press, 1963), vol. iv, pp. 356–68.

123. F.H. Brown, 'Indian Students in Great Britain', *Edinburgh Review*, January 1913, p. 138.

124. Mary Carpenter, *The Last Days in England of Rajah Rammohun Roy* (Calcutta, 1915), pp. 87–9; Sophia Dobson Collett, *Life and Letters of Rajah Rammohun Roy*, ed. D.K. Biswas and P.C. Ganguli (Calcutta, 1962), p. 312.

125. Margaret Morris Cloake, trans. and ed., *A Persian at the Court of King George* (London: Barrie and Jenkins, 1988), p. 90; *PA*, 1 January 1787; William Foster, *John Company* (London: John Lane the Bodley Head Ltd, 1926), pp. 267–8.

126. *DA*, 5 November 1777; Digby, 'Narrative', pp. 53–4; Spencer, ed., *Memoirs,* vol. ii, p. 408.

127. Hannay, *Chartered Companies*, p. 191; Penny, *Church*, vol. i, p. 507. After 1911 the term Anglo-Indian is used to describe Eurasians.

128. Alexander, *Shigurf*, p. 36; Head, *Sezincote*, pp. 12–17.

129. For Hélène Bennett: Desmond Young, *Fountain of Elephants* (London: Collins, 1959); Herbert Compton, *A Particular Account of the European Military Adventurers of Hindustan from 1784 to 1803* (London: T. Fisher Unwin, 1892); Lester Hutchinson, *European Freebooters in Moghul India* (New York: Asia Publishing House, 1964).

130. Khan, *Travels*, pp. 198–9.

131. Bashir Maan, *The New Scots* (Edinburgh: John Donald Publishers Ltd,

1992), p. 74; Kincaid, *Life*, p. 120; Spencer, ed., *Memoirs*, vol. iv, p. 466; Foster, *John*, p. 231; Spear, *Nabobs*, p. 63.

132. Benjamin Silliman, *A Journal of Travels in England, Holland, and Scotland* (Boston: 1812), vol. i, pp. 209–10.

133. BL Add. MS, 29, 178, Palmer to Hastings, 6 July 1802.

134. Michael H. Fisher, *The First Indian Author in England* (Delhi, OUP, 1996), p. 250. Pagoda was a south Indian coinage.

135. Spear, *Nabobs*, p. 63. For Anglo-Indians: H.A. Stark, *East Indian Worthies* (Calcutta, 1892); H.A. Stark, *Hostages to India* (Calcutta: Fine Art Cottage, 1926); C.J. Hawse, *Poor Relations* (Richmond: Curzon, 1996).

136. G.S. Mahomed, *Brighton Herald*, 11 August 1888; *Travels of Mahomet*, pp. 5–6, 9–21. The discrepancy regarding his birth date, 1759 or 1749, in part compounded by himself in his later work, *Shampooing*, published in 1822, has now been resolved by Fisher, *Author*, p. 284. The age, 101, on his death certificate and on the tombstone are incorrect.

137. For Mahomed's career in the Bengal Army, see *Travels of Mahomet*; Fisher, *Author*, pp. 146–92.

138. *Travels of Mahomet*, p. 127.

139. Fisher, *Author*, pp. 203, 237–8; *The Times*, 20 April 1813.

140. Persian translation in Fisher, *Author*, p. 240, and compare Stewart, Khan, *Travels*, vol. i, pp. 103–4; *Cork Gazette*, 20 July 1791; stereotypical descriptions, e.g. John Ovington, *A Voyage to Surat* (London, 1696), became part of the image of India for the next 250 years.

141. Only two Daly names are in the subscriber's list, both ruled out by Fisher as likely relatives, *Author*, fn. 27, p. 244.

142. Fisher, *Author*, p. 215.

143. Amelia, baptised 11 June 1809, and Henry Edwin, 6 January 1811, LMA: St Marylebone Parish Register. Interestingly, perhaps the first (and only?) mention of Mahomed's name as William Dean Mahomed appears in this register; Fisher, *Author*, pp. 251, 254–5.

144. The term is generally used for the post-Second World War immigrant enterprise, Robin Palmer, 'The Rise of the Britalian Culture Entrepreneur', in Robin Ward and Richard Jenkins, eds, *Ethnic Communities in Business* (Cambridge University Press, 1984); *The Times*, 27 March 1811; Marylebone Rate Book, 1810.

145. *The Epicure's Almanack or Calendar of Good Living* (London: Longman, Hurst, Rees, Orme & Brown, 1815), pp. 123–124; Khan, *Travels*, vol. i, p. 124, 1814 edn.

146. *The Times*, 20 April 1813; Fisher, *Author*, p. 262, fn. 58; *Shampooing*, preface; A.B. Granville, *The Spas of England* (1842), vol. ii, p. 563.

147. Brighton Baptism Register, 1813–37, East Sussex Record Office; *Cases Cured by Sake Deen Mahomed*, Written by the Patients themselves (Brighton, 1920), pp. 18–19; and compare Sir Evan Cotton, 'Sake Deen Mahomed of Brighton', *Sussex County Magazine*, vol. 13, 1939, pp. 746–50, who suggests 1786.

148. J.A. Erredge, *History of Brighthelmston* (Brighton: E. Lewis, 1862), pp.

234–5; C. Musgrave, *Life in Brighton* (London: Faber, 1970), pp. 201–3; Fisher, *Author*, p. 269.

149. Mahomed, *Shampooing,* p. 14; *Sussex Weekly Advertiser*, 24 April 1815 and 29 May 1815; Horatio Mahomed, *The Bath: A Concise History of Bathing* (London: Smith, Elder, 1843), pp. 54–8.

150. Mahomed, *The Bath*, p. 57; Mahomed, *Shampooing*, p. vii.

151. *Cases Cured*, p. v; *The Life and Adventures of George Augustus Sala* (London: Cassell & Co., 1895 edn), vol. i, pp. 201–2; Visitors' Signature Books, 3 vols, BRL.

152. *Shampooing*, preface; G.S. Mahomed claimed that Mahomed had been a medical student at the 'Hospital in Calcutta', *BH,* 11 August 1888. In a letter to Professor J.S. Cameron, 23 June 1995, Professor Sukumar Mukherjee, Head of the Department of Medicine at Medical College, Calcutta writes: Mahomed was 'apparently a dresser to one of those British Surgeons of the East India Company serving in Calcutta around 1792–93'. I am grateful to Professor J.S. Cameron for the letter. Could this refer to his elder brother?

153. A.H. Bevan, *James and Horace Smith* (London: Hurst & Blackett, 1899), p. 280; Fisher, *Author,* p. 283.

154. Quoted in Head, *Indian Style*, p. 51.

155. In 1818 Mahomed is recorded at Battery House Baths, Brighton, Baptism Register, 1813–37, ESRO; 1822 Boore's *Brighton Annual Directory* has Mahomed's Baths at 39 East Cliff; for the decor, Fisher, *Author*, pp. 279–81.

156. C. Wright, *Brighton Ambulator* (London: C. Wright, 1818), pp. 137–9; *Morning Advertiser*, 11 September 1828.

157. BRL: Visitors' Books; 'Lines to Mr Mahomed'; 'Lines' and 'Ode to Mahomed the Brighton Shampooer', in *Shampooing*; Horace Smith, ed., *Memoirs, and Letters and Comic Miscellanies* (London: Henry Colburn, 1840), vol. i, pp. 356–9; John Roles, 'Sake Deen Mahomed's Silver Cup', *The Royal Pavilion & Museums Review*, 1990, no. 3, pp. 4–5. The cup is in the Local History Collection.

158. Musgrave, *Brighton*, pp. 204–5; PRO: LC/11/49, 10 October 1825 and 5 January 1828; PRO: LC/3/69, September 1830.

159. *Brighton Gazette,* 27 December 1821 and 28 March 1822; *BG,* 2, 16, 30 January and 13 February 1834.

160. Quoted in Melville Lewis, *Brighton: Its History, Its Follies and Its Fashions* (London: Chapman & Hall, 1909), p. 135; *BH,* 4 August 1888; Fisher, *Author*, pp. 298–9.

161. *BG,* 27 February 1851; *Gentleman's Magazine*, vol. 189, January–June 1851, p. 444; Fisher, *Author*, pp. 294–6, 303; E.W. Gilbert, *Brighton Old Ocean's Bauble* (London: Methuen, 1954), p. 71; photograph in Rozina Visram, *Indians in Britain* (Batsford, 1987), p. 5.

162. Roles, *Silver Cup*; p. 3–4; Musgrave, *Brighton*, p. 204.

3 A COMMUNITY IN THE MAKING, 1830s–1914

1. P.C. Mozoomdar, *Sketches of a Tour Round the World* (Calcutta: S.K. Lahiri & Co., 1884), p. 6; *South Asian Lifetimes*, Croydon Clocktower; Ealing, Enumeration District 7, Schedule 131, p. 20; Gloucestershire Record Office, 26 July 1882 entry.

2. Alec Waugh, *The Lipton Story* (London: Cassell & Co., 1952), pp. 59–65; BPP, Cmd. 5134 (22), 1910, Qs 1316 and 1357; Maan, *New Scots*, p. 107. IOR: L/P&J/11/2–4 for passports. For pictures of the Sinhalese servants, see Sylvia L. Collicott, *Connections Haringey: Local-National-World Links* (Haringey Community Information Service, in Association with Multi-cultural Support Group, 1986), p. 106; Visram, *History*, p. 8, and front cover for Glasgow nannies.

3. Hurmat Ali, Abdul Karim's sister, was in the Queen's service, IOR: MSS EUR F 84/126a, telegram 3 April 1897.

4. Raymond Head, 'Indian Crafts and Western Design from the 17th Century to the Present', *RSA Journal*, vol. cxxxvi, no. 5378, January 1988, pp. 122–3; *Illustrated London News*, 12 August 1893.

5. David Duff, ed., *Queen Victoria's Highland Journals* (London: Webb & Brown, 1980), p. 217; M. Warner, *Queen Victoria's Sketch Book* (London: Macmillan, 1979), p. 198.

6. IOR: MSS EUR D/558/I, Victoria to Lansdowne, 11 July 1890; Arnold Florance, *Queen Victoria at Osborne* (London: English Heritage, 1987 edn), p. 49; Elizabeth Longford, *Victoria RI* (London: Weidenfeld & Nicolson, 1964), p. 508.

7. IOR: MSS EUR F 84/126a, confidential to Elgin, 30 April 1897; IOR: MSS EUR D/558/I, Queen to Lansdowne, 22 February 1889; Frederick Ponsonby, *Recollections of Three Reigns* (London: Eyre & Spottiswoode, 1951), p. 14.

8. Longford, *Victoria*, pp. 536–7; IOR: MSS EUR D/558/I, Queen to Lansdowne, 29 October 1890.

9. Ponsonby, *Recollections*, p. 15.

10. IOR: MSS EUR F 84/126a, Ponsonby to Babbington-Smith, 27 April 1897; SS to Elgin, 30 April 1897; Ponsonby, *Recollections*, p. 14.

11. IOR: MSS EUR F 84/126a; IOR: L/P&S/8/61, confidential memo, 14 September 1896; IOR: L/P/S19/168, Circular No. 7, Memo Anti-British Agitation.

12. IOR: MSS EUR F 84/126a, letters 27 and 30 April 1897; confidential to Elgin, 7 May 1897.

13. IOR: MSS EUR F 84/126a, memo 14 September 1896; letters 21 February 1896, 30 April 1897, telegram 3 April 1897; IOR: L/P/S19/168.

14. J.H. Plumb, *Royal Heritage* (BBC, 1977), pp. 281–2; IOR: MSS EUR F 84/126a, from SS, 7 May 1897, and postscript; Victoria to Salisbury, 17 July 1897, in Longford, *Victoria*, pp. 540–1.

15. Ponsonby, *Recollections*, p. 13; IOR: MSS EUR F 84/126a, Ponsonby to

Babington-Smith, 27 April 1897.

16. Quoted in Plumb, *Heritage*, p. 282.

17. See Visram, *Ayahs*, pp. 3–9; I have used Douglas Lorimer's definitions, see, *Colour*; J. Smith, *The Missionary's Appeal to British Christians on Behalf of Southern India* (1841), pp. 149, 153; quoted in E.J. Thompson and G.T. Garratt, *Rise and Fulfilment of British Rule in India* (London: Macmillan, 1934), p. 536. Thomas R. Metcalf, *Ideologies of the Raj* (Cambridge University Press, 1995).

18. Signed 'Britannicus', quoted in Kincaid, *Life*, p. 213.

19. Quoted in Krishna Kripalani, *Rabindranath Tagore* (Calcutta: Visva-Bharati, 1980), p. 291.

20. *London City Mission Magazine*, 1 November 1858, p. 291; ibid., 1 August 1877, p. 170; Augustus Muir and Mair Davies, *A Victorian Ship-Owner* (Cayzer, Irvine & Co., 1978), p. 31; Plomer, ed., *Kilvert*, vol. i, 1870–1, pp. 138 and 143; vol. iii, 1874–9, pp. 178 and 192; George Earl's painting, *Going North, King's Cross Station* (National Railway Museum), shows an ayah with a family.

21. For ayahs in India: IOR: MSS EUR D 1100/30; MSS EUR C 216; MSS EUR T 7; MSS EUR D 1197.

22. A.C. Marshall, 'Nurses of Ocean Highways', *The Quiver: The Magazine for the Home*, vol. 57, 1922, pp. 924–5. Edited version in *LCMM*, August 1922, pp. 104–6.

23. Marshall, *Nurses*, p. 923; BPP, No. 5134 (22), 1910, Q. 1316, evidence of Mrs Dunn; for ayahs in workhouses: IOR: L/P&J/6/395, f. 608, 16 April 1895, a 'Hindoo woman' in Manchester; L/P&J/6/209, f. 1399, 6 August 1887, Indian women in Camberwell and Hackney.

24. *Report of a Meeting for the Establishment of a 'Strangers'' Home*, 1855, pp. 13–14; *LCMM*, 1 November 1858, p. 29. The exact date is not recorded. An 1888 report suggests it had been in existence for the 'last 40 years', i.e. since 1848, which pre-dates the 1855 meeting; a 1921 report has the Home as established 'some thirty years ago', i.e. 1891, *LCMM*, 1 September 1888, p. 207 and December 1921, p. 140.

25. *LCMM*, 2 July 1900, pp. 172–4; ibid., December 1921, pp. 140–3; Kelly's *Street Directories*, Hackney and Homerton, 1894–1915; George Sims, *Living London* (London: Cassell, 1906), vol. iii, pp. 279 and 181; BPP, No. 5134 (22), 1910, Q. 1317.

26. *LCMM*, December 1921, p. 141; ibid., August 1932, p. 132; IOR: L/P&J/6/1482, f. 1552, April 1917; BPP, No. 5134 (22), 1910, Qs 1316, 1319, 1323, 1357.

27. BPP, No. 5134 (22), 1910, Qs 1327–39; *LCMM*, December 1921, p. 141; ibid., August 1929, p. 119; Marshall, *Nurses*, p. 924.

28. *LCMM*, August 1932, p. 132; ibid., 1934 Supplement, p. 7; and ibid., March 1934, pp. 42–3, including caption under the picture; Marshall, *Nurses*, p. 926.

29. *LCMM*, August 1932, p. 132; William Fletcher, 'A Haven for Oriental Women', *LCMM*, 1936, pp. 143–4.

30. Marshall, *Nurses*, p. 926; *LCMM*, December 1921, p. 143; ibid., March 1934, p. 43; Visram, *History*, p. 11, for photograph.

31. *LCMM*, December 1921, p. 140 and pp. 142–3; Plomer, ed., *Kilvert*, vol. i, p.143; Marshall, *Nurses*, p. 924; *LCMM*, August 1904, p. 222.

32. BPP, No. 5134 (22), 1910, Qs 871, 1323, 1329, 1346; *LCMM*, December 1921, p. 142; IOR: L/P&J/2/47, No. 7/264, memo Pakenham to SS, 4 September 1868; for stranded ayahs: IOR: L/P/&J/6/1482, f. 1552, dated 11 April 1917; *LCMM*, May and September 1927; *Stri Dharma*, vol. xi, no. 10, August 1928, p. 199.

33. *LCMM*, 2 July, 1900, p. 180; ibid., October 1926, p. 145; Plomer, ed., *Kilvert*, vol. iii., p. 178; Ina Taylor, *Helen Allingham's England* (Exeter: Webb & Bower, 1990), p. 56 and p. 58 for a reproduction of the painting with an ayah; Deborah Cherry, *Painting Women* (London: Routledge, 1993), p. 151 and plate 26.

34. BPP, No. 5134 (22), 1910, Q. 871, evidence of Shepherd, India Office; BPP, No. 5134 (22), 1910, Q. 1316; Fletcher, *Haven*, *LCMM*, 1936, p. 143; Marshall, *Nurses*, p. 923.

35. Anne Dunlop, 'Lascars and Labourers: Reactions to the Indian Presence in the West of Scotland during the 1920s and 1930s', *Scottish Labour History Society Journal*, no. 25, 1990, p. 41; F.J.A. Broeze 'The Muscles of Empire – Indian Seamen and the Raj, 1919–1939', *Indian Economic and Social Review*, vol. 8, no. 1, p. 46.

36. James L. Mowat, *Seafarers' Conditions in India and Pakistan* (Geneva: ILO, 1940), pp. 6–7; IOR: L/I/1/840, *Syren and Shipping*; Dinker Desai, *Maritime Labour in India* (Servants of India Society, 1939).

37. BPP, *Annual Statement of Trade and Navigation*, 1891–1914, reproduced in Visram, *Ayahs*, appendix, III, p. 297.

38. Broeze, 'Muscles', p. 44; BPP, No. 5134 (22), 1910, Qs 361 and 552; Desai, *Labour*, p. 93 for table of wages of whites, and Calcutta and Bombay rates.

39. For lascar food: IOR: L/E/7/940, f. 3127; IOR: L/E/7/604, f. 54; IOR: L/E/7/936, letter 18 May 1918 from Elliot; James Pegg, *Lascar's Cry to Britain* (London: T. Ward & Co., 1844), p. 12; for opposition to lascar accommodation, IOR: L/E/7/351, f. 680.

40. J. Walsh, 'The Empire's Obligation to the Lascar', *The Imperial and Asiatic Quarterly Review*, vol. 30, July–October, 1910, pp. 347–8, 408.

41. P&O circular, 1876, in Peter Padfield, *Beneath the House Flag of the P&O* (London: Hutchinson, 1981), p. 114; BPP, No. 545 (8), 1844, Q. 621; Walsh, 'Lascar', pp. 345–6; BPP, No. 5134 (22), 1910, Q. 341; BPP, No. 340 (20), 1848, Q. 2606; Tony Lane, *Grey Dawn Breaking* (Manchester University Press, 1986), testimonies from Captain Baillie and Noel Pereira, ex-pilot, p. 163. For ethnic stereotype, IOR: L/I/1/840, *Syren and Shipping*.

42. Walsh, 'Lascar', p. 347.

43. Muir and Davies, *Ship-owner*, p. 132; Caroline Adams, ed., *Across Seven Seas and Thirteen Rivers* (London: THAP books, 1987), p. 22.

44. Broeze, 'Muscles', p. 43.

45. IOR: L/E/7/936, File 2435, for summary of all relevant legislation. Lascars were defined as 'natives of India, including native states and foreign possessions in India', opinion of law officers, 8 January 1919. Compare Paul Gordon and Danny Reilly, 'Guest Workers of the Sea: Racism in British Shipping', *Race and Class*, vol. xxviii, no. 2, Autumn 1986, p. 74.

46. Hepple, *Race*, p. 44.

47. Salter, *Asiatic*, pp. 149–51; see also, Salter, *East*, pp. 127–9; PRO: CO. 77/46, ff. 223–31; BPP, No. 5134 (22), 1910, Q. 552; *Kentish Independent*, 12 August 1859.

48. *Glasgow Herald*, 10 January 1908; IOR: L/E/7/936, f. 2435, 14 August 1918, signed Hipwood.

49. *GH*, 21 April 1914.

50. *GH*, 15 June 1911; E.W. McFarland, 'Clyde Opinion on an Old Controversy: Indian and Chinese Seafarers in Glasgow', *Ethnic and Racial Studies*, vol. 14, no. 4, October 1991, pp. 506, 502; Tabili, *'We Ask for British Justice'* (Ithaca and London: Cornell University Press, 1994) p. 88. See also Baruch Hirson and Lorraine Vivian, *Strike Across the Empire* (London: Cleo Publications, 1992), pp. 37–8.

51. Pegg, *Lascar's Cry*, pp. 10–12; PRO: CO. 77/46, ff. 223–31; *Lascars and Chinese*, pp. 3–4; *Strangers' Home*, p. 9; Salter, *Asiatic*, pp. 21–2.

52. PRO: CO. 77/46; Peggs, *Lascar's Cry*, pp. 7–9; *MH*, 28 January 1842.

53. Subscribers' list in *Strangers' Home*, pp. 26, 28; Robert Miller, *From Shore to Shore* (R. Miller, 1989), p. 133.

54. For details of the Home, Visram, *Ayahs*, pp. 47–50. The Home was closed down in 1937 and West India House erected on its site.

55. *ILN*, 28 February 1857; BPP, No. 5134 (22), Q. 552; IOR: L/P&J/2/59, No. 7/567, from Hughes, 27 March 1879, Statistics: Working of the Home, June 1857 to 31 December 1877; Visram *Ayahs*, p. 50, and f/n 68 and 79; Salter, *Asiatic*, p. 69.

56. Dunlop, 'Labourers', p. 43; McFarland, 'Clyde', p. 498.

57. *St Andrew's Waterside Church Mission*, Reports, 1890–1914; *LCMM*; Salter, *East*, pp. 113–14. See also *GM*, January 1823, 'Internment of a Lascar' and May 1805, 'Mahommedan Jubilee'.

58. Proceedings of the East India Association, *The Imperial and Asiatic Quarterly Review*, vol. xxx, July–October 1910, p. 409; BPP, No. 5134 (22), 1910, Q. 551; *Indian Magazine and Review*, No. 477, September 1910; Miller, *Shore*, p. 134; *SAWCM*, report 1911, p. 32.

59. *SAWCM*, reports 1889–1905, 1910; Miller, *Shore*, pp. 133–4.

60. IOR: L/P/S19/168.

61. *Glasgow Post Office Directories*, 1888/9–1920/1; IOR: L/P/S19/168,

62. IOR: L/P/S19/168; Miller, *Shore*, p. 134; *Glasgow Post Office Directory*, 1900/1.

63. T.R. Underwood, 'Work among Lascars in London', *East and West*, vol. 4, 1906, p. 467; IOR: L/P/S19/168; *Glasgow Post Office Directory*, 1904/5, 1925/6.

64. Salter, *Asiatic*, pp. 116, 221; quoted in Anne Dunlop, 'Recovering the

History of Asian Migration to Scotland', *Immigrants and Minorities*, vol. 9, no. 2, July 1990, p. 147; Henry Mayhew, *London Labour and the London Poor* (London: Griffin, Bohn & Co., 1861), vol. iv., pp. 423–4; for instance, W.M. Thackeray, *The Newcomes* (Oxford University Press, 1995 edn) and Wilkie Collins, *The Moonstone* (Penguin Popular Classics, 1994 edn).

65. Salter, *East*, pp. 38, 111; Mayhew, *London*, vol. i, pp. 241–2; *KI*, 31 March 1855; ibid., 19 October 1861; *Punch*, vol. xiv, January–June 1848, p. 181; ibid., vol. 30, January–June 1856, p. 34.

66. *LCMM*, 1 November 1858, p. 286; ibid., 1 January 1867, p. 13; IOR: L/P&J/6/1482, f. 1552; Salter, *Asiatic*, pp. 69–70, 235.

67. *LCMM*, 1 November, 1858, pp. 289–90, 1 January and 1 November 1867; J. Thomson, *Street Incidents* (London, 1881), p. 48; Salter, *East*, p. 38; Salter, *Asiatic*, pp. 170–1.

68. *LCMM*, 1 January 1867, p. 9; ibid., 1 May 1899, p. 88; Salter, *East*, pp. 20–4, 41; Salter, *Asiatic*, pp. 208 and 227.

69. Mayhew, *London*, vol. i, opposite p. 206; IOR: L/P&J/2/50, No. 7/345, letter from S.B. Ivatts, 24 November 1870; Salter, *East*, p. 38.

70. Salter, *Asiatic*, pp. 26, 30–1, 159, 224; *LCMM*, 1 January 1867, p. 6, 1 August 1857, pp. 217, 221–2 and 1 November 1858, p. 267; *KI*, 7 January 1871.

71. For oculists: *Croydon Advertiser and Surrey County Reporter*, 22 November 1890; *The Times*, 21 September, 1893; IOR: L/P&J/6/339, No. 241; L/P&J/6/315, No. 991; L/P/&J/6/323, No. 1066; L/P&J/6/325, No. 1180; L/P&J/6/356 No. 1832; L/P&J/6/365, No. 77; L/P&J/6/373, No. 828; L/P&J/6/375, No. 1016; L/P&J/6/401, No. 1264 and L/P&J/6/322; and Visram, *Ayahs*.

72. Mayhew, *London*, vol. iii, pp. 188–9; ibid., vol. iv, pp. 424–5.

73. Salter, *Asiatic*, pp. 182, 236–9; *LCMM*, January 1867, p. 4.

74. *LCCM*, 1 August 1857, p. 217.

75. Salter, *Asiatic*, pp. 27, 227; Mayhew, *London*, vol. iv, p. 424.

76. *LCMM*, 1 August 1857; Salter, *East*, p. 20; Edward Said, *Orientalism* (Penguin edn, 1985), p. 26; Barry Milligan, *Pleasures and Pains* (Charlottesville and London: University Press of Virginia, 1995), p. 89. I am grateful to Cathie Bretschnider for this reference.

77. Richard Rowe, *Picked Up in the Streets* (London: W.H. Allen, 1880), p. 39; 'Opium Smoking', LMA: John Burns Collection; Virginia Berry, 'East End Opium Dens and Narcotic Use in Britain', *The London Journal*, vol. 4, no. 1, 1978, pp. 3–28.

78. IOR: L/P&J/6/158, f. 1282, letter No. 52, 1869; BPP, Cmd. 5133 (22), 1910, pp. 24, 19–20. See also, Visram, *Ayahs*, pp. 21–9 for the state's attitude to performers and petitioners.

79. Albert J. Mahomet, *From Street Arab to Pastor* (Cardiff: J.B. Thomasson, nd); J.E. Shephard, *A.J. Mahomet: From Street Arab to Evangelist* (Ventnor: W.B. Tomkins, nd). This is a 're-moulded' edition.

80. Mahomet, *Pastor*, pp. 2–6.

81. Mahomet, *Pastor*, pp. 4–18, 21–7, 73–5; Shephard, *Mahomet*, p. 25.
82. Mahomet, *Pastor*, pp. 30–43, 83–6, 91; Shephard, *Mahomet*, p. 63.
83. 'A.J. Mahomet, Wells', was one of the 47 preachers on the 1906 Plan, *Methodism in Wells: The Story so Far* (Centenary Souvenir Booklet, 1991), p. 4. I am grateful to Revd P.J. Collingwood for the booklet.
84. Kelly's *Norfolk Directory*, 1896, lists Mahomet as the only photographer; A.F. Reid, however, appears in 1892; Cyril Jolly, 'Street Arab to Pastor: A Wells Mahomet', *Eastern Daily Press*, 1969. I am grateful to Tom Sands for telling me that Mahomet was a photographer and for providing me with photocopies of the article and the booklet, '28 Photographic Views of Wells and District'.
85. Jean Stone, *More Memories of Wells* (1996); letters from Mrs Kathleen Francis, received 5 and 14 November 1998 and 9 January 1999.
86. Mahomet's photograph in Shephard, *Mahomet*, shows him as a younger man, without beard and more pronounced Indian features; the fact that Mahomet's father was an Indian from Calcutta, however, is omitted, p. 4.
87. IOR: MSS EUR F 170, from Gandhi, 14 August 1914.
88. Fisher, *Author*, pp. 262, 266 f/n 58; 303–5, and 314, f/n 126. Deen married Mary Ann Malthus in 1834.
89. *The Times*, 27 and 30 March 1844 for his insolvency; *Post Office Directory*, 1862; *GM*, June 1848, p. 656; his first wife, Francis Maria Owen (1819–43) died shortly after their marriage. There were four children by the second marriage: Clara (1852–?); Gertrude (1835–1943); Henry Pelham (1857–1919), described as 'masseur' in the will, and Lizzie (1862–?); *The Bath* and *Short Hints on Bathing* (London: Ryder Street, 1844).
90. Fisher, *Author*, pp. 318–19; Visitor's Books, BRL, testimonial, 30 October 1854.
91. *BH*, 4 August 1888; 1851 Census; *BH*, 27 January 1844.
92. *BH*, 27 January 1844; *SCM*, No. 9, January–December, 1935, p. 131; *BH*, 17 June 1848. Page's *Brighton Directory*, 1884; Leppard and Co.'s *Brighton and Hove Directory*, 1845–6; Folthorp's *Directory*, 1856 and 1864; *BH*, 13 July 1839; ibid., 19 September 1840 and 4 August 1888; Sala, *Life*, vol. i, p. 201.
93. *BH*, 13 July 1839 and 19 September 1840; recollections of Mrs H.W. Dixon to T.W. Bagshawe, 29 April 1954, BRL; *Sussex Daily News*, 16 January 1935; *The Times*, 29 July 1913; Kelly's *Norfolk Directory*, 1912. Arthur G.S. Mahomed's daughter, Phyllis Bell, was proprietor of the Punch and Judy Cafe in Verwood, Wimborne, Dorset in the 1950s, her daughter Joan lived in Kent. I am grateful to Dr Anthony Batty Shaw for this information, letter 18 September 1998.
94. *BH*, 4 August 1888; *SCM*, No. 9, January–December 1935, letter from Edith Ohlson.
95. In 1882, Mahomed requested the Royal College of Physicians, the letter is in their library, to drop his two 'superfluous' names as he 'invariably' signed himself F.A. Mahomed.

96. Guy's Hospital Academic Register records his work as 'very good indeed'; Mahomed's hand-written manuscript of his presentation on the sphygmograph is in the records of the Physical Society at Guy's Hospital. For technical details and Mahomed's important modification of the instrument, see A. Batty Shaw, 'Frederick Akbar Mahomed and his Contribution to the Study of Bright's Disease', *Guy's Hospital Reports*, vol. 101, nos 1–4, 1952, pp. 159–60; J. Stewart Cameron and J. Hicks, 'Frederick Akbar Mahomed and his Role in the Description of Hypertension at Guy's Hospital', *Kidney International*, vol. 49, 1996, pp. 1491–3.

97. J.F. Goodhart and W.H.A. Jacobson, 'In Memoriam', *GHR*, vol. 43, 1885–6, pp. 1–10; Samuel Wilks and G.T. Bettany, *A Biographical History of Guy's Hospital* (London: Ward, Lock, Bowden & Co., 1892), pp. 306–7, 309; *GHR*, vol. 25, 1881, pp. 295–416 for his thesis; Cameron and Hicks, *Frederick Akbar*, p. 1498; H.C. Cameron, *Mr Guy's Hospital: 1726–1948* (London: Longmans, Green & Co., 1954), p. 212. Mahomed's tombstone only records his MB, as does his death certificate, which also oddly, makes him only MRCP; his will, on the other hand, mentions his MD only.

98. Shaw, 'Akbar', pp. 162–3; J.D. Swales, 'Frederick Akbar Mahomed (1849–1884) Pioneer of Clinical Research', *Journal of Human Hypertension*, vol. 10, 1996, pp. 139–40; J.D. Swales, 'The Growth of Medical Science: The Lessons of Malthus', *The Harveian Oration* (London: Royal College of Physicians, 1995), p. 7; Cameron and Hicks, *Frederick Akbar*, p. 1494.

99. *GHR*, vol. 43, 1885–6, pp. 1–10; Shaw, 'Akbar', p. 169; 201; Swales, 'Malthus', pp. 7–8; Swales, 'Pioneer', p. 141;

100. From 1880 Mahomed lived at 12 St Thomas Street (1881 census), later moving to 24 Manchester Square. He is buried at Highgate Cemetery in a plot purchased for 20 guineas by Ada Chalk, his second wife and the sister of Ellen, who is also remembered on the tombstone.

101. *Medical Press and Circular*, 26 November 1884; *BMJ*, 29 November 1884, p. 1099; Swales, 'Pioneer', p. 137. The only serious study was in 1952 by Shaw. It is only now that Mahomed's work is given due recognition in the work of Swales and Cameron and Hicks.

102. Shaw, 'Akbar', p. 166; *GHR*, vol. 43, 1885–6, pp. 1–10; Mrs Dixon to Bagshawe, 29 April 1954, BRL; Cameron and Hicks, *Frederick Akbar*, p. 1503.

103. *BMJ*, 29 November 1884, p. 1099; *DNB*, vol. 12, p. 777–8; Wilks and Bettany, *Guy's*, p. 306; quoted in Shaw, 'Akbar', p. 158.

104. *Munk's Roll 1826–1925*, vol. 4; *BMJ*, 29 November 1884, p. 1099; Wilks and Bettany, *Guy's*, only refer to 'his papers on Bright's disease' and to his 'power as an original worker and thinker', pp. 306–11; see also *DNB*, vol. 12, pp. 777–8 and *The Times*, 24 November 1884.

105. Allbutt only cited Mahomed's student paper of 1872 in which his ideas were not yet fully developed. Cameron and Hicks, *Frederick Akbar*, p. 1503; Shaw, 'Akbar', p. 166.

106. Aberdeen University, *Roll of Graduates, 1901–1925;* for change of name

to Deane, *The Times*, 7 November 1902; *BMJ*, 25 December 1948; I am grateful to Dr Anthony Batty Shaw for this information, 4 September 1998.

107. John Callaghan, *Rajani Palme Dutt* (London: Lawrence & Wishart, 1993), pp. 9–12.

108. Maan, *New Scots*, p. 77; *Bombay Chronicle*, 28 October 1927; information from Sehri Saklatvala; IOR: L/P&J/7/1433; G.N. Nadkarani, *Journal of a Visit to Europe in 1896* (Bombay: Taraporevala & Sons, 1903), p. 271.

109. *Umpire*, 11 November 1906.

110. E.g. the six-line obituary in *The Times*, 24 May 1918, identified him only as the father in the case; *Daily Telegraph*, 11 January 1907; *Umpire*, 18 November 1906; Leslie Hale, *Blood on the Scales* (London: Jonathan Cape, 1960), p. 114.

111. Sir Arthur Conan Doyle, *Memories and Adventures* (Oxford University Press, 1989 edn), p. 216; *DT*, 11 January 1907; *Umpire*, 11 November 1906; Hale, *Blood*, p. 115; C.G.L. Du Cann, *Miscarriages of Justice* (London: Frederick Muller, 1960), pp. 201–2.

112. Shapurji Edalji, *A Miscarriage of Justice* (London: The United Press, 1905). The only copy available, as far as is known, is in the Staffordshire Record Office, Stafford. For details of events, see: *Umpire*, 11 November and 18 November, 1906; *DT*, 11 January 1907; Hale, *Blood*, pp. 115–22; J.D. Carr, *The Life of Sir Arthur Conan Doyle* (London: John Murray, 1959), pp. 218–26; R. and M. Whittington-Egan, eds, *The Story of Mr George Edalji* (Grey House Books, 1985) , pp. 14–15.

113 *Umpire*, 11 November–9 December 1906; *DT*, 11–12 January 1907. Doyle says he became interested after he saw the articles, but Edalji, writing in 1934, confirmed he had sent them to Doyle, *Daily Express*, 7 November 1934.

114. House of Commons, Cmd. 3507, 1907. See also, Edalji, *Miscarriage.*

115. Doyle, *Memories*, p. 219; House of Commons, Cmd. 3503, 1907, pp. 411–12.

116. Du Cann, *Justice*, p. 201.

117. Edalji, *Miscarriage*, p. 9; *Umpire*, 11 November, 1906; Doyle, *Memories*, p. 218; Rosemary Pattenden, *English Criminal Appeals 1844–1994* (Oxford: Clarendon Press, 1996), p. 30.

118. M. Mukherjee, *W.C. Bonnerjee: Snapshots From His Life and His London Letters* (Calcutta: Deshbandhu Book Depot, 1944), vol. i, pp. 9, 11, 25; J.N. Gupta, *Life and Works of R.C. Dutt* (London: J.M. Dent, 1911), p. 15.

119. Agnes Janaki Majumdar, *Pramila: A Memoir* (London: Privately Published, nd). I am grateful to Anita Money, a great-grand daughter of W.C. Bonnerjee, for a copy.

120. *Pramila*, pp. 9, 6–7. The memoir is circumspect, but see, *Family History*, in Antoine Burton, 'House/Daughter/Nation: Interiority, Architecture, and Historical Imagination in Janaki Majumdar's "Family History" ', *The Journal of Asian Studies*, vol. 56, no. 4, November 1997, pp. 929, 934.

121. *Pramila*, pp. 9–11, 13–24; Burton, *Family History*, pp. 935–7.

122. R.P. Masani, *Dadabhai Naoroji, the Grand Old Man of India* (London:

George Allen & Unwin, 1939), p. 71; Salter, *Asiatic*, pp. 195–8; *The Times*, 7 September 1918.

123. IOR: POS 5945, report March–October 1909; IOR: POS 8966, report 21 December 1910; IOR: Neg., 9830, report 21 November 1911; IOR: V/27/262/1; David Garnett, *The Golden Echo* (London: Chatto & Windus, 1953), p. 148; IOR: L/P/S19/168.

124. IOR: E/1/186; I am grateful to David Wilson for sharing his family research with me. Marriage certificate, 10 February 1835, St Leonard's Shoreditch, LMA; Robson's *London Directory*, 1837; Parish of St Botolph Bishopsgate Rate Book, 1837; death certificate, July 1855; *LG*, 29 August 1919.

125. IOR: MSS EUR T 109; Mukherjee, *Bonnerjee*, p. 2; S.K. Bhuyan, *London Memories* (Assam: Gauhati Publication Board, 1979), p. 1; M.K. Gandhi, *An Autobiography*, trans. Mahadev Desai (Penguin edn, 1984), p. 57; S. Satthianadhan, *Four Years in an English University* (Madras: Srinivasa, Varadachari & Co., 1893), p. 22; IOR: L/P&J/6/845, p. 197; M.C. Chagla, *Roses in December* (Bombay: Bharatiya Vidya Bhavan, 1978), p. 3. For Gandhi in London, see, P.D. Fraser, 'Observing the Empire: Gandhi, Malabari, Tagore and Edun, 1888–1928', in Anthony Copley and Rozina Visram, eds, 'Indians in Britain: Past and Present', *Indo-British Review A Journal of History*, vol. xvi, no. 2, June 1989, pp. 7–15; Stephen Hay, 'The Making of a Late-Victorian Hindu: M.K. Gandhi in London 1888–1891', *Victorian Studies*, vol. 33, no. 1, Autumn 1989, pp. 74–98.

126. J. Nowrojee and H. Merwanjee, *Journal of a Residence of Two Years and a Half* (London: William Allen & Co., 1841); Ardaseer Cursetjee, *Diary of an Overland Journey from Bombay to England* (London: Hennington & Galabin, 1840); Election Certificate, 27 May 1841, Royal Society; *Minutes of the Proceedings of the Institute of Civil Engineers*, vol. 51, 1878.

127. Chuckerbutty, known as Dr 'Goodeve', died in England in 1874 and is buried at Kensal Green Cemetery. Brown, 'Students', pp. 138–9; Das, 'Visitors', pp. 101–4; H. Das, *Life and Letters of Toru Dutt* (London: OUP, 1920); Clem Seecharan, *India and the Shaping of the Indo-Guyanese Imagination 1890s–1920s* (Leeds: Peepal Tree, 1993), p. 25.

128. Anon., 'Indian Students in England', *Journal of the National Indian Association*, January 1885, no. 169, pp. 1–9; Brown, 'Students', p. 144; *Indian Magazine and Review*, no. 231, March 1890; IOR: V/24/832, Indian Students' Department Records; BPP, No. 5133 (22), 1910, p. 17.

129. Brown, 'Students', p. 142; IOR: L/P&J/6/845, p. 198; Cornelia Sorabji, *India Calling* (London: Nisbet & Co., 1934), p. 52; Sorabji Papers, IOR: MSS EUR F 165/1, 1 October 1889; 165/7, 13 December 1892; 165/2, 2 April 1890. For an exploration of this point, see Antoinette Burton, *At the Heart of the Empire* (Berkeley: University of California Press, 1998), pp. 110–52; for a comparable situation, see Rozina Visram, 'Kamal A Chunchie of the Coloured Men's Institute: The Man and the Legend', *Immigrants & Minorities*, vol. 18, no. 1 March 1999, pp. 29–48.

130. IOR: MSS EUR F 111/281, 1903, letters 7 August 1903; 15 December

1902; 18 May 1903; 2 April 1903 and note by W.R. Hamilton; IOR: L/P&J/6/845, p. 9; Brown, 'Students', p. 148; *The Times*, 1 September 1908.

131. IOR: MSS EUR F 111/281, Curzon's minute, 6 September 1903; IOR: L/P&J/6/845, pp. 53, 108 and internal minute on the Report; *The Times*, 1 September 1908.

132. IOR: L/P&J/6/845, GOI to IO, 3 and 13 March 1908; enclosure, 1 July 1909; GOI to IO, 8 July 1909 and enclosures, IO to Mir Sultan Mohidin, 6 December 1909; *The Times*, 1 September 1908 and ibid., 1 April 1909.

133. *First Annual Report: Journal of the National Indian Association*, September 1885, re-named *Indian Magazine & Review* in 1886; IOR: V/24/832; IOR: L/P&J/3/250, report of the Political ADC, Gerald Fitzgerald, 5 April 1884; Brown, 'Students', p. 143.

134. Satthianadhan, 'Indian Students in English Universities', *JNIA*, November 1880; Ali Hamid, 'The Cost of Living in London', *JNIA*, February 1882; Mary Bhore, 'Some Impressions of England', *IM&R*, November and December 1900; IOR: MSS EUR F 165/1, 1 and 8 October 1889; IOR: L/P&J/6/845, p. 108.

135. *Edinburgh Indian Association, 1883–1983* (Centenary Issue, 1983), p. 13; Seecharan, *India*, pp. 25–6; IOR: V/24/832.

136. Gandhi, *Autobiography*, p. 56; BPP, No. 5133 (22), 1910, pp. 17 and 20; N.B. Wagle, 'Experiences of English Factory Life', *IM&R*, no. 361, January 1901, pp. 12–27; IOR: V/24/832, report for 1916–17.

137. IOR: L/P&J/6/845, evidence pp. 103–4, 191–201, 288, 162; IO to heads of Colleges, 21 January and 19 March 1909; from Balliol, 17 March 1909; Magdelen College, 20 February 1909; Report, pp. 11–15, 161–78; Lala Baijnath, *England and India* (Bombay: Jehangir B. Karani, 1893), p. 29.

138. Nowrojee and Merwanjee, *Journal*, pp. 35 and 451–2; Rakhal Das Haldar, *The English Diary of an Indian Student, 1861–62* (Dacca: The Asutosh Library, 1903), pp. xiv and 85; Satthianadhan, *University*, pp. 47, 49; Krishna Dutta and Andrew Robinson, *Rabindranath Tagore* (Bloomsbury, 1995), pp. 75–6; IOR: L/P&J/6/845; Wagle, 'Experiences', pp. 18, 20, 24–5; Dorothy Norman, ed., *Nehru: The First Sixty Years* (London: The Bodley Head, 1965), vol. i, p. 353.

139. Sorabji, *India Calling*, pp. 3–9, 38, 15–18, 64, 84.

140. Sorabji, *India Calling*, pp. 20–2; *The Queen*, 21 and 24 August 1889; IOR: MSS EUR 165/16, Sorabji to Hobhouse, 10 May 1888; *The Times*, 12 June 1889, for subscribers.

141. IOR: MSS EUR F 165/1, 26 September and 15 October 1889; 165/2 9 March 1890.

142. MSS EUR f 165/1, 15 October, 3 November 1889; 165/3, 2 November 1890; Pauline Adams, *Somerville for Women* (OUP, 1996), pp. 85, 117; Sorabji, *India Calling*, pp. 22–4.

143. IOR: MSS EUR F 165/3, 2 November 1890; 165/6, 14 February 1892; 8 and 26 May and 16 June 1892; Sorabji, *India Calling*, p. 28.

144. IOR: MSS EUR F 165/6, 22 June 1892; Sorabji, *India Calling*, pp. 34–5.

145. *The Women's Who's Who* (London: Shaw Publishing Co., 1934–5 edn), p. 355; IOR: MSS EUR F 165/5, 9 August 1891. See also 165/4 7 January 1891.

146. IOR: L/I/1/1520, Amery to Brendan Bracken, 4 December 1941; Sorabji to Macgregor, 16 August 1934 and miscellaneous Sorabji correspondence in same file; IOR: L/P/&J/12/455, Sorabji to Morrison, 21 January 1943, is a vicious attack on Menon.

147. Allan Ross, *Ranji Prince of Cricketers* (London: Collins, 1983), pp. 39–41.

148. Ross, *Ranji*, illustration opposite p. 64; p. 77.

149. E.g. Ogden's Cigarettes; Charles T. West's song, 'Ranji', was issued around 1895 by Lyon and Hall of Brighton, David R. Allen, *A Song for Cricket* (London: Pelham Books, 1981), pp. 50–4; Ross, *Ranji*, pp. 65, 109.

150. For Ranji's cricket record, season by season, Ross, *Ranji*, pp. 245–9; Chris Harte, *A History of Australian Cricket* (London: Andre Deutsch, 1993). Ranji succeeded to the throne of Nawanagar in 1907.

151. Ross, *Ranji*, pp. 135–6. Ranji's other book, *The Jubilee Book of Cricket*, published for Victoria's Jubilee, is dedicated to 'Her Majesty the Queen-Empress' (Blackwood, 1897); in Kusoom Vadgama, *India in Britain* (London: Robert Royce, 1984), p. 125; S. Satthianadhan, *A Holiday Trip to Europe and America* (Madras: Srinivasa, Varadachari & Co., 1897), p. 65; Clem Seecharan, *Tiger in the Stars* (Warwick University Caribbean Studies, 1997), p. 312.

152. IOR: MSS EUR F 111/159, Curzon to Hamilton, 29 August, 18 July, 25 July, 1900; 28 November and 1 October 1900. For a wider discussion on the perception and official attitude to the Princes, see, Visram, *Ayahs*, pp. 172–7; Shompa Lahiri, 'British Policy Towards Indian Princes in Late Nineteenth-Century and Early Twentieth-Century Britain', *Immigrants and Minorities*, vol. 15, no. 3, November 1996, pp. 214–32.

153. Quoted in M. Alexander and S. Anand, *Queen Victoria's Maharajah Duleep Singh, 1838–1893* (London: Weidenfeld & Nicolson, 1980), p. 13; for financial arrangements, IOR: L/P&S/18D/18 pt 1; for Sikh Wars, J.S. Grewal, *The Sikhs of the Punjab* (Cambridge University Press, 1990).

154. Rishi Ranjan Chakrabarty, *Duleep Singh: The Maharajah of the Punjab and the Raj* (Birmingham: D.S. Samara, 1988), p. 51; Alexander and Anand, *Duleep Singh*, pp. 25, 30 and 37.

155. Alexander and Anand, *Duleep Singh*, pp. 43–4; 59–60; Winterhalter gave him the height he would eventually acquire, although Duleep Singh never grew any taller, Visram, *History*, p. 17, for photograph.

156. Alexander and Anand, *Duleep Singh*, p. 82; IOR: L/P&S/18D/17, Minute by Dalhousie, 15 February 1856; *The Graphic*, 28 October 1893. Jindan died in England in 1863.

157. Alexander and Anand, *Duleep Singh*, pp. 111–12, 17; John Lord, *The Maharajahs* (London: Hutchinson, 1972), pp. 24–5.

158. *Vanity Fair*, 26 June 1878; E. Farrer, ed., *Portraits in Norfolk Houses* (Norwich: Jarrold & Sons, 1927), Preface, p. xiv.

159. *The Times*, 13 August 1882; Evans Bell, *The Annexation of the Punjab and*

the *Maharajah Duleep Singh*, 1882, was also critical of the conduct of the British government; for financial negotiations and inquiry, IOR: L/P&S/18 D/18, pt 1–6 and L/P&S/18D/19–25.

160. IOR: L/P&S/18D/18 pt iv, GOI, 17 August 1883; Alexander and Anand, *Duleep Singh*, p. 214; IOR: R/I/I/44, demi official, 22 July 1886; Khushwant Singh, *History of Sikhs* (New Delhi: Oxford University Press, 1997), vol. ii, p. 87, f/n 6.

161. Kelly's *Norfolk Directories*, 1896–1912; *Prince Duleep Singh*, Breckland District Council, Department of Industrial Development and Tourism; Somerville College Register. For a group photograph dated 1891, showing the two princesses and Sorabji, Visram, *Indians*, p. 27; IOR: L/P&S/18/ D/105, pecuniary position of the family of the late Maharajah Duleep Singh.

162. Alexander and Anand, *Duleep Singh*, pp. 23, 34,64, 84–6, 102; *ILN*, 17 July 1852.

163. Zoroastrian Archives, *The Zoroastrian Trust Funds of Europe* (1983); B.M. Malabari, *The Indian Eye on English Life* (Bombay: Apollo Printing Works, 1895), p. 228; *ILN*, 9 November 1889; John Wolffe, ed., *Religion in Victorian Britain* (Manchester University Press in Association with the Open University, 1997), vol. v, pp. 243–65; *The Baptist* (London), 24 April 1891, p. 265.

164. *IM&R*, no. 543, 1 November 1891, no. 470, February 1910.

165. Mary Louise Pratt describes 'contact zones' as 'social spaces where disparate cultures meet, clash, and grapple with each other, often in highly asymmetrical relations of domination and subordination – like colonialism, slavery ...' *Travel Writing and Transculturation* (London: Routledge, 1992), pp. 4–6.

4 THROUGH INDIAN EYES

1. Khan, *Travels*; Alexander, *Shigurf*. For Munshi Ismail, see Digby, 'Narrative'; for Mir Muhammad Hussain, see Gulfishan Khan, *Indian Muslim Perceptions of the West During the Eighteenth Century* (Karachi: Oxford University Press, 1998).

2. Baijnath, *England*, p. 1.

3. Cursetjee, *Diary*; Nowrojee and Merwanjee, *Journal*; E.W. West, ed., *Diary of the Late Rajah of Kolhapoor During his Visit to Europe in 1870* (London: Smith Elder & Co., 1872); Satthianadhan, *University;* Haldar, *Diary*; Bhore, 'Impressions'.

4. Alexander, *Shigurf*, pp. 37–9; Chs 10–12; Claudia Liebeskind's Review of Khan's *Muslim Perceptions*, in *Journal of the Royal Asiatic Society*, 3rd Series, vol. 10, pt 1, April 2000, p. 112.

5. Alexander, *Shigurf*, pp. 42–8, 63–5; Digby, 'Narrative', p. 57.

6. Alexander, *Shigurf*, pp. 52–4, 159.

7. Alexander, *Shigurf*, p. 140; Liebeskind's Review, p. 113.

8. Khan, *Travels*, vol. i., pp. 161–3, 216–23, 173, 197.

9. Khan, *Travels*, vol. ii.

10. Khan, *Travels*, vol. i, pp. 206–9, 212–13.

11. Khan, *Travels*, vol. i, pp. 118, 169, 189–90, 223, 230, 244.

12. Khan, *Travels*, vol. i, pp. 306–8, 225.

13. Khan, *Travels*, vol. i, pp. 259–61 and Appendix B: 'On the Vindication of the Liberties of the Asiatic Women'.

14. Nowrojee and Merwanjee, *Journal*, p. 91; Bhagvat Sinh Jee, Thakore Saheb of Gondal, *Journal of a Visit to England in 1883* (Bombay: Education Society's Press, 1886), p. 29.

15. Jhinda Ram, *My Trip to Europe* (Lahore: Mufid-i-am Press, 1893), pp. 10, 62; T.N. Mukharji, *A Visit to Europe* (Calcutta: W. Newman & Co., 1889), pp. 99–101; Malabari, *Indian Eye*, pp. 237–8; N.L. Doss, *Reminiscences English and Australasian* (Calcutta, 1893), p. 37.

16. G.P. Pillai, *London and Paris Through Indian Spectacles* (Madras: The Vaijayanti Press, 1897), pp. 10, 100; Ram, *My Trip*, p. 86; Haldar, *Diary*, p. 54; Baijnath, *England*, p. 21.

17. P.M. Choudry, *British Experiences* (Calcutta: New Britannia Press, 1889), p. 6; Doss, *Reminiscences*, p. 2; Mozoomdar, *Sketches*, p. 6; Nadkarani, *Journal*, p. 381; Mukharji, *Visit*, pp. 106, 6, 101; Ram, *My Trip*, p. 79; Baijnath, *England*, p. 39; Mehdi Hassan Khan, 'London Sketches by an Indian Pen', *IM&R*, no. 230, February 1890, p. 73.

18. Malabari, *Indian Eye*, p. 65.

19. Doss, *Reminiscences*, p. 98; Nadkarani, *Journal*, p. 46.

20. Ram, *My Trip*, pp. 42, 73; T.B. Pandian, *England to an Indian Eye* (London: Elliot Stock, 1897), p. 29; Doss, *Reminiscences*, p. 56; A.L. Roy, *Reminiscences England and American, Pt II: England and India* (Calcutta: Royal Publishing House, 1888), p. 35; Baijnath, *England*, pp. 23, 25–6; Hajee Sullaiman Shah Mahomed, *Journal of My Tours Round the World 1886–1887 and 1893–1895* (Bombay: Duftur Ashkara Oil Engine Press, 1895), p. 279.

21. Satthianadhan, *Holiday*, pp. 23, 74, 83; Ram, *My Trip*, pp. 17, 65–6; Pillai, *London*, pp. 23–4, 50; Baijnath, *England*, p. 34; Mahomed, *Tours*, p. 266.

22. MSS EUR F 165/3, 23 March 1890; Nowrojee and Merwanjee, *Journal*, p. 182; Baijnath, *England*, p. 69; Malabari, *Indian Eye*, pp. 202, 221–2, 46; Khan, *Sketches*, p. 69; Satthianadhan, *Holiday*, p. 75; Ram, *My Trip*, p. 26.

23. Pandian, *England*, pp. 5–13; Baijnath, *England*, p. 40.

24. N. Ramanujaswami, *My Trip to England* (Madras: Ananda Press, 1912), p. 35; Pillai, *London*, pp. 4–8, 11–13; Baijnath, *England*, pp. 29, 46; Khan, *Sketches*, p. 65. See Wellcome Library MS 5853, Mrs M.H. Turnbull's Nineteenth-Century Recipe Collection; MS 711, Leeds Apothecary's Cash and Recipe Book; *Blackheath Local Guide and District Advertiser*, 18 November 1893 for 'The Banyan Curry Powder' advertisement. I am grateful to Neil Rhind for a copy.

25. Malabari, *Indian Eye*, p. 48.

26. Roy, *Reminiscences*, p. 29.

27. Pillai, *London*, p. 2; Pandian, *England*, p. 35; Satthianadhan, *Holiday*, p.

72; Doss, *Reminiscences*, pp. 39, 86; Khan, *Sketches*, p. 63; Mukharji, *Visit*, p. 33; Ram, *My Trip*, p. 20; Baijnath, *England*, p. 34; Malabari, *Indian Eye*, p. 184.

28. Pillai, *London*, pp. 26–9; Ram, *My Trip*, pp. 76–7; Doss, *Reminiscence*, p. 40; Pandian, *England*, pp. 4–5, 23; Malabari, *Indian Eye*, p. 174.

29. Pandian, *England*, p. 21; Ram, *My Trip*, p. 18; Mukharji, *Visit*, pp. 39–40; Mahomed, *Tours*, p. 266; Pillai, *London*, pp. 34–5.

30. Malabari, *Indian Eye*, pp. 202–4; Pillai, *London*, p. 21; A Hindu, *Three Years in Europe* (Calcutta: Thacker, Spink & Co., 1873), p. 14; Baijnath, *England*, p. 31; Pandian, *England*, p. 50.

31. Baijnath, *England*, p. 32; Malabari, *Indian Eye*, p. 53; Pandian, *England*, p. 92; Pillai, *London*, pp. 46, 32.

32. Satthianadhan, *Holiday*, p. 61; Mahomed, *Tours*, p. 265; Pillai, *London*, pp. 10, 58; Pandian, *England*, pp. 79–83; Mukharji, *Visit*, p. 171; Roy, *Reminiscence*, pt ii, pp. 32–3.

33. Malabari, *Indian Eye*, pp. 46, 186; Baijnath, *England*, pp. 23, 35, 185; Pillai, *London*, pp. 68, 72, 78–9; Doss, *Reminiscences*, p. 81; Satthianadhan, *Holiday*, p. 99; A Hindu, *Europe*, p. 12; Pandian, *England*, p. 41; Jee, *Journal*, pp. 30, 99.

34. Khan, *Travels*, vol. i., pp. 106–7.

35. Pandian, *England*, p. 18; Pillai, *London*, p. 32; Nadkarani, *Journal*, p. 393.

36. Malabari, *Indian Eye*, p. 85.

37. Roy, *Reminiscences*, pt ii, pp. 30–1; Ram, *My Trip*, p. 13; Baijnath, *England*, p. 32; Malabari, *Indian Eye*, pp. 86–7, 122–6, 145; Pillai, *London*, p. 32.

38. Ram, *My Trip*, p. 81; Pillai, *London*, p. 60; Bhore, 'Impressions', p. 288; Satthianadhan, *Holiday*, p. 61; T. Ramakrishna, *My Visit to the West* (London: Fisher Unwin Ltd, 1915), p. 28.

39. Malabari, *Indian Eye*, pp. 76, 149–71, 217–18.

40. Pillai, *London*, p. 100; Ram, *My Trip*, p. 80; Jee, *Journal*, pp. 170, 176–8; Malabari, *Indian Eye*, pp. 67–9, 90.

41. Mukharji, *Visit*, p. 78–9, 81, 83–4.

42. Mukharji, *Visit*, p. xi; Khan, *Travels*, vol. ii, p. 27.

5 PARLIAMENTARIANS, REVOLUTIONARIES AND SUFFRAGETTES

1. See Dutta and Robinson, *Rabindranath*, pp. 8, 24–6; Tagore died in London in August 1846 and is buried in Kensal Green Cemetery.

2. Harish Kaushik, *The Indian National Congress in England 1885–1920* (New Delhi: Research Publications in Social Sciences, n.d.), p. 4; R.C. Majumdar, *History of the Freedom Movement in India* (Calcutta: Firma K.L. Mukhopadhyay, 1962), pp. 316 and 384; S.R. Mehrotra, *The Emergence of Indian National Congress* (Delhi: Vikas Publications, 1971), p. 16; J.H. Bell, *British Folks and British India Fifty Years Ago* (London: John Heywood, 1891), p. 65.

3. Majumdar, *Freedom*, pp. 384–5; Masani, *Naoroji*, p. 110.

4. Kaushik, *Congress*, p. 6; C.L. Parekh, ed., *Essays, Speeches, Addresses and Writings on Indian Politics of the Hon'ble Dadabhai Naoroji* (Bombay: Caxton Printing Works, 1887).

5. E. Kulke, *The Parsees in India* (New Delhi: Vikas Publishing, 1974), p. 218.

6. Majumdar, *Freedom*, p. 385.

7. Majumdar, *Freedom*, p. 386.

8. Kaushik, *Congress*, pp. 12–13, 63; Stanley Wolpert, *A New History of India* (Oxford University Press, 1989), p. 259; Bipan Chandra, *India's Struggle for Independence* (Penguin Books, South Asian edn., 1989), p. 136.

9. For membership and finance, see Kaushik, *Congress*, pp. 15–28; Mary Cumpston, 'Some Early Indian Nationalists and their Allies in the British Parliament, 1851–1906', *English Historical Review*, vol. 76, no. 299, April 1961, pp. 294–5.

10. Masani, *Naoroji*, pp. 71–80; for biographical details, see also Omar Ralph, *Naoroji The First Asian MP* (London: Hansib, 1997); S.P. Sen, ed., *DNB* (Calcutta: Institute of Historical Studies, 1973).

11. 27 March 1866, in Parekh, *Essays*, pp. 1–25.

12. Quoted in Wolpert, *History*, pp. 251–2. Racial exclusion is further highlighted in the furore over the 1883 Ilbert Bill.

13. Chandra, *Independence*, p. 91.

14. R.C. Dutt, *The Economic History of India Under Early British Rule* (London: Kegan Paul, Trench, Trubner & Co., 1906, 2nd edn); Parekh, *Essays;* Dadabhai Naoroji, *Poverty and Un-British Rule in India* (London: Swan Sonnenschein & Co., 1901).

15. C.A. Bayly, *The Raj* (National Portrait Gallery, 1991), p. 130.

16. S.B. Saul, *Studies in British Overseas Trade 1870–1914* (Liverpool, 1960), p. 62; quoted in E.J. Hobsbawm, *Industry and Empire* (London: Pelican Books, 1969), p. 149. For India and the British economy: also Hobsbawm, Ch. 10; P.J. Cain and A.G. Hopkins, *British Imperialism: Innovation and Expansion 1688–1914* (London: Longman, 1993), Ch. 7.

17. Kaushik, *Congress*, pp. 34, 51–5.

18. Kaushik, *Congress*, pp. 19; 40–1.

19. Kaushik, *Congress*, p. 4; Kulke, *Parsees*, p. 219. Ranade established the All People's Association, *Sarvajanik Sabha*, in Poona in 1870.

20. *KI*, 15 November 1884.

21. *Kentish Mercury*, 8 May and 16 October 1885; *KI*, 21 November 1884.

22. 1885: Evelyn 3,927, Ghose 3,560, turnout 79.9 per cent; 1886: Evelyn 3,682, Ghose 3,055, a slightly larger margin, but on a reduced turnout of 71.9 per cent, see F.W.S. Craig, ed., *British Parliamentary Election Results 1885–1918* (London: Macmillan, 1974). R.C. Dutt, *Three Years in Europe* (Calcutta: S.K. Lahiri & Co., 1890), pp. 142–3 for a description of the election.

23. *The Graphic*, 10 July 1886; Ram, *My Trip*, pp. 84–5; S. Banerjea, *A Nation*

in the Making (London: Humphrey Milford, 1925).

24. Election manifesto in Parekh, *Essays*, p. 303; Naoroji polled 1,950 votes, Duncan 3,651, turnout 57.1 per cent.

25. Henry Pelling, *Social Geography of British Elections* (London: Macmillan, 1967), p. 28. Naoroji: 2,961 votes, Penton: 2,956, turnout 71. 2 per cent. In 1886 the Conservative candidate had won by five votes; Bonnerjee won 2,355 to Cayzer's 3,192.

26. Quoted in Kaushik, *Congress*, p. 120; Masani, *Naoroji*, pp. 231, 234.

27. *Pall Mall Gazette*, in Masani, *Naoroji*, p. 243; 'Fairplay', 'India and Mr. D. Naoroji, MP' (1893); *The Times*, quoted in *Lord Salisbury's Blackman* (Lucknow: G.P. Varma and Bros. Press, 1889) pp. 63–5.

28. Quoted in *Blackman*, p. 1.

29. Masani, *Naoroji*, pp. 263–7.

30. Quoted in *Blackman*, pp. 1, 9–10, 15, 32–3, 43, 84–6, 112 and 114. Dyce Sombre, a 'Eurasian', had been elected in 1841 without fuss.

31. Naoroji received 49 votes to Eve's 45, *Daily News*, 17 August, 1888; IOR: MSS EUR D 767/1, Schnadhorst to Naoroji, 18 August 1888; D. Naoroji, *Mr D. Naoroji and Mr Schnadhorst* (London; 1892), p. 4.

32. Masani, *Naoroji*, pp. 268, 262–3; Naoroji, *Schnadhorst*, pp. 6 and 8–11.

33. IOR: MSS EUR D 767/1, Naoroji to Digby, 27 June and 19 August 1891; Naoroji, *Schnadhorst*, pp. 11–12. 'Invisible' in *Finsbury and Holborn Guardian*, 27 June 1891, claimed that Ford had been asked to stand and between 1,100–1,200 signatures had been obtained without canvassing support; ibid., 23 May 1891.

34. Masani, *Naoroji*, p. 271; Naoroji, *Schnadhorst*, pp. 12–15; IOR: MSS EUR D 767/1, Naoroji to Digby, 29 April 1892 and 26 March 1892; Naoroji in *Weekly News and Chronicle*, 1 August 1891.

35. Wolpert, *History*, p. 287; IOR: L/P&J/12/201.

36. *Address to his Fellow Electors*, July 1895, Finsbury Archives.

37. Quoted in Kaushik, *Congress*, p. 75; *The Times*, 3 June 1893.

38. *The Times*, 13 February 1895; Naoroji also gave evidence to the Royal Commission, Kaushik, *Congress*, p. 128.

39. In 1906 Hon H. Legg polled 4,264 votes against Mallik's 2,191, turnout 69 per cent; in 1910 Mallik won 4,286 votes, his opponent's 9,005, turnout 75.9 per cent; Morden polled only 16.4 per cent of the vote in 1918 and 1.7 per cent in 1922. Morden's *Address to Finsbury Electors*, FA.

40. *The Times*, 7 July 1892 and 3 July 1917; Duse Mohamed Ali, 'About it and About ... ' in *The Comet*, Lagos, Nigeria, 3 July 1937.

41. Quoted in A.K. Majumdar, *Advent of Independence* (Bombay: Chowpatty, 1963), p. 368; in Kaushik, *Congress*, p. 126.

42. Cumpston, *Nationalists;* Chandra, *Independence*, p. 98.

43. For Indian reaction in British Guiana, see Seecharan, *India*, pp. 20–1; Kulke, *Parsees*, p. 222. The casket is in the Local History Collection, FA; IOR: L/P&J/12/456, 13 March 1946. The portrait hangs at the India Club, the Strand; Insurance Street, WC1 was renamed Naoroji Street, Transport Sub-Committee, 9 March 1993, Islington Technical Services, FA.

44. O.C. Mathurin, *Henry Sylvester Williams and the Organisation of the Pan-African Movement, 1869–1911* (Westport, CT: Greenwood Press, 1976), p. 79; B.A. Kosmin, 'London's Asian MPs: The Contrasting Careers of Three Parsee Politicians', in Copley and Visram, 'Indians', p. 29.

45. H. Tinker, *A New System of Slavery* (Oxford University Press, 1974), pp. 201, 300; pp. 112–16; Masani, *Naoroji*, Foreword by Gandhi.

46. Quoted in R.P. Patwardhan, *Dadabhai Naoroji Correspondence* (Bombay, 1977), vol ii, p. xxxiv.

47. *India*, 2 September 1904; *The Late Dadabhai Naoroji on Swaraj* (Bombay Home Rule Series No. 6), p. 9.

48. Bhownaggree had set aside £3,000 for a lecture hall at the Imperial Institute, letter 4 January 1893, IOR: MSS EUR F 216/47; *The Times*, 21 November 1933.

49. IOR: MSS EUR F 216/65 (b), 30 March 1894. For biographical details: *The Times*, 15 November 1933; *DNB*, 1931–40 (Oxford University Press, 1949), pp. 75–6.

50. *The First Indian Member of Imperial Parliament* (Madras, 1892), p. 83.

51. IOR: MSS EUR F 216/65 (b), 9 March 1894.

52. IOR: MSS EUR F 216/65 (b), 9 March and 13 July 1894; letters dated Sunday, May 1894, and 31 August 1894; Bhownaggree's speech at his victory banquet, *The Times*, 14 November 1895; ibid., 15 November 1933;

53. Hamilton to Elgin, 2 April 1897, quoted in Majumdar, *Advent*, Appendix vi, pp. 368–9.

54. *The Times*, 14 November 1895; Masani, *Naoroji*, p. 370; *The Times*, 15 November 1933; *DNB*; *Eastern Argus*, 4 May 1895.

55. *The Times*, 15 November 1933. Bhownaggree won 2,591 votes, Howell 2,431 on a 67.6 per cent poll.

56. Letter 26 December 1905, in F.M. Leventhal, *Respectable Radical* (London: Weidenfeld & Nicolson, 1971), p. 212.

57. *EA*, 13 July 1895 and 4 July 1895.

58. *EA*, 3 August and 4 May 1895; *Bethnal Green News*, 18 November 1933; Earl of Meath's speech, *EA*, 29 June 1895.

59. Masani, *Naoroji*, p. 370; *The Political Estimate of Mr Bhavnagri* (Bombay, 1897) gives press coverage of his visit; Visram, *History*, p. 23 for a cartoon depiction; IOR: MSS EUR F 216/65 (b), letter to Birdwood, 9 March 1894.

60. *The Times*, 6 August 1897; *BGN*, 18 November 1933; Bhownaggree: 2,988 to Lawson's, 2,609, turnout 69.9 per cent.

61. *The Times*, 27 January, 5 July and 6 August 1897; ibid., 14 August 1896.

62 *The Times*, 4 April 1900 and 22 June 1905.

63. Quoted in Kulke, *Parsees*, p. 228; Patwardhan, *Correspondence*, vol. ii, p. 550; Masani, *Naoroji*, p. 370.

64. *The Times*, 14 August 1896, 17 August 1901, 22 July 1904, 22 June 1905.

65. *DNB*; *The Times*, 15 November 1933; quoted in J.R. Hinnells and O. Ralph, *Bhownaggree* (London: Hansib, 1995), p. 23.

66. Robert A. Huttenback, 'No Strangers within the Gates: Attitudes and Policies towards the Non-White Residents of the British Empire of

Settlement', *Journal of Imperial and Commonwealth History*, vol. i, no. 3, May 1973, pp. 271–302.

67. Masani, *Naoroji*, p. 370; Hinnells and Ralph, *Bhownaggree*, pp. 19–21.
68. *The Times*, 17 August 1901, 13 August 1904, 22 June 1905.
69. *The Times*, 6 August 1897, 17 August 1901 and 22 June 1905.
70. *Morning Leader*, 29 August 1905; Bhownaggree received 2,130 votes, Cornwall, 4,127.
71. IOR: L/P&J/6/1443, No. 2322; Mancherjee M. Bhownaggree, *The Verdict of India* (London: Hodder & Stoughton, 1916).
72. Bhownaggree to Saklatvala, 30 June 1930, Zoroastrian House Archives.
73. *The Times*, 4 August 1928; *DNB*; *Heroes of our Freedom Movement Syed Ameer Ali* (Karachi: Department of Films and Publication, Government of Pakistan, 1970).
74. *The Times*, 4 August 1928.
75. Syed Razi Wasti, ed., *Memoirs and Other Writings of Syed Ameer Ali* (Lahore, People's Publishing House, 1968), p. 44; M. Rahman, *From Consultation to Confrontation* (London: Luzac & Co., 1970), pp. 8, 163.
76. *Heroes*, p. 6; Majumdar, *Advent*, p. 48.
77. Syed Ameer Ali, 'India and the New Parliament', 1906, quoted in Wasti, ed., *Memoirs*, p. 236; Rahman, *Consultation*, pp. 33, 82.
78. Wolpert, *History*, 278; Wasti, ed., *Memoirs*, pp. 75–6.
79. *The Times*, 20 December 1908, 14 January and 6 July 1909; Rahman, *Consultation*, p. 135.
80. *The Times*, 4 August 1928.
81. Chandra, *Independence*, p. 142. 'Extremists' led by B.G. Tilak (1856–1920) was a more radical wing within the Congress.
82. C.H. Philips, ed., *The Evolution of India and Pakistan 1858–1947* (Oxford University Press, 1965), p. 151; Chandra, *Independence*, p. 137; Wolpert, *History*, p. 275.
83. Cama's message in *Bande Mataram*, IOR: POS 6052 Proceedings, July 1913; J.C. Ker, *Political Troubles in India, 1907–1917* (Calcutta: Superintendent Government Printing, 1917), viii.
84. V.N. Datta, *Madan Lal Dhingra and the Revolutionary Movement* (New Delhi: Vikas Publishing House, 1978), p. 7.
85. IOR: L/P/S19/168; Dhanajay Keer, *Savarkar and his Times* (Bombay: A.V. Keer, 1950), p. 28. The lectureship still endures.
86. Indulal Yajnik, *Shyamaji Krishnavarma* (Bombay: Lakshmi Publication, 1950), p. 122; IOR: L/P&J/6/891, for a copy of *The Indian Sociologist*.
87. Datta, *Dhingra*, p. 9; Yajnik, *Krishnavarma*, pp. 123–4; IOR: L/PARL/2/4 44, p. 11.
88. M.K. Gandhi, *Hind Swaraj*, ed., Anthony J. Parel (Cambridge University Press, South Asian edn, 1997), p. xxvi; Yajnik, *Krishnavarma*, p. 123.
89. Gandhi, *Hind*, p. xxvi; Ker, *Troubles*, p. 174; Valentine Chirol, quoted in Keer, *Savarkar*, p. 9.
90. Yajnik, *Krishnavarma*, p. 250; Garnett, *Echo*, p. 149.
91. Yajnik, *Krishanavarma*, p. 217.

92. IOR: V/27/262/1, *Indian Agitators Abroad*, Criminal Intelligence Office, Simla, 1911; IOR: POS 6052, Proceedings July 1913, *History Sheet of Madame Bhikaji Cama*. Another copy, dated August 1913, in IOR: Neg 9836 Proceedings Part B; Nawaz B. Mody, 'Madame Bhikaji Rustom Cama – Sentinel of Liberty', in Nawaz B. Mody, ed., *The Parsis in Western India: 1818–1920* (Bombay: Allied Publishers Ltd., 1998), pp. 47–8. For biographical details: *DNB*, ed., Sen, vol. i, pp. 240–3; Panchanan Saha, *Madame Cama 'Mother of Indian Revolution'* (Calcutta: Manisha, 1975).

93. Quoted in Yajnik, *Krishnavarma*, p. 229; IOR: POS 6052, July 1913. For a photograph, see Rozina Visram, *Women in India and Pakistan* (Cambridge: Cambridge University Press, 1992), p. 18.

94. Mody, *Cama*, p. 65; a copy of *Bande Mataram* is in IOR: Neg 9836, August 1913.

95. IOR: POS 6052 July 1913; IOR: Neg 9837 Proceedings, Part B, December 1914; Margaret Ward, *Maud Gonne* (London: Pandora, 1993), pp. 91, 155.

96. Geraldine Forbes, 'The Politics of Respectability: Indian Women and the National Congress', in D.A. Low, ed., *The Indian National Congress Centenary Hindsights* (Oxford: Oxford University Press, 1968), p. 61; IOR: POS 8966, Proceedings November 1910 and IOR: POS 8969, Proceedings June 1911.

97. IOR: POS 6052 July 1913; quoted in Yajnik, *Krishnavarma*, p. 217.

98. IOR: Neg 9836; IOR: POS 6052, July 1913.

99. *Indian Sociologist*, September 1908, vol. iv, no. 9.

100. Yajnik, *Krishnavarma*, p. 164; Ker, *Troubles*, p. 172; IOR: L/P/S19/168.

101. Ker, *Troubles*, p. 174; IOR: L/P/S19/168; IOR: V/27/262/1; IOR: L/P&J/6/871, No. 1956; *The Times*, 23 May and 2 June 1908; *Daily Mail*, 9 May 1908; IOR: L/P/&J/6/845, evidence of S.D. Bhabha; Garnett, *Echo*, p. 143.

102. IOR: L/P&J/6/891, f. 3430; Ker, *Troubles*, p. 175; IOR: V/27/262/1.

103. Yajnik, *Krishnavarma*, pp. 259–66.

104. *The Times*, 23 May 1908; IOR: L/P/S19/168; Ker, *Troubles*, pp. 176–8, 181; IOR: L/PARL/2/444; IOR: POS 5945, Political Proceedings, 1909; IOR: POS 6052; IOR: POS 8966.

105. IOR: POS 5945, 4 March 1909; see Chapter 3 for Lee Warner Committee Report.

106. IOR: L/P&J/6/890; IOR: POS 8962; Weekly Report of the Director of Criminal Intelligence Office, Simla, e.g. IOR: V/27/262/1.

107. IOR: POS 5945, demi-official from De Boulay to Sir Harold Stuart, 8 May 1909; telegram Viceroy to SS, 15 May 1909 and telegram 19 May 1909 from SS to Viceroy; IOR: POS 8962, Proceedings 1909, Weekly Report 17 July 1909; Ganesh Savarkar was arrested for Nasik Murders, IOR: L/PARL/2/444.

108. In recognition of Lalcaca's 'heroism' a memorial fund was begun in Bombay to which the Government of India contributed Rs. 1,500 (£100) from Indian revenues, IOR POS 8962, 6 August 1909; Weekly Report 3 July 1909, in IOR: POS 5945.

109. *The Times*, 2 July 1909; PRO: CRIM/1/113/1 and CRIM 10/99 95136; IOR: POS 5945 and POS 8962. Dhingra's statement found in his pocket, IOR POS 8962, Ker, *Troubles*, pp. 179–80, and *DN*, 18 August 1909. For Koregaonkar's testimony, IOR: L/P&J/6/986.

110. IOR: POS 5945, C.L. Dhingra's letter in the *Civil and Military Gazette*, May 1908; letters 7 July 1909 from Mohan Lal and Behari Lal Dhingra, and 4 July 1909, from the father, Dr Sahib Ditta Mal.

111. IOR: POS 5945, letter 3 July 1909; IOR: POS 8962, reports 31 July and 7 August 1909; Ker, *Troubles*, p. 181; Garnett, *Echo*, pp. 145–6; PRO: CRIM 10/99, pp. 461–2.

112. *The Times*, 2 July 1909; IOR: POS 5945, letter 3 July 1909 and telegram 31 July 1909; IOR: POS 8962, letter 31 July 1909.

113. IOR: POS 5945, Weekly Report 5 July 1909; IOR: POS 8962, 31 July 1909; Ker, *Troubles*, p. 179.

114. IOR: POS 5945, Weekly Report, 5 July and 13 July 1909; IOR: L/PARL/2/444; IOR: POS 8962, Weekly Report 31 July 1909; Ker, *Troubles*, pp. 180–1. The alleged 'grudge' went back to 1895 when Wyllie had been instrumental in removing Krishnavarma from the service of Udaipur state.

115. IOR: POS 5945, letters 4 July 1909 from Sahib Ditta Mal, J.R. Dunlop Smith, 7 July 1909, M.L. Dhingra and B.L. Dhingra, 7 July 1909; telegram 5 July 1909, PRO: CRIM 1/113/1.

116. Ker, *Troubles*, p. 180; *The Times*, 2 July 1909; PRO: CRIM 10/99, Trial transcript, p. 463.

117. Dhingra's statement in Ker, *Troubles*, pp. 179–80; IOR: POS 8962 and *DN*, 18 August 1909; PRO: CRIM 10/99, p. 464; Garnett, *Echo*, p. 148.

118. IOR: POS 8962, Weekly Report 31 July 1909; PRO: CRIM 10/99, pp. 461, 463 and 465.

119. PRO: CRIM 10/99, p. 464.

120. IOR: L/P&J/6/986, Confidential from the Home Department, Calcutta, 20 January 1910; the suggestion that Dhingra had been hunting Lords Morley and Curzon – and Wyllie for the 'last seven months' corresponds with the Weekly Report 31 July 1909, IOR: POS 8962.

121. *The Times*, 2 July 1909; IOR: L/P&J/6/986, p. 5; IOR: L/P&J/6/908, Cambridge meeting.

122. IOR: L/P&J/6/903, Wyllie to Judicial and Public Dept, 5 November 1908; IOR: L/P&J/6/896, p. 5.

123. *The Times*, 2 July 1909; IOR: POS 8962; Datta, *Dhingra*, pp. 70, 73; quoted in Gandhi, *Hind*, p. xxvii.

124. The editorial was written by Har Dayal, *Bande Mataram*, 10 September, 1909, in Ker, *Troubles*, pp. 114 and 180; IOR: POS 8962, Weekly Report 31 July 1909.

125. IOR: POS 8962, note by A.B. Barnard and telegram from Viceroy to SS, 3 August 1909; Garnett, *Echo*, pp. 153–4; IOR: POS 6052, *History Sheet;* Ker, *Troubles*, p. 183.

126. IOR: MSS EUR D 573/49, Ponsonby to Morley, 23 August 1909.

127. The *Ghadar* Party was founded in 1913 by Punjabi migrants on the West coast of America. IOR: POS 6052, July 1913; Weekly Reports 1907–14; IOR: POS 5947, Proceedings, May 1910; IOR: POS 8968, Proceedings April 1911; IOR: Neg 9837, Proceedings 1914; IOR: L/P&J/12/49, reports 27 May, 29 December 1924 and IPI note 18 June 1924; IOR: L/P&J/12/50, report 24 March 1925.

128. IOR: Neg 9837, Proceedings Part B 1914; Yajnik, *Krishnavarma*, pp. 317–18. Nehru saw Cama in Paris and the Krishnavarmas in Geneva in 1926, Jawaharlal Nehru, *An Autobiography* (New Delhi: Jawaharlal Nehru Memorial Fund, 1982), pp. 148–55.

129. Datta, *Dhingra*, p. 74.

130. IOR: POS 8969, Proceedings June 1911; IOR: V/24/832, High Commissioner for India, Indian Students' Department Reports; *The Indian Students' Union and Hostel, 1920–1953* (Commemorative Brochure, 24 March 1953).

131. IOR: L/P&J/12 series; Patrick French, *Liberty or Death* (London: Flamingo edn, 1997), pp. 12–13; see also Humphrey Jennings and Charles Madge, *May the Twelfth* (London: Faber & Faber, 1987 edn), pp. 333–4.

132. Forbes, 'Politics', p. 64; A. Linklater, *An Unhusbanded Life* (London: Hutchinson, 1980), pp. 141, 152; Hilary Francis, ' "Pay the Piper, Call the Tune!": The Women's Tax Resistance League', in M. Joannou and J. Purvis (eds), *The Women's Suffrage Movement* (Manchester: Manchester University Press, 1998), pp. 66 and 67. See also James D. Hunt, 'Suffragettes and Satyagraha: Gandhi and the British Women's Suffrage Movement', St Louis, Missouri, October 1976, copy in the Fawcett Library.

133. *Votes for Women*, 30 June 1911, p. 640. Photograph in Visram, *History*, p. 24.

134. *VfW*, 26 May 1911, p. 561. Mrs Unwin was first reported to have taken charge in the 5 May issue, being joined by Hanson by 19 May.

135. *VfW*, 2 June 1911, p. 583; 9 June 1911, p. 598; 23 June 1911, p. 630.

136. *VfW*, 12 May 1911, p. 533 and 2 June 1911, p. 583; and ibid., 30 June 1911, p. 640; *The Star*, 19 June 1911.

137. Catherine was a member of Esher and Molsey branch of the NUWSS, see Elizabeth Crawford, *The Women's Suffrage Movement: A Reference Guide* (London: UCL Press, 1999), entry on Sophia Duleep Singh. I am grateful to Elizabeth Crawford for allowing me sight of the entry prior to publication of the *Guide*.

138. IOR: L/P&S/18/D/105, for pecuniary position of the family. IOR: MSS EUR E 377/3–10 comprise letters from *c*. 1900–10, the diary of her visit to India and miscellanea ephemera, including Victor Duleep Singh's valuation for insurance and papers relating to the sale of Elveden.

139. IOR: MSS EUR E 377/6, 377/4 and 377/5, letters from Catherine and Bamba; 377/10 has dog registration certificates, vet's bills and dog show certificates and receipts, as well as bills for photographic equipment. *The Times* carried notices of her travels, e.g. 2 October 1913.

140. Bamba's preface in ed., Farrer, *Portraits;* IOR: MSS EUR E 377/4–8; the loose sheet of paper with the genealogy is in IOR: MSS EUR 377/8.

141. *The Times*, 2 July 1909; IOR: MSS EUR F 143/91, 24 February 1916 from a Sikh soldier in hospital in Milford-on-Sea; IOR: MSS EUR F 143/93, report 25 April 1916.

142. *Annual Reports of the WSPU*, MOL Collection; Margaret Kineton Parkes, *The Tax Resistance Movement in Great Britain* (London: J. Francis, n d), p. 44, FL collection.

143. *Suffrage Annual*, pp. 131–3; *VfW*, 17 March 1911, p. 384 and 6 December 1912, p. 158; Francis, *Piper*, pp. 68–70, and for an analysis of social class of the resisters; for a list of active resisters, see Parkes, *Tax*, pp. 42–4.

144. *VfW*, 25 November 1910, pp. 120–2 and 21 July 1911, p. 688; *Suffragette*, 29 November 1912, p. 105 and 18 April 1913, p. 447.

145. E.g. *VfW*, 7 April 1911, p. 451, 11 October 1912, p. 29; *Suffragette*, 10 January 1913, p. 193, 7 March 1913, p. 336; 4 April 1913, p. 412, 12 September 1913, p. 838, and 13 February 1914, p. 405.

146. *VfW*, 8 July 1910, p. 672; ibid., 16 December 1910, 5 May 1911, p. 516 and 19 May, 1911; *Suffragette*, 6 March 1914 and 20 March 1914; see also G.D. and Joan Heath, *The Women's Suffrage Movement in and around Richmond and Twickenham* (Borough of Twickenham Local History Society, Paper No. 13, December 1968), p. 25.

147. *VfW*, 2 June 1911; ibid., 26 May 1911, pp. 558, 566.

148. *VfW*, 28 July 1911, pp. 702 and 714; Warrant of Distraint, 15 July 1911, MOL Collection.

149. *VfW*, 2 January 1914, p. 209; *The Times*, 30 December 1913.

150. *VfW*, 23 January 1914, p. 254 and 30 January 1914, p. 270; and compare, Francis, 'Piper', p. 71.

151. Crawford, *Guide*; obituary notice, *Calling All Women: News Letter of the Suffragette Fellowship*, February 1949, p. 7.

152. Heath, *Suffrage*, p. 39; *Who's Who*, p. 155.

6 INDIANS IN THE FIRST WORLD WAR

1. D.C. Ellinwood and S.D. Pradhan, *India and World War I* (New Delhi: Manohar Publications, 1978), p. 2.

2. Total British and Indian troops sent from India: 1,338,620. Of these 242,607 were British and 1,096,013 were Indian, IOR: L/MIL/17/5/2383, p. 98 and p. 200.

3. IOR: L/MIL/5/738.

4. IOR: L/MIL/17/5/2383; K.G. Saini, 'The Economic Aspects of India's Participation in the First World War', in Ellinwood and Pradhan, eds, *War*, pp. 141–77.

5. IOR: L/MIL/17/2383, pp. 176; 179–86.

6. IOR: L/E/7/1154, file 1229 and file 1221; IOR: L/E/7/1073, Memo, Basu to Holderness, 5 February 1919.

7. Wolpert, *History*, p. 289; *India and the War*, with an introduction by Lord

Sydenham of Combe (London: Hodder & Stoughton, 1915), pp. 63–9; Yusuf Ali, 'India's Rally Round the Flag', *Asiatic Review*, vol. vi, January 1915, pp. 26–33; D.N. Singh, 'The Indian Press and the War', *Asiatic Review*, vol. v, July–November 1914, pp. 396–402.

8.   A.C. Bose, 'Indian Revolutionaries during the First World War. A Study of their Aims and Weaknesses', in Ellinwood and Pradhan, eds, *War*, pp. 109–26.

9.   Yusuf Ali, 'India and the War' and Legislative Council debate, *Asiatic Review*, vol. v, July–November 1914, pp. 407–15, 274; Naoroji in *India and the War*, pp. 68–70.

10.   Quoted in *India and the War*, p. 55.

11.   Jeffrey Greenhut, 'The Imperial Reserve: The Indian Corps on the Western Front, 1914–15', *Journal of Imperial and Commonwealth History*, vol. xii, no. 1, October 1983, p. 54; quoted in Gregory Martin, 'The Influence of Racial Attitudes on British Policy Towards India during the First World War', *Journal of Imperial and Commonwealth History*, vol. xiv, no. 2, January 1986, pp. 92–3.

12.   Massia Bibikova, *Our Indians at Marseilles* (London: 1915); *Brighton Argus*, 2 October 1914. Their letters described their enthusiastic welcome: e.g. IOR: MSS EUR F 143/84, 15 February 1915 and IOR: MSS EUR F 143/926, August 1916.

13.   Lord Hardinge in the House of Lords, July 1917, IOR: L/MIL/17/5/2383, p. 19; Philip Mason, *A Matter of Honour* (London: Macmillan, 1986 Papermac edn), pp. 412–14.

14.   Charles Lucas, ed., *The Empire at War* (London: OUP, 1921–6) vol. v; Mason, *Honour*, pp. 405–43; for casualties, IOR: L/MIL/17/5/2383, p. 176.

15.   IOR: MSS EUR F 170, Gandhi to IO, 14 August 1914; Gandhi, *Autobiography*, pp. 316–18; Wolpert, *History*, pp. 291–2; *Asiatic Review*, vol. v, July–November 1914, pp. 524–6; IOR: MSS EUR F 143/74; IOR: V/24/832, Report, 1916–17; IOR: MSS EUR F 143/66.

16.   PRO: WO 32/8651, Naoroji–WO correspondence and minutes, 1896; PRO: WO 372; Masani, *Naoroji*, pp. 187–8.

17.   Claude was A.G.S. Mahomed's son, PRO: WO 339/66754; the RFC Mahomed was James Kerriman Mahomed's son, *SDN*, 16 January 1935.

18.   Ranbir Singh, *In the Footsteps of Our Legends* (Noida: Book Mates Publishers, 1998), pp. 8–10; Norman Macmillan, *Offensive Patrol* (London: Jarrolds, 1973), p. 70.

19.   A.H. Mead et al., eds, *St Paul's School Registers* (London: 1990), pp. 90 and 103; PRO: WO 339/115198, Roberts to Brancker, 21 February 1917; Roy's brother, Lolit Kumar, who had a similar experience, remained with the HAC in France; PRO: WO 339/108859, Welinkar file.

20.   C. Shores, N. Franks and R. Guest, *Above the Trenches* (Canada: Fortress Publications, 1990), pp. 327–8; PRO: AIR 1/1222/204/5/2634/40 Sqdn Roy is buried within Estevelles Communal Cemetery, Pas de Calais, France.

21.   Mason, *Honour*, pp. 341–61; Ellinwood and Pradhan, eds, *War*, pp.

179–80; David Omissi, *The Sepoy and the Raj* (London: Macmillan Press, 1994), pp. 12–30.

22. Greenhut, *Imperial Reserve*, p. 55.
23. Mulk Raj Anand, *Across the Black Waters* (London: Jonathan Cape, 1940).
24. Report on 12 months' working of the Indian Mail Censorship, by Howell, 7 November, 1915, IOR: L/MIL/5/828, Pt I, and MSS EUR F 143/84. The Extracts and Howell's weekly reports are in the OIOC, the British Library. There are two copies: L/MIL/5/825 series and Walter Lawrence Papers, MSS EUR F 143/83 series.
25. Rozina Visram, 'The First World War and the Indian Soldiers', *Indo-British Review*, vol. xvi, no. 2, June 1989, pp. 17–26; Visram, *Ayahs*, Ch. 6.
26. IOR: L/MIL/5/825, Pt I, Howell's report, 3 February 1915; IOR: MSS EUR F 143/84, reports 31 July 1915 and 9 August 1915; IOR: MSS EUR F 143/90, 13 February 1916; S.D. Pradhan, 'The Sikh Soldier in the First World War', in Ellinwood and Pradhan, eds, *War*, p. 219. For *Komagata Maru* incident and the Canadian immigration policy: Joan M. Jensen, *Passage from India* (Yale University Press, 1988), especially, Chs 3 and 6.
27. IOR: MSS EUR F 143/84, from Faqir Khan, 24 August 1915; IOR: MSS EUR F 143/83, 28 February 1915.
28. IOR: L/MIL/5/828, Pt II, from a Brahmin, 11 September 1915; 23 March and 26 March 1915, and 21 January 1915; IOR: MSS EUR F 143/83, 23 April 1915; 2 March and 19 May 1915.
29. IOR: MSS EUR F 143/84, from Khan Bhadur, 17 June.
30. IOR: L/MIL/5/828, Pt II, Howell's report, 23 January 1915; MSS EUR F 143/83, report for March–June 1915; L/MIL/5/825, Pt I, 23 January 1915.
31. IOR: MSS EUR F 143/83, reports 5 May and 27 May 1915, and from Jemadar Sher Singh, June 1915.
32. Greenhut, *Imperial Reserve*, p. 57; and compare Gordon Corrigan, *Sepoys in the Trenches* (Staplehurst: Spellmount, 1999); IOR: L/MIL/5/828, Pt II, 23 March 1915.
33. IOR: MSS EUR F 143/83, 26 May 1915 from Yusuf Khan and Jalal Khan; from Lal Chand, May 1915; from Himal Chand, June 1915; Ratan Singh, June 1915 and Report 29 May 1915.
34. IOR: MSS EUR F 143/66, 17 March 1915; Greenhut, *Imperial Reserve*, p. 56.
35. IOR: MSS EUR F 143/92, 8 March 1915.
36. IOR: L/MIL/5/828, Pt II, 3 April 1918; IOR: L/MIL/5/825, Pt I, 19 January 1915; IOR: MSS EUR F 143/83, 26 February 1915.
37. IOR: L/MIL/5/825, Pt I; IOR: MSS EUR F 143/83, May 1915.
38. IOR: L/MIL/5/828, Pt II, letters 23 March 1915.
39. IOR: MSS EUR F 143/83, May 1915; 10 May and 17 May 1915; 25 May 1915.
40. IOR: MSS EUR F 143/84, from Haider Khan, 20 July 1915; IOR: MSS EUR F 143/85, from Havildar Yusuf Khan, 25 August 1915; Omissi, *Sepoy*, p. 118.
41. IOR: MSS EUR F 143/83, Censor's report, 1 May 1915; IOR: MSS EUR F

143/88, letter December 1915.

42. IOR: MSS EUR F 143/83, 23 April 1915 and May 1915; IOR: MSS EUR F 143/86, 22 September 1915.

43. A parcel of *bhailawa* was discovered. Experiments showed that the juice produced irritation and sores on the skin. IOR: MSS EUR F 143/83, May 1915; IOR: MSS EUR F 143/86, 14 October 1915, and IOR: L/MIL/5/828, Pt II, 12 January 1916.

44. IOR: MSS EUR F 143/83, 1 March, 3 March and 13 May 1915; 27 May 1915; Howell's report, 29 May 1915.

45. IOR: MSS EUR F 143/86, 6 October 1915; IOR: L/MIL/5/825, Pt I, from a British ASC Motor driver, 20 January 1915, and the Censor's comment.

46. IOR: L/MIL/5/825, Pt I, Censor's comment, 26 December 1914; letter 21 January 1915.

47. IOR: MSS EUR F 143/90, 2 February 1916; IOR: MSS EUR F 143/84, 25 June 1915; IOR: L/MIL/5/828, Pt II, 31 March 1915.

48. IOR: MSS EUR F 143/88, 1 December 1915; IOR: MSS EUR F 143/84, May 1915; IOR: MSS EUR F 143/86, 21 October 1915.

49. IOR: MSS EUR F 143/83, 3 March 1915; IOR: L/MIL/5/826, Pt I, 10 November 1915; IOR: L/MIL/5/828, Pt II, 22 January 1916; IOR: MSS EUR F 143/84, August 1915.

50. IOR: MSS EUR F 143/92, 5 September 1916.

51. Ellinwood and Pradhan, *War*, p. 185.

52. *Neuve Chapelle: India's Memorial in France, 1914–1918* (London: Hodder & Stoughton, 1927); IOR: L/MIL/17/5/2383, pp. 264–5.

53. Mir Dast's interview in the *Times of India*, reprinted in *Brighton and Hove Gazette*, 22 January 1916; IOR: MSS EUR F 143/83, 15 March 1915; Pradhan, *Sikh Soldier*, p. 220.

54. IOR: MSS EUR F 143/83, 13 March 1915; IOR: L/MIL/5/825, Pt I, 15 January 1915.

55. IOR: L/MIL/5/828, Pt II, 23 March 1915; and 22 January 1916.

56. IOR: MSS EUR F 143/83, 20 May; IOR: MSS EUR F 143/84, from Mohammed Ali Bey.

57. IOR: L/MIL/5/828, Pt II, 8 April 1915; IOR: L/MIL/5/825, Pt I, from a Hindu student, 28 January 1915.

58. V. Chirol in *Asiatic Review*, vol. v, July–November 1914, p. 274; German soldier in *Frankfurter Zeitung*, quoted in Mason, *Honour*, p. 413.

59. In V.G. Kiernan, *European Empires from Conquest to Collapse, 1815–1960* (London: Fontana Paperbacks, 1982), pp. 185–6; IOR: MSS EUR F 143/86, 22 May 1915.

60. In Greenhut, *Imperial Reserve*, p. 61; IOR: L/MIL/5/825, Pt I, note by Howell, 23 January 1915; Martin, *Racial Attitudes*, pp. 99–110.

61. Crewe to Hardinge, 19 November 1914, quoted in Martin, *Racial Attitudes*, p. 94. There were hospitals for Indian wounded in France.

62. IOR: MSS EUR F 143/66; *The Indiaman*, 17 December 1915, copy in IOR: MSS EUR F 143/96; Janet Gooch, *A History of the Brighton General Hospital* (London: Phillimore & Co., 1980.

63. IOR: MSS EUR F 143/74.

64. IOR: MSS EUR F 143/66; IOR: MSS EUR F 143/81, Report on Indian Section, Royal Victoria Hospital, Netley.

65. IOR: MSS EUR F 143/94.

66. IOR: L/MIL/5/825, Part I, note by Howell, 23 January 1915; IOR: MSS EUR F 143/66, Fitzgerald to Lawrence, 21 July 1915.

67. Colonel Arthur Lee, MP, to Lord Kitchener, 13 December 1914; S. White, 'Hindu Cremations in Britain', in P.C. Jupp and G. Howarth, eds, *The Changing Face of Death* (London: Macmillan, 1997), p. 135.

68. Hardinge to Lawrence, 14 April 1915, in Martin, *Racial Attitudes*, pp. 93–4.

69. IOR: MSS EUR F 143/80, Mosque at Woking, 1915. Before 1915, Muslim burials took place at the Muslim civilian cemetery in Brookwood. Nineteen soldiers were buried at the Horsell Common cemetery between 1917 and 1920. In 1923, they were re-buried at Brookwood. For the Ghat at Patcham, IOR: MSS EUR F 143/81, and *The Times*, 16 October 1915; for the Netley Ghat, *The Indiaman*, 15 January 1915, MSS EUR F 143/96.

70. Quoted in White, *Cremations*, p. 136, on which this interpretation of crematoria law is based. For the picture of the Chatri at Patcham today, see Visram, *Indians*, p. 43.

71. IOR MSS EUR F 143/66, MacLeod to Lawrence, 1 September 1915; IOR: MSS EUR F 143/94.

72. IOR: MSS EUR F 143/66, MacLeod to Lawrence, 30 March 1915; IOR: MSS EUR F 143/94, p. 4.

73. IOR: L/MIL/5/825, Pt I, Howell, 16 January 1915; Musgrave, *Brighton*, p. 371.

74. IOR: MSS EUR F 143/83, 30 April 1915 and 5 May 1915; IOR: MSS EUR F 143/ 87, 10 November 1915; IOR: L/MIL/5/828, Pt I, 10 January 1916; IOR: MSS EUR F 143/66, Fitzgerald to Lawrence, 14 July 1915.

75. IOR: L/MIL/5/828, Pt I, 13 August 1915; see also IOR: MSS EUR F 143/75, *Akbar i Jang.*

76. IOR: MSS EUR F 143/77, 5 July 1915.

77. IOR: L/MIL/5/825, Pt I, Howell to Barrow, 15 January 1915; Howell to Barrow, 3 February 1915; IOR: MSS EUR F 143/86, Howell's report, 11 October 1915.

78. IOR: MSS EUR F 143/66, 'The Visit of Convalescent Indian Troops to London', Major P.G. Shewell, October/November 1915. The total cost is not given. But for 1,752 individuals, exclusive of railway warrants for the Underground, the India Office spent £468.11.3 out of Indian revenues.

79. IOR: MSS EUR F 143/66, R.C. Volkers, 14 October 1915.

80. IOR: L/MIL/5/738, Ampthill to Bayley, 15 October 1917.

81. IOR: MSS EUR F 143/80, Lawrence to Kitchener, 'Arrangements for Indian Sick and Wounded in England and France', Report to the Secretary for War, 8 March 1916; see also statement by the Mulvie, Sadr-ud-Din, 27 August 1915.

82. IOR: MSS EUR F 111/160, Curzon to Hamilton, 15 November 1901.

83. Nawab Nazim of Bengal, too, was similarly condemned, Visram, *Ayahs*, pp. 174–5 and 176.

84. Lawrence to Hardinge, 18 March 1915, quoted in Martin, *Racial Attitudes*, p. 94; IOR: MSS EUR F 143/83, report by Howell, 19 June 1915. See also K. Ballhatchet, *Race, Sex and Class Under The Raj* (Weidenfeld and Nicolson, 1980).

85. At Barton over 5,000 patients had passed through the Home; at the Kitchener, 4,000 cases had been admitted, IOR: MSS EUR F 143/66 and 143/82; IOR: L/MIL/17/5/2016.

86. IOR: L/MIL/7/17316, Barrow to the War Office, 29 October 1914; Swain to Roberts, 6 November 1914.

87. IOR: L/MIL/7/17316, 29 October 1914, 3 November 1914 and reference paper signed Charles Havelock, 28 October.

88. IOR: L/MIL/7/17316, minute in connection with WO letter, 24 June 1915, and letter 17 June 1915 from Hewett, ISF Chairman.

89. *BH*, 26 December 1914; IOR: L/MIL/7/17316, 17 June 1915 and marginal minute in the Reference Paper, 30 June 1915; IOR: MSS EUR F 143/66, 7 January 1915 from Sharman, Commander, Netley Hospital.

90. IOR: L/MIL/7/17316, 4 June 1915; Joyce Collins, *Dr Brighton's Indian Patients* (Brighton Books, 1997), p. 21.

91. IOR: MSS EUR F 143/66, Broacha to Dunlop-Smith, 2 July 1915; Visram, *Ayahs*, p. 129, repeats Broacha's error.

92. IOR: L/MIL/7/17316, Proceedings of the Committee of the ISF, attached to Reference Paper, Military Department 25 June 1915; IOR: MSS EUR F 143/66, Broacha to Dunlop-Smith, 2 July 1915.

93. IOR: L/MIL/7/17316, Proceedings of the Committee of the ISF, attached to Reference Paper, Military Department 25 June 1915; letter 13 June 1915 from W.E.W. Bedford, Surgeon General, Southern Command to the WO, and letter 17 June from Hewett.

94. IOR: MSS EUR F 143/66, Dunlop-Smith to Lawrence, 12 January 1915; Lawrence to Keogh, 14 January 1915.

95. IOR: MSS EUR F 143/66, Holderness to Lawrence, 14 January 1915; Keogh to Lawrence, 15 January 1915 and Lawrence to Keogh, 14 January 1915.

96. IOR: MSS EUR F 143/66, Dunlop-Smith to Lawrence, 12 January 1915; Holderness to Lawrence, 2 February 1915.

97. IOR: MSS EUR F 143/83, report by Howell, 19 June 1915.

98. IOR: MSS EUR F 143/84, reports from Howell, 26 June 1915. IOR: MSS EUR F 143/90, 28 February 1916. Daba Chand (17 July 1915), Ramnath Singh (2 August 1915), and Dhunji Bhoy (note 2 August 1915), were seen by an officer and had to apologise for their letters, IOR: L/MIL/5/828, Pt I; from a Parsi, 23 January 1915, IOR: L/MIL/5, Pt I.

99. Quoted in Martin, *Racial Attitudes*, p. 94.

100. *BH*, 5 December 1915; Musgrave, *Brighton*, p. 371.

101. IOR: MSS EUR F 143/94, p. 13; IOR: MSS EUR F 143/66, report from Chief Constable Gentle, to Lawrence, 31 January 1915.

102. Quoted in Martin, *Racial Attitudes*, p. 94.

103. IOR: MSS EUR F 143/66, confidential, from White to Barrow, 14 December 1915.

104. IOR: MSS EUR F 143/82 and L/MIL/17/5/2016, A Report on the Kitchener Indian Hospital by Seton.

105. Testimony of Mrs Stiebel, wife of Lt Charles Stiebel, IMS, in Gooch, *History*, p. 106.

106. IOR: MSS EUR F 143/82 and L/MIL/17/5/2016; IOR: MSS EUR F 143/87, 16 November 1915 from Godbole giving details of the regime at the Kitchener Hospital.

107. IOR: MSS EUR F 143/82 and L/MIL/17/5/2016; IOR: MSS EUR F 143/85, August 1915.

108. *B&HG*, 17 July 1915.

109. IOR: MSS EUR F 143/66, 14 December; IOR: MSS EUR F 143/94; and MSS EUR F 143/66, report dated 11 July 1915.

110. IOR: MSS EUR F 143/66, Neve to Lawrence, 30 November 1915; Censor's reports 19 June 1915, IOR: MSS EUR F 143/83 and dated 31 July 1915, IOR: MSS EUR F 143/84; Seton's comments, IOR: MSS EUR F 143/82 and in L/MIL/5/828, Pt I, dated 2 August 1915.

111. Gooch, *History*, p. 109; IOR: MSS EUR F 143/96, signed 'Justitia', in *The Indiaman*, 30 April 1915; Howell's report 31 July 1915, IOR: MSS EUR F 143/84 and dated 11 September 1915, IOR: MSS EUR F 143/85.

112. For a selection of letters, see, IOR: MSS EUR F 143/83–87 and IOR: L/MIL/5/828, Pt I.

113. IOR: MSS EUR F 143/88, Mithan Lal, 2 December 1915.

114. IOR: MSS EUR F 143/87, from Godbole, 16 November 1915; IOR: MSS EUR F 143/89, 14 December 1915 and Censor's report, 2 January 1916.

115. *BH*, 13 March 1915, 5 December 1914; *Evening Herald*, 8 January 1916.

116. IOR: L/MIL/5/825, 23 January 1915 and 16 January 1915.

117. IOR: L/MIL/5/825, letter originally in English and undated; IOR: MSS EUR F 143/87, 1 November 1915.

118. IOR: L/MIL/5/828, Pt II, 13 March and 28 March 1916; IOR: MSS EUR F 143/84, 23 and 27 June 1915.

119. IOR: L/MIL/5/828, Pt II, 28 March 1915, 3 January 1916, 6 August 1916; and 6 January 1917, in L/MIL/5/828, Pt III.

120. IOR: MSS EUR F 143/90, letter 14 February 1916; IOR: L/MIL/5/828, Pt II, letters 3 April 1916, 2 January 1916.

121. IOR: L/MIL/5/828 Pt II, 27 December 1916, and the Censor's comment 4 January 1917.

122. IOR: L/MIL/5/828, Pt II, 16 January 1917; IOR: MSS EUR F 143/89, 5 January 1916.

123. IOR: MSS EUR F, 143/83, 4 June 1914, from a Pathan, Subedar Mahammad Azim; 15 May, from a Punjabi Muslim, Havildar Abdul Rahman; and from Bishan Singh, 14 May 1915; IOR: L/MIL/5/828, Pt II, 15 April 1915.

124. IOR: MSS EUR F 143/84, 17 July 1915 and MSS EUR F 143/85, 31

August 1915; IOR: MSS EUR F143/83, report 29 May 1915.

125. IOR: MSS EUR F 143/83, 9 June; IOR: MSS EUR F 143/92, 16 March 1916; IOR: L/MIL/5/828, Pt III, 20 January 1917.

126. IOR: L/MIL/5/825, Pt I, 12 February 1915; see also IOR: MSS EUR F 143/84, 18 July 1915, and L/MIL/5/828, Pt II, 26 June 1916.

127. IOR: L/MIL/5/828, Pt II and Pt III, 20 March 1916; see also 13 March 1916 and 11 March 1916; 17 January 1917.

128. IOR: L/MIL/5/828, Pt II, 27 May 1918; IOR: MSS EUR F 143/90, 7 February 1916; IOR: MSS EUR F 143/88, report 18 December 1915.

129. IOR: L/MIL/5/828, Pt II, 12 February 1915.

130. IOR: L/MIL/5/828, Pt II, 17 April 1915, and IOR: MSS EUR F 143/87, 16 November 1915.

131. IOR: MSS EUR F 143/92, 16 September 1916; Pradhan, *Sikh Soldier*, in Ellinwood and Pradhan, eds, *War*, p. 222.

132. IOR: L/MIL/5/ 828, Pt II, 3 July 1916 and 9 August 1916.

133. IOR: MSS EUR F 143/87, from a Sikh, 1915 and MSS EUR F 143/85 from a Dogra, 6 September 1915.

134. IOR: MSS EUR F 143/86, 26 September 1915.

135. IOR: MSS EUR F 143/89, 19 January 1916.

136. IOR: MSS EUR F 143/92, 26 August 1916; IOR: MSS EUR F 143/86, 30 September 1915.

137. Quoted in Pradhan, *Sikh Soldier*, p. 224, in Ellinwood and Pradhan, eds, *War*.

7 CITIZENS OR ALIENS?

1.   IOR: L/E/7/809, file 5454, BoT to IO, 28 December 1914; IOR: L/E/7/1377, file 536.

2.   IOR: L/E/7/1073, file 2391, 23 May and 24 July 1916; Handbill, No. 378, August 1916.

3.   IOR: L/P&J/6/1462, file 4505, 2 November 1916, Lash to IO; *Stratford Express*, 11 August and 22 September 1917; IOR: L/E/7/1073, file 2391, from Lever Bros, 25 September and 11 October 1916; BoT, 21 October 1916.

4.   IOR: L/E/7/1073, file 2391, from Lever Bros, 11 October 1916 and BoT to Lever Bros, 14 August 1917.

5.   IOR: L/E/7/1073, file 2391, from MMO, Greenock, 25 October 1917; from John Walker, 16 January 1918.

6.   IOR: L/E/7/1073, file 2391, from Basu to Holderness, 5 February 1919; from MMO, Greenock, to BoT, 25 February 1918; IO to BoT, 4 March, 30 July 1918 and minutes.

7.   For a list of lascars discharged in Britain, see IOR: L/E/7/1103, file 8231.

8.   Jacqueline Jenkinson, 'The 1919 Race Riots in Britain: A Survey', in R. Lotz and I. Pegg, *Under The Imperial Carpet* (Crawley: Rabbit Press, 1986), pp. 182–207; Roy May and Robin Cohen, 'The Interaction Between Race and Colonialism: A Case Study of the Liverpool Race Riots of 1919',

Race and Class, vol. xvi, no. 2, 1974, pp. 111–26; Jacqueline Jenkinson, 'The Glasgow Race Disturbances of 1919', *Immigrants & Minorities*, vol. iv, no. 2, July 1985, pp. 43–67; Neil Evans, 'The South Wales Race Riots of 1919', *Llafur*, 3, 1980, pp. 5–29; Fryer, *Staying Power*, pp. 298–311; PRO: HO 45/11017/377969.

9. May and Cohen, 'Colonialism', p. 115.

10. From a 'Philipino', 11 June 1919, in May and Cohen, 'Colonialism', p. 115; Fryer, *Staying Power*, pp. 298–311; *The Times*, 30 May 1919.

11. May and Cohen, 'Colonialism', p. 113; *Western Mail*, 13 June 1919; *DN*, 16 June 1919; *Manchester Guardian*, 16 June 1919.

12. IOR: L/E/7/1073, file 2391, Basu to Holderness, 5 February 1919; IO to Marine Department, BoT, 13 April 1921; quoted in May and Cohen, 'Colonialism', p. 119.

13. Dunlop, 'Labourers', pp. 49, 51.

14. *GH*, 5 March 1920.

15. *Hansard*, 30 June 1920, cols 432–7 and 7 July 1920, col. 1418; *GH*, 1 July 1920.

16. *Motherwell Times*, 21 January 1921.

17. *MT*, 11 February 1921; IOR: L/P&J/6/1462, file 4505, Lash to IO, 2 November 1916.

18. *MT*, 11 February 1921; *MT*, 4 March 1921 and 11 March 1921.

19. *GH*, 12 February 1921; *MT*, 11 February 1921.

20. PRO: HO 45/11017/377969, Assistant Constable Liverpool, 10 June 1919; Chief Constable Cardiff City Police to HO, telephone message, 12 June 1919, letters 13 and 18 June 1919.

21. PRO: HO 45/11017/377969: HO to Chief Constable Liverpool, 17 June 1919 and draft letter to Cardiff; minutes on HO Memo, 13 June 1919, signed HRS; Marwood to HO 14 June 1919; Note on the Conference, 19 June 1919; Ministry of Shipping to HO, 28 June 1919; letter to Salford, Liverpool, Cardiff, Hull, South Shields, London and Glasgow, 25 June 1919.

22. PRO: HO 45/11017/377969, letter to Salford, Liverpool, etc., 25 June 1919; Conference Report; draft letter June 1919, from HO to NSFU panel.

23. PRO: HO 45/11017/377969, Principal Naval Transport Office, Cardiff to MoS, 15 July 1919; Jacqueline Jenkinson: 'Repatriation to the West Indies: A Repercussion of the 1919 Race Riots in Britain', *Inter Arts*, Spring 1987, pp. 11–13.

24. *GH*, 3 March 1921.

25. IOR: L/E/7/1103, file 8231, Oliver to IO, 16 March 1921; letter from nine Indians and Adenese, 20 July 1921.

26. IOR: L/E/7/1103, file 8231, report C.S. Gilchrist, MMO Swansea, 23 July 1921; note by Baines, 25 March 1922.

27. IOR: L/E/7/1103, file 8231, Oliver to IO, 16 March 1921; Memo 1/4/21; see also IOR: L/E/7/936, file 2435, from IO to CO, 26 May 1921.

28. PRO: HO/45/11897, Bosanquet, King George Fund for Sailors, 10 June 1921. Of the 1,110 British seamen, 710 were Indians, Arabs and Somalis;

250 West Indians, and the rest from West Africa; see also IOR: L/E/7/1103, file 8231, NSFU to IO, 25 February 1921.

29. PRO: HO/45/11897, Bosanquet 10 June 1921, and correspondence in the same file; IOR: L/E/7/1103, file 8231, Oliver to IO, 9 June 1921, on behalf of Mrs Mahomed Ahmed and other Cardiff boarding-house masters; minute by Baines, 16 June 1921.

30. PRO: HO 45/11897, Cardiff Town Clerk, 21 April 1921 and undated from the Immigration Officer; HO minutes, April 1921, and draft letter May 1921; Bosanquet 10 June 1921. By then appeals for funds for relief were being rebuffed both by the CO and IO.

31. IOR: L/E/7/1103, file 8231, Report on unemployed Aden seamen, 7 July 1921.

32. IOR: L/E/7/1103, files 8230 and 8231; see also L/E/7/1102, file 8227; IOR: L/E/7/1098, file 6990.

33. IOR: L/E/7/1103, file 8231, minute Baines, 16 June 1921; Report 7 July 1921. See also L/E/7/1103, file 8230 and L/E/71102, file 8277.

34. IOR: L/E/7/1103, file 8230, telegram from Aden, 1 October 1921. Initially, of the 430 on board, reportedly, 80 or 90 were Indians, IOR: L/E/7/1103, file 8231. See also PRO: HO 45/11897.

35. IOR: L/E/7/1103, file 8231; IOR: L/E/9/962, note of meeting at the BoT, 5 May 1930; and compare Dunlop, 'Labourers', p. 51.

36. For details: PRO: HO 45/11897, 23 January 1920; CO to Sir John Pedder, 15 September 1920; memo IO, 4 March 1920; BoT to Consul-General at Marseilles, September 20 1920; Arab seamen arriving in UK, letter to W. Haldane Porter, 4 December 1920; Circular SI 284, 31 December 1920, signed W. Haldane Porter, Chief Inspector Alien's Branch. See also IOR: L/E/7/936 file 2435, from Société Internationale de Philologie, Sciences et Beaux-Arts, to FO, 15 November 1920 on behalf of 25 Arab sailors, and BoT's response, 26 November 1920; Circulars in the same file.

37. PRO: HO 45/12314.

38. IOR: L/E/9/953, draft letter, n d, IO to GOI, and memo dated 1942, signed M.J. Clarson.

39. IOR: L/E/9/953, Aliens and Nationality Committee Memo No. 185, 9 November 1925; PRO: HO 45/12314, HO to CO 14 August 1925. For extension of 'Lascar Articles' to 'Adenese': IOR: L/E/7/1098, file 7339, IO to BoT, 12 November 1921 and minute; IOR: L/E/7/936, file 2435, IO to BoT, 29 July 1920 and minute; letter from GOI, 27 December 1922.

40. IOR: L/E/9/953, HO confidential letter to Chief Constables, 23 March 1925.

41. IOR: L/E.9/953 and PRO: HO 45/12314, HO to CO, 14 August 1925, signed Blackwell.

42. Fryer, *Staying Power*, p. 356; Kenneth Little, *Negroes in Britain* (London: Routledge and Kegan Paul, 1972 edn), pp. 84–9; Ron Ramdin, *The Making of the Black Working Class in Britain* (London: Wildwood House, 1987), pp. 74–7.

43. Colin Holmes, *John Bull's Island* (London: Macmillan Education, 1988),

p. 154; Paul B. Rich, 'Philanthropic Racism: The Liverpool University Settlement, the Anti-Slavery Society and the Issue of "Half-Caste" Children, 1919–51', *Immigrants & Minorities*, vol. 3, 1984, p. 70.

44. This questioning is based on a reappraisal of the official PRO and OIOC documents. See, Laura Tabili, 'The Construction of Racial difference in Twentieth-Century Britain: The Special Restriction (Coloured Alien Seamen) Order, 1925', *Journal of British Studies*, 33, January 1994, pp. 54–98, and *We Ask*, Chapter 6; Tony Lane, 'The Political Imperatives of Bureaucracy and Empire: The Case of the Coloured Alien Seamen Order, 1925', *Immigrants and Minorities*, vol. 13, nos 2–3, July/November 1994, pp. 104–29; Gordon and Reilly, 'Guestworkers', pp. 75–6. And also, Marika Sherwood, 'Race, Nationality and Employment among Lascar Seamen, 1660–1945', *New Community*, vol. 17, no. 2, January 1991, pp. 234–5; Paul B. Rich, *Race and Empire in British Politics* (Cambridge University Press, 1990 edn), pp. 122–30.

45. PRO: HO 45/12314, internal minute, signed E.N. Cooper, 14/2/25; IOR: L/E/9/953 and PRO: HO 45/13392, Haldane Porter's explanation at the Conference on 13 December 1926, that 'the accumulation of coloured seamen … led the Board of Trade to press for stricter control of new arrivals'.

46. IOR: L/E/9/953 and PRO: HO 45/12314, 14 August 1925, signed Blackwell.

47. PRO: HO 45/11897, January 1923; IOR: L/E/7/936, file 2435.

48. IOR: L/E/7/1103, file 8231, IO memo, 16 June 1921.

49. IOR: L/E/9/953, *SS Tenbergen*, 7 March 1925; IOR: V/26/750/4, Native Seamen Committee Report, 1884, outlining the system operating at Bombay, recommended its adoption at Calcutta; IOR: L/E/9/971, IO minute, 1/12/1943, confirms the practice.

50. IOR: L/E/9/953, *SS Tenbergen* case; IO to HO, 2 July 1925 and minute. PRO: HO 45/12314, letter on *SS Tenbergen* case, 22 May 1925, has been destroyed. Case of Porah Deen in same file.

51. IOR: L/E/7/1390, file 2503, rejection slip signed by Thomas, 1 April 1925, and extract from the report, 2 April 1925; Rowley, to FO, 15 April 1925; HO to FO, 21 May 1925; report from Thomas, 2 April 1925.

52. IOR: L/E/7/1390, file 2503, minute 4 June 1925 and from IO to GOI, 11 June 1925; minute by E.J. Turner, 5 June 1925; IOR: L/E/9/972, HO to A.N. Rucker, 21 October 1935, for the phrase.

53. IOR: L/E/7/1390, file 2503, IO minute by Turner, 5 June 1925.

54. IOR: L/E/9/953, Mary Fazel, 7 September 1925.

55. IOR: L/E/9/953, 14 September 1925; application for passport was submitted on 16 September 1925 and verification of birth was finally received on 24 August 1926; undated from Mary Fazel to IO, and reply, 27 August 1926.

56. IOR: L/E/7/1494, file 1182, from Fitzgerald and Gani, 11 February 1927; FO to IO, 12 March 1927 and HO to IO, 24 March 1927; Gani's Registration Book, 1920.

57. Fryer, *Staying Power*, p. 356; PRO: HO 45/12314, Chief Inspector Aliens Branch, Conference Memo, 3 April 1925, attended by Chief Constables, Superintendents MMO and Immigration staff, Liverpool, 2 April 1925.

58. IOR: L/E/7/1494, file 1182, Gani, 11 February 1927; both were sent to the Asiatic Home on their arrival in March, from where, in May 1927, Gani worked his passage back.

59. IOR: L/E/7/1465, file 5170, letters 6 and 29 August 1926 to India HC; copy of notes by Shipping Master, Calcutta, 9 November 1926; from E.S. Davies, 10 August 1926; IO to HO, 14 January 1927.

60. IOR: L/E/7/1438, file 395, Gloag to HO and IO, 20 January 1926.

61. PRO: HO 45/12314, report from Glasgow City police, 10 September 1925; letter from Chief Constable, 11 September 1925 and HO internal note, 'its extension elsewhere also is about ripe for consideration'.

62. IOR: L/E/7/1438, file 395, S.W. Harris, HO to IO, 19 February 1926; Report from Glasgow City police, 11 February 1926. Gloag's 'further letter' to HO with 56 names of his clients is missing. Curiously, the entire Gloag correspondence in the PRO file, mentioned only as a minute, has been weeded out, PRO: HO 45/12314.

63. IOR: L/E/7/1438, file 395, Report 11 February 1926, Glasgow City police; IOR: L/E/9/953 and PRO: HO 45/12314, 17 February 1926, to IO.

64. IOR: L/E/9/953 and PRO: HO 45/12314, GIU to IO, 17 February 1926. The GIU is listed in the students' societies section of Glasgow University Calendar only from the academic year 1926/7 onwards. But it pre-dated its inclusion in the calendar; its first mention in surveillance reports comes in a report dated 23 January 1923, which lists its office bearers and their length of residence in Scotland, some as long as 10 years, IOR: L/P&J/12/159.

65. *Negro World*, 30 January 1926, in HO 45/12314; IOR: L/E/9/953, *New India* reproduced GIU's letter to IO, with details of Glasgow Indians and the 1925 Order.

66. The list of 63 Indians is in PRO: HO 45/12314 and IOR: L/E/9/953.

67. IOR: L/E/7/1438, file 395, HO to IO, 19 February 1926 and to Gloag, of the same date; PRO: HO 45/12314, HO minute, 2 March 1926 and draft letter to GIU, 16 April 1926; IOR: L/E/9/953, HO to GIU, 26 April 1926.

68. IOR: L/E/9/953, Parliamentary Notice, 14 April 1926; HO to Wardlaw-Milne, 15 April 1926 and Parliamentary reply 28 April 1926. The Wardlaw-Milne correspondence and Parliamentary notice have been weeded in the PRO file, HO minute 14/5/26, HO 45/12314; and *Hansard*, 1926, vol. 194, cols 195–6, 2030.

69. IOR: L/E/9/953, GIU letter in *New India*, *Forward* and editorial statement; GOI to IO, 1 April 1926; IO to HO, 3 May 1926; HO to IO, 1 June 1926 and minutes, and IO to GOI, including unofficial letter 28 June 1926. Also in PRO: HO 45/12314.

70. IOR: L/E/9/953, IO minute, signed Donaldson, 22 April 1926; IO to GOI, 22 June 1926 and private letter to GOI, 28 June 1926; PRO: HO 45/12314, HO to IO, 1 June 1926.

71. *Workers' Life*, 13 May 1927, in IOR: L/E/9/953.

72. IOR: L/E/9/953, GIU to *Forward* and *New India.*

73. IOR: L/E/9/953, 2 July 1925, signed L.G. Walton, and minutes.

74. IOR: L/E/9/953, minutes and confidential letter, 12 December 1925, IO to GOI. See also minutes, 5 November 1925 and Memo No. 186, Aliens and Nationality Committee, 13 November 1925; PRO: HO 45/12314, memo, 24 September 1925, signed Cooper.

75. IOR: L/E/9/953, IO to GOI, 12 December 1925; Memo No. 186, 13 November 1925; HO to Chief Constables, 7 December 1925 and IO to HO, 4 May 1926. For application form and Certificate, see IO to HO, 27 March 1926, PRO: HO 45/12314.

76. IOR: L/E/9/954 and PRO: HO 45/14299, Pt 2, memo of an Inter-Departmental Conference, 12 March 1931.

77. IOR: L/E/9/962, Adams to Baines, IO, 25 November 1930; IO to GOI 26 November 1931.

78. IOR: L/E/9/962, Adams to Baines, 12 February 1931 and IO to GOI, 26 November 1931; PRO: HO 45/14299, Pt 1, HO to India H C, 4 July 1930. For cases of cessation of the issue of certificates, see HO minutes, 23 June 1930, in same file.

79. Lane, 'Bureaucracy', p. 104.

80. IOR: L/E/9/953, 9 November 1925, Memo No. 185; IOR: L/E/9/954, for July 1931 returns and IOR: L/E/9/972, returns 1936–9.

81. IOR: L/P&J/12/234, minutes 15 and 16 June 1927; IOR: L/E/9/954, clarification on the position of BPP in Britain, Adams to Baines, 25 November 1930; IOR: L/E/9/955, Aliens Department to Waterlow and Sons, solicitors, 18 July 1935, in reply to query on behalf of the Indians from Mirpur district, which confirmed that under 'section 27 of British Nationality Act and Status of Aliens Act, 1914, a BPP is an alien and not a British subject'; and internal minute, if BoT replied to Waterlow and Sons, re BPP being aliens, they would commit themselves to 'a principle of discrimination'.

82. IOR: L/E/9/953, minute signed, M.J. Clarson, 1942.

83. IOR: L/E/9/962, BoT to IO, following a deputation from the NUS to BoT and HO, 15 April 1930; report Immigration Officer, Port of Liverpool, signed P.R. Fudge, 27 October 1930; report CID, Special Branch Liverpool, signed J. Lawson, 26 November 1930 and report signed George Wallace; Adams to IO, 12 February 1931; PRO: HO 45/14299 Pt 2, HO, signed Cooper, to Hoskins, BoT, 15 April 1931.

84. IOR: L/E/9//962, report signed Fudge, 27 October 1930; report signed Lawson on the role of Ethel Mohamed, wife of Noah Mohamed, tea-shop owner, 16 November 1930; note of a meeting at the BoT, attended by representatives from IO, HO, India HC, 5 May 1930; MMO Liverpool to BoT, 5 December 1929; complaint from the Hall Line to BoT, 30 July 1930.

85. PRO: HO 45/14299 Pt 2, Cooper to Hoskins, BoT, 15 April 1931 and to Adams, India HC, 24 April 1931.

86. PRO: HO 45/14299, Pt 1, HO minute, 23 June 1930; applications then

received 'closer scrutiny', IOR: L/E/9/962, India HC to HO, 5 November 1930; BoT circular to LTOs, 26 August 1930.

87. IOR: L/E/9/955, minute, signed J.R. Gibson, 12/4/1935; IOR: L/E/9/972, Ghulam Rasul correspondence, March–October 1933; minute, signed, Baines, 19 May 1933.

88. IOR: L/E/9/954, Adams to Robinson, 11 March 1929.

89. IOR: L/E/9/962, HO *Police Bulletin*, Notice May 1930.

90. IOR: L/E/9/962, report from Liverpool, signed Fudge, 27 October 1930; CID Special Branch, signed Lawson, 26 November 1930; PRO: HO 45/14299, Pt 1, from Brocklebank Ltd, 29 July 1930, and P. Henderson Ltd, 25 July 1930.

91. IOR: L/E/9/962, Adams to IO, 12 February 1931; PRO: HO 45/14299, Pt 1, Ellerman and Bucknall Steamship Co. to BoT, 23 July 1930; Mercantile Marine Department to Cooper, 14 October 1930; IOR: L/E/9/962, BoT to IO, 14 October 1930; BoT to IO, 6 March 1931.

92. C.B.A. Behrens, *Merchant Shipping and the Demands of War* (London: HM Stationery Office and Longmans, Green & Co., 1955), p. 179; IOR: L/E/9/962, India HC, signed Montgomery to GOI, dated 26 November 1931; GOI to Secretaries of the Government of Madras etc., and to IO, 31 May 1932, and Notice of Warning.

93. IOR: L/P&J/12/645, IPI to Silver, 29 April 1943; Conference Report, 25 March 1943; cable IO to GOI, 19 October 1943 and telegram 20 October 1943; IOR: L/P&J/12/630, IPI to Silver, 5 October 1944 and minute, 9 October 1944 signed Wood; IPI to Silver, paper on desertions, 5 January 1945 and note dated 5 January 1945; John Barnes and David Nicholson, *The Empire at Bay* (London: Hutchinson, 1988), diary entry, 12 December 1944, p. 1022, gives Amery's reaction: 'I shall not regret their departure.'

94. PRO: MT 9/2737, British Shipping Assistance Bill.

95. IOR: L/E/9/955, Qayum to IO, 3 April 1935; Mohamed to IO, 8 and 22 February 1935; Bhader to IO, 6 March 1935; Mohamed Star [sic] 9 May 1935; Waterlow and Sons, solicitor, 9 July 1935.

96. Tabili, *We Ask*, p. 158. Alley's background is disputed: IPI described him as 'ex-Bengali seaman', but associates doubted he was a Muslim, see IOR: L/P&J/12/630, Indian Organisations in the UK, A Review 1942–3, 19 November 1943; Qureshi in Adams, *Seven Seas*, p. 158; Anant Ram, *Reminiscences of a Panjabi Migrant in Coventry* (typescript of interview by A. Chandan and D.S. Tatla, 1991). I am grateful to Amarjit Chandan for a copy.

97. Tabili, *We Ask*, pp. 158–9; IOR: L/P&J/12/373.

98. IOR: L/P&J/12/384; MRC: MSS 292/655/6 for Conference circular. No report of the conference has been traced. However, IOR: L/P&J/12/452, Misc 8, 1 August 1939, suggests a conference at Transport House organised by Menon.

99. IOR: L/E/9/955, Mehta's statement to the *Statesman*, 2 May 1935; extract from the Trade Union Record (Bombay) July and August 1935; extract from Indian Legislative Assembly, 6 September 1935.

100. IOR: L/E/9/955, Star [sic] to IO, 9 May 1935; Parliamentary Debates, 2 April 1935; *DT*, 2 April 1935.

101. IOR; L/E/9/955, Adams to IO, 15 April 1935.

102. IOR: L/E/9/955, report of Meeting on Employment of Protected Persons on ships in receipt of subsidy, 15 November 1935; Thomson to Hawkins, Secretary, Cardiff and Bristol Channel Ship Owner Association, 7 March 1935; and BoT to IO, 9 May 1935.

103. IOR: L/E/9/955, IO to BoT, 17 April 1935 and minutes; BoT to IO, 9 May and 6 June 1935; Tramp Shipping Subsidy Committee to NMB, 5 July 1935 and minutes; BoT to IO, 6 August 1935; Report, 25 November 1935, for views of BoT.

104. IOR: L/E/9/955, IO to CO, 14 August 1935.

105. IOR: L/E/9/955, Report, 25 November 1935; Memo from CO, February 1936 and internal minutes; additional letter from IO to BoT, 21 February 1936.

106. IOR: L/E/9/955, Tramp Subsidy Committee, 19 March 1936, signed Thomson.

107. IOR: L/E/9/955, BoT, signed Carter, to IO, 6 June 1935; resolution of Sailor's and Firemen's Panel of NMB on manning of vessels applying for subsidy, 27 June 1935, and reply by Subsidy Committee, 5 July 1935; Memo, Tramp Shipping Subsidy Committee: Employment on Ships Qualifying for Subsidy, BoT, July 1935.

108. IOR: L/E/9/955, Parliamentary Debates, 4 May 1937, and House of Lords Debates, 9 March 1937; PRO: MT 9/3083.

109. PRO: HO 45/14299, Pt 2, Kent Chief Constable, 20 December 1930; Police Inspector, Limehouse, London, 14 January 1931; *GH*, 1–4 September 1925; IOR: L/E/9/962, HO to Adams, 31 December 1931.

110. IOR: L/E/9/954, Circular, T 10179/6202/378, 4 September 1931.

111. IOR: L/E/9/954, Circular, T 3491/144/378, 15 April 1930 and Circular, T 10179/6202/378, 4 September 1931.

112. IOR: L/E/9/962, Liverpool CID Branch report, signed Lawson, 26 November 1930; PRO: HO 213/242, R. Wilkie, Chief Constable, South Shields to Holderness, Aliens Department, 30 June 1934 and minutes, 15 and 16 June 1934; quoted in Martin, 'Racial Attitudes', p. 101.

113. IOR: L/E/9/962, Report signed Blagg, 21 October 1930; for a differing account, see Report of CID Special Branch, signed Lawson, 26 November 1930 and report signed Wallace. See also *Manchester Evening Chronicle*, 21 March 1931; PRO: HO 213/353 and HO 45/14299 Pt 2.

114. IOR: L/P&J/12/69–71, for 'stop lists'.

115. IOR: L/E/9/962, HO to Adams, 31 December 1931 and Adams to IO, 20 January 1931; PRO: HO 45/14299, Pt 2, Memo of Inter-Departmental Conference, 12 March 1931; IOR: L/E/9/972, India HC to IO, 18 August 1933; IOR: L/E/9/457, Hunter Report on Seamen's Welfare in Ports, 1939, p. 253.

8 LASCAR ACTIVISM IN BRITAIN, 1920–45

1. PRO: MT 9/2737, Stat 19, 1919–33; Behrens, *Merchant*, p. 157 for 1938.
2. Broeze, 'Muscles', p. 48; e.g. Sir William Mackinnon and James Mackay (Lord Inchcape); several MPs acted as the Federation's lobbyists. Not all lines belonged to the Shipping Federation.
3. Statistics from Desai, *Labour*, pp. 17 and 58; IOR: L/E/9/457, GOI to IO, 7 October 1937.
4. PRO: MT 9/2778, minute 1, 11 January 1938 and document 15, 22 April 1938; minute 3, 16 February 1938 and document 29; IOR: L/E/9/977 for modification to lascar limit line, 6 March 1935, meeting with Anchor-Brocklebank line; for objections, IOR: L/E/9/956, IOR: L/E/7/1125, file 2139 and IOR: L/E/7/1350, file 2928.
5. *The Special Fund for Seamen, Commonly Called the Lascar Fund*, reports 15 July 1912–31 December 1922, 31 December 1924 and 31 December 1925. I am grateful to Geraldine Charles for copies. The 'Asian Levy' survived into the 1980s, Gordon and Reilly, 'Guestworkers'; PRO: MT 9/2778, Documents 32, 26 May 1938, and 28, 19 May 1938.
6. PRO: MT 9/2778, documents 31 (with tables) and 28, 29 and 15; PRO: MT 9/3657, minute 2, 6 January 1942; IOR: L/E/7/351, file 680.
7. PRO: MT 9/3083, additional document 4; IOR: L/E/9/977, 17 December 1936, Parliamentary question by 'Mr Smith'.
8. IOR: L/E/7/1152, file 727, question by J.D. Gilbert, 11 December 1922; Dr Menzies to Lawrence, 9 May 1922; Report by H.A. Jury, 5 May 1922; notes by Captain T.G. Segrave, 30 November 1922; Menzies to Cobb, MP, 15 June 1922. Nairoolla's in Poplar charged 25 shillings a week to 28 shillings at the Strangers' Home.
9. IOR: L/E/7/1152, file 727, attended by representatives from lines, the Shipping Federation, BoT and BFSS.
10. IOR: L/E7/1152, file 727, Conference Report, 22 February 1923, notes by Segrave, 30 November 1922; *KM*, 20 February 1920.
11. IOR: L/E/7/1152, file 727, Report and resolutions; draft and final letter to Hon. Alexander Shaw, MP, 1 January 1923; IO to BoT, 6 March 1924; *The Times*, 7 July 1923; PRO: HO 45/11897, report by Cooper, 17 February 1921, for 'leakage' and action; IOR: L/E/7/1360, file 3847, for 'approved' lodging-houses.
12. IOR: L/E/9/967, Adams to GOI, 28 February 1935; IOR: L/E/9/457, Hunter Report, 1939.
13. IOR: L/E/9/973; IOR: L/E/9/961 and L/E/7/940, file 3127 for more examples.
14. Desai, *Labour*, Ch. 2; Mowat, *Seafarers*, Ch. 2; Broeze, 'Muscles', pp. 52–4; IOR: L/E/9/957 and IOR: L/E/7/1364, file 4884, extract from the Legislative Assembly, 19 September 1927.
15. Desai, *Labour*, p. 192; for non-ratification of ILO Conventions, *MP*, 7 July 1920; IOR: L/E/9/957, telegram from GOI, 25 May 1926, International

Labour Conference, June Session (Seamen's Articles of Agreement); IOR: L/E/9/457, GOI instructions to Indian delegates at 21st and 22nd Session, International Conference, October 1936 (welfare in ports); GOI to IO, 7 October 1937, draft convention and recommendation (maximum hours of work); GOI to IO, 23 February 1939 (liability of ship-owners for sickness, injury, etc.); see also IOR: L/E/7/1163, file 2886; IOR: L/E/7/1364, file 4884.

16. For a history of seamen's unions in India: Desai, *Labour*, Ch. 11; Mowat, *Seafarers*, Ch. 10; Broeze, 'Muscles', pp. 50–67; PRO: MT 9/3657, AISF letter head; IOR: L/E/9/976, IO to F.H. Norman, 9 April 1940, omits NSUI and BSU from its membership.

17. Desai, *Labour*, p. 205. Police often cited this as evidence of lascar duplicity and dishonesty.

18. This brief reconstruction is based on: IOR: L/P&J/12/46; IOR: L/P&J/12/1 59; IOR: L/P&J/12/47; IOR: L/P&J/12/238; IOR: L/P&J/12/143; IOR: L/P&J/12/49; D. Petri, *Communism in India 1924–1927* (Calcutta: Government of India Press, 1927 and 1972 edns); Cecil Kaye, *Communism in India with Unpublished Documents from the National Archives of India (1919–1924)*, ed. S. Roy (Calcutta: Editions India, 1926 and1971 edns). Both Kaye and Petrie, who succeeded him as Director of the Intelligence Bureau (DIB) in India, and IPI in London, viewed Communism and the activity of the Left from their own perspectives, as a threat to the Raj. These records, though valuable in themselves, provide a rather limited and at times a contradictory picture.

19. Kaye, *Communism* (1926 edn), pp. 64, 72, 112–13; documents, pp. 54, 85, 233–4 and 354 (1971 edn); Petrie, *Communism* (1927 edn), pp. 37, 40, 54–5, 255, 257 and 330; pp. 34, 37 and 511(1972 edn); IOR: L/P&J/12/49, L/P&J/12/143 and L/P&J/12/238.

20. IOR: L/P&J/12/233, Knight to Saklatvala, 14 December 1924; IOR: L/P&J/12/234, Upadhyaya History Sheet. Petrie suggests he 'went to England' in November 1922 and came to notice in December 1925; IOR: L/P&J/12/50, reports 20 January and 15 July 1925.

21. IOR: L/P&J/12/233 and L/P&J/12/234; IOR: L/P&J/12/468, McInnes to Turnbull, 1 March 1934; Petri, *Communism*, pp. 258–9, 376 (1927 edn).

22. IOR: L/P&J/12/234 and L/P&J/12/233; Petri, *Communism*, p. 259; IOR: L/E/9/953 for Liverpool rally. From here Upadhyaya went to Birkenhead where he was seen issuing ISU membership cards to Indian seamen. Subscription was 7d. a year.

23. IOR: L/P&J/12/234 and L/P&J/12/233.

24. IOR: L/P&J/12/234, Upadhyaya to Hall, 1 May 1927; minute dated 15 July 1927; Saklatvala to MPs, 2 June 1927; *Hansard*, vol. 206, cols 1652–3, 23 May 1927.

25. IOR: L/P&J/12/233 and L/P&J/12/234.

26. *The Worker*, 1 July 1927.

27. IOR: L/P&J/12/233, report, 31 May 1931; from Sgt Charles Taylor and Chief Inspector H. Moore, 30 June 1927.

28. IOR: L/P&J/7/1408; Petri, *Communism*, p. 259 (1927 edn); IOR: L/P&J/12 /234. Upadhyaya could travel to Paris because British passport holders did not require a visa.

29. IOR: L/P&J/12/234, IO to Haig, personal and secret, 17 November 1927; GOI to IO, 22 December 1927, 9 March, and 15 March 1928; IO to IPI, 3 April 1928 and draft letter from IO to HO nd, recommending deportation; IO to IPI, 24 May 1928; IPI to IO, 30 May 1928 and IO to GOI, 4 June 1928.

30. IOR: L/P&J/12/233; PRO: MT 9/2084, report Metropolitan Police, Special Branch, 10 April 1931; IOR: L/P&J/12/50, report 20 January 1925.

31. Upadhyaya was running the Indian Seamen's Club in Albert Road, Woolwich in 1932. He was next heard of as a salesman, first of 'eastern goods', later, in 1936 as a paper salesman. By 1938, as 'N. Paddy', he was trading as printer, stationer, paper and paper bag merchant from 16 Meadow Road, Fentiman Road in Lambeth, IOR: L/P&J/12/233.

32. Tony Lane, *The Merchant Seamen's War* (Manchester University Press, 1990), p. 8.

33. PRO: MT 9/3150, minute 1, 1 September 1939; document 26a, 5 September 1939.

34. PRO: MT 9/3150, minute 2, 1 September 1939; IO to GOI, 1 September 1939; Shipping Master, Calcutta, 5 September; GOI to IO, 6 September 1939.

35. PRO: MT 9/3150, minutes 1 and 3, and document 21, 1 September 1939; 15 September 1939, signed Harold Cayzer; IOR: L/P&J/12/630, Unrest among Indian Seamen, 23 November 1939.

36. PRO: MT 9/3150, minute 7, 5 September 1939 and document 19, 12 September 1939; Minute 8, 6 September 1939; from Cayzer, 15 September 1939.

37. PRO: MT 9/3150, minutes 8 and 9, 6 and 8 September 1939.

38. PRO: MT 9/3150, minute 10, 9 September 1939 and document 9, 8 September 1939. See also minute 12, 10 September 1939 for settlements on other ships.

39. PRO: MT 9/3150, minute 8, 6 September and document 19, 12 September 1939; minute 17, 16 November and telegram from GOI, 15 September 1939. See also minute 7, 5 September 1939, and minute 26 November 1940.

40. PRO: MT 9/3150, minute 10, 9 September 1939, and talk with India HC, 14 September 1939.

41. PRO: MT 9/3150, minutes 17 and 18, 16 November 1939.

42. *Daily Worker*, 23 October 1939; IOR: L/P&J/12/630, 16 November 1939; reports from the Police Office, West India Dock, to the Chief Police Officer, 28–30 October, 1–2 November 1939.

43. IOR: L/P&J/12/630, reports 16, 23, 29 November and 7 December 1939; PRO: MT 9/3150, documents 38 a–e.

44. IOR: L/P&J/12/630, reports 23, 29 November and 7 December 1939.

45. MRC: MSS 292/655/6, cutting from *Advance*.

46. IOR: L/P&J/12/630, reports 7, 17, 23 November, and 5, 7 December 1939; IOR: L/P&J/12/452, report 15 November 1939; PRO: MT 9/3150, document 75, 20 January 1940.

47. PRO: MT 9/3150, document 19, 12 September 1939; document 74a, 13 December 1939; IOR: L/P&J/12/630, reports dated 1, 9, 17, 23 and 29 November 1939.

48. PRO: MT 9/3150, document 66, 13 December 1939; IOR: L/P&J/12/630, minute 23 November 1939, reports 16 November and 7 December 1939 and India HC's letter, 11 January 1940.

49. IOR: L/P&J/12/630, notice by India HC, 8 December 1939; MRC: MSS 292/655/6, 6 December 1939.

50. IOR: L/P&J/12/630, message from *Reuters*, 1 December 1939; PRO, MT 9/3150, document 58; MRC: MSS 292/655/6, *Advance*, 1 December 1939.

51. MRC: MSS 292/655/6, *Advance*, 1 December 1939; Sir Walter Citrine, TUC, to Philip Allen, Private Secretary, HO, 18 December 1939; IOR: L/E/9/976, note to Sir J. Woodhead, 16 March 1940; minute, signed EWRL, 15 March 1940

52. *Journal of Commerce*, 21 November 1939 in PRO: MT 9/3150; IOR: L/P&J/12/630, from DIB, 17 April 1944; IOR: L/I/1/1062, note by F.F. Turnbull, 28 August 1944; Broeze, 'Muscles', f/n 80, p. 65; IOR: L/E/9/958, IO to GOI, 22 June 1944, signed Wood.

53. PRO: MT 9/3150, document 75, 20 January 1940; document 74, Norman to Atkins, IO, 10 January 1940.

54. IOR: L/P&J/12/630, 7 December 1939; MRC: MSS 292/655/6, Alley to Citrine, 2 December; memo of interview, 6 December 1939; Citrine to Snedden, Shipping Federation and Anderson, HO, 11 December and 18 December 1939; Spence to Citrine, 11 December 1939; PRO: MT 9/3150, document 74a.

55. MRC: MSS 292/655/6, HO, to Citrine, 20 December 1939; IOR: L/P&J/12/630, meeting 13 December 1939; PRO: MT 9/3150, document 74a; IOR: L/E/9/976, Press Note, 22 February 1940; IOR: L/E/9/977, Greany to Norman, 27 December 1939.

56. IOR: L/E/9/976, Norman to IO, 24 April 1940; minute signed Lumby, 25 April 1940; IOR: L/E/9/977, Greany to Norman, 27 December 1939; Norman to IO, 29 December 1939; GOI to IO, telegram 6 February 1940; Norman to IO, 4 October 1940; PRO: MT 9/3150, Norman to Greany, 29 December 1939.

57. IOR: L/E/9/976, IO minutes signed A. Dibdin, 15 March 1940; minute signed EWRL, 14 March and 25 April 1940 and IO to Norman, 9 April 1940; PRO: MT 9/3150, documents 64 and 74a, minutes and notes, 13 December 1939; documents 74, 10 January 1939, to Walsh Atkins, and 75, 20 January 1940; see also PRO: MT 9/3657, minute 5, 12 January 1942. For official view on Alley, see IPI confidential memo, Notes on ISU/AISF in L/P&J/12/630, 4/12/39, and PRO: MT 9/3150, document 62a.

58. IOR L/P&J/12/630, IPI report, 26 January 1940; PRO: MT 9/3150, document 75, 20 January 1940 and Norman to Greany, 29 December 1939;

IOR: L/E/9/976, Norman to IO, 11 March 1940.

59. PRO: MT 9/3150, minute 24, 23 February 1940; IOR: L/E/9/976, Greany to Norman, 1 March 1940 and Norman to IO, 11 March 1940; IOR: L/E/9/977, Greany to Norman, 27 December 1939.

60. IOR: L/E/9/976, GOI telegram 31 March 1940; Norman to IO, 11 March 1940 and 24 April 1940; PRO: MT 9/3150 and IOR: L/P&J/12/630, meeting 13 December 1939.

61. IOR: L/P&J/12/630, IO minute signed A.D., 23 May 1940 in IPI to Silver, 22 May 1940; IOR L/E/9/976, IO to Norman, 4 May 1940; PRO: MT 9/3150, document 64, minutes and notes, 13 December 1939. See also minute 6, 12 January 1942, PRO: MT 9/3657.

62. IOR: L/P&J/12/630, meeting 13 December 1939 and PRO: MT 9/3157 document 74a; IOR: L/E/9/457, Hunter Report November 1939; note on Seamen's Welfare Officer's Conference, 27 August 1941; IOR: L/E/9/976, IO to MoS, 4 May 1940; IOR L/I/1/840, *Syren and Shipping*, 24 December 1941.

63. IOR: L/E/9/977, GOI to India HC, telegram 31 July 1940; Lumby to Adams, 6 August 1940; IOR: L/&J/12/630, IPI to Silver, 13 February 1941, and minute signed, W.D.C., 13 February 1941; Adams to Lumby, 20 March 1941.

64. IOR: L/P&J/630, IPI to Silver, 13 February 1941 with a note, 11 February 1941; IPI to Silver, 16 June 1941; IOR: L/E/9/976, Bukht's report on the All-India Seamen's Centre, 13 September 1943.

65. IOR: L/I/1/840, Memo: Indian Seamen in the British Merchant Navy, December 1941; relevant extracts from LWO Reports, IOR L/E/9/457 and L/E/9/458.

66. IOR: L/E/9/457, Ministry of Labour and National Service to S.T. Ally, 9 October 1941; S.T. Ally to IO, 14 October 1941 and extract from Progress Report of Seamen's Welfare Board, 16 October 1943; IOR: L/P&J/12/630, reports of SWOs, August 1941 and December–January 1941; PRO: MT 9/3657, document 22, Lord Leathers, MOWT to Huque, 24 August 1942 and document 23, Huque to Lord Leathers, 25 August 1942.

67. PRO: MT 9/3150, documents 66, 13 December 1939 and 68, 16 December 1939; document 75, 20 January 1939; for drafts, see documents 67, 69 and 70a.

68. IOR: L/P&J/12/630, Statement issued by HC's office; PRO: MT 9/3150, document 72; IOR: L/I/1/840, Bureau of Public Information, New Delhi, letter 2 July 1943; memo and India HC's amendments, 5 December 1941; see also letter from IO to Webster, British Library of Information, New York, 16 December 1941.

69. IOR: L/I/1/840, tribute to Indian seamen, 3 January 1942; *Shipping World*, 21 January 1942; quoted in Lane, *Seamen's War*, p. 178.

70. Lane, *Seamen's War*, pp. 179–80; PRO: MT 9/3657, Alley's Memo, Indian Seamen in the Merchant Navy; *ELA*, 20 December 1941.

71. IOR: L/E/9/457, extracts for week ending 27 September 1941; note on SWOs' Conference, 27 August 1941.

72. For lascar voices: Adams, ed., *Seven Seas;* and fictional account, Mulk Raj Anand, 'A Lascar Writes Home', *Our Time*, vol. 1, no. 2, April 1941, pp. 20–3.

73. IOR: L/E/9/977, P&O to Noon, 17 September 1940; Shipping Federation to owners carrying lascar crews, 2 October 1940; PRO MT 9/3150, cable to Mackinon, Mackenzie & Co., Calcutta, 13 September 1940; IOR: L/P&J/12/630, IO to Adams, 12 March 1941; cutting, *Newstatesman and Nation*, 15 February 1941; PRO: MT 9/3657, document 18, 8 May 1942; Lane, *Seamen's War*, p. 164.

74. IOR; L/P&J/12/630, GOI telegram, 25 February 1941; IOR: L/E/9/977, Superintendent MMO, Glasgow, prosecution of Indian seamen from the *SS Karanja*, 19 May 1941; Norman to Lumby, 30 May 1941.

75. IOR: L/P&J/12/630, e.g. *SS Cedarbank*, 3 April 1940; from City of Glasgow Police, 23 May 1941; IPI note on unrest, 11 February 1941; India HC to Lumby, 20 March 1941; PRO: MT 9/3423, *SS Prome*; *Liverpool Daily Post*, 1, 3 and 4 February 1941; IOR: L/E/9/977, *SS Macharda* and *SS Karanja*; PRO: MT 9/4747; IOR: L/P&J/12/645, Conference 25 March 1943.

76. Desai, *Labour*, pp. 62–3.

77. IOR: L/P&J/12/630, *News*, May 1940; report City of Glasgow Police, 23 May 1941; *DW*, 6 January 1941; IOR: L/E/9/457, Parliamentary Session, 1940–41.

78. IOR: L/I/1/890, Conference Report, 1941; *GH*, 8 September 1941; IOR: L/P&J/12/630, Le Burn to IO, 8 October 1941; Ministry of Pensions to IO, 22 October 1941.

79. *ELA*, 20 December 1941; PRO: MT 9/3657, AISF memo.

80. PRO: MT 9/3657, AISF memo.

81. *ELA*, 20 December 1941; PRO: MT 9/3657, documents 1–2, 6–6a, 11 December 1941; minute 1, 31 December 1941; IOR: L/I/1/840, Booker to Adams, 2 January 1942; Adams to Booker, 19 January 1942.

82. PRO: MT 9/3657, document 5, Shipping Federation to MOWT, 15 January 1942; minute 1, 31 December 1941; document 12, MOWT to ITF, 21 February 1942 and minute 10, 19 February 1942; document 6, India HC to MOWT, 19 January 1942; IOR: L/E/9/977, GOI to IO, telegram 30 October 1940; IOR: L/I/1/840, India HC to Booker, 19 January 1942.

83. PRO: MT 9/3657, minutes 1, 31 December 1941 and 3, 7 January 1942; document 19, ITF, Lascar Wage, 2 May 1942; document 5, 21 May 1942.

84. PRO: MT 9/3657, documents 10, 12, 13 and 16, and minute 15, 7 April 1942.

85. PRO: MT 9/3657, document 2, 11 May 1942; document B, AISF Supplementary Memo, 11 May 1942; minute 2, 6 January 1942; document 6, Kneale to Adams, 22 May 1942.

86. PRO: MT 9/ 3657, document 5, 21 May 1942.

87. PRO: MT 9/3657, documents 8, 9, 11 A, and minute 5, 22 June 1942 and document 12, Guttery to IO, 24 June 1942.

88. PRO: MT 9/3657, minute 5, 22 June 1942; minute 7, 6 July 1942;

document 17, IO to GOI, 15 July 1942; see also document 20, 25 August 1942.

89. PRO: MT 9/3657, document 18, 8 May 1942; UNL: TUC Library Collection, HE 879, 1943, Memo All-Indian Seamen's Centre, 5 October 1943, Table III; for white seamen's wages, Behrens, *Merchant*, p. 174, f/n 1.

90. IOR: L/E/9/457, Alley to Curran, 13 December 1942, intercepted by postal and telegraph censorship, released 26 December, 1942; IOR: L/P&J/12/630 DIB, shortage of seamen, IPI to Silver, 25 February 1944; PRO: MT 9/3657, documents 25, 25a and 25b; minutes 13 and 14, dated 26 October 1942.

91. IOR: L/E/9/976, Bukht's report, 13 September 1943, membership card, Durant's Press cuttings, 13 and 14 September 1943 and extract from Reuters, 12 September 1943; *Daily Herald*, 13 September 1943.

92. IOR: L/E/9/976, India HC to IO, 9 December 1943; Ali to Alley, 8 October 1943; censored cable, Oldenbroek and Alley to Ali, 22 December 1943.

93. IOR: L/P&J/12/630, Ali to Alley, 24 May 1944 and Notice, 10 June 1944; IOR L/E/9/976, 10 October 1944, to Shipping Master, Calcutta.

94. IOR: L/P&J/12/646, IPI reports on Indian Organisations in the UK, 27 May and 19 November 1943; 22 January, 8 March and 5 August 1944 and 4 March 1945; IOR: L/E/9/976, AISC News Bulletin, 1 May 1944; IOR: L/P&J/12/630, case of *Jisadane*, 19 June 1944 and Wood to Silver, 5 September 1944.

95. UNL: TUC Library Collections, HE 879, 1943, AISC Memo.

96. IOR: L/E/9/976, Alley to India HC, 22 December 1943; Oldenbroek and Alley to Ali, cable 22 December 1943; Alley to Secretary of State for India, 14 January and 24 January 1944.

97. IOR: L/E/9/976, India HC to IO, 30 December 1943; minutes, signed Rumbold, 29 January 1944 and A. Baxter, 17 February 1944; minutes signed Rumbold, 24 January and 14 February 1944.

98. IOR: L/P&J/12/630, IPI to Silver, 8 March 1944; IOR: L/E/9/976, Ali to Alley, 8 October 1943.

99. IOR: L/E/9/977, GOI to IO, cypher telegram, 25 February 1944; IOR: L/E/9/976, Zaman to GOI to IO, 23 May 1944; IO to Kneale, 29 July 1944; meeting at the High Commission held on 23 February 1944, IOR: L/E/9/976, IO to Adams, 26 February 1944. The transcript is now missing, but see Tabili, *We Ask*, pp. 172–3 and f/n 34, p. 242.

100. IOR: L/P&J/12/630, report 28 June 1944 from Central Intelligence Office, Simla; IOR: L/E/9/976, MOWT to IO, 20 December 1945; IO to Ernest Bevin, nd; IOR: L/E/9/458, Guttery to Desai, 20 February 1946.

101. IOR: L/E/9/976, Reuters cable, 23 December 1945; MOWT to IO, 20 December 1945; Rumbold to Lumby, 4 January 1946; IO to Guttery, draft letter 31 December 1945; Ernest Bevin (?) to Pethick-Lawrence, 11 January 1946; IO minute to Rumbold, 29 December 1945; MOWT to IO, 3 January 1946.

102. IOR: L/E/9/976, IO to Guttery, draft letter 31 December 1945; minute,

Rumbold to Lumby, 4 January 1946; IO to Bevin, nd.
103. IOR: L/P&J/12/646, IPI report 4 March 1945; Mowat, *Seafarers*, pp. 56–7.

9 ASIANS IN BRITAIN, 1919–47

1. N.V. Rajkumar, *Indians Outside India* (New Delhi: All-India Congress Committee, 1951); C. Kondapi, *Indians Overseas 1938–1949* (New Delhi: Indian Council of World Affairs, 1951), p. 360; Dilip Hiro, *Black British, White British* (Paladin, 1992 edn), p. 111.

2. Maan, *New Scots*, p. 124; Kapur, *Irish Raj*, pp. 66–7; Ram, *Reminiscences*; IOR: V/24/832; Hiro, *Black British*, p. 111; PRO: HO 45/14299 Pt 2, Limehouse Station 'K' Division, 7 February 1931, signed Tuck.

3. F.A. Richardson, *Social Conditions in Ports and Dockland Areas* (Joint Council of the British Social Hygiene Council and the British Council for the Welfare of the Mercantile Marine, 1934–5), p. 17; PRO: HO 45/14299, Pt 1, Immigration Report, Liverpool, 27 and 28 October 1930.

4. Little, *Negroes*, p. 62; *DH*, 10 January 1929, in PRO: HO 45/13392; IOR: L/E/7/1360, file 3847; IOR: L/E/7/1152, file 727; IOR: L/P&J/12/409; Phyllis Young, *Report on Investigation into the Conditions of the Coloured Population in a Stepney Area* (London: privately published, 1944), p. 24. Typescript in IOR: L/E/9/458 and PRO: MT 9/3952; Lodging Houses file, Tower Hamlets Archives. See also IOR: L/E/9/457, Hunter Report, 1939; Yousuf Choudhury, *The Roots and Tales of the Bangladeshi Settlers* (Birmingham: Sylheti Social History Group, 1993).

5. Adams, ed., *Seven Seas*, pp. 44 and 152–3; street directories, 1927–9; 1938–9; IOR: L/P&J/12/630, report 21 February 1940; for Ally's lodging-house application, 14 July 1938, at 137 Leman Street: Lodging House File, THA; for P&O scheme to trace deserters, PRO: HO 45/14299, Pt 1.

6. IOR: L/E/7/1103, Oliver to IO, 9 June 1921; PRO: HO 45/11897, report by Bosanquet, 10 June 1921; IOR: L/E/7/1152, file 727, Segrave's report, 1 December 1922.

7. Ayub Ali died in Sylhet in 1980. In 1947, S.T. Ally returned to Sylhet with his English wife and a car, the first to be shipped to Sylhet, a symbol of his success and wealth. But he did not live long to enjoy his status. He died in 1948. Adams, ed., *Seven Seas*, pp. 40–7; IOR: L/P&J/12/646, IPI: Indian activities in the UK.

8. Maan, *New Scots*, pp. 139–41; Ram, *Reminiscences*; IOR: L/P&J/12/645, History Sheet: Kartar Singh Nagra; *LCMM*, September 1936; Kapur, *Irish Raj*, p. 112.

9. IOR: L/P&J/12/159, weekly report Indians in Glasgow, 23 January 1923; IOR: L/E/9/962, report Sgt Lawson, 26 November 1930; Kapur, *Irish Raj*, p. 92.

10. Bradford Heritage Recording Unit (BRHU), *Here to Stay* (City of Bradford Metropolitan Council, Arts, Museum and Libraries, 1994), pp. 34–5.

11. Adams, ed., *Seven Seas*, p. 45; Keith Waterhouse, *City Lights* (London:

Sceptre, 1995), p. 30; Bert A. French, *Boyhood Memories of Plumstead 1920–1928* (London: Clare Corner Publications, 1994), p. 34; Bertha Sokoloff, *Edith and Stepney* (London: Stepney Books Publications, 1987), p. 155.

12. IOR: L/E/9/962, Chief Constable to HO, 12 January 1931; Adams, ed., *Seven Seas*, pp. 73, 134 and 154; Young, *Report*, p. 12; M.E. Fletcher, *Report on an Investigation into the Coloured Problem in Liverpool and Other Ports* (Liverpool Association for the Welfare of Half-Caste Children, 1930), p. 48; Sokoloff, *Edith*, p. 155; *City and East London Observer*, 27 August 1938; IOR: L/E/9/457, Hunter Report, 1939, appendix, xvii.

13. IOR: L/P&J/12/468, History Sheet: Said Amir Shah; IOR: L/P&J/12/645, History Sheet: Akbar Ali Khan; MRC: MSS 292/91/108, Alley to Harris, 15, 17 March and 12 April 1939, including 'A True Copy' of Agreement.

14. IOR: L/E/9/457, Hunter Report, 1939, Appendix, xvii; BHRU, *Here to Stay*, pp. 33, 34–5; Ram, *Reminiscences*.

15. Meg Henderson, *Finding Peggy* (Corgi Books, 1994), pp. 28–9; G.S. Aurora, *The New Frontiersmen* (Bombay: Popular Prakashan, 1967); De Witt John, *Indian Workers' Association in Britain* (Oxford University Press, 1969), p. 4; Hiro, *Black British*, p. 110; Visram, *Ayahs*, p. 192.

16. Maan, *New Scots*, Ch. 4; Kapur, *Irish Raj*, pp. 78–87; McFarland, 'Clyde', p. 511; IOR: L/P&J/12/645, note: Indians on suspect list, 15 May 1942; IOR: L/E/9/962, India HC to Baines, 20 January 1932; IOR: L/E/7/1512, file 3843, memo from Commissioners in Sind, 13 April 1927.

17. IOR: L/E/9/972, HO to IO, 4 August 1933 and Kirkcaldy Burgh Police, 27 September 1933; IOR: L/E/9/962, Chief Constable to HO, 12 January 1931; Kapur, *Irish Raj*, p. 91.

18. Pedlar Acts 1871 &1881; Ram, *Reminiscences.*

19. This section is based on Ram, *Reminiscences*; Maan, *New Scots*, pp. 122–38; Kapur, *Irish Raj*, pp. 79–94; *Glasgow Weekly Record*, 18 October 1930; 'The Mohammeds of Lewis', BBC R4, 16 September 1986.

20. IOR: L/P&J/12/468, History Sheets; IOR: L/P&J/12/500, report 4 November 1936; IOR: L/E/9/962, Scotland Yard to HO, 4 June 1932; *LCMM*, September 1936.

21. Maan, *New Scots*, pp. 117–18; Kapur, *Irish Raj*, pp. 169, 82 and 151; PRO: HO 45/14299, Pt 2, Kent County Constabulary report, 19 December 1930, signed Richdale; IOR: L/E/9/962, note 5 May 1930.

22. PRO: HO 45/14299 Pt 2, reports Limehouse Station, 'K' Division, 14 January and 7 February, 1931; report from the Kent Chief Constable, 20 December 1930, and minutes; Maan, *New Scots*, pp. 136–7.

23. Fryer, *Staying Power*; Ramdin, *Black Working-Class*; Michael Banton, *The Coloured Quarter* (London: Jonathan Cape, 1955).

24. Maan, *New Scots*, pp. 132–3, 137, 141 and 149; IOR: L/E/9/457, Hunter Report, 1939, appendix, xiv; *GH*, 1 February 1941.

25. Maan, *New Scots*, p. 146; IOR: L/P&J/12/646, Review 1942–3, cites the date of the Majlis as 1941.

26. PRO: HO 213/353; IOR: L/E/9/457, Hunter Report, 1939; IOR: L/E/9/962,

CID Special Branch, 26 November 1930; Dhani Prem, *The Parliamentary Leper* (Aligarh: Metric Publications, 1965), p. 6; Tabili, *We Ask*, p. 140; IOR: L/E/9/955, letters from Indian seamen to IO; PRO: HO 45/14299, Pt 2, minutes attached to the report, 20 December 1930 from the Kent Chief Constable.

27. IOR: L/E/9/457, Hunter Report, 1939; PRO: HO 213/353, Scotland Yard report, signed Inspector 'G' Division, 19 June 1937; IOR: L/E/9/962, Commercial Street, 'H' Police Division, report 11 July 1932; Limehouse Station 'K' Division, report, 28 July 1932; PRO: HO 45/14299, Pt 2, Limehouse Station 'K' Division, report 7 February 1931; Young, *Report*; *LCMM*, September 1936 and September 1939; Sokoloff, *Edith*, p. 155.

28. Adams, ed., *Seven Seas*, pp. 43 and 163; Scotland Yard reports, 7 July 1943 and 27 September 1944, IOR: L/P&J/12/630; IPI Notes on Indian Organisations, 27 May 1943 and IOR: L/P&J/12/646, 1945, nd.

29. Flyer, THA; IOR: L/P&J/12/630, IPI report 13 December 1939.

30. Adams, ed., *Seven Seas*, p. 158; IOR: L/P&J/12/630, IPI to Silver, 22 May 1940; IOR: L/P&J/12/454, report 4 February 1942.

31. First Report, THA; Sokoloff, *Edith*, pp. 156–7; IOR: L/E/9/457, Hunter Report, 1939.

32. Adams, ed., *Seven Seas*, p. 48; Kapur, *Irish Raj*, pp. 92, 82 and 150; Maan, *New Scots*, pp. 143–4.

33. Henderson, *Peggy*, pp. 28–9; Maan, *New Scots*, pp. 144, 111–14; Kapur, *Irish Raj*, pp. 150–1; Young, *Report*, p. 10; *GH*, 1–4 September 1925.

34. *Manchester Evening News*, 20 March 1931; *Daily Dispatch*, 20, 23 and 24 March 1931; *MEN*, 21 March 1931; *MG*, 21 March 1931.

35. *GWR*, 18 October 1930.

36. PRO: HO 45/14299, Pt 2, Kent County Constabulary, Chatham Division, signed Richdale, 19 December 1930; Kapur, *Irish Raj*, p. 82; IOR: L/E/9/457, Hunter Report, 1939.

37. PRO: HO 213/353, Cardiff City Police, 7 June 1937; IOR: L/P&J/12/645, note on suspect list, 15 May 1942; notes on IWA, 14 April 1942; Ram, *Reminiscences*.

38. Ram, *Reminiscences*.

39. IOR: L/P&J/12/645, Birmingham Conference, 25 March 1943; note on suspect list, 15 May 1942. See also IOR: L/P&J/12/ 646.

40. IOR: L/P&J/12/645, History Sheets; Adams, ed., *Seven Seas*, p. 77; Maan, *New Scots*, p. 151; Young, *Report*, p. 11.

41. Ram, *Reminiscences*; Adams, ed., *Seven Seas*, p. 198; Young, *Report*, pp. 11–12; IOR: L/P&J/12/646, IPI: Indian activities in the UK, 8 March 1944.

42. IOR: L/P&J/12/645, IPI note on IWA, 14 April 1942; History Sheets.

43. IOR: L/P&J/12/645, IWA meeting at Bradford, 22 February 1942; Prem, *Leper*, p. 7; Ram, *Reminiscences*; *DW*, 1 August 1940; IOR: L/I/1/597, cutting from *Indian Review*; confidential telegram GOI to IO, 8 August 1940; telegram IO to GOI, 5 September 1940 and draft letter, together with cancelled paragraphs.

44. IOR: L/P&J/12/645, IPI to Silver, 29 July 1943, a speech by Jan

Mohammed at Birmingham, 11 July; Conference, 25 March 1943; Chief Constable, Johnson to HO, Aliens Department, 31 March 1943.

45. E.g. Hiro names Udham Singh, Ujjagar Singh and Akbar Ali Khan; Josephides suggests that Singh has acquired leadership status posthumously. Anant Ram, who moved to Coventry from London in 1942 and became branch secretary in 1945, confirms that Singh was not associated with the IWA 'at any stage', his leadership role being 'a complete fabrication'. IWA membership has variously been described as 'Punjabi pedlars' from the Midlands and 'factory workers in Coventry'. Josephides claims that 'most of the early settlers were not workers', which does not accord with the historical record. Desai includes professionals and students. See, Hiro, *Black British*, p. 138; Sasha Josephides, *Towards a History of the Indian Workers' Association* (Warwick University: ESRC, Research Paper in Ethnic Relations, No. 18, 1991), pp. 1, 10; Ram, *Reminiscences*; John, *Indian Workers*, p. 45; Mark Duffield, *Black Radicalism and the Politics of De-Industrialisation* (Aldershot: Avebury, 1988), p. 74; Rashmi Desai, *Indian Immigrants in Britain* (Oxford: Oxford University Press, 1963), pp. 102–3; IOR: L/P&J/12/645; and IOR: L/P&J/12/ 646.

46. IOR: L/P&J/12/645, IPI Note on IWA, 14 April 1942; History Sheets; IPI to Silver, 28 April 1945; IOR: L/P&J/12/646, Indian Organisations in the UK: A Review 1942–1946; Ram, *Reminiscences*; Prem, *Leper*, p. 6. Office bearers in 1942: Sastry (secretary), Sardar Shah of Birmingham (treasurer), Akbar Ali Khan, Coventry (president), Natha Singh (Bradford) and Thakur Singh Basra (Coventry).

47. IOR: L/P&J/12/645, IWA, 17 December 1942; History Sheets; Note on IWA, 14 April 1942; IOR: L/P&J/12/646, Review, 1942–3; IOR: L/P&J/12 /454, Indian Organisations, 8 September 1942.

48. IOR: L/P&J/12/646, Indian Activities in the UK, March–May 1945. Office holders in 1945: president, Mohammed Fazal Hussein (Bradford); vice-president, Charan Singh Chima (Coventry); general-secretary, Ali Muhammad (Birmingham); assistant secretary, J.R. Maini (Birmingham); treasurer, Ujjagar Singh (Coventry).

49. IOR: L/P&J/12/646, Review: 1942–3; Indian Notes, 17 April 1942; IOR: L/P&J/12/645, IWA meeting, Coventry, 24 May 1942; report on IWA, 17 December 1942; report Birmingham CID, 12 April 1943; Ram, *Reminiscences*.

50. Ram, *Reminiscences*; IOR: L/P&J/12/645, IWA 17 December 1942.

51. IOR: L/P/&J/646, Indian Organisations, 27 May 1943; June–July 1943; Review, 1942–3; 22 January and 8 March 1944; IOR: L/P&J/12/645, League and IWA meeting, Birmingham, 25 January 1942.

52. IWA meetings, IOR: L/P&J/12/645–6; Barnes and Nicholson, eds, *Empire*, p. 1022. For Udham Singh, PRO: CRIM 1/1177; IOR: L/P&J/7/3882; IOR: L/P&J/7/3610; IOR: L/P&J/11/2/354 for passport; and IOR: L/P&J/12/500. Roger Perkins, *The Amritsar Massacre Legacy* (Chippenham: Picton Publishing, 1989), claims Singh was a double agent.

53. IOR: L/P&J/12/645; IOR: L/P&J/12/646, Indian Notes, 15 December 1942.

54. IOR: L/P&J/12/645, IPI to Silver, 11 June 1942; IWA, 17 December 1942; reports 19 June 1947 and 2 July 1947.

55. Photograph in Visram, *History*, p. 36; Kapur, *Irish Raj*, p. 121; Maan, *New Scots*, p. 125; IOR: L/P&J/12/645, History Sheet: Dr Diwan Singh; Savitri Chowdhary, *I Made My Home In England* (Laindon: Grant-Best Ltd, nd); MOL Oral Archives Collection; *The Mercury*, 23 May 1991.

56. IOR: L/E/9/457, Hunter Report, 1939, p. 171 and appendix, xi and xvii; IOR: L/P&J/12/645, Conference Report, 25 March 1943; IPI to Silver, 29 April 1943.

57. Rich, 'Philanthropic'; Banton, *Coloured Quarter*, pp. 36–8. Fletcher, *Report*; Nancie Sharpe [Hare], *Report on the Negro Population of London and Cardiff* (nd, ?mid-1930s); Richardson, *Conditions*.

58. IOR: L/E/9/457, Hunter Report, 1939, p. 171; IOR: L/P&J/12/645, IPI to Silver, 29 April 1943; Conference, 25 March 1943; Chief Constable Johnson to Tudor, Aliens Department, 31 March 1943; IO to GOI, cable 19 October 1943; Young, *Report*, pp. 21–3; Adams, ed., *Seven Seas*, p. 48.

59. Young, *Report*, pp. 9–10, 26. The committee comprised, Revd St John Groser, Rector of St George's, Stepney (chairman), Edith Ramsay, Miss E. Shepherd of Stepney Moral Association, Margaret Wrong, secretary to the International Committee on Christian Literature for Africa, A.K. Lewis, and Shahibdad Khan, Jamiat-ul-Muslmin. Its estimate of the 'coloured' population was derived from the National Registration and ARP statistics; Sharpe, *Report*; for photograph of 'half-caste Indian boys', *LCMM*, October 1931.

60. Young, *Report*, pp. 10 and 29; Sharpe, *Report*. See also Sokoloff, *Edith*, p. 155; Edith Ramsay Papers, THA; Banton, *Coloured Quarter*, pp. 76–88.

61. D.F. Karaka, *I Go West* (London: Michael Joseph, 1938), pp. 12, 36, 41–2; D.F. Karaka, *All My Yesterdays* (Bombay: Thacker & Co., 1943); A.S.P. Ayyar, *An Indian in Western Europe* (Madras: C. Coomaraswamy Naidu & Sons, 1942), pp. 134–5; *Hansard*, 19 May, 1927, col. 1370, 31 May 1927, col. 349 and 2 June 1927, col. 603–4; *GH*, 1 and 3 June; *Edinburgh Evening News*, 20–24 May, 1927.

62. *Oxford Mail*, 29 April 1938; *MG*, 13 July 1938; IOR: L/I/1//598, Polak to Stuart, IO, 15 June 1938.

63. IOR: L/I/1/598, 26 October 1938, signed Townend.

64. IOR: L/I/1/597 and IOR: L/I/1/598.

65. IOR: L/I/1/597, Shah in *The Listener*, 8 December 1938; Vijayaraghavacharya quoted in *MG*, 4 July 1938; also 'Tail-Skid' in the *Aeroplane*, 13 April 1938; IOR: L/I/1/598, Kakar to India HC, 4 February 1938; Polak to Stuart, 15 June 1938. See also Noon to Sir Findlater Stewart, 19 February 1938; Victoria League to Stewart, 27 May 1938; *Hansard* extract, 14 February 1938; Legal Adviser to J. Chidell, 23 February 1938.

66. IOR: L/I/1/598, Stewart to McPherson, 3 June 1938, and reply 6 June 1938; Victoria League to Stewart, 5 March 1938; undated draft from Victoria League to Hotels and Restaurants Association.

67. IOR: L/I/1/597, Joyce to Townend, 14 September 1938; IOR: L/I/1/598,

Townend to Joyce, 8 and 11 December 1938 including minutes and drafts; Symon to Noon, 12 December 1938; *The Star*, 30 December 1938; list of hotels and boarding houses; letter from Lionel Aird, East–West Friendship Council to Stewart, 14 March 1939; minute signed SFS, 9 December 1938 and Zetland, 12 December 1938.

68. IOR: L/I/1/598, Victoria League to Symon, 15 February 1939; IOR: L/I/1/597, Lord Willingdon's speech at the East India Association; IO to GOI, draft telegram, ID 1918/41; Ministry of Information to Joyce, 4 July and Joyce to Leech, 8 July 1941.

69. Quoted in Holmes, *John Bull's*, p. 134; *Kelly's London Directory*, 1938, p. 3165; IOR: L/P&J/12/453, 27 June 1941; IOR: L/P&J/12/468, History Sheet: Shahibdad Khan; IOR: L/P&J/12/364; IOR: L/P&J/12/302; Kapur, *Irish Raj*, p. 174.

70. IOR: L/P&J/12/467, Sinha file; *Indian Student*, vol. 1, May–July 1937, copy in IOR: L/P&J/12/475.

71. *Indian Student*, vol., 1, May–July 1937; *Asian Times*, 2 September 1995; *Oriental Post*, No. 28, December 1944, copy in Edith Ramsay Papers, THA; *Guardian Guide*, 5–11 September 1998; Maan, *New Scots*, p. 137.

72. S. Natrajan, *West of Suez* (Bombay, The Indian Social Reformer Ltd, 1938), p.107; Ayyar, *Indian*, p. 117; Palmer Family History Document. I am grateful to Namita Punjabi for a copy; photograph of an 'at home' at Veeraswami's in 1928, Visram, *Indians*, p. 28; Choudhury, *Tales*, pp. 64–66; Shafi's proprietor was Lal, a Punjabi.

73. *Indian Student*, vol. 1, May–July 1937; IOR: L/P&J/12/186; IOR: L/P&J/12/42; *Oriental Post*, December 1944; Adams, ed., *Seven Seas*, pp. 49–51. See also Choudhury, *Tales*, pp. 64–7.

74. Adams, ed., *Seven Seas*, 52; McFarland, 'Clyde', p. 511; IOR: L/P&J/12/4 54, 8 September 1942; *Indian Student*, vol. 1, May–July 1937.

75. Kondapi, *Indians*, p. 360; IOR: L/P&J/12/441, Misc 744, 2 February 1932.

76. Elsie Goldsmith-Goading, *Dr Rochi Hingorani* (privately published, n d); *Medical Directory*, 1930; *West London Observer*, 27 September 1935, p. 9.

77. MOL Oral Archives Collection; *The Mercury*, 23 May 1991; *Health Service Journal*, 3 December 1998, p. 31; IOR: L/P&J/12/231, Bhatt file; IOR: L/P&J/12/497.

78. Garnett, *Echo*, pp. 141, 143; IOR: V/27/262/1; IOR: L/P&J/6/986; Rohit Barot, *Bristol and the Indian Independence Movement* (Bristol Branch Historical Association, 1988), pp. 12–21.

79. Barot, *Bristol*, pp. 21–6; see relevant sections in IOR: L/P&J/12/646.

80. HO, Civil Defence Department, 5 March 1945. I am grateful to George Chowdharay-Best for a copy; *Hackney Gazette*, 12 March 1945. See also, *BGN*, 20 July 1935; *DT*, 18 July 1992.

81. His brother, Dhani Ram (d. 1974), joined his practice in 1931. The Saggar practice continued under Dr Karam Saggar (nephew). Jainti Saggar and Jane had two daughters, Maan, *New Scots*, pp. 127–9.

82. Family Papers and information from George Chowdharay-Best and Shakun Banfield; Chowdhary, *Home*, for an account of his life as a doctor; *Laindon*

Times and Recorder, 6 January 1960; *BMJ*, 6 February 1960.

83. *LT&R*, 6, 13 and 20 January 1960; Savitri Chowdhary, *In Memory of my Beloved Husband* (Laindon: Grant-Best Ltd, nd); for Chowdhary School, see *Basildon Recorder*, 13 July 1966; school photo albums, Essex County Council Archives. The brass plaque is in the possession of Laindon Conservation Centre for eventual display at the Dunton Plotlands Museum, letter from Janet Smith, Assistant County Archivist, ECCA, 7 February 1997.

84. *BMJ*, 22 July 1967. One of Gulati's sons is a doctor.

85. *Holborn Guardian*, 4 November 1938; *Medical Directories*, 1928–45; *Post Office Directory*, 1929.

86. *News Chronicle*, 19 June 1948; *Islington Gazette* 11 June 1948.

87. Kay Beauchamp, in John Allan, *Berthold Lubetkin* (RIBA Publications, 1992), p. 368, f/n 42; ibid., p. 333.

88. Official Minutes, 25 June and 26 November 1935; 18 February and 5 March 1936, Finsbury Borough Council, FA; Allan, *Lubetkin*, pp. 118, 331.

89. *IG*, 25 October 1938; *Opening of the Health Centre*, 21 October 1938; Finsbury Borough Council, official minutes, 20 October 1936; 'Finsbury makes a Programme', *The Architectural Review*, January 1939, pp. 5–22; Metropolitan Borough of Finsbury, Annual Report on Public Health, 1938, all FA.

90. Allan, *Lubetkin*, p. 333.

91. *IG*, 11 June 1948; *IG*, 26 October 1938; *NC*, 19 June 1948; *Finsbury Citizen*, November and December 1937.

92. *IG*, 11 November 1938; *HG*, 4 November 1938; *Medical Directories*, 1939–45; *IG*, 8 November 1940; recollection of Monica Pearson, *DT*, 23 October 1975.

93. Special Council Meeting, 8 June 1948, FA; *IG*, 11 June 1948; *DT*, 31 October 1975.

94. Sarvepalli Gopal, *Radhakrishnan* (Delhi: Oxford University Press, 1989); Maan, *New Scots*, pp. 129–30; *The Keys*, vol. 1, nos. 1–3; IOR: L/P&J/12/646 Indian activities in the UK, 5 August and 28 December 1944.

95. IOR: L/P&J/12/302, Karandikar file; Petrie, *Communism*, p. 370; IOR: L/P&J/12/186, Seal file; IOR: L/P&J/12/262–263, Khan files; *Oriental Post*, No. 28, December 1944.

96. J. Maclaren-Ross, *Memoirs of the Forties* (Penguin Books, 1984), pp. 135–52; *Poetry London*, vol. 1, no. 1, February 1939; vol. 3, No. 11, September–October 1947; Cedric Dover, *Half-Caste* (London: Secker & Warburg, 1937); E.M. Forster and others, *Talking to India* (London: George Allen & Unwin, 1943); George Orwell, *The Complete Works* (London: Secker & Warburg, 1998), vol. 13, p. xxiv.

97. Mulk Raj Anand, *Conversations in Bloomsbury* (New Delhi: Oxford University Press, 1995 edn); *The Bubble, A Novel* (New Delhi: Arnold Heinemann, 1984); Alastair Niven, *The Yoke of Pity* (New Delhi:

Arnold-Heinemann, 1978); *Independent*, 3 January 1997; *Guardian*, 8 January 1997; IOR: L/P&J/12/639.

98. Twentieth Century Library series includes J.A. Hobson, *Democracy*; N. Bentwich, *The Jews*, J.H. Drabber, *The Black Races*, Ralph Fox, *Communism*, and W. Holtby, *Women*; for Penguin–Pelicans, see, *Penguins: A Retrospect 1935–51* (Penguin Books, 1951); Sir Emrys Williams, *The Penguin Story 1935* (Penguin Books, 1956); *The Times*, 7 October 1974. Pelicans edited by Menon included, G.D.H. Cole, *Practical Economics*; E. Halevy, *A History of English People in 1815*; J.B.S. Haldane, *The Inequality of Man*; Roger Fry, *Vision and Design*, and H.G. Wells, *A Short History of the World*, first issued as a Penguin.

99. Callaghan, *Rajani*, p. 7; R. Palme Dutt, *Problems of Contemporary History* (London: Lawrence and Wishart, 1963); IOR: L/P&J/12/30. The Dutt family was on the 'Stop List' for passports for India, IOR: L/P&J/12/69; L/P&J/12/29 and 31; *Guardian*, 9 November 1993; IOR: L/P&J/12/518, Angadi file.

100. *Guardian*, 19 October 1988; Paul Rapoport, ed., *Sorabji A Critical Celebration* (Aldershot: Scolar Press, 1992), on which this section is based.

101. *The Times*, 17 October 1988; *Guardian*, 19 October 1988; quoted in Rapoport, ed., *Sorabji*, pp. 36, 284.

102. Rapoport, ed., *Sorabji*, pp. 260, 69.

103. *The Congregational Yearbook*, *1949*; Obituary notice; *Reuters*, 12 June 1943.

104. Family Papers, courtesy Muriel Simpson; *Twenty-Five Years Among Coloured People in London Docklands* (CMI Report, 1945–6), p. 3; *Joyful News*, 25 February 1926.

105. SOAS: WMMS Home and General, Box 672, FBN 18, No. 908; address: 'Coloured Students' Problems', Royal Empire Society, 1938, Family Papers; *Foreign Field*, November 1923; QVSR, Reports 1921–4; *Methodist Recorder*, 28 January 1926.

106. Letters in CMI *Annual Reports*, Family Papers; the petition, 24 June, to Revd E. W. Thompson, from Mrs Williams of 35 Catherine Street, E 16 and members, in SOAS: WMMS, FBN 18, No. 907; *The Negro World*, 3 July 1936.

107. SOAS: WMMS, FBN 18, No. 908, confidential statement, 21 April 1933; No. 909, record of conversation, 30 August 1934; No. 910, Shaw to Chunchie, 12 July 1935; *Christian Herald*, 8 May 1924; *FF*, November 1923. For a wider discussion of relations between the Methodists and Chunchie, see Visram, 'Chunchie'.

108. CMI *Annual Reports* 1933–52; SOAS: WMMS, FBN nos 908 and 906. For Shoran Singha, *MT*, 18 March 1921 and IOR: L/I/1/1516.

109. *Sunday Circle*, 18 April 1936; CMI *Annual Reports*, 1933–52 and photograph albums; *The Keys*, vol. 4, nos 3 and 4; *Young India Abroad*, Annual Report of Indian Students' Union Hostel, 1936; Family Papers: fragment of newspaper cutting; letter to *West Africa* from a 'visitor', 14 January 1937.

110. CMI, *Annual Reports*, auditors' report, signed Messrs M.L. Bhargava, 1949–50; CMI, *Annual Reports* from 1935. Detailed analysis of his work in Visram, 'Chunchie'.

111. Chowdhary, *Home*, pp. 3, 7–9, 13, 24–5, 64–5; see also, Anand, *Bubble*; Ayyar, *Indian*.

112. Chowdhary, *Home*, pp. 15, 19 and 29.

113. Chowdhary, *Home*, pp. 68–90; Savitri Chowdhary, *Indian Cooking* (London: André Deutsch, 1954); Shakun Banfield, Introduction (1999 edn); letters from George Chowdharay-Best, 13 and 19 April 1997.

114. Chowdhary, *Home*, pp. 46–9.

115. Chowdhary, *Home*, p. 90; IOR: L/E/9/967, 26 April 1935.

116. Sheila Allen, *New Minorities*, *Old Conflicts* (New York: Random House, 1971), p. 34.

117. Secretary, Indian Social Club to Town Clerk, Poplar Borough Council, 22 November 1938, THA; *ELA*, 20 October 1933; *EEN*, 20 October 1933; and compare Sehri Saklatvala, *The Fifth Commandment* (Salford: Miranda Press, 1991), pp. 424–5; *Yorkshire Post*, 30 March 1984; Prem, *Leper*, p. 6.

118. See relevant reports in IOR: L/P&J/12/455–6 and L/P&J/12/646; Prem, *Leper*; IOR L/P&J/12/4.

119. Hinnells and Ralph, *Bhownaggree*, pp. 29–30.

120. IOR: L/P&J/12/468, *The East London Mosque and Islamic Cultural Centre*, Opening Ceremony, 1 August 1941; Scotland Yard report, 6 August 1941; Suhrawardy to Amery, 27 July 1942; IPI fact sheet, 30 October 1943; IOR: L/P&J/12/646, Indian Notes, 25 September 1944.

121. IOR: L/P&J/12/497.

122. Ayyar, *Indian*, p. 298.

10 RADICAL VOICES

1. IOR: L/P&J/12/256, reports 29 July, 18 November 1925, 24 March and 14 July 1926; IOR: L/P&J/12/257, 12 October 1927; IOR: L/P&J/12/258, reports 28 December 1927, 27 June 1928.

2. IOR: L/P&J/12/256–258; IOR: L/P&J/12/409, Gunewardena file; IFL booklet and letterhead, L/P&J/12/258.

3. IOR: L/P&J/12/256, IFL circular; report 24 March 1926; IOR: L/P&J/12/2 58, IFL booklet; reports 13 June and 11 July 1928; Franklin to Garvey, 12 June 1928; IOR: L/P&J/12/259, 29 March 1929; IOR: L/P&J/12/260, 22 July 1931; IOR: L/P&J/12/261, 8 June and 6 July 1932.

4. IOR: L/P&J/12/257, 13 February and 23 March 1927.

5. IOR: L/P&J/12/257, letter 11 March 1927; IO to IPI, 19 March 1927; IPI to Monteath, secret and personal, 25 April 1927; IOR: L/P&J/12/258, IO to Mrs Fitzroy-Clarke, 6 September 1928; reports 5 September and 28 November 1928.

6. IOR: L/P&J/12/257, Metropolitan Police Report on Katwaroon, 12 October 1927; IO correspondence on Das and Pathy, 19 September, 8 November

and 2 December, 1927; IO to Lloyd, CO, 9 December 1927 and Lloyd to IO, 16 December 1927; IOR: L/P&J/12/258–61, reports.

7. IOR: L/P&J/J/12/258, IFL to Saklatvala, signed Khan, 4 July 1927; IOR: L/P&J/12/259, 3 April 1929; IOR: L/P&J/12/262, report 23 July 1930.

8. Present among the 63 were: Tarini Prasad Sinha (Convenor), N.R. Lotwala, Dr Saeed Mohamedi, Clemens Dutt, Nur Jehan Mohammed Yusuf, Mrs Hansa Sen, Dr Vakil, M.A. Khan, Dr Pardhay, Upadhyaya and Saklatvala. IOR: L/P&J/12/361, Scotland Yard special report 17 June 1928; IOR: L/P&J/12/362, 18 March 1929 and affiliation letter, 8 May 1929; for its constitution, office holders and membership, IOR: L/P&J/12/363 and 361. LBINC offices: 30 St John Street, Chancery Lane.

9. IOR: L/P&J/12/361, 14 November 1928; IOR: L/P&J/12/363, reports 28 March 1929, 22 January, 2 April, 14, 28 May, 12 November 1930; IOR: L/P&J/12/364, 18 July 1931.

10. Ayyar, *Indian*, pp. 78–9; IOR: L/P&J/12/361, 17 October 1928; IOR: L/P&J/12/363, draft Resolution Students' Commission, 23 July 1930; IOR: L/P&J/12/42, note Indian Students' Hostel; reports 1 December 1926, 20 August 1930; IOR: L/P&J/12/4, confidential note, nd, 'Situation in Cambridge', H.L.O. Garrett; IOR: L/P&J/12/252, IO, nd to Vice-Chancellor, Pembroke College.

11. IOR: L/P&J/12/363, 15 October 1930; draft resolution Political Commission, 23 July 1930; 2 April and 17 September 1930; *Workers' Life*, 26 July 1929, IOR: L/P&J/12/362; IOR: L/P&J/12/364, 4 March 1931.

12. IOR: L/P&J/12/362, reports 20 March 1929, 17 April 1929 and circular; 'Oral Answers', quoted in Saklatvala, *Commandment*, pp. 393–4.

13. Saklatvala, *Commandment*, p. 3; *Hansard*, vol. 213, col. 2274, 25 November 1927.

14. Saklatvala, *Commandment*, pp. 26–7; Mike Squires, *Saklatvala* (London: Lawrence & Wishart, 1990), p. 4; Panchanan Saha, *Shapurji Saklatvala* (New Delhi: People's Publishing House, 1970), pp. 2–3.

15. Saklatvala, *Commandment*, pp. 31–3; Squires, *Saklatvala*, pp. 5–6; Saha, *Shapurji*, p. 3; Marc Wadsworth, *Comrade Sak* (Leeds: Peepal Tree, 1998), p. 21; *Sunday Worker*, Saklatvala's interview in 1925; PRO: FO 372/2561, memo to Arthur Henderson, November 1929.

16. *DW*, 20 January 1936; IOR: MSS EUR D 1173, Saklatvala Papers, 15 March 1937 from Mrs S. Richards and 2 March 1937 from Clynes, secretary, GMWU.

17. The League's Minute Book impounded by the police in November 1917 records among its members a 'Mr Saklatarals', most probably a misprint, see Partha Sarathi Gupta, 'British Labour and the Indian Left 1919–1939', in B.R. Nanda, ed., *Socialism in India* (New Delhi: Vikas Publications, 1972), p. 73, f/n 13.

18. *DH*, 19 April 1913; S.V. Bracher, *The Herald Book of Labour Members*, 1922.

19. Petri, *Communism*, p. 367: Petri claims Saklatvala's association with Indian revolutionaries began in New York, before his arrival in England; IOR:

POS 8966, B series, weekly report 6 December 1910; IOR: V/27/262/1.

20. IOR: POS 8969, 11 April 1911; Arthur Field, writing to Beram Saklatvala in 1937, claimed the WWLI was founded in 1917 by C.F. Ryder and himself, and Saklatvala joined 'within a year', IOR: MSS EUR D 1173. However, the actual date was 1916, the initiative coming in 1911, see Saklatvala, 'India in the Labour World', *Labour Monthly*, November 1921; Sant Nihal Singh, 'When the Deputation arrives in London', *Commonweal*, 25 April 1919 and 2 May 1919. The WWLI had two committees: Saklatavala headed the Indian section, and John Arnall the English committee; Field was general-secretary, J.M. Parikh, president (later K.S. Bhatt) and K.P. Mehta, a Tata employee and Saklatvala's friend, treasurer.

21. Statement of Principles, 1918, in Saklatvala, *Commandment*, pp. 92–6.

22. Statement to the Joint Committee, 25 January 1919, in Squires, *Saklatvala*, p. 159.

23. Saklatvala, *Commandment*, pp. 112–21.

24. Saklatvala, *Commandment*, pp. 112–13; for WWLI and AITUC, see Marjorie Nicholson, *The TUC Overseas* (London: Allen & Unwin, 1986), pp. 151–5.

25. *Labour Leader*, 4 December 1915, 1 January 1920; *ILP Annual Conference*, 1918; Squires, *Saklatvala*, p. 16.

26. *LL*, 26 April 1917 and 24 July 1918.

27. *ILP Annual Conference*, 1918 and 1919. T.P. Sinha, ILP research worker, became secretary of its Advisory Committee, IOR: L/P&J/12/303, Sinha file.

28. G.R. Williams, *London in the Country* (London: Hamish Hamilton, 1975), p. 105; Michael Ward, *Red Flag Over the Workhouse* (Wandsworth History Workshop, 1992), p. 5; for Battersea's radical tradition, see Barry Kosmin, 'Political Identity in Battersea', in Sandra Wallman, *Living in South London* (Aldershot: Gower, 1982); Richard Price, *An Imperial War and the British Working Class* (London: Routledge & Kegan Paul, 1972).

29. *South Western Star*, 3 February 1922; and ibid., 22 July 1932 and 24 March 1922; George Padmore, *Pan-Africanism or Communism?* (London: Dennis Dobson, 1956), p. 29; Saklatvala's 1922 Election Address, Wandsworth Local History Library.

30. *Daily Graphic*, 30 October 1924; *British Weekly*, 11 December 1924; *DH*, 3 December 1923; *DG*, 30 October 1924.

31. *BW*, 11 December 1924; *Communist*, 25 November 1922.

32. Letter 7 October 1925, in Wadsworth, *Comrade*, p. 150; Kulke, *Parsees*, p. 230 and f/n 21; *DE*, 21 May 1929; see for instance, *MP*, 28 February 1926.

33. Kosmin, 'Battersea', p. 29; *DH*, 11 May 1929.

34. Foreword by Dutt, in Saha, *Shapurji*, p. viii; *Daily Chronicle*, 28 November 1923; *DE*, 4 December 1923.

35. *Evening Standard*, 26 November 1923; *DT*, 19 November 1923 and ibid., 1 December 1923; *DC*, 28 November and 1 December 1923; *MP*, 30 November 1923; *DN*, 1 December 1923; *DH*, 3 and 4 December 1923.

36. *Hansard*, 23 November 1923.

37. *Hansard*, 5 July 1923; *The Times*, 6 July 1923; Saklatvala, *The British Labour Government and India*, TUC and the Labour Party, No. 9 July 1924, in Wadsworth, *Comrade*, pp. 144–9.

38. Saklatvala to Joshi, 10 March 1926, in Gupta, 'British Labour', p. 81; Saklatvala to Bhownaggree, 23 June 1930, ZHA.

39. *Hansard*, 9 July 1925; Simon Commission debate, in Saklatvala, *Commandment*, Ch. 19.

40. IOR: MSS EUR D 1173, Prabhuram and Saratkumari Chatterjee, 13 February 1937; quoted in Hakim Adi, *West Africans in Britain 1900–1960* (London: Lawrence & Wishart, 1998), p. 44; *Hansard*, 9 July 1925; e.g. Saklatvala, *Socialism and 'Labourism'* (CPGB, 1928).

41. *MG*, 3 May 1926; *The British Gazette*, 5 May 1926.

42. Quoted in Fryer, *Staying Power*, p. 352; *MG*, 7 May 1926; Saklatvala, *Commandment*, pp. 313, 316.

43. PRO: FO 372/2561, memo to Henderson.

44. *Evening News*, 29 August and 17 September 1925; *DT*, 18 September 1925.

45. *DT*, 17 and 19 September 1925, ibid., 16 January 1929; *SW*, 20 September 1925; *DH*, 18 September 1925 and 22 January 1929; *The Times*, 3 January 1927; *DW*, 21 February 1926.

46. *DG*, 11 August 1925; *BC*, 17 January 1927. Indian newspapers in WLHL and IOR: MSS EUR D 1173.

47. *BC*, 15, 17 and 24 January 1927; *Ibid*, 21 February 1927; *Ibid*, 7 March 1927; Nicholson, *TUC*, p. 124.

48. *BC*, 27 and 29 January 1927; ibid., 5 February 1927, Lala Rajpat Rai's reply; *The Times*, 11 October 1927; *BC*, 1 March and 19 January 1927.

49. "Who is this Gandhi?", *LM*, 1930; *LM*, November 1921.

50. Chandra, *Independence*, p. 506; B.S. Josh, *Comrade Sak* (Channel 4, 1990), IOR: MSS EUR R 204, for video cassette.

51. IOR: MSS EUR C 152/3, vol. ii, Irwin to IO, 16 March 1927; 9 October 1927.

52. IOR: MSS EUR C 152/3, vol. i, Birkenhead to Irwin, 22 September 1927 and 8 December 1927; IOR: L/P&J/12/363, 11 December 1929.

53. IOR: MSS EUR D 1173, Saklatvala in Nottingham, 17 December 1926; Thomas Bell, *Pioneering Days* (London: Lawrence & Wishart, 1941), p. 265; Saklatvala, *Commandment*, pp. 332, 315.

54. *DW*, 18 January 1936.

55. IOR: L/P&J/12/362, 23 June 1929; IOR: L/P&J/12/363, 8 January 1930; IOR: L/P&J/12/364, IPI report 28 January 1931; IOR: L/P&J/12/381, 3 April 1929; Saklatvala, *Commandment*, pp. 426–35.

56. *NC*, 5 August 1931; IOR: L/P&J/12/364, Nehru's letter, 16 September 1931; Saklatvala's open letter, 10 June 1931, and Manifesto attached to 28 October 1931 report; IOR: L/P&J/12/372, 21 June 1933; *DW*, 26 June 1931.

57. IOR: L/P&J/12/362, IPI report 29 October 1929; IOR: L/P&J/12/356, 10 December 1930; IOR: L/P&J/12/364, 8 July 1931; IPI report 4 August

1931; reports 5 August, 28 October and 11 November 1931; *DW*, 26 and 29 June 1931; IOR: L/P&J/12/356, 20 January, 1932.

58. See files L/P&J/12/441 and L/P&J/12/371; for Rienzi, IOR: L/P&J/12/252, from GOI to IO, 14 November 1932 and IPI to Clauson, 2 December 1932.

59. IOR: L/P&J/12/364, IPI report 15 September 1939; *DW*, 9 July 1932; IOR: L/P&J/12/372, reports 27 September and 11 October 1933; Squires, *Saklatvala*, p. 197.

60. *DW*, 7 July 1934; e.g. his late son, Beram, see Squires, *Saklatvala*, p. 204; Comintern Archives: 495/100/938.

61. CA: 495/100/938.

62. He also received a pension. *Daily Mirror*, 23 July 1927; *DG*, 18 September 1925; *The Times*, 13 July and 14 September 1925.

63. *LM*, February 1936; *BC*, 15 February 1936; Padmore, *Pan-Africanism*, p. 29; G.D. Overstreet and M. Windmiller, *Communism in India* (Berkeley: University of California Press, 1959), p. 175; Hugh Thomas, *The Spanish Civil War* (London, 1965), pp. 487–8.

64. IOR: L/P&J/12/646, IPI Indian Notes 5 August 1944; T.J.S. George, *Krishna Menon* (London: Jonathan Cape, 1964), p. 150; also for biographical details, Suhash Chakravarty, *V.K. Krishna Menon and the India League* (New Delhi: Har-Anand Publications, 1997) vol. i, pp. 13–88; *DNB* (Oxford University Press), vol. i, 1971–80, pp. 560–61.

65. IOR: L/P&J/12/455, the date for its founding is given as 1912, report 23 December 1942; IOR: L/P&J/12/356, minute and letter signed Peel, 7 December 1931; George, *Krishna*, p. 53.

66. IOR: L/P&J/12/356, reports 25 June and 12 November 1930; IOR: L/P&J/12/448, 16 March 1932; League letterhead 8 November 1932; George, *Krishna*, pp. 53–7; Chakravarty, *Menon*, vol. i, Chs 1–2.

67. IOR: L/P&J/12/356, Cleaver to IO, 1 December 1931 and reply, 7 December 1931; report 3 February 1932; IOR: L/P&J/12/448, 16 March 1932; League letterhead 8 November 1932; Julius Silverman, 'The India League', in *A Centenary History of the Indian National Congress 1885–1985* (New Delhi: Vikas Publishing), vol. iii.

68. Barnes and Nicholson, eds, *Empire*, pp. 97–8, 104; Churchill to Stuart, 16 September 1931, quoted in Chakravarty, *Menon*, vol. ii, pp. 31, 26–9; IOR: L/P&J/12/448, IPI to Clauson, 30 November 1932.

69. IOR: L/P&J/12/450, reports 21 April and 5 May 1937; IOR: L/P&J/12/453, national delegates' conference 10 August 1941; IOR: L/I/1/890, Flyer, 'Let the People of Britain Speak', and conference programme; IOR: L/P&J/12/3 56, 29 October 1930.

70. Chagla, *Roses*, p. 232; IOR: L/I/1/2457; recollections of Nawab Ali, in Adams, ed., *Seven Seas*, p. 78; surveillance files, IOR: L/P&J/12/323; IOR: L/P&J/12/448–56.

71. George, *Krishna*, pp. 63–4.

72. Chakravarty, *Menon*, vol. i, p. 285; IOR: L/P&J/12/631, Bhicoo Batlivala in *Los Angeles Examiner*, 5 March 1940; IOR: L/I/1/890, *India Pictorial*, 1945; Alex Sloan, MP, at the Glasgow conference 5–6 September 1941.

73. IOR: L/P&J/12/323, IPI to Silver, 15 June 1937; George, *Krishna*, pp. 65–6.

74. IOR: L/P&J/12/455, 23 December 1942; note by Williamson, 14 March 1933, quoted in Gupta, 'British Labour', pp. 108–9.

75. IOR: L/P&J/12/448, League letterhead, November 1932; IOR: L/P&J/12/4 78, reports 23 December 1942, 20 January, 17 February, 3 March, 1943; IPI to Silver, 24 November 1941; Silverman, 'India League', p. 848; George, *Krishna*, p. 69.

76. IOR: L/P&J/12/453–5.

77. IOR: Neg. 9837, part B, 5 May 1914; IOR: L/P&J/12/42, reports 1 December 1926, 30 April 1930; IOR: L/P&J/12/4, IPI to Silver, 23 November 1937; report 11 August 1937; IOR: L/I/1/144, minute signed EMB, 12 March 1948; Sonia Gandhi, ed., *Freedom's Daughter* (London: Hodder & Stoughton, 1989); D.F. Karaka, *The Pulse of Oxford* (London: J.M. Dent & Sons, 1933), pp. 35–9. For surveillance files on student organisations, IOR: L/P&J/12/4; L/P&J/12/42; L/P&J/12/405–7; L/P&J/12/475; see also IOR: L/I/1/143; and *Memoirs of T. Subasinghe* (unpublished), Institute of Commonwealth Studies Library, London.

78. IOR: L/P&J/12/384, Note Misc., No. 17/IPI, 29 July 1940; IOR: L/P&J/12 /42, IPI to Silver, 27 September 1940; Subasinghe, *Memoirs*; League files, IOR: L/P&J/12/453–6 and IOR: L/P&J/12/646. For the Subject People's Conference, IOR: L/P&J/12/658, annual report Swaraj House, 1945.

79. IOR: L/I/1/1457; IOR: L/P&J/12/456, Special Branch report 25 October 1944; for national officers and executive committee, IOR: L/P&J/12/454, report 5 August 1942; for office bearers in the provincial branches, 1942–3, IOR: L/P&J/12/646; for membership, IOR: L/I/1/890, invitation card, and K.C. Arora, *Indian Nationalist Movement in Britain, 1930–1949* (New Delhi: Inter-India Publications, 1992), pp. 211–15; for the East End branch, IOR: L/P&J/12/455, report 23 June 1943.

80. IOR: L/P&J/12/454, 25 November 1942; IOR: L/P&J/12/455, 18 September 1943; IOR: L/P&J/12/451, Misc. No. 14, 20 October 1938; George, *Krishna*, pp. 71–4, 120.

81. George, *Krishna*, p. 97; Gandhi, ed., *Daughter*, pp. 354 and 388; IOR: L/P&J/12/456, Menon to Nehru, 22 September 1945; IOR: L/P&J/12/478, Vaidya file. For surveillance files on these organisations, IOR: L/P&J/12/4 28, L/P&J/12/658, and L/P&J/12/646.

82. IOR: L/P&J/12/448, 2 March 1932; letter to the Council, reproduced in Silverman, 'India League', pp. 849–50.

83. *Condition of India* (London: Essential News, 1933), pp. 155–6; 195, 162.

84. *Condition*, pp. 245, 247, 182–3.

85. *Condition*, pp. 464; 271 and 354–5; IOR: L/P&J/12/448, IPI to Clauson, 28 November 1932 and League Conference, 26 November 1932.

86. IOR: L/P&J/12/448, IPI to Clauson, 28 November 1932; conference report, 7 December 1932; IOR: L/I/1/50, London Conference, private report.

87. IOR: L/I/1/50, Commons Adjournment (Xmas) India debate; IOR: L/ P&J/12/448, letter and list dated 29 July 1932, together with minutes and

replies; weekly DIB reports and letters, e.g. 6 October 1932 and from Hallet, 3 October 1932.

88. IOR: L/P&J/12/448, memo 16 October and telegram 24 October 1932; government's case against the League delegation; IOR: L/I/1/50, Director of Public Information, GOI, to MacGregor, IO, 24 October, 13 and 26 November 1932.

89. IOR: L/I/1/50, cutting from *Hindustan Times*, 1 December 1932; Stephens to MacGregor, 12 December 1932; minutes 22 March, 13 and 14 October 1933; MacGregor to Davies of the Newspaper Society, 18 October 1933 and MacGregor to Crawford of *DM*, 31 March 1934; IOR: L/P&J/12/449, cypher telegram GOI to IO, 25 March 1934; Note by Williamson, quoted in Gupta, 'British Labour', p. 110.

90. *Condition*, p. xiii.

91. Quoted in George, *Krishna*, pp. 110–11.

92. IOR: L/P&J/12/451, League circular 'National Independence Demo, 1938'; reports 12 January and 9 February 1938; George, *Krishna*, pp. 115–16; Nehru, *Autobiography*, p. 601.

93. *DW*, 29 June 1938; Martin Bauml Duberman, *Paul Robeson* (London: The Bodley Head, 1989), pp. 225, 266; Subasinghe, *Memoir*.

94. IOR: L/P&J/12/451, 15 June 1938; IOR: L/P&J/12/456, reports 19 January 1944, 28 February 1945, and 24 October 1946; Gandhi, ed., *Daughter*, pp. 319, 321, 324 and 346–7.

95. IOR: L/P&J/12/323, reports 14 July 1937 and 6 April 1938; IOR: L/P&J/12/456, 2 February 1944.

96. George, *Krishna*, 87.

97. Council Minutes, 1934–47, Camden Local Studies and Archives; George, *Krishna*, p. 88.

98. George, *Krishna*, pp. 121–2; Special Meeting, Metropolitan Borough of St Pancras and Order of Proceedings, 28 January 1955, CLS&A; *Hampstead and Highgate Express*, 4 February 1955.

99. *DW*, 29 April 1940; *Dundee Telegraph and Post*, 18 April 1940; IOR: L/P&J/12/323, 1 May 1940; V.K. Krishna Menon, 10 June 1940. See also *DT*, May 1940.

100. *MG*, 9 January 1941; *DW*, 3 January 1941.

101. IOR: L/P&J/12/323, telegram Joyce to Puckle, 14 January 1941; IOR: L/I/1/890, Byrt to *Times of India*, 2 January 1941; *The Times* obituary, 7 October 1974, refers to Menon's 'communist leanings'.

102. IOR: L/P&J/12/323, V.K. Krishna Menon, 10 June 1940; IOR: L/I/1/890, Leach to Joyce, 29 August 1941; draft, nd, and Leach to Joyce, 19 August 1941; George, *Krishna*, pp. 130–1.

103. *MG*, 9 January 1941; *DW*, 3 January 1941.

104. IOR: L/P&J/12/323, interview with Nehru, 10 May 1940.

105. *India, Britain and Freedom* (India League, 1941); IOR: L/P&J/12/323, Menon's note on 'India and the War', 18 September 1939; R.J. Moore, *Escape from Empire* (Oxford: Clarendon Press, 1983), pp. 7–10; Barnes and Nicholson, *Empire*, pp. 636–7.

106. IOR: L/P&J/12/453, reports 15 January–1 July 1941; IPI to Silver, 25–6 September 1941; cypher telegram IO to GOI, 24 June 1941.

107. IOR: L/P&J/12/453, IPI to Silver, with details and reports of the conference: 19 July, 7 August, 15 August 1941, and minute to the SS on the conference; IOR: L/I/1/890, for programme, resolutions and report by Sir Frank Brown.

108. IOR: L/I/1/890, conference report; IOR: L/P&J/12/454, 4 February 1942; IOR: L/P&J/12/453, meeting hosted by Rebecca Sieff, IPI notes 11, 14, 20, 28 October 1941.

109. Moore, *Empire*, pp. 11–12.

110. IOR: L/I/1/890, Morley to Brock, 27 June 1942; IOR: L/P&J/12/323, Indian Notes 9 May 1942; Menon's activities, 5 August 1941; IOR: L/P&J/12/646, Indian Notes 15 December and 10 June 1942; and activities for 1942–6.

111. IOR: L/P&J/12/454, IPI to Silver, 28 September and 1 October 1942; Scotland Yard report 3 February 1943, IOR: L/P&J/12/455.

112. IOR: L/I/1/890 for flyers and copy of *India Pictorial*; IOR: L/P&J/12/454, IPI to Silver, 28 September and 1 October 1942; Special Branch report 25 August 1942; IOR: L/P&J/12/455, 3 February 1943; IOR: L/P&J/12/454, 4 February 1942.

113. IOR: L/I/1/890, Edwards to Amery, 29 June 1942; League Birmingham Branch flyers; IOR: L/P&J/12/454, circular 12 June 1942, signed Prem; Executive Committee meeting, Birmingham Branch, 19 August 1942; Shop Stewards Conference Conway Hall, 6 June 1942; IOR: L/P&J/12/456, Birmingham City Police, 25 January 1944; IOR: L/P&J/12/646 Indian Notes, 10 June 1942; Silverman, 'India League', p. 857.

114. IOR: L/P&J/12/456, Menon's memo.

115. IOR: L/P&J/12/631, Batlivala file; IOR: L/P&J/12/453, IPI to Silver, 25 August and 12 September, 1941; IOR: L/P&J/12/455, IPI to Silver, 'most secret', 28 June 1943; draft letter, IO to Butler, July 1943 with minutes, 30 July 1943 and 13 June 1944; PRO notice, 23 October 1996.

116. IOR: L/I/1/890, undated draft letter from Munster to Kemsley and report by a Special Representative, 22 June 1942; IOR: L/P&J/12/639.

117. IOR: L/I/1/890; IOR: L/P&J/12/455, internal notes: League counter-propaganda, nd signed VWS, minute and note 'antidote to the poison', 12 February 1943.

118. IOR: L/I/1/890, MacGregor to Robieson, *GH*, and Waters, *Scotsman*, 6 July 1942; draft letter, nd, Munster to Kemsley; draft letter, Watson and minute, Joyce, 10 July 1942; IOR: L/P&J/12/455, Ministry of Supply, Paper Control to Judd, 20 July 1942; Edwards to Amery, 1 February 1943; IPI to Silver, 'Position with regard to India League', 1 February 1943.

119. IOR: L/P&J/12/455, League counter-propaganda, signed VWS; minute 12 February 1943; IOR: L/I/1/890, letter nd from Munster to Kemsley; Joyce to Edwards, 8 July 1942; Morley to Huxley, 11 January, 12 and 16 February 1943.

120. IOR: L/I/1/890, minute signed HM, 8 April 1942; Morley to Gillam, 9 July

1943; IO to Brooks, 4 September 1942; 'Questions suitable for putting to Krishna Menon', 1942; IOR: L/I/1/1520, Sorabji file; IOR: L/P&J/12/455, Sorabji to Morrison, 21 January 1943; IOR: L/I/1/57, Joyce to Basu, 14 July 1936.

121. IOR: L/I/1/890, MacGregor to Robieson, 6 July 1942; Joyce to Suhrawardy, 3 July 1942; Moore, *Empire*, p. 8; IOR: L/P&J/12/631, minute to Joyce, signed CEN, 1 December, 1942; 'Talk with Mr Yusuf Ali', signed CEN, 17 December 1939.

122. IOR: L/I/1/890, Leach to Joyce, 19 and 29 August 1941, with confidential draft, n. d.; IOR: L/P&J/12/630, Viceroy's telegram, 21 Novemer 1939 and minutes; IOR: L/P&J/12/323, Linlithgow to Amery, 23 June 1942, and minute, 8 July 1942; Linlithgow to Amery, 20 November 1942, *Transfer of Power* (HMSO, 1972), vol. ii, document 233; IOR: L/P&J/12/455, IPI to Silver, 1 February 1943, 'Possible Action'.

123. *Labour Party Annual Report*, 1944. To prevent the resolution on India being lost for lack of time, a deputation requested Laski, Conference chairman, to bring it forward in the agenda, Scotland Yard report, 20 December 1944, IOR: L/P&J/12/456.

124. Quoted in Silverman, *India League*, p. 865; IOR: L/P&J/12/478, Nehru's letter to Swaraj House, report 29 August 1946.

125. IOR: L/P&J/12/455, 23 December 1942; Conference report 13 October 1943.

126. Mountbatten to Menon, 10 July 1947; Viceroy's Personal Report 11 July 1947; Mountbatten to Listowel, 25 July 1947, *Power*, vol. xii, documents 55, 65 and 227, pp. 70, 92, 330.

127. IOR: L/P&J/12/456, Metropolitan Police reports 10 October, 21 November, 1945; Manchester City Police, 22 November 1945; IOR: L/P&J/12/65 8, 21 November 1945.

128. *Camden and St Pancras Chronicle*, 4 and 18 March 1977; *Camden Journal*, 6 December 1974. Camden Council contributed the plinth for a bronze head of Menon unveiled in Fitzroy Square by Michael Foot in 1977. The memorial no longer exists, having being stolen in 1981.

11 CONTRIBUTIONS IN THE SECOND WORLD WAR

1. IOR: L/MIL/17/5/4263; IOR: L/I/1/837 and L/I/1/836; IOR: L/I/1/858; Bisheshwar Prasad, ed., *Official History of the Indian Armed Forces in the Second World War* (Combined Inter-Services Historical Section: India and Pakistan, 1960), vols i–iv.

2. IOR: L/I/1/978.

3. *The Times*, 7 and 28 December 1940; IOR: L/I/1/978; IOR: L/P&J/12/643. Despite glowing publicity and PR, surveillance reports hint at trainee dissatisfaction with the 'elementary' training and control exercised over them, IPI note, 23 June 1941, Review, 12 September 1941 and Report, n.d. in IOR: L/P&J/12/643.

4. IOR: L/I/1/903; IOR: L/I/1/836; *The Times*, 25 January and 7 March 1941.

5. IOR: L/MIL/17/5/4263; IOR: L/I/1/858.

6. IOR: L/MIL/17/5/4278; IOR: L/I/1/836.

7. IOR: L/MIL/17/5/4263; IOR: L/I/1/837; D.F. Karaka, *With the Fourteenth Army* (London: Dorothy Crisp & Co., 1945).

8. IOR: L/MIL/17/5/4261-4262; IOR: L/I/1/903; IOR: L/I/1/836; quoted in S.L. Menezes, *Fidelity and Honour* (New Delhi: Oxford University Press, 1999), p. 347; *Birmingham Post*, 11 September 1941; *OM*, 14 March 1941; Forster, *Talking to India*.

9. Dharm Pal, *The Campaigns in Italy 1943–45*, pp. xxv, 143, in Prasad, *History*, vol. iv.

10. Pal, *Italy*, vol. iv, pp. 143, 273; IOR: L/MIL/17/5/4281; IOR: L/MIL/17/5/4 280, pp. 72, 189; *The Times*, obituary, 21 July 1999.

11. Menezes, *Fidelity*, pp. 347, 357 and 371; and IOR: MSS EUR T3.

12. IOR: L/I/1/836; IOR: L/I/1/903; IOR: L/MIL/17/5/4263; Subasinghe, *Memoir*.

13. IOR: L/MIL/17/5/4261.

14. IAF appointment, August 1940; personal interview, September 1986; Visram, *Indians*, p. 46.

15. IOR: L/I/1/858; Singh, *Legends*, pp. 57–69.

16. PRO: MT 9/3657, document 12; *Our Merchant Seamen* (Government of India, 1947); IOR: L/I/1/840, memo, December 1941; IO to Director General, MOWT, July 1945.

17. Quoted in Adams, ed., *Seven Seas*, p. 38; GOI, *Seamen*.

18. Quoted in Adams, ed., *Seven Seas*, pp. 34, 37; PRO ADM 199/2147, *Sutlej* 18 July 1944. The compliment to the 'two natives', however, is back-handed.

19. Quoted in Lane, *Seamen's War*, pp. 178–9; in Adams, ed., *Seven Seas*, p. 35.

20. GOI, *Seamen*.

21. IOR: L/I/1/840, memo, December 1941; GOI Bureau of Information, 2 July 1943, signed Bhatt; GOI to IO, 26 June 1945; IOR: L/I/1/837; IOR: L/I/1/978, broadcast by Huque, 23 February 1943.

22. L/I/1/1056, liability for military service.

23. IOR: L/I/1/118.

24. Subasinghe, *Memoir;* IOR: L/I/1/120, Education Department report, 1939–40; Prem, *Leper*, p. 7.

25. IOR: L/I/1/1042.

26. IOR: L/I/1/837, Indian Comforts Fund, 1939–45.

27. IOR: L/P&J/12/323, IPI to Silver, 14 April 1942.

28. IOR: L/I/1/837; IOR: L/I/1/1520.

29. Jean Overton Fuller, *Noor-un-nisa Inayat Khan* (The Hague: East-West Publications, 1971, first published as *Madeleine*, 1952), p. 37.

30. Fuller, *Noor-un-nisa*, pp. 95, 114.

31. M.R.D. Foot, *SOE The Special Operations Executive 1940-46* (London: BBC, 1984), p. 138.

32. Fuller, *Noor-un-nisa*, p. 110.
33. *Continental Daily Mail*, 6 April 1949, in Khan file, IWM; Fuller, *Noor-un-nisa*, pp. 89, 104, 119.
34. M.R.D. Foot, *SOE in France* (London: HM Stationery Office, 1966), p. 292; Fuller, *Noor-un-nisa*, pp. 130, 141.
35. Foot, *SOE*, p. 337; Jean Overton Fuller, *Double Agent?* (London: Pan Books, 1961), p. 25; *Noor-un-nisa*, pp. 127–8, 131 and 133.
36. Foot, *SOE*, p. 337; newspaper report, 'Chosen for Pluck', 5 April 1949; *CDM*, 6 April 1949, cuttings in Khan file, IWM; Fuller, *Noor-un-nisa*, p. 111.
37. Fuller, *Noor-un-nisa*, p. 150; *LG*, 5 April 1949.
38. Fuller, *Noor-un-nisa*, pp. 150–5; *LG*, 5 April 1949; Foot, *SOE*, p. 338.
39. Fuller, *Noor-un-nisa*, pp. 155-172; IWM: Khan files.
40. *LG*, 5 April 1949; Foot, *SOE*, pp. 339–40; Fuller, *Noor-un-nisa*, pp. 206–7.
41. Fuller, *Noor-un-nisa*, pp. 208–9; p. 185 and f/n 1. Foot, *SOE*, pp. 428, 339.
42. Foot, *Operations*, p. 139; *SOE*, p. 341.
43. *LG*, 5 April 1949; Foot, *SOE*, pp. 334, 428–9; Fuller, *Noor-un-nisa*, 241–9.

12 CONCLUSIONS

1. IOR: L/E/9/457, Hunter Report, 1939; *LCMM* 1 August 1857.
2. Head, *Indian Style*, pp. 67–8, 71; *The Maharajah's Well at Stoke Row* (published by the Restoration Appeal Fund, 1979).
3. BPP, No. 122 (7), p. 36.
4. Official Citation, 5 March 1945.
5. Royal Society: Citation from the Printed List of Candidates, 1918; *Proceedings of the Royal Society of London*, Series A, vol. xcix, September 1921, for obituary; Paul Hoffman, *The Man Who Loved Only Numbers* (London: Fourth Estate, 1999 edn), pp. 82–91.
6. *DNB*, ed., S.P. Sen, vol. iv, pp. 245–6.
7. Sorabji, *India Calling*, p. 28.
8. P.S. Sastri, *Ananda K. Coomaraswamy* (New Delhi: Arnold-Heinemann, 1974).
9. Nick Merriman and Rozina Visram, 'The World in a City', in Nick Merriman, ed., *The Peopling of London* (Museum of London, 1993).

Select Bibliography

1 MANUSCRIPTS AND RECORDS

All manuscripts, record collections and series details are fully cited in the footnotes. Here only some of the main collections and archives are listed.

Oriental and India Office Collections, The British Library, London (IOR)
Court Minutes: B series.
Economic and Overseas Department: L/E/7 and L/E/9 series.
European Manuscripts: MSS EUR series.
Home Miscellaneous: H/Misc. series.
Home Political Proceedings: Part A and B (microfilm).
Information Department: L/I/1 series.
Marine Records: L/MAR/B and L/MAR/C series.
Military Department: L/MIL/5 and L/MIL/7 series.
Public and Judicial Department: L/P&J/6 and L/P&J/12 series.
Political and Secret Department: L/P&S series.

Public Records Office, Kew, London (PRO)
Board of Trade Mercantile Marine Department: MT 9.
Home Office Aliens Department: HO 45; HO 213.
Treasury Letters: T1/630 etc.
War Office: WO 338 etc.

Modern Records Centre, University of Warwick, Coventry (MRC)
TUC records: MSS 292/655; MSS 292/91.

The British Library, London
BM Add. MS. 34, 282; BM Add. MS. 29, 178.

Other Repositories
The British Library Newspaper Library, Colindale, London.
BRL: Brighton Reference Library.
CLS&A: Camden Local Studies Library and Archives.
ECCA: Essex County Council Archives, Chelmsford.
ESRO: East Sussex Record Office.
FA: Finsbury Archives.

FL: Fawcett Library, London.

Guildhall Library, London.

GLHL: Greenwich Local History Library.

Hammersmith and Fulham Archives.

Institute of Commonwealth Studies, London.

IWM: Imperial War Museum, London.

King's College London (Guy's Campus).

Lewisham Local History Centre.

LMA: London Metropolitan Archives.

London City Mission Archives.

MOL: Museum of London.

Newham Local Studies Library.

Norfolk Record Office, Norwich.

Royal Commonwealth Society Library, Cambridge University.

SOAS: School of Oriental and African Studies, London.

Staffordshire Record Office, Stafford.

THA: Tower Hamlets Archives.

The Family Record Centre, London.

The Royal Society, London.

The Wellcome Library for the History and Understanding of Medicine, London.

UNL: University of North London, TUC Library Collection.

WLHL: Wandsworth Local History Library.

ZHA: Zoroastrian House Archives, London.

2 PARLIAMENTARY PAPERS

House of Commons Sessional Papers of the Eighteenth Century, Lambert, Sheila, ed., (Wilmington, Delaware, 1975), vol. 67, 1789.

Papers presented to the House of Commons from the East India Company, and also from the Commissioners for the Affairs of India, respecting the trade between India and Europe, BPP, No. 122 (7), 1801.

Reports and papers on the policy of employing India built ships in the trade of the East India Company and admitting them to the British Registry (London 1809).

Papers Relating to the East India Company, BPP, No. 357 (5), 1810.

Fourth Report from the Select Committee on the Affairs of the East India Company, Appendix No. 47, BPP, Nos 152 and 182, 1812.

Minutes and evidence taken before the Committee of the whole House and the Select Committee on the Affairs of the East India Company, BPP, No. 122, 1813.

Report from the Committee on the State of Mendicity and Vagrancy in the Metropolis, BPP No. 471, (3), 1814–15.

A Bill to Make Further Regulation for the Registry of Ships built in India, BPP, No. 281, (2), 1814–15.

A Bill as Amended by the Committee to make Further Regulation for the Registry of Ships built in India, BPP, No. 360, (2), 1814–15.

Report from the Committee on Lascars and other Asiatic Seamen, BPP, No. 471 (3), 1814–15.

Copy of all Correspondence between the Commissioners for the Affairs of India, and any other Public Body, Relative to the Care and Maintenance of Lascar Sailors, BPP, No. 279, (10), 1816.

East India Shipping: An Account of the Crews of the several ships from the East Indies and China, BPP, No. 491 (17), 1823.

East India Company Affairs: Report of the Select Committee of the House of Lords appointed to inquire into the Present State of the Affairs of the East India Company, BPP, No. 646 (6), 1830.

Report from the Select Committee on Manufactures, Commerce and Shipping, BPP, No. 690, (6), 1833.

Report from the Select Committee on British Shipping, BPP, No. 545 (8), 1844.

Fourth Report from the Select Committee on Navigational Laws, BPP, No. 556 (20), 1847.

First Report from the Select Committee of the House of Lords appointed to inquire into the Policy and Operation of Navigational Laws, BPP, No. 340 (20), 1848.

Second Report from the Select Committee of the House of Lords appointed to inquire into the Policy and Operation of the Navigational Laws, BPP, No. 431, (20), 1848.

Third Report from the Select Committee of the House of Lords appointed to inquire into the policy and operation of the Navigational Laws, BPP, No. 754 (20), 1848.

Papers Relating to the Case of George Edalji, Cmd. 3507, 1907.

Report from the Committee on Distressed Colonial and Indian Subjects, Cmd. 5133 and 5134 (22), 1910.

3 BOOKS, ARTICLES AND MEMOIRS

Adams, Caroline, ed., *Across Seven Seas and Thirteen Rivers* (London: THAP Books, 1987).

Adams, Pauline, *Somerville for Women* (Oxford: Oxford University Press, 1996).

Adi, Hakim, *West Africans in Britain 1900–1960* (London: Lawrence & Wishart, 1998).

Alexander, James E., *Shigurf Namah i Velaet … the Travels of Itesa Modeen* (London: Printed for Parbury, Allen & Co., 1927).

Alexander, M. and Anand, S., *Queen Victoria's Maharajah Duleep Singh*,

1838–1893 (London: Weidenfeld & Nicolson, 1980).

Allan, John, *Berthold Lubetkin* (London: RIBA Publications, 1992).

Allen, David R., *A Song for Cricket* (London: Pelham Books, 1981).

Allen, Sheila, *New Minorities, Old Conflicts* (New York: Random House, 1971).

Anand, Mulk Raj, *Across the Black Waters* (London: Jonathan Cape, 1940).

—— 'A Lascar Writes Home', *Our Time*, vol. 1, no. 2, April 1941, pp. 20–23.

—— *Letters on India* (London: George Routledge & Sons, 1942).

—— *Conversations in Bloomsbury* (New Delhi: Oxford University Press, 1995 edn).

—— *The Bubble, A Novel* (New Delhi: Arnold Heinemann, 1984).

Apcar, Amy, ed., *Life and Adventures of Joseph Emin, an Armenian* (Calcutta: Baptist Mission Press, 1918).

Archer, M., Rowell, C. and Skelton, R., *Treasures from India* (London: The Herbert Press in association with the National Trust, 1987).

Arora, K.C., *Indian Nationalist Movement in Britain, 1930–1949* (New Delhi: Inter-India Publications, 1992).

Aurora, G.S., *The New Frontiersmen* (Bombay: Popular Prakashan, 1967).

Ayyar, A.S.P., *An Indian in Western Europe* (Madras: C. Coomaraswamy Naidu & Sons, 1942).

Baijnath, Lala, *England and India* (Bombay: Jehangir B. Karani, 1893).

Ballhatchet, Kenneth, *Race, Sex and Class under the Raj* (London: Weidenfeld & Nicolson, 1980).

Banerjea, S., *A Nation in the Making* (London: Humphrey Milford, 1925).

Banton, Michael, *The Coloured Quarter* (London: Jonathan Cape, 1955).

Barnes, John and Nicholson, David, *The Empire at Bay* (London: Hutchinson, 1988).

Barot, Rohit, *Bristol and the Indian Independence Movement* (Bristol Branch of the Historical Association, 1988).

Bayly, C.A., ed., *The Raj* (London: National Portrait Gallery, 1990).

Behrens, C.B.A., *Merchant Shipping and the Demands of War* (London: HMSO and Longmans, Green & Co., 1955).

Bell, J.H., *British Folks and British India Fifty Years Ago* (London: John Heywood, 1891).

Bell, Thomas, *Pioneering Days* (London: Lawrence & Wishart, 1941).

Berry, Virginia, 'East End Opium Dens and Narcotic Use in Britain', *The London Journal*, vol. 4, no. 1, 1978, pp. 3–28.

Bevan, A.H., *James and Horace Smith* (London: Hurst & Blackett, 1899).

Bhore, Mary, 'Some Impressions of England', *Indian Magazine & Review,* November 1900, pp. 286–91; December 1900, pp. 309–14.

Bhownaggree, Sir Mancherjee M., *The Verdict of India* (London: Hodder & Stoughton, 1916).

BHRU, *Here to Stay* (City of Bradford Metropolitan Council, Arts, Museums and

Libraries, 1994).

Bhuyan, S.K., *London Memories* (Assam: Gauhati Publication Board, 1979).

Bibikova, Massia, *Our Indians at Marseilles* (London: Smith, Elder & Co., 1915).

Braidwood, Stephen J., *Black Poor and White Philanthropists* (Liverpool: Liverpool University Press, 1994).

Broeze, F.J.A., 'The Muscles of Empire – Indian Seamen and the Raj, 1919–1939', *Indian Economic and Social Review*, vol. 8, no. 1, pp. 43–67.

Brown, F.H., 'Indian Students in Great Britain', *Edinburgh Review*, January 1913, pp. 138–56.

Burton, Antoinette, 'House/Daughter/Nation: Interiority, Architecture, and Historical Imagination in Janaki Majumdar's "Family History"', *The Journal of Asian Studies*, vol. 56, no. 4, November 1997, pp. 921–46.

—— *At the Heart of the Empire* (Berkeley: University of California Press, 1998).

Cain, P.J. and Hopkins, A.G., *British Imperialism: Innovation and Expansion 1688–1914* (London: Longman, 1993).

Callaghan, John, *Rajani Palme Dutt* (London: Lawrence & Wishart, 1993).

Cameron, H.C., *Mr Guy's Hospital: 1726–1948* (London: Longmans, Green & Co., 1954).

Cameron, Stewart J. and Hicks, Jackie, 'Frederick Akbar Mahomed and his Role in the Description of Hypertension at Guy's Hospital', *Kidney International*, vol. 49, 1996, pp. 1488–506.

Carpenter, Mary, *The Last Days in England of Rajah Rammohun Roy* (Calcutta, 1915).

Carr, John Dickson, *The Life of Sir Arthur Conan Doyle* (London: John Murray, 1959).

Chagla, M.C., *Roses in December* (Bombay: Bharatiya Vidya Bhavan, 1978).

Chakrabarty, Rishi Ranjan, *Duleep Singh The Maharajah of the Punjab and the Raj* (Birmingham: D.S. Samara, 1988).

Chakravarty, Suhash, *V.K. Krishna Menon and the India League* (New Delhi: Har-Anand Publications, 1997) vols i and ii.

Chandra, Bipan, *India's Struggle for Independence* (Penguin Books, South Asian edn, 1989).

Cherry, Deborah, *Painting Women* (London: Routledge, 1993).

Choudhury, Yousuf, *The Roots and Tales of the Bangladeshi Settlers* (Birmingham: Sylheti Social History Group, 1993).

Choudry, P.M., *British Experiences* (Calcutta: New Britannia Press, 1889).

Chowdhary, Savitri, *I Made My Home In England* (Laindon: Grant-Best Ltd, nd).

—— *Indian Cooking* (London: André Deutsch, 1954); revised edn, with introduction by Shakun Banfield, 1999.

—— *In Memory of My Beloved Husband* (Laindon: Grant-Best Ltd, nd)

Cloake, Margaret Morris, trans. and ed., *A Persian at the Court of King George* (London: Barrie & Jenkins).

Collett, Sophia Dobson, *Life and Letters of Rajah Rammohun Roy,* ed., D.K. Biswas and P.C. Ganguli (Calcutta, 1962).

Collicott, Sylvia L., *Connections Haringey: Local-National-World Links* (Haringey Community Information Service, in Association with Multi-Cultural Support Group, 1986).

Collins, Joyce, *Dr Brighton's Indian Patients* (Brighton Books, 1997).

Compton, Herbert, *A Particular Account of the European Military Adventurers of Hindustan from 1784 to 1803* (London: T. Fisher Unwin, 1892).

Condition of India: Being the Report of the Delegation Sent to India by the India League in 1932 (London: Essential News, 1933).

Copland, Revd Patrick, *Virginia's God be Thanked* (London, 1622).

Copley, Anthony and Visram, Rozina, eds, 'Indians in Britain: Past and Present', *Indo-British Review: A Journal of History*, vol. xvi, no. 2, June 1989.

Corrigan, Gordon, *Sepoys in the Trenches* (Staplehurst: Spellmount, 1999).

Cotton, Sir Evan, 'Sake Deen Mahomed of Brighton', *Sussex County Magazine*, vol. 13, 1939, pp. 746–50.

—— *East Indiamen The East India Company's Maritime Service* (London: The Batchworth Press Ltd, 1949).

Craig, F.W.S., ed., *British Parliamentary Election Results 1885–1918* (London: Macmillan, 1974).

Crawford, Elizabeth, *The Women's Suffrage Movement: A Reference Guide 1866–1928* (London: UCL Press, 1999).

Cumpston, Mary, 'Some Early Indian Nationalists and their Allies in the British Parliament, 1851–1906', *English Historical Review*, vol. 76, no. 299, April 1961, pp. 279–97.

Cursetjee, Ardaseer, *Diary of an Overland Journey from Bombay to England, and of a Year's Residence in Great Britain* (London: Hennington & Galabin, 1840).

Dabydeen, David, *Hogarth's Blacks* (Manchester: Manchester University Press, 1987).

Das, Harihar, *Life and Letters of Toru Dutt* (Oxford: Oxford University Press, 1921).

—— 'Early Indian Visitors to England', *The Calcutta Review,* 3rd series, vol. 13, October–December 1924, pp. 83–114.

Datta, V.N., *Madan Lal Dhingra and the Revolutionary Movement* (New Delhi: Vikas Publishing House, 1978).

Desai, Dinker, *Maritime Labour in India* (Bombay: Servants of India Society, 1939).

Desai, Rashmi, *Indian Immigrants in Britain* (Oxford: Oxford University Press, 1963).

Digby, Simon, 'An Eighteenth-Century Narrative of a Journey from Bengal to England: Munshi Ismail's *New History*', in Christopher Shackle, ed., *Urdu and Muslim South Asia* (London: SOAS, University of London, 1990).

Dixon, Conrad, 'Lascars: The Forgotten Seamen', in R. Ommer and G. Panting, eds, *Working Men Who Got Wet* , Proceedings of the Fourth Conference of the Atlantic Canada Shipping Project, 24–6 July, 1980 (Maritime History Group, University of Newfoundland, 1980).

Doss, N.L., *Reminiscences English and Australasian* (Calcutta: M.C. Bhowmick, 1893).

Dover, Cedric, *Half-Caste* (London: Secker & Warburg, 1937).

Doyle, Sir Arthur Conan, *Memories and Adventures* (Oxford: Oxford University Press, 1989 edn).

Duberman, Martin Bauml, *Paul Robeson* (London: The Bodley Head, 1989).

Du Cann, C.G.L ., *Miscarriages of Justice* (London: Frederick Muller, 1960).

Duff, David, ed., *Queen Victoria's Highland Journals* (London: Webb & Brown, 1980).

Duffield, Ian, 'London's Black Transportees to Australia', paper presented at a Conference on the History of Black People in London, University of London Institute of Education, 27–9 November 1984 (with tables and appendices).

Duffield, Mark, *Black Radicalism and the Politics of De-Industrialisation* (Aldershot: Avebury, 1988).

Dunlop, Anne, 'Lascars and Labourers: Reactions to the Indian Presence in the West of Scotland during the 1920s and 1930s', *Scottish Labour History Society Journal,* no. 25, 1990, pp. 40–57.

—— 'Recovering the History of Asian Migration to Scotland', *Immigrants and Minorities*, vol. 9, no. 2, July 1990, pp. 145–67.

Dutt, R.C., *Three Years in Europe* (Calcutta: S.K. Lahiri & Co., 1890).

—— *The Economic History of India Under Early British Rule* (London: Kegan Paul, Trench, Trubner & Co., 1906, 2nd edn).

Dutt, Rajani Palme, *Problems of Contemporary History* (London: Lawrence & Wishart, 1963).

Dutta, Krishna and Robinson, Andrew, *Rabindranath Tagore* (London: Bloomsbury, 1995).

Edalji, Revd Shapurji, *A Miscarriage of Justice: The Case of George Edalji* (London: The United Press, 1905).

Edinburgh Indian Association, 1883–1983 (Centenary Issue, 1983)

Edwardes, Michael, *The Nabobs at Home* (London: Constable & Co., 1991).

Egan, Pierce, *Life in London* (London: Sherwood, Heeley & Jones, 1821).

Ellinwood, D.C. and Pradhan, S.D., *India and World War I* (New Delhi: Manohar Publications, 1978).

Equiano, Olaudah, *The Interesting Narrative of the Life of Olaudah Equiano, or Gustavus Vassa, the African* (London, 1789, 2nd edn), vols i and ii.

Erredge, J.A., *History of Brighthelmston* (Brighton: E. Lewis, 1862).

Evans, Neil, 'The South Wales Race Riots of 1919', *Llafur,* 3, 1980, pp. 5–29.

Farrer, E., ed., *Portraits in Norfolk Houses* (Norwich: Jarrold & Sons, 1927).

Fay, Eliza, *Original Letters from India*, E.M. Forster, ed., (London: Hogarth Press, 1986 edn).

Fisher, Michael H., *The First Indian Author in English* (New Delhi: Oxford University Press, 1996).

Fletcher, M.E., *Report on an Investigation into the Coloured Problem in Liverpool and Other Ports* (Liverpool Association for the Welfare of Half-Caste Children, 1930).

Florance, Arnold, *Queen Victoria at Osborne* (London: English Heritage, 1987 edn).

Foot, M.R.D., *SOE in France* (London: HM Stationary Office, 1966).

—— *SOE The Special Operations Executive 1940–46* (London: BBC, 1984).

Forbes, Geraldine, 'The Politics of Respectability: Indian Women and the National Congress', in D.A. Low, ed., *The Indian National Congress Centenary Hindsights* (Oxford: Oxford University Press, 1968).

Forbes, Thomas Roger, *Chronicles from Aldgate* (New Haven, CT: Yale University Press, 1971).

Forster, E.M., et al., *Talking to India* (London: George Allen & Unwin, 1943).

Foster, William, ed., *The Embassy of Sir Thomas Roe to India, 1615–1619* (revised edn, Oxford University Press, 1926).

—— *John Company* (London: John Lane the Bodley Head Ltd, 1926).

Francis, Hilary, ' "Pay the Piper, Call the Tune!": The Women's Tax Resistance League', in M. Joannou and J. Purvis, eds, *The Women's Suffrage Movement* (Manchester: Manchester University Press, 1998).

French, Bert A., *Boyhood Memories of Plumstead 1920–1928* (London: Clare Corner Publications, 1994).

French, Patrick, *Liberty or Death* (London: Flamingo edn, 1997).

Fryer, Peter, *Staying Power* (London: Pluto Press, 1984).

Fuller, Jean Overton, *Noor-un-nisa Inayat Khan* (The Hague: East-West Publications, 1971).

Gandhi, M.K., *An Autobiography*, trans. Mahadev Desai (Harmondsworth: Penguin paper edn, 1984).

—— *Hind Swaraj*, Anthony J. Parel, ed. (New Delhi: Cambridge University Press, South Asian edn, 1997).

Gandhi, Sonia, ed., *Freedom's Daughter* (London: Hodder & Stoughton, 1989).

Garnett, David, *The Golden Echo* (London: Chatto & Windus, 1953).

George, Dorothy M., *Life in the Eighteenth Century* (London: Penguin Books, 1979 edn).

George, T.J.S., *Krishna Menon* (London: Jonathan Cape, 1964).

Gilbert, E.W., *Brighton: Old Ocean's Bauble* (London: Methuen, 1954).

Gooch, Janet, *A History of the Brighton General Hospital* (London: Phillimore & Co., 1980).

Goodhart, James F. and Jacobson, W.H.A., 'In Memoriam Frederick Horatio Akbar Mahomed', *Guy's Hospital Reports*, vol. 43, 1885–6, pp. 1–10.

Gordon, Paul and Reilly, Danny, 'Guestworkers of the Sea: Racism in British Shipping', *Race and Class*, vol. xxviii, no. 2, Autumn 1986, pp. 73–82.

Granville, A.B., *The Spas of England* (London: Henry Colburn, 1842), vols i and ii.

Greenhut, Jeffrey, 'The Imperial Reserve: The Indian Corps on the Western Front, 1914–15', *Journal of Imperial and Commonwealth History*, vol. xii, no. 1, October 1983, pp. 54–73.

Grewal, J.S., *The Sikhs of the Punjab* (Cambridge: Cambridge University Press, 1990).

Grose, John-Henry, *Voyage to the East Indies* (London, S. Hooper & A. Morley, 1757).

Gupta, J.N., *Life and Works of R.C. Dutt* (London: J.M. Dent, 1911).

Gupta, Partha Sarathi, 'British Labour and the Indian Left 1919–1939', in B.R. Nanda, ed., *Socialism in India* (New Delhi: Vikas Publications, 1972).

Guy, J. and Swallow, D., eds, *Arts of India 1550–1900* (London: Victoria & Albert Museum, 1990).

Haldar, Rakhal Das, *The English Diary of an Indian Student, 1861–62* (Dacca: The Asutosh Library, 1903).

Hale, Leslie, *Blood on the Scales* (London: Jonathan Cape, 1960).

Hannay, David, *The Great Chartered Companies* (London: Williams & Norgate Ltd, 1926).

Hay, Stephen, 'The Making of a Late-Victorian Hindu: M.K. Gandhi in London 1888–1891', *Victorian Studies*, vol. 33, no. 1, Autumn 1989, pp. 74–98.

Head, Raymond, 'Sezincote, a Paradigm of the Indian Style' (MA thesis, Royal College of Art, London, 1982).

—— *The Indian Style* (London: George Allen & Unwin, 1986).

—— 'Indian Crafts and Western Design from the 17th century to the Present', *RSA Journal*, vol. cxxxvi, no. 5378, January 1988, pp. 116–31.

Heath, G.D. and Heath, Joan, *The Women's Suffrage Movement in and around Richmond and Twickenham* (Borough of Twickenham Local History Society, Paper No. 13, December 1968).

Hecht, J.J., *Continental and Colonial Servants in 18th-century England* (Smith College Studies in History, vol. xl, Northampton, Massachusetts, 1954).

Heiton, John, *The Castes of Edinburgh* (Edinburgh: John Menzies, 1859).

Henderson, Meg, *Finding Peggy* (London:Corgi Books, 1994).

Hepple, Bob, *Race, Jobs and the Law in Britain* (London: Allan Lane/The Penguin Press, 1968).

Heroes of our Freedom Movement (Karachi: Department of Films and Publication, Government of Pakistan, 1970).

A Hindu, *Three Years in Europe* (Calcutta: Thacker, Spink & Co., 1873)

Hinnells, J.R. and Ralph, Omar, *Bhownaggree Member of Parliament 1895–1906* (London: Hansib, 1995).

Hiro, Dilip, *Black British, White British* (London: Paladin, 1992 edn).

Hirson, Baruch and Vivian, Lorraine, *Strike Across the Empire* (London: Cleo Publications, 1992).

A History of the Black Presence in London (London: Greater London Council, 1986).

Hoare, Prince, *Memoirs of Granville Sharp* (London, 1820).

Hobsbawm, E.J., *Industry and Empire* (London: Pelican Books, 1969 edn).

Hoffman, Paul, *The Man Who Loved Only Numbers* (London: Fourth Estate, 1999 edn).

Holmes, Colin, *John Bull's Island* (London: Macmillan Education, 1988).

Holzman, James M., *The Nabobs in England* (New York, 1926).

Hughes, Lt Col. R.M., *Laws Relating to Lascars and Asiatic Seamen Employed in the British Merchant Service* (London: Smith, Elder & Co., 1855).

Hunter, William, *An Essay on the Diseases Incident to Indian Seamen, or Lascars, on Long Voyages* (Calcutta: Printed at the Honourable Company's Press, 1804).

Hutchinson, Lester, *European Freebooters in Moghul India* (New York: Asia Publishing House, 1964).

Huttenback, Robert A., 'No Strangers within the Gates: Attitudes and Policies towards the Non-white Residents of the British Empire of Settlement', *Journal of Imperial and Commonwealth History*, vol. 1, no. 3, May 1973, pp. 271–302.

India and the War, with an introduction by Lord Sydenham of Combe (London: Hodder & Stoughton, 1915).

India, Britain and Freedom (India League, 1941).

Irwin, J. and Schwartz, P.R., *Studies in Indo-European Textile History* (Ahmedabad: Calico Museum of Textiles, 1966).

Jee, Bhagvat Sinh, Thakore Saheb of Gondal, *Journal of a Visit to England in 1883* (Bombay: Education Society's Press, 1886).

Jenkinson, Jacqueline, 'The Glasgow Race Disturbances of 1919', *Immigrants & Minorities*, vol. 4, no. 2, July 1985, pp. 43–67.

—— 'The 1919 Race Riots in Britain: A Survey', in R. Lotz and I. Pegg, *Under the Imperial Carpet* (Crawley: Rabbit Press, 1986).

—— 'Repatriation to the West Indies: A Repercussion of the 1919 Race Riots in Britain', *Inter Arts,* Spring 1987, pp. 11–13.

Jennings, Humphrey and Madge, Charles, *May the Twelfth* (London: Faber & Faber, 1987 edn).

Jensen, Joan M., *Passage from India* (New Haven, CT: Yale University Press, 1988).

John, De Witt, *Indian Workers' Association in Britain* (Oxford: Oxford University Press, 1969).

Josephides, Sasha, *Towards a History of the Indian Workers' Association* (Warwick University: ESRC, Research Paper in Ethnic Relations, No. 18, 1991).

Kapur, Narinder, *The Irish Raj* (Northern Ireland: Greystone Press, 1997).

Karaka, D.F., *The Pulse of Oxford* (London: J.M. Dent & Sons, 1933).

—— *I Go West* (London: Michael Joseph, 1938).

—— *All My Yesterdays* (Bombay: Thacker & Co., 1943).

Kaushik, Harish, *The Indian National Congress in England 1885–1920* (New Delhi: Research Publications in Social Sciences, nd).

Kaye, Cecil *Communism in India* (1919–1924), ed. S. Roy (Calcutta: Editions India, 1926; 1971).

Keer, Dhanajay, *Savarkar and his Times* (Bombay: A.V. Keer, 1950).

Ker, J.C., *Political Troubles in India, 1907–1917* (Calcutta: Superintendent Government Printing, 1917).

Khan, Abu Talib, *The Travels of Mirza Abu Talib Khan, in Asia, Africa, and Europe* Charles Stewart, trans., (Longman, Hurst, Rees & Orme, 1810; 1814) vols i and ii.

Khan, Mehdi Hassan, 'London Sketches by an Indian Pen', *Indian Magazine & Review,* February 1890, pp. 61–73; March 1890, pp. 139–48.

Kiernan, V.G., *European Empires from Conquest to Collapse, 1815–1960* (London: Fontana Paperbacks, 1982).

Kincaid, Dennis, *British Social Life in India 1608–1937* (London: Routledge & Kegan Paul, 1938; 1973).

Kondapi, C., *Indians Overseas 1838–1949* (New Delhi: Indian Council for World Affairs, 1951).

Kosmin, Barry A., 'Political Identity in Battersea', in Sandra Wallman, *Living in South London* (Aldershot: Gower, 1982).

Kripalani, Krishna, *Rabindranath Tagore* (Calcutta: Visva-Bharati, 1980).

Kulke, E., *The Parsees in India* (New Delhi: Vikas Publishing, 1974).

Lahiri, Shompa, 'British Policy Towards Indian Princes in Late Nineteenth-Century and Early Twentieth-Century Britain', *Immigrants and Minorities*, vol. 15, no. 3, November 1996, pp. 214–32.

Lane, Tony, *Grey Dawn Breaking* (Manchester: Manchester University Press, 1986).

—— *The Merchant Seamen's War* (Manchester: Manchester University Press, 1990).

—— 'The Political Imperatives of Bureaucracy and Empire: The Case of the Coloured Alien Seamen Order, 1925', *Immigrants and Minorities*, vol. 13, nos 2–3, July–November, 1994, pp. 104–29.

Lascars and Chinese: A Short Address to Young Men of the Several Orthodox Denominations of Christians (W. Harris, 1814).

Lawson, Philip, *The East India Company* (London: Longman, Studies in Modern History series, 1993).

Leventhal, F.M., *Respectable Radical* (London: Weidenfeld & Nicolson, 1971).

Life of William Allen, with a Selection from his Correspondence (London: Charles Gilpin, 1846), vol. i.

Linklater, A., *An Unhusbanded Life* (London: Hutchinson, 1980).

Little, Kenneth, *Negroes in Britain* (London: Routledge & Kegan Paul, 1972 edn).

Lives of the Most Remarkable Criminals ... from 1720–1735, Collected from the Original Sources and Memoirs (1874), vol. i.

Lockyer, Charles, *An Account of the Trade in India* (London, 1711).

Longford, Elizabeth, *Victoria RI* (London: Weidenfeld & Nicolson, 1964).

Lord, John, *The Maharajahs* (London: Hutchinson, 1972).

Lord Salisbury's Blackman (Lucknow: G.P. Varma & Bros. Press, 1889).

Lorimer, Douglas A., *Colour, Class and the Victorians* (Leicester: Leicester University Press, 1978).

Lucas, Charles, ed., *The Empire at War* (London: Humphrey Milford/Oxford University Press, 1921–6), vol. v.

Maan, Bashir, *The New Scots* (Edinburgh: John Donald Publishers Ltd, 1992).

Maclaren-Ross, J., *Memoirs of the Forties* (Harmondsworth: Penguin Books, 1984).

Macmillan, Norman, *Offensive Patrol* (London: Jarrolds, 1973).

McFarland, E.W., 'Clyde Opinion on an Old Controversy: Indian and Chinese Seafarers in Glasgow', *Ethnic and Racial Studies*, vol. 14, no. 4, October 1991, pp. 493–515.

McNeill, Mary, *The Life and Times of Mary Ann McCracken, 1770–1866* (Dublin: Allen Figgis).

Mahomed, George S., *The Treatment at the Bournemouth Mont Dore* (London: Bailliere, Tindall & Cox, 1889).

Mahomed, Hajee Sullaiman Shah, *Journal of My Tours Round the World 1886–1887 and 1893–1895* (Bombay: Duftur Ashkara Oil Engine Press, 1895).

Mahomed, Horatio, *The Bath: A Concise History of Bathing* (London: Smith, Elder, & Co., 1843).

—— *Short Hints on Bathing* (London: 7 Ryder Street, 1844).

Mahomed, S.D., *Cases Cured by Sake Deen Mahomed* (Brighton, 1920).

—— *Shampooing, or, Benefits Resulting from the Use of the Indian Medicated Vapour Bath* (Brighton, 1822; 1826; 1838).

Mahomet, Albert J., *From Street Arab to Pastor* (Cardiff: J.B. Thomasson, nd).

Mahomet, Dean, *The Travels of Dean Mahomet* (Cork: Printed by J. Connor, 1794).

Majumdar, Agnes Janaki Penelope, *Pramila: A Memoir* (London: Privately Published, nd).

Majumdar, A.K., *Advent of Independence* (Bombay: Chowpatty, 1963).

Majumdar, R.C., *History of the Freedom Movement in India* (Calcutta: Firma

K.L. Mukhopadhyay, 1962).

Malabari, B.M., *The Indian Eye on English Life* (Westminster: Archibald Constable & Co., 1893; Bombay: Apollo Printing Works, 1895).

Marshall, A.C., 'Nurses of Ocean Highways', *The Quiver: The Magazine for the Home*, vol. 57, pp. 923–6.

Marshall, Peter J., *East India Fortunes* (Oxford, 1976).

Martin, Gregory, 'The Influence of Racial Attitudes on British Policy Towards India during the First World War', *Journal of Imperial and Commonwealth History*, vol. 14, no. 2, January 1986, pp. 91–112.

Masani, R.P., *Dadabhai Naoroji, the Grand Old Man of India* (London: George Allen & Unwin, 1939).

Mason, Philip, *A Matter of Honour* (London: Macmillan, 1986 Papermac edn).

Mathurin, O.C., *Henry Sylvester Williams and the Organisation of the Pan-African Movement, 1869–1911* (Westport, CT: Greenwood Press, 1976).

May, Roy and Cohen, Robin, 'The Interaction Between Race and Colonialism: A Case Study of the Liverpool Race Riots of 1919', *Race and Class*, vol. xvi, no. 2, 1974, pp. 111–26.

Mayhew, Henry, *London Labour and the London Poor* (London: Griffin, Bohn & Co., 1861), vols i–iv.

Mehrotra, S.R., *The Emergence of Indian National Congress* (New Delhi: Vikas Publications, 1971).

Melville, Lewis, *Brighton: Its History, Its Follies and Its Fashions* (London: Chapman & Hall, 1909).

Menezes, Lt Gen. S.L., *Fidelity and Honour* (New Delhi: Oxford University Press, 1999).

Merriman, Nick, ed., *The Peopling of London* (Museum of London, 1993).

Metcalf, Thomas R., *Ideologies of the Raj* (Cambridge: Cambridge University Press, 1995).

Miller, Robert, *From Shore to Shore* (R. Miller, 1989).

Milligan, Barry, *Pleasures and Pains* (Charlottesville and London: University Press of Virginia, 1995).

Mody, Nawaz B., 'Madame Bhikaji Rustom Cama – Sentinel of Liberty', in Nawaz B. Mody, ed., *The Parsis in Western India: 1818–1920* (Bombay: Allied Publishers Ltd, 1998).

Moore, R.J., *Escape from Empire* (Oxford: Clarendon Press, 1983).

Mowat, James L., *Seafarers' Conditions in India and Pakistan* (Geneva: ILO, 1940).

Mozoomdar, P.C., *Sketches of a Tour Round the World* (Calcutta: S.K. Lahiri & Co., 1884).

Muir, August and Davies, Mair, *A Victorian Ship owner* (Cayzer, Irvine & Co., 1978).

Mukharji, T.N., *A Visit to Europe* (Calcutta: W. Newman & Co., 1889).

Mukherjee, M., *W.C. Bonnerjee: Snapshots from His Life and His London Letters*

(Calcutta: Deshbandhu Book Depot, 1944).

Musgrave, C., *Life in Brighton* (London: Faber, 1970).

Myers, Norma, 'The Black Presence through the Criminal Records, 1780–1830', *Immigrants and Minorities*, vol. 7, no. 3, November 1988, pp. 292–307.

—— *Reconstructing the Black Past* (London: Frank Cass, 1996).

Nadkarani, G.N., *Journal of a Visit to Europe in 1896* (Bombay: Taraporevala & Sons, 1903).

Naoroji, Dadabhai, *Mr D. Naoroji and Mr Schnadhorst* (London, 1892).

—— *Poverty and Un-British Rule in India* (London: Swan Sonnenschein & Co., 1901).

Natrajan, S., *West of Suez* (Bombay, 1938).

Nehru, Jawaharlal, *An Autobiography* (New Delhi: Jawaharlal Nehru Memorial Fund, 1982).

Neill, Edward D., *Memoir of Reverend Patrick Copland* (New York: Charles Scribner & Co., 1871).

Neuve Chapelle: India's Memorial in France, 1914–1918 (London: Hodder & Stoughton, 1927).

Nicholson, Marjorie, *The TUC Overseas* (London: Allen & Unwin, 1986).

Niven, Alastair, *The Yoke of Pity* (New Delhi: Arnold-Heinemann, 1978).

Norman, Dorothy, ed., *Nehru: The First Sixty Years* (London: The Bodley Head, 1965), vol. i.

Norton, Paul F., 'Daylesford: S.P. Cockerell's Residence for Warren Hastings', *Journal of the Society of Architectural Historians*, vol. 22, no. 3, October 1963, pp. 127–33.

Nowrojee, J. and Merwanjee, H., *Journal of a Residence of Two Years and a Half* (London: William Allen & Co., 1841).

Omissi, David, *The Sepoy and the Raj* (London: Macmillan Press, 1994).

Orwell, George, *The Complete Works* (London: Secker & Warburg, 1998).

Our Merchant Seamen (Government of India, 1947).

Overstreet, G.D. and Windmiller, M., *Communism in India* (Berkeley: University of California Press, 1959).

Padfield, Peter, *Beneath the House Flag of the P&O* (London: Hutchinson, 1981).

Padmore, George, *Pan Africanism or Communism* (London: Dennis Dobson, 1956).

Palmer, Robin, 'The Rise of the Britalian Culture Entrepreneur', in Robin Ward and Richard Jenkins, eds, *Ethnic Communities in Business* (Cambridge: Cambridge University Press, 1984).

Pandian, T.B., *England to an Indian Eye* (London: Elliot Stock, 1897).

Parekh, C.L. ed., *Essays, Speeches, Addresses and Writings on Indian Politics of the Hon'ble Dadabhai Naoroji* (Bombay: Caxton Printing Works, 1887).

Parkes, Margaret Kineton, *The Tax Resistance Movement in Great Britain* (London: J. Francis, nd).

Pattenden, Rosemary, *English Criminal Appeals 1844–1994* (Oxford: Clarendon Press, 1996).

Patwardhan, R.P., *Dadabhai Naoroji Correspondence* (Bombay, 1977), vol. ii.

Pegg, Revd James, *Lascar's Cry to Britain* (London: T. Ward & Co., 1844).

Pelling, Henry, *Social Geography of British Elections* (London: Macmillan, 1967).

Penguins: A Retrospect 1935–51 (Penguin Books, 1951).

Penny, Revd Frank *The Church in Madras* (London: Smith, Elder & Co., 1904).

Perkins, Roger, *The Amritsar Massacre Legacy* (Chippenham: Picton Publishing, 1989).

Petri, D., *Communism in India 1924–1927* (Calcutta: Government of India Press, 1927; 1972).

Philips, C.H. ed., *The Evolution of India and Pakistan 1858–1947* (Oxford: Oxford University Press, 1965).

Pillai, G.P., *London and Paris Through Indian Spectacles* (Madras: The Vaijayanti Press, 1897).

Plomer, William, ed., *Selections from the Diary of the Reverend Francis Kilvert* (London: Jonathan Cape, 1969), vols i and ii.

Plumb, J.H., *Royal Heritage* (BBC, 1977).

Ponsonby, Frederick, *Recollections of Three Reigns* (London: Eyre & Spottiswoode, 1951).

Prasad, Bisheshwar, ed., *Official History of the Indian Armed Forces in the Second World War* (Combined Inter-Services Historical Section: India and Pakistan, 1960) vols i–iv.

Pratt, Mary Louise, *Travel Writing and Transculturation* (London: Routledge, 1992).

Prem, Dhani, *The Parliamentary Leper* (Aligarh: Metric Publications, 1965).

Price, Richard, *An Imperial War and the British Working Class* (London: Routledge & Kegan Paul, 1972).

Rahman, M., *From Consultation to Confrontation* (London: Luzac & Co., 1970).

Rajkumar, N.V., *Indians Outside India* (Delhi: All-India Congress Committee, 1951).

Ralph, Omar, *Naoroji: The First Asian MP* (London: Hansib, 1997).

Ram, Anant, 'Reminiscences of a Panjabi Migrant in Coventry' (Typescript of interview by A. Chandan and D.S. Tatla, 1991).

Ram, Jhinda, *My Trip to Europe* (Lahore: Mufid-i-am Press, 1893).

Ramakrishna, T., *My Visit to the West* (London: Fisher Unwin Ltd, 1915).

Ramanujaswami, N., *My Trip to England* (Madras: Ananda Press, 1912).

Ramdin, Ron, *The Making of the Black Working Class in Britain* (London: Wildwood House, 1987).

Rapoport, Paul, ed., *Sorabji: A Critical Celebration* (Aldershot: Scolar Press, 1992).

Report of a Meeting for the Establishment of a 'Strangers' Home', for Asiatics,

Africans, South-sea Islanders, and Others Occasionally Residing in the Metropolis (1855).

Rich, Paul B., 'Philanthropic Racism: The Liverpool University Settlement, the Anti-Slavery Society and the Issue of "Half-Caste" Children, 1919–51', *Immigrants & Minorities*, vol. 3, 1984, pp. 69–88.

—— *Race and Empire in British Politics* (Cambridge: Cambridge University Press, 1990 edn).

Richardson, F.A., *Social Conditions in Ports and Dockland Areas* (Joint Council of the British Social Hygiene Council and the British Council for the Welfare of the Mercantile Marine, 1934–5).

von la Roche, Sophie, *Sophie in London 1786*, trans. Clare Williams (London: Jonathan Cape, 1933).

Roles, John, 'Sake Deen Mahomed's Silver Cup', *The Royal Pavilion & Museums Review*, 1990, No. 3, pp. 4–5.

Ross, Allan, *Ranji: Prince of Cricketers* (London: Collins, 1983).

Rowe, Richard, *Picked Up in the Streets* (London: W.H. Allen, 1880).

Roy, A.L., *Reminiscences England and American Pt II, England and India* (Calcutta: Royal Publishing House, 1888).

Saha, Panchanan, *Shapurji Saklatvala* (New Delhi: People's Publishing House, 1970).

—— *Madam Cama 'Mother of Indian Revolution'* (Calcutta: Manisha, 1975).

Said, Edward W., *Orientalism* (Harmondsworth: Penguin edn, 1985).

Saklatvala, Sehri, *The Fifth Commandment* (Salford: Miranda Press, 1991).

Sala, G.A., *The Life and Adventures ...* (London: Cassell & Co., 1895 edn), vol. i.

Salter, Joseph, *The Asiatic in England* (London: Seeley, Jackson & Halliday, 1873).

—— *The East in the West* (London: S.W. Partridge & Co., 1896).

Sastri, P.S., *Ananda K Coomaraswamy* (New Delhi: Arnold-Heinemann, 1974).

Satthianadhan, S., *Four Years in an English University* (Madras: Srinivasa, Varadachari & Co., 1893).

—— *A Holiday Trip to Europe and America* (Madras: Srinivasa, Varadachari & Co., 1897).

Saul, S.B., *Studies in British Overseas Trade 1870–1914* (Liverpool: Liverpool University Press, 1960).

Scott, A.F., *Every One a Witness: The Stuart Age* (London: White Lion Publishers, 1974).

Seecharan, Clem, *India and the Shaping of the Indo-Guyanese Imagination 1890s–1920s* (Leeds: Peepal Tree, 1993).

—— *Tiger in the Stars: The Anatomy of Indian Achievement in British Guiana 1919–29* (Warwick University Caribbean Studies, 1997).

Sen, S.P., ed., *Dictionary of National Biography* (Calcutta: Institute of Historical Studies, 1973).

Sermoneta, Duchess of [V Caetani], *The Locks of Norbury* (London: John Murray, 1940).

Shade, Sarah, *A Narrative of the Life...* (London: Knight & Compton, 1801).

Sharpe [Hare], Nancie, *Report on the Negro Population of London and Cardiff* (typescript, nd).

Shaw, Anthony Batty, 'Frederick Akbar Mahomed and his Contribution to the Study of Bright's Disease', *Guy's Hospital Reports*, vol. 101, nos 1–4, 1952, pp. 153–73.

Shephard, Revd J.E., *A.J. Mahomet from Street Arab to Evangelist* (Ventnor: W.B. Tomkins, nd).

Sherwood, Marika, 'Race, Nationality and Employment among Lascar Seamen, 1660–1945', *New Community*, vol. 17, no. 2, January 1991, pp. 229–44.

Shores, Christopher, Franks, Norman and Guest, Russell, *Above the Trenches* (Canada: Fortress Publications, 1990).

Shyllon, F.O., *Black People in Britain 1555–1833* (Oxford: Oxford University Press, 1977).

Silliman, Benjamin, *A Journal of Travels in England, Holland, and Scotland* (Boston: 1812), vol. i.

Silverman, Julius, 'The India League', in *A Centenary History of the Indian National Congress 1885–1985* (New Delhi: Vikas Publishing), vol. iii.

Sims, George, *Living London* (London: Cassell, 1906), vol. iii.

Singh, Khushwant, *History of Sikhs* (New Delhi: Oxford University Press, 1997), vol. ii.

Singh, Ranbir, *In the Footsteps of Our Legends* (Noida: Book Mates Publishers, 1998).

Sitwell, Osbert, *Great Morning* (London: Macmillan & Co. Ltd, 1948).

Smith, Horace, ed., *Memoirs, and Letters and Comic Miscellanies in Prose and Verse on the late James Smith* (London: Henry Colburn, 1840), vol. i.

Smith, J., *The Missionary's Appeal to British Christians on Behalf of Southern India* (1841).

Smith, J.M., *Mendicant Wanderers through the Streets of London* (Edinburgh: William P. Nimmo & Co., 1883).

Sokoloff, Bertha, *Edith and Stepney* (London: Stepney Books Publications, 1987).

Sorabji, Cornelia, *India Calling* (London: Nisbet & Co., 1934).

Spear, T.G.P., *The Nabobs* (Oxford: Oxford University Press, 1932).

Spencer, Alfred, ed., *Memoirs of William Hickey* (London: Hurst & Blackett, 1913), vols i–iv.

Squires, Mike, *Saklatvala* (London: Lawrence & Wishart, 1990).

Stone, Jean, *More Memories of Wells* (1996).

Strandes, Justus, *The Portuguese Period in East Africa* (Dar es Salaam and Nairobi: East African Literature Bureau, 1968).

Subasinghe, T., *Memoirs of T. Subasinghe* (unpublished; copy ICS Library, London).

Swales, John D., 'The Growth of Medical Science: The Lessons of Malthus', *The Harveian Oration* (London: Royal College of Physicians, 1995).

—— 'Frederick Akbar Mahomed (1849–1884): Pioneer of Clinical Research', *Journal of Human Hypertension*, vol. 10, 1996, pp. 137–42.

Tabili, Laura, *'We Ask for British Justice': Workers and Racial Difference in Late Imperial Britain* (Ithaca, NY and London: Cornell University Press, 1994).

—— 'The Construction of Racial Difference in Twentieth-Century Britain: The Special Restriction (Coloured Alien Seamen) Order, 1925', *Journal of British Studies*, 33, January 1994, pp. 54–98.

Taylor, Ina, *Helen Allingham's England* (Exeter: Webb & Bower, 1990).

Tennant, Revd William, *Indian Recreations* (Edinburgh: John Anderson etc., 1803), vol. i.

Thackeray, W.M., *The Four Georges* (Leipzig, 1861).

The Epicure's Almanack: or Calendar of Good Living (London: Longman, Hurst, Rees, Orme & Brown, 1815).

The First Indian Member of the Imperial Parliament (Madras, 1892).

The Late Dadabhai Naoroji on Swaraj, 1906 (Bombay Home Rule Series, No. 6).

The Maharajah's Well at Stoke Row (Published by the Restoration Appeal Fund, 1979).

The Political Estimate of Mr Bhavnagri or the Bhavnagri Boom Exposed (Bombay, 1897).

The Women's Who's Who (London: Shaw Publishing Co., 1934–5 edn).

Thomas, Hugh, *The Spanish Civil War* (Harmondsworth: Penguin, 1965).

Thompson, E.J. and Garratt, G.T., *Rise and Fulfilment of British Rule in India* (London: Macmillan, 1934).

Thomson, J., *Street Incidents* (London, 1881).

Tinker, Hugh, *A New System of Slavery* (Oxford: Oxford University Press, 1974).

Transfer of Power (HMSO, 1972).

Underwood, T.R., 'Work among Lascars in London', *East and West*, vol. 4, 1906, pp. 451–68.

Vadgama, Kusoom, *India in Britain* (London: Robert Royce, 1984).

Visram, Rozina, *Ayahs, Lascars and Princes* (London: Pluto Press, 1986).

—— *Indians in Britain* (London: B.T. Batsford, 1987).

—— 'The First World War and the Indian Soldiers', *Indo-British Review*, vol. 16, no. 2, 1989, pp. 17–26.

—— *Women in India and Pakistan* (Cambridge: Cambridge University Press, 1992).

—— *The History of the Asian Community in Britain* (Hove: Wayland, 1995).

—— 'Kamal A. Chunchie of the Coloured Men's Institute: The Man and the Legend', *Immigrants & Minorities*, vol. 18, no. 1 March 1999, pp. 29–48.

Wadia, R.A., *The Bombay Dockyard and the Wadia Master Builders* (Bombay, 1935).

Wadsworth, Marc, *Comrade Sak* (Leeds: Peepal Tree, 1998).

Wagle, N.B., 'Experiences of English Factory Life', *Indian Magazine & Review*, No. 361, January 1901, pp. 12–27.

Walsh, J., 'The Empire's Obligation to the Lascar', *The Imperial and Asiatic Quarterly Review*, vol. 30, July–October, 1910, pp. 341–53.

Ward, Margaret, *Maud Gonne* (London: Pandora, 1993).

Ward, Michael, *Red Flag Over the Workhouse* (London: Wandsworth History Workshop, 1992).

Warner, M., *Queen Victoria's Sketch Book* (London: Macmillan, 1979).

Wasti, Syed Razi, ed., *Memoirs and Other Writings of Syed Ameer Ali* (Lahore: People's Publishing House, 1968).

Waterhouse, Keith, *City Lights* (London: Sceptre, 1995).

Waugh, Alec, *The Lipton Story* (London: Cassell & Co., 1952).

West, E.W., ed., *Diary of the Late Rajah of Kolhapoor During his Visit to Europe in 1870* (London: Smith Elder & Co., 1872).

White, Stephen, 'Hindu Cremations in Britain', in Peter C. Jupp and Glennys Howarth, eds, *The Changing Face of Death* (London: Macmillan, 1997).

Whittington-Egan, Richard and Whittington-Egan, Molly, eds, *The Story of Mr George Edalji by Sir Arthur Conan Doyle* (London: Grey House Books, 1985).

Wilberforce, R.I. and Wilberforce, S., *Life of William Wilberforce* (1838).

Wilks, Samuel and Bettany, G.T., *A Biographical History of Guy's Hospital* (London: Ward, Lock, Bowden & Co., 1892).

Williams, Sir Emrys, *The Penguin Story 1935* (Penguin Books, 1956).

Williams, G.R., *London in the Country* (London: Hamish Hamilton, 1975).

Wolpert, Stanley, *A New History of India* (Oxford: Oxford University Press, 1989).

Woods, John A., ed., *Correspondence of Edmund Burke* (Cambridge: Cambridge University Press, 1963) vol. iv.

Wright, C., *The Brighton Ambulator* (London: C. Wright, 1818).

Yajnik, Indulal, *Shyamaji Krishnavarma* (Bombay: Lakshmi Publications, 1950).

YMCA Indian Students' Union and Hostel, 1920–1953 (March 1953).

Young, Desmond, *Fountain of Elephants* (London: Collins, 1959).

Young, Phyllis, *Report on Investigation into the Conditions of the Coloured Population in a Stepney Area* (London: privately published, 1944).

4 NEWSPAPERS AND PERIODICALS
(Abbreviations Only)

BC	*Bombay Chronicle*
BG	*Brighton Gazette*
BGN	*Bethnal Green News*
BH	*Brighton Herald*
B&HG	*Brighton and Hove Gazette*
BW	*British Weekly*
CDM	*Continental Daily Mail*
CMI	*Coloured Men's Institute*
DA	*Daily Advertiser*
DD	*Daily Dispatch*
DE	*Daily Express*
DG	*Daily Graphic*
DH	*Daily Herald*
DN	*Daily News*
DT	*Daily Telegraph*
DW	*Daily Worker*
EA	*Eastern Argus*
EEN	*Eastern Evening News*
ELA	*East London Advertiser*
FF	*Foreign Field*
GH	*Glasgow Herald*
GHR	*Guy's Hospital Reports*
GM	*Gentleman's Magazine*
GWR	*Glasgow Weekly Record*
HG	*Holborn Guardian*
IG	*Islington Gazette*
ILN	*Illustrated London News*
IM&R	*Indian Magazine and Review*
JNIA	*Journal of the National Indian Association*
KI	*The Kentish Independent*
KM	*The Kentish Mercury*
LCMM	*London City Mission Magazine*
LG	*The London Gazette*
LL	*Labour Leader*
LM	*Labour Monthly*
LT&R	*Laindon Times and Recorder*
MC	*Morning Chronicle*
MC&LA	*Morning Chronicle and London Advertiser*
MEN	*Manchester Evening News*
MG	*Manchester Guardian*
MH	*Morning Herald*
MP	*Morning Post*
MP&DA	*Morning Post and Daily Advertiser*
MT	*Motherwell Times*
NC	*New Chronicle*
OM	*Oxford Mail*
PA	*Public Advertiser*

QVSR	Queen Victoria's Seamen Rest
SAWCM	St Andrew's Waterside Church Mission
SCM	Sussex County Magazine
SDN	Sussex Daily News
SW	Sunday Worker
SWS	South Western Star
VfW	Votes for Women

Index

Compiled by Peter Fryer